Human rights, plural legalities and gendered realities
Paths are made by walking

**Other titles in the Women's Law Series
available through Weaver Press**

**Pursuing grounded theory in Law
South-North experiences in developing women's law**
*Agnete Weis Bentzon, Anne Hellum, Julie Stewart, Welshman Ncube and
Torben Agersnap*
1998: 220 x 140mm 311pp
ISBN 1 77906 026 2
Written by five experts from southern Africa and Scandinavia, this book
covers research design skills in data collection, fieldwork methods,
interpretation of fieldwork data and integration of the findings into a
framework of legal analysis. Useful for researchers – both lawyers and
social scientists – who want to gain an insight into changing law and
gender relations in plural systems of law in southern and eastern Africa.

**Women's human rights and legal pluralism in Africa
Mixed norms and identities in infertility management in Zimbabwe**
Anne Hellum
1999: 220 x 140mm 469pp
ISBN 1 77906 017 3
This book analyzes the United Nations Women's Convention as a tool for
women's development in the African context to focus specifically on the
practical matter of gender equality. The study examines how different
groups of women manage their procreative problems in everyday life.
How families, chiefs, traditional healers and local courts respond to
tensions between different norms and expectations is also explored.

**Taking law to the people
Law reform and social change in Zimbabwe
Amy Tsanga**
2003: 210 x 148mm 307pp
ISBN: 1 77922 013 8
This timely book analyzes the challenges that confront rights-awareness
organizations that take on the task of transmitting laws to the people.
Using the example of the Harare Legal Projects Centre in Zimbabwe, the
author examines the multiple factors that impact on the reception of state
law, ranging from culture, gender and communication methods to
organizational models.

WEAVER PRESS

ANNE HELLUM, JULIE STEWART, SHAHEEN ALI AND AMY TSANGA

Human rights, plural legalities and gendered realities
Paths are made by walking

Published by
Southern and Eastern African Regional Centre for Women's Law (SEARCWL)
University of Zimbabwe
P.O.Box MP167, Mt Pleasant, Harare, Zimbabwe
with
Weaver Press
P.O.Box A1922, Avondale, Harare, Zimbabwe
© 2007 Anne Hellum, Julie Stewart, Shaheen Sardar Ali, Amy Tsanga
ISBN: 978-1-77922-062-2

Publishing consultant: Margo Bedingfield
Cover photo: Biddy Partridge

Printed in Mauritius by Précigraph Ltd

Contents

Part III

The legal and political accommodation of women and girls' bodies

Part IV

At the crossroads between human rights, constitutions, laws, culture and religion

Preface

This is the fourth book in the North-South Legal Perspectives Series and the second on the theme of human rights within the overall series. This book reflects the evolutionary process in our thinking within the realms of women's law as to how human rights can be used to improve the position of women, and tangentially men, within the global realm. As individual researchers and lecturers, the editors – and self evidently the authors of these 17 chapters – have struggled with the problem of making human rights real for *all* those they are supposed to benefit. There was a point in our collective time when we each closely questioned the capacity of a human rights based approach to deliver change. Yes, we were aware of the rhetoric and the theoretical potential of a rights based approach to issues that affected women from the most basic relating to delivering the fruits of development to the right to self actualization and pleasure, which is the ultimate accomplishment for human rights.

Thus we asked ourselves individually and collectively: Is a human rights based approach viable? To which our collective answer seemed to be *Yes, but...*! *But* being the operative point of intervention as it is clear that a human rights based approach doesn't work merely by the statement of the rights in a convention or by continuing to make yet more statements of their rights in documents such as the Protocol to the African Charter on the Rights of Women. There has to be action and there has to be grounded realism as to what needs to be done and what can realistically be done in different contexts and settings. This book seeks from a variety of perspectives derived from Southern and Eastern Africa, Europe and South Asia to map the gap between promise and delivery but also and most importantly to fill in the methodological and conceptual 'spaces' to show how paths can be created between the promise of rights and a deliverable reality.

The first book in the North-South Legal Perspectives series, Bentzon, Hellum, Stewart *et al.*'s (1998) *Pursuing grounded theory in law,* used the analogy of the dung beetle to demonstrate how a grounded exploratory approach to issues that affect women in relation to the law can reveal new and beneficial approaches to improving their position or at the very least understanding the reality of their lives and why they do or do not engage with the law at a variety of levels. That book, which set out a framework for explorations of the options and limits of legal pluralism from a woman's law and gender perspective, clearly demonstrated the need for further analysis of the relationship between human rights and legal pluralism.

Increasingly through research and teaching on undergraduate and masters programmes dealing with women's and gender issues at the universities of Zimbabwe, Oslo and Warwick it became apparent that using human rights as benchmarks or aspirational tools in the quest for the improvement of women's lives gave us a range of commonalities and comparators that enhanced our understanding of the global and local interactions of laws and entitlements that worked for or against women. Most significantly it led us to ask the key question: 'What else is needed to make rights materialize and deliver for women?' This is a question that this book seeks to address.

In between these two books the series explored through Anne Hellum's *Women's human rights and legal pluralism in Africa* (1999) the mixed norms and influences, ranging from human rights instruments like the Convention on the Elimination of All Forms of Discrimination of Women, to Zimbabwean state law and custom that determined how different groups of women dealt with issues of fertility and childlessness in complex social, legal and family settings. What mediated and directed their decisions greatly expanded our understanding of the relationship between human rights, legal change and women's powers and capacities to negotiate outcomes that suited their needs.

Amy Tsanga's study of the problems, difficulties and opportunities incurred in *Taking law to the people* helped us understand the significance of a thorough analysis of how and why we pressure for law reform and how, what, where and why we disseminate information about law reform (Tsanga, 2003). Tsanga aptly demonstrated to us all that if we are to make a human rights approach relevant to the perceived needs of women themselves we have to locate our engagements with women in women's perceptions of their own needs and their daily realities.

It is these grounded realities and their significance in our quest for change that has informed our thinking, researching, teaching and theorizing on women's and gender issues across three continents so far, Africa, Europe and Asia (south). Each of the editors has supervised remarkable postgraduate and undergraduate research that cries out for an audience. We have been surprised individually and collectively by the methodological and theoretical similarities in our approaches. We have each experienced the power of being able to hold an informed dialogue with those antagonistic to women's rights exposing the flawed nature of the oppositional arguments and fervently hope that others may gain some insights from the approaches and methodologies presented in the various chapters.

What is striking, looking back at the book in its finished form, are the similarities of concerns, needs and issues that affect women on all three continents. The contexts may be different but the similarities will become glaringly obvious to the reader. Thus we see the significance of documenting our own work, that of our students and our colleagues in a quest to generate greater insights into gendered realities, plural legalities and the potential of a human rights based approach to change women and girls' lives. The final form of the book seems to justify our early conviction that these multiple locations, settings and circumstances, if we could draw them together into addressing the global human rights agenda and women's concerns, would yield valuable crosscutting insights.

We have many people to thank in the production of this book, not least each other, for tolerance, patience and support. Each of us over the writing, collection and editing processes needed to draw on the group's collective reserves, we each experienced the trauma of family deaths, serious life-threatening illnesses of family members, personal exhaustion and stress but we are still talking to each other and continue to draw on our collective ethos for intellectual and personal survival.

Margo Bedingfield our long suffering managing editor has been eternally patient and tolerant; lawyers are picky people, fiddling endlessly with words and their meanings, tuning and retuning sentences and paragraphs and never leaving punctuation alone, but she coped in her usual quiet, accommodating but incisive manner.

Given that we were working from at various times up to four continents and relying on variable email connections the process has been surprisingly congenial and efficient. Of course the best times were when we were all together, including Margo, editing, discussing, arguing, (maybe we should be p.c. and calling it dialoguing) and pushing out the conceptual boundaries. Lest anyone is mistaken these were also opportunities for fun, laughter and sheer intellectual pleasure.

Our long suffering authors especially deserve our thanks; editor one might be more than happy with a piece only to discover that editor two had somewhat different expectations while editors three and four could see a whole range of new or different possibilities for the chapter. Authors quietly accepted our comments and made appropriate adjustments and additions to their chapters as they saw fit, with remarkable tolerance and perspicacity.

Books of this nature need various forms of support, especially financial, thus to the Norwegian Development Agency, NORAD, to the Norwegian Ministry of Foreign Affairs and especially to the staff of the Royal Norwegian Embassy in Harare Zimbabwe we proffer our gratitude for consistent, generous, friendly and never flagging financial and administrative support.

This book demonstrates the significance of building long-term transnational university programmes both academically and administratively. The administrative teams at the Southern and Eastern African Regional Centre for Women's Law (SEARCWL), University of Zimbabwe and the Institute of Women's Law and the Department of Public and International Law, University of Oslo, have ensured that we are free to get on with our academic work and teaching in the context of the accelerating economic, political and social crisis in Zimbabwe. They have dealt with the mammoth task of administration under extremely difficult circumstances. Thus we give special recognition to Blessing Tsomondo, Rudo Makunike-Bonzo in Harare and to Else Vera Aas in Oslo.

'Where is the little blue book I was using yesterday?' is a not infrequent style of question directed at librarians – we all thank Cecilie Butenschon-Mariri, SEARCWL librarian, and Beate Heileman from Oslo for coming to our rescue and frequently, but politely, telling us that 'it wasn't a blue book, it wasn't yesterday and I will see if I can get it back for you from a loan'. Their involvement was especially valued towards the end of the processes as they stalwartly tracked down missing and muddled references.

A favourite question to ask female students is how many women does it take to keep you in the classroom? Well we might ask how many men does it take to support us in our work to try and improve the lot of women? Strictly in alphabetical order we would like to thank to Alastair, Ali and Bill and the men who supported the authors in their work. We deeply appreciate and acknowledge your involvement in the pursuit of women's rights. Although it is invidious to single out any one man, I think the authors will forgive the editors if we nominate Geoff Green (Ann Stewart's partner) as the man of the book[1] for the way in which he supported and proactively assisted Ann in the care of her parents – see chapter 2.

---

[1] Cricket fans will appreciate this appropriation of the man of the match award, believe us (as they always say when the award is being made) it was a close run decision, we hold back on a man of the series at this point as there are more books to come.

About the editors

Professor dr. juris Anne Hellum

Anne Hellum is professor at the Department of Public and International Law and Director of the Institute of Women's Law. Her doctoral thesis was 'Women's human rights and legal pluralism in Africa'. Her areas of research are women's law, human rights and development and anthropology of law. She has been visiting professor at the Human Rights Study Centre at the University of Peshawar and at the Southern and Eastern African Centre for Women's Law at the University of Zimbabwe.

Professor Julie Stewart

Julie Stewart is the Director of the Southern and Eastern African Centre for Women's Law, formerly the Women's Law Centre, at the University of Zimbabwe. Her research interests lie in exploring customary law and drawing the threads of different systems of law together to create a more holistic approach to law especially as it affects the lives of women. One of the critical aspects of this overall research theme is devising appropriate research methods and analytical tools which facilitate activist research on all aspects of the law with all kinds of different groups and individual needs.

Professor Shaheen Sardar Ali

Shaheen Sardar Ali is Professor of Law at the University of Warwick, United Kingdom and Professor II at the Women's Law Institute, University of Oslo. She was formerly Professor at the University of Peshawar, Pakistan and visiting Professor at Washington University School of Law, St Louis Missouri in the United States. She has served as cabinet Minister for Health, Population Welfare and Women's Development in the Government of the North West Frontier Province of Pakistan and Chair of the National Commission on the Status of Women. Her teaching and research interests include gender and human rights including women and children's rights, Islamic law, Islamic Law and Jurisprudence and gender and the law. She has served as consultant to a range of international organizations including NORAD, DFID, UNIFEM, UNICEF, ILO and UNDP.

Dr Amy Tsanga

Amy Tsanga is the Deputy Director of the Southern and Eastern African Centre for Women's Law. Her doctoral thesis completed in 1998 examined issues of social activism and rights awareness within an African context. An aca-activist, Amy has broad experience in human rights activism, teaching and action research in the area of women's rights and social action strategies. She also has wide experience in consultancy work on women's rights and human rights issues.

About the contributors

Ann Stewart is Reader in Law and Director of Undergraduate Admissions at the School of Law, University of Warwick, United Kingdom. Her research interests are in the area of gender and the law. She has a particular interest in gender issues in the developing world and has been involved in a number of internationally based gender and law projects.

Tove Bolstad is a farmer and freelance researcher who has worked with the Institute of Women's Law at the University of Oslo for many years. Her main area of research is women and land in Norway. She has written a number of books that disseminate information about married women's land rights in the event of marriage, divorce and death of the husband.

Henrietta Wolayo Ssemmanda is currently Registrar of the Supreme Court of Uganda. Her Masters in Philosophy dissertation was entitled 'Social arrangements, guardianship and children's rights. Confronting the best interests of the child principle in the law with social reality'. Previous areas of study have included women and children in armed conflict and the enforcement of court orders. She is also actively involved in the Jurisprudence of Equality project of the International Association of Women Judges.

Ellen Sithole is currently Deputy Dean of the Faculty of Law and a lecturer in the Department of Procedural Law, Faculty of Law, University of Zimbabwe. Ellen has been a WLSA researcher and has specialized in procedural law at all levels especially in issues of customary law procedure.

Anne Griffiths has a chair in Anthropology of Law in the School of Law at the University of Edinburgh. Her major research areas include anthropology of law, African law and gender, culture and rights. She is currently president of the International Commission on Folk Law and Legal Pluralism.

Patricia Kameri-Mbote is associate professor and Dean of the Faculty of Law of the University of Nairobi. She has published widely in the field of international law, environmental and natural resources law and policy, women's rights and property rights.

Jacinta Anyango Oduor is an advocate of the High Court of Kenya and a senior practising lawyer. She holds a masters degree in Women's Law from the University of Zimbabwe.

Rie Odgaard is a Mag. Scient researcher at the Danish Institute of International Studies. She is a social anthropologist and has specialized in land rights and land tenure, land institutions and gender issues.

Agnete Weis Bentzon is professor emeritus at the Faculty of Law at the University of Copenhagen. She is Dr Juris in Sociology of Law from the University of Oslo and was Professor of Sociology of Law at Roskilde University Centre in Denmark.

Reena Patel is a lecturer at the University of Warwick and teaches courses on Gender and the Law; Gender, Law and Poverty; Gender, Law and Economic Relations; and Comparative Perspectives on Gender, Law and Development. Her research interests are in the area of gender, law and development and land rights.

Ingunn Ikdahl is Research Fellow at the Faculty of Law at the University of Oslo. Her main research area is human rights and women's land rights. Her areas of teaching are international women's law, equal status law and property rights.

Anne Lene Staib Knudsen is legal advisor in the Ministry of Justice in Norway. She was a research assistant at the Institute of Women's Law.

Gro Hillestad Thune is a human rights advisor and was previously a practising lawyer. She was member of the European Commission of Human Rights for 15 years.

International and regional legislation

Paths are made by walking:
introductory thoughts

Anne Hellum, Julie Stewart,
Shaheen Sardar Ali and Amy Tsanga

Human rights, a grounded approach

A human rights based approach to development brings promise of increasing access to justice, equality and freedom, and ultimately, the elimination of poverty. Until now there has been an apparent failure to deliver the projected human rights benefits and protections to individuals, especially the poor and vulnerable. This has given rise to contestation over whether a human rights framework can deliver on its own promises. By locating ourselves at the intersection of theory and practice, rhetoric and reality, our aim with this book is to grapple with current challenges in making human rights attainable entitlements for those they are designed to benefit. There is, our authors contend, potential to transform the rhetoric of human rights into implementable entitlements.

The subtitle of the book, *Paths are made by walking* comes from a Shona[2] proverb. It provides a metaphor for the processes we argue need to be undertaken to actualize rights and effectively deliver them to the envisioned beneficiaries, especially in the case of women and girl children. In developing a grounded human rights based approach we emphasize the need to constantly take human rights from the plane of abstract principles and place them in dialogue with local problems and practices. In keeping with the ethos of this book, the authors revisit recent human rights achievements in the context of women and girl children's daily struggles for education, health, land, water and food. Through the examination of individual life situations, women and girls' concerns are brought back into human rights discourses and practices.

The case studies show how women and girls in their quest for basic human rights have to negotiate the shifting and contested boundaries between public and private rights and responsibilities. The first thematic section deals with the tension between the delivery of care and the right to work and education. How human rights, state laws and customs are balanced in the context of declining economies leading to private and family-based solutions for appropriate care is addressed. The second section turns its attention to the concern for women as producers of food in relation to land and water resources and reforms. It addresses the

---

[2] The Shona are the largest ethnic group in Zimbabwe they have a rich oral tradition of proverbs about life and how to live it.

need for greater recognition of women's work as family providers and explores how women negotiate access at the interface between international human rights standards, state laws and status hierarchies embedded in marriage and kinship. How women and girls manoeuvre to attain the right to education, work and participation in public spaces by trying to overcome social, cultural and moral constructions of biological difference is dealt with in the third part. The authors turn their attention to the relationship between ratification of human rights treaties, legislative enactments and budgetary allocations.

Drawing all these threads together into a coherent, manageable framework revealing what informs the intersecting factors and forces that converge on women and girls' lives is not an easy task. The comparative evidence offered by this book demonstrates the weaknesses of too much of the human rights literature which offers blueprint approaches. The case studies show that what works in one context may not work in another. What is needed, the case studies also show, is knowledge that can facilitate the translation of the complex realities and legalities of women's lives into human rights measures that respond to the situation at hand. Underlying the contributions to this volume is thus a research strategy that seeks to engage the tension between the complexities of women's lived realities and achieving basic universal rights through exploring locally appropriate implementation approaches. In identifying this strategy we emphasize the following seven elements:

- In translating the human rights based approach to development into a grounded and responsive strategy, a practice-oriented actor approach is adopted. Thus the individual woman and the girl-child are treated as the subjects of rights and the actors in change in the local, national and international arenas. They become, using this approach, the starting point for legal and human rights analysis.

- We appreciate that gender is often implicated in perceptions of value of work and identities have implications for the interpretation and application of seemingly gender-neutral reforms, regulations or entitlements. While new laws and policies, in line with international legal standards, often are moulded on a seemingly gender-neutral model, there is an interrelated need to systematically address the gendered division of labour and the gendered uses of public spaces, land and water. Unless dealt with through socio-legal analysis, gendered constructions of space, bodies, work and resources will sustain and reinforce existing discrimination between men and women.

- Recognizing that women suffer hardships and injustices not only because they are discriminated against as women but also because of their class, race, age, religious or ethnic backgrounds or sexual orientation, calls for closer consideration of intersectionality. In conceptualizing human rights or delivering them to women it has to be taken into account that while women are individuals, as assumed by the international and national citizenship law, they are also embedded in family relationships as well as relationships within religious, ethnic, economic or political communities.

- In dealing with women's multiple positionalities, human rights and legal pluralist approaches need to be combined. This involves engaging a normative human rights framework with a descriptive analysis of its interaction with official and unofficial national and local norms in different contexts. Such a relational and contextual gender perspective epitomizes and reveals the complex, ambiguous and often contentious relationship between human rights and legal pluralism.

- Instead of offering a wholesale theory on the requirements and conditions for change, this book demonstrates the need for a contextualized analysis of the specific local and natural conditions which mediate women and girls' lives. Thus the chapters, individually and collectively, show the importance of contextualizing human rights within the complex and varied gendered realities and the plural legalities within which they operate.

- Yet throughout the book there is an acute awareness that the dangers inherent in a contextual human rights approach should not be underestimated. Thus, there is an appreciation that there is always a risk that findings on the harsh realities of women and girls' lives and the consequent analysis of their needs will be overridden or compromised in the local, national and international processes in which rights, culture and religious values are negotiated. The book thus addresses areas of resistance and prepares researchers to work out the appropriate strategies to assert, claim and 'defend' human rights initiatives in the context of different argumentation paradigms and cultures.

All in all the book constitutes a compilation of micro-level studies combining gendered understandings about people's local experiences, problems and practices in a continuous dialogue with evolving human rights principles and implementation strategies. It constitutes a concerted effort to build a responsive human rights approach from below and within. Through this compilation, it offers a body of knowledge to be brought to the table where international, regional and national law and its bearing on women's lives is negotiated and to be used by local activists around the world who seek to define their problems in human rights terms.

Human rights in context

The intersection of the human rights and women's movements has produced an impressive portfolio of human rights instruments at international and regional levels. Most states, as members of the United Nations and regional bodies, have signed or gone further and ratified major human rights treaties, declarations and platforms of action.[3]

At the regional level a similar normative development is taking place. As a supplement to the African Charter of Human Rights, a protocol to the African Charter on the Rights of Women had by January 2006 been ratified by the required 15 signatories and entered into force. In terms of regional African policies, the Gender and Development Declaration was agreed by the heads of state or government of the Southern African Development Community (SADC) with an addendum on the 'Prevention and eradication of violence against women and children'. Islamic states have agreed upon instruments such as the Cairo Declaration on Human Rights in Islam and the Universal Islamic Declaration of Human Rights. In Europe, the European Convention on Human Rights with its non-discrimination principle is being paralleled by the European Union Human Rights Charter.

Some national governments have 'domesticated' human rights instruments; others have enacted laws incorporating them wholly or partly into national legislation. Elsewhere, states which have not responded to human rights agendas or have done so inadequately are under pressure from a variety of sources to effect such agendas and actively implement human rights provisions internally.

There is increasing multifaceted pressure for change that comes from women's international and national lobby groups as well as from women's grassroots movements. International women's non-governmental organizations have become a forceful pressure group within the United Nations and at the regional, national and local levels (Merry, 2005). The CEDAW committee, for example, plays a significant role in highlighting human rights abuses against women, noting areas of non-compliance with human rights standards and indicating areas for improvement of human rights delivery for individual states and, more generally, the lessons to be learnt or new initiatives to be taken up. Yet, despite signifi-

---

[3] The most noteworthy of these for women is the United Nations Convention on the Elimination of All Forms of Discrimination Against Women 1979 (CEDAW) which places women's rights in a global normative framework of non-discrimination and equality. CEDAW has over the years been supplemented with a series of international and regional declarations and platforms of action such as the Declaration on the Elimination of All Forms of Violence Against Women, the Vienna Platform of Action and the Beijing Platform of Action.

cant progress in raising the profile of women's human rights needs, women's rights on paper do not match the situation of women on the ground. This reality has prompted us to try to identify the missing links in the effort to actualize women's human rights, ending poverty that denies women and girl children the opportunity to meaningfully participate in and benefit from development.

There are constant debates, conferences and international agendas seeking new approaches that will deliver the benefits of development initiatives and ensure human rights compliance as part of the development package.[4] In order to integrate human rights into development planning, the Secretary-General of the United Nations called for mainstreaming of human rights across the entire United Nations system in 1997. As a follow-up, in 1998 the United Nations Development Programme (UNDP) issued a policy paper entitled 'Integrating human rights with sustainable development' (UNDP, 1998) in which it views human rights and sustainable development as inextricably linked. In its 10 May 2001 statement on poverty, the United Nations Committee on Economic, Social and Cultural Rights described poverty as a multidimensional denial of human rights and strongly advocated a human rights approach, emphasizing elimination of discrimination as linked to poverty reduction. Reflecting this trend, there is a growing body of literature integrating development aid with human rights (Hauserman, 1998; Andreassen *et al.*, 2006; Frankovits, 2005; Nowak, 2005). Yet the stark reality is that in much of the world poverty is increasing and women have not attained the promised equality with men.

The failure of the human rights norms and machineries to bring about meaningful change in the lives of individuals, in particular those of women and girls, has spawned an increasingly robust critique on the sterility of human rights from feminist development oriented activists in the still (under)developing south as well as from feminists in the north (Mohanty, 1991; Charlesworth, Chinkin and Wright, 1991; Orford, 1999; Stewart, 2000; Kapur, 2006). The critique questions the efficacy of the language of law and rights as an effective tool for empowerment by highlighting the dissonance between 'having' a right and being able to access it (Nyamu-Musembi and Cornwall, 2004). Further, there is contestation and tension about the nature, form and content of these human rights norms rather than dialogue and context-based interpretation and application of the norms (Ali, 2000 and 2002; Hellum, 1999; Nyamu-Musembi 2002).

---

[4] The Beijing Declaration and Platform for Action, adopted at the Fourth World Conference on Women 15 September 1995 (A/CONF.177/20).

If we are to address these critiques, the first step is to identify where the obstacles are in the 'delivery chain' of human rights to women and their use of these rights. Is it in the formulation of human rights norms at international or regional level? Is it in the translation of human rights norms into national laws and local practices? Is it in the political contestations over acceptance of external normative orders? Is it in contestations over national sovereignty? Is it patriarchal hostility, a resistance to women's entitlements because they challenge male power and hegemony? Is it in the language of law? Is it in the application of the laws? Is it in the interpretation of the laws? Is it in the implementation and 'enforcement' of laws? Is it because women lack awareness of their legal rights? Is it because, even if all other factors are satisfied, women choose not to use the laws? Are the formulations of the laws insensitive and inappropriate to the actual needs of the women they are intended to benefit? Arguably it is all of these issues but to a greater or lesser extent depending on the social, economic, cultural, religious or perhaps geographical or educational context in which the right is 'presented' and the beneficiary woman or girl child is expected to use and engage with it.

Most of the authors of this book contextualize human rights norms and explore what works and what does not in a particular context. One of the challenges they address is how to bring the human rights framework from the plane of abstract principles and turn it into practical responses to women and girls' concerns on the ground. Towards this end, a practice-oriented actor approach is adopted which sees the individual woman and the girl-child as the subjects of rights and actors for change in the local, national and international arenas. Based on case studies ranging from trouble-free cases at the family and village level to cases dealt with by local, national and international courts, the chapters explore, document and or theorize about the preconditions required for the creation and realization of attainable and deliverable rights to women, whoever and wherever they are.

At the gendered interface of law and practice
Seeing women as the subjects of rights and actors for change, the first step of research usually is a gendered analysis of the situation under investigation. Thus key questions to be addressed and researched have to be formulated such as: What are the implications for both women and men and different groups of women in the operation of a particular law, custom or practice? Do gendered and classed differentials emerge? How can those differentials be corrected or addressed? Is the problem that seemingly adequate legal provision becomes discriminatory in application or in lived reality? Are there fundamental, inescapable differences, such as sex-based differences, that need to be factored into national plan-

ning to achieve a level playing field for men, women, boys and girls in their life journeys?

The book's authors take into account the seemingly obvious but often legally obscure reality that human rights norms, as embodied in national constitutions and laws, are in a state of constant interaction and often tension with social, cultural and religious norms and values. The various chapters, set in a variety of contexts, demonstrate that women suffer hardships and injustices not only because they are discriminated against as women but also because of their class, race, age, religious or ethnic backgrounds or sexual orientation. Thus in conceptualizing human rights or delivering them to women it has to be recognized that while women are individuals, as assumed by the international and national citizenship law, they are embedded in family, religious, ethnic, or political communities. A bare-bones assessment of women's human rights entitlements and attainment is a sterile exercise without understanding the relationships which have significant bearing on their life situations, their life choices and their capacity to make and effectively pursue their options.[5]

Seeking to identify a suitable or negotiated entry point into interpretation, enforcement or application processes in relation to human rights agendas is an approach situated in the ambiguities and dilemmas faced by individual women and those working at the 'development and human rights coal-faces'. In practice, they have to contend with the persistent charges that are made by those (often men but also women) who feel threatened by change and believe that women's human rights norms are the creation of western feminists, reflect western, radical feminist aspirations and are out of tune with 'other' cultural, religious, social and economic orders. The chosen entry points for dialogue thus throw up their own points of resistance and inter-cultural and inter-religious tensions. By mapping the effects of multiple intersecting factors shaping women's lives and responses, the authors illustrate and further develop the linkages between implementing women's human rights and stimulating development processes.

The case studies in this collection demonstrate the dynamic, complex and varied relationships between international, national and local law and how the differences can be addressed, minimized or at least recognized and strategized around. Identifying similarities and differences between international and local norms and practices, the case studies speak to the options and limits of a human rights based developmen-

---

[5] Realistically we also argue that precisely the same considerations, with the necessary sex and gender adjustments would also apply to men and boy children's human rights entitlements and aspirations.

tal approach. Looking for entry points for dialogue can unexpectedly reveal that the rights it is sought to implement may already be recognized in a different form and sourced in different ways from the western patterns. This makes them no less significant or enforceable; it is the mechanisms that may differ. Ikdahl's analysis of women's land rights (chapter 10) and Odgaard and Bentzon's chapter on customary processes for women's access to land (chapter 8) illustrate the potential for a middle ground of similar outcomes from different perspectives between so-called western human rights norms and customary responses to similar issues. To use a wildlife analogy, they may be camouflaged within a cultural or religious context, perhaps they are buried under a pile of (historical) leaves and detritus.

For example, in access to basic life resources, such as clean drinking water, local norms and practices in Zimbabwe point to a right to water that is more clearly defined at the local level than in international human rights law (Hellum, chapter 5). Yet modes of acquiring or asserting access to resources in local norms and practices often reflect a status hierarchy based on gender, marriage, kinship, procreative capacity or ethnic belonging (Griffiths, Kameri-Mbote and Oduor, chapters 6 and 7). In some instances, concern for the welfare of the family overrides gender-based status hierarchies to enable the family to cope with changing social and economic circumstances (Odgaard and Bentzon, chapter 8). Other studies on land and land rights explore women's indirect access to land and, challenging male-centred interpretations of rights, support initiatives to tackle and secure their land rights within cultural contexts (Patel, chapter 9). While positive cultural values emerge, such as the value of women's work, spaces for negotiation can be identified as grounded information reveals issues requiring further dialogue. In Zimbabwe, documenting norms and practices protecting widows' continued access to family property has given rise to inheritance reform based on gender equitable norms emerging from local adjustments (Stewart and Tsanga, chapter 16). In Uganda the government has formally recognized customary practices by putting children who are brought up by extended family members on an equal footing with biological children (Ssemmanda, chapter 3).

Yet the dangers inherent in a culturally sensitive human rights approach should not be underestimated. There is always a risk that findings on the harsh realities of women and girls' lives and the consequent anlaysis of their needs will be overridden or compromised in the local, national and international processes in which rights, culture and religious values are negotiated. Thus researchers need to be able to anticipate areas of resistance and prepare the appropriate arguments to 'defend' these new initiatives – an example of this is to be found in Stewart and Tsanga's chapter on changing the laws of inheritance in Zimbabwe (chapter 16). Likewise emphasizing the indivisibility of human rights and the interrelatedness of the right to life, health, education and work, as Hellum and Staib do in their chapter on women and girls' right to reproductive choice, leads to taking a clear position that access to reproductive choice and information on sexuality and education in given situations must be given priority when there are economic or religious constraints or arguments raised against such initiatives (chapter 13).

Women's human rights, development and legal pluralism
– mapping links, identifying gaps

The human rights based approach to development has gained momentum as a guiding framework for development cooperation ranging from state to state partnerships to international institutions such as the United Nations and, to a certain extent, the World Bank and the International Monetary Fund. This approach emphasizes the interconnection between the right to resources that are basic for livelihood and the right to participate in allocating and managing these resources with the existence of institutions that actively ensure a non-discriminatory, transparent and accountable distribution process (Nyamu-Musembi and Cornwall, 2004; Ikdahl *et al.*, 2005, Andreassen *et al.*, 2006). This shift is reflected in a rapidly growing body of internationally required reporting procedures and indicators as international donors and economic institutions mainstream human rights into their policies. In the same vein, women's organizations, non-governmental organizations and international human rights bodies are directing their attention towards states' responsibilities to respect, protect and fulfil basic social and economic human rights of women and children, including the right to health, education, livelihood, food and water on a non-discriminatory basis.

All these efforts are, undoubtedly, enhancing state accountability to the international human rights community. Yet the complex implications and consequences for individuals who are the primary subjects of the international system of human rights law and the main actors in development, may easily get lost in a top-down and state-based approach. A problem with the approaches of international development agencies and non-governmental organizations is that they often lack grounding in empirical knowledge derived from gendered and sexed life situations and the plural legalities involved in local struggles. Scholars within the legal pluralist camp have pointed to the failure of western-style law in addressing the concerns of women in non-western social, cultural and economic contexts (von Benda-Beckman, 1991; Griffiths, 1997; Whitehead and Tsikata, 2003). Conversely, from a human rights perspective, legal pluralism with its focus on empirical description of the multiplicity of norms that are at work in different contexts has been criticised for its lack of moral and political direction (Baxi, 2005; Banda, 2005).

Socio-legal women's law scholarship adopts a middle ground in this theoretically contested terrain. In order to describe, understand and improve women's position in law and society, authors within this tradition engage in identifying and analyzing the (often) complex, ambiguous and contentious relationship between women's human rights and legal pluralism (WLSA Zimbabwe, 1994; Mehdi and Shaheed, 1996; Bentzon *et al.*, 1998; Hellum, 1999; Ali, 2000; Tsanga, 2003). This book seeks to go a step further by exploring how identifying locally appropriate 'plural sources of regulatory norms' and engaging them with human rights imperatives may move us beyond the abstract rhetoric and negation that is often referred to as western-style law versus custom and religion. Thus, the authors turn their attention to the complex, ambiguous and often contentious relationship between men and women in terms of unequal distribution of power and resources within different social, ethnic and religious communities. Combining a human rights and legal pluralist approach, they critically examine recent international and national policy initiatives, building on the potential of local knowledge and institutions as part of the search for a more equitable distribution of natural resources with the quest for poverty elimination and economic growth. The struggle of the Ogiek people for access to the Mau forest in Kenya, Kameri-Mbote's and Oduor's analysis (chapter 7), for example, reveals that men, in a situation where the Ogiek have taken their land claims to court with the support of the non-governmental organization community, represent the generic community's voices while women's concerns as users of the land and carers of children and elderly are not articulated. The case of the Ogiek demonstrates how the quest for cultural rights, unless situated in its gendered context, can result in a restatement of patriarchy and the entrenchment of patriarchal norms of dominance over women.

The need to critically examine both a human rights based and a legal pluralist approach to development is demonstrated by recent debates on formalization, privatization and devolution of power in relation to basic resources such as land and health services. The World Bank policy research report, *Land policies for growth and poverty reduction*, for example, points to the potential for building upon local customs, norms and institutions in securing land rights and promoting production (World Bank, 2003). Along with the neo-liberal privatization policy in the health sector there is increased emphasis in United Nations policies on social service provision by, for example, the family, non-governmental organizations, faith-based organizations, and traditional and religious leaders (UNFPA, 2004).

How women fare within this neo-liberalist resort to the local in terms of access to land, water, health, caring facilities and education, is a critical issue that calls for a concerted analysis of the relationship between human rights and legal pluralism. Whereas the authors conclude that understanding and appreciation of local norms and customs can be a tool for engaging in meaningful change, there is a need to be constantly alert to the risk of uncritically buying into customary and religious approaches and losing out on human rights entitlements. As pointed out by several authors in this book, women and girl children's rights are often overruled by conflicting concerns and priorities in the implementation process. Teenage girls' rights to reproductive information, education and services have not been translated into real rights because of poverty, illiteracy and religious, cultural and economic constraints. This illustrates the need to sharpen the human rights tools to enable more effective engagement with, for example, economic and religious constraints (Hellum and Staib, chapter 13).

How African states mix and merge obligations under human rights law, state law and custom in an attempt to 'dump' caring challenges beyond their capacity on women and girls in the family is demonstrated in several chapters. Sithole's analysis (chapter 4) of home-based AIDS care in Zimbabwe shows how informal gendered caring obligations by implication fill the public welfare gap and go hand in hand with a decline in women and girls' access to education and paid work. Ssemmanda's finely tuned analysis (chapter 3) of the legal recognition of social caring arrangements in Ugandan child law points to both options and limits for girl children as far as the rights to housing, care and education are concerned. Even seemingly strong western welfare states have, as demonstrated by Stewart and Bolstad (chapters 1 and 2), increasingly adopted an avoidance of responsibility approach towards public caring services.

Towards a responsive non-discrimination approach – from abolition to recognition

An important issue which emerges throughout the chapters is the inherent bias of laws, policies and practices not taking issue with the gendered construction of public spaces, bodies, health, work and natural resources, including land and water. How the failure to accommodate women and girls' bodies in public spaces results in discrimination in access to resources essential for human development, such as health, education and work, is highlighted in several contributions. Gender is implicated in perceptions of value which in turn have implications for the interpretation and application of seemingly gender-neutral regulations or entitlements. In Pakistan, as pointed out by Ali (chapter 12), the lack of female toilets affects women as judges and litigants, as teachers and pupils, as health service providers and users of health services. On the African continent, as shown by Stewart, Hellum and Staib (chapters 11 and 13), inadequate management of adolescent girls' sexual and reproductive maturation and menstruation by schools may affect their access to education, health and work.

While new laws and policies in Africa, Asia and Europe are moulded on a seemingly gender-neutral model, the contributions in this book demonstrate the need to take into account that natural resource management is highly gendered. By overlooking the gendered division of labour and uses of land and water, laws, policies and court rulings often discriminate against women. Patel's study (chapter 9) of the recognition of women's work unravels how consideration of who constitutes the subject groups of 'farmers', 'tillers' or 'tenants' within the law is premised upon the male as the active worker or producer and the consequent ignorance of the nature and extent of women's work and of their contributions to the family's survival as a result of such work. Hellum's study of water management in the communal lands in Zimbabwe (chapter 5) uncovers the class and gender bias inherent in the Zimbabwean water reform that overlooks women's small-scale irrigated gardens that are critical to ensure rural livelihoods.

In their search for a responsive non-discriminating approach, many of the authors point to CEDAW and the Protocol to the African Charter's potential in valuing and respecting biological, social and economic differences between men and women. The links between discrimination, disentitlement and lack of recognition of women's work and use of natural resources as family providers is pointed out. As such the book sets out a non-discrimination strategy that, by recognizing and valuing women's work and contributions to family caring and food security, gives legitimacy to their rights claims when they seem to come into conflict with local customs and practices.

The main themes of the book

The book is divided into four thematic sections briefly described in the introduction.

I Who cares? Implications of caring and caring arrangements
This section is about caring – who does it, who receives it and who monitors and determines levels of support and intervention by the state and its agencies in the provision of care. The four chapters each present examples of different roles women fulfil as carers. All the stories that inform the chapters emanate from the family and its multifaceted responses to care needs within its midst. However, the stories are not only

about the family, they are also about states' promises and obligations in the delivery of services – nationally and in terms of their international commitments. They tell a story of the state's failure to deliver on promises and facilitate access to the resources it is obliged to provide. This failure has a profound effect on women and girls' attainment of equality with their male counterparts since, as a general rule, caring and domestic duties fall upon them. Of significance is how women and girls' lives are affected by the state systems' failure and indifference in carrying out the groundwork for provision of services and resources to facilitate sex and gender equality.

The authors further expose the conflicts that riddle female lives – conflicts between embracing change, eschewing predetermined gender roles and meeting the needs of the wider family; conflicts of serving family needs while satisfying their own needs. They also expose the state's internal conflicts about resources and prioritizing their allocation. Although none of the authors dwells directly on the state's allocation of resources to health, social services or education sectors, the availability and suitability of services in these sectors profoundly affect the choices made within families or by individual women – about education, employment rights, caring needs and, thus, about women and girls' lives. The spectre of women's traditional domestic role comes back to haunt individual women in mid-life who were educated and acculturated to escape it, just as it haunts the educational and career prospects of younger women and girls when their lives are mediated and directed by family needs and demands.

Sithole (chapter 4) aptly reveals these dynamics, mainly using research carried out by students doing the Diploma in Women's Law at the Women's Law Centre, University of Zimbabwe. She poses a range of questions about the impact of home-based care for AIDS patients on the lives of women and girls who bear the burden of the carer's role within the family. She tackles this issue not only from the perspective of care work and the health risks involved but also from the perspective of the carers' rights to education, career choices, health, leisure and self actualization. The state's abrogation of its human rights based obligations to provide care and appropriate support to carers in these situations affects not just the right to health but a plethora of other rights. Sithole's graphic examples show how the rights of the carees, the carers and their families are profoundly affected by the AIDS epidemic.[6]

---

[6] Sithole reveals that, like virtually every other family in Zimbabwe and the eastern and southern African region, her own extended family has been affected by the HIV/AIDS pandemic. She is acutely aware of the silence that pervades the family on the treatment and care of patients and the risks that are attendant upon their carers because of the refusal to recognize the disease and its implications.

The dynamics of caring for elderly parents or nursing chronically and terminally ill relatives may cause a girl or woman to abandon her ambitions, put her career on hold or perform complex and stressful juggling acts of life and work to undertake caring duties. In the sub-Saharan Africa context, the gap in the middle-aged section of society created by people aged between 25 and 50 years dying leaves the elderly with caring obligations for the young. Furthermore, young people – often girls in rural areas – take on the task of caring for those affected by AIDS and are as much victims of the pandemic as are those who are infected.

We tend to see the carer phenomenon through the lens of poor women and girls who have few options but even in welfarist or social welfare states, caring is shuffled off to the family by bureaucratic ineptitude, caps on funding and complicated assessment procedures. Ann Stewart (chapter 1) describes the tribulations of undertaking the care of an elderly and ailing family member within the ambit of the state 'welfare' system in England. Her tale, initially told at an intensely personal level, is particularly poignant when she analyzes what took place, the rights of the various parties and the complexities of the legal and bureaucratic processes from the perspective of an academic lawyer, well-versed in a rights-oriented feminist legal discourse. It is painfully clear how difficult it must be for anyone without her knowledge, bargaining and lawyer's skills, financial and personal resources, contacts and negotiable employment arrangements, to obtain assistance, provide appropriate care and steer a way through the minefields of bureaucracy. The conflicts she exposes in the intersection of family privacy and state monitoring and evaluation of caring and needs are evident, and not readily resolvable.

Caring arrangements can, however, also be a way of coping with extended family needs and finding opportunities for children to be educated. We cannot prejudge cases on a simplistic, competing and antithetical basis. Coping strategies abound – what may seem oppressive or questionable from an outsider perspective may provide pragmatic solutions. Ssemmanda (chapter 3) exposes a potential rights-based conflict when she investigates and analyzes families seeking educational opportunities for girl children in Uganda. The girls may be placed in social arrangements where they earn their keep and education by caring and domestic work in a 'surrogate' family. The children take on what could be perceived as adult roles that are prejudicial to their full enjoyment of childhood. Ssemmanda describes the importance to her own life of the family-based arrangement that placed her in her aunt's home for the purposes of obtaining an education – an education which her own natal family would, by her account, not have been able to provide. She contextualizes and problematizes the needs of the child against the rights of the child to give us a balanced perspective of such care arrangements.

What is especially significant about this chapter is the interface between traditional, social and cultural practices within families and communities and the recent legislative interventions in the form of the Children's Act in Uganda. The Act now recognizes these social arrangements and treats those with children in their care as de facto guardians who have obligations akin to those of parents or de jure guardians. The statute is new and assessment of its efficacy premature but it points a way forward and indicates how positive African values can be harnessed into the human rights agenda.

Although Ssemmanda does not pursue the issue, her chapter raises the perennial issue of the fine divide between chores that children are required to carry out and child labour – especially considering the additional chores that children in social arrangements undertake to earn their keep. Such arrangements largely escape regulation because the state does not have the person power or even the will to intervene and families resist intervention.[7] But self-evidently there is need for regulation and the Ugandan approach couples recognition with the creation of frameworks for intervention and protection of the rights of the child.

Family expectations or acceptance of family-based obligations dominate this section. From a northern perspective, Bolstad (chapter 2) analyzes the ways in which women's time and lives are appropriated by her marital family to satisfy caring needs in rural Norway. She looks at the situation of women absorbed into kår contracts. The woman is not herself a party to the contract but she acquires the obligations to provide care, domestic support and catering, usually to her husband's parents, as part of the agreement made between male family members on the transmission of rights to the family farm from an older man to a younger man, usually a son. The bargain is simple, the son takes over the farm and its economic potential in return for continuing occupation rights of residential premises on the farm and other agreed services that will be provided to the 'retiring' party. The agreement might be made even before the younger man is married and well before his parents need care. But who does the caring and bears the brunt of tensions, anger and family frustrations? Inevitably, this falls upon the acquirer's wife who is not privy to the contract but is the gender role determined provider of services. The connection between the gender-determined division of labour in agriculture, with its rigid expectations as to which duties devolve upon

---

[7] Research experience throughout eastern and southern Africa in trying to track down and interview girls and boys in domestic service or other family-based arrangements can be extremely difficult. Everyone in the homestead is described as family and, technically, correctly so, but there is no equality within the family in terms of access to resources or benefits.

men and women respectively, and the contents of agreements seen in the light of women's experience of kår contracts, illuminates a new aspect of the gendered systems in agriculture in the European context.

II Livelihood, land and water: engendering property relations

Land and related natural resources form a critical part of many communities' lifelines. Conflicting concerns such as economic growth, democracy, equality and secure livelihoods are today reflected in national land and water reforms across the globe (Ikdahl, Hellum, Kaarhus *et al.*, 2005; Derman and Hellum, 2003). Through case studies from southern and eastern Africa and India the six contributions in this section seek to voice the concerns of women who rely on access to land and water as family providers. A crosscutting issue is how women's engagement with land and water is valued, respected and protected in local, national and international law. By engaging abstract human rights principles with women's uses of land and water the different contributions pinpoint critical dimensions that a human rights based approach needs to address in the quest for substantive equality with regard to land, water and related natural resources.

The perspective from below and within takes us into the complex interface between rights, status hierarchies embedded in marriage and kinship, recognition of women's work and concerns for family welfare and local livelihoods. Griffiths (chapter 6), on the basis of her fieldwork among the Bakwena in Botswana, shows how power relations informed by marriage status determine women's access to property under both statutory and customary law. Yet structural power relations within marriage and kinship are not absolute. Water management practices in the communal lands in Zimbabwe, as observed by Hellum (chapter 5), illustrate how the concern for access to basic livelihood resources may overrule gendered status hierarchies. In the same vein, Odgaard and Bentzon's study of the Hehe in Tanzania (chapter 8) demonstrates how patrilineal inheritance principles, in a situation where sons migrate to urban areas, are modified by the recognition of daughters' work as family carers. Patel's study of female rice workers in Orissa (chapter 9) highlights the significant role that peasant women play within the household and in overall agricultural production. Addressing the potential for change she emphasizes that this role needs to be an important determinant in defining women as the subjects of ownership rights within law. It is a forward-looking contribution pointing to the potential of giving social legitimacy to women's land claims through recognition of their work.

While new laws and policies, in line with international legal standards, often are moulded on a seemingly gender-neutral model, land and water uses are, as demonstrated in this section, highly gendered. Overlooking the gendered division of labour and the gendered uses of land and water, laws, policies, non-governmental organization advocacy and court rulings often lead to discrimination against women. Starting out with the struggle of the Ogiek people for access to the Mau forest in Kenya, Kameri-Mbote and Oduor (chapter 7) interrogate the gendered perception of the group's relationship with the state, the forest and its resources. The analysis reveals that men, in a situation where the Ogiek have taken their land claims to court with the support of non-governmental organizations, represent the generic community's voices while women's concerns as users of the land are not articulated. The case of the Ogiek demonstrates how the quest for cultural rights, unless situated in its gendered context, can result in a restatement of patriarchy and the entrenchment of patriarchal norms of dominance over women. In a similar vein, Patel's study of the recognition of women's work (chapter 9) seeks an explanation of why, despite official assurances that all leases and allocations under the Orissa Land Settlement Act 1959 would be issued on an equal basis, men received more than twice as many as women in 1995. How the consideration of who constitutes the subject group of 'farmers', 'tillers' or 'tenants' within the law is premised upon the male as the active worker or producer is unravelled. She points to the ignorance of the nature and extent of women's work and its contribution to the family's survival. Hellum's study of water management in the communal lands in Zimbabwe (chapter 5) uncovers the class and gender bias inherent in the Zimbabwean water reform. The new policy overlooks women's gardens which are a form of agriculture that, in ensuring rural livelihoods, cuts across the division of domestic and productive land and water.

The underlying argument of the authors in this section is that the gap between laws, policies, court rulings, registration practices and women's actual uses of land and water reflects the non-recognition of women as significant actors in agricultural production within the wider society, the state and its laws. Gender is, as demonstrated, implicated in perceptions of value, which in turn have implications for the interpretation and application of seemingly gender-neutral regulations or entitlements. The case studies point to CEDAW's potential to emphasize that women's contributions, in terms of both domestic and productive work, be recognized as a means of acquiring access to basic livelihood resources that are a form of marital, family or local community property. In addition to the significant overlaps in the themes, each of these chapters addresses specific concerns that a human rights based approach needs to consider to lay a foundation for substantive equality with regard to land, water and related natural resources.

Independent and effective land rights for women have been identified by researchers and policy makers as vital for family welfare, food security, gender equality, empowerment, economic efficiency and poverty elimination (Agarwal, 1994 and 2002). Hellum's study of women's gardens in three villages in Mhondoro communal land in Zimbabwe (chapter 5) emphasizes the mutual importance of land and water in ensuring rural livelihoods. Here, as elsewhere in Africa, land and water uses are interwoven through highly gendered patterns of use. While irrigated cash crop agriculture is often controlled by men, women, assisted by their children, are usually in charge of hand-irrigated vegetable gardens. This integrated form of agriculture that cuts across the domestic and productive domain is often overlooked when policies and investment plans are made, resulting in irrigation of commercial crops, controlled mostly by men, being favoured. The case of women's gardens thus points to the importance of overriding the dichotomous perception of productive and domestic work to promote non-discriminatory and pro-poor models of land and water reform.

Customary law is often seen as a barrier to equal land rights for women. Questioning this assumption, Odgaard and Bentzon (chapter 8) explore ways in which women among the patrilineal Hehe in Iringa rural district and the Sangu in Mbarali district in Tanzania access land and other property. The chapter illustrates how general changes in the society and in gender relations influence the way property rights are perceived and articulated among the Hehe and Sangu peoples over time. As regards distribution within the family, the authors uncover crosscutting alliances and conflicts between fathers, their daughters and their sons. Building on an understanding of customary law as dynamic, contingent on time and space, the authors explore how daughters' access to family property is being enhanced. To make higher courts sensitive to this dynamism of the living customary law, the authors suggest systematic efforts to make research on the living customary law available to judges at all levels of the courts system.

In her discussion of the options and limits of independent land rights for women, Griffiths (chapter 6), like Kameri-Mbote and Oduor, explores how power relations are informed by marriage status which in turn determines women's access to property. Both in law and practice questions arise as to who has the power to construct, shape, transform or contest the terms of reference upon which the negotiation of claims to land rest and what implications this has for women's use of law. Unlike other contributors in this volume who point to the flexibility of local norms, Griffiths emphasizes the structural constraints embedded in the gendered construction of marital status and its implications for access to social and material resources. An interesting question is whether and to what extent local practice has responded to the changing social, economic and legal environment over the last 15 years.

Ikdahl (chapter 10) discusses the status of women's land use and the recognition and protection of their work and uses of the land in relation to international human rights law. Taking the contested status of women's engagement with land reflected in Tanzania's land reform process as a starting point, Ikdahl asks what the human rights protection of property clause has to offer women. Applying a responsive and dynamic approach, Ikdahl links protection of property to broader human rights issues such as the rights to non-discrimination, integrity and livelihood. The human rights arguments, as developed in this chapter, provide a legal backdrop for further recognition of rural women's quest for tenure security, not only as individuals but as providers of livelihood and food security for children and the elderly in the family.

III The legal and political accommodation of women and girls' bodies
The four chapters in this section attempt to stretch the boundaries of human rights discourse by critically assessing the constituent elements of a range of women's human rights that are crucial to their effective realization and enjoyment. The authors argue that to actualize women's human rights to health, education, a clean and healthy environment, sanitation, human dignity, privacy and employment, more is required than legislative enactments, ratification of human rights treaties, budgetary allocations and physical structures. A number of themes and crosscutting issues emerge in the contributions highlighting the centrality of simple, grounded substantive measures to breathe life into human rights.

Stewart (chapter 11) explores a possible contributory cause to the limited number of girls progressing to higher levels of education. Drawing upon research findings in the FEMED study conducted on schoolgirls in Zimbabwe, she postulates that inadequate management of sexual maturation and menstruation in schools, including lack of adequate sanitary protection wear, causes girls to drop out of school (Stewart, 2004). While this is not the only reason girls drop out of school, it can be a factor in their attendance and retention in school and must be addressed as a component of the right to education as well as other human rights. The main thrust of Stewart's chapter lies in the deconstruction of what constitutes an emerging right to development (within which lie the right to education and health) and identifying elements of the right that are clearly management rather than content issues of the right to education or health. Thus she deals with menstruation not as an issue impinging on young girls' right to health per se but as possibly barring or inhibiting fulfilment of their right to education.

Ali (chapter 12) poses a similar dilemma regarding effective implementation of women's human rights. Her chapter draws on her experiences as Minister for Health in the North West Frontier province of Pakistan (1999–2001) where women professionals in the Department of Health and other government departments brought to her attention the difficulties they face in performing their jobs due to the lack of a toilet in the workplace. Lack of access to a toilet restrains the capability of women both as users of public space and as professionals in service delivery and provides an example of how poor planning and management can cancel out effective enjoyment of human rights, including the right to health. Ali points out that in a deeply segregated society, such as Pakistan, accommodating women's bodies in public spaces becomes a human rights and discrimination issue. Whether it is women judges in court buildings, women teachers and girl pupils in schools, government functionaries in office blocks or women users and service providers in health facilities, their basic human right to access to health, education, employment, and so on, is under siege.

Staib and Hellum (chapter 13) address the protection of teenagers' reproductive health in the context of human development. They adopt a holistic approach in their analysis of the right to protection from unwanted pregnancies and sexually transmitted diseases and the right to access to health information, education and services. A major challenge for the human rights based development approach is to work out ways of ensuring that women and girls' rights are not jeopardized in the process of negotiating rights and cultural and religious values. Emphasizing the indivisibility of human rights and the interrelatedness of the rights to life, health, education and work, the authors conclude that access to reproductive and sexual information and education in given situations needs to be given priority when confronted with economic or religious constraints.

Thune (chapter 14) draws on the controversial issue of female circumcision to illustrate the challenges of implementing human rights among immigrant communities in Norway. Recognizing the significance that the United Nations Convention on Rights of the Child places on the elimination of this phenomenon as well as the call of the CEDAW committee on states to actively pursue measures to eradicate the practice, her concern is with the efficacy of the methods that the Norwegian government has embraced to address the reality of female circumcision amongst its immigrant communities. What emerges from Thune's chapter is that a top-down approach to human rights – seeking to pass legislation at the national level without embracing the realities of the target group – may roll back the gains of human rights activism. She focuses on a Bill that overrides confidentiality and requires members of specific professions to report and prevent female circumcision – failure to do so would result in punishment, including imprisonment. Thune points out that while a variety of professionals, including nurses, teachers and religious officials, voiced concern about its implementation, some of the strongest concerns came from immigrant women who had made real gains in attitudinal change and felt that the punishment aspect would serve to alienate communities.

A number of cross-cultural comparisons emerge from the four contributions in section III. In Stewart's chapter the inhibiting factor for girls' education is not the absence of toilets but the lack or non-availability of sanitary pads. Stewart's evaluation points to the struggles of young girls accommodating their bodies without resources in a desegregated environment. Building schools and announcing free and compulsory schooling are pointless without adequate or appropriate supporting mechanisms such as toilets with space for cleaning up and affordable sanitary pads which are the management and procedural mechanisms that act as catalysts in transforming lifeless rights into real entitlements. Ali, on the other hand, brings to our attention the absence of toilets (or few functional ones) in public spaces. She argues that in a segregated society, such as Pakistan, women's bodies and their visibility is a problem per se; hence the virtual absence of women from public spaces and the failure to identify or fulfil her basic needs such as a toilet. On the contrary, in the Zimbabwean context, women are visible and participate in the public space. This comparison exposes the varying shades of patriarchy – which raises the question, does visibility in and of itself become more empowering?

The chapters in this section also reveal that discrimination may and does arise when sex-based needs and realities are ignored in the name of gender mainstreaming. Thus, laws calling for equality and non-discrimination often mean men and women are assumed to start from the same point in the mainstreaming exercise so run the risk of unwittingly perpetuating discrimination against women because the necessary preconditions for their inclusion have not been understood let alone taken into account.

IV At the crossroads between human rights, constitutions, laws, culture and religion

The three chapters in section IV discuss the relationship between human rights and legal pluralism in relation to women's access to law. How the courts balance the plurality of norms at work is explored at different levels of the judicial system. The role of legal awareness programmes addressing both right holders and duty bearers is addressed. These chapters provide a wider understanding of how human rights concepts fare from an implementation perspective, particularly when they encounter religious and customary norms and practices that may be at variance with human rights standards.

A common theme addressed in the chapters is that, in advancing the rights of women and if human rights are to gain significance and acceptance beyond the instruments which they constitute, there is need to engage effectively with legal pluralism. This manifests itself in many contexts, for example, where received laws operate alongside customary laws or religious laws, or from the plethora of cultural and religious norms that shape people's lives. The authors also address the role of the legislature in passing laws in consonance with human rights standards as contained in international and regional human rights instruments. They touch on the issue of human rights norms and the courts' application of the laws at different levels of the judicial system and discuss raising awareness about women's rights as human rights among diverse groups, from members of society and law reformers to judicial officers but, more significantly, how to do so by engaging effectively with the cultural context in which these rights seek fulfilment.

Recognizing the role that religious and customary laws continue to play in women's lives, the authors call for an approach to human rights and development that acknowledges the inherent dynamism that informs these laws and practices. In view of the dominance of human rights ideology as an interpretative tool and the proliferation of human rights instruments adopted by state parties, all the chapters in this section deal with the need to engage with this normative framework in the development of religious and customary laws.

In addition to these common themes, each chapter addresses specific nuances that expose the multiple challenges and realities that confront parliamentarians, practitioners, academics, activists and researchers in giving meaning to human rights within plural, cultural and legal settings.

Using cases that have come before the courts in Pakistan, Ali (chapter 15) focuses on the controversial issue of crime and punishment under Islamic criminal law in instances where women have been accused of engaging in extra-marital sexual relations (Hudood Laws). Her chapter traces the origins of the Islamic law on extra-marital relations and notes the dangers that have arisen for women's rights from the selective interpretation of the relevant verses of the Quran and the total neglect, in most cases, of the requirement that those who accuse women unjustly of immorality should be punished. This is in light of the findings that allegations of inappropriate conduct are often made out of the need to settle personal vendettas or to prevent or punish women who have chosen their own marriage partner. The rigid and patriarchal interpretations infringe on fundamental women's rights such as freedom from non-discrimination, dignity, equality and freedom of life.

Her chapter also deals with the interpretative role of the courts. She exposes the divergence in the manner of dealing with such cases between the lower and the upper courts. From the cases analyzed, she observes that lower courts are more inclined to convict in such cases while upper courts are more likely to reverse convictions on appeal, largely due to their visibility and willingness to give meaning and effect to human rights principles and treaties to which Pakistan is party. She identifies continuing legal education as a key strategy in exposing members of the lower courts to human rights principles impacting on women. Providing information, examples, models and opportunities for discussion are all important in contributing towards changing people's attitudes, including those of the judiciary.

Using inheritance by widows and girl children in Zimbabwe as an example, Stewart and Tsanga (chapter 16) analyze the ways in which customary law was misinterpreted to create the notion of a single male heir, despite the flexible wording of the relevant legislation regarding estates of deceased persons governed by customary law. They tackle the role of judicial activism in advancing women's rights and examine a variety of cases that have come before the Zimbabwean courts to illustrate the rough and uneven terrain women have traversed in asserting their inheritance rights. Unlike in Pakistan where the lower courts have tended to display an unhealthy conservatism in interpreting women's rights under Islamic law, Stewart and Tsanga illustrate that in Zimbabwe the lower courts tend to be more progressive than the higher courts in their approach to women's rights under customary law. They attribute this to the exposure of lower court judicial officers to issues of women and the law in their training since inheritance matters are not dealt with by chiefs but by trained judicial personnel who are increasingly alive to the debates on gender and equality. They note that the Supreme Court started off on a progressive path at independence but veered off this path when conservative and patriarchal forces took the helm. Their chapter locates women's inheritance within the current human rights framework, more particularly in relation to the Protocol to the African Charter on Women's Rights which takes an unequivocal stance on women's inheritance rights. They also analyze the new law on the administration of estates under customary law in Zimbabwe and its compliance with human rights principles.

Given the reality that attitudes are often most difficult to change at societal level, Tsanga (chapter 17) calls for legal literacy or legal information dissemination programmes that recognize the centrality of plurality in people's lives. She concedes that mileage can be gained from the human rights framework but also emphasizes the need to seek solutions from the positive elements in customary and religious laws. In the case of customary law she argues that its conciliatory and informal method of dispute resolution can be harnessed in the development of African legal systems and the fulfilment of human rights in African cultural contexts. Rights awareness implementers need to engage more squarely with the various aspects of feminist thought in framing arguments for the improvement of women's lives. Unless people have participated in formulating new constitutions that incorporate human rights principles, they may regard them as alien. In the final analysis she emphasizes the importance of multiple strategies which include building on positive elements of both customary and religious laws, engaging a human rights framework, especially the use of regional instruments, and the need to build on the spirit of historic struggles for freedom that have shaped people's consciousness.

Recognizing the significant role that courts play or stand to play in human rights education, the Pakistani and Zimbabwean examples from the courts offer interesting comparisons. We gain some understanding of the factors leading to lower courts being more conservative in Pakistan and more open to change in Zimbabwe and, conversely, the upper courts being more open to change in Pakistan as far as the hudood laws are concerned while the upper courts in Zimbabwe vacillate towards the conservative when it comes to women's rights to inheritance. The comparisons underscore the importance of raising awareness amongst the various strata that comprise the judiciary. Progressive interpretation and use of a human rights interpretative framework cannot be left to judicial officers' chance awareness of the issues at stake. Clearly, continuing human rights and gender awareness programmes are vital at all levels of the judicial system.

Walking the talk

In summation, walking these human rights paths has been a challenging yet fulfilling process for the editors and contributors of this book. It has been in many ways revisiting a landscape explored time and again – but with a difference! It has taught us to stop and think and ask ourselves where a human rights based approach may lead us. The sheer diversity of intersecting plural legalities and gendered realities emerging from different places indicates commonalities and divergence in conceptualizing as well as operationalizing human rights.

Mapping the links between discrimination, disentitlement, and lack of recognition of women's work and contributions to welfare and food security provides the basis for a contextual and responsive non-discrimination approach. By recognizing and valuing women's work it gives legitimacy to their rights claims when they seem to come into conflict with local customs and practices.

Uncovering how discrimination and disenfranchisement arises when gendered constructions of bodies and spaces are ignored in the name of gender mainstreaming, the authors demonstrate the dangers of unwittingly perpetuating discrimination through this process. Men and women cannot be assumed to start from the same point in the mainstreaming exercise. The non-discrimination principle implies that necessary preconditions for women and the girl child's inclusion must be considered.

In demonstrating the indivisibility of the rights to water, food, reproductive health, education and work; women and girl child's caring roles; use of natural resources; and the (non) accommodation of women and girls' bodies, the chapters show how rights can and should play an important role in development. Such an appreciation of the interrelated and indivisible character of human rights forcefully speaks to the lived realities of women and girls. Likewise it raises the importance of recognizing and addressing cultural and historical concerns about individuals and communities' rights to livelihood.

Among the many lessons learnt from the field studies, one stands out: that even the most careful and meticulous formulations of human rights will only come to life if they speak to the woman whose life is touched by it. The devil is in the details of everyday life!

Selected bibliography

Ali S. S. (2000) *Gender and human rights in Islam and international law*, Kluwer Law International, the Hague/London/Boston.

Agarwal B. (1994) *A field of one's own*, Cambridge University Press, Cambridge.
– (2002) *Are we not peasants too? Land rights and women's claims in India*, Population Council, SEEDS series, No. 21, New York.

Andreassen, B. A. and S. P. Marks (eds) (2006) *Development as a human right. Legal, political and economic dimensions*, FXB Centre for Health and Human Rights/Harvard University Press, Cambridge.

Banda, F. (2005) *Women, law and human rights: An African perspective*, Hart, Oxford.

Banda F. and C. Chinkin (2004) *Gender, minorities and indigenous peoples*, Minority Rights Group International, London.

Baxi U. (2005) 'Legal pluralism in India: An Introduction', *Indian Socio-Legal Journal*, XXXI.

Bentzon A. W., A. Hellum, J. Stewart, W. Ncube and T. Agersnap (1998) *Pursuing grounded theory in law: South-North experiences in developing women's law*, Mond Books/ Tano Aschehoug, Harare and Oslo.

Charlesworth H., C. Chinkin and S. Wright (1993) 'Feminist approaches to international law', *American Journal of International Law* Vol. 85, 613–645.

Derman B. and A. Hellum (2003) 'Neither tragedy nor enclosure: Are there inherent human rights in water management in Zimbabwe's communal lands?', pages 31–50 in T. Benjaminsen and C. Lund (eds) *Securing land rights in Africa*, Frank Cass, London.

Frankovits A. (2005) 'Introduction', pages 1–14 in M. Scheinin and M. Suksi (eds), *Empowerment, participation, accountability and non-discrimination: Operationalizing a human rights-based approach to development. Human rights in development yearbook 2002*, Martinus Nijhoff/ Nordic Human Rights Publications, Dordrecht.

Griffiths A. (1997) *In the shadow of marriage: Gender and justice in an African community*, University of Chicago Press, Chicago and London.

Hellum A. (1999) *Women's human rights and legal pluralism in Africa*, Mond Books/ Tano Aschehoug, Harare and Oslo.

Hellum A. (2001) 'Towards a human rights based development approach: The case of women in the water reform process in Zimbabwe', *Law, Social Justice & Global Development*, 2, www2.warwick.ac.uk/fac/soc/law/elj/lgd.

Hellum A. and B. Derman (2004) 'Land reform and human rights in contemporary Zimbabwe: Balancing individual and social justice through an integrated human rights framework', *World Development*, 32(10):1785–805.

Ikdahl I., A. Hellum, R. Kaarhus and T. A. Benjaminsen (2005) *Human rights, formalization and women's land rights in southern and eastern Africa*, Studies in Women's Law No. 57, University of Oslo, Oslo.

Kapur R. (2006) 'Revisioning the role of law in women's human rights struggles', pages 101–116 in S. Meckled-Garcia and B. Cali (eds) *The legalization of human rights multidisciplinary perspectives on human rights and human rights law*, Routledge, London.

Koskinen P. (2005) 'To own or to be owned: Women and land rights in rural Tanzania', pages 145–86 in M. Scheinin and M. Suksi (eds), *Empowerment, participation, accountability and non-discrimination: Operationalizing a human rights-based approach to development. Human rights in development yearbook 2002*, Martinus Nijhoff/ Nordic Human Rights Publications, Dordrecht.

Mehdi R. and F. Shaheed (1997) *Women's law in legal education and practice in Pakistan*, North South Cooperation in Women's Law, New Social Science Monographs, Copenhagen.

Merry S. E. (2005) *Human rights and gender violence: Translating international law into local justice*, University Of Chicago Press, Chicago.

Moore S. F. (1978) *Law as process*, Routledge & Kegan Paul, London.

Nowak M. (2005) 'A human rights approach to poverty', pages 15–36 in M. Scheinin and M. Suksi (eds) *Empowerment, participation, accountability and non-discrimination: Operationalizing a human rights-based approach to development. Human rights in development yearbook 2002*, Martinus Nijhoff/ Nordic Human Rights Publications, Dordrecht.

Nyamu-Musembi C. (2002) *Towards an actor-oriented perspective on human rights*, IDS Working Paper 169, Institute of Development Studies, Brighton.

Nyamu-Musembi C. and A. Cornwall (2004) *What is the 'rights-based approach' all about? Perspectives from international development agencies*, IDS Working Paper 234. Institute of Development Studies, Brighton.

Office of the United Nations High Commissioner for Human Rights (OHCHR) (2002) *Draft guidelines on a human rights approach to poverty reduction*, www.unhchr.ch/html/menu6/2/povertyE.pdf.

Orford A. (1999) 'Contesting globalization: A feminist perspective on the future of human rights', pages 157–186 in B. H. Weston and S. P. Marks (eds) *The future of international human rights*, Transnational Publishers Inc New York.

Southern African Development Community (SADC) (1997) *Gender and development declaration*, 8 September 1997.

Stewart (ed) (2004) *Life skills, sexual maturation and sanitation: What's (not) happening in our schools – An exploratory study from Zimbabwe*, Weaver Press and Women's Law Centre, UZ, Harare.

Tsanga A. (2003) *Taking law to the people*, Weaver Press, Harare.

United Nations (2003) 'The human rights based approach to development cooperation: Towards a common understanding among the UN agencies', statement from an inter-agency workshop held in May 2003, www.crin.org/hrbap/index.asp?action=theme.docitem&item=4689.
– World Summit on Sustainable Development (2002) *The Johannesburg Declaration on Sustainable Development*, adopted 4 September 2002, Johannesburg.
– The *Beijing Declaration and Platform for Action* (1995) adopted at the Fourth World Conference on Women 15 September 1995. A/CONF.177/20.
– *Vienna Declaration and Plan of Action*, adopted by the World Conference on Human Rights, 25 June 1993, A/CONF.157/23.
– *Statement on Poverty and the International Covenant on Economic, Social and Cultural Rights* (2001) adopted by the United Nations Committee on Economic, Social and Cultural Rights, UN doc. E/C.12/2001/10.

United Nations Development Programme (1998) *Integrating human rights with sustainable human development: A UNDP policy document*, http:// magnet.undp.org/Docs/policy5.html.

United Nations Fund for Population Activities (2004) *Working from within: Culturally sensitive approaches in UNFPA programming*, New York.

von Benda-Beckman K. (1991) 'Development, law and gender skewing', *Journal of Legal Pluralism and Unofficial Law*, 30&31: 87–130.

World Bank (2003) *Land policies for growth and poverty reduction: A World Bank policy research report*, World Bank and Oxford University Press, Oxford.

Whitehead A. and D. Tsikata (2003) 'Policy discourses on women's land rights in sub-Saharan Africa: The implications of the re-turn to the customary', *Journal of Agrarian Change*, 3(1–2):67–112.

Women and Law in Southern Africa Research Project (WLSA) Zimbabwe (1994) *Inheritance in Zimbabwe: Law, customs and practices*, WLSA Trust, Harare.
–(1997) *Paradigms of exclusion: Women's access to resources in Zimbabwe*, WLSA Trust, Harare.

Part I

Who cares?
Implications of caring and caring arrangements

1

Families and feminism:
Caring for mum and dad

Ann Stewart

I am going to tell a story of caring for two ordinary, decent human beings coming to the end of their long lives. It is a case study of caring about the elderly from personal experience.[8] The story also shows how one family and a European welfare state in 'late modernity' struggle to value their elderly members. The second section provides the social and legal context and gender politics. It reinterprets the story through the legal and administrative provisions. I then consider whether human rights discourse provides an adequate framework for the provision of social care. I will argue that the dominant human rights discourse, which assumes that the human subject is an autonomous, independent individual rather than vulnerable and interdependent, is predicated on an ethic of work. A better starting point for conceptualizing the issues associated with caring is provided by the feminist analysis of the ethic of care.

1 Families

Mum was born in London in 1911. Her father, an alcoholic, died young. Consequently, she was obliged to leave school at 13 and a half to work as a nanny. Dad was born in 1912, in Scotland into a farming family. The economic depression of the 1930s and the flooding of the farm by the river Tay led to its sale. The family moved to a smallholding in England. My dad's schooling also finished before he was 14. He worked on the land thereafter.

They met as a result of the war, married in 1944 and moved into a tied cottage[9] on the farm where Dad was working as a dairyman, the job he continued to do until he fully retired at 68. Mum ceased paid employment and became a housewife and mother.

---

[8] This is only one story of caring. I leave out my brother who loved and cared for his parents. It is about caring over a short time. Many care for lifetimes under incomparably more difficult circumstances. It is also about one way of caring and is not intended as a model for caring generally.

[9] Accommodation provided by an employer for the duration of employment.

The long retirement

The last two jobs that Dad had were in the same village in the south of England. When Dad was of retirement age at 65, they accepted the tenancy of a state-owned bungalow in the village, thereby ending a lifetime of housing insecurity.[10] Mum and Dad were poor, living solely on the basic state pension and additional means tested benefits, although they were better off than they had ever been in their lives. Mum and Dad were generally wary of public authorities: the attention of the state for their social class and generation would usually signal trouble. The only significant contact was through their public sector landlord.

Their southern village transformed over the 30 years they lived there into an affluent commuter community. However, the village retained a significant degree of social cohesion. Mum and Dad had few friends but neighbours watched out for them. In an emergency there was always someone around to help. This degree of social care was valuable, particularly because their family lived far away.

Mum and Dad enjoyed good health well into their retirement. In his late eighties, Dad's sight deteriorated, he had heart failure and anaemia but these conditions of ageing were not substantially incapacitating. Mum was generally well until her mid-eighties when she was diagnosed with cancer. She received treatment and went into remission. However thereafter her arthritic hip deteriorated which restricted her mobility, thereby frustrating her and sapping her confidence.

Family revisited

During my childhood, the family relied on Dad's meagre weekly pay (agricultural wages were low) but Mum was a good manager and Dad a good worker. Both invested in their children. I went to grammar school,[11] then university and became an academic lawyer. I left home to go to university and thereafter lived in urban areas far away. However, despite the substantial social and physical distance between us, we remained close emotionally.

I was born late in my mother's life: she was 41. My children were born when I was relatively young (26 and 30) by professional middle class standards. I was 49 when Dad was 89 and Mum 90. My children were 23 and 19.

---

[10] The Labour government's social housing legislation in the 1970s provided occupants of tied housing with the opportunity to gain access to state-owned rented accommodation. Rent (Agriculture) Act 1976 now the Housing Act 1988 provided for security of tenure for those living in farm cottages. If the farmer needs the cottage she or he may apply to the local housing authority to have the protected worker rehoused.

[11] A selective state school.

Crisis

In the year before the crisis, Mum had fallen a couple of times, breaking her wrist once. She was hospitalized on both occasions. Mum was becoming increasingly anxious and compulsive in her behaviour. She was restricting both her own and Dad's diet and refusing to heat the bedroom. She was not able to go out and she was restricting Dad's movements, not wanting him to be out of the house. Dad was losing weight and finding it difficult to cope with caring. He was hospitalized once. The bungalow was dirty and the bedroom damp. Village community support was no longer sufficient.

In the summer of 2001, when Mum was almost 90, she was admitted to the small local hospital. She had a range of infections and was very frail. After an initial improvement in her overall condition, she deteriorated, became more immobilized, confused and compulsive. I realized after about six weeks that she was not going to be allowed home. Dad refused to accept this. He was not looking after himself. He spent every possible minute at the hospital, which fed him in the evening out of compassion.

I started looking around for nursing homes, secretly and guiltily. There were two near the village. Neither had places available. No privately-run[12] home was obliged to take applicants and, in an open market, could choose those they perceived as less difficult. Mum was classed as difficult. The homes were expensive, between £450 and £600 per week, whereas mum was eligible for public support of approximately £390 a week.[13] This would purchase a shared room in a nursing home miles away on the outskirts of a city. Dad would have great difficulty visiting. I visited the homes: some seemed reasonable, others frightened me. Generally, I was asked whether I could 'top up' (make up any difference in costs). I was able and prepared to pay. The good homes told me it took new residents up to four months to lose the confusion produced solely by the move. The consultant estimated that mum probably had between three and six months to live.

Mum was assessed as needing nursing care but what of Dad? He was nearly 89, had poor sight, was subject to blackouts, very weak from not eating and worn out with care and anxiety about Mum but he did not need nursing care. It was doubtful whether he would be seen by the public authority as in need of, and therefore financially eligible for, residential care.[14] If he was not then we would be obliged to pay approxi-

---

[12] There were no public homes.

[13] Their total weekly welfare income was about £140.

[14] Care homes are classified as either nursing or residential. Nursing homes have staff and facilities to nurse while residential homes provide general domestic and social care.

mately £250 extra a week. In any case there were no combined nursing and residential homes so he would be unable to live with Mum even if we could support the top-up for Mum and the total cost for Dad which was unrealistic.[15]

The hospital ward consisted of ten beds all occupied by the elderly waiting for institutional care. No one had left in two months. If one of the far-off homes had a place and were willing to take her, would the hospital authority deem it unreasonable to turn it down? Would social services insist on transferring her? I feared state discretion as I struggled to understand all the issues and deal with my dad's emotional turmoil as I finally took him to visit the local good homes with no places. He looked, answered politely when asked his opinion but saw and heard nothing.

In October I started my year-long sabbatical leave. It was impossible to concentrate when I felt so powerless to assist two hugely vulnerable people in what seemed likely to be the last few months of their lives together. I decided to move into their bungalow and look after them with any additional assistance I could muster. Because of the generation gap, my children had left home. My partner was slightly startled but wholly supportive. I told my university employers what I wanted to do: to take unpaid leave of absence for an uncertain period (based on the prognosis of the consultant). My head of department reacted in an exemplary way: quickly, positively and creatively. There was no questioning my actions. That I was on sabbatical leave and therefore had no teaching commitments made the practicalities easier.

First skirmishes

The consultant was supportive and agreed to discharge Mum, clearly happy to gain one bed back. Her general practitioner concurred. Both saw the issues as social and therefore not their concern. Mum had been provided with a social worker as a result of hospitalization who was responsible for putting the 'package' of social care together and gaining financial authorization.

I discussed adaptations, aids and handling with the National Health Service (NHS) occupational therapy team and they taught me how to move and handle Mum. I learned to nurse her from nursing staff. I found it difficult to establish who would be responsible for supplying the specialized equipment although I established that some came from NHS stores, some from social services and some came from a voluntary scheme run by the local Red Cross.

The first serious problem came with the paid care package. Mum

---

[15] A modest top up of £110 plus £250 a week would account for over 70 per cent of my net salary.

was assessed as needing 45 minutes assistance a day (one morning visit to wash and dress, one evening visit, to be put to bed). The small private agency that was to provide this on behalf of social services specified that, because of her limited mobility, she would need two workers for each visit. This ignored me. Social services would fund one worker because I was there. The agency was not willing to work with me because I was a family carer although I was going to provide 23.25 hours of care every day. I finally persuaded the owner of the agency that I would be an ally: reliable, professional and crucially not 'trouble-making family'.

Skills and life quality in a village

Mum was duly discharged. The bungalow was clean, warm and equipped. I received first-rate support from the occupational therapy team and quickly established a very good relationship with the care agency. The individual carers worked on their own, not wanting my assistance. The community nurse came regularly for three months to attend to the pressure sore mum gained in hospital. She and the carers checked informally that I was coping.

I was now an unpaid carer, with no professional identity, living in a southern village, 200 miles from my home, in a tiny two-roomed bungalow, with my parents after 30 years apart. I lived on a tiny state allowance available to carers.[16] However the combined resources (state pension and allowances) available to the household more than met our immediate needs. My existing financial commitments were modest. I had no mortgage and a partner to pay utilities bills at home. I had savings set aside to support one son at university.

We got on well but there were huge emotional and psychological challenges. Dad and I had to negotiate responsibilities because he saw it as his job to take care of Mum. She was very frail physically but much more problematic was her mental state. The battle, and I did see it as a battle, was to re-establish a firm, familiar routine to their lives which would gradually reconnect them with the wider world. Mum started to enjoy eating again, put on weight, gained strength and alertness, lost all signs of asthma and chest infections; her pressure sore, cuts and tears healed.

Mum had never used a wheelchair but to gain any mobility this was essential. Very reluctantly she agreed to go in it and we started to venture outside. She was ashamed of her physical disabilities, worried about peoples' reactions to her speech difficulties. However we were soon going out for walks around the village twice a day, in almost all weathers. I discovered a voluntary service that provided transport for disabled peo-

---

[16] £42 approximately – 18 per cent of the minimum state weekly pension.

ple so once a week we collected their pension, an important activity, and went shopping in the local market town. We would have tea and cakes in a cafe.

Dad gained weight and became visibly happier. He had lost confidence in negotiating the wider world on his own but he started to enjoy going out and meeting people because Mum was with him. Mum also re-engaged with the world. In hospital the doctor had talked of dementia as well as terminal frailty but both of these states were a result of insufficient care before hospitalization and, importantly, a product of hospitalization.

Relocation and the stroppy daughter

For Mum and Dad this was an ideal solution although they both worried about my job and my absence from home and family. I genuinely did not miss my paid job. However, it had played a very significant part in my life. How long would my employers tolerate my absence? Would I have to give up my professional life? What would I live on? Could I manage both jobs?

The only possible longer-term arrangement which would allow them to remain together outside institutional care and me to undertake paid work involved moving us all to my home in the north of England. However, many things needed to occur to enable such a move, including the installation of a disabled shower room and wheelchair access, as well as provision of all the specialist equipment (the existing equipment had to be returned) and paid care. All of this had to be arranged at long distance on the telephone or by post.

Our existing social worker advised me about a newly introduced scheme of direct payments whereby social services provided a sum of money, based on an assessment of needs, which enabled the individual to buy their own care. This scheme would give us flexibility.

Most functions fell within the responsibility of the social services department of the city council where I live. I began to encounter huge problems. I prepared a detailed written statement of the current position, the proposed action and a list of key contacts but I didn't know to whom to send it. It was pointless addressing it to a huge department but it was impossible to gain access to anyone to establish even this first step. There was one external line available to anyone who needed to contact any section (for a city of half a million). I rang endlessly but never managed to get through. I could not visit the department because I was 200 miles away and unable to leave.

In the end my partner took time off work and sat in a queue for half a day after which he managed to speak to a general information officer who promised to pass my statement on. He was told that they were very busy and everything was difficult. We finally obtained the contact details via another route. After many attempts to contact the specified person, I was told that Mum would need a social worker before anything could be done. I was given the number of the relevant social work team. They were never in the office or they were off sick. Finally I was told to whom to send my statement and Mum was eventually allocated a social worker whose first words to me were, 'So you are the stroppy[17] daughter.' This was after approximately three weeks of fruitless attempts to contact anyone.

We quickly established that although Mum would be eligible in principle for assistance for adaptations, it would be impossible to give any time-scale for undertaking these. It would be impossible to provide her with any equipment or care until she had been assessed by the appropriate team. This would be done after she arrived although it would then take up to a month to arrange because the department was so overworked.[18] I explained that their fellow professionals had undertaken such an assessment recently and that they could fax it through to the department, thereby avoiding any duplicate work. This was not acceptable. I was told that finances to support care were very tight but that Mum would require two paid carers all the time and under no circumstances would I be included in any care assessment. Nobody had heard of the direct payment scheme.

Undaunted, I decided that I would finance the adaptations, generally available specialist equipment[19] and temporary ramp (a total cost of £6,750). I appealed to the community nursing service for help with the other equipment. They were happy to have a list faxed through to them and to track it down.

There was no way of avoiding social services if I wanted financial support for paid care. I persisted with our assigned social worker and persuaded her that I wasn't a demanding troublemaker but a person who was going to make minimum demands and take responsibility for my

---

[17] A colloquialism meaning bossy and argumentative with overtones of irrationality!

[18] She would therefore have been totally confined to a normal bed unable to move, vulnerable to chest infections, pressure sores and total immobility: all the conditions we had worked so hard to recover from.

[19] The total cost amounted to approximately 20 per cent of my annual salary.

[20] I had found out independently that the city council was not using the scheme sufficiently to meet its targets so I reasoned that if I pressed the case, the authority would react positively. The 12th annual report of the Chief Inspector of Social Services 2002–3 reported on the reluctance of social services departments to make use of these provisions for the elderly and urged them to overcome 'organizational and cultural barriers' to their use. There were only 1032 nationwide. New direct payment regulations in 2003 require all local councils to make direct payments to all individuals who are eligible and want them.

parents' care, particularly if we could use the direct payments scheme.[20] She agreed to put an emergency case to the appropriate panel while she found out more about direct payments. This care package, which provided Mum with the same level of care as she had been receiving but with two agency carers, was approved.

Finally after two months of immense frustration and anxiety, there were sufficient elements in place to risk the move. Mum and Dad reluctantly gave up the tenancy of their home in the country. It was frightening for them, becoming totally dependent on my good will. A Red Cross ambulance we hired brought us north.

Care, work and carework

The next few weeks were consumed with intense work and anxiety. Mum's social worker visited shortly after we arrived. She was keen to find ways to facilitate my return to paid work and had established that the direct payments scheme would be the best vehicle. Mum's needs were assessed by an elderly care team. The social worker prepared a proposal on the basis of this assessment for the relevant committee to release the funds for 98 hours of paid care per week (49 hours each for two workers). This was a high level of formal support and enough to enable me to return to full-time paid work. I thought that the requirement of two full-time carers wholly unnecessary. In retrospect, I am glad that I did not refuse this level of support. The assessors understood that caring is an endurance activity with an almost inevitable intensification of needs.

We advertised for carers through the government-run employment agency. They offered one candidate stating 'this was a good one'. I did not recognize the significance of this statement. We recruited the 'good one', our first and only full-time worker who stayed until Mum died. We were provided subsequently with a number of additional potential candidates to consider, none of whom were remotely suitable. After many frustrating and distressing attempts, we gave up trying to recruit from the unemployed because there was no pool of labour, even though the pay rate was significantly above the national minimum wage.[21]

We considered part-time workers because there was interest in such work in our poor inner city area but in all cases the individual would have been economically disadvantaged by accepting the job.[22] We therefore needed part-timers not in receipt of state benefits so we recruited

---

[21] Care work in the private sector is almost always at or just above the minimum statutory wage.

[22] Although the Labour government has made efforts to ensure that people who work in low paid work are no worse off than if they remained on state welfare (the benefit trap), there are still problems.

three excellent postgraduate students, all of whom had undertaken care work before and been trained on moving and handling.

The transfer from my care to paid care went reasonably smoothly. Dad and Mum were now living in someone else's house and being cared for with little privacy by strangers but they were in a familiar home and the carers were employed solely to meet their needs. I cared for them in the evenings and the weekends. They were stoical and adapted.

I had two jobs now: unpaid carer and surrogate employer. For most of the next two years we had four direct employees and a contract of services with an agency. I organized wages, national insurance and tax, weekly rotas, holidays, sick leave, invoices, accounts and staff grievances: in effect all the strains of running a small business. In addition I had to grapple with frequent problems with the benefits agency which provided Mum and Dad's range of state benefits.

There were daily uncertainties. I never knew how long any arrangement would last. One example of this was the sudden withdrawal of the agency carers who continued to come night and morning so as to extend our hours of coverage. I received a letter that arrived on 2 April to say that they would no longer be providing the service from the 31 March. Luckily their workers had alerted me informally to difficulties the week before.

Nonetheless, the arrangements worked, precariously. My employers had continued to be supportive of my prolonged absence putting me under no pressure at all. Four months after the move north I notified them that I was returning to my sabbatical work. I now added a third job, paid work. It was not easy given I was a full-time carer for over 100 hours a week. It was much worse when I returned from sabbatical leave in the autumn of 2002. The combination of the uncertainties of care with the imperatives of teaching was exhausting, intellectually and emotionally, in addition to the physical demands of caring on my own and running a complex operation as soon as I stopped paid work.

The community nursing service played a key role throughout. At each stage when I felt that the arrangements were reaching breaking point, the senior nurse offered constructive, proactive support. In time, she arranged respite care. Every two months, Dad and Mum would go to a nursing home run by the community nursing service (and therefore free) for two weeks. My carefully prepared care plan was breezily ignored with comments about over protective or interfering families yet Mum would return with significant cuts and bruising, weakened by infections. The situation was worse after Dad died. I felt guilty but this arrangement was vital: it gave me a break. In 2003 the NHS informed us that they were withdrawing the service at the end of year due to staff shortages. I was devastated.

Ramps, lifts and brick walls

Very shortly after we arrived we were visited by the aids and adaptations liaison officer of social services. The temporary moveable ramp that we had purchased[23] was far too steep and dangerous for carers, Mum and Dad. The officer was helpful, quickly establishing that Mum was eligible for financial support, and recommended the installation of an electronic step lift as an emergency priority. The authority however was incapable of translating this recommendation into action. Myriad processes had to be completed involving three departments: adaptations in social services for technical specifications, housing for financial support, planning for building permission.[24] The working practices involved were literally impossible to believe, more appropriate in a nineteenth century Dickensian novel.

Finally after social services and then housing departments had ground through their procedures, the planning officer objected to the step lift and wanted a wooden ramp. Social services were not willing to consider a ramp because the gradient was too steep (1:11 instead of the required 1:12 while our temporary ramp, in use for eight months by then, was 1:7). My partner (who has been a senior officer in this and a number of other local authorities) and I had used every conceivable skill we possessed to try to cut through these processes. We had chased progress systematically and relentlessly and used all forms of leverage, including local politicians. It was all fruitless.

Eight months into the process, after our full-time carer had fractured her skull by slipping off the temporary ramp with Mum in the wheelchair, we arranged a site meeting between social services and planning departments on our doorstep. There seemed to be no recognition of the consequences of their bureaucratic impasse. We gave up and the next week built a wooden ramp with a 1:11 gradient without planning permission (which we obtained retrospectively). This cost £1,100, compared to the proposed £13,500 step lift. It solved all problems instantly. My greatest regret is that I had not done this at the start.

The end of an era

Dad, aged 90, died instantly of heart failure in our home while helping to move Mum in November 2002. Mum lived on with worsening but still reasonable quality of life until October 2003 when she died peacefully in her bed in our home on Dad's birthday, aged 91.

---

[23] The only access to our house is via very steep steps.

[24] We live in a conservation area: specific permission is required from the local authority before external changes to properties can be undertaken.

2 The legal context

Although the activity of caring for the elderly is contained within a policy framework of 'social care' or 'care in the community', the legal framework is widely recognized as fragmented, even chaotic (Mandelstam, 2001; McDonald, 2001). In contrast to the care of children, there is no single originating statute to provide legal clarity or to encapsulate the values which might inform any policy or procedures (McDonald, 2001). The relevant legal provisions are spread out in legislation dating back as far as 1948.

Historically, health care has been provided by the NHS and social care by local government. The 1970 Local Authority (Social Services) Act established local government social services departments to provide an organizational focus for a range of duties and responsibilities owed to, among others, children, the disabled and the elderly. While the NHS is provided free at the point of use and funded through insurance levied on the working population, local government services are not necessarily free at the point of service and are funded through a combination of revenue transfers from central government, locally raised taxation and charges. Both these areas of welfare state activity have been subject to major changes in the last 25 years. Conservative governments have changed the relationship between the welfare state and the market through the privatization of public services and the creation of market mechanisms within the public sector in an attempt to reduce public expenditure but also to change the relationship between the providers and recipients of services. The aim has been to oblige providers to treat users more as consumers. One mechanism for this has been the provision of financial assistance in the form of state cash for individuals to enable them to purchase care in the market (Lewis, 1998: 3).

These changes brought a considerable reduction in the autonomy of local government with increased regulation from the centre. The return of a Labour government in 1997 has resulted in substantially greater funding of the NHS and some areas of local government responsibilities. There has been no relaxation in the drive towards privatization and 'marketization' of public services[25] or of central government supervision which takes the form of management by a plethora of centrally-imposed and specific performance targets for service provision.

---

[25] Dean (1996:16-18) describes these processes as promoting the commercial welfare sector through the use of new public management doctrines (treating users of services as customers); introduction of 'quasi-markets' (separating bureaucratically and financially the commissioning of services and their provision within local authorities); linking payment of services to quality of services (the competent citizen becomes the successful consumer by getting the best out of services).

Social care has been in the epicentre of these changes. Historically the NHS cared for both acute and chronic illness. The elderly who were deemed to be in need of nursing care could be catered for by long-term and free at the point of use geriatric facilities. Social services offered social care support to the elderly through the provision of a range of services, including help with domestic activities, the provision of prepared meals, day centres and residential homes. Local authorities had the power to charge for these services and some would exercise their discretion to levy a means-tested contribution.

During the 1980s the Conservative government provided financial incentives to stimulate the development of a private market in nursing and residential care homes (Palmer, 2000; Ginn and Arber, 1999). This was achieved by providing individual elderly people with the funds to cover the costs through a means-tested benefit funded from general taxation. Thus the poor elderly had state funds to purchase domiciliary care. Financial pressure was also brought to bear on local government to privatize existing residential facilities. Many elderly were moved from NHS hospitals into the private sector,[26] while many more poor elderly people entered residential care rather than receiving home-based services provided through local authority budgets.[27] The result was a massive explosion in capitalized, private provision. While the policy achieved the dual objectives of producing a flourishing private alternative to the public sector, albeit heavily reliant on state funds, and establishing the concept of choice for the poor, it also resulted in an unlimited bill for the central exchequer.[28]

All of these changes were carried out under the existing legislation on social care. However, by 1989 there was mounting concern over costs and also about the impact of the incentives to institutionalize the poor elderly. The White Paper (Department for Health, 1989) heralded a change in policy to support the elderly within the community wherever possible. The 1990 NHS and Community Care Act gave responsibility for all such care to local authority social services departments. The funds which were providing individuals with means-tested benefits were reallocated as revenue grants to local authorities to provide services in the area of social care. Local authorities were expected to charge for services provided although the level of these charges was left to their discre-

---

[26] In 1999 more than half a million people were in private nursing and residential homes. Only 27 per cent funded themselves entirely (Palmer, 2000: 464).

[27] The number of NHS long stay beds reduced by 38 per cent between 1983–99 (a loss of 21,300 beds) and the number of private nursing home places increased by 900 per cent (an increase of 141,000 beds) (Sutherland, 1999: chapter 4).

[28] Expenditure grew from £350m in 1985 to £2.5bn in 1993–4 (Sutherland, 1999: chapter 4).

tion. However funds were made available on the basis that 85 per cent would be spent in the private sector (Land and Lewis, 1998: 55).

The explicit aim of the policy was to produce a needs-led rather than a service provision driven system (Mandelstam, 2001:17). However another, implicit, aim of the policy was to curb expenditure – each authority had a finite yearly budget to fulfil their duties which meant that meeting all needs would be impossible. The NHS and Community Care Act contained just one new legal provision to introduce the new system and to attempt to balance needs and resources. Section 47 introduced a duty to undertake an assessment of needs and to consider the provision for these needs which would be met using the existing legislative provisions. Thus needs were separated from provision but linked through eligibility criteria which each local authority established independently in such a way that the threshold for eligibility was set according to available funds (Lewis and Land, 1998). Social services could meet needs by providing their own services or through funding provision by others. The latter was encouraged.

While social services had a duty to assess the needs of anyone who met the criteria, individuals would be means tested to establish their financial eligibility. The numbers of elderly entering residential homes dropped and the number of those receiving care at home increased. The distinction between nursing and social care, never a very clear one in the context of the elderly, became even more blurred. The expectation that nursing care in old age would be provided through the NHS and therefore would be free was thwarted for all those who were not the poorest. This led to considerable public outcry (Sutherland, 1999: chapter 4). There is evidence to suggest that the quality of services provided within the private sector dropped because of the capping of funds from local authorities (Palmer, 2000).

While these changes required little primary legislation, they were accompanied by a plethora of secondary legislation, policy and practice guidance (Department for Health, 1990, 1998, 2001 and 2003), the legal status of which is often extremely hard to determine (Mandelstam, 2001). Local authorities or other appropriate bodies are given duties, powers and responsibilities with varying degrees of discretion. The complexity and sometimes contradictory nature of these provisions is reflected in the difficulties encountered with enforceability (Mandelstam, 2001: chapter 3). Overseeing public bodies is generally undertaken through forms of regulation such as guidance, internal organization procedures, inspection and public accounting procedures (Braye and Preston-Shoot, 1999). Individual redress is limited to access to internal complaint procedures and to the relevant ombudsman. While individuals may be able to use public law procedures to challenge the decision-making process, the courts have been reluctant to become involved, particularly where there are policy tensions between needs and resources. In recent years individuals, who are deeply affected by changes in policies which have led to withdrawal or profound changes in services, have increasingly resorted to public law (Palmer, 2000). Private law remedies are usually not available because there is no privity of contract and no concept of a 'public service contract' in English law (Palmer, 2000: 461). New statutory provisions may change this position.

Did Mum have a right to 'choose' to go home?

When Mum was hospitalized, she was allocated a local authority social worker who undertook an assessment of her needs in accordance with section 47, NHS and Community Care Act 1990. She was assessed as needing considerable levels of care when she left hospital. Her pre-hospitalization arrangements of informal (spousal) care supported by a limited amount of paid care and some neighbourhood support was now inadequate. However the second element of section 47 involves a consideration of provision. While she met the eligibility criteria for provision, the level of support that would have been necessary to meet her needs at home would be deemed not feasible because of cost and the absence of providers. In the affluent south, there was a limited supply of paid carers for the authority to purchase. The authority would deny her choice and meet her needs through meeting costs in a home. Mum would have had no legal grounds to challenge this decision.[29] Thus she has no right to choose where and how she should be looked after. The legislation provides her with an inferred right to a local authority conducted needs assessment (Dean, 1996: 15).

Could mum have chosen her institutional home?

Despite the guidelines (Department for Health, 1990) urging maximum choice, in practice she would have had no choice. Firstly because she was not able physically to leave the hospital. Secondly, and importantly, the sum allocated would only purchase a bed in a shared room at distance. Thirdly, the courts have confirmed that publicly-funded residents have no right to choose a home.[30]

Could Mum have refused to leave the hospital?

Hospital discharges are a matter of considerable bureaucratic tensions between the NHS and social services departments. To meet its own gov-

---

[29] The courts allow a local authority to take account of its own resources in making an assessment *R v Sefton CC ex p. Help the Aged and Blanchard* (1997) 4 All ER 449. See also *R v Gloustershire CC ex p Barry* (1997) 2 All ER 1.

[30] *R v Wandsworth London Borough ex p. Beckwith* (1996) 1 All ER 129.

ernment performance targets, the NHS needs a high turnover in bed occupancies but these will not be met if the elderly's socially-defined needs are not provided for swiftly through the assessment process. However, the duty to assess and, where appropriate, to meet the individual's needs may take time. Delayed discharge is known colloquially as 'bed blocking'. There has been mounting government pressure in the form of guidance on the two organizations to cooperate and to ensure swift onward passage of the elderly. This pressure has recently been formalized into the Community Care (Delayed Discharges) Act 2003 which imposes penalties on social services departments for delayed discharges. So Mum would not have been able to refuse to leave unless she could demonstrate to the satisfaction of a court that the section 47 process had not been undertaken appropriately.

Could Mum have discharged herself and gone home?
Mum was not obliged legally to accept an assessment so she could have discharged herself and gone home although she would not have survived long at home.[31] In practice she would not have had the power to challenge the judgement of the professionals that it was too risky.[32]

Could Dad have stayed with Mum by accompanying her to a home?
The social worker would also have had the duty to assess Dad under section 47 in two ways: first, as in need of care himself but, secondly, as a carer. It is not clear whether the first of these occurred. Dad was not aware of it. I can deduce that he was assessed as having needs for social care but that he did not meet the eligibility thresholds because with the pressure on resources, the eligibility level is set very high in most authorities. Thus he would not have been eligible for residential accommodation which might have allowed him to accompany Mum if an appropriate home existed. This would have had to be 'dual registered' under the Care Homes Act 1984.[33]

---

[31] This point begs many moral and philosophical issues about personal choice. Who determines whether someone is managing? What criteria are used? Mum and Dad might have preferred to live a very poor quality life together without outside interference. They would have sustained injury or succumbed to infections but that would have been their choice although the extent to which Mum should rely on Dad to care even if he was willing to do it raises further issues.

[32] There can be compulsory admission to hospital under the Mental Health Act 1983 and for those who are not mentally disordered, compulsory removal from home under section 47 of the National Assistance Act. It is very unlikely that she would have met either criterion.

[33] The home meets the requirements for registration as a residential and nursing home. The 1984 Act has been replaced by the 2000 Care Standards Act, see note 25.

Did Dad and I have rights as carers?

Dad was entitled to have his needs assessed under section 47 of the NHS and Community Care Act 1990 as a carer willing to provide 'substantial and regular care'. This assessment was conditional on Mum's assessment. When I arrived there was also a similar duty to assess my needs and to reassess Mum. The 2000 Carers and Disabled Children Act also provides for the independent assessment of carers.[34] My unpaid labour as carer changed the needs assessment; the provision requirements and costs were substantially reduced, the policy guidelines encouraging 'home care' rather than 'care home' could be met and the arrangement was low risk to social services as long as I coped.

The decade between the two Acts has brought about more recognition, encapsulated in the National Strategy for Carers document, of the importance of informal care to the care in the community policy which could not function without it (Department for Health, 1999, chapter 2).[35] The aim of the assessment is to support carers in their caring role and to help the carers maintain their own health and wellbeing.[36] Social services are empowered under the 2000 Act to provide modest grant funds directly to carers to purchase services such as respite care.[37] As Dean points out, the citizen's right to receive a substantial service (rather than a formal needs assessment) can be contingent on the imposition of an obligation on a close relative as an informal carer (1996: 15). The aim is to ensure that this care is 'sustainable' and that the carer, wherever possible, retains a relationship with the labour market.

When we moved north, the assessment and subsequent care plan recognized my wish to return to paid work while continuing to provide substantial care. I was also able to obtain, as a carer, free respite care because it was organized through the district nursing service.

---

[34] 1995 Carers (Recognition and Services) Act introduced the carer's right to assessment in tandem with the service user.

[35] Britain has 5.7 million carers; one in six households contains a carer; 3.3 million women; 2.4 million men; most likely to be aged 45–64; 9 out of 10 care for a relative; 2 out of 10 for a partner or spouse; 4 out of 10 for parent(s); half look after someone aged over 75 (Department for Health, 1999:17).

[36] The rights of carers have been strengthened by the enactment of the Carers (Equal Opportunities) Act 2004. It will come into force in April 2005. This places duties on local authorities to inform carers of their rights and to consider their wishes to work, study or have leisure activities. It also gives local authorities powers to obtain assistance for carers from health, housing and education authorities.

[37] The government increased funds available in 2004/5 and also introduced more flexibility, see www.carers.gov.uk/2004_05carers_grant_guidance.pdf (accessed 30/07/04).

Are care plans transferable?

The guidelines (Department for Health, 1990) require social services to draw up a care plan that documents needs and provision. While this must have been undertaken, we never saw such a document. When Mum moved to a metropolitan district authority (MDC), policy guidelines required a reassessment of the care plan in the light of new circumstances. Each local authority is an autonomous body setting its own eligibility criteria, albeit acting within national guidelines. The county council assessment had no validity for the metropolitan district authority whose social services were obliged to undertake their own section 47 assessment which they could not do until Mum was physically present.

Could mum choose and 'control' or trust her carers?

When this assessment took place, the carer element in the assessment of Mum's needs had changed. Dad was still available, although disturbed by moving, but the quantity of informal care was reduced by my stated aim of returning to paid work. Mum was assessed as needing 49 hours of paid care from two carers per week and my informal care for the rest of the time. She met the metropolitan district authority's eligibility criteria for both levels of need and financial support.

The new element was the method of provision. In the county council the paid care was provided by a private care agency and funded directly by social services. In the metropolitan district authority Mum had access to the direct payments scheme. This scheme, when first introduced in 1996 under the then Community Care (Direct Payments) Act, was designed to enable disabled people whose needs had been assessed under section 47 to purchase directly the services they needed with funds provided by social services. Initially the scheme had an upper age limit of 65 but was extended in 1999 to the elderly.[38] Mum was deemed eligible. At the age of 90 Mum became an employer. She entered into a contract for services (the provision of care workers) with a care agency and employment contracts with her carers.

The aim of the direct payments scheme as set out in the guidelines (Department for Health, 2000, now 2003) was to increase choice, flexibility and independence for the disabled. The scheme reflects the approach of the disability movement that campaigns for rights for rather than duties owed to the disabled. However the scheme also highlights issues relating to service quality control and the abuse of power in the

---

[38] The present legal framework is provided by section 57 of the Health and Social Care Act 2001, section 17A of the Children Act 1989 and the Community Care, Services for Carers and Children's Services (Direct Payments) England Regulations 2003. Local Authorities in England are also provided with guidance (Department for Health, 2003).

care sector. When social services provide care services directly or contract with an agency for these, the user of the services has no contractual relationship with the provider. Contract terms are enforced by social services. This is an area of considerable concern for users if the quality of the service is poor or if the parties change the terms of the contract. Palmer (2000) has discussed the limited legal redress available to users. Any complaint from the user over quality must be directed towards the social services care manager rather than the supplier of the services although this is not, in my experience, made clear to users. As Dean points out:

> 'The *business* of service provision is uncoupled from the *politics* of welfare: policy-makers may evade responsibility for policy failures (because customers are encouraged to blame the providers of services)' (1996: 18).

These difficulties also arise, often in acute form, with residential care arrangements with residents, funded and placed in homes through social services, powerless to enforce care plans or to resist changes negotiated between the purchaser and provider (Palmer, 2000: 468–71). The introduction of the 1999 Third Party Contracts Act may provide some improvement by allowing users to be parties to the contract (Palmer, 2000: 472).

Under the direct payments scheme the user is in a direct contractual relationship with the provider of services and therefore able to negotiate and enforce the terms of the contract, at least in theory.[39] Mum's experience shows the interplay of market and state in this area. The agency employed by the county council social services was small, new and dependent on building up a good reputation with the purchaser. It was responsive to user needs. The agency employed directly by Mum in the metropolitan district authority was big, suffered from acute labour supply problems and had what seemed to be an unproductive relationship with its main purchaser, the authority.[40] So when the agency lost its metropolitan district authority social services contract, it was no longer viable and withdrew unilaterally, without notice, from its private contract with Mum. Undoubtedly it was in breach of contract but Mum was not in a position to seek redress.

The power relations with the four directly employed carers were

---

[39] Some commentators have argued that this type of cash transfer is evidence of the development of the concept of social rights (Lewis, 1998), others (Dean, 1996) argue that it is a strengthening of civil rights at the expense of social and political rights.

[40] All the available agencies seemed to be in same position.

different. The job specifications clearly spelt out not only the terms of the employment but also stressed the requirement to respect Mum's wishes and her relationship with Dad. The ability to 'hire and fire' was important but so also was the need to develop trust because she was dependent on the carers. There was a need for a management function which I undertook because she was unable to do this. Employing a range of staff minimized their exhaustion and frictions. It also guarded against the potential for abuse. There has been alarming evidence in recent years of abuse of vulnerable people, including the elderly, in care homes but also within their own homes (Sutherland, 1999; Walker and Maltby, 1997: 99; Brammer and Biggs, 1998).[41] There is potential for the recipient of care to abuse the provider particularly when the care is undertaken within a 'private' domestic setting. However the shortage of carers in the market provides the wider context: choice once again becomes an illusion.

Could Mum have remained at home under any circumstances?
Mum's final involvement with the assessment process occurred at the time of Dad's death when her circumstances changed. There is a duty under section 47 and under the guidelines to undertake regular reviews of the care plan. I gather in our case that this was every three months although it did not happen which was perfectly acceptable to both sides. However, I triggered this process inadvertently after Dad died by raising the issue of care when I was away. Our social worker very quickly intimated that a home would probably be cheaper if Mum required more finance and in any case if she put forward a case for more resources the relevant committee might review the existing resources. The authority has the power to do this if, after it has undertaken the review procedure appropriately and taken account of all relevant circumstances, it determines that the balance between needs and available resources has changed. Mum would have been unlikely to succeed in any legal challenge to this decision (Palmer, 2000; *R v Lancashire* CC ex p RADAR [1996]: *The Times* 12 July). This nightmare prospect was averted by inertia. Through overwork or tacit understanding our social worker did not undertake the review procedure and after a few weeks of agonizing uncertainty we continued as before. I funded the extra care.

---

[41] General regulation of homes has been undertaken through annual inspections by social services. The Care Standards Act 2000 establishes a new independent regulatory body, the National Care Standards Commission to cover homes and home care provision. It provides for the provision of a national protection of vulnerable adults list which will document any worker who has been deemed to have abused a vulnerable adult.

Did Mum have a right to adaptations in her home?
Part I of this chapter told the story of aids and adaptations. The impenetrable arrangements for the provision of aids are reflected in the legislative context. Various statutes require the provision of aids under different, discretionary circumstances. Some aids must be provided free through the NHS, others must be paid for. Some aids can be provided under the Chronically Sick and Disabled Act 1970 and can be subject to social services means tested charge.

Mum's inability to obtain adaptations in my home turns out to be wholly consistent with the national picture. This 'service' is a true and enduring nightmare (Mandelstam, 2001: 30–31). One key reason lies in the origins of the care in the community policy. While there are specific powers to provide services within a number of Acts,[42] housing issues were not included within the ambit of the 1990 community care policy. There has been therefore a split function within authorities and in some cases between authorities, between housing and social care with no duty to cooperate despite a torrent of policy and practice guidelines from central government.[43] The position has once again been reviewed and as of 2003 new regulations required collaboration between NHS and local authorities.[44]

Rights to social welfare?
Has social welfare been the subject of human rights measures? The Universal Declaration of Human Rights provides a right to social security (article 22) and a right to an adequate standard of living, including medical care and necessary social services (article 25). Article 9 of the International Covenant on Economic, Social and Cultural Rights covers the provision of social security including social insurance. CEDAW provides equal access to health care (article 12) and rights to family benefits (article 13) but nothing specific on social care. The United Kingdom has incorporated the European Convention on Human Rights into domestic legislation through the Human Rights Act 1998.[45] However its

---

[42] 1948 National Assistance Act, 1970 Chronically Sick and Disabled Act.

[43] In county council areas social services are a county function but housing is a district council function. Metropolitan district areas undertake both functions. The 1999 Health Act creates a new duty of cooperation between NHS bodies and local authorities in England and Wales. The Local Government Act 2000 requires public authorities to collaborate on financing services.

[44] In our own authority the woeful position has been recognized and reorganization has taken place to try to tackle the problems of delivery to targets. Tough new targets have been imposed by central government through the Performance Assessment Framework.

[45] It came into force in 2000.

substantive provisions relate to civil and political, not social, rights.[46] It is not clear to what extent the procedural legal culture underpinning the human rights framework will permeate the highly discretionary policy area of social care provision. There is some evidence that it is having an impact on the courts' willingness to intervene in public law cases (Preston-Shoot, Roberts and Vernon, 2001:11).

The European Union[47] has gradually developed its own approach to human rights.[48] In 2000 it proclaimed a Charter of Fundamental Rights of the European Union which draws on both the European Convention on Human Rights and the Council of Europe's Social Charter. However there is scant reference to social welfare.[49] Legislation outlawing discrimination on the basis of age, introduced in 2006, is limited to the area of employment.[50]

While none of the provisions relating to care are constructed as the rights of individuals, they constitute the social rights of citizens in a welfare state. Marshall (1950) saw these rights to education, health and social care, housing and income maintenance as the unique achievement of the twentieth century, building on the civil and political rights obtained in the eighteenth and nineteenth century. Citizenship is constituted through their provision. In the United Kingdom welfare state these entitlements have been provided collectively, based on politically-determined criteria. Most are discretionary. Classical liberalism has always been uneasy about positive rights (requiring the state to ensure provision) preferring negative rights (protecting individual freedoms and property rights). Reich (1964) attempted to redefine this 'government lar-

---

[46] The United Kingdom is also a signatory to the European Social Charter adopted by the Council of Europe 1961 part 11 (revised 1996 and in force 1999). Paragraph 24 requires retired workers to have access to pensions affording a decent standard of living, paragraph 25 requires other retired persons to have access to social assistance to meet needs. Both are state obligations not individual rights and redress is through collective complaint via a trade union or non-governmental body.

[47] The United Kingdom is a member of the European Union and as such is bound by its enactments.

[48] It has concentrated on rights to support the economic objectives of the union. 'The European Union Charter of Fundamental Social Rights of 1989 and Social Protocols (or Social Chapters) to the 1993 and 1997 Maastricht and Amsterdam treaties ... sought to build upon earlier measures in the Treaty of Rome relating to freedom of movement, health and safety at work and the equal treatment of men and women' (Dean, 2004: 12).

[49] Article 34: the union recognizes and respects the entitlement to social security benefits and social services (where these have been established by member states).

[50] The legislation is required to implement a European Employment Directive. Anti-discrimination rights are also provided under the Disability Discrimination Act 1995, Sex Discrimination Act 1975 and Race Relations Act 1976. The focus is on securing equal civil and political rights.

gesse' as the new property, as part of the logic of individual ownership. Benefits, available from the state once eligibility is established, are entitlements not gifts. Eligibility is based on principles that do not depend on individual personality or status.

However in the last decades of the twentieth century, welfare provision in this form came under increasing critical pressure. Neo-conservatives sought to reduce the role of the state in the provision of social rights, on the presumption that the market was a better method of provision. Through the introduction of markets and quasi-market mechanisms, the more emancipatory (in the sense of removed from the commodified form of the market) social rights are transformed into civil rights (based upon purchasing). Welfare rights activists were also critical of the discretionary, bureaucratic method of provision and argued from the standpoint of doctrinal human rights that individuals should have a right to social care and an adequate income. Their suspicion of the range of powers available to the state is echoed in the analysis of post-modernists such as Foucault (1979). He argued that power in a modern state is not exercised purely through force but by sophisticated surveillance and disciplinary processes associated in part with the administration of welfare rights and social legislation. The processes of governance have entered all areas of our lives, dissolving the liberal boundaries between public and private, constructing us as particular types of individuals: informal carers, care workers, active citizens who purchase and choose their care. To exercise rights, citizens must submit to legal definitions and pinpointed regulatory forms. Welfare pluralism involving the provision of services through informal, voluntary and commercial mechanisms while funded by the state has not lessened this form of governance. It has simply added new processes of standard setting, monitoring and regulation.

Our story can be set within these wider debates relating to caring in a 'late modern' welfare state. We all benefited substantially from the availability of social rights provided by the state, Mum in particular because she was poor and physically vulnerable but I did too. I would not have been able to care for her and return to paid work without these. However we had to expend huge amounts of emotional and intellectual energy to wrestle with the discretionary nature of state provision and limitations in implementation. Being 'stroppy' substituted for the exercise of rights. Even then with all our skills, we were defeated in some areas. My economic power largely ameliorated the consequences of the inability of the state to deliver, thus insulating Mum and I from the dire consequences. We were beneficiaries of new forms of welfare pluralism, through the direct payment scheme, but the responsibilities of formal employment were an enormous cost to pay to achieve some control over the methods of care. Civil rights are in the end no substitute for functioning exercisable social rights. We experienced the overwhelming power of governance, social control, in all aspects of our lives; our home became a public space, surveilled and regulated, occupied by carers, accessible to many more on demand, the rhythms of our lives were moulded by external processes, our minds were colonized. We had to struggle to define care and responsibility to meet our social norms in spite of the rules, in Fraser's (1997) terms, to engage in the politics of needs interpretation.

Rights, justice or care?

It would be possible to conclude that this has been a tale about the lack of individual rights or the gap between rights and their implementation or an example of Foucaultian governmentality. Depending on the approach it might lead to a call for more individual rights, stronger legal provisions to limit discretion or suggestions of strategies to limit the power of governance. However I want to place this study of 'actual' caring within the wider feminist concept of the ethic of care in an era of globalization.

While economic globalization based on neo-liberal market economics is challenging the ability of states to protect their welfare policies, political globalization is entrenching a particular discourse of human rights, based on a liberal individualist conception of rights (Dean, 2004: 7). This human subject is self-interested, competitive and wholly autonomous and in need of rights to maintain order. Such an approach focuses on the rights associated with a free market and the ability to own property, and seeks to harness the state to the pursuit of these goals. This orthodoxy has been challenged within the global policy arena by Sen (1997; UNDP, 2000) who has argued that human freedoms are the goals rather than the side effects of development. The aim of development is therefore to enhance human capabilities. Martha Nussbaum (2002) has also considered the relationship between gender, justice and development. While recognizing that the 'language of rights has proven enormously valuable to women', she thinks that the 'rights framework is shaky' because: it is intellectually contested (there are many different conceptions of what rights are); it has been 'associated historically with political and civil liberties and only more recently with economic and social entitlements'; it has ignored the specific claims of women; it has been associated with negative liberty; and it is insensitive to non-western traditions of thought (2002: 47-48). Instead she too argues strongly in favour of capabilities. The central question to be asked is 'What is a woman actually able to do and to be?' Nussbaum considers there are some central human functional capabilities that should be available to every individual. These are life, bodily health, bodily integrity, sense, imagination and thought, emotions, play, practical reason, affiliation and control over one's environment (2002: 60–62). Thus the questions in relation to emotions are 'Is she able to love those who love and care for her?'; 'How can this capability be provided?'

Nussbaum's capability approach is rooted in the abstract universal individual which has been the subject of trenchant critiques from feminist legal scholars (see Barnett, 1998). Another view of the human subject, that it is vulnerable and requires mechanisms for mutual cooperation and support to survive and that there is a need for rights to recognize human interdependence, is one associated with feminist approaches. Feminist work on the political concept of the ethic of care (Gilligan, 1982; Tronto, 1994; Sevenhuijsen, 1998; Williams, 2001; Ellis, 2004; Drakapoulou, 2000) provides further insights into this conception. At present, as Dean (2004) argues, human rights are constructed upon an ethic of work and a set of assumptions about the role of work in the maintenance of human society while failing to accommodate any corresponding ethic of care.

> 'Work is seen … as the primary responsibility of the individual and the first bulwark against poverty or social exclusion. Care … is seen at best as something that must be accommodated to work' (2004: 18–19).

Williams argues that care 'should be recognized as a central political and intellectual issue for social policy' (2001: 469) while Sevenhuijsen calls for a 'democratic ethic of care' that 'starts from the idea that everybody needs care and is (in principle at least) capable of care giving' (2000: 15). The citizen must be understood not as an abstract individual or 'equal rights holder' but as a 'self in relationship'. Vulnerability is part of ordinary human subjectivity (2000: 19) and care is as much a daily practice as work.

> 'A feminist ethic of care displaces the dominant discourse of human rights in favour of an understanding that human freedom is built upon interdependency: it is our need for, and capacity to care that precede and shape our rights and responsibilities' (Dean, 2004, 19).

Wærness (2001) argues that this approach allows us to understand both autonomous and involved aspects of human life and avoids constructing a dichotomy in welfare policy between dependence and autonomy or between justice and care.

Fisher and Tronto (1990) have distinguished four phases of the ethic of care, each accompanied by different competences and values. Their scheme provides a way of analyzing the justice of existing care arrangements in terms of both process and outcome (Ellis, 2004: 31). 'Caring about' (value of attentiveness) is not conditional on love; it is an orientation rather than a motivation. It involves recognizing others' needs for care. 'Caring for' (value of responsibility) means taking responsibility for meeting identified needs. It requires more detailed knowledge than caring about. 'Taking care of' (value of competence) is the concrete work of directly meeting others' needs for care to a competent standard. 'Care receiving' (value of responsiveness) consists in providing care in ways that are responsive to the needs and interests of the care receiver (Sevenhuijsen, 1998; Ellis, 2004). These phases are often gendered: powerful (male) policy makers undertake the first two while far less powerful women undertake the latter two.

Policy makers in the United Kingdom, including central government and the Equal Opportunities Commission, are developing the concept of work/life balance[51] to validate caring activities. However, caring is placed firmly within the demands of the market: the balance is equal opportunities for workers with family responsibilities. Thus while caring is central to late modernity it is still devalued. Ellis has used Fisher and Tronto's framework to consider United Kingdom care policy generally. She concludes that:

> '...an overarching emphasis on the obligation to engage in paid work obscures the extent to which citizenship rights may be reciprocated in other ways, such as care giving or providing insights into the experience of managing age and impairment which most of us face at some point in our lives' (2004: 44).

She argues that:

> '...only care policy based on the precepts of relational autonomy might enable citizens to manage the ethical dilemmas they face in balancing responsibilities to self and others' (2004, 44).

This story illustrates these dilemmas, developing the ethic of care and integrating it with an ethic of rights and justice to create new ways of understanding human rights may start to provide the answers.

Bibliography

Barnett H. (1998) *Introduction to feminist jurisprudence*, Cavendish Press, London.

Boyd S. (1999) 'Family, law and sexuality: Feminist engagements', in *Social and Legal Studies* 8: 369.

Brammer A. and S. Biggs (1998) 'Defining elder abuse' in *Journal of Social Welfare and Family Law*. 20 (3): 285-304.

---

[51] This concept is found in the revised Social Charter of the Council of Europe (article 27) and the Charter of Fundamental Rights of the European Union (article 34).

Braye S. and M. Preston-Shoot (1999) 'Accountability, administrative law and social work practice: Redressing or reinforcing the power imbalance?', in *Journal of Social Welfare and Family Law* 21(3): 235-256.

Dean H. (1996) *Welfare, law and citizenship*, Prentice Hall, Harvester, London.

Dean H. (ed) (2004) *The ethics of welfare: Human rights, dependency and responsibility*, Policy Press, Bristol.

Department for Health (1989) *Caring for people: Community care in the next decade and beyond*, Cm 849, HMSO, London.
– (1990) *Community care in the next decade and beyond: Policy guidance*, Department for Health, London.
– (1998) *Modernizing social services: Promoting independence, improving protection, raising standards*, White Paper, Cm 4169, HMSO, London.
– (1999) *Caring about carers: Carers national strategy document*, Department for Health, London.
– (2000) *The community care (Direct Payments Act) 1996: Policy and practice guidance*, Department for Health, London.
– (2001) *Fair access to care guidelines*. Department for Health, London.
– (2002–3) *The 12th annual report of the Chief Inspector of Social Services 2002–3*, available at: http://www.dh.gov.uk/ PublicationsAndStatistics/Publications/AnnualReports/ChiefInspectorAnnualReportsDocument/fs/en?CONTENT_ID=4098545&MULTIPAGE_ID=4941746&chk=HciGG0
– (2003) *Community care, services for carers and children's services (direct payments) guidance, England*, Department for Health, London.

Department for Trade and Industry (1998) *Fairness at work*, London.

Drakapoulou M. (2000) 'The ethic of care, female subjectivity and feminist legal scholarship', in *Feminist Legal Studies* 8: 199-226.

Ellis K. (2004) 'Dependency, justice and the ethic of care', in H. Dean (ed) *The ethics of welfare: Human rights, dependency and responsibility*, The Policy Press, Bristol.

Equal Opportunities Commission (2004) 'Carers and work/life balance', http://www.eoc.org.uk/cseng/policyandcampaigns/carers_and_worklife_balance_.asp (accessed 30/07/04).

Fisher B. and J. Tronto (1990) 'Towards a feminist theory of caring', pages 35–62 in E. K. Abel and M. Nelson (eds) *Circles of care: Work and identity in women's lives*, State University of New York Press, Albany.

Foucault M. (1979) *Discipline and punish*, Penguin Books, Harmondsworth.

Fraser N. (1997) *Justice interruptus: Critical reflections on the 'postsocialist' condition*, Routledge, London & New York.

Gilligan C. (1982) *In a different voice: Psychological theory and women's development*, Harvard University Press, Cambridge MA.

Ginn J. and S. L. Arber (1999) 'Playing politics with pension statistics: Legitimating privatization', pages 152–167 in D. Dorling and L. Simpson (eds) *Statistics in society,* Arnold, London.

Lewis J. (ed) (1998) *Gender, social care and welfare state Restructuring in Europe,* Ashgate, Aldershot.

Land H. and J. Lewis (1998) 'Gender, care and the changing role of the state in the UK', in J. Lewis (ed) *Gender, social care and welfare state restructuring in Europe,* Ashgate, Aldershot.

Mandelstam M. (2001) *Community care practice and the law,* second edition, Jessica Kingsley Publishers, London.

Marshall T. H. (1950) 'Citizenship and social class', in T. Marshall and T. Bottomore (1992) *Citizenship and social class,* Pluto, London.

McDonald A. (2001) 'Care in the community', in L. Cull and J. Roche (eds) *The law and social work: Contemporary issues of practice*, Palgrave and Open University, Buckingham.

Nussbaum M. (2002) 'Women's capabilities and social justice' in M. Molyneux and S. Razavi (eds), *Gender justice, development and rights*, Oxford University Press, Oxford.

Palmer E. (2000) 'Residential care: Rights of the elderly and the Contracts (Rights of Third Parties) Act 1999', in *Journal of Social Welfare and Family Law* 22 (4): 461-476.

Preston-Shoot M., G. Roberts and S. Vernon (2001) 'Values in social work law: Strained relations or sustaining relationships?' *Journal of Social Welfare and Family Law* 23(1): 1-22.

Reich C. A. (1964) 'The new property', 73 *Yale LJ* 733.

Sen A. (1999) *Development as freedom,* Oxford University Press, Oxford.

Sevenhuijsen S. (1998) *Citizenship and the ethics of care: Feminist considerations on justice, morality and politics*, Routledge, London.
– (2000) 'Caring in the Third Way: The relation between obligation, responsibility and care in Third Way discourse', in *Critical Social Policy* 20 (1): 5-37.

Sutherland (1999) Royal Commission on Long-term Care, *With respect to old age: Long term care – Rights and responsibilities*, Cmnd 4192–1, HMSO, London.

Tronto J. C. (1994) *Moral boundaries: A political argument for an ethic of care,* Routledge, London and New York.

United Nations Development Programme (UNDP) (2000) *Human development report 2000,* Oxford University Press, Oxford.

Wærness K. (1984) 'Caring as women's work in the welfare state', in H. Holter (ed), *Patriarchy in a welfare state,* Universitetsforlaget, Oslo.

– (2001) 'Gender equality and social security system in an era of globalization', paper presented at the 'Policy Dialogue on Gender Equality', Saga Conference Tokyo November 20–25.

Walker A and T. Maltby (1997) *Ageing Europe*, Open University Press, Philadelphia.

Williams F. (2001) 'In and beyond New Labour: towards a new political ethics of care', in *Critical Social Policy* 21(4): 467-93.

List of cases
R v Lancashire CC ex p RADAR [1996]: *The Times* 12 July
R v Sefton CC ex p. Help the Aged and Blanchard (1997) 4 All ER 449
R v Gloustershire CC ex p Barry (1997) 2 All ER 1.
R v Wandsworth London Borough ex p. Beckwith (1996) 1All ER 129

List of legislation
United Kingdom

Care Homes Act 1984
Carers and Disabled Children Act 2000
Children Act 1989
Chronically Sick and Disabled Act 1970
Community Care (Delayed Discharges) Act 2003
Community Care (Direct Payments) Act 1996
Community Care, Services for Carers Children's Services (Direct Payments) England Regulations 2003
Disability Discrimination Act 1995
Health Act 1999
Health and Social Care Act 2001
Housing Act 1988
Human Rights Act 1998
Local Authority (Social Services) Act 1970
Local Government Act 2000 22
Mental Health Act 1983 17
National Assistance Act 1948
NHS and Community Care Act 1990
Race Relations Act 1976
Rent (Agriculture) Act 1976
Sex Discrimination Act 1975
Third Party Contracts Act 1999

International

European Convention on Human Rights 1950
Council of Europe's Social Charter 1961
Charter of Fundamental Rights of the European Union 2000
Universal Declaration of Human Rights 1948

2
Kår contracts in Norway
Agreements made by men concerning
women's work, ownership and lives

Tove M. Bolstad

This chapter examines an age old contractual arrangement entered into by, usually, men in succeeding generations of a family on farms in Norway to provide for accommodation and care of the seller (farm owner) and his wife as the older couple enter retirement or semi-retirement. The performance of the care requirements as set out in these kår-contracts, is described and analyzed from the perspective of the wife of the purchaser of the farm who, although not formally a party to the contract, is the person who ends up taking on the primary care duties created by the contract. The chapter makes a significant historical contribution to this book as it investigates and documents critical elements in complex relationships between official assumptions about the penetration of law into the family arena and the imperatives at work within families and communities on compliance with tradition which, in this instance, are played out in a modern, strongly welfarist, state, namely contemporary Norway.

1   Introduction

This chapter emanates from the author's own experiences of growing up on a farm in Norway and her subsequent experiences of being married to a farmer. The research data was collected through archival research and qualitative interviews with women married to farmers who, as the next generation farmer, had entered into kår-contracts with their parents. The field research was initially carried out in 1989 and at that time it was commonly assumed that kår-contracts were a matter of history and that the few that remained would peter out with time. The belief that they would fall away was largely based on the assumption that the Norwegian welfare state, with its economic and institutional provisions for the elderly, had surplanted the age-old role of women as caregivers to the elderly within families. The original research did not proceed from a human rights analysis but from an analysis of the women's position from

---

[52]   Translated by Michael Kromberg

a legal rights perspective. The problem is not absence of rights for women or the state's lack of awareness of women's right to formal legal entitlements in such situations, rather it is the extent to which women are unaware of such rights or unprepared to actively pursue them. The issue is women's acceptance of the social and cultural norms that prevail in farming communities and families and, more particularly, the pressure to accept, comply and conform to the gendered dynamics of farms, farming and family lives on farms.

As the chapter shows, a plurality of caring situations clearly coexisted in 1989 and continues today within the seemingly unified, comprehensive and uniform law and policy that regulates the Norwegian welfare system. Admittedly kår-contracts are dwindling in numbers but they persist, even in the twenty-first century. Thus, although the information is not recent, it reflects the persistence of a private contractual arrangement entered into between men which can have profound effects on the lives of women who are not strictly parties to it. At the end of the chapter there is a brief discussion about the changes which had taken place by 2005, largely prompted by economic developments in Norway and new production imperatives on the farms to meet global market demands.

Background

A farmer who sold his farm on retirement – usually to a son or sometimes to a daughter – would enter into a contract at the time of transfer securing rights to accommodation and possibly care. This is a specialized contract called a kår-contract (kår pronounced 'core'). Such an agreement is a legally-binding document often appended to the deed of transfer. Kår-contracts represented the farmer's old-age pension and, although the need for such contracts partially fell away with the introduction of national insurance, kår-contracts are still entered into when farm property changes hands.[53]

As this chapter shows, kår-contracts have consequences for women's rights and determine the work they perform on the farm. It is traditionally expected that women who move onto a farm after marriage will participate in many kinds of farm labour and that this will be their chief occupation. The woman has a background and support role, according to Thorsen (1993):

'The farmer's wife is not only to be industrious and enterprising, she should also make no demands of her own.'

The kår concept has been variously defined, but a working dictionary definition is:

---

[53] Agreements which are set up today are first and foremost related to residential or occupational rights.

'Kår arises first and foremost in connection with the transfer of farming property, and entails that the seller secures certain regular services (usually in kind) from the purchaser for the maintenance of both himself and his wife for the rest of their lives' (Gulbrandsen, 1984).

It might be assumed that, in a state like Norway, such contracts are now only of historical interest, partly because old age pensions have replaced kår-contracts. But this is an oversimplification; new legislation cannot simply replace traditional arrangements without further ado. Kår-contracts are still being entered into although there is a decreasing need for them. To fully appreciate kår-contracts it is important to realize that generational communal living on farms is different from and more integrated than the city's 'generation dwelling',[54] in which work in the home and salaried jobs are often distinct. In agriculture, private life and work are played out in the same arena. The farmer takes over a place of work for himself and his family. The farmer's parents often continue to live on the farm and may have considerable control over the working of the farm, both in the household and with respect to the commercial aspects of the farm, 'in the spirit of the family traditions'.

Thus, an investigation of kår-contracts provides an insight into women's legal, factual and unequal status on the farm. Such contracts often last until the death of the seller and the obligations created often increase in scope during the contract period. Even today there are women who are struggling to fulfil outdated contracts – agreements which were made in a different age and under different circumstances with conditions suited to life in the old agrarian culture with extended families and a barter economy. Analysis of these contracts helps highlight the norms which govern daily life on the farm and which differ from, for example, latter-day government regulation on intra-family rights.

Sometimes the agreements appear to relate to men but through them the real principal actor, the 'woman who married into the family', may be discerned. The males of both generations – buyers and sellers – have made agreements affecting the daily lives of the women which may threaten their self-determination and integrity. Women may feel controlled by others and powerless and the conditions contained in the agreement may undermine their self-esteem and be restrictive in a situation where broad-mindedness and flexibility would be for the common good.

---

[54] A working life and a generation occupy differing time-spans. If it is assumed that a working life commences at 25 and continues until 67 years of age, at which time old age pension takes over, and that the oldest children take over when they are 25 to 30 years younger than the parents, then two generations have overlapping interests in the farm for 15–20 years. In some instances the farm can provide for all who live on it; in others the older members of the family, the younger, or both, must contribute income from other sources.

A sense of family closeness and communal spirit promotes a high quality of life and may thus be worth preserving but it has to be perceived to be worthwhile by all parties.

Kår-contracts

Kår-contracts have ancient roots, although they were not prominent in Norwegian legislation. The Allodial or Freehold Law of 1821 mentions kår-agreements and they are also mentioned in 1888 marriage legislation but little attention is paid to this sphere in legal literature. However, among the earliest private documents surviving from the middle ages are a number of contracts of this nature. The kår-contract is also discussed as an example of obligations to a third person[55] in instances involving the seller reserving for himself and his wife certain rights, and kår is mentioned as a basic right[56] relating to property. Erik Solem (as well as others) has described these contracts as hazardous:

> 'Through the kår-contract the farmer has secured a natural and necessary pension arrangement, but it is not based on statistics and probability calculations. Because the risk cannot be evened out by numbers of cases, as with other insurance, it is subject to a strong element of hazard, which in the case of persons covered by a kår-contract, is to some degree neutralized by the fact that they are relatively unaffected by variations in monetary value and by the security inherent in the ownership of fixed property' (Solem, 1942).

There is little source material from recorded legal praxis on adjudication on such contracts and it is assumed that disputes arising from kår-contracts, to the extent that they are brought to court, were and still are handled by the lower courts. In instances which have been submitted for adjudication at higher levels, the claims and the circumstances related to performance are dealt with from the point of view of the contracting parties and not from that of the woman who in many instances fulfils the conditions in practice.

Kår contracts are interpreted in accordance with standard contractual principles. The foundation of Norwegian contract law is contractual freedom; one may choose whether or not to enter into contractual arrangements and determine what content the agreements are to have. They may be brought before a court of law in the event of disputes so that the parties can have the content of the agreement clarified and fulfilled with

---

[55] Promise on the part of a person (here the kår-provider) to another (here the kår beneficiary) which aims at securing justice not only for the kår-beneficiary but also for a third party (here the kår-beneficiary's wife).

[56] Obligation devolving on a fixed property, entailing that the possessor at any given time shall produce certain fixed, periodic benefits to the holder of the rights.

the assistance of the courts. Contractual freedom presupposes that contracts are entered into between free and equal parties. Should there be disparity in the relative strengths of the parties, the law often intervenes and regulates the contractual conditions, wholly or in part to protect the rights of the weaker party. If, for instance, one of the contracting parties has exploited another's lack of independence in order to gain an advantage, the agreement may be invalidated in terms of the law.

In the event of disagreement between contracting parties, it is the contract's wording in accordance with normal linguistic usage which provides the basis for interpretation. If the agreement specifies that milk, pork and corn are to be supplied out of the farm's production, the obligation to supply such items may be suspended if production undergoes change. If, on the other hand, the conditions are formulated in general terms, there are good grounds for supposing that the buyer of the farm will be expected to continue supplying the items even though he has to purchase them in a shop. Other considerations open to interpretation, such as prevailing traditions in the area, may lead to different results. The intentions of the parties at the time of signing the agreement are important but difficult to prove.

As a general rule, kår-contracts apply only to the contracting parties and to no others. Third parties may sometimes gain rights through agreements entered into by others, for example, in insurance contracts in which the woman is accorded rights to benefits resulting from an agreement between the husband and his employer. This also applies to kår-contracts. It is usual for the seller's spouse to have rights to the same kår benefits as the seller. The rights of third parties are, however, dependent on the contracting parties. Should the seller and the buyer wish to renegotiate the agreement, the third party is in a weak position unless the agreement was irrevocable.

Obligations embodied by the contracts do not normally encompass third persons (Knoph, 1981). When women have fulfilled contractual obligations entered into by others, it is not as a result of legal compulsion but because of social bonds. But if women feel that they are obliged to carry out labour which they are traditionally expected to perform, is it possible to talk about 'third women duties'? I shall return to this later.

2   Research sources and methods

Kår contracts as source material

The source material consists of 100 deeds of transfer selected because they contain specific provisions relating to the right to support on a farmer's retirement. The task of collecting the documents was carried out in 1989.

'Better than anything else, the source material throws light on the internal structure of the agrarian community in olden times. Here one comes face to face with powerful internal coherence' (Hovdhaugen, 1984).

Further transfers may have been made subsequent to 1989, rendering some documents historical but that is not significant here.

The perspective of the women
Discussions were held with women at seminars and conferences on women-related legislation, and their views both on retirement conditions generally and on issues related to family rights were ascertained. Some of these discussions were recorded on tape. Four interviews from the counties of Trøndelag and Hedmark were also taped. Some quotations taken from this material are used in this chapter.

Furthermore, two questionnaire investigations were carried out. One questionnaire was sent to all female representatives of the Norwegian Farmers' Association at the county level and the Norwegian Farmers' and Smallholders' Association. Approximately half, altogether 57 women, answered all the questions concerning their association with the farm and with the marriage partner, concerning their upbringing and how far they had moved away from home, and so on.[57]

The other investigation was in the form of a questionnaire on the ownership of the farm and the marriage partners' financial arrangements, to the extent that women knew about this, and how they perceived their situation. The questionnaires were distributed and filled in at two regional meetings of farmers' wives and at a course for women in agriculture in a total of three counties and 97 women between the ages of 26 and 85 responded. The conversations and questionnaires provided insight into women farmers' daily experiences.

A women-oriented analytical perspective
Arising from overarching legal and ethical concepts, integrity, dignity and power of self-determination are crucial considerations in assessing women's human rights status. Essential to women's integrity, dignity and self-determination is the extent of their control in respect of their own labour, time and money. Such determinants can be particularly important in tightly-knit communities. On farms, productive income-generating work and work on behalf of the family are performed at the same

---

[57] Various concepts concerning women in these organizations are used. In the Farmer and Smallholders' Association or Farmers' Wives Association the term 'farmer's wife' is used. It is tempting to ask whether this implies emotional differences in connection with the land and the farmer, respectively.

location. There may be no distinction between income generated in the family interest and privately owned or earned money; it all goes into the same 'family treasury'. Such intense community life does not always function well or in an egalitarian manner. An indication of pressures in the closed family circle is provided by Kari (aged about 50) who refers to her small additional area of work off the farm premises as her 'mental health protection'.

For a woman on the farm determining what constitutes *her*[58] work, *her* time and *her* money can be problematic. The extent of a woman's choice in determining the parameters of her life on the farm is often a matter of tradition and is culturally determined. Marrying is first and foremost a matter of forming a close attachment to another person. But a marriage contract, especially in this context, automatically makes a woman into a full-time, part-time or overtime housewife and, where there is a kår-contract, into a carer and 'domestic worker' for others beyond her own immediate family.

Work on the farm is gendered and that affects the nature and form of not only the work but the value that is attributed to it. Tordis Borchgrevink looked at women's culture in the close-knit rural community and concluded that a woman's honour and dignity were associated with duties which in turn were related to domestic and caring functions. Labour which was defined as salaried work for men was defined as a leisure occupation for women. Initiating further education to equip a woman with qualifications for the labour market was interpreted as her 'only thinking of herself' (Borchgrevink, 1989).

All cultures contain spheres in which it is impossible for the members 'to think that they are thinking wrongly' – things are regarded as self-evident and natural even though others may perceive them as violations of rights. Such spheres are arenas of silence, of non-articulation, arenas into which discussion does not intrude or in which it is forbidden to speak. Cultural competence consists in knowing when 'to keep one's mouth shut' (Bourdieu, quoted by Borchgrevink, 1989).

For example, the right to income derived from one's own labour in a common enterprise was granted to women in 1969 (in relation to the Income Tax Act, §16.5). Legally, married couples in Norway may now share income according to the proportion of income-generating labour performed but the farmer's wife does not automatically earn income through her labour on the farm. She has to negotiate an income with her husband. Labour conflicts may be experienced as marital conflicts (Labugt, 1987). The same applies to wage bargaining.

---

[58] Emphasis added (eds).

In instances where married couples share income, it has often been a purely 'paper convenience', with the husband continuing to manage both incomes (Øien, 1990). Farmers' wives know that the needs of a farm, which are defined by men, have priority over individual needs, as the farm in turn provides for the people living on it. Some have not formally shared the income (on income tax returns) for fear of losing out on joint old age pensions, assuming that the couple were equally long-lived. Statistically, women live longer than men and all income therefore ought strategically to be entered under her name (Dale, 1991).

Domestic and care functions do not entitle the woman to income. Work performed in the home for the husband and children is, in accordance with the Marriage Act, seen as a way of fulfilling the spouses' mutual duty of support. A woman who fulfils this duty in care and kind is entitled to a monetary contribution from her husband. Investigations show that there are large variations in how readily women have access to such money. It is moreover not just a matter of having access to her own money but the manner in which money is obtained which is of crucial importance to a woman's dignity and integrity. To feel that she is a recipient of a gift has a negative impact on her self-esteem (Hellum, 1985). Many farmers' wives have made do with 'egg money'.

The wife's work for her in-laws does not give rise to any individual economic entitlement unless agreed upon in the contract. The in-laws' right to care and support is usually seen as a part of the son's payment for the farm. She, in other words, pays for the farm by caring for his parents. The sum of the tangible work performed forms the basis for assessing whether a woman who married into the farm has gradually established joint ownership rights to the farm with her husband.

3   Entering into kår-contracts

The contracting parties

An analysis of who enters into agreements reveals the contracting parties and who is obliged to fulfil the conditions. In the material forming the basis of this study, 79 of the purchasers of farms are men, ten are women, eight are couples, and three are designated 'other'. The civil status of the purchasers is seldom mentioned in the contracts but the ages vary between 24 and 56 years, indicating that many were probably married at the time of transfer. There is no obligation to state the family relationship between seller and purchaser in the contract but it is often indicated. Information contained in the source material reveals that children of the seller purchased the farm on their own in 60 of the 100 instances: namely 53 sons and 7 daughters. In 12 cases, the buyer is a more distant relative of the seller – a grandson, granddaughter or nephew, for example. In 19 of the cases there is no information about the male purchasers' familial relationship but there are reasons to assume that the buyer is the seller's son-in-law – the special rights spelled out in the agreement indicate a familial connection. Also in these instances the age difference between seller and buyer corresponds to a generation. While collecting the source material I paged through other contracts in which the family connection is known and it was evident in several instances that the son-in-law was the sole purchaser of the farm. That it has not been unusual to sell the farm to the son-in-law is the consequence of a particular provision in allodial (granting preferential or superior inheritance rights) legislation. There is a deadline, now one year, for a person who has superior allodial right to press his or her claim to be the purchaser. In the event of a farmer selling the farm to a son-in-law instead of to the daughter or to the daughter and the son-in-law jointly, he in effect sells the farm 'out of the lineage'.

Of the eight couples who purchased farms jointly, five represent cases in which the purchasers are the daughter and son-in-law of the seller. In one instance the son and the daughter-in-law bought the farm in community of property. In the two remaining cases the relationships are not stated. Difference in names between seller and the purchasing couple indicate that the female purchaser may be a daughter (it has been customary for women to take their husband's surname). The age difference between buyer and seller and provisions governing sustenance rights tend to support this conclusion.

The sellers in the source material include 57 men, 20 women, 14 couples and eight classified as 'miscellaneous', for example the farm accruing to the deceased's estate. There are presumably some widows among the 20 female sellers as sustenance provisions are mentioned for only one person. Sellers in this category vary in age between 56 and 85 years.

No particularly discernable changes in this picture have taken place over the years. In the 1960s, three couples bought farms jointly, while one couple purchased a farm together in the 1980s. The small noticeable change with respect to couples purchasing farms jointly in the 1980s is compensated for in respect of women by an increase in the number of women who became single owners of farms. Of a total of 27 buyers, five were women in the 1980s. There was a small increase in the number of couples who jointly sold their farms in the 1970s and 1980s. It may be concluded that it is mainly men who sell and buy farms and that the sale and purchase of farms is predominantly a male preserve. The sellers and the purchasers' spouses (mostly wives) do not figure as contracting parties and are referred to as 'third parties'.

How agreements are made

In the source material, it is mainly men who are the contracting parties. The seller and purchaser of the farm are often father and son, and they may be 'socially and morally' bound and not free in relation to the agreement. The son has grown up with the expectation that he will exercise his 'birth right of inheritance' or allodial privilege, an honourable right, but he may have other interests which are difficult to combine with running a farm. Should he nevertheless fulfil his 'duty of inheritance' as expected of him by his parents, he will be in a strong negotiating position. Dependence can be double-edged but usually the father is the stronger party since all his life he has bred attitudes into his son consistent with his own expectations for himself and for the farm. Kår-contracts within the family are seldom brought before the courts and there is reason to suppose that the obligations contained in such contracts are also fulfilled in real life, even though the contract in question might be set aside by a court if there was litigation because of its onerous conditions.

The negotiating process has undergone change. Buyers and sellers of farms in more recent years could attend courses on transfer of ownership together with the rest of the family and with others in the same situation. There is a tendency to be more open and for real negotiations between equal partners. Thus elements of control are moderated and the favourable aspects enhanced. But at the time of the initial research, kår-agreements were still being made in the traditional format:

> 'It is usual to repeat what has been customary, so that terms are stipulated without the parties involved really thinking about what is happening' (Brit, about 40 years old).

4   Contents of kår-contracts

In definitions of kår-contracts, the concept of 'support' often appears. This concept and that of 'sustenance' are used interchangeably and sometimes indiscriminately. 'Support' is defined as providing the resources which are essential to the maintenance and continuation of the individual's life (Ketscher, 1990). Such essentials are housing, food and clothes, and it is normal for continuing rights of residence on the farm to be secured. Although a variety of conditions may be agreed at the time of transfer of the farm, we shall confine ourselves to the most typical of such conditions. These will be examined in two ways: firstly, by analyzing the conditions as they appear in kår-contracts; secondly, by assessing how women have experienced these conditions as played out in day-to-day situations. We commence with the matter of accommodation.

Accommodation, rights of continuing residence
Residential rights occur with greatest frequency in the source material –
81 times in all – and reflect changing social and economic conditions.
The provision is usually formulated in the contract as follows:
–   the seller's right to use the entire main dwelling;
–   the right to sections of the main dwelling;
–   the right to share the use of rooms; or
–   the right to one's own dwelling, often referred to as the 'kår-dwell-
    ing'.

The most usual form this took in the 1950s was for seller and buyer to
each occupy his or her own section of the main dwelling. In the 1960s,
the seller often reserved the right to occupy the entire main dwelling but
it was almost as common for the seller and buyer to occupy their own
sections of the main dwelling. Only in the 1970s did it become usual for
the seller to occupy a separate house on the farm. Most of the agreements in which the seller reserves the right of occupancy without speci-
fying precisely where or in which the deed of ownership refers to separate kår-agreements, stem from this period. In the 1970s, relatively few
sellers reserved the right to occupy the entire main dwelling but in the
1980s this once more became the largest group. During the 1980s, reservations concerning a separate house and unspecified conditions appear
with equal frequency. There are still several instances in which the seller
and the purchaser share the main dwelling.

In a majority of kår-contracts the right of a woman's parents-in-law
to live on the farm is of lifelong duration. A situation in which relationships become problematic cannot be resolved by giving notice to the
'tenant'. The parents-in-law live there during work and leisure time.
Residential rights may entail the buyer's wife having her parents-in-law
living in the same house or in a neighbouring dwelling through many of
life's phases. The first phase in which the parents-in-law may be experienced as domineering, then in a more egalitarian phase and finally in a
phase where the parents-in-law are dependent on the help of others (usually, the daughters in-law). The daughter-in-law may have a corresponding but opposite development through the different phases. She is inex-
perienced and often unskilled in the establishment phase, then she becomes more self-assured and finally she is dominant. The changing nature of women's lives, their greater exposure to the world at large, their
initial youthful vigour and their increasing self-confidence and level of
education, may help today's newly married woman to get off to a more
confident and self assertive start in a kår arrangement.

As Mette (30) expressed the potential for the future:

'When we make the purchase, we have right of determination.'

Ideally, the new owner moves in at the time of transfer and this demarcates the transition of authority on the farm and in farming activities. However, such clearly demarcated transitions are more complicated in the realm of women's roles and interactions on the farm. The main dwelling and its uses present greater problems than a division of male labour on the farm – the new woman's 'nest-building' takes place here, where the former 'woman's' life and family raising took place. In the source material, the seller often reserves the right to lifetime occupancy of the main dwelling. Thus, two women may be defining the uses of the same space and where there are lifetime occupancy rights these delineate the older woman's dominant position.

Many parents-in-law do not wish to get involved in the lives of the younger people but the sense of always being 'visible' may create self pressure to behave in a particular way. Brit, who has parents-in-law in the kår-dwelling in the farm courtyard, explains how she always took the rake with her when she sunned herself behind the house. She believed she had to legitimize the break in the eyes of her mother-in-law and show that she was doing something useful.

A sense of intrusion and lack of privacy may also be present. Gro (about 35) recounts how her father-in-law, a widower, had not planned his retirement as a pensioner. He was over 70 when he transferred the farm. The right of residence which he had secured was arranged in such a way that he should have his own bedroom and two 'lodges' at his disposal but with a shared entrance and kitchen. In this instance the father-in-law's place at the kitchen table was a part of his residential rights. Gro describes her father-in-law as good-natured and gregarious, nonetheless she came to feel that the shared household was trying so they installed a kitchenette for him to make his own light meals. When her husband's brothers and sisters came visiting, he and Gro often participated in comradely 'coffee sessions' with the father-in-law but Gro reacted adversely to the others freely fetching extra cups from 'her' cupboard, helping themselves to newspapers and magazines, and the like:

> 'My husband didn't notice this and didn't view it in the same way as I did but I often felt put upon. I had nothing which I could call my own and was not respected as housewife and owner of the home.'

Out of consideration for her father-in-law, the furniture was left in place at the time of transfer. It became progressively oppressive for Gro to be surrounded by furniture 'belonging to others' as well as other items from the previous generation that remained in the home. But Gro continues:

> 'We should also constantly remember the positive aspects of living together like this. We had assistance with baby-sitting and other help;

yes, we felt it was good for the children to have grandfather close at hand. He was clear of mind for a good many years. I still recognize many fine things in our eldest son, who bears the same name, which he got from my father-in-law. I can see them going for a walk, they had the same gait, with their hands behind their backs, loping along. Even now the eldest has something of the old man's characteristics– brooding on words and expressions, he was skilled with words. Very lyrical, he was, my father-in-law.'

The close contact of the children with the grandparents was emphasized by many of the interviewees as a special quality of this intimate, shared living arrangement. Mette also says that it was good for the youngsters to be in close contact with the older generation but simultaneously expresses the need to draw the line:

'I feel that it is we who should teach the youngsters what is right and what is wrong, and not the father-in-law. He wants to bring them up, it is a role to which he had been accustomed all along.'

There are also examples where such contact with the grandparents did not always go according to plan. Brit says:

'This relationship with the grandchildren was a very sensitive area – the children were not always welcome and they were scolded. We experienced this when we were invited into their part of the house with visiting relatives for coffee. The youngsters had been told that it was only for grown ups and if there was anything left over, the children would have it served on the kitchen steps afterwards.'

Mother-in-law problems are cited in divorce cases in the farming community as a serious cause of conflict (Dahlen and Metlid, 1989). Whereas many women struggle under difficult circumstances, examples were also found of mothers-in-law and daughters-in-law developing excellent, even intimate relationships. Mette says that she felt an urge to protect her mother-in-law who had a domineering husband. She could hear him scolding his wife as he felt there should have been some household money left even though it might be months since she had last shopped or been given money. Mette says:

'One felt tempted to intervene and put things straight. But one can't do that, and the best thing one can do is to provide comfort.'

However, she drew the line at her father-in-law's meddling in her own affairs:

'Why should our marriage go to pieces because of him? It was better to talk back at him.'

Food

Right to food and provisions is mentioned in 56 instances. During the 1950s, 67 per cent of transfer agreements contained provisions concerning food, for example:

> 'The purchaser shall provide in kind the following items as the need arises: 125 kilos of meat and pork; up to 300 kilos of bread flour; up to 400 kilos of potatoes per year. Furthermore, 3 litres of milk daily; 2 score eggs per month; fruit, berries and vegetables for own consumption out of the farm's produce.'

In 33 per cent of the cases, the conditions were linked to need and in 27 per cent of the cases, provisions are unspecified – they are to have 'normal kår-conditions'.

The provision of food is most frequently mentioned (83 per cent) in the 1960s. Provisions such as 'sellers have the right to full board at the purchaser's table' and 'free dinner which is eaten with the rest of the household' also occur. Detailed conditions concerning the supply of produce are most common. In 43 per cent of the cases, these are linked to a needs assessment but in 24 per cent, the level or type of provisions are not specified. In the 1970s, there were fewer detailed food specifications and in the 1980s conditions relating to the provision of food were mentioned in only six out of 27 cases, all of them non-specific.

As can be readily envisaged, the nature and form of food can present considerable problems within families, even within nuclear families. In kår-contracts some of the conditions linked to food can be met without difficulty. Quantity, type and time of delivery are specified annually. In some cases the seller has reserved the right to determine time of delivery 'in accord with detailed requests' and as this is not interpreted by the court but by 'the old man himself', he is actually in a position, for instance, to decide that the pig is to be slaughtered at the new moon so that the pork might go a long way, even though it is at the busiest time of the year for the young people. Daily supply of milk may pose problems. The delivery of milk usually takes place at fixed times. Delays may be interpreted as a breach of both contract and work ethics and set in train negative feelings and, less frequently, perhaps open disagreements, for in agrarian society 'silence is golden' (Thorsen, 1989).

Brit, who did not grow up in a farming community, says:

> 'I was perhaps allowed to talk more freely about such things (during my upbringing), get it out of my system but I have married into a family where everything has to be rosy in the garden. Everything has to be so pretty, everybody just has to smile all the time while everyone is really fed up with everyone else. My husband never dares take up anything with his mother, that's just not done.'

The stipulation 'according to need' is an imprecise concept which allows a wide variety of interpretations. Does it refer to the seller's own needs or to the household's need for milk, including family and guests who may be visiting? Brit described how her mother-in-law fetched milk from the barn. When she visited the other children, she took along both milk and butter, as she said:

'It annoys me endlessly, for this is really a gift from us to my husband's brothers and sisters.'

The stipulation 'full board at the seller's table' is comprehensive. First, it embraces all categories of food and at set times. But meals mean more than that; they are the gathering point of the nuclear family. Loving concern for the family is expressed through the preparation of food. Women are faced with significant challenges when others have a contractual right to participate in the innermost life of the family, not only on weekdays but every day. As Gro described:

'When we had evening guests, he came in and sat down with us and got a little Saturday treat also, so we didn't have much private life, to put it that way.'

That extra meals, Saturday treats and Sunday coffee with neighbours are included in the conditions of sale seems unreasonable but it is not easy to breach the custom and say: 'We are eating this meal without you'.

Irrespective of the solution chosen, one is resentful or one's conscience nags. As is demonstrated in one case that went as far as litigation, food and food-related issues can be a source of profound tension. This case (RG, 1970: 461) is discussed further in section 5 on page 48.

Firewood

Right to firewood is a normal kår-condition and it occurs in 73 per cent of the transfer documents from the 1950s and in 82 per cent of those dating from the 1960s. The figures for the other decades are 57 per cent in the 1970s and 56 per cent in the 1980s. The following examples illustrate these contracts:

'Firewood when it is needed. Chopped wood',

'... dry, sawn and chopped, and stacked inside, good quality wood, if necessary, carried in for the convenience of warming the house.'

Firewood was a crucial contractual condition. Wood was a source of warmth and was used for preparing food and, even now, wood fuel represents a special feeling of security and comfort (especially in long, cold, dark winters). A series of provisions concerning quality are linked with the conditions regarding wood fuel. For those who have the raw materials and wood for cooking food there is always a way out. Labour associated with wood is a man's task. Procuring good firewood for heating the house also endows the man with a certain positive quality. A man who procures raw wood which gives off smoke does not show real concern for his family.

The man's task is associated with collecting wood, fetching it in from the forest, chopping and drying it, and stacking it in a shed. Many contracts, however, stipulate that the wood is to be distributed to the various fireplaces. To carry in wood is traditionally the contribution of children to the family circle but children have to be organized and that responsibility falls on the mother. Carrying in wood by implication entails many other tasks. Bark and shavings are spread in the passages and stairs. Where stairs and passages are shared, sweeping and washing associated with firewood is typical woman's work. Gro describes how her father-in-law took upon himself responsibility for firewood, and 'made a terrible mess' – often, unfortunately, when Gro had just washed the floors.

Services

Provisions concerning services do not appear as frequently as the conditions discussed above, but they cover most of the time periods. As services are associated with physically demanding tasks, they merit discussion. The following are some examples of services and treatment specified throughout the period in the documents examined:

'…proper care during sickness and a decent burial';

'During times of sickness the kår-people are to be provided with necessary care';

'Loving care during illness and a proper funeral';

'Care and help when old age is upon us';

'The seller and his brother demand to be treated with respect.'

The most important duties are associated with the provision of care and nursing. Trine (about 65) recalled how she only later reflected on the burden of care she had assumed. While it was being carried out, it seemed to be appropriate and was needed, such labour was in many instances felt to be a meaningful and rewarding task. It was moreover the custom on the farms. Providing such services is seldom included today but there are still women who bear heavy responsibilities because parents-in-law had such rights stipulated in kår-contracts, rights which had been established many years previously, in another age and under other circumstances.

'Normal residential and kår-rights'

In more recent contracts, kår-conditions are often less precise. All that appears is 'normal living and kår-rights' or something similar. It is up to the parties to determine the contents of the concept and here there may be divergence of opinion due to generational differences.

What the concept 'usual kår-rights' implies in addition to residential rights is hard to determine. Perhaps food produced on the farm is included. Is the meat from elk hunting to be shared? If so, is it to be supplied automatically or upon request? There are many unclear formulations in these contracts. The parties may have made special arrangements but it is not unusual for there to be certain expectations and for the recipient to be disappointed or pleased depending on whether such expectations are met or not. Can a cheerful giver be compelled to continue delivery of supplies because she has once shared something spontaneously? Expressed and unexpressed expectations may function as the seller's method of control and change of the circumstances of the young folks should they conflict with the seller's interests. For instance, if a woman who married onto the farm wants to spend part of her time outside the farm, these rights may be used as a way of attempting to restrict her activities. In this context it has to be realized that expectations as to behaviour are an implicit (albeit unwritten and unarticulated) part of the farming tradition (Thorsen, 1993).

Also in cases where the typical conditions are not spelled out in the kår-contract, the duties are perceived as real. Peder (about 25 years) felt that it was wise to define conditions precisely so that the parents could not make additional demands later. However, Gro says that the contract did not contain special provisions on maintenance. It just seemed natural and obvious that her father-in-law should eat with them. He often came in to warm the coffee kettle. It simply didn't occur to him to knock on the door 'at home'. He arrived early for dinner, stood next to Gro and sniffed and asked if the food would be ready soon.

In a decision in a case involving 'care and nursing' which came before the Supreme Court in 1953, the court ruled that the proviso was neither unreasonable nor unusual (Rt, 1963: 337). It is doubtful whether the Supreme Court would have arrived at the same conclusion today, and care and nursing would probably not be embraced by the concept of 'normal kår-provisions' now. But the attitudes of the older generation presumably do not change so quickly. Discord can lie like a curse over the farm as few conflicts are brought to court. There are reasons to suppose that many women are complying with agreements which would have been declared invalid today.

The 1980s

Detailed provisos concerning the provision of food are absent from the contracts signed in the 1980s. This may be due to more specialization in farming in the districts in which the contracts originate and to the fact that the cash economy had taken over on the farms.

Provisos related to firewood still appeared in the 1970s and 1980s, while the associated work duties are not mentioned in more recent contracts. This may be due to many sellers feeling that they are physically fit enough to fetch the wood themselves and, in the event of growing weaker, there are alternative methods of heating. One is no longer so dependent on firewood, it is now more to create a cosy atmosphere. It was not at all unusual for the seller to supply firewood for the whole farm.

The task of nursing altogether disappeared from the contracts in the 1980s. But there are some duties which had been agreed to earlier which are only now to be carried out. The age of the youngest sellers in the 1950s was 62 and in the 1960s was 57. In most cases, the wives, who also have kår-rights, are younger. One should not overlook the possibility that 'debt obligations' which were imposed in contracts signed 30 years earlier are only being 'paid off' today. As these duties devolve on steadily fewer, they may be felt as particularly heavy burdens for those to whom they apply.

Most of the sellers in the source material reserve the right to continue living on the farm but it is no longer so usual to share the same house, though this still occurs. It may be more prevalent in other parts of the country (also Rt, 1953:337). In the 1980s sellers continued to have rights to the main dwelling – this may be due to the younger set preferring to build a more modern house to the standards they desired or the seller's wish to retain the family home.

A number of work responsibilities rest on the people on the farm, out of consideration for the family and the close-knit collective. Traditions associated with the kår-conditions may make the duties seem particularly onerous. But also in cases where duties and responsibilities are happily carried out within the close community, residential rights are the precondition for a number of tasks which it would not otherwise be natural to perform.

5   The implications of kår-contracts for women

The following lower court ruling (RG, 1970: 461) is included here to illustrate that it is not always easy to distinguish between women's legal obligations associated with kår-contracts and the duties she is performing anyway.

In 1970, a conflict concerning the performance of kår-responsibilities was tried by the High Court. The purchaser took upon himself the obligation of providing kår-services when he acquired the deed to the farm on 14 June 1961. The wife of the purchaser was not a party to the agreement. The kår-obligations were:

'The seller is to have the following rights during his lifetime:

1 Free use and disposal of the south lounge with corresponding loft;
2 Free and adequate firewood;
3 Free electricity for own purposes;
4 The seller has the right to eat at the purchaser's board;
5 Necessary washing and cleaning.

'The above-mentioned rights are assessed at a five-year value of kr.3,000 – three thousand. '

The seller claimed that rights 2, 4 and 5 had not been fulfilled. The district court concluded that the purchaser had not defaulted on any of these provisions.

This determination was appealed to the High Court.

'Madam Purchaser'[59] is married to her husband in community of property. With respect to the claim pertaining to right 4, it is clear that it applies only to the afternoon mealtime and the seller complained that he was not informed of this. It appears that an afternoon meal is taken on the farm within a clearly defined timeframe. The court therefore concluded that the seller did not need to be notified when the meal was ready to be served. The court was unable to establish that, in terms of the deed, 'Madam Purchaser' had the duty of running around and searching the neighbourhood to tell him that food was ready. With regard to the washing and cleaning duties contained in right 5, the court assumed that the non-performance of this proviso by 'Madam Purchaser' was due to circumstances created by the seller himself.

'Several witnesses describe the seller as an aggressive and difficult person who, on several occasions, had been violent towards the buyer's wife and daughters without cause. One Saturday dinnertime the seller started an argument with 'Madam Purchaser' concerning firewood. He became angry and pulled out several hair curlers which she had on her head that day, so that tufts of hair came away and curlers and hair lay strewn all over the floor. Then he grabbed her by the throat and started choking her. He pushed her against a table on which the radio stood so that it overturned...and so the story continued. She

---

[59] She was, as stated previously, not a party to the agreement.

got away and warned a neighbour who in turn informed the local chief constable. He advised her to move elsewhere, which she did until her husband came home from work for a week. He was a construction worker and thus away from home a great deal.'

In the judgment above, the deed of the farm was in the man's name only. The wife was nonetheless a party to the contract. That the couple are legally regarded as joint owners does not give sufficient cause for her to be regarded as a party on whom the fulfilment of contractual obligations devolves. The husband is essentially regarded as the sole owner of the farm. In terms of conjugal legislation, each owns what he or she brought into the marriage at the time when it was solemnized as well as what they contributed to it subsequently. Each is only obliged to pay her or his own debts. Kår responsibilities are compensation for the value of the property, representing a debt which is owed by the partner who purchased the farm and which the other partner is not obliged to discharge. This applies whether they are married in community of property or not. In other words, the wife is in principle not legally obligated.

A strict reading of kår-contracts?
It can be argued, based on a strict reading of the source material, that the men who entered into such contracts with their parent or parents formally undertook to wash the clothing and sweep the floors, serve food to the seller and his wife, and moreover provide loving care. The purchaser in the judgment cited above had obligated himself to feed the seller, a duty he had, seemingly, never discharged himself or could not have done as he was away for days at a time in connection with his job as a construction worker. The implication of such contracts is that the wives of the purchasers are clearly expected to fulfil the kår-obligations, yet they struggle to acquire equity in the farm.

Arguably, women, through the performance of kår-duties and other work, should be able to accrue joint property rights. In order to establish joint ownership in relation to a farm which is in principle owned by only one of the marriage partners, emphasis is placed on who has participated in paying off the mortgage. Given the gendered nature of work on the farm and the apparent lack of direct income-generating work on the part of the wife, it has not been easy for farmers' wives to produce evidence of income-generating labour on the farm. However, their labour is a significant contribution towards attainment of ownership. The problem is that there is no express rule on such contributions and a specific assessment has to be carried out in every instance. The possibilities of such a claim being sustained are fair. Also the Norwegian Marriage Act confirms that work in the home may convert to right to ownership. It might be argued that as the farm dwelling represents an integral part of the 'business premises', joint ownership of the home as part of the business is legally feasible.

An important and difficult question thus arises: does joint ownership entail the obligation to perform duties enjoined by the sales contract and or does fulfilment of kår-obligations confer joint property ownership? The question is raised here but is beyond the immediate scope of this chapter although this is a matter requiring a further discussion of the legal implications of various aspects of such contracts. In theory, when the woman who marries onto the farm is an 'active' party to a subsequent kår-agreement, it is her responsibility to decide during negotiations whether she wishes to obligate herself to having the seller living on the farm and eating at her table for the rest of his or their lives.

However, women who purchase farms together with their husbands are unfortunately seldom involved in the negotiations. They just sign on the dotted line. The husband acts on behalf of both and is tacitly her 'authorized representative' up to the moment of signing. The women, even though they might be able to avoid the obligation vis a vis their husbands, because there is nothing specific agreed as to which of the purchasers is to carry out the duties, nonetheless meet the obligations out of moral and perceived legal duties. But there are also examples of women who think otherwise. Brit, who had not grown up in a farming community, bought the farm in joint ownership with her husband but regarded the kår-conditions as her husband's responsibility and as something which she did not feel obligated to carry out. However, she was an exception.

Most women appearing in the source material make few demands and accept responsibility for carrying out the agreed duties. In one instance, the woman bound herself by signing the kår-agreement (which in this case was appended to the contract) but without any right to recompense. In the deed, the man appears as sole owner. In several deeds, separate kår-agreements are referred to but not appended, thus it is impossible to determine whether more women in the source material have formally obligated themselves in relation to kår-duties.

Formal requirements and actual duties

Conditions specified in the kår-contract may be used to keep young farmers' wives in their 'accustomed' place. That supplies are to be delivered at predetermined times, the right to demand a lift to the shops when the need arises (there are still many elderly women without a driver's licence), the right to dinner which is eaten together with the young family, all provide the elderly with a contractual right to be taken notice of – in addition to the moral basis which underlies familial relationships. By virtue of this, the older folk possess a means of preventing women from taking paid employment or obtaining further education.

Kristin (about 55) related how her husband, his brothers and sisters and her parents-in-law felt that she had nursing duties even though she married after her husband had taken over the farm and was not acquainted with the conditions under which he had purchased the farm. Kristin is not alone in performing such work today which tradition, not legal obligation, has enjoined upon wives.

Hanne (about 50) wrote that a kår-contract which she had never signed had determined her life for 22 years:

> 'I feel used, exploited. It was automatically assumed that I would accept responsibility for everything and there was no money for hiring help. I felt that it was expected of me. At any rate, I was criticized when I didn't manage to perform all my duties. This was women's work, for that's the way it was for mother and for mother-in-law and for women before them again.'

This reflects attitudes which are more in harmony with the marriage legislation before 1888 than now. In terms of these regulations, women once more became 'minors' in the eyes of the law when marrying. Her husband became her guardian and was authorized to make legal dispositions on her behalf and in respect of her labour. They had joint ownership, the husband having free right of disposition. In return, the husband was obliged to provide for the woman (Mejdell, 1979). After 1888, married women's authority to act on their own behalf was established but the joint family estate was still to be under the control of the husband. When society underwent changes and the former concept of an extended family living in a barter economy made way for a nuclear (or kår) family living in a cash economy, it was seen that there were economic advantages in giving the woman access to her own finances. This represented a guarantee that the money would be used to the greater benefit of the family.

Since 1927, partners have in principle had separate finances within the marriage. Nevertheless, men still function as the family's external representative, interpreting the rules of society for the family and being its 'legal face'. There may be several reasons why the man has continued to decide over the woman's labour as if the relationship between them had not undergone changes in the eyes of the law. The concept of 'community of property' in many ways clouds the legal economic relations between the marriage partners, leading to conceptual differences of interpretation.

To questions regarding who has the title to the farm, which arrangements they have with respect to financial assets and how they view the ownership issue, most women answer that the husband has signed the contract on his own, that they are married in community of property and that they own the farm jointly. This may be one of the reasons for women acceding to fulfilling the obligations undertaken by the husband and which may later make it possible for them to be legally adjudged as co-owners. The obligations moreover represent a 'normal' gendered division of labour between the partners and reflect a sense of belonging and solidarity and the wish to help each other, as is the case within good marital relations.

Kår-contracts may be seen as inevitable or normal in farming families. 'Does one not have to have a kår-contract?' asked Mette in surprise and pondered whether there could possibly be other solutions than that the husband's parents continue to live on the farm. To pose this question was for her an unexpected, almost dangerous, thought. One does not throw away 'the good life' in the form of contact between the generations and the sense of belonging, particularly when the rest of society 'longs for such qualities of life'. But while one often experiences the cities as impersonal, people in rural areas can feel closeness as oppressive. Social control can stultify personal growth (Garbo, 1992). Relationships on the farm can be particularly stifling and many women have experienced this over the generations.

Why do women conform?
Even though women may be aware of their legal status, they may still fulfil obligations they know do not rest upon them. Why do they do this?

In a manner similar to that discussed in other chapters in this book one always needs to ask: are there other normative systems in a society, existing alongside and in addition to the official legal system? Women act first and foremost out of a feeling of care and concern – this is the concept of 'care rationality' (Wærness, 1975). They are concerned that daily life should be favourable for all those under their care. Hanne Petersen has demonstrated the existence of several legal systems called 'informal laws' in women's workplaces in the public sector in Denmark. Informal laws are rules which are adhered to because they are perceived as a moral duty and because they may be sanctioned by, for instance, some people becoming angry if such duties are not fulfilled. Such informal regulations arise readily in semi-autonomous spheres (Petersen, 1975). Family life and farm life in particular is precisely such an area. Women fulfil duties because they give priority to what they feel is right, just and important; and perhaps one can ask whether, for example, the concept of freedom has too often had its tangible expression shaped by male values. Women's freedom can readily become 'dignified dependence' where togetherness and belonging are important values which put the collective values ahead of the individualistic ones and which form the premise for the decisions made by women. Women on the farms seem still in some instances to conform to age old patterns of performance and adhere to traditional values and norms by which women are 'judged' socially.

6   And as to the future?

The purchase and sale of farms in the source material took place mainly between men and most of them were close relatives, often father and son. In instances where family ties are not indicated, the buyer may be the seller's son-in-law. When a couple buys a farm jointly, men are most often co-purchasers in cases where the women have prior right of inheritance. This shows that women and men establish ownership rights in different ways. The man secures his right first, as purchaser and co-owner. Women may only come to obtain or assert the right of ownership which has accrued as a result of their efforts after their involvement has been evaluated, usually at divorce. While the marriage exists, the woman's legal ownership rights are often unarticulated, unrecognized and unclear.

There are adverse implications for the farm and the woman herself where this is the case. An unclear ownership situation may demotivate active, self-confident involvement in the business of the farm. A loss for the woman herself but also a loss for society to the extent that it may be possible to speak of a female administrative role in agriculture which builds on greater respect for nature's own values (Avdem and Sundan, 1991).

Women farmers are participants in lifelong 'changes of ownership' scenarios, from their husbands' birth as entitled to allodial privilege, right up to the death of the seller. Some women are still burdened by having to fulfil obligations contracted in the distant past. The agreement governing transfer may render the situation of women farmers extremely unequal, depending on the existence of kår-agreements, their character, who is legally obligated and who fulfils the conditions in practice.

Men's legally protected prior right to land was abolished as from 1 January 1975. This has resulted in more women buying farms in accordance with the Act of Allodial Privilege. But it is dubious whether we shall see a complete about-turn so that men who marry into a farming family will automatically find themselves in the position formerly occupied by women. This has not happened before. Male superiority in terms of sheer muscular strength and the farm's need for brute force before the age of technology have strengthened the bargaining position in transfer negotiations of men marrying into farming families. Liv (aged about 40) told of how a son-in-law, who some generations ago was to marry a girl with allodial right, demanded that 'the oldies' should leave the farm before he drove onto the farm. He waited down by the road until he saw them slink away along the edge of the forest.

Relationships will now be different between the people on the farm. Mother and daughter will be observed in the same farm courtyard. This could lead to new kinds of interaction. Relationships between men may change character. It is possible that goodwill, which one takes for granted between father and son until the opposite has been demonstrated, will have to become more prominent in the new relations between men. What will be completely new is the feeling of having 'ousted' the brother or a daughter with allodial right. The source material has demonstrated that it takes longer to change attitudes than laws.

The youngest among the older generation play with the idea of moving to an 'old age collective' at the time of transfer. But tradition, suitable existing dwellings and economic considerations probably ensure that the generational community on farms will survive, and if people manage to break the silence and discuss their own and others' needs and expectations, it will provide a solid foundation for continued communal living.

August 2005

To identify the individual young woman in the farm household, to understand her gendered role and obligations, legal or otherwise, and to analyze her rights was my purpose in working with kår-contracts in the 1980s. In considering her position and her options it became clear that a woman should involve herself actively in the conditions of a contract if she intends to participate actively in running the farm. If the woman is not a party to the contract of sale, it should be because of her personal and conscious choice. The question also arose, as alluded to earlier, as to whether the right of joint ownership of her 'own' farm can be incorporated in the concept of gender equality?

Many changes have occurred in the last 16 years. Before 1989 it was important to be self-sufficient in basic agricultural products at all levels of the economy. The new global market economy has changed the way consumers and thereby politicians look at agriculture. Low prices for food are important now. That means more efficient, industrial agriculture and less remuneration from farming. The farmers are increasingly competing in a global market whereas they used to compete only with other Norwegians

Less income means low incomes on farms – often no higher than a normal family household. Now it is quite normal for farmers' wives to also work outside the farm. Many farms have changed from being family concerns to being individual concerns. The trend that the parents move to more central areas continues, making kår-contracts superfluous. Instead of service and food, the parents need money to buy their new flat. New tax-rules mean that parents sell the farm to their son or daughter only if they buy it as a couple, if they do not the tax burden is not spread and thus the tax would be much higher.

Since 1965 women and men have been in equal positions concerning the allodial (preferential) right but it is still mainly men who take over from the parents, Farming as a profession is more open to women now but the incomes from farming are lower and it is far harder work than in other areas. There are many better jobs to choose from in society so it is probably easier for women not to fulfil parents' expectations that they will take over the farm, especially if they have older or younger brothers. On many farms it is quite 'natural' that the farmer is a man, even if a woman now has the allodial priority. A thousand year old tradition takes time to change. The Allodial Act is now under revision. The Minister of Agriculture wanted to abolish the Act since many in the liberal government look at it as restricting the freedom to sell and buy farms. Some farmers wanted to abolish the Act too, possibly to make it easier to sell their farms to the younger son.

It would be interesting to extend this study and look at farms where kår-contracts are still in place and to collect and analyze documents on the transfer to the next generation. Other questions arise: How many continue the tradition with kår-contracts and how many do not? And what is the situation and main focus among parents, children and their new families now? My assumption is that there will be many different solutions to elderly parents' need for care in a changing farming community. The kår-contracts are likely to be of a more informal character and not, as earlier, formalized through the deed of transfer.

Bibliography

Avdem A. J. and B. Sundan (1991), 'Landbruk; Pengane eller livet?' ('Agriculture; Your money or your life!'), *Nytt om Kvinneforskning*, 3:51-61.

Bolstad T. M. (1991), *Bondekvinne – liv og lov*, (*Farmers wife – the life and the law*) Landbruksforlaget, Oslo.
– (1994) 'Om kårkontrakter og om tilgiftede kvinners eiendomsforhold til gårder' ('About kår-contracts and about married women's property right to her husbands farm'), *Institutt for offentlig retts skriftserie* nr. 6, Oslo.
– (2003) 'Odel i spenn mellom slekt, familie og marked' ('Allodial right in tension between relatives, family and market'), *Kvinnerettslige arbeidsnotater* nr. 60, Oslo.

Borchgrevink T. (1989) *Mye arbeid – liten innflyteIse?* (*Much work – little influence*), Landbruksforlaget, Oslo.

Dahl T. S. (1976) 'Ekteskapet, den moderne husmannskontrakten' ('Marriage, the modern serf's contract'), in I. T. Støren and T. S. Vetlesen, red., *Kvinnekunnskap*, Gyldendal, Oslo.

– (1985) 'Innledning til kvinneretten' ('Introduction to women's law'), in I. T. Stang Dahl, red., *Kvinnerett I*, Universitetsforlaget, Oslo.

Dahlen S. and B. Metlid (1989), 'Hvordan er skilsmissesituasjonen i landbruket - og hvorfor?' ('Divorce in the agricultural community, whys and wherefores'), MA thesis, Institute of Agricultural Economy, As-NLH.

Dale K. (1991) 'Fortjener kvinnene i jordbruket mer inntekt?' ('Do women in agriculture deserve better pay?'), *Norsk Landbruk* 11:34-36.

Garbo G. L. (1992) 'Stadig flere deprimerte' ('Steadily more depressed'), *Apollon*, 5:23-25.

Gulbrandsen E. (1984) *Juridisk leksikon*, Kunnskapsforlaget, Oslo.

Hellum A. (1985) 'Penger og verdighet etter ektefelleloven, Paragr. 1,' ('Money and dignity in §1 of the Marriage Act'), in I. T. Stang Dahl, red., *Kvinnerett ll,* Universitetsforlaget, Oslo.

Hovdhaugen E. (1984) *På kår. Den gamle føderådsskipnaden*, Det norske Samlaget, Oslo.

Ketscher K. (1990) *Offentlig børnepasning i retlig belysning* (*Communal child care in the light of the law*), Jurist- og Økonomiforbundets Forlag, Copenhagen.

Knoph R. (1981) *Oversikt over Norges Rett* (*Overview of Norwegian law*), Universitetsforlaget, Oslo.

Labugt I. (1987), 'Generasjonsforhold i landbruket' ('Generational relations in agriculture'), Memorandum No. 17, Institute of Agricultural Economy, As-NHL.

Mejdell K. (1979) 'Våre oldemødres rett til penger' ('Our great grandmothers' right to money'), Kvinnerettslige studier nr. 9, Institute of Women's Law, Oslo.

Øien E. S. (1990) *Faktorer som påvirker praktiseringen av ektefelledelt ligning i jordbruket*, Nord-Trøndelagsforskning, Steinkjer.

Petersen H. (1991) *Informel ret pa kvinnearbejdsplasser* (*Informal law at women's places of work*), Akademisk Forlag, Copenhagen.

Skard Ø. E. (1990) *Faktorer som påvirker praktiseringen av ektefelle-delt ligning i jordbruket* (*Factors which influence the practice of shared income tax declarations in agriculture*) Report No. lO, Steinkjer:NTF.

Solem E. (1942) 'Føderåd – Bondens alderstrygd' ('Kår-contracts – the farmer's old age pension'), *Tidsskrift for rettsvitenskap* 249-291.

Thorsen L. E. (1993) *Det fleksible kjønn: Mentalitetsendringer i tre generasjoner bondekvinner 1920-1985 (The flexible sex: Attitudinal changes spanning three generations of farm women, 1920-1985)*, Universitetsforlaget, Oslo.

– (1990) *Det fleksible kjønn : mentalitetsendringer i tre generasjoner bondekvinner, 1920-1985*, Institutt for etnologi, Universitetet i Oslo, 1989. - 514 s. : ill.; Avhandling (doktorgrad) - Universitetet i Oslo, 1990.

Wærness K. (1975) 'Kvinners omsorgsarbeid i den ulønnede produksjonen' ('Women's caring role in unpaid production'), Workpaper No. 801 from *Levekårsundersøkelsen (Study of living conditions)*, Bergen.

List of cases
Rt, 1953:337
RG, 1970: 461

List of legislation
Norway
Act of Allodial Privilege 1987
Allodial or Freehold Law of 1821
Income Tax Act, §16.5, 1948
Marriage Act 1991

3
Working with custom
Promoting children's rights to livelihood by making de facto guardians responsible

Henrietta Wolayo Ssemmanda

In this chapter I examine the prevalent practice in Uganda of placing children in the care of extended families for reasons ranging from lack of economic means to pursue education within their own families to addressing a relative's need for children. Whatever the reasons for the variety of social arrangements involving children, of particular interest is the manner in which the official law in Uganda has responded. Legislation recognizing de facto guardians and making them legally responsible for the upbringing of young relatives in their care within the framework of the best interests of the child has been put in place. I argue that this recognition is an example of how formalization of custom can be used to enhance human rights. The notion of rights of the child has been introduced with minimum disruption to social practices and values since the existing custom provided a soft landing for the introduction of formal legal concepts. I explore the child care norms underlying social arrangements against the backdrop of international and domestic law standards. In the light of qualitative case studies I undertook on child care social arrangements, I also examine the strengths and weaknesses of the 'cross fertilization' of custom and statute that has taken place in Uganda.

1 Introduction

The upbringing of children in social arrangements within the extended family is widespread in Ugandan society. By upbringing of children in social arrangements, I am referring to situations where the parents agree that the child should be brought up by relatives even though both parents are alive. It is the agreement between the biological and social parents, and the physical relocation of the child to the new home that constitutes a social arrangement. I refer to the children in such arrangements as social children.

---

[60] In the article, 'Food and sadza. Custody and the best interests of the child', Alice Armstrong uses the term 'fluctuating custody' to describe custody arrangements within the extended family network (Armstrong, 1994).

In 1972 after I sat for my primary school leaving examinations, I recall my parents putting their heads together and deciding that my mother's sister, who had access to more resources owing to the nature of her employment, should be approached to request that she fund my secondary education. My aunt responded favourably to the request. Life was not easy for us at the time as we were a family of six children and I was the eldest at 12 years old. My father was a prisons officer while my mother was the typical housewife, getting up early to till the gardens and making handicrafts for sale.

I secured a place to pursue secondary school education at Mt St Mary's, a first-class senior school in Namagunga, Uganda. Of note is that I was not consulted about the decision to send me to live with my aunt. I was merely told that my maternal aunt would pay for my secondary education. More important was my father's confidence that I could make it through secondary education. In other words, my being female did not deter him from ensuring that I got formal education. Contrary to the widely held belief that girls' access to education is constrained by beliefs in their socially ascribed subordinate status in society, it never occurred to me that, as a girl, education was a privilege. My aunt paid for my entire secondary education. Without her, I may never have gone beyond primary education to become a lawyer, simply because of scarce resources. During the time I lived with her, I was given food, clothing, medical attention and shelter. Although I performed domestic chores, I had time for leisure, just like her biological children.

As a framework for analyzing child care norms under customary practices, I not only draw from my own experience, as captured above, of being brought up in a social arrangement but more significantly from research which I carried out for my MPhil dissertation on social arrangements, children's rights and guardianship, and confronting the best interests of the child in light of lived social realities (Ssemmanda, 2001).

The primary motivation for my empirical study was to take a closer look at the actual child care arrangements that people are making. I was interested in whether the girls get sufficient time for leisure and schoolwork and whether they are treated like the de facto guardian's biological children as regards care, food and medical treatment. Through qualitative research carried out in rural Mpigi and urban Kampala in Uganda, I obtained insights into the different models of contemporary arrangements, explored the different models across the generations, and ascertained the models that have persisted across generations and those that are extinct. Respondents comprised de facto guardians – both middle class and the rural poor – in contemporary arrangements, social children living in current arrangements, elderly folk of 80 years old and children who had left arrangements and were living in the Children Reception Centre, Naguru.[61]

In-depth interviews with selected de facto guardians gave insight into the different social values informing the upbringing of social children in the arrangements. Focus group interviews were instrumental in unearthing some of the negative ideology that informs some arrangements. By identifying children in arrangements, I was able to observe differences and similarities between the arrangements – those that promoted the welfare and rights of the social child and those that did not. Taking the girl-child's lived realities as a starting point, I was curious as to whether de facto guardians in current arrangements had embraced new positive social values or whether the widely held belief that the girl child's destiny in life was domestic labour had persisted.

This chapter is divided into five parts, beginning with this introduction to the study. In part two I examine the different models of social arrangements that emerged from my fieldwork. Given that customary childcare norms continue to regulate the position of children in social arrangements, in part three I examine these practices against the backdrop of formal international and domestic law using the Convention on the Rights of the Child and the Children's Act of 1996 as standard setting instruments. In part four, exploring the interface between national law and international law on the one hand and the practice of upbringing of children in social arrangements on the other, I raise questions on whether child care arrangements protect the human rights of the child in general and the girl child in particular. In part five, I conclude with an assessment of the strengths and weaknesses of the integrated approach as a model in promoting human rights and as a strategy for law reform which works with custom.

2   Social arrangements in practice

The nature of social arrangements

What emerged from my research is that social arrangements take different forms which are often triggered by a variety of social situations. The nature of the problem giving rise to the need for the arrangement generally influences its form as will be illustrated in discussing the basis for social arrangements. Through my field work, I found that models of social arrangements have also evolved across generations. For instance, I found grandparent/grandchild model arrangements were common in the rural area of Mpigi but I also came across some in the urban area of

---

[61]   This is a reception centre for children in need of care and protection. The children are normally sent to the centre through a court order. The centre is located in Kampala, Uganda.

Kampala. Grandparents considered it a customary obligation to bring up grandchildren, a duty they perceived as arising from the process of childbirth. Having produced the parents of these children, it followed that they had to take care of the grandchildren as well.

I also found that social arrangements are generally negotiated within extended family relationships. For example, they include situations where a child is placed in the care of a paternal aunt (a paternal aunt/niece and or nephew arrangement), with a maternal aunt (a maternal aunt/niece and or nephew arrangement) and in the care of a paternal uncle (a paternal uncle /niece and or nephew type of arrangement). The de facto guardians in these arrangements had a duty to provide food, clothing, education, shelter, medical attention and moral guidance to those in their care.

Cohesion of the extended family is a factor influencing arrangements that combine the needs of the different parties. However, some arrangements, especially those that are prompted by the need for domestic help, are negotiated among non kin. Extended family arrangements are often based on reciprocity while arrangements made by non-relatives tended to reflect the more narrow interests of the parents and the receiving family in terms of labour.

Also, whereas past arrangements for bringing up children were entered into as a customary obligation, in contemporary arrangements they are entered into by mutual consent. In the past, the arrangements led to permanent transfer of parental responsibility while in arrangements of today, there is fluctuating custody. Fluctuating custody means that the child's residence in the home of the relative is not permanent. He or she may change residence to another relative or back to the parents as the need arises.

The need for education in light of limited financial resources
The desire for formal education for one's children was a factor that influenced some incidences of social arrangements. Parents who cannot afford a good education for their children place them in social arrangements. My own experience bears this out. Tied to this is the reality of poverty and economic constraints.

In a case study of a woman called Reste, I found that she lived with her brother's five children and two of her own. She said she took custody of the five children as a gesture to relieve her needy brother in spite of the fact that she was needy herself.

In another case study involving a legal practitioner, whom I shall call Mary, the need to provide education was also central as a basis for the social arrangement. Mary, a successful legal practitioner, took over responsibility for educating her brother's son after the brother lost his job. A factor that influenced her decision was her nephew's academic brilliance. Another was that her brother had a large family. This case not only gives a male dimension to a social arrangement but also underscores the importance attached to the value of formal education. Social arrangements where the de facto guardians have embraced the value of formal education often lead to the realization of the right of the child to education.

De facto guardians in need of domestic help sometimes seek young children they can send to school and at the same time address their own needs for domestic help. One of the cases I came across involved Mrs K and three girls aged between 11 and 15 years old.

Mrs K, a woman in her fifties, lives in a rural area. In addition to her niece and nephew, she also had in her custody three young girls whom she called domestic workers. Two of the girls were sisters, Olivia aged 15 years and Miria aged 11 years. These two girls were brought to the respondent from some remote village by a friend of the respondent called Nabirye. The girls were said to come from a very needy family. The agreement with Nabirye was that the respondent would bring up the girls and when they were old enough, they would repay by performing domestic chores in the home. Miria was eight years old when she came to stay while Olivia was twelve years old. At the moment, their father collects Olivia's pay while Miria is paid in kind. With the advent of universal primary education, Miria receives free education, while the respondent caters for educational requirements like books and school uniforms in lieu of a wage. The girls, who appeared well looked after, said they had a brother and three sisters who lived with their parents. The girls sometimes went home to visit. They said their grandmother (respondent) catered for all their needs including clothing and medical needs. The third girl, Damallie, was 11 years old. Her mother took her to the respondent because she was poor and also had a large family. Damallie says she has six sisters and two brothers. The agreement between the respondent and Damallie's mother was that the respondent would bring up the girl and when she was old enough, she would repay through domestic chores. The respondent used to pay graduated tax for the girl's father but since the advent of universal primary education, the respondent now funds scholastic requirements for the girl. The work the girls do includes collecting water, cooking, collecting firewood, cleaning the house and washing dishes.

This case study shows the reciprocal relationship underlying the agreement between the parties: provision of a form of labour in return for maintenance and education. I found that poverty on the part of a child's parents is a major factor influencing such social arrangements. All the girls came from needy families. The agreement between their parents and Mrs K was that they perform domestic work while in her custody as they accessed formal education and the provision of scholastic materials by Mrs K.

These cases illustrate how social arrangements serve an important social function in enabling access to education for children who might otherwise fail to access formal education and the benefits that flow from it. My personal experience is a good example of fulfilling the need for education and reciprocity through domestic work as a basis for a social arrangement. The fact that I received education, food, clothing, shelter and medical attention points to the positive attributes of the practice of children in social arrangements. I performed domestic chores but this was a form of reciprocity for maintenance. It was a minor consideration compared to the short and long term benefits I received from the arrangement. Without it, my life history would have been different.

Reproductive consequences and marital concerns
Teenage pregnancies and preservation of the marriage institution emerged as other social situations giving rise to the need to enter into social arrangements for the care of a child. Often, in situations where young mothers are deemed incompetent in the role of parenting, the child may be looked after by a more able adult. In some situations the young woman will have fallen pregnant from a married man and the fear is that his wife will abuse the child from the extra-marital union.

In one of the cases I came across, Susan, a 40 year old housewife, told me she was asked by her brother to take custody of his five year old son as the new wife was abusing the boy and the boy's mother had left the matrimonial home. This paternal aunt/nephew social arrangement was between a brother and a sister and was brought about by the need for marital harmony in the brother's house. The sister was looking after her brother's child out of a sense of compassion and perhaps because she was at ease with a mothering role. Another social function offered by social arrangements is therefore the provision of a home to children from teenage mothers and children from extra-marital unions.

The study also showed that the state of being childless is an important factor in bringing about social arrangements. I came across Kate who is married but childless. She took custody of her brother's two children. This is another example of a paternal aunt/niece or nephew social arrangement. Although she cited the abject poverty her brother lived in as the reason for taking in his two children, another motive for the arrangement was addressing her childlessness. Another important basis for social arrangements is therefore that they can offer a ready solution to childless women. The women are able to perform the mothering role while at the same time the children in the arrangements receive the benefit of a good upbringing.

Underlying all the arrangements is also the social value attached to reciprocity. In some cases, actors are expected to take custody and care of social children as a gesture of reciprocity for those actors having grown up in such arrangements themselves. Within the extended family, reciprocity could be based on anticipated or possible future arrangements. Another aspect of reciprocity is the anticipation of social and economic security for the de facto guardian. In terms of domestic work, children in social arrangements are expected to perform domestic work in return for their care and upkeep.

3 Assessing customary practices in child care arrangements in the light of international and national law

The best interests of the child principle
Analyzing the different models of child care arrangements under customary practices also involves assessing how they measure up to domestic as well as international standards in addressing the best interests of the child. The Convention on the Rights of the Child is the basic document regulating the position of children in international law. It sets standards for the treatment of children in all aspects of their lives. The convention is an outcome of a consensus among different nations and different cultures. As Pais (1999:23) aptly notes, the fact that the convention has been so widely ratified illustrates the universality of the values and norms it represents and the acceptance of human rights standards as a strategy for transforming the lives of children.

Of significance, article 3 of the convention enjoins states to ensure:

'In all actions concerning children, whether undertaken by public or private social welfare institutions, courts of law, administrative authorities or legislative bodies, the best interests of the child shall be a primary consideration.'

In a similar vein, article 4 of the African Charter on the Rights and Welfare of the Child, a regional instrument, reiterates the best interests principle as the basic standard for all actions concerning children, thus embracing the same normative basis for the rights of the child as in international law.

The best interests of the child as a cornerstone for children rights is also embodied in Uganda's national law which deals with children. Section 3 of the Children Act[62] provides that:

---

[62] The Children Act Chapter 59 Volume III, Laws of Uganda 2000. Prior to the latest revision of the laws of Uganda, the Act was referred to as the Children Statute 6 of 1996.

'The welfare principle and the children's rights set out in the first schedule shall be the guiding principles in the making of a decision based
on the provisions of the Act.'[63]

The first schedule to the Children Act reinforces section 3 and gives
guiding principles in the implementation of the Act. Part of the text of
the schedule states as follows:

'Whenever the State, a court, local authority or any person determines
any question with respect to:

a) the upbringing of a child or

b) the administration of a child's property or the application of any
income arising from it, the child's welfare shall be of the
paramount consideration.'

The best interests principle is therefore the normative basis for all actions concerning children in both national and international law. In en-
acting the Children Act the legislature sought not only to comply with
Uganda's Constitution of 1995 but also with the spirit of article 3 of the
Convention on the Rights of the Child and article 4 of the African Charter on the Rights and Welfare of the Child.

The Children Act not only introduced the notion of the rights of the
child in the area of upbringing of children but also bridged the gap between custom and formal law.

Section 5 of the Children Act places the same legal obligations concerning the upbringing of a child on de facto as well as de jure guardians. It provides that:

'(1) It shall be the duty of a parent, guardian, or any person having
custody of a child to maintain that child and, in particular, that duty
gives a child the right to:

---

[63] The use of the term 'welfare' is simply a matter of semantics otherwise the term
means one and the same thing as the 'best interests'. In *Pulkeria Nakagwa v
Dominico Kigundu* (1978) HCB 310, a judge of the High Court of Uganda echoed
the vagueness in the welfare principle. Citing dictum in *Lourgh v Ward*, (1945)
ALL ER 338, he had this to say:
'The term welfare though incapable of exact definition, means in relation to custody of children, that all circumstances affecting the wellbeing and upbringing of
the child have to be taken into account and the court has to do what a wise parent
acting for the child ought to do.'
The court in that case held that the father's natural and superior right to custody of
the child as against the mother's, the claim of other relatives, as well as the conduct of the parties, all have to be taken into account along with the paramount
importance of the welfare principle. The judge noted that the father's natural right
to the custody of his children could be interfered with because it was considered
better for a child of tender years to live with the mother. Therefore, the law evolved
in such a manner that children in social arrangements were excluded from the
operation of the principles that developed in parent/child relationships.

(a) education and guidance
(b) immunization;
(c) adequate diet;
(d) clothing;
(e) shelter; and
(f) medical attention

(2) Any person having custody of a child shall protect the child from discrimination, violence, abuse and neglect.'

Section 5 of the Children Act introduced legal regulation in the area of upbringing of children in three main ways:

1   By imposing duties on any person with custody of social children. Those with custody of social children became de facto guardians;
2   By conferring rights of the child on all children;
3   By recognizing social arrangements for children.

By conferring on all guardians duties and specific responsibilities towards children in their care, the Act can be said to have taken an integrated approach to customary practices and formal law in that it recognized a customary practice of care through a variety of social arrangements, and simultaneously expanded it by introducing the notion of rights of the child. The Children Act confers the status of de facto guardian on relatives who have custody of social children within the framework of the extended family. It imposes duties on them towards the children and confers rights on children in such arrangements. In so doing, the Children Act can be said to draw on custom to ensure the realization of the modern notion of the rights of the child. The Act recognizes the positive aspects of social arrangements which lead to the realization of the rights of the child. In recognizing de facto guardianship as embodied in customary practice, the law is clearly acknowledging the positive aspects of the practice of children brought up in arrangements following agreements between adults of the extended family. The integration of customary based child care arrangements into mainstream law is also an example of how legal pluralism can be accommodated within a unified legal system through cross fertilization.

In several incidents I came across, the social values embraced by the actors led to the realization of the rights of the child. In my own experience, narrated at the commencement of this chapter, the agreement for me to live with my maternal aunt demonstrated the capacity of the actors (parents and aunt) to draw on custom in coping with the dynamics of change – embracing the value of formal education in a manner that was beneficial to the child. The arrangement also demonstrated an attribute of custom: that it can be mobilized to suit situations as they arise – in this case the need to access education for the girl child. In readily accepting to fund my education and take me into her custody, my aunt was not only responding to the agreement with my parents but also to custom and the children's right to education. Nanyonga, a grandmother in her sixties had this to say:

> 'I have lived with my grandchildren peacefully. I show them love as their mother would have done. I give them shelter and food, and attend to their health needs. I teach them how to relate to people. I have lived with children of both sexes. When a child misbehaves, I contact the parent or school authorities for correction. Currently, I have in my custody a grandson. The rest are now grown up and married.'

In this case study, the right of the child to be protected from discrimination, violence, abuse and neglect are realized through the attitude of the grandmother. Obviously, the children who have passed through her hands benefited from her care. Considerations of maintaining good relations with the wider family deterred the mistreatment of the social child. The role of the wider community is to act as a deterrent to the mistreatment of the children in these arrangements. Respondents said they did not mistreat the social children in their care because of fear of hostility from members of the extended family. The welfare of the child was therefore an important factor in the upbringing of the social child.

The central concern of how social arrangements, in reality, interface with principles embodied in international and domestic law is examined below.

4   The interface between national and international law and the practice of bringing up children in social arrangements

Having outlined the various situations giving rise to social arrangements and noted that the quest for education in light of limited resources is often one of the factors bringing about child care social arrangements, it is of interest to analyze how such social arrangements measure up to the expected standard in as far as the rights of the child to education are concerned and also in so far as the prohibition against child labour is a fundamental right of the child.

The right to education and prohibition against child labour
Article 32 of the Convention on the Rights of the Child lays down the principle against child labour. It prohibits economic exploitation of the child and any work that is harmful and hazardous to the child's holistic development. The value system in African settings is that domestic work is an obligation and doubles as socialization in gender roles and survival

skills. In western construction, taken to extremes, it is viewed as a form of child labour. The African position is reinforced by article 27 of the African Charter on Human and Peoples' Rights which confers duties on individuals towards the family and community. In my understanding, 'individuals' include children.

The child's right to education is set out in section 6(a) of the Children Act which provides that:

> 'It shall be the duty of a parent, guardian or any person having custody of a child to maintain that child and in particular that duty gives a child the right to education and guidance, immunization, adequate diet, clothing, shelter and medical attention.'

The right of the child not to be subjected to hazardous and exploitative employment is also recognized in section 8 of the Act, which states that:

> 'No child shall be employed or engaged in any activity that may be harmful to his or her health, education or mental, physical or moral development.'

A further analysis of social arrangements that are founded on the provision of education in return for domestic labour is of interest given the perspective among some scholars that children engaged in domestic labour miss out on good education. Can we say that such social arrangements founded on domestic labour in return for education are nonetheless problematic and exploitative from a child's rights perspective? My own case study as well as that of Mrs K discussed earlier demonstrate the interface between the social value of reciprocity, the right to education and the performance of domestic work in light of the right of the child not to be subjected to hazardous and exploitative employment. It highlights the need to be sensitive to individual situations and to understand the social context of the realization of the rights of the child.

The choice of missing out on education because of scarce resources on the part of parents on the one hand or combining an opportunity for education and domestic work in a reciprocal arrangement on the other, makes the latter the better of the two evils. Even with the advent of universal primary education, there are children who miss out on education because the parents cannot afford the scholastic materials. Therefore, embracing the social value of education by actors in social arrangements often leads to the realization of the child's right to education.

In short, I would argue that the reciprocal arrangement where a child benefits from education while engaged in the performance of domestic duty offers a middle position which allows us to perceive the value of performing domestic work while at the same time recognizes the right of the child not to be subjected to harmful or hazardous activity. Surely, where a child is able to access formal educational institutions while helping out with domestic chores, the rights of the child to education, health, shelter and clothing are being realized. In fact, in such arrangements, the best interests principle standard is met. Therefore, understanding the social context of the right of the child to be protected against economic exploitation and hazardous activity is an important stage in the promotion of human rights. Hellum brings out this point when she discusses the management of procreative problems among childless Shona women and the principle of gender equality:

> 'In an attempt to reconcile conflicting human rights values like gender equality and cultural diversity in a dynamic, flexible and situation-sensitive manner, the emerging pluralist alternative is trying to define a space between universalism and relativism...' (Hellum, 1999: 421)

This is not to say that in the African context performance of domestic work is only within the framework of reciprocal arrangements. Some children are engaged in domestic work as paid domestic workers. These children do not access school and some are exploited because the children are not paid regularly (Ssemmanda, 1995). It is these arrangements that are in conflict with the best interests principle and that should be the target of law enforcement initiatives against child labour and not those situations where the child is able to access education, albeit carrying out domestic chores in return.

Not all cases of social arrangements work out in the best interests of the child or promote the rights of the child as envisaged by international and domestic law. Rosemary's experiences are a case in point.

In contrast to the arrangements that promote the rights of the child, Rosemary's experience is one of trauma, abuse and dehumanization. I found eight year old Rosemary at the Children Reception Centre, Naguru in Kampala. She was committed to the centre by a magistrate as a child in need of care and protection. She had been brought to Kampala from Masaka, some 100kms away, by her paternal uncle who promised her father that he would get her into school. On reaching Kampala, she was regularly assaulted by her uncle and made to perform domestic chores every day which included washing dishes and clothes and tending to the children. For an eight year old, it was child abuse to subject her to such work. When it became too much for her, she fled her uncle's home. Rosemary's case shows the capacity of de facto guardians to reject positive social values in the upbringing of social children in their care thereby leading to a denial of the rights of the child.

In practice, there are many children, including those sent to nonrelatives and relatives alike, who are exploited by their caretakers. This is often the case when the law is not supported by social norms. Although many children in Uganda live with their parents, many also live on the streets, in orphanages, as domestic workers with their employers and with their relatives. Child abuse, polygamy, single parenthood, poverty and death of parents are some of the causes for having many street children who obviously have limited if any access to education in Uganda.[64]

In many instances work obligations may amount to exploitation. For example, I recently came across a case where a sister with a total of 10 children but with no definite means of livelihood gave custody of her 14 year old daughter, Rose, to her younger sister with modest means. The agreement between the two sisters was that the girl would perform domestic chores as she pursued her secondary education at a nearby school. The arrangement did not last for long because the girl complained to the mother that the maternal aunt gave her too many chores thereby exhausting her, she was very harsh and discriminated against her in terms of letting her eat only after her own children had had their fill. I knew the aunt and she complained that her sister's daughter was lazy. The two sisters lived in the same town so the girl's mother was in constant touch with her daughter. In the end, the girl had to return to her parents' home.

The right to non-discrimination
How do child care social arrangements hold up against the backdrop of section 5 (2) of the Children Act which provides for protection of the child against discrimination by imposing a duty on any person with custody of a child to protect the child from discrimination, violence, abuse and neglect? While the welfare of the child is crucial there is, however, a hierarchy within the family – a hierarchy between insiders and outsiders, sister and brother's children and between girl and boy children.

The right of the child not to be discriminated against can be discussed in the light of three dimensions, namely:
- socially ascribed gender roles;
- cultural construction of a social and biological child;
- different rankings in value attached to sons and daughters.

In my extended case study of Rose's situation, three of the dimensions above are manifest. There is the dimension of discrimination in terms of gender; the girl, Rose, was accepted in the home because she could perform domestic chores and being female disposed her to this belief on the part of her mother and her sister. There is also the dimension of discrimination on account of being a social child; because she was a social

---

[64] See, for instance, the study by Nansakusa Penn, 'The problem of street children in rural /urban areas: A case study of Mbale municipality' (unpublished dissertation, Makerere University, Faculty of Arts, 2004).

child, she was treated differently from her aunt's biological children. At the same time, the principle of non-discrimination was manifested by her access to formal education in spite of the fact that she was female. These dimensions are examined more fully below.

Socially ascribed sex roles and protection against discrimination
The preference for girls on account of their ability to perform domestic chores is a reflection of society's perception of the role of the girl child. In rural Uganda girls have been socialized to perform domestic roles like child rearing, cooking and cleaning.

In earlier models of arrangements, the paternal aunt took custody of her niece principally to socialize her in gender roles. The fact that performance of domestic work by the girl child is still considered a social value indicates that there is continuance of the notions of gender roles with some arguably positive and some obviously negative consequences for the girl child. The positive factor is that the girls receive formal education and the negative factor is that the girls may be easily exploited. Ultimately, some people have embraced new values and ideas in combination with the old gender roles. Others have rejected such new ideas and denied the girl child education.

The specific nature of discrimination envisaged by the Children Act against which children are to be protected is not spelt out. However, guidance can be found in the Convention on the Rights of the Child as well as in the Convention on the Elimination of all forms of Discrimination Against Women (CEDAW) as to what kind of conduct amounts to discrimination. For example, article 5 of CEDAW provides that:

> 'State parties shall take all appropriate measures:
>
> (a) To modify the social and cultural patterns of conduct of men and women, with a view to achieving the elimination of prejudices and customary and all other practices which are based on the idea of the inferiority or the superiority of either of the sexes or on stereotyped roles for men and women.'

Sex or gender role stereotyping is discrimination within the meaning of article 5 of CEDAW. Therefore, preference for girls on account of their ability to perform domestic chores can be said to be a contravention of this article. However, grounded realities present problems for the realization of such principles. Whereas the principle against stereotyping demands that expression be given to the idea of non-discrimination, social reality may call for tacit approval of discrimination due to advantages that may accrue to some girls in the arrangements by way of accessing education. Under such circumstances, the best interests of the child serve as a guiding principle in balancing out the performance of domestic work and the principle against discrimination.

Exploring other means of alleviating the workload in the home to free girls from the association with domestic work is one way of tackling such problems. Another answer lies in opening child day care centres so that people do not seek girls from needy families as a source of cheap labour. Strengthening enforcement mechanisms on the rights of the child would also go a long way in eliminating practices that keep young girls away from school to perform domestic chores.

Discrimination between biological and social children

The wider community plays an important role in defining attitudes towards social children. Respondents in a focus group discussion were of the view that adults tended to differentiate between their own natal children and the social children. This discrimination was epitomized in a Luganda[65] proverb which, translated into English, means:

> 'When you give a saucepan of groundnut sauce to your child to lick, it is out of love. When you give it to a social child, it is termed as mistreatment.'

Metaphorically translated, the proverb means that a parent's love can never be substituted.

A common feature about all the arrangements, both current and older models, is that the social children are referred to as *abawereke*. Whereas some elderly respondents in the rural area said the term means 'those who are carried' and who turn out successful owing to the harsh life they undergo, some urban folk considered the term to be derogatory as in 'tethering goats'. I concluded that the term *abawereke* represents the dichotomy prevalent in people's attitudes towards the children in arrangements. It represents the prevalence of arrangements that are in the best interests of the child and those against them.

The belief that it is impossible to love a social child meets with a principle of law which commands the opposite of the belief. The social construction of the relationship with a social child appears to have continued over time. Proverbs take time to take root so it is likely that the belief has been around for sometime. The belief leads to a value system that goes against the grain for a child's welfare.

Preference of sons over daughters' children

As regards preference for sons' children over daughters' children in arrangements involving grandparents, the group interest of perpetuation of the lineage is the force behind this. This is discrimination within the meaning of article 5 of CEDAW. The social value of ranking the chil-

---

[65] Luganda is a language spoken by the Ganda ethnic community of Uganda.

dren based on the birth status of the parent is also discrimination within the meaning of article 2 of the Convention on the Rights of the Child and is incompatible with the principle of non-discrimination in law.

Patrilineal considerations and negative beliefs that undermine female children constitute a normative order which exists among other norms like that which is against discrimination of any kind. Addressing the undesirable normative order would be a starting point in getting people to change their beliefs and therefore their attitudes towards social children. The changed order would then be integrated in legislation.

It can be said that the non-discriminatory principle in legislation is in harmony with some social values and in conflict with others. The principle is in harmony with the social value of not discriminating against the girl child in terms of considering her welfare, including her access to formal education. The principle conflicts with the social value of preference for a son's children and the belief in discrimination against social children. The principle is contentious when it comes to the perception of domestic work as beneficial to a child. An integrated approach takes care of the various dimensions of the principle in real life by providing room for change. For it is only the positive social values which are presumed to be integrated in the law. It is assumed that social transformation will take place with regard to reconciling conflicting values in order to bring the social reality in harmony with the law.

5   Working with custom: an assessment of the integrated approach model in promoting human rights

The appropriateness of an integrated approach to promoting human rights that accommodates legal pluralism to foster change in human behaviour is important to examine.

An integrated approach combines law and life. As a tool for managing social change, the reinforcement of social arrangements through legal recognition and integration into written law is a worthy enterprise because the springboard for embracing change will already be in place. The social norm of concern for the welfare of the child is congruent with the best interests of the child principle. The positive values in the arrangements are consistent with the elements of the specific rights of the child. Some of the arrangements presented interfaces between the statutory rights and exploitative and discriminatory values. Others were consistent with the best interests principle in terms of access to formal education and other statutory rights of the child. Some arrangements balanced the girl's domestic chores and her right to education and leisure. In other arrangements the girls were deprived of their rights. The arrangements themselves are 'social welfare' sensitive responses that foster the growth and development of the child. Bringing them under legal regulation is appropriate in view of the fact that they are widespread.

The integrated approach, in contrast with the dual model of colonial law or models based on unification through elimination of custom as has often been the case in post-colonial laws, offers an alternative method of regulating such social responses. This integrated method captured in section 5 of the Children Act, sees law and life as an integrated whole. The approach not only renders the law synonymous with the social values of the people but also offers a framework facilitating new values and ideas, harnessing the capacity of the people to adopt new values and thereby foster change.

The integrated approach model of the Children Act is also a realistic approach to law reform since, as Allot (1980) notes, through such an approach the legislature takes advantage of existing behaviour and the high regard for a particular aspect of life. An alternative model of regulation is introduced in the hope that social transformation will occur as the new model is accepted.

The approach recognizes that there may be common values underlying different forms of law. As such, it does not seek to substitute indigenous norms with statutory norms through a wholesale dichotomous approach. It recognizes that in spite of difference, there are overarching values and sanctions are put in place when there is a breach of standards. Statutory norms and customary norms are not seen as incompatible but as a process of interacting and intersecting principles. The approach may be termed pluralist because it allows for continuity and change in a 'situation-sensitive manner'. This mode is neither relativist nor universalist but represents an in-between position (Hellum, 1999).

The pluralist approach has been operationalized through the integrated approach of section 5 of the Children Act. The positive social values on the upbringing of children have been merged in the Act with a notion of the child as an individual with specific rights. It demonstrates an effort at using existing resources to effect change. A new norm is emerging – one which promotes human rights through working with custom rather than treating the two as distinct and conflicting systems.

The approach allows room for change in values drawing on the capacity of the actors to adopt new values which are compatible with the rights of the child. The integrated approach therefore facilitates social and legal change. It demonstrates that recognizing positive values obtaining in African communities as a resource can be channelled towards promoting human rights and at the same time act as a basis for acceptance of the notion of rights. As the English legal scholar Michael Freeman (1997: 25) asserts:

'Rights are important because those who lack them are like slaves, means to the end of others and never sovereigns in their own rights. Those who claim rights or for whom rights may be claimed, have a necessary precondition to the constitution of humanity, of integrity, of individuality, of personality.'

Conclusion

This chapter demonstrates a grounded approach to law reform. The integration of existing positive customs that are consistent with international norms into the formal law is one approach to introducing new ideas with minimum disruption of social life. The Uganda legislature introduced the notion of rights of the child by making de facto guardians responsible for the social children in their custody. The de facto guardians had been responsible for their young relations for generations. Taking advantage of the positive aspects of social arrangements for children within the framework of the extended family is an innovative approach to law reform.

However, the reform is not without challenges. Child abuse takes place within family and non-family arrangements. In the final analysis, arrangements that were informed by customary obligations turned out to be for the welfare of the child, for example, grandparents/grandchild arrangements. Where the arrangements were based on mutual agreements, for example, a paternal uncle/niece arrangement, there was a risk of the actors rejecting the positive social values informing the arrangements thereby exposing the children in them to abuse and denial of rights. Ultimately, the success of social arrangements depended on the capacity of the actors to embrace positive social values and reject those values that undermine the rights of the child.

The main challenge is enforcement of the Act. Providing children with information is important as are appropriate conflict resolution forums. Although breaches attract some sanctions, tougher sanctions or responses to the breaches of the Act are needed. Expecting the executive committee courts to enforce the rights is not enough, owing to the limited sanctions available to them, among other things.[66] There is need for more research into dispute resolution within the framework of the extended family and social arrangements so that an input can be made in the formal dispute resolution mechanisms.

---

[66] The village committee courts were initially set up by the Resistance Committee (Judicial Powers) Statute 1/1988. After several amendments, they have been renamed 'executive committee courts' and the enabling law is the Executive Committee (Judicial Powers) Act Chapter 8, Laws of Uganda 2000. The courts are composed of the elected executive committees of the village, parish and sub-county. Executive committees are local administrative units under the Local Government Act Chapter 243 Laws of Uganda.

Bibliography

Allott A. (1980), *The limits of law*, Butterworths & Co Ltd, London.

Armstrong A. (1994) 'School and sadza. Custody and the best interests of the child', *International Journal of Law and family*, 8:151–190.

Freeman M. (1997), *The moral status of children*, Martinus Nijhoff Publishers, London, the Hague.

Hellum A. (1999), *Women's human rights and legal pluralism in Africa*, Mond Books, Harare.

Pais S. M. (1999) 'A new vision for a non-violent world', in A. M. Traham (ed), *A new vision for a non-violent world: Justice for each child*, Thomson Professional Publishers, Canada.

Penn N. (2004) 'The problem of street children in rural /urban areas: A case study of Mbale municipality', unpublished dissertation, Makerere University, Faculty of Arts, Nairobi.

Rosaldo Z. M. and L. Lamphere (eds) (1989) *Women, culture and society*, Stanford University Press, Stanford.

Ssemmanda W. H. (2001) 'Children's rights, social arrangements and guardianship: Confronting the best interests principle: A Kampala and Mpigi based study', thesis submitted to the University of Zimbabwe for the award of Master of Philosophy Degree.
– (1995), 'The legal position of young female domestic workers in Kampala', Women's Law Diploma Dissertation, University of Zimbabwe, Harare.

Website cited

www.sos-childrensvillage.org

List of cases
Lourgh v Ward, (1945) ALL ER 338
Pulkeria Nakagwa v Dominico Kigundu (1978) HCB 310

List of legislation
Uganda
Constitution of Uganda 1995
Children Act, Chapter 59 2000
Children Statute 6 of 1996
Executive Committee (Judicial Powers) Act Chapter 8, 2000
Local Government Act Chapter 243
Resistance Committee (Judicial Powers) Statute 1/1988

Regional and international
United Nations Convention on the Rights of the Child 1989
Convention on All Forms of Discrimination Against Women (CEDAW) 1979
African Charter on the Rights and Welfare of the Child 1990
African Charter on Human and Peoples' Rights 1981

4
Women's burden: Women, HIV/AIDS and home-based care in Zimbabwe

Ellen Sithole

HIV/AIDS has taken its toll of lives, especially in the southern African region. But, as this chapter illustrates it is not only affecting those who are ill. Women and girls who are forced by cultural and economic imperatives to provide care to family members affected by HIV/AIDS have their lives and life opportunities eroded by the care-giving roles they take on. Governments' human rights and development related obligations to eliminate harmful cultural practices that adversely affect women and girls' rights to equality are engaged as components in the overall strategies to address the impact of the HIV/AIDS pandemic, especially in developing or under-developing countries.

1   Introduction

his chapter is partly based on an empirical study conducted by students of the then Post-Graduate Diploma in Women's Law[67] at the University of Zimbabwe under my supervision in April 2001.[68] The study was carried out in Kadoma, a small town about 140 kilometres from Harare.[69] I also draw from literature written on the Zimbabwean situation and the situation in southern Africa and on my own observations of events that took place within my extended family and those of a work colleague. I use cumulative data from these sources to critically examine the concept of home-based care with specific focus on its impact on the human rights of women.

---

[67] Since 2003 the programme has been upgraded to a Masters in Women's Law. In both programmes students are required to carry out a mini field research in groups at the end of the first semester of the programme.

[68] The students were Lavender Makoni, Ndangariro Perpetua Moyo, Nonkululeko Ngwenya (all from Zimbabwe), Grace Mutenyo and Everse Ruhindi (from Uganda) and are referred to as 'the student researchers' throughout this chapter. The work has not been published.

[69] Kadoma is situated on the Harare-Bulawayo highway. Kadoma is surrounded by commercial farms with maize and cotton being the major crops. It is also a mining town being home to several large-scale gold mines such as Rio Tinto and Eiffel Flats. Apart from mining, the town's major industries include a textile factory, meat and dairy processing plants and some light engineering. Commercial entities include supermarkets, hotels and transport businesses.

Background

The HIV/AIDS pandemic has brought about serious socio-economic and cultural challenges for Zimbabwe and other developing countries. The challenges are exacerbated by the continuing decline in Zimbabwe's economy which had commenced before the severe onset of the pandemic. According to the *Zimbabwe human development report 2003*, extreme poverty increased significantly during the 1990s. The authors of the report cite the Poverty Assessment Study Survey (PASS 1) of 1995 which revealed that an estimated 45 per cent of households were living below the food poverty line which is the level at which people can meet their basic foods needs, compared to about 25 per cent in 1990. The survey also revealed that, based on the total consumption poverty line, poverty increased from about 40 per cent of total households in the late 1980s to 61 per cent by 1995. The report also notes that the rate of increase of formal employment declined from 4.3 per cent in 1988 to a negative -1.8 per cent in 1995. By 2002, it had further declined to -10.2 per cent. Inflation continues to rise; it peaked at more than 600 per cent at the end of 2003, declined to around 125 per cent, and rose again to about 254 per cent in July 2005. The increase between June and July 2005 was 90 per cent. The problem of poverty is further compounded by the high prevalence of HIV/AIDS in Zimbabwe. The number of people infected with HIV (and still alive) in Zimbabwe rose from 390,000 in 1988 to nearly 1.8 million in 2003. In 2003 approximately 10 per cent of the infected persons had developed AIDS. AIDS is responsible for about 9 out of every 10 deaths in the 15–49 age group (Ministry of Health and Child Welfare, 2004:27–28, 31).

The prevalence of poverty in Zimbabwe's urban and rural areas is not disputed. The following description of Rimuka (an urban residential area in Kadoma which was the focus of the Kadoma study) is typical of high density suburbs in many of Zimbabwe's urban areas:

'It is a densely populated urban area that is largely composed of old house models from the colonial era. Rudimentary structures have been constructed in order to house the expanding population.[70] Most of the people live in absolute to relative poverty and are employed in the informal sector, with a small percentage that is formally employed' (Kadoma study).

---

[70] Many of these structures were deemed to be illegal and pulled down by the Zimbabwe government when in May/June 2005 it embarked on *Murambatsvina* (reject trash/restore order) in which informal settlements and businesses were destroyed. Kadoma was also affected by this exercise which has been widely condemned by the international community, including the United Nations Envoy on Human Settlement Issues, Anna Kajamulo Tibaijuka who carried out a fact-finding mission.

Thus it is not surprising that families do not have the means to meet their basic needs such as food, housing, health and education. The state has not coped with the overwhelming demand for assistance in accessing these services. The result is that the burden of caring for those affected by AIDS falls on families regardless of their economic status. This study will reveal that it is mainly women and girls who bear this burden. Their ability to cope with this burden depends on their access to the necessary legal, socio-economic and cultural resources.

Rationale for home-based care

The Zimbabwe government produced what at face value appears to be a feasible rationale for placing the emphasis and responsibility for the care and management of terminal AIDS patients on families. According to the government's *National HIV/AIDS strategic framework 2000–2004* (Zimbabwe government, 1999:17):

> 'The home-based care concept provides an opportunity and channel for education/training, resource provision, attitude/behaviour change, positive influence on customs and traditions surrounding the care of the sick as well as the management of bereavement etc.'

The *National community home-based care standards of 2004* state that home-based care is part of the 'continuum of care' which is defined as:

> 'A comprehensive multi-level response from the hospital to the home and vice versa, covering a wide range of medical, emotional and social support needs of chronically ill patients and their families' (Zimbabwe government, 2004: xi).

The same document provides the following as the advantages of home-based care:

> '1 Patients are cared for in familiar home environments until they die, as opposed to being isolated during hospitalization.
> 2 The entire family works together to support the patient.
> 3 Families and communities begin to understand HIV and AIDS better, helping to make prevention initiatives more effective and providing experience and skills for coping with future cases in the family or community.
> 4 Communities adopt more supportive attitudes and an awareness that AIDS in Africa is a family disease.
> 5 A comprehensive home care programme facilitates planning by identifying households where orphans and other dependants will be left behind to fend for themselves.
> 6 Home care frees up hospital beds and reduces the cost to the conventional health care system while maintaining a strong link with it' (Zimbabwe government, 2004: 2–3).

The *National community home-based care standards* also recommend that needs assessment and situational analysis of care and support for the patient and family should be carried out before a patient is released under the home-based care programme. The assessment should, inter alia, address the following issues:

'The patient's family primary caregivers including: family structure, emotional status, interaction patterns within and outside the family, decision-making processes surrounding the terminal illness, problems and resource needs, experience in caring for the terminally ill. The capacity of the community to understand the nature of HIV or AIDS related illness, providing care, mobilizing resources and responding to patient needs: including the socio-cultural environment and coping mechanisms during illness and at the time of bereavement' (Zimbabwe government, 2004: 8).

The policy documents on home-based care give the impression that it was a well-planned policy introduced by the Zimbabwe government in order to deal with the HIV/AIDS pandemic. Yet the home-based care programme was not pre-planned; the state was faced with a crisis, hospitals were overcrowded and could not cope with the increase in numbers of patients due to the AIDS pandemic. Families thus had no alternative except to care for them by themselves. The state latched onto this practice as a way of managing the crisis and started encouraging home-based care for AIDS patients. However, the state did not provide adequate resources for home-based care and experience on the ground is that families often have to find their own resources for drugs, gloves, detergents and other needs of home-based care patients. Nor does the state provide adequate support from health personnel. Patients are supposed to be assessed prior to discharge from hospital or for inclusion in the assistance programme, in most cases they are simply discharged remain unassessed as does the anticipated home-based care environment. The promised continuum of care is non-existent in most cases. The lack of proper planning for home-based care and failure to provide adequate resources for the programme have led to the conclusion that hospit are dumping patients on families and the state is using families to subsidize it in the provision of health care services.

The 'advertised' standards paint an ideal situation which is far removed from the grounded reality as will be made clearer by the articulation of the burden of care on women and girls (as primary care-givers) and how it is made worse by the underlying social, cultural, economic and legal inequalities. Five aspects of the burden of care will be dealt with namely:
- Poverty and the economic consequences of care;

- Cultural factors influencing care;
- The psychological burden;
- Lack of support from health and other service providers;
- Policy and legal issues.

2 Poverty and the economic consequences of home-based care

To illustrate the realities of the situation I present the experiences of four women who undertook home-based care. Three of these women told their stories to the student researchers in the Kadoma study. The fourth one is a workmate who was willing to share the experience. Fictitious names have been used. Betty's story graphically illustrates the stress and problems experienced by home-based carers, especially young carers.

Betty (aged 15 years in 2001)[71]

Betty's father died in 1996 when she was 11 years old and in grade 4 at school. One week after the father's death, her mother gave birth to a baby girl. Shortly afterwards, her mother fell ill and was hospitalized. The doctor advised her to stop breastfeeding the baby. The baby was taken home to be looked after by Betty for the three weeks that her mother was in hospital. She did not attend school for those three weeks because she was looking after the baby. Betty resumed school when her mother was discharged from hospital but she would occasionally miss school because her mother and the baby often fell ill. The baby died two years later. Her mother continued to fall ill from time to time complaining of fever and tuberculosis.[72] Betty's performance in school declined due to the frequent absences. However, she still managed to pass her grade 7 (the last level of primary school) but failed to proceed to secondary school due to lack of school fees and her mother's illness.

Before Betty's mother became ill, she was an informal trader who sold groundnuts and mealie-meal at the bus terminus. Betty took over the task from her mother when she fell ill.

Betty has three brothers, two older and one younger than her. The older brothers were (at the time of the study) engaged in informal

---

[71] At the time the research was carried out.

[72] Prior to the advent of the HIV/AIDS pandemic, tuberculosis had become rare in Zimbabwe. In fact nurses at Kadoma General Hospital told the student researchers that the tuberculosis ward was about to be closed before HIV/AIDS brought increased cases of tuberculosis. Tuberculosis is the most prevalent opportunistic infection associated with HIV/AIDS in Zimbabwe.

income-generating activities. One was selling firewood whilst the other was carrying people's luggage (at the bus terminus) for a fee. The younger brother was at school (grade 7). The income derived from Betty's trading and the brothers' income-generating activities was being used to meet the family's basic needs and pay the school fees for the boy in grade 7. The trading and other income-generating activities did not bring in much and the family struggled to survive and sometimes had to borrow food from neighbours.

Betty was responsible for cooking the family's meals and looking after her ill mother. Betty and her brothers were not receiving any help from the extended family. The mother was from Malawi and most of the relatives from her side were in that country although she and her brothers did not have any contact with them. The relatives from the father's side had simply broken ties with Betty and her brothers. The last time they had seen any of them was when a paternal uncle attended their father's funeral.

Betty's main desire was to go back to school. Her older brothers had gone to school up to form 4 – O-level (she did not say whether they passed their O-levels). She felt hurt by being deprived of education and broke down in tears when she spoke to the student researchers about this issue.

The economic impact – for the home and for the nation
The economic impact of HIV/AIDS (and the subsequent home-based care) at household level includes substantial income reduction due to loss of opportunities to earn money and diversion of labour from activities that are crucial for survival such as income-generating activities and food production. In addition, savings and assets are depleted in order to meet the cost of care. The result is poor families often spiral from acute or seasonal poverty to chronic poverty and food insecurity (Zimbabwe government, 1999: 43–44). Agricultural output has been observed to decline by as much as 50 per cent among households affected by AIDS illness and death (Ministry of Health and Child Welfare and National AIDS Council, 2004: 38). Women provide the bulk of agricultural labour in rural areas and are thus faced with competing demands to maintain crop production and care for family members suffering from AIDS-related illnesses (Ministry of Health and Child Welfare and National AIDS Council, 2004).

Urban women and women employed outside the home are also affected by the problem of competing demands. Women who are informal traders or are engaged in other income-generating activities in the informal sector have had to stop or curtail these activities due to their care responsibilities. The case of Rose who had to give up her tuckshop business, is a typical example of this predicament.

Rose

Rose, a 30 year old woman from Rimuka, was initially interviewed in the presence of her husband, who was the patient. Rose's husband dominated the interview and answered questions which were directed at his wife. The student researchers got around this problem by asking her to accompany them to the local shopping centre where they would buy food for the family (they had no food to eat that day). The husband was very pleased to let her go and the student researchers were able to interview her more freely.

Rose's husband was 34 years old and they had two children of school-going age. The husband was suffering from tuberculosis and boils. The couple believed he had been bewitched although he was receiving conventional treatment for the tuberculosis. Rose would press out the boils with her bare hands.

Prior to his illness, Rose was running a small grocery store (known as a tuckshop in local parlance) but it collapsed because she could not cope with the demands of running the business due to her care responsibilities. She had resorted to using her meagre savings but these had now been depleted leaving the family in abject poverty.

Rose summarized her reaction to the difficulties as follows:

'There was a time when it was too much for me. I wanted to run away but by that time I had committed my life to God and was born again. I then thought that it would not please God and I decided to stay. I am telling you life can really be hard' (translation of the Shona words used).

Women who are formally employed have had to give up their employment in order to take up care responsibilities. Martha gave up her secretarial job in order to care for her husband.

Martha (aged 25 years in 2001)

Martha, who has three children, was married in 1996 and her husband fell ill in 1997. She said her husband and herself were initially 'rumoured' to have AIDS and were shunned by the community. She said her husband was then said to have tuberculosis and that came as a relief to her because 'tuberculosis is a curable disease'.[73] Her husband was still ill at the time of the study.

---

[73] It is very likely that the husband was HIV positive and tuberculosis was an opportunistic infection, particularly given the length of his illness (more than 3 years).

Martha and her husband lived in her father-in-law's house. When the student researchers visited the house they found the father-in-law, Martha's sister-in-law (the wife of Martha's husband's brother), Ms M's husband and a friend (a woman) in the house. Most of the questions asked by the researchers were answered by Martha's husband despite being addressed to Martha. When Martha tried to respond, her husband would interrupt and give his own response until Martha gave up. Martha was uncomfortable. Towards the end of the interview, the student researchers overheard Martha's sister-in-law say to the friend:

'This woman cannot talk. If she does so she would be sure of a beating' (translated version of the Shona words used).

The student researchers made arrangements for Martha to be called to the local clinic (under the pretence that the baby was needed for check-up) where they were able to interview her more freely.

Martha told the student researchers that she was employed as a secretary but had to give up her job to look after her husband when he fell ill. She told them that the workload at home was such that she could not cope with employment outside the home.

A study in eastern Zimbabwe revealed that one in seven care-givers had to give up formal employment to provide care for sick family members (Mushati, 2004).

The economic burden of care is worsened by poverty. Women are disproportionately affected by poverty (Poverty Reduction Forum, 2003). The socio-cultural definition of gender roles in Zimbabwe results in women bearing the brunt of the economic burden of care despite their resource constraints. Girls are often in a worse position than women because, like Betty who had to leave school to care for and fend for the family, they are in a more vulnerable position, socially and economically. In order to survive some girls end up engaging in commercial sexual activity, either of their own volition or at the instigation of adults (Zimbabwe government, 1999:10).

Elderly women also experience greater social vulnerability and poverty. The *Zimbabwe human development report 2003* carries a narrative on the plight of a widow from Zimbabwe's eastern border city of Mutare aged over 80 years (Mrs B).

'Mrs B lives in Mutare's oldest high-density suburb. She and her late husband are of Malawian origin. Her husband died of natural causes in 1990. Four of her five sons died one after the other in 1994, 1995, 1999 and 2002, with their wives following them. They left ten children (six boys and four girls) aged between four and thirteen years.

She suspected that some of the younger children were HIV positive because they were constantly sick. Her surviving son was working in South Africa. She was being stigmatized by the community and was accused of being a witch who caused the death of her own children. The son in South Africa was not visiting her for fear of her alleged witchcraft. She was getting a meagre pension from her late husband's employers and some few contributions from the employers of one of her deceased sons (the other deceased sons were not formally employed). She was also getting a small stipend from the state's Department of Social Welfare. She was supplementing these meagre resources by leasing two rooms in her four roomed house and two wooden structures constructed in her yard' (Zimbabwe government, 1999:92).

The burden of care experienced by women caring for those affected by HIV/AIDS is worsened by the lack of support (in practice) from health and other service providers.

The weakening of the traditional safety-net of the extended family (due to poverty and other socio-cultural factors) has increased the economic burden of care on women and girls.

Traditionally, the extended family was a social safety-net in the event of illness, death and other situations of need. Extended family members would provide psychological support by visiting the sick person or the bereaved and provide counselling. They would provide materially for the sick person's needs or funeral expenses. They would also provide shelter and care for sick relatives. The breakdown of the extended family network means the family no longer provides these services and the burden falls squarely on the immediate family members (parents, brothers, sisters and children). Where the immediate family members lack the necessary resources, the burden becomes unbearable.

Coping with resources – still a struggle

How extended family members step in to provide social, medical and material support in times of illness is clearly illustrated by the case of Jane who provided care for her niece.

Jane's story[74]

My niece was 34 years old. She was separated from her husband and had left her two sons with her mother-in-law. The children were in

---

[74] Jane works for a university-based women's rights organization where she is a highly valued employee. Her story starkly illustrates the complex nature of problems faced even by families who have resources, guaranteed employment and sympathetic employers. Jane's husband owns and runs his own business.

secondary school. She was staying in one of Harare's low-density sub-urbs making a living by selling vegetables. Her health started to deteriorate until finally she suffered a stroke[75] which left her paralyzed on the right side of her body. She was immobile and lost her power of speech. She could only beckon with signs and shriek.

She was admitted to hospital for two weeks. At the time of discharge, the doctor advised us that she would take a long time to heal. My husband did not wait to be asked if he could accommodate her. He volunteered. We had a three-bedroomed house. She shared a bedroom with our live-in domestic worker and other relatives who would come to visit. The children shared the other bedroom.

The patient was bedridden so we had to hire a nurse aide from 7 am to 5 pm for five days a week – over weekends we managed without outside assistance. She required medication from time to time and had a catheter accompanied by urinary bags. The catheter had to be changed regularly by an expert and, since it was difficult for us to take her to see a doctor regularly, we hired a qualified nurse to visit once a week to change the catheter (if necessary) and check on the patient generally. We bought, inter alia, gloves and detergents. We were advised to buy 'adult pampers' (disposable diapers) but we could not afford them.

The hospital wanted us to take her for physiotherapy every week but this proved difficult because we could not always ask to be excused from work.[76] The only option was to engage a physiotherapist who could treat her at home which we could only afford twice a week because of the high cost. We had a wheelchair which we had purchased earlier on with the intention of donating it to our church community and it proved invaluable for our immobile patient. Disposable gloves were too expensive so we improvised by using re-usable household gloves which raised doubts as to whether they were safe.

My niece had two sisters who were both employed. They assisted greatly. They would pay the nurse aide, source medicines, food and toiletries, especially gloves. I would take over from the nurse aide during weekends and the sisters sometimes assisted me. The three of us were studying and our studies were adversely affected because some-

---

[75] Strokes are a not uncommon side effect of HIV/AIDS and comparatively young people suffer such strokes.

[76] *Editor's comment* – such time would have been given if requested. However, Jane was reluctant to ask feeling that she was already taking too much time off work with the problem. Jane and her husband were also taking care of her husband's nephew who was orphaned by AIDS. Fortunately there was a pension and insurance available for his care.

times we could not attend lectures due to our care-giving role.[77]

During the period of shortages of essential foodstuffs,[78] such as mealie-meal,[79] in the shops, we resorted to home-grown reserves.[80] We had enough maize of our own for mealie-meal, we kept chickens for eggs and meat and kept rabbits for meat too. We also grew our own vegetables. Food consumption was very high because of the constant flow of visitors (relatives, church members and workmates) who came to comfort us.[81] We had our small car to run errands and take the patient to hospital. We also had a telephone line to keep in touch with the nursing staff.

A few years before, we had looked after my niece's mother in a similar condition although she was mobile and could converse. She had passed away in our care.

Morally we were in high spirits and ready to deal with our ailing niece. On the financial side, my husband and I combined earnings to meet the medical bills and her requirements such as food, gloves, detergents and so on. We would run out of money on payday as the cost of living soared and we saved no money at all. In fact the money we had was barely enough to cater for our own needs and those of our patient. Sometimes we were forced to stagger payment of our bills. We did not get any assistance from relatives except for my niece's two sisters.

The next section examines the socio-cultural factors that impact on home-based care.

3 Socio-cultural factors that impact on home-based care

The extended family's social safety-net is critical in Zimbabwe because there is no state-funded social security net. The state offers limited as-

---

[77] In Jane's case the studies were part-time degree studies. Although not directly related to the caring role, Jane's studies were interrupted for a year after she required emergency surgery and thereafter suffered an embolism. She is now fully recovered and about to finish her degree.

[78] At the time these events took place Zimbabwe was in a period of steep economic decline and there was a shortage of commodities – in part due to unrealistic price controls which meant that goods were not available but could be bought on the black market at a premium.

[79] Maize meal which is the staple for most Zimbabweans.

[80] Jane and her husband have a two and a half acre plot which made food growing activities possible.

[81] Although emotionally beneficial the strain on family resources of needing to provide hospitality when visitors arrive can be a significant burden on families already suffering financial strain in coping with those who are ill.

sistance in cases of extreme destitution, usually for aliens (because they have no family network to fall back on), orphans and the disabled. The orphans assisted are mainly those whose families cannot be traced. In all other cases of need, such as unemployment, sickness and bereavement, the family (immediate and extended) is expected to provide the necessary support.

Home-based care in Zimbabwe is informed by the culturally constructed gender ideology that perceives women and girls as the primary providers of services in the home, including caring for the sick. Women and girls are expected to take on the caring role in addition to all other household chores. A consequence of this approach is that most care-givers involved in home-based care are women. The Kadoma study did not come across a single male care-giver. Respondents emphasized that care giving was primarily a woman's role although one key informant (a community health worker) indicated that she had come across four men who had cared for their sick wives (at different times) but they had all died (together with their wives) by the time that the research was conducted. In practice, women tend to be the ones who take care of sick husbands and other family members while men will send their sick wives to their natal families to be taken care of by their mothers or sisters. Married women are sometimes forced by family pressure or their own 'family oriented conscience' to temporarily leave their marital homes in order to provide care for sick mothers or sisters. This can strain their marital relationships as the husbands may accuse them of abandoning them and may resort to extra-marital affairs (Zimbabwe government, 1999:84–85). Women may end up leaving employment or worrying about the time they spend in caring and thus potentially risking the security of their employment. This must impact adversely on both the work and home environment and also create high stress levels which can lead to physical and psychological problems. Jane's experience of a husband who is supportive of his wife's caring roles for her own family members is remarkable by its rarity, no doubt he was influenced in part by her role in caring for his own nephew but he was the one who suggested that they take care of her niece.[82]

For girls, one of the consequences of the gendered care roles is that they are forced to drop out of school in order to provide care to sick family members. Betty, who had to take over her mother's roles in the family, aptly illustrates this problem. Girl children who are forced to provide care are often fairly young (most of them are aged between eight

---

[82] A part of the tale that Jane did not relate is that she was wondering how to broach the subject of bringing her niece into the home when her husband in the very early hours of one morning made the suggestion to her.

and eleven years) because the older children tend to leave home (UNAIDS, 2000). This means that when they drop out of school they are deprived of basic (primary) education making it very difficult for them to function in a society that requires literacy skills.

In addition to the socio-cultural factors, women also experience psychological burdens associated with the care role.

4   The psychological consequences of home-based care

To understand the psychological consequences of the burden of care, one has to realize that HIV and AIDS in Zimbabwe is still surrounded by many myths, denial and stigmatization. Martha recounted how she and her husband were shunned by the community when it was 'rumoured' that they had AIDS. Rose and her husband believed that the husband was ill because he had been bewitched.

The Kadoma study revealed that most AIDS cases are being treated as cases of tuberculosis by the affected families and the community. The belief that it is tuberculosis puts carers at risk of cross infection if they do not take appropriate safety measures in providing care. In my own extended family,[83] people have died of AIDS-related illnesses but it has never been discussed openly in the family or revealed to outsiders.

Helen Jackson makes the following pertinent observation:

> 'AIDS ... often leads to marital and family conflict, arousing blame and suspicion regarding the source of infection and the cause of death' (Jackson, 2002:26).

The problem of blame is worsened by the fact that most of the HIV cases in adults are a result of sexual transmission of the infection. Knowledge of this fact results in accusations of infidelity whenever a diagnosis of AIDS is made. Women are often the ones accused, especially if they are the first to be diagnosed, a likely event because most of the testing is linked with antenatal care and the prevention of mother (parent) to child transmission of HIV. The resultant tension, anger or guilt makes the caring role more stressful for women. The situation is worsened by the fact that the husband's family often becomes involved in the dispute by joining him in accusing the wife of infidelity.

Even where there are no accusations of infidelity, providing care to a sick family member under circumstances of extreme poverty and lack of support can be extremely stressful for women. The 30 year old woman from Rimuka (see above) indicated that the burden of caring for her sick husband was so unbearable that at one point she considered running away from home.

---

[83]   A family which includes medical personnel and other professionals.

Accusations of witchcraft are sometimes made against women in their capacity as wives of those infected with HIV or as mothers, grandmothers or other female relatives. Sometimes these accusations are targeted at elderly women who are doing care work under extreme conditions of poverty, lack of support and stigma, such as was the case for Mrs B, whose story is recorded above.

5   Lack of support from health and other service providers

The burden of care experienced by women caring for those affected by HIV/AIDS is aggravated by the lack of support (in practice) from health and other service providers.

The resource constraints faced by the state are well known in Zimbabwe. The health services is one of the most affected sectors due to the HIV/AIDS pandemic. Public hospitals and clinics are facing critical shortages of staff, drugs and other health facilities. There is a serious brain drain as staff leave the public sector for the private sector or for other countries such as Australia, Botswana, South Africa and the United Kingdom.

Private health care is unaffordable for most Zimbabweans because few people are formally employed (thus few are covered by employer-subsidized health insurance) and there is no national public health insurance. Most of those engaged in informal sector income-generation activities are struggling to make ends meet. Health insurance is beyond their reach.

In the light of the above, the support to the home-based care programme from the health sector is minimal. A nurse at a public health institution in Kadoma told the student researchers that she had given up doing follow-ups for home-based care patients because the institution was unable to supply the patients and carers with the requisite materials such as gloves, disinfectants, and so on, and the extreme poverty of most of the families meant that they were unable to purchase these materials on their own. Some, as evidenced from the women's stories, could not even afford to purchase adequate food for themselves and the patients.

The *Zimbabwe human development report 2003* aptly summarises the effect of operating the home-based care programme without the necessary support services:

> 'It is assumed that home and family are synonymous with love and care but this is not always so for all people. Among the poor, there are no detergents for basic hygiene, let alone disinfectants for the protection of the patient and the care-givers. There are no sanitary towels to deal with the incontinence. It is in these austere conditions that home-based care programmes are supposed to work. Often, specialists do

not come by and there are no intravenous fluids and lines to feed individuals who cannot eat on their own. Home-based care, therefore,
becomes a subsidy for cash-strapped hospitals in the face of neo-liberal policies and their emphasis on cost recovery (Jackson, 2002:156).

A question of resources?
As Jane's story indicates, women with economic resources can afford to
seek health care services thus mitigating the burden of care. They can
afford to take the patients to nursing homes for care and or to hire private nurses to provide care in the home. Jane and her husband were able
to hire a private nurse aide and nurse to attend to their niece at home.
However, those who are formally employed would still require a sympathetic approach to their plight from their employers so that they can
take time off to visit the patients in hospitals or nursing homes or to
make arrangements for home-based care by private nurses and monitor
such care. Jane was reluctant to keep asking for time off in order to
attend to her niece, even though time would have been freely given.
Negotiable work opportunities are not readily available and less skilled
or unskilled workers may well find that they are dismissed, plunging the
family into even further poverty and difficulties.

Non-governmental organizations, such as the Red Cross and some
churches, are providing assistance to those involved in home-based care.
They offer food and other material support and some of them have trained
volunteers (known as community home-based care volunteers) who work
within communities and assist families by teaching them how to care for
the patients and by providing relief care where necessary. However, these
interventions do not meet the need for support services and most carers
are working with no support services and no critical advice on care and
carer welfare and protection.

There are state-based resources for HIV/AIDS care but these are
notoriously difficult to access. The AIDS levy which was introduced in
1999 places a three per cent surcharge on income tax and is intended to
assist in addressing the problem of HIV and AIDS, including assisting
those involved in home-based care. However, the funds are inadequate
in relation to the demand and can only be accessed where there is medical proof of the patient's HIV status. As can be seen from the Kadoma
research and from Mrs B's experience, proof of HIV status is not easy to
obtain, nor, it would seem, are people aware of how they can access
state-based support. This lack of access to assessment and to resources
means that carers are dealing with a serious disease without adequate
knowledge of the patient's needs or their own protection, let alone the
necessary medical and financial resources.

The next section discusses the implication of the burden of care for women's human rights.

6 Caring, care-giving and women's rights

There is no doubt that the notion of caring for others is a norm and value which is accepted by most Zimbabweans. The cultural practices of the indigenous people of Zimbabwe emphasize the idea of family solidarity within the extended family structures. Family members, as in Jane's case, support each other financially, materially and psycho-socially in times of crises such as illness (chronic or otherwise), old age and death.

Internationally, there are human rights instruments which embody the value of protection of the wellbeing of the family whilst respecting the rights of women and children. The preamble to the African Charter on Human and People's Rights (the African charter) emphasizes that the concept of human rights should take into account 'the values of African civilization'.[84] Article 18.1 creates an obligation for states parties to take care of the physical health and moral welfare of the family. In article 18.2, the family is described as 'the custodian of morals and traditional values recognized by the community'.[85]

Article 18.3 provides for the elimination of discrimination against women and the protection of the rights of women and children in accordance with international human rights instruments.

The African charter takes an unusual approach to human rights because, unlike most human rights instruments, it does not only provide for the rights to be protected and the obligations of states parties to ensure their protection, it goes further by stating the duties of individuals to ensure the protection of certain values. Article 29.1 imposes the following duty on individuals:

> 'To preserve the harmonious development of the family and to work for the cohesion and respect of the family, to respect his parents at all times, to maintain them in case of need.'

On further analysis the approach of the African charter appears to be contradictory. On one hand the duty of care for family members and family values are emphasized, on the other hand the state's obligation to secure the protection of the rights of women and girls (including their rights within the family) is emphasized. As discussed below, in the con-

---

[84] The preamble to the African Charter on the Rights and Welfare of the Child contains a similar provision.

[85] Article 18.1 of the African Charter on the Rights and Welfare of the Child provides that the family is 'the natural unit and basis of society' which should enjoy the protection and support of the state for its establishment and development.

text of the state's devolution of health care provision down to the level of home-based care, the gendered reality of the care-giving role may result in the violation of the rights of women and girls.

The provisions of CEDAW take cognisance of the apparent contradiction between upholding culturally constructed family values and norms on one hand and protecting the rights of women and girls on the other. Article 5 requires states parties to take appropriate measures to modify social and cultural patterns in order to eliminate prejudices and customary practices that are based on stereotyped roles for men and women. The preamble to CEDAW reinforces this approach where it states that the parties to the convention were:

> '…aware that a change in the traditional role of men as well as women in society and in the family is needed to achieve full equality between men and women.'

In the African context, the provisions of the African charter on women's rights have been strengthened and clarified by the Women's Protocol.[86] The preamble to the protocol states that states parties to the protocol:

> '1 Recognize the crucial role of women in the preservation of African values based on the principles of equality, peace, freedom, dignity, justice, solidarity and democracy;
>
> 2 Are concerned about the continuation of discrimination against women despite the ratification of the African charter and other international human rights instruments by the majority of state parties;
>
> 3 Are firmly convinced that any practice that hinders or endangers the normal growth and affects the physical and psychological development of women and girls should be condemned and eliminated.'

Despite these international human rights provisions (and some national laws), upholding the values of family solidarity and caring for one another within the family which are epitomised by the home-based care concept on one hand and observance of the human rights of women and girls on the other, in practice the rights of women and girls in Zimbabwe are being violated as a result of the economic and socio-cultural context in which they are providing care.

The culture of caring is under serious threat due to increasing poverty and other social pressure. Research by Women and Law in Southern Africa Research Trust (WLSA), Zimbabwe highlights some of the

---

[86] The Women's Protocol has now received the necessary 15 ratifications to come into operation. However, although Zimbabwe is a signatory, it has not as yet ratified the document.

changes that have occurred within the family and the struggles for scarce resources that are occurring within the family (WLSA Zimbabwe, 1997 a and b). The resource constraints at both family and national level have resulted in women carrying a disproportionate share of the burden of care. Women's burden has been worsened by the gender roles that assign responsibility for caring for the sick to women and girls. This has increased the disadvantages suffered by women and girls as they lose out on opportunities to improve their status through education and income-generating activities. Thus, a cycle of poverty is being perpetuated.

The right to school education is provided for in the Zimbabwe Education Act.[85] The provision is silent on the state's obligation to provide school education for children whose parents cannot afford to pay the school fees. It is also silent on the issue of girl children being forced to drop out of school in order to provide care for sick family members.

Furthermore, section 5 of the Education Act imposes the duty to provide for school education on parents without making any provision for assistance for parents who lack the means to provide for their children's education. Compulsory primary education is stated as an 'objective' in the section, thus making it an unenforceable right. The section does not even indicate the measures which the state must take to progressively realize this objective.

The Children's Act[88] has a provision which protects children from harmful employment for gain but does not make any reference to unpaid care work. However, the definition of a 'child in need of care' in the Children's Act includes a child 'whose parent or guardian makes him (or her) perform child labour' (section 2). The definition of child labour includes work 'which is likely to jeopardise or interfere with the education of (a) child'.[89] A child in need of care may be removed from the custodian and placed in the custody of a suitable person or institution.[90]

---

[87] Chapter 25:04, section 4(1). Internationally, it is provided for in article 10(f), the Women's Convention article 28.1 of the United Nations Convention on the Rights of the Child and article 11 of the African Charter on the Rights and Welfare of the Child. However, it should be noted that these international human rights instruments (and all the others cited in this study) have not been incorporated into Zimbabwe's domestic law as required by section 11B(1) of the Constitution of Zimbabwe.

[88] Chapter 5:06, section 10A

[89] The concept of child labour is very difficult to define in the Zimbabwean (and African) context because children are expected to perform household chores as part of their normal upbringing. The imposition of duties to the family upon the individual by the African Charter compounds the problem. However, it should be accepted that withdrawing a child from school so that she may perform care duties is an unacceptable form of child labour.

[90] See Part IV of the Children's Act

In practice, this is not an appropriate option for girls forced to provide care for sick family members because, in most cases, there are no suitable alternative custodians and Zimbabwe's children's institutions are overcrowded. In any event, the separation of the children from their family members would further traumatize them. A solution has to be found which allows girl children to receive the necessary support services so that they can remain in school and stay with their families. The necessary support services should include support from health service providers, financial and material support, counselling and assistance in providing care to the family members.

Women lose out on opportunities for employment and other income-generating activities as a result of their engagement in unpaid care work. Women who are formally employed are having to abandon employment in order to take up care work because of the competing demands on their time. Women who are involved in income-generating activities in the informal sector cannot continue with those activities because of home-based care responsibilities. The problem stems from women being assigned, and when problems arise, being unquestioningly expected to take up the role of primary care-givers within the home. This is a culturally-constructed role which needs revisiting in view of the HIV/AIDS pandemic and the need to provide home-based care. Men must also be involved in care-giving. This is in line with the right to equality which is enshrined in section 23 of the Constitution of Zimbabwe and various international human rights instruments.[91]

In order to achieve a state of equality between men and women with respect to the care-giving role, there is need to overhaul the legal, macro-economic and health provision framework. Concurrent with such overhaul is the need to change the social and cultural context which imposes, almost without question, the care burden on women and girls. The state has taken advantage of the social obligations of women to provide care, and the importance of women's caring as a value adopted by the state is frequently emphasized. The wife of the president is frequently to be heard extolling the importance of women undertaking these duties, even to the point where they give up their own life opportunities to provide such care. The solutions to the problems are not simple but the state has to become far more proactive and responsible in the handling of the consequences of the pandemic.

---

[91] See article 18.3 of the African Charter on Human and People's Rights (the charter), article 10 of CEDAW and article 2.1 (c) and 2.2 of the Protocol to the African Charter on Human and People's Rights on the Rights of Women in Africa (the African Women's Rights Protocol).

7   Conclusion and recommendations

The burden faced by women in providing home-based care to AIDS patients will be considerably lessened by realization of the right to health. The United Nations Covenant of Economic, Social and Cultural Rights provides that everyone is entitled to the 'highest attainable state of mental and physical health'.[92] The state is obliged to take the necessary measures to ensure the enjoyment of this right. The Beijing Platform for Action strategic objective C3–108 sets out a list of key strategies and interventions to enhance women's, and especially girls', capacity to manage their roles within the pandemic; in this context special attention is drawn to 108(g) which highlights the need for provision of services and resources to women and girls who find themselves in the position of principal care-givers. Objective 108(i) deals with the critical need for information on the pandemic to be provided to women. As with many of the other initiatives and rights discussed in this book, there is no shortage of directions and suggestions as to solutions, however the bottom line is good governance and good national budgetary management without which nothing actually happens to improve the lives of citizens.

In the context of HIV/AIDS, access to proper health infrastructure and adequately trained personnel as well as the necessary medicines would alleviate the health problems of AIDS patients by enabling them to live longer, better quality lives, thus lessening the burden on care-givers. I do not intend to delve into the details of the debate on the availability of anti-retroviral drugs (ARVs) and their ability to mitigate the impact of HIV/AIDS. All I need to state is that ARVs have been shown to prolong life and reduce the symptoms of AIDS. Therefore, their availability would lessen the burden experienced by women in providing care. However, ARVs are currently not widely available in Zimbabwe (and other developing countries) and despite the efforts to change the situation, the global social-legal and political context is not favourable to efforts towards making ARVs more widely available.[93] The restrictive provisions of the World Trade Organization's Agreement on Trade Related Aspects of Intellectual Property (TRIPS) have further exacerbated the situation. The struggles experienced by the Treatment Access Campaign of South Africa in seeking to make ARVs more accessible in the face of opposition from international pharmaceutical companies are indicative of the impact of these restrictive conditions.

Despite the hostile global context, the state still has the obligation to

---

[92] Article 16(1) of the African charter states the same.
[93] *Murambatsvina* (get rid of rubbish campaign) deprived many people receiving ARVs of accommodation and they had to disperse thus losing contact with their ARV providers.

take the necessary legislative and other measures, within its available resources, for the progressive realization of the right to health.[94] The state must create conditions for all people, including the poor and marginalized, to access adequate healthcare. The measures to be taken will be legal and policy measures, administrative measures as well as measures aimed at removing the operational and financial hurdles that hinder people's access to healthcare.

From a legal perspective, the right to health should not remain an ideal entrenched in international instruments that has no relationship with domestic reality. There is need to incorporate this right, and the concomitant obligation of the state to ensure its progressive realization into domestic law, including the constitution. Legal measures, such as compulsory licensing and the authorization of generic substitutes, can also be taken in order to reduce the cost of medicines, thus making them more accessible. Budgetary allocations for health must be prioritized and increased so that health infrastructure can be adequately provided and or maintained and trained health personnel can be retained. The state cannot simply plead lack of resources and watch the situation deteriorate.

Below are some specific recommendations as to what the Zimbabwean state can do to lessen the burden of care on women, in addition to addressing the broader issue of the realization of the right to health.

The state must take immediate steps to create an enabling legal and policy environment that alleviates the burden on women and girls. The national HIV/AIDS policy strategies on gender that include addressing issues of women's equality and access to education (primary, secondary, tertiary), credit, skills training and employment should be implemented in the home-based care programme and all other public and private sector programmes. The national community home-based care standards should be amended so as to specifically address the gender dimensions of home-based care, particularly the legal and socio-cultural factors that result in women and girls bearing a disproportionate share of the burden of care.

Practical measures should be taken to ensure that girls do not drop out of school in order to take up home-based care responsibilities. Employers should be encouraged to develop policies that support employees (women and men) who are engaged in home-based care activities in order to ensure that they are not compelled to give up their employment due to the competing demands on their time.

Finding solutions to the burden of care, given Zimbabwe's constantly

---

[94] Section 27(1) and (2) of the Constitution of the Republic of South Africa provides for such an obligation.

declining economy, is particularly difficult. However, failure to address these needs means a continuing decline in both development and human rights entitlements to individuals, especially women and girls. Whatever the national budgetary constraints might be argued to be, it is critical for the future of the nation that individuals' education is not halted or adversely affected by care obligations. Basic healthcare has to be provided nationwide to stem the adverse affects of HIV/AIDS which is manageable with ARVs. Zimbabwe has lost medical personnel at all levels and a once-effective primary health care system has declined along with the general economic decline. The HIV/AIDS pandemic has exacerbated the overall economic decline which has in turn exacerbated the adverse affects of HIV/AIDS, medically, socially and emotionally.

Thus, as a national priority, serious efforts have to be made to find practical and implementable programmes which provide the necessary medical assessments, care advice and basic resources to families caring for HIV/AIDS victims. Urgent measures have to be taken to ensure that women who are currently engaged in care-giving within the home-based care programme receive adequate medical and financial resources and the necessary emotional and psychological support. In this regard, given the poverty of government-based responses, the concept of community home-based care, where communities are encouraged to mobilize resources and offer material and moral support to care-givers and their families, should be strengthened and encouraged. Programmes aimed at dissemination of information on HIV and AIDS and destigmatization of HIV and AIDS need to be strengthened as they raise community awareness about the issues which helps mobilize community support. They are also concomitant with the right to information as enshrined in CEDAW and the Women's Protocol.

Ideally, relief care services[95] should be made available to women who are care-givers in order to reduce the stress from the care-giving role. Women who are compelled to give up income-generation activities in order to provide unpaid care should receive public social assistance (possibly from the AIDS levy) in order to prevent their further impoverishment. But without realistic national budgetary allocations and a serious commitment to good and stable governance, these are just exhortations.

Labour-saving initiatives such as the provision of piped water and electricity could assist in reducing the burden of care (and other household chores) on rural women (Jackson, 2002:279). Although there are rural electrification plans on paper and a levy for rural electrification on

---

[95] The *Zimbabwe human development report (2003*: 167-8) recommends the establishment of care centres offering inter-disciplinary care where care-givers can temporarily leave their patients to give themselves respite. Community home-based care volunteers can also provide relief care.

electricity bills, rural electrification is at a very low level, so alternative means for electricity generation could be considered and implemented, as well as better means of communication using cell phone technology. Women and girls in rural areas are especially addressed in article 14(2)(h) of CEDAW which requires that they:

> '…enjoy adequate living conditions, particularly in relation to housing, sanitation, electricity and water supply, transport and communications.'

HIV/AIDS adds new dimensions to the roles and obligations of women; it threatens to curtail their access to new opportunities for employment and to benefit from development. Girls are especially at risk of losing out on education and of carrying an excessive burden of home-based caring obligations. Communities can assist, families can broaden the base of care-giving but governments, as in the case of Zimbabwe, have to accept their caring obligations. Governments have to facilitate the basic conditions for caring for the population, provide the basis for economic stability and put in place affordable, accessible and, where necessary, free basic health care including access to ARVs to improve the quality of life, prolong the lives of AIDS patients and relieve the obligations placed on carers. Investment in national AIDS care is an investment in the nation itself.

Bibliography

Jackson H. (2002) *Aids Africa: Continent in crisis*, Southern Africa HIV/AIDS Information Dissemination Service (SAFAIDS), Harare.

Ministry of Health and Child Welfare (Zimbabwe) and National AIDS Council (Zimbabwe) (2004) *The HIV/AIDS epidemic in Zimbabwe: Where are we? Where are we going?*, Harare.

Mushati P. *et al.* (2004) cited in 'Appendix D Selected sources' in *The HIV/AIDS epidemic in Zimbabwe: Where are we? Where are we going?*, Ministry of Health and Child Welfare (Zimbabwe) and National AIDS Council (Zimbabwe), Harare.

Poverty Reduction Forum (2003) *Zimbabwe human development report, 2003: Redirecting our responses to HIV and AIDS*, Institute of Development Studies, UZ, Harare.

UNAIDS (2000) cited in Poverty Reduction Forum (2003) *Zimbabwe human development report, 2003: Redirecting our responses to HIV and AIDS*, Institute of Development Studies, UZ, Harare.

WLSA Zimbabwe (1997a) *Continuity and change: The family in Zimbabwe*, WLSA, Harare.

WLSA Zimbabwe (1997b) *Paradigms of exclusion: Women's access to resources in Zimbabwe*, WLSA, Harare.

Zimbabwe government (1999) *National HIV/AIDS strategic framework 2000-2004*, Harare.

– (2004) *National community home-based care standards,* Harare.

Internet documents

AIDS Law Project *wwww.alp.org.za/* accessed May to June 2004

– Pamphlet titled *HIV/AIDS current law and policy*

– 'HIV/AIDS in prison: treatment, intervention and reform: A submission to the Jali Commission'

– 'The legal framework of South Africa in relation to HIV/AIDS'

– 'Chaffed and waxed sufficient: Drug access, patents and global health'

ILO, 'HIV/AIDS and work: global estimates, impact and response 2004', www.ilo.org/public.

The Herald (online edition) 20 September 2004, news item titled, 'Home-based caregivers should get a minimum wage: Activists', www.herald.co.zw.

– 21 September 2004, comment titled 'Look into welfare of caregivers', www.herald.co.zw.

UNAIDS (2005) 'HIV/AIDS, human rights and law', www.unaids.org accessed on 27/05/2005.

UNIFEM, 'Turning the tide: CEDAW and the gender dimensions of the HIV/AIDS pandemic', www.gender *and aids.org,* accessed on 30 August 2004.

List of legislation

Zimbabwe

Children's Protection and Adoption Act, Chapter 5:06, 1972

Constitution of Zimbabwe

Education Act, Chapter 25:04, 2004

South Africa

Constitution of the Republic of South Africa

Regional and international

African Charter on Human and People's Rights 1981

African Charter on the Rights and Welfare of the Child 1990

Protocol to the African Charter on Human and People's Rights on the Rights of Women in Africa 2003

United Nations Convention on the Elimination of all forms of Discrimination against Women (CEDAW) 1979

United Nations Convention on the Rights of the Child 1989

Part II

Livelihood, land and water: Engendering property relations

5

Human rights encountering gendered land and water uses

Family gardens and the right to water in Mhondoro communal land

Anne Hellum

How does a human rights approach to development, which sets universal standards, respond to the diverse realities of women? How can a balance be achieved between the concerns of women and the poor against the quest for more efficient and productive uses of land and water? As governments in southern and eastern Africa have in recent years initiated water reforms based on the user-pay principle and moves to privatize water,[96] struggles against considering water as a commodity have intensified. The human right to water, as expressed in General Comment No. 15 on the human right to water by the United Nations Committee on Economic, Social and Cultural Rights, provides a bottom line to privatization and World Bank strategies. By analyzing family gardens in Mhondoro communal land in Zimbabwe this chapter explores the potential for linking local customs and the human right to water in framing pro-poor, gender-sensitive water laws and policies. The hand-irrigated family gardens in Mhondoro communal lands, where women grow vegetables both for consumption and sale, serve as a window into local water management norms and practices. How local considerations, emphasizing that no-one should be denied water and land that is necessary for life, are resonated in national and international laws and policies explored. The potential for international and regional human rights legislation to improve rural livelihoods is discussed in the light of existing plural legalities and gendered realities.

---

[96] Shifting from considering water as a social service to an economic good, many governments have in recent years made moves to privatize water. The record of privatization is mixed as international companies, engaged by national governments, in many instances have exploited the poor for profit. WHO (2000) estimated that 1.1 billion people (80 per cent in rural areas) had no access to an improved water supply of at least 20 litres of safe water per person a day.

1   The right to water and livelihood: Towards a grounded, gendered and situation-sensitive approach

Water deprivation is often intrinsic to poverty (IWMI, 2004). In southern and eastern Africa, lack of adequate and clean water intensifies poverty and poor health. Poor women and men often lack the resources to capture water for improved productive water uses through cropping, livestock and water-dependent, small-scale activities.

Water's centrality for basic needs led the United Nations Committee on Economic, Social and Cultural Rights in General Comment No. 15 of July 2002 to address the right to water under the right to livelihood in articles 11 and 12 of the International Covenant on Economic, Social and Cultural Rights.[97] As inseparable from the right to an adequate standard of living 'including adequate food, clothing and housing', the committee concluded that the right to water falls within the category of resources essential for the right to life and human dignity. The human right to water, according to the committee, implies that priority in water allocation must be given to water for personal and domestic uses and furthermore for water that is necessary to prevent starvation and disease. In a similar vein the Johannesburg Declaration of 4 September 2002 underscores the role of human rights in sustainable development.[98] It calls for integration of human rights into development processes to facilitate access to basic livelihood resources, such as food, water, housing and health being respected, protected and fulfilled on a non-discriminatory basis in strategies towards more sustainable natural resource uses.[99] Even the World Bank, which was in the forefront of arguing that water was not a human right but an economic good that required proper financing (World Bank, 2002 and 2003), has shifted towards examining human rights and equity.

General Comment No. 15 on the human right to water provides a tool for international and national policy makers and planners to integrate human rights into development planning. It is also a follow up of the Statement on Poverty of 10 May 2001, where the United Nations

---

[97] Its 29th session in Geneva 2002.

[98] Adopted at the 17th plenary meeting on 4 September 2002 (United Nations, 2002).

[99] Article 17 of the Johannesburg Declaration states: 'We welcome the Johannesburg summit focus on the indivisibility of human dignity and are resolved, through decisions on targets, timetables and partnerships, to speedily increase access to basic requirements such as clean water, sanitation, energy, health care, food security and the protection of biodiversity. At the same time, we will work together to assist one another to have access to financial resources, benefit from the opening of markets, ensure capacity building, use modern technology to bring about development, and make sure that there is technology transfer, human resource development, education and training to banish forever underdevelopment.'

Committee on Economic, Social and Cultural Rights[100] considered poverty as a multidimensional denial of human rights and strongly advocated a human rights approach to poverty reduction:

> 'Anti-poverty policies are more likely to be effective, sustainable, inclusive, equitable and meaningful to those living in poverty if they are based upon international human rights.[101]

Addressing the human right to water the committee sets out a framework that intends to assist international law and policy makers, international organizations and civil society in translating human rights norms into equitable and pro-poor policies and practices. General Comment No. 15 gives concrete content to the human rights based approach to poverty. It also supplements the general principles embedded in the document, *Draft guidelines: A human rights based approach to poverty* (OHCHR, 2002).

To rectify existing racial, social and gender injustices in water distribution a number of former African settler colonies have put in place uniform regulatory systems focusing on water permits and levies. The existence and effectiveness of local community-based arrangements in supporting members' rights to life, health, food and livelihood have largely been ignored in recent water reforms (Meinzen-Dick and Bruns, 2000; Derman and Hellum, 2003). The need to go beyond state law and start from the local perspectives of those who use water, their daily experiences, how they conceive water and rights, and the options they have to acquire and defend their access to water, has been documented by a vast body of water research informed by legal pluralism (Spierz, 1995; von Benda-Beckman *et al.*, 1997a and b; Meinzen-Dick and Bruns, 2000). Studies of natural resources management show that women in communal lands and resettlement schemes rely on a mixture of water sources that are regulated by both statutory and customary law. Local use rights to land and water, such as riverine gardens and *dambo* cultivation, are particularly important for the vegetable production of large groups of women and, as such, for the livelihood of poor families (Derman, 1997; Sithole, 1999). Yet local norms and practices also entail male prerogatives in controlling access to and distribution of land and water.

---

[100] The Secretary-General of the United Nations in 1997 called for mainstreaming human rights across the entire United Nations system. The United Nations Development Programme (UNDP) in 1998 issued a policy paper titled 'Integrating human rights with sustainable development'. Human rights and sustainable development are, in this document, viewed as inextricably linked.

[101] United Nations Committee on Economic, Social and Cultural Rights: 'Statement on Poverty and the International Covenant on Economic, Social and Cultural Rights', UN doc. E/C.12/2001/10.

To explore the potential of linking local customs and practices to international and national laws and policies this chapter takes the situation of female communal farmers struggling to fend for their families as the departure point. It begins in Mhondoro communal land where the main sources of livelihood are: maize, cotton and tobacco cropping; cattle; cash income from seasonal and permanent labour; remittances from family members in towns and abroad; and last but not least women's produce from hand-irrigated seasonal vegetable gardens. Land and water uses in Mhondoro, as elsewhere in Africa, are highly gendered. Maize and cotton cropping is mainly controlled by men while women provide for their families largely through produce for both consumption and sale from seasonal vegetable gardens. Gardening is an economic activity that highlights the mutual interdependence of land and water in ensuring rural livelihoods in terms of food, health and education.

Family gardens provide an insight into the significance of the gendered uses of common pool land and water resources as one of multiple rural livelihood strategies. They provide a starting point for exploration of whether and how local, national and international laws and policies respond to women's concerns as family providers. An overall theme in this chapter is how the uniform and gender-neutral water laws and policies, such as the user-pay principle that in recent years has been put in place, correspond to the human right to water and the integrated, gendered land and water uses on the ground.

By using grounded theory, empirical knowledge about people's local experiences, problems and practices is employed in a continuous dialogue with the constantly evolving human rights principles encompassing the right to water, the right to livelihood and the right to food.[102] The human rights principles, and national laws and policies that have a bearing on people's access to resources are discussed in the light of 'the living laws' and realities of male and female land and water users. The aim is to contribute to a gendered, contextual and situation-sensitive human rights approach to water, livelihood and poverty elimination.

The chapter is divided into six parts. The first part is the introduction to the study. The second part describes family gardens in three villages in Mhondoro. The third part examines local norms and practices to see if they express a right to livelihood and water. The fourth part explores how national water laws and policies in Zimbabwe respond to local norms, practices and concerns. The fifth part analyzes the human right to water in the light of the rights to livelihood and non-discrimination embedded in the Convention on Social, Economic and Cultural

---

[102] About grounded theory in law see Bentzon, Hellum, Stewart *et al.* (1998) and Hellum (1999).

Rights and the Protocol to the African Charter on Human and Peoples' Rights on the Rights of Women. Linking the right to water and livelihood without discrimination to existing plural and gendered realities and legalities, the last part points to the potential for international and regional human rights law to improve rural livelihoods.

2 Family gardens in Mhondoro: A source of livelihood

Mhondoro communal land is situated in Chegutu district, which is made up of large-scale and small-scale commercial, communal, resettlement and urban areas 120kms west of Harare. The major river that flows through this high plateau area is the Mupfure. It is part of the larger Sanyati catchment area south of Harare. The Mupfure flows through communal and commercial farming land and the town of Chegutu.

Since 1999 I have been taking part in a study examining how primary water is managed locally in the three villages of Bangira, Murombedzi and Kaondera in the chieftainship of Mashamayombe (Derman and Hellum, 2003; Hellum and Derman, 2004a; Derman, Hellum and Sithole, 2005). This local qualitative study was part of a wider study of national water reform in Zimbabwe that was undertaken by the Centre for Applied Social Studies at the University of Zimbabwe.[103] It started in 1999 when water was plentiful and was continued through the drought and the political and economic crises in 2002, 2003 and 2004. Apart from dry season vegetable gardens located along streams, rivers, seasonally flooded grasslands (*vleis*) and, increasingly, boreholes, agriculture in this area is primarily rainfed maize and cotton with an expansion of irrigated fields of tobacco seedlings. We selected this area due to a rapid and recent increase in tobacco growing, a relatively high number of private wells and the existence of a dam project.

In Mhondoro, as elsewhere in Zimbabwe, people's livelihoods rely on a number of sources. Reflecting the social and economic integration between the rural and urban areas, these sources include: maize, cotton and tobacco cropping; cattle; cash income from seasonal and permanent labour; remittances from family members in towns and abroad; and pro-

---

[103] I am grateful to the team at the Centre of Applied Social Sciences (CASS) at the University of Zimbabwe for undertaking a broader study of the water reform process as part of natural resources management. CASS's study is titled 'Broadening access to water in Zimbabwe'. It is a part of the Land and Water in Southern Africa BASIS CRSP programme (BASIS = broadening access and strengthening input systems). It was funded by the United States Agency for International Development. The co-principal investigators were Francis Gonese (CASS) and Professor Bill Derman, Michigan State University. The fieldwork was conducted in cooperation with CASS researchers, Stanley Vombo and Pinnie Sithole.

duce from seasonal vegetable gardens. Land and water uses are, as mentioned, highly gendered. While the sale of maize, cotton and tobacco produce is mainly controlled by men, women are usually in charge of the output of seasonal vegetable gardens. In different parts of Zimbabwe crops grown in gardens generate income that pays for children's education, food, clothing and farm equipment and provides vegetables for household consumption and nutrition (Derman, 1997; Sithole, 1999).

Almost every family in the three villages had gardens when we began our study in 1999. A quantitative survey of water management in the area showed that 90 per cent of households had some form of dry season garden which required hand irrigation.[104] In those areas where underground water was plentiful many households had dug private wells and established small gardens in their homesteads. In areas where underground water was scarce or non-existent, there were neither private wells nor boreholes. In these areas many villagers had been allocated land on seasonally flooded areas, *vleis* and *dambos*, or close to the river.

A number of elderly people told us they were the first villagers to start gardening in the 1950s. They were taught to grow vegetables by an agricultural extension officer in the colonial administration, at that time, the Department of Conservation and Extension (CONEX). After independence in 1980 gardening was facilitated by a government home well building programme that increased and improved water supplies through inputs like free cement for wells. The Zimbabwean government began withdrawing from rural areas during the 1990s under the combined policies of structural adjustment and decentralization. People in Mhondoro, as local communities elsewhere, have since been left to find alternative economic sources for expanding water supplies for drinking water, watering cattle and irrigation. The Centre for Applied Social Studies survey indicated that 70 per cent of the households in the three villages had invested work and money in private wells and other water resources.

The crops grown in the gardens are kovo, rape, onions, tomatoes, beans, groundnuts and cabbage. They rely heavily on common pool water resources including rivers, boreholes and shallow wells. The gardens are as much a source of income as of food for the family. The income is often used to meet household needs, including food, education, clothing and medical expenses. Thus there is no clear distinction between domestic and productive land and water uses or between livelihood sources in terms of in kind and cash. The case of Mrs Madhuku illustrates this:

> Mrs Madhuku started gardening in 1987. She and her husband are full-time farmers. They have four boys of twelve, nine, five and two

---

[104] Centre for Applied Social Sciences, University of Zimbabwe, BASIS survey data (CASS, 2000–2001).

years old. The family garden is close to the river, adjacent to gardens belonging to other families in the village. According to Mrs Madhuku it was the *sabhuku* (headman) in Kaondera who allocated the land upon the request from the men in the family. He said that the land belonged to all the families who had farms along the rivers. According to Mrs Madhuku no tribute was paid. The headman encouraged people to have gardens so they could be self reliant. There was no competition since there was plenty of land along the river. Mrs Madhuku told us that she had taken up gardening because of the increasing prices of vegetables. They used to buy vegetables at one of the nearby commercial farms and neither she nor her husband had grown vegetables before. Her husband went on a course arranged by the agricultural extension officers. She was taught by her husband as they were working together in the garden. The garden is very labour intensive requiring water at least three times every week and weeding. The children take part in the work in the garden. They use water from the river and a shallow well they have dug. The first year they grew sugarloaf, rape, onions, charlottes and kovo. Now they have an all-year-round garden with a greater variety of crops. In addition to maize, the garden is their most important source of cash income. In 2002 Mrs Madhuku sold vegetables for Z$30 per bundle,[105] amounting to Z$500 per month. Groundnuts sold for up to Z$1500 per bag. With the income she buys clothes, pays school fees and buys food such as oil, bread and sugar. In addition they consume vegetables on a daily basis.

The land used for gardens was seen as community property controlled by the chiefs and headmen on behalf of the villagers. Allocations to families or community gardens usually went through the headman.

Bangira village had community gardens similar to those described. All villagers who were interested joined the garden club that obtained land adjacent to the dam. A locally-elected garden committee was in charge of distribution. If the land allocated to the committee on behalf of the villagers was insufficient the headman saw it as his duty to allocate more land, we were told. All the households had community gardens. On most of the plots people grew kovo that they ate with sadza. Some gardens also had tomatoes. Many households, we observed, also had private gardens at their homestead. In an effort to save wood for fencing materials, to place the gardens closer to a permanent water source and to protect the wetlands, a communal garden project was funded in Bangira village. The initiator was a knowledgeable and well-connected local woman, Mrs Moyo. She was concerned about the poverty of local

---

[105] In 2002 50 Zimbabwe dollars were equivalent to one United States dollar.

women and saw the growth of her own farm as dependent on broader infrastructural investment for the whole area.[106] She approached Africa 2000, a UNDP sponsored non-governmental organization, which constructed a dam for cattle and gardens in Bangira.

The gardens are maintained and irrigated by women with the help of their children and sometimes their husbands. There is considerable variation as to women's degree of control, particularly over the economic output. Some married women, like Mrs Madhuku, told us that she and her husband made joint decisions. Other married women were subject to more control. One example was Mrs Sekremai:

> Mrs Sekremai lived with her husband Robert, her mother-in-law who was a widow and three children. Her husband had dug a well on the farm land his father had been allocated. Water from this well was used for domestic purposes and to irrigate the vegetable gardens. Robert, who saw himself as in charge of the family land, told us that he had allocated land for three vegetable gardens: one for himself, one for his mother and one for his wife. It was his wife, with the help of the children, who watered and weeded the three gardens. He is in charge of selling the produce and handles cash if there is any surplus. Most of the vegetables are, according to his wife, used to feed the family.

In times of drought and hardship the significance of gardens increased. Our visit to Mhondoro communal lands in January 2003 and February 2004 showed significant changes from earlier years in land and water management. In 2002 food shortages set in due to the government's general economic mismanagement, the fast-track government takeover of most commercial farms and repeated drought.[107] In Chegutu, as elsewhere in Zimbabwe, virtually all previously white-owned commercial farm land has been divided into intact commercial farms whose new owners are now either resettlement model A1 farmers (providing primarily for non-commercial farming) or resettlement model A2 farmers on

---

[106] Earlier, Africa 2000, a UNDP sponsored non-governmental organization, had constructed a dam for cattle and gardens in Mhondoro. Heifer International had provided cattle for a livestock project in Bangira. The Zimbabwe Tobacco Association (ZTA) had built a borehole in Bangira village to irrigate tobacco seedlings and their transplantation, and also provided seeds and fertilizer in the first year. The government provided cement and personnel to construct individual wells on homestead property in Kaondera. These efforts were based upon increasing opportunities for rural residents to improve their incomes through commercial activity. It appeared to us that the development of what seemed to be private wells on individual homesteads was part of this process.

[107] For further analysis of the relationship between the fast-track government takeover of land and the water reform at national and local level, see Hellum and Derman (2004b).

subdivided commercial farms (meant to be commercial in operation).[108] There is now a marked shortage of maize in the area, even for those with resources, resulting partly from the local drought and partly from the nation-wide fall in maize production due to the fast-track land reform. When we last visited in February 2004 all the villagers received food aid. Most residents have less cash to buy food or they cannot keep up with inflation. This is due to growing unemployment in the cities and an inflation rate which was close to 350 per cent in August 2004. Fast-track land reform has affected seasonal jobs on the adjacent commercial farms and diminished local markets for garden produce.

A statement made by a local farmer in Murombedzi village succinctly summarizes the gardens' current importance and the difficult times: 'Our gardens are now our butcheries.' By this he meant that vegetables now substituted for meat which had become too expensive.

Single, divorced and widowed women with dependants who do not receive cash from family members rely increasingly on their gardens. It is in this group we found the most vulnerable among the poor, both in the communal lands and in the resettlement areas. Yet there are also differences between the women:

> Mrs Maboreke is a divorced woman who must find income for her children's school fees, clothing and other household needs. She produces vegetables and markets them as well as sewing clothes with her ancient sewing machine. She sells vegetables for up to Z$800 per week. She also farms cotton and maize during the rainy season. She suffers greatly from the inflation despite all her hard work. Her children water her garden daily on their return from school.

Elderly widows, whose children lack education and are out of work, struggle to make ends meet. They are at the mercy of their husband's relatives who control the land they live on:

> Palestine is a widow with a 19 year old son and 18 year old daughter who are both unemployed. She is struggling for their survival. To grow food she took up a field that was initially allocated to her late husband. This garden is situated next to her late husband's brother's land. Although her husband's brothers inherited the land, none of them ploughs for her, she complained. She gets water from a shallow well she and her daughter dug themselves. Her brother-in-law, who has a large garden with sugar cane and maize nearby, does not help her even though he uses the water from her shallow well. She is so poor that

---

[108] Zimbabwe's post-independence land reform is analyzed in Roth and Gonese (2003). For a broader political analysis, see Hammar, Raftopoulos and Jensen (2003). For analysis of Zimbabwe's land reform from a human rights perspective see Hellum and Derman (2004a) and (2005).

she cannot afford to buy seeds to plant vegetables. People give her surplus seeds when she asks. The produce from the garden is used for consumption. She and her children eat mainly kovo and rape with sadza made from the mealie-meal (ground maizemeal) they get through food aid.

There are significant differences in the gardens and therefore their importance and income-generating capability. Due to the crisis, people have to change their cropping strategies. Gardens on *vleis* and wetlands are expanded as people turn to cash crops. With the drought in 2002 and the economic crisis, the expansion of gardens has increased pressure on the existing water sources in the area. There is a considerable difference between the situation of widows and widowers:

A retired employee from Harare has turned his garden on the *vlei* into a commercial maize and sugarcane field. Due to inflation his pension is almost worthless. He is a widower living with his two daughters who are still at school. His son is studying law in South Africa. The main crops grown in the garden are sugarcane and maize. The produce is sold for a good price but he works 'from dawn till sunset' to fend for his children whose education he sees as important. During the drought his shallow well dried up. He increased his water supply by using water from an elderly widow's garden nearby and from the common borehole. With great difficulty, the community headman managed to stop him from using the borehole water that, according to local norms, were to be used strictly for drinking water. The headman also reported him to the chief for chopping down a large number of trees to fence his garden.

3 Livelihood, equality, land and water in 'local law'

We now turn to the norms and values underlying the way in which land and water was shared in the three villages. Sources of everyday practice but also cases of contestation and statements made by the villagers are used to explore the content and outreach of the norms underlying local water management. To supplement our own observations we have examined a series of Zimbabwean monographs on natural resource management including water, wetlands, forests and land (Matondi, 2001; Sithole, 1999; Derman, 1997; Nemarundwe, 2003; Walker, undated; Cleaver 1998). These works provide empirical records from communal areas in Shamva, Mutoko, Chiduku, Dande, Masvingo, Guruve and Matabeleland.[109] The normative overlap between these practices in terms of geographic, social and institutional space is here termed 'local law'

---

[109] For a thorough account of this literature see Derman, Hellum and Sithole (2005).

(Hellum, 1999, 2000). It refers to the blend of normative and practical impulses that inform the ways in which people under changing circumstances manage land and water sources that are essential for livelihood.

A significant feature of local water management practices in Mhondoro was the villagers' overall concern about people's livelihoods. The consideration that people cannot be denied access to resources that are essential for livelihood cuts across the sharing of both water and land. That women managed most water for household and garden needs suggests that their fundamental concerns for basic needs are reflected in patterns of cooperation and the norms and practices evolving around the use of this critical resource.

Drinking water

As regards drinking water, our study in Mhondoro demonstrated a surprising degree of consistency over time and space in upholding the norm that no one can be denied drinking water (Derman and Hellum, 2003). The obligation to share drinking water extended to all water sources, including those on private land. In Murombedzi most villagers fetched their drinking water from a well in the garden of a widow. The duty of sharing extended to boreholes constructed for principally commercial or dedicated use. It cut across kinship and village borders and increased rather than decreased during drought periods. A factor upholding the right to clean drinking water was the strongly-held view of most villagers that they risk having the water source poisoned if it was not shared.[110] Our research findings from Mhondoro are consistent with our readings of a series of Zimbabwean monographs on natural resource management including water, wetlands, forests and land (Matondi, 2001; Sithole, 1999; Nemarundwe 2003). The empirical record from communal areas in Shamva, Mutoko, Chiduku, Dande, Masvingo, Guruve and Matabeleland all suggest that water for drinking can and should be made available for all. Nemarundwe in her doctoral thesis reports from the Romwe catchment area in Chivi district, south Zimbabwe, that drinking water is made available to all no matter what the source of water. No matter what the tenurial status, whether publicly or privately owned, the water sources are available for drinking water. In a powerful and clear manner she writes:

> 'Because water is considered *hupenyu* (life), there has been no case of denying another village access to water during drought, although rules of use are enforced more stringently during drought periods' (2003: 108).

---

[110] The norms of sharing and potential sanctions exist in those areas of the three catchments where the CASS water research team has been working.

The study points to actual incidents where this general ideal was challenged. One example was a well owner who prevented others from accessing his well. Two days after he locked the gate to the well he found a dead dog. In response to this he later unlocked the gate (2003:113) In parallel fashion, Dr Bevlyne Sithole's research in Mutoko and Chiduku communal areas in eastern Mashonaland and Manicaland summarizes farmers' views on water as follows:

> 'Water should be available to all, rich or poor, but the person who impounds the water is the one who makes the river dry' (Sithole, 1999: 195).

Water has been given scarce attention in the anthropological literature from Rhodesia and Zimbabwe so it is difficult to know how consistent this practice has been over time. Good or poor rains were historically indicators of social wellbeing or social conflict (Bourdillon, 1987; Lan, 1985; Maxwell, 1999; and many others). Droughts were said to be caused by serious breaches of conduct both in general and in people's dealing with water. Good communication needed to be maintained with the ancestors to ensure good water supplies and rainfall.

Water for crops

There is a difference between sharing water for drinking and cooking on the one hand, and irrigating gardens and watering livestock on the other. Access to the water from wells that had safe drinking water was not for watering gardens or washing clothes, everyone emphasized. Where groundwater was available people had dug shallow wells to provide water for the crops grown in the gardens. This water, people emphasized, was only for garden use for the family itself or close relatives. Unlike clean drinking water, which was seen as common property, shallow wells used to irrigate gardens were treated as family property. In Mhondoro, as elsewhere in Zimbabwe, fencing vegetable gardens along rivers or on wetland to protect crops from cattle is common practice. Once allocated for gardening, the land and the water available for irrigation is seen as family property. Access to both land and water for gardening may, unlike clean drinking water, be restricted on the basis of kin.

Garden land with available water

In Mhondoro there was, however, an overall concern for ensuring people's access to water resources vital for livelihood. Water from rivers was considered a resource to be shared among the villagers. Furthermore, those who needed it were allocated land for gardens in areas with available water sources. In Kaondera all the villagers we talked to told us that they had the headman's explicit or implicit approval to access land for gardens on *vleis* or close to rivers. We did not come across a single incidence of anyone being denied access. The *sabhuku* confirmed that he had not denied anyone land for gardens. The gardens, he said, were an important source of livelihood and self reliance. That was why he had not taken action when people allocated themselves gardens without his permission. Another reason, he told our local research assistant, was fear of revenge in terms of bad spirits, *zrishiri*. In a similar vein the headman in Bangira told us that he saw it as his duty to allocate land to the community gardens upon the request of the garden committee. Like safe drinking water, gardens in terms of land close to a water source were seen as something people could not be denied.

These practices can be seen as an expression of a norm that people should be given land with available water resources necessary for their livelihood. This norm of sharing was expressed through the day-to-day allocation and apparently upheld through the belief that denial of such a right was associated with spiritual revenge. *Dambo* areas and land close to water were abundant in the three villages we studied in Mhondoro. Research from other areas in Zimbabwe suggests that the norm of sharing in situations of scarcity is narrowed down to the kin group. Sithole, in her work on *dambos*, documents increased desiccation in Mutoko and Chiduku communal areas. According to Sithole (and also Matondi, 2001) the main mechanism for sharing scarce livelihood resources under these conditions is subdivisions among kin within the household.

The concern for livelihood in Kaondera, Bangira and Murombedzi, as elsewhere in Zimbabwe, appears to be so strong that it in many instances it overrules national law criminalizing wetland and streambank cultivation. Assuming that these practices disturbed the river flow and caused erosion, the Water Act of 1927, the Natural Resources Act and the Streambank Regulation of 1952 prohibited wetland, streambank or riverine cultivation (Beinart, 1984; Bullock, 1995). Although newer hydrological and agricultural research shows that sustainable wetland and *dambo* farming under proper management by communal farmers is possible and economically viable, these laws are still in force (Matiza, 1992). They have, however, been randomly enforced. In some instances, the local authorities have used the regulations as a means of moving people away from river banks. This has to a large extent been the case in the Zambezi valley where large areas were designated for cotton production (Derman, 1997). In other instances the practice has been tolerated (Sithole, 1999). One reason is that some natural resources officers in charge lack the resources to enforce the prohibition against streambank and wetland cultivation[111] but there is also significant evidence that many public servants, who themselves have a rural background, see these practices as important for rural livelihoods.

---

[111] The enforcing officials for the Natural Resources Act streambank regulations.

'Local law', the right to livelihood and non-discrimination
The integrated land and water uses in Mhondoro provide a window into the complex and multifaceted character of 'local law'. The right to safe drinking water in many ways resembles the human right to water. It is something people cannot be denied and breach of the norm is associated with sanctions. The case of safe drinking water in Mhondoro thus points to a morally based duty rather than a negotiable and reciprocity-based notion of property as often pointed to as a characteristic feature of the fluid and flexible African customary laws, sometimes characterized as 'negotiated law' (Berry, 1993; Bentzon, 1994). Extending to men and women as well as insiders and outsiders it also points to a notion of equality and non-discrimination in as far as access to resources that are vital for livelihood are concerned.

While the case of access to gardens with available water resonates a concern for livelihood, unlike the right to safe drinking water, it is not available on a universal and non-discriminatory basis. Outsiders don't have access and in situations of scarcity the duty to share is limited to kin. Land for gardens is, as a main rule, allocated to the male head of household on behalf of the family. Yet livelihood concerns crosscut the male status rule so as to make land available to single and childless women, widows and divorcees who are able to garden. Married women are, due to these formalities, often seen as lacking control of the land they use for their production. Yet there is also evidence suggesting recognition of women's right to control the produce of the land they use for family maintenance. In the three villages in Mhondoro there were considerable variations ranging from women being the main managers and decision-makers to joint management and decision-making and finally to those men who asserted they were in control. Sithole observed that women seem to be acknowledged by most men as owners of the garden (1999: 80). This suggests that ownership within the family is not acquired through status rules but by actual use and work on the land. Yet this is not straightforward. Sithole observes that it seemed impossible for women, and men for that matter, to think about ownership in terms of this belonging to this person or that one (1999: 80).

In general, despite the growing investment in water and new forms of cropping in the Mhondoro area, the above described principles of allocation of garden land and water reflected deep concern for broader household needs and capacities. No distinction was made between domestic and productive land and water use where the aim was to ensure the fundamental needs of the family. Neither the site of more commercialized agriculture and growing investment in water up to 2002 nor the existing crisis had led to the enclosure of resources. It appears that in this area, local norms and institutions have been able to respond to multiple needs while maintaining a focus on ensuring resources for liveli-hood in a broad sense.[112] When we visited in 2003 and 2004, however, we noticed increasing inequalities in distribution of land for gardens. As the social and economic crisis accelerates people are changing their cropping strategies by converting their gardens into irrigated fields. We sense a pattern of increasing inequality as villagers who are in command of social and economic resources are accessing two or more gardens for themselves. Important resources in this respect are labour, access to seeds and fertilizer, and equipment to transport water from available sources in other villages in the event of drought. While we have noted the strength of local management systems, we may also fear that the systems may be adversely affected by the general breakdown of law and order that has taken place at all levels of law and society as a result of the ongoing economic and political crisis (Hellum and Derman, 2005).

4 Water reform, user-pay, primary and commercial water

In 1997 the Zimbabwe government embarked on water reforms setting out to create broad-based economic growth, build democratic and participatory water management systems, and redress race, class and gender inequities in water distribution. Under the Water Act of 1998 all water is vested in the president and no person can claim private ownership of any water. In presenting the first reading of the new draft Water Bill, the then Attorney General Patrick Chinamasa emphasized that:

> 'What the existing legislation has done is that the water is the president's water but the president then put in legislation to give permission to people to exploit it and that is what is peculiarly known as the water right' (Zimbabwe Parliamentary Debates, 1998: 1566).

In defending the abolition of the concept of private water Chinamasa also asserted the common Zimbabwean understanding of water:

> 'Water is a public resource. It is a gift from God. None of us here are rainmakers and that includes commercial farmers. The rainmaker is God. He provides His people and that water forms part of the hydro-logical cycle (Zimbabwe Parliamentary Debates, 1998: 1562–1563).

This is consistent with Zimbabwe's history as a centralized state while appearing to incorporate new global water-management policies (Derman, Ferguson and Gonese, 2001). In Zimbabwe, as elsewhere in Africa, the Dublin Principles for water management, such as water as a social and economic good, has arguably been the most widely recog-

---

[112] Platteau (2000) suggests that local institutions perform better than state ones, and that individualization is not necessarily best for land tenure evolution in Africa.

nized axiom for reform.[113] The thinking behind this principle has been incorporated into policy documents authored by the World Bank and other donor organizations (World Bank, 1993). In Zimbabwe the user-pay principle was adopted with little knowledge and concern for local water management systems and principles. The 1998 water legislation transferred national planning functions to a new parastatal agency, the Zimbabwe National Water Authority (ZINWA) that was to be funded primarily through the sale of water behind government dams, the provision of water to cities and the levying of water to large-scale users. It follows from the Zimbabwe National Water Authority Act Section 41 that only permitted water is subject to the user-pay principle in terms of the new water levy. Under the new Water Act of 1998, it is only water used for commercial purposes that requires a permit in terms of section 34. Commercial water use is an economic concept including agriculture, mining, livestock, hydroelectric power, and so on. Thus water development is viewed as increasing the number of commercial water users and pays far more attention to the business side of water than to the local concerns and the human rights concerns that in later years have gained momentum.

Water for basic needs is, however, given high priority in Zimbabwe's Water Act of 1998. In the new Act, not substantially different from earlier ones, primary water is defined as water used for:

1) domestic human needs in or about the area of residential premises;
2) animal life; 3) making of bricks for private use and 4) dip tanks (Water Act, section 32.1).

To access primary water, no permission is needed. Zimbabwe's waters have been divided into the categories of commercial and primary since the beginning of the colonial era (Derman and Hellum, 2003). The first regulation of water was by the Order in Council, 1898, Section 81 pertaining to the British South Africa Company. It required the company to ensure that the 'natives or tribes' had a fair and equitable portion of springs or permanent water. This was in the areas assigned to the tribes for their agricultural and pastoral pursuits (Hoffman, 1964). Primary water was an introduced concept stemming from the earliest southern African water laws. Throughout the colonial period the Water Acts required the colonial authorities to respect the primary use rights of tribal trust land inhabitants. This principle is embedded in the Water Acts of 1927, 1964,

---

[113] This is one of the four Dublin Principles, the guiding international document for water reform. The other three are: (1) Freshwater is a finite and vulnerable resource, essential to sustain life, development and the environment; (2) Water development and management should be based on a participatory approach involving users, planners and policy-makers at all levels; and (3) Women play a central part in the provision, management and safeguarding of water.

1976 and also the new Water Act of 1998. This division of water seems to reflect the core land tenure division between commercial (formerly European) lands and communal lands (formerly tribal trust lands).

A key future concern in the implementation of Zimbabwe's water reform is how to alleviate poverty and promote small-scale production within the existing law and policy framework. New innovative forms of commercial cropping emerging within the common property regimes in the communal lands, such as women's gardens in Mhondoro, represent a challenge with regard to drawing a dividing line between commercial and primary water uses embedded in the new laws and policies. These uses render problematic the legal division between commercial and primary water.

The new stakeholder-based water management implies that the planning for the water management of a catchment area rests in the hands of catchment councils.[114] In order for catchment councils to issue water permits they must have an approved catchment plan requiring a fairly detailed accounting of actual water use. This is where primary water for the first time needs to be conceptualized and accounted for. The implementation of the user-pay principle requires a clear separation of what is primary and what is commercial since this is not specified in the definition of primary water in the Water Act of 1998. Consultants looking into the implications of the user-pay principle have now started a discussion on whether borehole users should pay for their water since they are being encouraged to use water for productive purposes (more commercial purposes) (Robinson, 1998: 37). This lack of conceptual and policy clarity has provided space for further commercialization of water (Manzungu and Marchiridza, 2005). Manzungu reports how catchment and sub-catchment councils eager to raise revenue overlook the concerns of the poor. In Gwai catchment area there was a suggestion to levy a charge for every head of cattle. In Save catchment area, levies were proposed for any water use where some income was realized. The Mazowe catchment council's debate as to what constitutes commercial water illustrates the issues that the increasingly market-driven water discourse is giving rise to. When drawing a dividing line between commercial and primary use they relied upon a technological answer. If the water is moved by hand, it is, according to this view, not commercial. If it is moved by some of form of machine, it will be considered commercial.[115]

These discussions on how to draw the boundary between primary

---

[114] Water Act 1998 section 21

[115] Research notes, February 2000. At a Mazowe catchment council meeting there was a discussion on whether to ask the Centre for Applied Social Sciences to suggest a definition for commercial water. This discussion ended when the chairperson suggested the technological definition.

and commercial water is far removed from the integrated way land and water is shared and managed in Mhondoro. People we talked to in Bangira wanted to get funding to install a pump so that water could be moved to their gardens. While emphasizing that women's gardens were not solely for domestic use, they were reluctant to pay for water if it was moved from the dam to their gardens by a pump. The products that were grown in these gardens were both for family consumption and sale. A wealthy couple who had worked hard to establish funding for the dam so as to raise the living standard of their own and other families argued that since the surplus was used for livelihood essentials, such as clothes, school-fees or medicine, the water use should not be seen as commercial.

It was hoped that broadening stakeholder representation beyond white commercial farmers to include black communal area farmers, members of rural district councils and indigenous commercial farmers, would lead to more efficient and locally appropriate priorities. The Centre of Applied Social Sciences team's surveys have, however, indicated that key stakeholders identified at the village level are not represented on councils. Observations at catchment council meetings indicate that the few women present are usually either technocrats or secretaries. Neither in the new water laws nor in the statutory instruments implementing the water reform has any mention been made of how to incorporate women more fully as stakeholders in water management and development (Hellum, 2001). This is despite women's heavy involvement in agricultural production and household water provisioning featuring significantly in the Dublin Principles.

While bridging inequalities between commercial white and black water users the Zimbabwean reform gives little thought to the situation in communal areas and resettlement schemes where poor women and men often lack resources to capture water for improved productive water uses through cropping, livestock and water-dependent, small-scale activities such as gardens. If there is to be a significant change in access to water, then representation patterns will have to be altered in terms of gender and class, not just race.[116] The dramatic increase in the number of Zimbabwean poor calls for better coordination between water policies

---

[116] Zimbabwe has one of the highest rates of inflation in the world, combined with a shrinking economy – assessed by a series of macro-economic measures including gross domestic product, economic growth, formal sector employment, and so on. Its index has fallen from a high in 1985 (UNDP: 243) to 90th out of 94 developing countries. In the past several years Zimbabwe has fallen from a medium human development nation to a low one (Human Development Report, 2003). It was ranked 145th in the world in its human development index and it is this high only because of high rates of schooling. Due to AIDS it is projected to have only a 0.2 per cent annual growth rate – from 12.8 million people in 2001 to 13 million in 2015. One third of the population is reported to be sick with AIDS or HIV positive (page 260). Life expectancy at birth has fallen from 56 to 33.1.

and poverty elimination strategies. Equally important is to rectify the mismatch between the unified law and policy framework that the water reform has put in place over the plural, gendered and socially-differentiated reality. While the notion of primary water speaks to respecting basic needs, the division between commercial and primary water does not sit well with the way of sharing, both with regard to safe drinking water and to dry season gardens with available water sources that we observed in Mhondoro. To deny someone drinking water and, to a certain extent, land with available water for vegetable gardens necessary for livelihood was in local practice associated with different kinds of sanctions. By overlooking social and gender differentiation in relation to allocation and uses of water, the seemingly neutral water laws and policies may easily be to the effect that existing social and gender inequalities are reinforced and increased. To promote substantive equality and poverty elimination this gap between the seemingly class and gender neutral user-pay principle and the gendered and social reality where poor women fend for their families by growing vegetables both for consumption and sale needs to be addressed.

5   Converging international and local concerns

In striking a balance between the quest for more effective and productive uses of land and water resources and the concerns of the poor, the human rights based approach to development leans towards international legal standards such as the right to water, the right to livelihood and the right to equality and non-discrimination. This approach provides a bridge between centralized and free-market economic models, being concerned with promoting the freedoms denied under communism and the substantive equity which is often missing in an unrestrained, free-market system (Hausermann, 1998). Access to fundamental resources such as food, health, education, water and land are regarded as central development issues embedded in the three interrelated categories of rights sometimes referred to as the three generations of human rights.[117] These are:

- Civil and political rights such as the right to participation, the right to protection of bodily integrity and property and the right to equality and non-discrimination;
- Social, cultural and economic rights such as the right to health, the right to food, the right to water and the right to livelihood; and
- Solidarity rights such as the right to development and the right to a healthy environment.

---

[117] For a comprehensive overview of social, economic and cultural rights, see Eide, Krause and Rosas (2001).

The human rights based development approach overlaps and supplements other development theories and policies seeking to balance liberalist and welfarist values and concerns. Like the human development approach, worked out by the economist Amartya Sen and the philosopher Martha Nussbaum, it emphasizes human agency and entitlements as core factors in poverty elimination and development. Both the rights based and the capability approach place the individual with his or her capacity to pursue personal, social, political and economic goals at the core of the development process. The capabilities approach initiated by Sen and Nussbaum sets international standards for measuring development in terms of quality of life adapted by United Nations Development Programme (Sen, 1993 and 1999; Nussbaum, 1999). Unlike the capabilities approach, the human rights based approach provides a legally binding framework based on the indivisibility of people's civil, political, social and economic human rights. With regard to poverty elimination the right to resources that are vital for livelihood on a non-discriminatory basis, with corresponding legal obligations for national governments to respect, protect and fulfil these rights, is a core element (Nowak, 2005; Hauserman, 1998; Sengupta, Eide, Marks and Andreassen, 2003; Frankovits, 2005). The document, *Draft guidelines: A human rights based approach to poverty*, which also has a bearing on water rights, sets out the following framework to advance the goal of poverty reduction (OHCHR, 2002:42–4):

a By urging speedy adoption of a poverty reduction strategy, underpinned by human rights, as a matter of legal obligation;

b By broadening the scope of poverty reduction strategies so as to address the structures of discrimination that generate and sustain poverty;

c By urging the expansion of civil and political rights which can play an instrumental role in advancing the cause of poverty reduction;

d By confirming that economic, social and cultural rights are binding international human rights, not just programmatic aspirations;

e By adding legitimacy to the demand for ensuring meaningful participation of the poor in decision-making processes;

f By cautioning against retrogression and non-fulfilment of minimum core obligations in the name of making trade-offs; and

g By creating and strengthening the institutions through which policy makers can be held accountable for their actions.

Laying down the actual obligations of states to respect, protect and fulfil basic rights on an equal basis, the human rights approach makes women subjects of international law and a direct voice through individual and group-based complaint procedures.[118]

The right to livelihood and water
The year 2003 saw an international breakthrough for the human right to water. The Committee on Economic, Social and Cultural Rights, in General Comment No. 15 on the right to water, made a plea to extend the obligation to respect, protect and fulfil the right to water beyond the nation state. The right to water, like any other human right, imposes on states parties an obligation to ensure that the right to water is respected, protected and fulfilled on a non-discriminatory basis in laws and policies. States parties must ensure that new laws, policies and programmes do not lead to segments of a population being denied this right either de jure or de facto. As with other human rights, water becomes everyone's right in the capacity of being human. It is a right that constitutes an end in itself and not a means towards other ends such as increased economic growth.

The human right to water has evolved through piecemeal international law-making, dynamic interpretation by human rights treaty bodies, such as the Committee on Social, Economic and Cultural Rights and to a certain extent through state practice. There is a growing body of legal literature addressing the human right to water (McCaffrey, 1992; Gleick, 1999; Hellum, 2001, Salman and McInerney-Lankford, 2004; WHO, 2003). The right to water is embedded in the South African Constitution.[119] It is already explicitly and implicitly recognized in a wide range of international conventions, declarations and other standards. The Convention on the Rights of the Child gives all children a right to clean drinking water.[120] Article 14.2(h) of the Convention on the Elimination of All Forms of Discrimination against Women (CEDAW) states that rural women have a right to 'enjoy adequate living conditions, particularly in relation to housing, sanitation, electricity and water supply, transport and communications'. The Protocol to the African Charter on Human and Peoples' Rights of Women in Africa goes one step further.[121] Article 15 on the right to food security obliges states parties to 'provide women with access to clean drinking water, sources of domestic fuel, land and the means of producing nutritious food'.

The right to water is furthermore embedded in the Bill of Rights in

---

[118] See Knop (1994) and Oloka-Onyango and Tamale (1995).
[119] The Constitution of the Republic of South Africa, 1996, chapter 2 section 27.
[120] The Convention on the Rights of the Child, article 24.
[121] The protocol was adopted by the Second Ordinary Assembly of the African Union, Maputo, 11 July 2003 and by 10 July 2005 was not yet in force.

section 27(1)(b) of the South African constitution stating that everyone has the right to access sufficient water. Article 12 of the Zambian constitution states that the state shall endeavour to provide clean and safe water. According to article 90 of the Ethiopian constitution every Ethiopian is entitled, within the country's resources, to clean water. The preamble to the Namibian sixth draft Water Resources Management Bill of 2001 states the government's overall responsibility for and authority over the nation's water resources and their use, including equitable allocation of water to ensure the rights of all citizens to sufficient safe water for a healthy and productive life, and the redistribution of water. There is also a growing body of national case law recognizing the right to water as intrinsically linked to the right to life and the right to environment.[1220]

The Committee on Social, Economic and Cultural Rights has on several occasions recognized that water is a human right contained in article 11(1) of the International Covenant on Economic, Social and Cultural Rights defining the right to an adequate living standard 'including adequate food, clothing and housing'.[123] The term 'including', in accordance with the dynamic interpretation of the committee, indicates that the catalogue of rights encompassing the right to livelihood is not exhaustive but must be adapted to changing social and economic concerns such as the global water crisis.[124] Concluding that water is a human right, the committee emphasizes the interdependence between human rights in general and between access to water and the right to health in article 12.1, the right to food in article 11 and the right to life and human dignity enshrined in the International Bill of Human Rights.

Recognizing that water is required for a range of different purposes that are essential for human life, the Committee on Economic, Social and Cultural Rights sets water allocation priorities embedded in the human rights system itself. According to the committee, priority should be given to the right to water for personal and domestic uses as well as water resources required to prevent starvation and disease (6). Furthermore, the committee notes the importance of ensuring sustainable access to water resources for agriculture to realize the right to adequate

---

[122] In the *Vellore Citizens Welfare Reform v Union of India, 1996 A.I.R. (S.C) 2715,* the Supreme Court held that tanneries had violated citizens' right to life by discharging untreated effluents into agricultural areas and local drinking water supplies. In the salt miners case the Supreme Court of Pakistan expanded article 9 of the right to life in the Constitution to encompass unpolluted water – *General Secretary, West Pakistan Salt Miners Labour Union, Khwra Khelum v The Director, Industries and Mineral Development, Punjab Lahore, Human Rights Case No. 120 of 1993.*

[123] See General Comment No. 6 (1995) and General Comment No. 15 (2002)

[124] See also Eide *et al.* (2001).

food.[125] According to Comment 15, attention should be given to ensuring that disadvantaged and marginalized farmers, including women farmers, have equitable access to water and water management systems, including sustainable rain harvesting and irrigation technology. Taking note of the duty in article 1, paragraph 2, of the covenant, which provides that people may not 'be deprived of their means of subsistence', states parties should ensure that there is adequate access to water for subsistence farming and for securing the livelihoods of indigenous peoples. This aspect of the human right to water is also expressed in the Statement of Understanding accompanying the United Nations Convention on the Law of Non-Navigational Uses of Watercourses (A/15/869 of 11 April 1997) which declares that, in determining vital human needs in the event of conflicts over the use of watercourses, 'special attention is to be paid to providing sufficient water to sustain human life, including both drinking water and water required for production of food in order to prevent starvation'.

The human right to water thus cuts across the division between primary and commercial water use or the economic division between domestic and productive water uses. Provided water is necessary for livelihood it is irrelevant whether the water is moved by hand or by a pump or machine. Whether the water is used for vegetables that are consumed by the family or sold to provide cash to raise money for nutrition or medicine is also irrelevant. Implementing the user-pay principle, national and international water managers are thus obliged to respect, protect and fulfil the human right to water. This implies ensuring that water required for drinking and production of food necessary for livelihood is given priority. The right to water thus goes beyond clean drinking water encompassing water for irrigating crops that are essential for food, nutrition and health. The integrated character of the human right to water calls for careful consideration of the user-pay principle so as to ensure that poor water users are exempted.

The right to non-discriminatory access
States parties are also obliged to ensure that the right to water is enjoyed without discrimination on the grounds of sex, class, colour, religion or political opinion. The non-discrimination principle embodies an obligation to ensure that the allocation of water resources and investments in water facilitate equal access to water for all members of society. Inappropriate resource allocation can lead to discrimination that may not be overt. Investment should, according to Comment 15, not disproportionately favour expensive water supply services and facilities that are only

---

[125] See General Recommendation No. 12 (1999).

available to a small fraction of the population.

Article 26 of the International Covenant on Civil and Political Rights implies that water reform must be carried out without any discrimination based on race, class, sex or ethnicity:

> 'All persons are equal before the law and are entitled without any discrimination to the equal protection of the law. In this respect, the law shall prohibit any discrimination and guarantee to all persons equal and effective protection against discrimination on any ground such as race, colour, sex, language, religion, political or other opinion, national or social origin, property, birth or other status.'

The principle of non-discrimination is also embedded in the International Covenant on Economic, Social and Cultural Rights, the African Charter of Human and Peoples' Rights, the International Convention on the Elimination of all forms of Racial Discrimination, the Child Rights Convention, the Convention on the Elimination of all forms of Discrimination against Women and the Protocol to the African Charter on Human and Peoples' Rights on the Rights of Women in Africa.

The Convention on the Elimination of All Forms of Discrimination against Women (CEDAW), the International Covenant on Economic, Social and Cultural Rights and the Protocol to the African Charter on Human and Peoples' Rights on the Rights of Women in Africa all substantiate the principle of non-discrimination in relation to water, land and food security. Discrimination in relation to CEDAW means:

> '…any distinction, exclusion or restriction made on the basis of sex which has the effect that they impair or nullify, on a basis of equality between men and women, human rights in the political, economic, social, cultural, civil or any other field'.[126]

Taking into account that gender neutral laws in a situation where resources such as time, money, land and water are unevenly distributed between men and women, article 1 of CEDAW, article 3 of the covenant and article 1 (f) of the protocol oblige states parties to take measures to eliminate both direct and indirect discrimination. Direct discrimination occurs when a difference in treatment relies directly and explicitly on distinctions exclusively based on sex and characteristics of men or women, which cannot be justified objectively.[127] Indirect discrimination occurs when a law, policy or programme does not appear to be discriminatory on the face of it but has a discriminatory effect when implemented. This can occur, for example, when women are disadvantaged compared to men with respect to the enjoyment of a particular opportunity or ben-

---

[126] CEDAW, article 1.

[127] General Comment No. 16 (2005), article 3: The equal right of men and women to the enjoyment of all economic, social and cultural rights, E/C.12/2005/3.

efit due to pre-existing inequalities. Applying a gender-neutral law may leave existing inequality in place or exacerbate it.

Indirect discrimination encompasses development policies and programmes that on face value are gender-neutral but in practice have the effect that large groups of female water users are disfavoured in comparison with male water users. Policies, programmes and plans for improvements and investments in water that are based on a division between domestic and productive water use, will often have a discriminatory effect. A series of recent research projects on gender, water and development have documented systematic marginalization of female water users as a result of gender-insensitive approaches from technical agencies assuming household unity (Cleaver and Elson, 1995; Cleaver, 1998; Zwarteveen, 1997; Ferguson, 1998; Van Koppen, 2000; Schreiner and Van Koppen, 2003). One problem is that water sources used by female small farmers, for example to irrigate vegetable gardens by borehole water, have been seen as unproductive by conventional economic standards. As a result of the gendered character of land and water uses, seemingly gender-neutral investment policies have often disproportionately favoured expensive water supply services controlled by men. This may result in indirect discrimination in terms of both CEDAW and the protocol.

Article 14.1 of CEDAW substantiates the concept of indirect discrimination by explicitly stating that work in the monetarized and non-monetarized sectors shall have equal status. It states that:

> 'States parties shall take into account the particular problems faced by rural women and the significant roles which rural women play in the economic survival of their families, including their work in the non-monetarized sectors of the economy.'

In General Recommendation No. 21,[128] the CEDAW committee states that financial and non-financial contributions to property 'should be accorded the same weight' (paragraph 32). In a similar vein, article 13(h) of the protocol says that states parties shall 'take the necessary measures to recognize the economic value of the work of women in the home'.

This implies that states parties, in accordance with article 2 in CEDAW are obliged to take appropriate measures to eradicate legal, social, economic and cultural barriers that impede women's access to water on an equal basis with men. In accordance with article 26 of the Protocol to the African Charter, states parties undertake to 'adopt all necessary measures and in particular shall provide budgetary and all other resources for the full and effective implementation of the rights'.

---

[128] 'Equality in marriage and family relations', from the CEDAW Committee (1994), reference A/49/38.

Taking the human right to water beyond the nation state, the Committee on Social and Economic Human Rights also recommends that United Nations agencies and other international organizations concerned with water, such as the World Health Organization, Food and Agriculture Organization and United Nations Development Programme, should co-operate effectively with states parties in relation to the implementation of the right to water. It is also recommended by the committee that international financial institutions, notably the International Monetary Fund and the World Bank, should take into account the rights to water in their lending policies, credit agreements, structural adjustment programmes and other development projects.

6   Options and limits of the globalization of law

Demonstrating the mutual interdependence of land and water in local resource management and its significance for rural livelihoods, the case of women's gardens in Mhondoro is not unique. It raises general questions about women's rights to justice, equality and dignity as family providers in international, national and 'local' law. To effectively contribute to equality and the elimination of poverty, a human rights based approach must, as demonstrated, be sensitive to the existing plural gendered realities and legalities that actually frame people's allocation and management of land and water.

The integrated character of the human right to water in terms of civil, political, social, economic and cultural rights speaks to rural women's lived realities and is sensitive to the concerns embedded in local norms and practices. Both local practices and international human rights call into question the division between primary and commercial water in international and national water policies such as Zimbabwe's. CEDAW, the International Covenant on Economic, Social and Cultural Rights and the Protocol to the African Charter on Human and Peoples' Rights on the Rights of Women in Africa cut across the division between primary and commercial water. These instruments provide protection against discrimination caused by laws and policies that overlook the plural and gendered character of local land and water uses. This development points to the role of international human rights bodies such as the Committee on Economic, Social and Cultural Rights, the Committee on the Elimination of All Forms of Discrimination against Women and the African Court of Human Rights in developing human rights standards that respond to women's diverse living conditions through cross-cultural dialogue.

International and regional human rights discourses, emphasizing women's right to resources and participation in resource management, speak to the plural and gendered realities and legalities on the ground. They resonate the increasing body of knowledge documenting the significance of African women's participation in local water management and the economic value of their uses of water for both domestic and productive purposes that has over the years been brought to the international and regional negotiating table by researchers and non-governmental organizations. Like the evolving body of human rights protecting women against violence, the human right to water represents a discourse that may be used by actors around the world who seek to define their problems in human rights terms (Merry, 2001).

As local concerns, discourses and practices are making their mark on international laws and policies, and vice versa, the boundaries between local and international laws are becoming blurred. This trend can clearly be observed in relation to international law's increased recognition of women and indigenous peoples' uses of water and land.[129] The concepts of 'local law', 'mobile law' and 'glocalization' draw attention to the interactive character of international law and policy making concerning the right to livelihood, water and land.[130] Focusing on interaction and interplay these paradigms move beyond the simplistic notion of international human rights and African customary laws as distinct, separate and opposing norms and values.

By setting standards that are binding for national laws, policies and practices, the human right to water sets a legal limit to free-market economic models. It balances the quest for more effective and productive water voiced by international actors like the International Monetary Fund and the World Bank, against people's right to life and the right to livelihood without discrimination. The human rights approach requires that national laws and policies undergo a gender impact analysis in order to identify potential discriminatory effects. Water investment policies that on the surface are neutral will have to be examined in the light of the gendered character of land and water uses to ensure that they do not disproportionately favour agricultural enterprises controlled by men. It also requires that transparent, representative and accountable water management institutions with appeals to an independent court are established.

The Zimbabwean case points to the lack of both enabling legislation and rule of law in the context of a centralized and élite ruled nation-state putting race before gender and social inequalities. Vesting all land and water in the president, the Water Act neither recognizes a right to water for communities nor for individuals. In countries where the right to wa-

---

[129] On the implications for women's local land use of the changing conception of property in international human rights law see Ikdahl's chapter in this volume.
[130] See von Benda-Beckmann, von Benda-Beckmann and Griffiths (2005).

ter is embedded in the constitution and the legislation of the country, such as South Africa, poor water users are challenging the legality of the user-pay principle through the national court system.[131] At the international and regional legal level the individual complaint procedures embedded in CEDAW and the African Charter offer the opportunity of further challenging national laws and policies that don't respect, protect and fulfil women's local water rights.

Bibliography

Beinart W. (1984) 'Soil erosion, conservationism and ideas about development: A southern African exploration, 1900–1960', in *Journal of Southern African Studies,* Vol. 11(1):52-83.

Bentzon A. W., A. Hellum, J. Stewart, W. Ncube and T. Agersnap (1998) *Pursuing grounded theory in law: South-north experiences in developing women's law*, Mond Books/ Tano Aschehoug, Harare and Oslo.

Bentzon A. W. (1994) 'Negotiated law', in H. C. Marcussen with C. Lund (eds*) Access, control and management of natural resources in sub-Saharan Africa*, Occasional Papers No. 13, International Development Studies, Roskilde University, Roskilde.

Berry, S. (1993) *No condition is permanent: The social dynamics of agrarian change in sub-Saharan Africa,* University of Wisconsin Press, Madison.
– (2002) 'Debating the land question in Africa', in *Comparative studies in society and history,* Vol. 44 (4): 638–668.

Bourdillon M. (1987) *The Shona peoples,* Mambo Press, Gweru.

Bruns B. and R. S. Meinzen-Dick (2000) *Negotiating water rights*, Vistaar Publications, New Delhi.

Bullock A. (1995) 'Hydrological studies for policy formulation in Zimbabwe's communal lands', pages 69–82 in R. Owen K. Verbeek, J. Jackson and T. Steenhuis, *Dambo farming in Zimbabwe: Water management, cropping and soil potentials for smallholder farming in the wetlands,* University of Zimbabwe Publications, Harare.

Centre for Applied Social Sciences (CASS, 2000–2001) *BASIS survey* data, University of Zimbabwe, Harare.

---

[131] The right to water is provided in Section 27 (1)(b) of the South African Constitution. Section 27(2) requires the state to take reasonable legislative and other measures, within its available resources, to achieve the progressive realization of the right. In the *Resident of Bon Vista Mansions v Southern Metropolitan Local Council,* (Unreported WLD judgement by Budlender AJ, case no: 01/312) the court found that the disconnection of water supply would constitute a breach of the state's duty to respect the right of access to water. The human right to water in South Africa is dealt with in the article 'Access to water' (Stein and Niclaas, 2002).

Cleaver F. and D. Elson (1995) 'Women and water resources: Continued marginalization and new policies', *Gatekeeper* Series No. 49, International Institute for Environment and Development.

Cleaver F. (1998) 'Choice, complexity and change: Gendered livelihoods and the management of water', in *Agriculture and Human Values* 15: 293-99, Kluwer Academic Publishers, Dordrecht.

Derman B. (1997) 'How green was my valley! Land use and economic development in the Zambezi valley, Zimbabwe', pages 331–380 in B. Isaac (ed) *Research in economic anthropology,* Volume 18, Greenwood, Greenwich, Ct.

Derman B., A. Ferguson and F. Gonese (2002) *'Decentralization, devolution and development: Reflections on the water reform process in Zimbabwe'*, BASIS CRSP Report, BASIS CRSP, Madison, WI.

Derman B. and F. Gonese (2003) 'Water reform: Its multiple interfaces with land reform and resettlement', pages 287–307 in M. Roth and F. Gonese (eds) *Delivering land and securing livelihood: Post-independence land reform and resettlement in Zimbabwe*, CASS, University of Zimbabwe and Land Tenure Centre, University of Wisconsin, Harare and Madison, WI.

Derman B and A. Hellum (2003) 'Neither tragedy nor enclosure: Are there inherent human rights in water management in Zimbabwe's communal lands?', pages 31–50 in T. Benjaminsen and C. Lund (eds) *Securing land rights in Africa*, Frank Cass, London.

Derman B., A. Hellum and P. Sithole (2005) 'Intersections of human rights and customs: A livelihood perspective on water laws', paper delivered at the international workshop on 'African water laws: Plural legislative frameworks for rural water management in Africa', 26–28 January 2005, Gauteng, South Africa.

Eide A. (2001) 'The right to an adequate standard of living including the right to food', in A. Eide, A. Krause and A. Rosas (eds) *Economic, social and cultural rights: A textbook*, Kluwer International, Dordrecht.

Ferguson A. (1998) 'Water reform in Zimbabwe: Gender equity dimensions', paper presented at the African Studies Association Meetings, Chicago, 29 October–1 November, 1998.

Frankovits A. (2005) 'Introduction', pages 1–14 in M. Scheinin and M. Suksi (eds) *Empowerment, participation, accountability and non-discrimination: Operationalizing a human rights-based approach to development: Human Rights in Development Yearbook 2002*, Martinus Nijhoff/ Nordic Human Rights Publications, Dordrecht.

Gleick P. (1999) 'The human right to water', in *Water Policy* Vol. 1 (5): 487–503.

Hammar A., B. Raftopolous and S. Jensen (2003) *Zimbabwe's unfinished business: Rethinking land, state and nation in the context of crisis*, Weaver Press, Harare.

Hauserman J. (1998) *A human rights approach to development: Rights and humanity,* Department for International Development, London.

Hellum A. (1999) *Women's human rights and legal pluralism in Africa. Mixed norms and identities in infertility management in Zimbabwe*, Tano Aschehoug/Mond Books, Oslo and Harare.

Hellum A. (2001) 'Towards a human rights based development approach: The case of women in the water reform process in Zimbabwe' in *Law, Social Justice and Global Development,* University of Warwick online journal, Available at http://elj.warwick.ac/uk/global/issue/2001-1/hellum.html.

Hellum A. and B. Derman (2004a) 'Re-negotiating water and land rights in Zimbabwe: Some reflections on legal pluralism, identity and power', pages 233–260 in J. Murison, A. Griffiths, K. King (eds) *Remaking law in Africa,* Centre for African Studies, University of Edinburgh, Edinburgh.
– (2004b) 'Land reform and human rights in contemporary Zimbabwe: Balancing individual and social justice through an integrated human rights framework', pages 1785–1805 in *World Development* 32(10).
– (2005) 'Negotiating water rights in the context of a new political and legal landscape in Zimbabwe', pages 177–199 in F. von Benda-Beckmann, K. von Benda-Beckmann and A. Griffiths (eds) *Mobile people, mobile law: Expanding legal relations in a contracting world*, Ashgate, Aldershot.

Hoffman H. J. (1964) *Water law in Southern Rhodesia*, Government Printers, Salisbury (Harare).

Ikdahl I. with A. Hellum, R. Kårhus and T. A. Benjaminsen (2005) *Human rights, formalization and women's land rights in southern and eastern Africa,* Noragric report, UMB/ Studies in Women's Law, University of Oslo, Oslo.

Ikdahl I. (2007) in this volume.

International Water Management Institute (IWMI) (2004) *Implications of customary laws for implementing integrated water resources management*, inception report, Pretoria.

Knop K. (1994) 'Why rethinking the sovereign state is important for women's international human rights law', in R. Cook (ed) *Human rights of women: National and international perspectives,* University of Pennsylvania Press, Philadelphia.

Lan D. (1985) *Guns and rain, guerrillas and spirit mediums in Zimbabwe,* University of California Press, Berkeley, CA.

Manzungu E. and R. Marchiridza (2005) 'Economic-legal ideology and water management in Zimbabwe: Implications for smallholder agriculture', paper delivered at the international workshop on 'African water laws: Plural legislative frameworks for rural water management in Africa', 26–28 January 2005, Gauteng, South Africa.

Matondi P. (2001) *The struggle for access to land and water resources in Zimbabwe: The case of Shamva district,* Phd thesis, Swedish University of Agricultural Sciences, Uppsala.

Matiza T. (1992) 'The utilization and status of *dambos* in southern Africa: A Zimbabwe case study', pages 91–104 in T. Matiza and H. N. Chabwela (eds) *Wetlands conservation conference for Southern Africa: Proceedings of the SADCC wetlands conference*, IUCN, Gland.

Maxwell D. (1999) *Christians and chiefs in Zimbabwe: A social history of the Hwesa people*, Praeger, Westport.

McCaffrey S. C. (1992) 'A human right to water: Domestic and international implications', in *Georgetown International Law Environmental Law Review*, V(1), 1–24.

Meinzen-Dick and Bruns (2000) 'Negotiating water rights: Introduction', in B. Bruns and R. S. Meinzen-Dick (eds) *Negotiating water rights*, Vistar Publications, New Dehli.

Merry S. E. (2001) 'Women, violence and the human rights system', in M. Agosin (ed) *Women, gender and human rights. A global perspective*, Rutgers University Press, New Brunswick.

Nemarundwe N. (2003) *Negotiating resource access: Institutional arrangements for woodlands and water use in southern Zimbabwe*, Phd thesis, Swedish University of Agricultural Sciences, Uppsala.

Nussbaum M. C. (1999) *Women and human development: The capabilities approach*, Cambridge University Press, Cambridge.

Oloka-Onyango J. and S. Tamale (1995) 'The personal is political or why women's rights indeed are human rights: An African perspective on international feminism', in *Human Rights Quarterly* 17: 534–548.

Office of the United Nations High Commissioner for Human Rights (OHCHR) (2002) *Draft guidelines on a human rights approach to poverty reduction,* available at www.unhchr.ch/html/menu6/2/povertyE.pdf.

Platteau J. P. (2000) *Institutions, social norms and economic development,* Harwood Academic Publishers, Amsterdam.

Robinson P. (1998) *Targeted water price subsidies*, Zimconsult, Harare.

Roth M. and F. Gonese (eds) (2003) *Delivering land and securing livelihood: Post-independence land reform and resettlement in Zimbabwe*, Centre for Applied Social Sciences, University of Zimbabwe and Land Tenure Centre, University of Wisconsin, Harare and Madison, WI.

Rhodesia government (1976) *The Water Act.*

Sen A. (1993) 'Capability and wellbeing', in M. Nussbaum and A. Sen (eds) *The quality of life*, Oxford University Press, New York.
– (1999) *Development as freedom*, Borzoi Books, Knopf.

Sengupta A., A. Eide, S. Marks and B. A. Andreassen (2003) 'The right to development and human rights in development', a background paper for 'The Nobel symposium' organized in Oslo 13–15 October, the Norwegian Centre for Human Rights, University of Oslo.

Salman S. and S. McInerney-Lankford (2004) *The human right to water: Legal and policy dimensions*, World Bank, Washington DC.

Schreiner B. and B. van Koppen (2003) 'Policy and law for addressing poverty, race and gender in the water sector: The case of South Africa', in *Water Policy* 5: 489–501.

Sithole B. (1999) 'Use and access to dambos in communal lands in Zimbabwe: Institutional considerations', a thesis submitted in partial fulfilment of the requirements for a PhD, CASS, University of Zimbabwe, Harare.

Stein R. and L. Niklaas (2002) 'Access to water', pages 733–739(7) in *Physics and chemistry of the Earth*, Parts A/B/C, Volume 27, Number 11.

Spierz H. L. J. (1995) 'State and customary laws: Legal pluralism and water rights', *FMIS Newsletter* 13: 1–7.

United Nations (2002) *Report of the World Summit on sustainable development, Johannesburg, South Africa, 26 August–4 September, 2002*, New York.

United Nations Committee on CEDAW
– (1991) *Measurement and quantification of the unremunerated domestic activities of women and their recognition in the GNP*, General Recommendation No. 17, reference: A/46/38.
– (1994) *Equality in marriage and family relations*, General Recommendation No. 21, reference: A/49/38.

United Nations Committee on Economic, Social and Cultural Rights
– (1999) *The right to adequate food*, General Comment No. 12, reference: E/C.12/1999/5.
– (2000) *The right to the highest attainable standard of health*, General Comment No. 14, reference: E/C.12/2000/4.
– (2002) *The right to water*, General Comment No. 15, reference: E/C.12/2002/11.
– (2005) *The equal right of men and women to enjoyment of all economic, social and cultural rights*, General Comment No. 16, reference: article 3: E/.12/2005/3.
– (2001) *Statement on poverty*.

United Nations Development Programme (UNDP) (2003) *Human development report: Millennium development goals: A compact among nations to end poverty*, Oxford University Press, New York and Oxford.
– (1998) *Integrating human rights with sustainable development*, a UNDP policy document.
UNESCO (2003) Water *for people, water for life: The United Nations world water development report*, UNESCO and Berghahn, Barcelona.

Van Koppen B. (2000) 'Gendered water and land rights in Rice Valley improvement, Burkina Faso', in B. Bruns and R. S. Meinzen-Dick (eds) *Negotiating water rights*, Vistar Publications, New Dehli.

von Benda-Beckman F. and K. (1991) 'Law in society: From blindman's buff to multilocal law', in 'Living law in the low countries', *Recht Der Werklijkheid,* special issue of the Dutch and Belgian Law and Society Journal.

von Benda-Beckman F and K. and A. Griffiths (eds) (2005) *Mobile people, mobile law: Expanding legal relations in a contracting world*, Ashgate, Aldershot.

von Benda-Beckman F. *et al.* (1997a) 'Local law and customary practice in the study of water rights', in R. Pradhan *et al. (ed) Water rights, conflict and policy,* International Irrigation Management Institute, Colombo, Sri Lanka.

von Benda-Beckman K. *et al.* (1997b) 'Rights of women to the natural resources of land and water', *Women and Development Working Paper 2*, Neda, the Hague.

World Health Organization (2000) *The global water supply and sanitation assessment*, WHO, Geneva.
– (2003) *Right to water*, Health and human rights publication series No. 3, WHO, Geneva.

World Bank (1993) *Water resources management: A World Bank policy paper*, Washington DC.
– (2002) *Bridging troubled waters*, Operations Evaluation Department, World Bank, Washington DC.
– (2003) *Water resources sector strategy: Strategic directions for World Bank engagement,* Washington DC.
– (2003) *World development report 2003: Sustainable development in a dynamic world,* World Bank and Oxford University Press, Washington and New York.

Zimbabwe government (1998) *Zimbabwe parliamentary debates*, Vol. 25, No. 26, Tuesday, 3 November, Harare.
– (1998) *Zimbabwe parliamentary debates*, Vol. 23, No. 8. 15 September.
– (2000c) *Towards integrated water resources management*, Government Printers, Harare.
– (2003) *Report of the Presidential Land Review Committee under the Chairmanship of Dr Charles Utete,* two volumes, Government Printers, Harare.

Zwarteveen M. (1997) 'Water: From basic need to commodity: A discussion on gender and water rights in the context of irrigation', in *World Development 25* (8) pp. 1335–1349.

List of cases
India
Vellore Citizens Welfare Reform v Union of India, 1996 A.I.R. (S.C) 2715
General Secretary, West Pakistan Salt Miners Labour Union, Khwra Khelum v The Director, Industries and Mineral Development, Punjab Lahore, Human Rights Case NO. 120 of 1993
South Africa
Resident of Bon Vista Mansions v Southern Metropolitan Local Council (Unreported WLD judgement by Budlender AJ, case no: 01/312)

List of legislation
Zimbabwe
National Water Authority Act No. 11/1998
Natural Resources Act 1952
Statutory Instrument 33: Water (Catchment councils) Regulations 2000a
Statutory Instrument 47 of 2000: Water (Subcatchment councils) Regulations 2000b
Streambank Regulation of 1952
Water Act of 1927
Water Act No. 31/1998

Namibia
Water Resources Management Bill of 2001 126

Constitutions
Constitution of the Republic of South Africa 1996
Constitution of the Federal Democratic Republic of Ethiopia 1994
Constitution of Zimbabwe

Regional and international

Organization of African Unity
African Charter on Human and Peoples' Rights 1981
Protocol to the African Charter on Human and People's Rights on the Rights of Women in Africa 2003 (entered into force November 2005)
United Nations
Agenda 21 Chapter 18 Protection of the Quality and Supply of Freshwater Resources: Water Resources 1992
Beijing Platform for Action 1995
Convention on the Elimination of all forms of Discrimination Against Women (CEDAW) 1979
Convention on the Law of Non-Navigational Uses of Watercourses 1997
Convention on the Rights of the Child 1989
Declaration on the Right to Development, adopted by General Assembly, resolution 41/128 f 4, December 1986
Dublin Statement on Water and Sustainable Development 1992
International Covenant on Civil and Political Rights 1966
International Covenant on Economic, Social and Cultural Rights 1966
Rio Declaration on Environment and Development 1992

6

Making gender visible in law: Kwena women's access to power and resources

Anne Griffiths

In exploring the links between human rights discourse, legal pluralism and women's lived experiences of law, the issue of power is omnipresent. For at whatever level empirical studies are carried out – detailing the ways in which international, regional, national and local laws, norms and values come together to situate individuals and groups' claims to resources and the gendered position that women occupy in differing economic, social and political contexts – questions always arise as to who has the power to construct, shape, transform or contest the terms of reference upon which the negotiation of such claims rests and what implications this has for women's use of law. This chapter explores how power shapes access to social and material resources in the context of family relationships involving Kwena women's relationships with men. It is based on an ethnographic study carried out in the village of Molepolole in Botswana between 1982 and 1989. This study, derived from social actors' perceptions and experiences of daily life, examined the role of marriage in the social construction of relationships between women and men and the ways in which marital status affects the kinds of claims that women pursue with respect to their male partners, such as compensation for pregnancy, maintenance and rights to property.[132] Although conducted in the 1980s, the study's methodological approach, centred on life histories, raises questions about how power is constructed and the gendered nature of its dimensions that are pertinent to Botswana today.

One aspect of property rights in Africa that has generated much controversy over the years concerns land tenure. Customary land tenure in Africa and its effects are the subject of ongoing debate, especially in the broader context of nation building and development (Berry, 2002; Juul and Lund, 2002; McAuslan, 2003; Manji, 2001, 2003a and b; Odgaard, 2003; Peters, 2003; Smith, 2003). In essence these debates have become polarized around the issue of whether or not customary land tenure stands in the way of national development and progress. This is because it is argued that customary law fails to provide for clearly defined and enforceable property rights that accompany the concept of the individual

---

[132] For a detailed account of this research see Griffiths (1997).

through registered rights of private ownership. On the contrary, 'communal' land tenure is viewed as lacking the necessary 'security' to ensure agricultural investment and the productive use of land in the quest for improved economic growth and the reduction of poverty. This view, predominantly upheld by international agencies like the International Monetary Fund and the World Bank, has been influential in exerting pressure on African governments that are dependent on aid to introduce or extend registration of land. It has generally ignored the gendered position of women that frames their access to and control over land. Nyamu-Musembi (2002), for example, documents how government policy – in formalizing and individualizing property rights in land in Kenya – is having an adverse effect on women. This is because land is now registered in the name of male heads of households as sole owners and while sole ownership is not a requirement of registration, the practice is followed and has led to women accounting for less than 5 per cent of registered landholders nationally. Manji (2003a) critically examines draft World Bank policy reports on land relations, especially their promotion of formal rural credit that is predicated on the assumption of the availability of women's unpaid labour, for this fails to acknowledge the impact that such policies will have on gender relations given the nature of its recommendations.

The move towards registration of title and privatization of land has not gone unchallenged. Scholars engaging in field research have questioned the underlying assumptions on which such moves are predicated, especially the validity of framing economic development on a paradigm derived from western European experience (Peters, 1997, 2002, 2003:3–15; Francis, 1984; Colson, 1971; Berry, 1975; Bruce, 1988; Guyer and Lambin, 1993; Netting, 1993; Linares, 1992; Moore, 1998). In addition, scholars (Berry, 1993, 2002; Moore, 1986) have highlighted positive aspects of customary land tenure which gives individuals scope for manoeuvre and social agency through its indeterminate character and negotiability which is integral to the system. This may work to the benefit of some women who find that social and economic change brings about changes in customary land tenure that are to their advantage (Bikaako and Ssenkumba, 2003). As Berry (1993:104) observes, it is:

> '…not so much that land rights are insecure and that land use, therefore, is inefficient but that people's access to land depends on their participation in processes of interpretation and adjudication, as well as their ability to pay.'

What this means is that:

> 'People's ability to exercise claims to land remains closely linked to membership in social networks and participation in both formal and informal political processes.'

However, in debating the advantages and disadvantages of customary land tenure in relation to land registration, the discussion remains entrenched, for the most part, in advocating for individual property rights to take precedence over customary land tenure or vice versa. By framing the debate in this way – in terms of the old, juridical form of legal pluralism that treats customary law as separate and distinct from western-style law (Hooker, 1975) – what is rendered invisible is the gendered world in which women and men live and how this shapes their access to and control over resources such as land. For this becomes obscured in playing one system off against the other and through general discussions at a more abstract level (focusing on formal legal characteristics) such as, what constitutes a 'right' in each system. Analysis at this level ignores what happens on the ground, where land rights are highly complex, and involve multiple and overlapping uses and claims. The reality on the ground gives rise to the need for a more comprehensive and informed understanding of legal pluralism that takes account of 'that state of affairs, for any social field, in which behaviour pursuant to more than one legal order occurs' (Griffiths, 1986:2), often referred to as the new or strong form of legal pluralism. It also necessitates a more sophisticated and concrete knowledge of the ways in which gender operates in legally plural contexts to constrain or facilitate access to and control over resources between and among the sexes.

The situation is rendered more complex by the imposition, at another level, of international human rights law that actively seeks to promote non-discrimination and equality of treatment for women in relation to men, through conventions and declarations, such as the Convention on the Elimination of all forms of Discrimination Against Women (CEDAW) and the Declaration on the Elimination of all forms of Violence Against Women. The discourse on international human rights has become caught up with questions of culture that tend to polarize debate in terms of opposing perspectives embracing a universalist or relativist conception of rights (Cowan, Dembour and Wilson, 2001). Banda (2004) observes the ways in which culture has been deployed in an African context either by feminists who challenge the universalism of human rights on the basis that it represents an idealized, northern male perspective that is ethnocentric, or by self-interested male élites from the south, who are anxious to promote African culture as inimical to a northern rights based discourse centred on the individual. Rather than engaging with the endless debates surrounding the universal or relative nature of rights, Banda highlights regional initiatives promoted by bodies such as the Southern African Development Community in drafting the Gender and Development Declaration 1997, its Addendum on Violence Against Women, as well as the Protocol on the Rights of African Women. The speed with which human rights discourse has had an impact at both global and local levels – as manifested through international conventions and instruments, an ever-proliferating range of supra-national institutions dealing with 'rights', and through the local mobilization of rights by individuals, associations and 'indigenous' groups – calls for a re-interpretation of the relationship between culture, rights and law. Rather than viewing culture in terms of social groups as discrete, clearly bounded and internally homogenous with relatively fixed meanings and values (a view that resonates with the old, juridical view of legal pluralism), such reinterpretation embraces culture as a 'network of perspectives' (Hannerz, 1992:265–266) or as a 'sociological fiction, a shorthand referring to the disordered social field of connected practices and beliefs which are produced out of social action' (Cowan, Dembour and Wilson, 2001: 14). Thus culture becomes reconceptualized in analytical terms which stress process, fluidity and contestation, a perspective which is in keeping with the new or strong form of legal pluralism.

To pursue this kind of analysis that acknowledges the need to integrate a gendered perspective on law, it is necessary to acquire a concrete understanding of the social basis upon which law operates through detailed field studies. These require encompassing both customary and western-style law (and any other law, such as religious law, that may apply) in research that goes beyond a formal study of the legal institutions, cases and personnel that feature in any particular empirical context. For this reason my chapter focuses on the way in which *Bakwena*[133] in Molepolole form part of networks which frame their world and channel their access to resources. Based on a local micro-study of women and men's lived experiences, drawn from life histories and disputes, it highlights the importance of the position which individuals occupy in their networks of kinship, family and community that is a crucial factor in facilitating or constraining their access to resources. These life histories derived from individuals in Mosotho *kgotla* document their experiences as well as their connections to the broader social polity to which they belong. Combined with others collected by Isaac Schapera in 1937 they provide a picture of continuity and change across two generations that highlights the differences between and among the sexes.

This grounded perspective is important because it foregrounds villagers' perceptions of law, the circumstances under which they do or do not have access to formal legal forums and, especially, the conditions under which individuals become silenced or unable to negotiate with

---

[133] In Setswana which is one of the official languages in Botswana (along with English) the prefix 'ba' is the plural modifier of nouns designating persons, so 'Bakwena' is the plural form of 'Kwena' (Kwena people/persons).

others in terms of daily life. Such information is crucial in promoting an understanding of who has the authority and power to negotiate in day-to-day social life for, as elsewhere, few negotiations extend beyond daily life that require handling in a formal legal arena, such as a court.

In particular, my analysis explores how Kwena women's relationships with land are mediated through the gendered networks of family and household in conjunction with the broader economic, political, ideological and social domains of which they form part. It highlights how these factors shape the power of individuals to negotiate with one another, the types of discourse they employ and, in particular, the difficulties that women encounter in accessing and using land, due to the gendered dimensions of the world in which they operate. Thus my discussion of land is situated within the broader context of property and access to resources because among *Bakwena* 'land' represents only one component, albeit an important one, in the constellation of assets that individuals and families rely on for their livelihood. For this reason my analysis views property in terms of social relations between people,[134] a perspective that requires it to be situated within wide-ranging political, economic and socio-cultural matrixes, rather than in terms of narrowly defined heritable or incorporeal, moveable rights associated with formalist analyses of law.

1   The household and the *kgotla*

As with any Tswana village, the organization of Molepolole is structured through administrative units, known as *kgotlas* and wards, which derive from households. In Tswana ideology, a household consists of a male head with a wife and their children; if a man has more than one wife there is a separate household for each wife. This ideal has long since ceased to be realized. National Development Plan 6 (NDP6), a government development plan comments, that 'females head a third of the households in urban areas and half in the rural areas.'[135] UNICEF (1989) has also commented on this in its observations on children, women and development in Botswana. A subsequent government development plan (NDP7:9) observes that 'women headed 40 per cent of households in urban areas and nearly half in the rural areas'. The term 'female-headed household', which appears in the literature on government planning and policy development in Botswana (Botswana government, 1982), is the subject of some controversy.[136] I use the term 'female head of household'

---

[134] See Gluckman (1965); Hann (1998:2); Hoebel (1966:424); Moore (1998:33); and Middleton (1988:xx).

[135] Botswana government (NDP6).

[136] See Peters (1983) and Kerven (1984).

to denote those households associated with Mosotho *kgotla* in which women are in de facto control of the household and lands attached to it and where no adult male of equivalent generational status, whether husband, partner or brother was present at the time of research. I use the term 'household' to represent a physical entity or domain which is located in or associated with a *kgotla*.

A ward is composed of a number of households organized by the chief around a *kgotla*. In precolonial times, all households of a ward were at least nominally descended from an eponymous founder but this has not been the case for several decades. It is through households that the political structure of the *morafe* (polity) maintains itself. A *kgotla* is the assembly centre (both the physical location and the body of members) of a group of households presided over by a male headman or ward head; in the past, all household heads were related through the male line but this is rarely the case today. It forms part of the organization of Tswana society that revolves around the construction of a *morafe*. The political community within Kwena society, like that of other Tswana *merafe* (plural of *morafe*, polities), is conceived of as a hierarchy of progressively more inclusive co-residential and administrative groupings, beginning with households and expanding to cover extended family groups in *kgotlas*, to wards.

Wards are the major units of political organization of a Tswana village; they are still presided over by men.[137] The most powerful ward is *kgosing*. The word *kgosing* is derived from the word *kgosi*, interpreted as 'chief'. *Kgosing* refers both to the chief's ward, which is the most senior of all Kwena wards in the polity over which it presides, and to the chief's *kgotla* (often, loosely, called the chief's court), which lies at the heart of *kgosing* ward, representing the most senior of all the *kgotlas* within the ward itself. The chief's *kgotla* in *kgosing* is the most senior and powerful in the polity and represents the apex of the administrative and political structure through which the *kgosi* exercises his power. When I began my research in Molepolole in 1982 there were six main wards[138] and 73 *kgotlas*.[139]

2   Women, households and access to resources

In material terms it is clear that those women who have access to the greatest resources are those who are married or who can draw on the support of adult males. According to UNICEF (1989:58), in Botswana:

---

[137] Since my study was completed Mosadi Seboko has been installed as a *kgosi* for the Balete of Ramotswa.

[138] These are Kgosing, Maunatlala, Mokgalo, Ratshosa, Ntoloedibe and Borakalalo.

[139] According to the 1982 list in tribal administration.

'Female-headed households with no male present had an annual income less than one-half that of male-headed households and just over half that of female-headed households with a male present.'

Given the range of factors affecting women's access to resources the same report (on page 58) concluded that 'household structure (male or female headed) is ... an important predictor of poverty patterns'. The government (Botswana government, 1991:16–17) also documents that 'households headed by women (which account for nearly half of all households) have generally lower incomes than male-headed households'.

At a local level, the 30 households associated with Mosotho *kgotla* in 1984 were on a par with the national profile for female-headed households as women ran most of them. Of these, 18 were headed by women at various stages in the life cycle and of varying status, including eight widows, four wives whose husbands were engaged in migrant labour, a deserted wife (whose husband left her years before) and five unmarried women over the age of 40. The remaining 12 households were headed by married men, most of whom had come to that stage in the life cycle when they had returned to their rural home to live out their later years. Among these households the best resourced were those of married couples who had the cash income to invest in livestock, sustain agricultural production and run small businesses in the informal sector. In considering resources my analysis links individuals with households and family groups to take account of both intra and supra household networks of cooperation and/or disaffection (Griffiths, 1988:289–316).

Membership within these differing networks has important consequences for individuals as it provides the contexts within which different forms of power may be negotiated. This is especially pertinent for women when it comes to negotiations over their status and rights to property. Such negotiations are predicated upon structures of ownership and control and access to resources, the most essential components of which are land, livestock and employment. Most women have access to land (which is held under customary tenure)[140] through pre- or post-mortem inheritance, through use rights accorded to them by others (who may or may not be kin) who have land but are not working it, through land boards, or through their husbands or male partners' rights to land.

---

[140] There are three main categories of land in Botswana: customary land, freehold land and state land. Customary land is administered by the land boards and covers 70 per cent of the total land area of the country; freehold land constitutes around 5 per cent of the total land area; and state land, which is administered by the Department of Lands, covers about 25 per cent of the total land area, comprising national parks and wildlife management areas (Botswana government, NDP9:332).

However, it is not so much access as the capacity to use that access that is important, as well as control over the products that derive from it. As an agricultural resource this depends on women's ability to raise cash to buy the seeds and other items necessary for its maintenance (Kerven, 1982) as well as their ability to mobilize the labour necessary for its cultivation (whether through kin or by hire) (Izzard, 1982:712; Cooper, 1982:14). In both respects women tend to be dependent on men (Solway, 1980; Kerven, 1984) especially where they form part of the peasantariat, because of the nature of the social system and their poorer prospects of employment as compared with those of men.

Gendered domains

Authority in households is based on age, sex and status. Children defer to adults who acquire status with marriage and age but women do not have the authority comparable with that of men. This is underlined by the fact that although they act as heads of households, they never qualify for the position of head of a group of households which form a *kgotla*, the basic unit in the political structure of the *morafe*. At each stage of her life a woman falls within the shadow of male authority. When unmarried, it is the authority of her father and her brothers; when married, it is that of her husband; and when widowed or in old age (if never married) it is that of her sons. Material and social circumstances combine to create a situation where it is hardly surprising that households of married men and women prove the most effective in agricultural production.

The agricultural domain is closely allied to that of livestock as many people still rely on draught power to plough the land. Once again, women find themselves at a disadvantage in acquiring stock. This is due, in part, to the laws of succession according to which the largest category of cattle, referred to as estate cattle, is handed down from father to sons. Although a daughter can and frequently does acquire some livestock (where such cattle exist) her share is never on a par with that of her brothers, especially her eldest brother who takes over responsibility for the family group on his father's death. Given the patrilineal nature of Tswana society where descent is traced through the male line – through the man's father where the parents are married, and through the woman's father where they are not – it is not surprising that male offspring have been privileged over female offspring when it comes to inheritance under customary law. This situation has been documented elsewhere in Africa, although recent research (Bikaako and Ssenkumba, 2003; Nyamu-Musembi, 2003) notes a change in practice that is to women's benefit. Women in Botswana may inherit livestock from their mothers but a mother's opportunities to acquire her own stock have tended to be limited, as these can only derive from certain sources of labour. Cattle owned by women are mainly produced from their own (not their husbands') inherited land which may be exchanged for livestock; or the produce of that land may be used to make beer, which in turn may be sold to provide the cash for cattle purchases.

As there is very often little surplus produce because most of what is grown is required for home consumption and any livestock acquired is liable to perish during drought years, it is extremely hard to acquire livestock in this way. Acquiring money to purchase stock is also difficult for women, given the low rates of pay that many of them receive even when they are fortunate enough to find employment (Datta, undated: 3; UNFPA, 1989:13). Even where such difficulties are overcome, women still have to contend with the reality of male control over animals, as it is boys and men who run the cattleposts where they are kept.

Access to wage employment is one of the most important factors affecting the social and economic position of women in Botswana (Brown, 1983; Kerven, 1984:267; UNICEF, 1993:12–20). This is because cash, so essential for survival, is generally less available to women for a number of reasons. In the formal sector, certain basic types of employment on which the majority of the male population rely, for example, in the mining and construction industry, are not open to women. Others, particularly those of a more professional nature, require a certain degree of education which limits their availability to both sexes. Only a minority of women have the necessary qualifications, yet they are beginning to outnumber the jobs available. Moreover, women in Botswana generally fall short of these qualifications compared with men (UNFPA, 1989:13). For most women the main kind of employment that was (at the time of my study) open to them tended to be at the level of domestic service (Alexander, 1991:49) or working as barmaids or shop assistants. There was competition for such work which in any case is insecure and poorly paid. In this situation women find it hard to negotiate or enforce their terms of service, even where these are laid down by law. Men also have these difficulties but have more options with regard to potential employment.

The informal sector provides a supplemental or alternative means of raising income on which many women depend (Datta, undated; Izzard, 1982: 702). It is mainly women who work in this sector but, as studies elsewhere have shown (Moore, 1988: 90), investment in this sector does not guarantee returns and, when it involves illegal activities such as prostitution, puts the individuals concerned at risk. Bakwena experience (author's own data and Datta, undated: 24) indicates that the returns women receive from this sector are insufficient on their own to provide for capital accumulation or personal enrichment.

In the years since independence there has been a 'remarkable economic transformation' in Botswana (NDP6: 13) which has been 'unmatched by any non-oil producing country in Africa' (NDP6: 16).[141] According to the United Nations Development Programme, in 1998 Botswana ranked fourth among African countries in terms of its human development index but not all have benefited equally from this development. The government recognizes that there is 'real poverty' (NDP6: 19) and from the data available on income distribution that there is:

> '… considerable evidence about the unequal distribution of the assets and opportunities upon which higher incomes depend. Poverty is more evident in rural areas than among the urban population; the households most affected … are those who do not have viable cattle herds, those without cattle at all, female-headed households, and those who do not engage in agriculture at all …These categories overlap, so that for example households which are both female-headed and non-livestock owning are likely to be especially impoverished' (NDP6: 21).

In contrast a minority has clearly benefited from Botswana's economic development. The beneficiaries are primarily descendents of nineteenth century *dikgosana* (royal families) who control vast tracts of land. They are the largest cattle owners and the higher income group of wage earners, both in public and private sectors (NDP6: 8).

3   Life histories

Life histories from Mosotho *kgotla* demonstrate that women's access to resources is heavily dependent upon the type of network to which they belong. Such networks embody two basic forms of existence that have emerged during the course of the encounter with colonialism and which mark the process of social differentiation in Botswana.[142] From these it is possible to chart not only the common points of reference but, more significantly, the variations that allow for different life courses. Kerven (1982) notes that:

> 'Tswana livelihoods are made within the minimal core of the family and the maximal universe of the southern African economy.'

The government of Botswana itself (1991:xxi, 95, 145) noted the ways in which the country's development is inextricably tied to decisions, processes and events that take place at a regional and international level beyond its national borders. In this environment families depend on a

---

[141] This is due to diamonds discovered in 1967. Botswana is now a major diamond producer in the world and is in partnership with De Beers in South Africa. Since completing the research, a diamond sorting plant has opened in Molepolole.

[142] For a detailed discussion of the historical, political and economic dimensions giving rise to this, see Griffiths (1997:17–27, 62–105).

combination of 'crops, cattle and wages' for their existence which are combined according to 'a family's class position and its stage of life cycle' (Kerven, 1982: 545). This interdependence among family groups, centred around subsistence agriculture, livestock and intermittent employment, gives rise to what Parson (1981) has termed the *peasantariat*, a social class that incorporates most families in Botswana today. Within this class the focus on resources is geared to subsistence agriculture, the raising of livestock and migrant labour which is generally of an unskilled nature and entered into on a contract basis (Cooper, 1979). However, there is a growing number of those who have been able to focus on other activities and to form part of an élite, referred to by Cooper (1982) as the *salariat*. The education (often to university level) of this class has enabled them to acquire skilled and stable forms of employment, generally within a government-based or affiliated organization which carries with it a range of benefits.

Within the *kgotla* there are families which span both these groups, highlighting the important consequences of membership within networks for individuals, especially women, when it comes to negotiating status and rights to property. These are, of course, not rigidly fixed categories – the salariat could not exist without the possibility of social mobility – and should be thought of as the polar regions (not end points) of an uneven continuum of socio-economic-political statuses. They do, however, reflect quite accurately the lived reality of the vast majority of *Batswana* (citizens of Botswana) lives, as the authors in Kerven (1982) demonstrate for the period of this study. From the life histories culled from over two generations of those living in Mosotho *kgotla*, certain patterns of existence are foregrounded which revolve around networks of varying kinds. These networks underline the ways in which power is constituted in the world of everyday life which is crucial to an individual's existence, as well as highlighting the important factors that inform people's actions before disputes arise or parties turn to courts to settle their differences.

The different life trajectories open to individuals are exemplified by the descendants of one of Mosotho *kgotla*'s founding ancestors, Koosimile, who had two sons (Radipati and Makokwe) by different wives. Makokwe's descendants, who represent most families in the *kgotla*, engage in subsistence agriculture, the raising of livestock and migrant labour of an unskilled type associated with the peasantariat. Radipati's descendants, however, have pursued another form of existence – one founded on education and skilled, secure employment – which has placed them among that élite salariat nationwide. Within these groups women find themselves differentially situated from men in terms of the kinds of claims that they can pursue with respect to status and property.

Not only that but their position in relation to one another also varies according to their affiliation within a particular group, as we shall see with three women – Olebeng, Diane and Goitsemang – who although of the same generation and related have had very different lives.

For those families in Botswana who focus on subsistence agriculture, the raising of livestock and unskilled, migrant labour, marriage still plays an important role in providing access to the broader networks of supra-household management and cooperation on which they rely for their subsistence. This was so for Makokwe's family in which there has been a relatively high rate of kin marriage among members of the older generation (ranging from 50–90 years old). When it comes to marriage within this group, women find their choices shaped by male networks and structures of authority which provide the resources and mainstay for their existence. So, for example, through male sibling support some women find themselves with the power of choice which is not available to other women who lack access to this type of network. This gives rise to a situation where those with choices, such as Olebeng, may opt not to marry, while those without access to the conditions under which such choice become available – like Diane, whose situation we shall examine – want to marry but are unlikely to do so because of the position in which they find themselves.

Olebeng: an unmarried woman with supportive male siblings

Life for the women in Makokwe's family revolves around the village and the lands where they engage in domestic and agricultural activities. Living in the village for much of the year they are able to attend school, unlike their brothers who are away herding cattle at distant cattleposts. This means that they are able to acquire a greater degree of formal education than their brothers, who in many cases among the older generation, have received none at all. Among this group, women's work is integrated with that of their male counterparts. Makokwe's only daughter, Olebeng, for example, has been part of a family network, exchanging her domestic and agricultural labour for her brothers' assistance with ploughing and support. She has never moved beyond this sphere of operations to undertake any form of paid employment, so that throughout life her activities have linked her into a network where she has had to rely on male support from her father, her brothers and her male partners for existence. Within this system, she has been fortunate because her five older brothers have been quite generous in providing support, assisting her with ploughing and upholding her welfare. They have, for example, consented to her taking over the natal household because they have all married and established their own households elsewhere in the village. Compared with other women, she was in a relatively strong position in that her circumstances permitted a certain degree of choice, including whether or not to marry. During her life she had several children (all of whom died at birth) with a number of male partners but has never married. This is out of choice, according to Olebeng, who maintains that from her very first pregnancy neither she nor her family had any interest in pursuing the issue of marriage.

But Olebeng's situation is unusual because in this environment – where emphasis is placed on subsistence agriculture, livestock and a cash input from migrant labour – marriage is particularly important for women who, as unmarried daughters and sisters, find themselves at the bottom of the social hierarchy in terms of power and access to resources. Such power derives not only from status and a point in the lifecycle but also includes an individual's capacity to generate or control resources. Among women, power devolves with age linked to status, so that a young unmarried childless woman is in a less influential position compared to her older married sister who has children. Both, however, deferred to their mother and even more so to their grandmother who, by virtue of her age and status, is considered to be in the most powerful position of them all. It is not age alone but the incidents that mark its passage, such as childbearing, that are integral parts of the lifecycle which create status; the combination of age with status fuels the dynamics of power. The same is true for men. A young childless man who has never experienced formal employment has less status than his older married brother who has children and has worked at the mines. Both should defer to their father and grandfather who have passed beyond these stages. However, this is not always done, especially where the older generation is dependent on the younger to provide for them through the cash that they remit back to the family from their earnings as migrant labourers.

In these circumstances, women are constrained by the gendered world they live in, where men have more control over resources, such as cash, on which all households depend. Money is not only required to support family members but to maintain the subsistence agricultural base. Women have fewer opportunities than men to generate the income required because they do not have access to the most common forms of male employment down the mines or on construction sites and the returns they receive from participation in the informal economy are insufficient on their own to provide the resources they require. Those who are most successful are married women whose husbands have paid out the cash necessary to promote and sustain their activities. Women selling fat cakes (fried bread dough), for example, need money to buy the flour with which they are made. Although women may have access to land and own livestock, the use of these resources is often mediated through men. This is because it is men or young boys who herd the livestock at the cattlepost and who are responsible for moving them to the lands for ploughing or to the village to sell. Not infrequently, a man will report that cattle have gone missing or died. Given the distances involved, it is hard to challenge a herder's claim, even though an owner may suspect that the herder has in fact appropriated them for his own purposes. When it comes to cultivation of land most people still rely on oxen to work the plough. Those that have a team or can contribute to one have control over ploughing and the sequence it may follow. In Mosotho *kgotla*, these are mostly married men who plough their own fields before those of their brothers, parents and, lastly, unmarried sisters.

Diane: a vulnerable unmarried female head of household
Within this kind of network, an unmarried woman finds herself at a disadvantage. While part of a group formed of her family and kin have responsibility for her – and thus obligations to plough for her – her position is vulnerable in that her interests are subordinated to those of other family members. This was the case with Diane and her unmarried daughters who found themselves greatly disadvantaged by the constraints inherent in a kinship network. Unlike Olebeng, Diane had a relationship fraught with conflict with her male kin. Her brothers abandoned her after their father's death. They not only left her to fend for herself but also appropriated for their own use the land that she was left by her mother. Without access to her brothers' network and powerless to challenge their actions (even in the local *kgotla*) she has found herself in a position where she has had to rely on a series of male partners for support, in relationships of *bonyatsi* (concubinage) that preclude marriage. Despite this, she still firmly expresses the view that 'it is natural with Batswana to marry. A woman must marry'. Her own life history, however, has placed her in a position where marriage is no longer a viable option given the number of children that she has had with different men.

By 1989 Diane had had ten children by four different fathers. As one of the poorest female heads of a household in Mosotho *kgotla*, her life history fits the national profile of the vulnerable female-headed household described by Kerven (1982), Izzard (1979), Brown (1983) and others which is so much at risk and with which the government of Botswana (NDP7) was and is so concerned. This is because of the highly impoverished position in which many female heads of households find themselves and which is often perpetuated in succeeding generations (Motzafi-Haller, 1986). This was the case with Diane's five eldest daughters who have all, like their mother, had to leave school early because of pregnancy in circumstances where marriage was non-negotiable.

Goitsemang: an unmarried woman with access to resources

Other women, however, who form part of an emerging salariat find themselves with a greater degree of power and control over the choices that are open to them. This is because within their family group they are less reliant on the type of male networks that peasantariat women depend on for their existence. Goitsemang was such a woman. Despite the fact that her father Radipati was Makokwe's half brother, members of Radipati's family have experienced very different life trajectories from that of Makokwe. Unlike his contemporaries, Radipati (who died in 1950) was an educated man who placed great emphasis on his children's education, which his wife Mhudi struggled to provide after his death. As a result, his three daughters were educated (at a time when many women only received a nominal education) and acquired formal employment. The eldest unmarried daughter, Goitsemang (aged 52 in 1989), worked as a nurse in South Africa and then in a management capacity for a construction company in Botswana so that she has been able to build a house in Gaborone. This is something which many people in the village aspire to but are unable to achieve. Her younger unmarried sister has also acquired a plot of land in Gaborone by working for the same company. Radipati's sons were also educated and two of them, most unusual for that time, went on to acquire university degrees. Through their access to education and skilled, stable employment, the family fits the kind of profile associated with the emerging salariat. Among the younger generation a number of women are employed as teachers or court clerks and the men are similarly situated within government employ. The family's activities differ from those associated with a subsistence agricultural base and they no longer plough.

Within this family group, Goitsemang, like her contemporaries Diane and Olebeng, has had children and remained unmarried. However, in her case, her relationships with men had the hallmarks of a potential customary marriage which failed to materialize. Such a marriage reflects a process that takes place over many years and involves reciprocal relations between the respective families. Unlike a civil or religious marriage which is registered, it is not necessarily predicated upon a specific, identifiable occasion. While some features, such as the transfer of *bogadi* (marriage payment), may be treated as definitive markers of marriage, their absence does not rule out social recognition of a relationship as a marriage. Among Bakwena, a ceremony, *patlo*,[143] is viewed

---

[143] This ceremony involves parents, relatives and friends of the man who come to the woman's *kgotla* to perform a ritual involving a public request for marriage and acceptance of this request by the woman's family. For further details see Griffiths (1997: 54–55).

as being central to the constitution of a customary marriage. But it is not the only definitive feature, so that relationships can and do acquire the status of a marriage without it. What is important is the degree to which both families have become involved in the relationship and accorded it public recognition through the giving of gifts and attendance at significant life events, such as celebrations for the birth of a child or funerals.

Goitsemang observed that with her first partner the families met, discussed and agreed to marriage on a number of occasions, although it never materialized. This relationship is a typical example of the kind of marital negotiations referred to by Comaroff and Roberts (1977), where the parties start out seriously exploring the potential of the relationship but over time one withdraws, usually to pursue another relationship.

In her subsequent relationship, Goitsemang found herself at odds with her family. The relationship also had the potential for a customary marriage but was rejected by Goitsemang's family because they did not want her to enter into a polygamous union.[144] Nonetheless, Goitsemang maintained this relationship against her family's wishes. She had the power to ignore her family then because her employment gave her access to a world in which she was beyond their control. What was crucial for Goitsemang was that she was removed from the kind of pressures that accompany dependence on domestic and agricultural labour and the networks that sustain them. Through her education and training she had access to alternative means of support. These resources empowered her to make decisions on her own account and made her less vulnerable to demands made by kin. Goitsemang has felt able to challenge her brother David's claims to control over the natal household under customary law and has received sufficient support from local *kgotla* members to continue running the household for the time being.[145]

The problem arose between Goitsemang and David because she was not prepared to accept that as the senior family representative, he had control over the household. This was because of the investment that she had made in the property that went beyond the normal kind of female labour and domestic activity associated with a household, which would be taken for granted and which could not be used as a bargaining tool for control in this context. Because of this investment she was able to challenge her brother's authority and to mobilize support from the *kgotla*. This support hinged on an alliance between old and new criteria, the

---

[144] In Botswana, individuals may marry according to customary law or register a civil or religious marriage under the Marriage Act 1970 (Chapter 29:09). Under customary law, a man may marry more than one wife but not if he is already married to a woman under the 1970 Act. Nor can he marry a woman under the 1970 Act if he is already married to another woman under customary law.

[145] See Griffiths (1998a).

former based on the notion that as an unmarried woman she should be allowed to remain in the natal household, the latter on the basis of consistent and direct financial investment of the kind that is not usually made by women. For his part, while David appealed to tradition he was also constrained by it. A married man of his age, with his skills, is expected to have built his own household and, according to Goitsemang, it reflected poorly on him that he wished to turn her and her other unmarried sisters out in order to take over the household for his own purposes. Several *kgotla* members supported her view that 'a man of his age and standing should not be fighting over what others have made'.

This is only one example of how changing conditions create the space to transform the norms that govern social life. In this case, Goitsemang was able to challenge her brother successfully because she was able to reconfigure aspects of customary law to her advantage by drawing on traditional practice, as well as by integrating a novel element into the discourse, that of direct financial investment in property. It is unlikely that either element on its own account would have been sufficient to shift the status quo in her favour. Her situation was very different from that of Diane who was unable to contest her brothers' actions or from that of Olebeng who survives on the basis of a cooperative relationship with her brothers. At her stage in life, Goitsemang has no desire to marry because, as she observes, 'marriage just brings quarrels'. This is a view shared by a number of educated and employed women who prefer to avoid the status of wife, given the ways in which gender impacts on spousal roles and rights to property.[146]

4   Ethnography and land reform

My discussion of data in this chapter has focused on how power and authority is constructed in daily life through individuals' access to resources and the networks to which they belong. I have highlighted the gendered position in which Kwena women find themselves which affects their access to property while at the same time underling how differential access to resources may empower some women, such as Goitsemang, more than others, like Diane, when it comes to negotiating their claims with men. The data reveal the conditions which give rise to differences between families and which foster gender relations. These differences have implications for women and for their power to negotiate access to resources and property, including marriage and land. Thus, women within the peasantariat find that power is mediated through their particular position in relation to male networks and structures of author-

---

[146] For discussion of this, see Griffiths (1997:134-210).

ity that provide the mainstay for their existence. So, for example, through male sibling support some women find themselves with the power of choice which is not available to other women who lack access to this type of network. Those with choices, like Olebeng, may opt to not marry while those without access to the conditions under which such choice becomes available, like Diane, still seek to marry but often in vain. In contrast, women associated with the salariat, who are not so reliant on these male networks, find themselves with a greater degree of power and control over the choices that are open to them that may enable them to shift the terms of the discourse to their advantage when it comes to making claims. Thus Goitsemang was able to make a breakthrough when it came to asserting her claim to the natal household over her brother while Diane found herself at odds with the system where she had no power to contest her brothers' appropriation of land or to influence events.

The difficulties women face in gaining access to or control over property, including land, under customary law are clearly derived from the gendered position they occupy in kinship networks and from the economic, political, ideological and social domains that shape the world in which they live. They are not unique to Bakwena. Studies elsewhere in Africa have documented the problems women face in the light of the above constraints (Whitehead and Tsikata, 2003; Muthoni, 2003; WLSA, 2001; Diop Tine and Sy, 2003; Bigombe and Bikie, 2003; Abdullah and Hamza, 2003). These studies also document how law reform may prove inadequate in addressing this problem because of its lack of implementation or failure to have an impact on prevailing social attitudes that militate against it.

I have written elsewhere (Griffiths, 1996, 1997, 1998a, 1998b, 2000, 2001,2002) on how membership of networks and access to resources affect individuals' access to and use of law under both customary and western-style law. I have chosen to focus on the former in this chapter because the narratives derived from life histories and disputes underline the extent to which social understandings, expectations and values permeate law – regardless of where it is situated in a customary or western-type of legal setting. Kwena ethnography not only demonstrates that the social contexts within which law is embedded cannot be ignored but also underscores the need to recognize the degree to which customary law and western-style law are mutually constitutive, being underpinned by the norms and values that operate in a social world in which people live. Such a perspective makes gender visible in law.

There have been many changes in Botswana since my Bakwena study in Molepolole was carried out. Women's organizations and non-governmental organizations, such as Emang Basadi (Stand Up Women), have generated more public awareness of women's issues and linked into international networks that have supported activism on the ground as, for example, in the case of Unity Dow where the Urban Morgan Institute for Human Rights, University Cincinnati College of Law lodged an Amicus Brief on Unity Dow's behalf. Botswana has now become a signatory to CEDAW and a woman, Mosadi Seboko, has been installed among Balete of Ramotswa as a *kgosi*. The AIDS epidemic has taken its toll. It is not possible to document all the changes that have taken place but it would be interesting to factor these changes into empirical research in the future to see in what ways, if any, these changes have contributed to shifting constellations of power and what impact this has had on gender relations.

How these social phenomena shape the relationship between culture, rights and law requires empirical research if the question of land reform and women's access to and control over land is to be adequately addressed. For law reform, if it is to be sensitive to gender, must be formulated on an informed comprehension of the social basis upon which law operates. As of June 2003 the Botswana government 'is in the process of reviewing its national land policy and the issues of women's land rights is said to be one of those being addressed' (Radijeng, 2004:207) with a view to removing 'all forms of discrimination against women and to make all policies and law gender neutral' (Lekula, 2003 quoted by Radijeng, 2004: 207). Yet, as the above discussion has shown, the introduction of gender neutral language and formal changes in law will achieve little if they do not reflect a grounded knowledge and understanding of how women and men find themselves differentially situated when it comes to access to and control over resources such as land. As Ngonola, Professor of Law, University of Botswana, has observed:

> 'Land boards[147] claim to follow a gender neutral policy on allocations. But it would be interesting to apply your type of analysis to the actual situation on the ground. There is not much information on how women have been faring in their dealings with land boards' (personal communication, 2003).

In the land debate Peters (2003) has argued for the need to find a way forward that goes beyond privileging western-style law with its emphasis on individual property rights over customary land tenure or vice versa. She warns against overplaying the negotiability of customary law and the power of human agency in a world where social inequality is growing and observes (2002:61) that:

> '… an overemphasis on ambiguity and open-endedness is in danger of deflecting research from the patterns of inequity in landholding and

---

[147] Land boards administer the allocation of customary land, see note 236.

the relations between the latter and broader processes of differentiation and class formation.'

 Ethnography provides the means of redressing the balance and of exploring in greater detail how class, ethnicity, gender and age contribute to relations of inequality that impact on individuals and families, especially women's access to, and control over, land.

Bibliography

Abdullah H. J. and I. Hamza (2003) 'Women and land in northern Nigeria: The need for independent ownership rights', pages 133–175 in L. Muthoni Wanyeki (ed) Women *and land in Africa: Culture, religion and realizing women's rights*, Zed books Ltd and David Philip Publishers, London and Cape Town.

Alexander E. (1991) *Women and men in Botswana: Facts and figures,* Ministry of Finance and Development Planning, Central Statistics Office, Government Printer, Gaborone.

Banda F. (2004) 'The end of culture? African women and human rights', pages 115–136 in J. Murison, A. Griffiths and K. King (eds) *Remaking law in Africa: Transnationalism, persons and rights,* Centre for African Studies, Edinburgh University, Edinburgh.

Berry S. (1975) *Cocoa, custom and socio-economic change in rural western Nigeria,* Clarendon Press, Oxford.
– (1993) *No condition is permanent: The social dynamics of agrarian change in sub-Saharan Africa,* University of Wisconsin Press, Madison.
– (2002) 'Debating the land question in Africa', *Comparative Studies in Society and History* 638–668.

Bikaako W. and J. Ssenkumba (2003) 'Gender, land and rights: Contemporary contestations in law, policy and practice in Uganda' pages 232–278 in L. Muthoni Wanyeki (ed) *Women and land in Africa: Culture, religion and realizing women's rights,* Zed books Ltd and David Philip Publishers, London and Cape Town.

Bigombe Logo P. and E. H. Bikie (2003) 'Women and land in Cameroon: Questioning women's land status and claims for change', pages 31–65 in L. Muthoni Wanyeki (ed) *Women and land in Africa: Culture, religion and realizing women's rights*, Zed books Ltd and David Philip Publishers, London and Cape Town.

Botswana government (1982) *Migration in Botswana: Patterns, causes and consequences,* final report of the National Migration Study, Vol. 3, Ministry of Finance and Development Planning, Central Statistics Office, Government Printer, Gaborone.
– (1985) *National development plan (NDP6) 1981–1991,* Ministry of Finance and Development Planning, Central Statistics Office, Government Printer, Gaborone.

– (1991a) *National development plan 1991–1997 (NDP7)*, Ministry of Finance and Development Planning, Central Statistics Office, Government Printer, Gaborone.
– (2003) *National development plan 2003/04–2008/09 (NDP9)*, Ministry of Finance and Development Planning, Central Statistics Office, Government Printer, Gaborone.

Brown B. (1983) 'The impact of male labour migration on women in Botswana', *African Affairs* 82(328), 367-388.

Bruce J. W. (1988) 'A perspective on indigenous land tenure systems and land concentration' in R. E. Downs and S. P. Reyna (eds) *Land and society in contemporary Africa*, University Press of New England, Hanover.

Colson E. (1971) *The social consequences of resettlement: The impact of the Kariba resettlement upon the Gwembe Tonga*, Kariba Studies, Vol. 4., Manchester University Press, Manchester.

Comaroff J. L. and S. Roberts (1977) 'Marriage and extramarital sexuality: The dialectics of legal change among the Kgatla', *Journal of African Law* 21(1):97–123.

Cooper D. M. (1979) *Economy and society in Botswana. Some basic national socio-economic coordinates relevant to an interpretation of national migration statistics,* National Migration Study, Working paper 2, Government Printer, Gaborone.
– (1982) *An overview of the Botswana class structure and its articulation with the rural mode of production: Insights from Selebi-Phikwe* (dated 1980) Centre for African Studies, University of Cape Town, Cape Town.

Cowan J. K., M. B. Dembour and R. A. Wilson (eds) (2001) *Culture and rights: Anthropological perspectives*, Cambridge University Press, Cambridge.

Datta K. (undated) *Research on women in the economy and its impact on policy making in Botswana,* Gender Research Programme, University of Botswana and National Institute of Development Research and Documentation, Gaborone.

Diop Tine N. and M. Sy (2003) 'Women and land in Africa: A case study from Senegal', pages 207–231 in L. Muthoni Wanyeki (ed) *Women and land in Africa: Culture, religion and realizing women's rights*, Zed books Ltd and David Philip Publishers, London and Cape Town.

Francis P. (1984) 'For the use and common benefit of all Nigerians: Consequences of the 1978 Land Nationalization Act, *Africa* 54(3):5-28.

Gluckman M. (1965) *Politics, law and ritual in tribal society,* Basil Blackwell, Oxford.

Griffiths A. (1988) 'Support among the Bakwena', pages 289-316 in F. von-Benda-Beckmann et (eds) *Between kinship and the state,* Foris Publications, Dordrecht.

– (1996) 'Between paradigms: Differing perspectives on justice in Molepolole, Botswana', special issue on *Popular justice: Conflict resolution within communities*, *Journal of Legal Pluralism and Unofficial Law* 36:195–214.

– (1997) *In the shadow of marriage: Gender and justice in an African community, University* of Chicago Press, Chicago.

– (1998a) 'Reconfiguring law: An ethnographic perspective from Botswana', *Law & Social Inquiry* 23(3):587–620; Mediation, Gender and Justice in Botswana, *Mediation Quarterly* 154:335–342.

– (1998b) 'Gender, power and legal pluralism in Africa', special issue on *Urban normative fields in contemporary Africa, Journal of Legal Pluralism and Unofficial Law* 42:123–138.

– (2000) 'Gender, power and difference: Reconfiguring law from Bakwena women's perspectives' *PoLAR (Political and Legal Anthropology Review)* 223(2): 89–106.

– (2001) 'Gendering culture: Towards a plural perspective on Kwena women's rights', pages 102–126 in J. Cowan, M. B. Dembour and R. A. Wilson, *Culture and rights,* Cambridge University Press, Cambridge and New York.

– (2002a) 'Women's worlds, siblings in dispute over inheritance: A view from Botswana', special issue on *Women, law and language in Africa, Africa Today* 49(1):61–84.

– (2002) 'Doing ethnography, living law, life histories and narratives from Botswana', pages 160–181 in J. Starr and M. Goodale (eds) *Practising ethnography in law: New dialogues, enduring methods*, Palgrave/St Martin's Press, New York.

Griffiths J. (1996) 'What is legal pluralism?', *Journal of Legal Pluralism and Unofficial Law* 24: 1–55.

Guyer J. and E. F. Lambin (1993) 'Land use in an urban hinterland: Ethnography and remote sensing in the study of African intensification', *American Anthropologist* 95(4):839–859.

Hann C. M. (ed) (1998) *Property relations: Renewing the anthropological tradition,* Cambridge University Press, Cambridge.

Hannerz U. (1992) *Cultural complexity: Studies in the social organization of meaning,* University of Columbia Press, New York and Oxford.

Hoebel E. A. (1966) *Anthropology: The study of man,* McGraw Hill, New York.

Hooker M. (1975) *Legal pluralism: An introduction to colonial and neo-colonial laws,* Oxford University Press, Oxford.

Izzard W. (1979) *Rural-urban migration of women in Botswana,* final fieldwork report for National Migration Study Botswana, Government Printer, Gaborone.

– (1982) 'The impact of migration on the roles of women', pages 654–707 in *Migration in Botswana: Patterns, causes and consequences*, final report of the National Migration Study, Vol. 3, Ministry of Finance and Development Planning, Central Statistics Office, Government Printer, Gaborone.

Juul K. and C. Lund (eds) (2002) *Negotiating property in Africa*, Heinemann, London and Portsmouth.

Kerven C. (1982) 'The effects of migration on agricultural production', pages 526–622 in *Migration in Botswana: Patterns, causes and consequences*, final report of the National Migration Study, Vol. 3, Ministry of Finance and Development Planning, Central Statistics Office, Government Printer, Gaborone.
– (1984) 'Academic, practitioners and all kinds of women in development: A reply to Peters', *Journal of Southern African Studies* 10(2), 259–268.

Linares O. F. (1992) *Power, prayers and production: The Jola of Casamance, Senegal,* Cambridge University Press, Cambridge.

Manji A. (2001) 'Land reform in the shadow of the state: the implementation of new land laws in sub-Saharan Africa', *Third World Quarterly* 22(3)327–342.
– (2003a) 'Capital, labour and land relations in Africa: a gender analysis of the World Bank's policy research report on land institutions and land policy', *Third World Quarterly* 24(1):97–114.
– (2003b) (Remortgaging women's lives: The World Bank's land agenda in Africa', *Feminist Legal Studies* 11:139–162.

McAuslan P. (2003) *Bringing the law back in: Essays in land, law and development,* Ashgate, Aldershot and Burlington.

Middleton J. (1988) 'Foreword' in R. E. Downs and P. Reyna (eds), *Land and society in contemporary Africa,* University Press of New England, Hannover.

Moore S. F. (1986) *Social facts and fabrications; 'Customary law' on Kilimanjaro 1880–1980,* Cambridge University Press, Cambridge.
– (1998) 'Changing African land tenure: Reflections on the incapacities of the state', *The European Journal of Development Research.* 10(2):33–49.

Motzafi-Haller P. (1986) 'Whither the "true Bushman"?: The dynamics of perpetual marginality', pages 259–328 in F. Rotland and R. Vossen (eds) *Proceedings of the International symposium on African hunters and gatherers,* Sprache und Geschichte in Afrika, Vol. 7.1, Monastery of Sankt Augustin, Sankt Augustin.

Muthoni W. L. (ed) (2003) *Women and land in Africa: Culture, religion and realizing women's rights*, pages 133-175, Zed books Ltd and David Philip Publishers, London and Cape Town.

Netting R. M. (1993) *Smallholders, householders: Farm families and the ecology of intensive, sustainable agriculture,* Stanford University Press, Stanford.

Nyamu-Musembi C. (2002) 'Are local norms and practices fences or pathways? The example of women's property rights', pages 126–150 in A. A. An-Na'im (ed) Cultural *transformation and human rights in Africa,* Zed Books, London and New York.

Odgaard R. (2003) 'Scrambling for land in Tanzania: Processes of formalization and legitimization of land rights', pages 71–88 in A. Tor and C. Lunds *(eds) Securing land rights in Africa*, Frank Cass, London and Portland.

Parson J. (1981) 'Cattle, class, and state in rural Botswana', *Journal of Southern African Studies* 7, 236–255.

Peters P. (1983) 'Gender, developmental cycles and historical process: A critique of recent research on women in Botswana', *Journal of Southern African Studies* 10(1): 100–122.
– (1997) 'Against the odds', *Critique of Anthropology* 17(2):189–210.
– (2002) 'The limits of negotiability: Security, equity and class formation in Africa's land systems', pages 45–66 in K. Juul and C. Lund (eds) *Negotiating property in Africa*, Heinemann, Portsmouth.
– (2003) 'Beyond embeddedness: A challenge raised by a comparison of the struggles over land in African and post-socialist countries', paper presented at International Conference on Changing Properties of Property, Max Planck Institute for Social Anthropology, July 2–4, 2003, Halle, Germany.

Radijeng G. O. (2004) 'Customary law and gender equality : the legal status of women in Botswana', PhD thesis, University of Botswana.

Smith R. E. (2003) 'Land tenure reform in Africa: a shift to the defensive', *Progress in Development Studies* 3(3):210–222.

Solway J. (1980) *People, cattle and drought in the Western Kweneng District,* Rural Sociology Report Series 16, Gaborone.

United Nations Population Fund (UNFPA) (1989) *Gender, population and development,* report on the High-Level Seminar for Chiefs and District Commissioners, edited by L. Divasse and G. Mookodi, Macmillan Botswana, Gaborone.

UNICEF (1989) *Children, women and development in Botswana: A situational analysis,* consultant's report compiled for the joint GOB/UNICEF Programme and Planning and Coordinating Committee, UNICEF and Ministry of Finance and Development Planning, Gaborone.
– (1993) *Children, women and development in Botswana: A situational analysis,* report prepared by Mandeleo (Botswana) for the Government of Botswana and UNICEF, Gaborone.

Whitehead A. and D. Tsikata (2003) 'Policy discourse on women's land rights in sub-Saharan Africa: The implications of the re-turn to the customary', *Journal of Agrarian Change* 3(1-2):67–112.

Women and law in Southern Africa Research and Educational Trust (WLSA) (2001) *A critical analysis of women's access to land in the WLSA countries,* WLSA Regional Office, Harare.

List of legislation
Botswana
Marriage Act 1970
Regional and International
Southern African Development Community
SADC Gender and Development Declaration 1997
Addendum on Violence Against Women 1998
Organization of African Unity
Protocol to the African Charter on Human and People's Rights on the Rights of Women in Africa 2003
United Nations
Convention on the Elimination of all forms of Discrimination Against Women (CEDAW) 1979
Declaration on the Elimination of all forms of Violence Against Women 1994

7

Following God's constitution
The gender dimensions in the
Ogiek claim to Mau forest complex

Patricia Kameri-Mbote and Jacinta Anyango Oduor

This chapter looks at the Ogiek community, a minority Kenyan group, that has for some time been struggling for recognition as an indigenous people and for land and resource rights over the Mau forest complex. The government controls the forest by virtue of the Forest Act and the Ogiek claim is predicated on occupation and ancestral lineage. Ever since colonial times there have been attempts to evict the Ogiek from their ancestral forest, usually on the pretext that they are degrading it. When the Ogiek are removed, however, their forest is not protected but rather exploited by logging and tea plantations, some owned by government officials. The government plans to open up around one tenth of Kenya's forests – most of it in the Mau forest – to outsiders. This will open the way for more settlers, loggers and tea plantations.[148] In a scenario of legal pluralism and gendered division of labour, the study seeks to excavate Ogiek women's positioning vis-a-vis the land and resources and to distil the women's voices in a complex narrative that has seen the Ogiek go to court against the state. More specifically, the questions explored include whether women have been considered and whether their opinion resonates with that of other community members. This analysis reveals that while men usually champion the generic community's voices, as is the case in this research, women's voices are not necessarily articulated within that voice and the quest for cultural rights could result in a restatement of patriarchy and the entrenchment of patriarchal norms of dominance over women. From a human rights perspective, the research found that the rigour in pushing for the rights of the marginalized Ogiek community does not go as far as to include women's rights. The sentiments of women have been left out despite the fact that there are practical solutions to these problems.

---

[148] Electronic news from Survival International, a registered charity organization based in the United Kingdom supporting tribal peoples worldwide. Accessed at www.survival-international.org/latest.htm (24 March 2004).

I   Introduction

Land and the resources linked to it form a critical part of many communities' lifelines. Lack of access to these resources can lead to the decimation of affected communities. This is especially the case where the communities' life is linked to a particular ecosystem as is the case for the Ogiek. In a situation where the rights of the entire community are under threat, the weaker actors ordinarily stand to lose in so far as access to, control over and ownership of resources is concerned. Ogiek women are disadvantaged because they lack property ownership rights and generally tend to be poorer than men. They suffer from an illiteracy rate of more than 95 per cent. They are also subjected to female genital mutilation and early marriage (Minority Rights Group International, 2003). The work of the Ogiek women and children is gathering wild fruits, berries, roots and herbal barks for food and medicines. The women transmit their knowledge to the next generation and maintaining the richness of this traditional knowledge depends largely upon the Ogiek continuing to use their land. It is against this background that this chapter looks at the struggle of the Ogiek for access to the Mau forest in the face of competing actors. The metaphor 'following God's constitution' is adopted as a frame of reference to interrogate the Ogiek community perception of their relationship with the state, the forest and its resources. In a patriarchal setting, an understanding of God's constitution must be read in the context of male domination and socio-cultural and legal relations in which men as a class have power over women as a gender. Those power relations are social constructs and neither biological nor natural. This power can be ideological, social, political and economic. The cultural aspect of patriarchy in most cases takes the form of the devaluation of women's work or achievements while the ideological aspect portrays women as natural, biological creatures inherently different but inferior vis-a-vis men.

Who are the Ogiek?
Many historical works refer to the Ogiek as the 'Dorobo' which means poor people who cannot afford cattle. The name Dorobo is derived from a Maasai name *il torobo* which means a poor person who has no cattle and has to live on hunting and gathering. From documented literature, especially the works of W. A. Chandler, the Ogiek were first seen to have unique physical features and thought to be different from other tribes (Kamau, 2000). What followed was general speculation about the Ogiek and their neighbours and the conclusion reached by 1974 was that there is nothing in the traditional Ogiek life of hunting and gathering which indicates a prior adaptation to a plains environment, pastoral-

ism or agriculture (Blackburn, 1974). The Ogiek is one of the few remaining hunter-gatherer peoples of East Africa. It is arguably the largest hunter-gatherer community in Kenya. Their home since time immemorial has been the Mau mountain forest overlooking Kenya's rift valley. The population of the Ogiek is 20,000 (Central Intelligence Agency, 2006). They are scattered within the rift valley from Mount Elgon in north Uganda up to the northern part of Tanzania. Mr Taptich,[149] an Ogiek elder, says the word *Ogiek* means 'caretaker of the universe'.[150]

They depend mainly on hunting and gathering, while most Ogiek grow vegetables and keep livestock too. They traditionally hunted animals, such as antelope and wild pigs, which is now generally illegal. They gather not only wild plants but also honey from beehives which they make from hollow logs and place in the high branches of the forest trees. The honey plays a central part in Ogiek society. It is used for food and for brewing beer and also to trade with neighbouring people outside the forest.[151] The question remains as to why the Ogiek were never considered a tribal and distinct cultural entity and why everyone wanted them out of their habitat.

The link to the forest and land: A story of domination of a people
Throughout the period of colonialism, the Ogiek were seen as harmful and barbaric. Subsequently, the colonial government sanctioned a series of efforts to dispossess them of their land and exterminate, assimilate and impoverish them. In 1933, the colonial government set up the Carter Land Commission to examine the question of land. The Ogiek made several claims for their ancestral territories but all of them were rejected. Among the 42 tribes that the Carter Land Commission differentiated, the Ogiek were not listed.[152] They were considered 'just a wandering people' and thus not recognized as a distinct tribe. From that time on, the Ogiek became squatters on their own land. When Kenya became independent in 1963, things did not improve for the Ogiek as the independent governments adopted the colonial policy on ethnic minorities, including the Ogiek.

The Mau forest complex, the home of the Ogiek, has been considered a forest zone protected under the Forest Act. It covers about 290,000 hectares of land and is about 250kms from Nairobi, Kenya's capital city.

---

[149] Interview done on 24 October 2003.

[150] No assessment of the economic contribution of hunting and gathering by the Ogiek to the economy has been done as of today.

[151] Government bee-keeping projects initiated in the 1970s in Busia and Luo Nyanza in western Kenya and in Ukambani in eastern Kenya failed. Unlike the Ogiek, however, these communities had no knowledge of bee-keeping.

[152] The Carter Land Commission was set up in 1932 by the Secretary of State for Colonies, to consider the land requirements of the African population.

It is one of the largest continuous indigenous forests in Kenya. As a water catchment area, the forest traps, stores and releases rainwater thus regulating stream flows and has been responsible for much of the rain in the country. While the Ogiek were perceived as a danger to the forest environment and attempts were made to evict them from what, in essence, is their ancestral land, the government also started selling parts of the Mau forest to influential people of the dominant Kenyan tribes in the 1980s. The government allowed charcoal burning, logging, tea plantations and flower farming in the Mau forest. It is estimated that up to 60 per cent of the tree cover has been lost over the last 20 years.[153] Moreover the Ogiek way of life is being transformed from hunting and gathering to sedentary farming. Intermarriage with other communities is also reducing the numbers of authentic Ogiek community members as intermarriage with a person from a more dominant tribe leads to the subjugation of cultural tenets of Ogiek life.

Resisting domination

In this whole schema, a great animosity has emerged between the Ogiek and the government over the way in which the forest has been handled. For instance, in allocating forestland, the state did not give priority to the Ogiek and in May 1999 the government threatened to evict between 5,000 and 10,000 of the Ogiek community from Tinet Mau on the grounds that they were illegal squatters in the forest. Supported by the Roman Catholic church, they contested the eviction. In a ruling finally given in March 2000, the Nairobi High Court ruled that the Kenyan government was within its rights to evict the Ogiek. The judgment even denied that the Ogiek were indigenous to Mau Tinet (Wong, 2002). Even though Kenya has ratified several international treaties related to protection of rights of indigenous peoples – for example the International Covenant on Economic, Social and Cultural Rights and the International Convention on Civil and Political Rights – the recommendations have not been respected when concrete policies are being formulated and implemented (World Rainforest Movement, 2000).

The cases filed include: *Joseph Letuya & Others v the Attorney General & Others* (Nairobi HCCC No. 635 of 1997); *Joseph Letuya & 21 Others v the Minister for Environment & Natural Resources*, Nairobi HCCC NO.2280/0I; *Francis Kemei & 91 Others v Attorney General & three Others*, Nairobi HCCC No. 238 of 1999; *Simon Kiwape &19 Oth-*

---

[153] The *Daily Nation* quoted United Nations consultants as saying that the forest excisions will negatively impact on the Aberdare circuit and the Mau Hills catchment areas. They warned that, ultimately, communities in Nyanza Province and the planned Sondu-Miriu hydroelectric power project would be affected (see *Daily Nation*, 10 March 2001 www.nationaudio.com).

ers v Muneria Naimodu & two others, Civil Case No.19/97; *Narok and Representatives v Ministry of Environment & Ministry of Lands*, Nairobi HCCC No. 421/02. We will lay out the facts in two of the cases as a basis for the discussions on the gender nuances.

Joseph Letuya & Others v the Attorney General & Others (Nairobi HCCC No. 635 of 1997)

In this case, the community sued the government challenging the legality of the demarcation and alienation of their ancestral land. The decision will have to address the concept of ancestral land in Kenya, the issues of indigenous claims (not only for the Ogiek but other communities), the government's ownership of land with customary claims by the community and the concept of legal pluralism. The recognition of a people's right to their culture and the need to consult them when dealing with natural resources available to them will also have to be addressed. Conflicting statutes on forest resources, environmental management and various legislation dealing with land ownership can be interpreted so as to address the reality on the ground rather than as a theoretical framework. The environmental legislation includes a right to public participation in decision making. It will be interesting to see how this works in this particular case. This case was unfortunately still pending when this data was compiled.

Francis Kemei & 91 Others v Attorney General & three Others (Nairobi HCCC No. 238 of 1999)

The Ogiek living in Tinet Mau challenged an order for eviction from the forest. This case was determined at an interlocutory stage as it had sought a temporary injunction against the government. As a result, the ruling was based on legal arguments rather than *viva voce* evidence. The application was heard as a constitutional reference by a two-judge bench. On the argument that the Ogiek were hunters and gatherers the judges said:

> 'Hunting is illegal in Kenya. The eviction is for the purpose of saving the whole of Kenya from possible environmental disaster and it is being carried out for the common good within the statutory power since the Ogiek can make a living outside the forest.'

On the issue of a claim of dependence on the forest as a source of their livelihood for bee-keeping, the judges said:

> 'There is no reason why the Ogiek should be the only favoured community to own and exploit our natural resources, a privilege not enjoyed by or extended to other Kenyans.'

No international instruments were referred to in the ruling and the judges did not address the fact that other Kenyans do not use the forest in the same way as the Ogiek. No argument on their knowledge of conservation was, for instance, canvassed. Additionally, there were no women plaintiffs in any of the suits and the pleadings were couched in gender-neutral terms that covered the entire community. Gender as a variable has not been canvassed in the suits. This is a grave omission given that women, as a constituent part of a marginalized community, experience different forms of discrimination and the effects of constant eviction, lack of land ownership, and no protection of women's rights to found a family and live in peace or their children's right to education and their right to live in safety and freedom from discrimination are not addressed. The cases proceed as though matters being decided involve men who are busy hunting and destroying the forest while the reality on the ground is that there are several settlements where women keep homes and children attend school.

The Ogiek have resisted this assault over the years from colonial times to the present day. They have taken the contestation to court as well as organized themselves in groups to resist the assault. The groups include the Ogiek Rural Integral Projects and the Ogiek Welfare Council. They have come together as a group to assert their rights which they see as rooted in their identity as a distinct people and have the following to say about themselves.

They believe they are the only community in Kenya that follows 'God's constitution'. They live in the forest and maintain it with an in-born knowledge of conservation just the way God made it and wants it to continue to be.[154] According to Joseph Sang,[155] the tribe regard themselves as the only truly indigenous tribe of Kenya who did not migrate there. He also asserts that:

> 'The Ogiek lived with God in the forest a long time ago. When one killed an elephant, God left the Ogiek and went to heaven. And so we know that we cannot hunt big animals.'[156]

The gender dimension of domination and resistance
It is against this background that we investigate and examine the gender dimension in the Ogiek claim to the Mau forest complex. The chapter draws from research carried out towards a Masters' in Women's Law degree in 2004 (Oduor, 2004). The research centred on women's access to resources and used experiences of a marginalized community, the Ogiek, to problematize and interrogate discourses surrounding land and environmental resources. Cases filed in the courts were illustrative of the neglect of women's voices in the quest by a marginalized commu-

---

[154] Personal communication with Mr Towett, a member of the Ogiek community.
[155] Coordinator of Ogiek Welfare Society interviewed on 16 October 2003.
[156] Interview carried out on 21 November 2003.

nity to gain access to resources that are vital for their livelihood and performance of daily chores. Four themes emerged from that study, namely: environmental concerns; marginalization of the community; the forest as a symbol of culture; and land rights. Women have not been at the forefront and gender issues have not taken priority in the discourses. This highlights the intersectional discrimination that women suffer on account of being members of a marginalized community as well as being women. In these contexts barriers for women seeking to access justice are insurmountable as the seemingly more urgent and nagging community concerns take centre stage (Banda and Chinkin, 2004). For Ogiek women, the quest for land and forest rights as an assertion of the rights of the Ogiek as an indigenous group and their right to their culture, brings the issue of women and culture to the fore. Ogiek women are strongly controlled by culture. Paradoxically, the claim of the Ogiek to their cultural rights is seemingly a liberation struggle but Ogiek women's subjugation is rooted within the same culture. An analysis of the data collected enables us to distil women's voices. It also provides a lens through which to critically analyze and engage the human rights framework upon which claims to indigenous rights and cultural identity are predicated, in relation to women's lived realities.

As the Ogiek seek to negotiate space in the political, legal and economic spheres, a number of narratives can be discerned in their struggle. First is the struggle by a people for their cultural rights to land and to continue living in the forest. Second is the juxtaposition of community management of environment resources with the dictates of sustainable management of environmental resources. Third is the domination of the poor by richer and more powerful groups. Fourth and most importantly is the experience of these narratives by different members of the community. In this narrative, it is important to explore whether the vigour with which the Ogiek resist domination is the same vigour with which they protect weaker members of their community from domination by stronger members.[157] In this respect we will look at how women have fared in the Ogiek resistance against domination.

Rays of hope and windows of opportunity

Three major developments in Kenya have raised hopes in the Ogiek struggle for land rights. In 2001 the Constitution of Kenya Review Commission was formed and assigned the task of making a new constitution for Kenya, including the issue of division of land. The Ogiek took the opportunity to bring their demands to the commission but the new constitution is not yet finalized. The second development was the election

---

[157] See generally, Fox-Genovese (1991).

of President Mwai Kibaki at the end of 2002. Kibaki's Rainbow Coalition ended 25 years of Moi's moderate dictatorship and a more democratic government was put in place. The climate had never been so favourable for change. The third development is the ongoing national land policy formulation process which seeks to establish a framework of values and institutions to ensure that land and associated resources are held, used and managed equitably, efficiently, productively and sustainably. These three developments present an opportunity for the Ogiek to secure their legal rights over their ancestral lands.

The second part of the chapter comprises the historical background. The third part provides the legal and conceptual framework for the research and provides the context of the analysis of the Ogiek cases from a gender perspective in the fourth part. The final section comprises the conclusion and way forward.

2 Historical background

Land is central to most African communities, offering both a means of subsistence as well as the only readily available economic resource. In Kenya, the population's dependence on land is underscored by the high percentage of people engaged in agriculture and pastoralism, both anchored on land. Moreover, the main foreign exchange earnings are from agriculture (including horticulture) and tourism also based on land. The way in which rights in land are organized is therefore central to Kenyans' aspirations to alleviate poverty and create wealth.

The history of land rights in Kenya exemplifies a process of alienation and displacement of native Kenyans from their lands into reserves and the systematic acquisition of prime land for settler occupation and its designation as the 'white highlands'. Discriminatory policies were then set in motion to facilitate the exploitation of land resources and the institutionalization of colonial agriculture. Acquisition of land rights for settlers was mainly done through political processes that were followed by legal instruments giving the political acts the requisite binding force. Colonial land policy was thus not systematic. Decisions were made in the face of day-to-day problems whose resolution demanded swift action. This seems to have been the origin of the instrumentalist tradition in property law in Kenya.[158] Law played an instrumental role in the process of alienation of land rights and the determination of who could own

---

[158] Policies dealing with land in Kenya have rarely been systematic since colonial times. In most cases guidelines are circulated to relevant departments as working documents and later given legal authority after they have been in operation for some time. The subsequent legal instrument validates all actions previously taken pursuant to the guidelines. This leaves room for administrative abuse of power.

land and the quantum of rights that such ownership conferred.[159] In this whole scheme, Africans were considered incapable of owning land in the sense in which the concept of ownership is understood in English jurisprudence.[160] Customary law and rights under that law were treated as inferior to the newly introduced private property rights based on English law. This necessitated the maintenance of a dual system of land law with English law applying to areas occupied by white settlers and native law and custom applying in the reserves. The areas occupied by the settlers were expansive, more arable and more habitable than those occupied by the natives. Africans were concentrated in areas which were not immediately required for European settlement. This created social and economic problems in the reserves with poverty, disease, famine and ethnic tensions characterizing the lives of the natives.

The system of separate development for settlers and natives maintained by the colonial authorities cushioned them from the burgeoning quests for individualized tenure even though the conditions for it were already well developed. The reason for this was to allow the colonial administrators room to take as much land as the settlers needed by keeping the native rights to land usufructuary and consequently impermanent. The net effect of this process was suppression of individual initiative since African tenure was characterized as communal (equated with unregulated open access situations) notwithstanding clear pointers to the contrary.[161] It also masked the rights of individuals and communities who worked on land and justified uncompensated taking of that land for allocation to settlers on permanent terms.[162] It is important to point out that what the colonialists designated as an African land tenure system was actually a creation of the colonial authorities.

By 1940, there was severe land shortage within the reserves and the Africans were demanding the restoration of stolen lands. In 1952, these demands culminated in the Mau Mau revolts predominantly led by the

---

[159] This was, for instance, achieved through the promulgation of the two Crown Lands Ordinances of 1902 and 1905 respectively. Through these ordinances, first the commissioner, and later the governor, was empowered to make grants of leasehold or freehold to the settlers on very flexible terms. Similar strategies were adopted in Tanganyika, first by the German colonialists and later by the British.

[160] See for example, Okoth-Ogendo (1991) and Wanjala (2000).

[161] Among the Kikuyu, initiatives taken by family members were acknowledged by giving the individuals limited rights to the land in question and the produce of that land.

[162] See Sorrenson (1967) and Chanock (1991). Similar happenings in the Mt Kilimanjaro area of Tanzania where individual rights to land were so prevalent that even after the introduction of *ujamaa* (socialism) which designated all land as government land and that individuals were lessees of the government, people continued to deal with land as private property as they had done before. See Falk Moore (1991).

Kikuyu, thus awakening the colonial administration to the need for tenure reform (Okoth-Ogendo, 1991). Having constructed African tenure systems as communal (read 'open access'), colonial agronomic experts believed the solution to the African land problem lay in tenure, namely, the structure of access to the use of land in areas occupied by the natives. The factors of the traditional tenure system that made it inimical to proper land use and agricultural development were, in their view: encouragement of fragmentation which cut down on returns from labour and time expended on the land; incessant disputes which were a disincentive to long-term capital investment and an insecure basis for generating agricultural credit; and inheritance practices encouraging subdivision of the holdings into sub-economic units of production.[163] The solution to the problem was conceived in terms of individualized title to land and intensified agriculture in African areas through technological improvements. It was hoped that this would increase production and divert the attention of Africans away from the settler occupied areas (Okoth-Ogendo, 1991).

The assumption was that individual proprietorship would generate entrepreneurship, irrespective of the injustices occasioned by expropriation of African rights to land by the settlers. A commission was set up to investigate African tenure systems and make recommendations on ways of improving them and making them contribute to the economic development of the colony. The Swynnerton Plan recommended the consolidation of landholdings of families into one, followed by the adjudication of property rights in that land and the registration of individuals as absolute owners of land adjudicated as theirs. This process was to end the perceived uncertainty of customary tenure already considerably modified by years of European contact. The coincidence of the tenure reform process with a deteriorating political climate centred on the land issue presented an occasion for the colonialists to ingrain a political flavour within the process. Through tenure reform, the colonial administrators sought to create a stable landed gentry among the natives. This gentry was to act as a buffer between the settlers and political mavericks hankering for redistribution of land.[164]

The instrumentalist role of law perfected by the colonial administrators was useful in ensuring that rights granted to loyalists and settlers were protected through law from claims by the Mau Mau protagonists who had gone into the forests to fight for land rights. The administrative process of consolidation, adjudication and registration was formalized

---

[163] See Swynnerton (1954).

[164] See Sorrenson (1967) *supra* note 258. See also Osolo-Nasubo (1977) and Leo (1984 and 1960).

by the Native Land Tenure Rules of 1956.[165] To ensure that the rights granted through the process were not disturbed, the African Courts (Suspension of Land Suits) Ordinance was passed in 1957 to bar all litigation to which the 1956 rules applied. It is remarkable that a large part of Central Province was consolidated in 1956 with a state of emergency in place.[166] The net effect of these laws was to close avenues available to aggrieved landholders and dispossessed peasants. Subsequent laws on land tenure adopted these provisions. The Native Lands Registration Ordinance of 1959 spelt out the rights of the registered proprietor at § 37(a), namely, 'an estate in fee simple in such land together with all rights and privileges belonging or appurtenant thereto'.[167] While the rights of the registered proprietor were stated to be subject to duties that such proprietor had as trustee, it is instructive to note that customary notions of trusteeship, recognized under some Kenyan communities' native customs, were not included.[168] More specifically, according to the registration statute, a right of occupation at customary law would only be protected if noted on the register. Many families did not bother to note customary rights on the register because they saw no possibility of a piece of paper vesting any more rights in the family representative than he would have had at custom. Cases of such family representatives seeking to evict the other family members from the family land, however, esca-

---

[165] These rules empowered the Minister for African Affairs to set up machinery for the adjudication of areas of 'native' lands within which private rights to land were considered to exist.

[166] The Kikuyu districts of Kiambu, Nyeri and Fort Hall (now Murang'a) (comprising Central Province), and Embu and Meru (comprising part of Eastern Province) were among the first areas where tenure reform was carried out. See for example, figures given in MacArthur (1961). Consolidation consisted of the process of amalgamating all the pieces of land owned by one person to determine the acreage such person was entitled to. It would be followed by adjudication, namely, a determination of the rights of each person to that land and then registration that vested absolute rights in the registered proprietor to the land.

[167] See Colony and Protectorate of Kenya, Native Lands Registration Ordinance No. 27 of 1959. The aim of this ordinance, as stated in the preamble, was 'to provide for the ascertainment of rights and interests in, and for the consolidation of land in the native lands; for the registration of title to and transactions and devolutions affecting such land and other land in native lands and for purposes connected therewith and incidental thereto'. It was the precursor to the current Registered Land Act, Chapter 300 of the Laws of Kenya.

[168] Case law has dealt extensively with the issue of trustees and though there seems to be no general agreement, the removal of formal courts' jurisdiction to adjudicate on land matters and the transfer of that jurisdiction to local chiefs and elders seems to have been an acknowledgement of the need to consider the circumstances surrounding any registration in native areas to determine the interests of all potential beneficiaries. See the Magistrates' Courts Jurisdiction Act, Chapter 10 of the Laws of Kenya.

lated.[169] The ordinance moreover declared that a first registration was not to be challenged even if it had been obtained through fraud.[170]

The tenure reform process considered the rights of land owners, not the landless or those whose rights were not recognized by the colonialists.[171] Furthermore the ordinance limited the number of people who could be named as owners of any piece of land to five, illustrating commitment to individual as opposed to group tenure.[172] In most cases families designated someone, usually the eldest son or male head of household, to be registered as absolute owner, not realizing the latitude the 'owner' had to deal with the land so registered. Women and younger men with rights of use and occupation under customary law were unlikely to be chosen as representatives and were effectively excluded from controlling land and the resources that go with it. The elder male owners were given immense power to deal with land and could mortgage or even sell it without recourse to other members of the family who, though not owning the land legally, had access rights at customary law.[173]

The colonial government alienated land suitable for its citizens which became known as the 'white highlands'. At independence when land was given back to indigenous Africans, it found its way into the hands of those Kenyans who had seen the light earlier through exposure and hence tribal territory collapsed within the white occupied land. Similarly, in an open market of willing buyer/willing seller, ancestral land now belongs to non-tribal members. Certain groups like the Ogiek and Maasai realized that they could claim rights over this kind of land but their claims to areas where there are forest and wildlife resources have become more complex with the growing concern for environmental sustainability. The process of alienation of land and the demarcation of rights largely took place before sustainable development was internalized as a guiding principle in land management.[174]

---

[169] See *Obiero v Opiyo* (1972) East African Law Reports 227; *Mwangi Muguthu v Maina Muguthu* Civil Case No. 377 of 1968 (Unreported) and *Esiroyo v Esiroyo* (1973) East African Law Reports 388.

[170] *See* § 89 (1) of the Native Lands Registration Ordinance.

[171] This process marginalized categories of people such as the 'Ahoi' among the Kikuyu who lived and worked on other people's lands for generations. See Jomo Kenyatta, *Facing Mount Kenya* (1938).

[172] § 66 of the Native Lands Registration Ordinance.

[173] See, for example, Kanogo (in Khasiani, 1992). In the process of consolidation, adjudication and registration, the major targets were heads of households (invariably male) who got absolute rights to the land in total disregard of the rights enjoyed by other members of the population.

[174] World Commission on Environment and Development (1987). Sustainable development has been adopted by later environmental conventions and declarations and in many national environmental laws. Kenya's Environment Management and Coordination Act 2000 has it as a guiding principle.

3   Legal and conceptual framework

Women the world over have been at the centre-stage of economic production, including agricultural, livestock and business sectors. In Africa, where the mainstay of most economies is farming or agriculture and livestock production, women contribute to over 80 per cent of the workforce (Boserup, 1989). In most parts of the continent, women are closely associated with production of food and raw materials for the industrial sector. Women are also more directly involved in small-scale crafts and localized industries, trade and general business. This has until recently been ignored or obscured in national production statistics.

However, women, who comprise over half of the world's population, rarely own any reasonable forms of property, do not have adequate access to the same and do not even make major decisions pertaining to allocation and use of such property. According to a United Nations Commission on Women's Status, women constitute 60 per cent of the global population, perform nearly two-thirds of working hours, receive one-tenth of the global income and own less than 1 per cent of global property.[175]

Traditionally among various Kenyan communities, most women do not own land or other immovable property. At best, they have *usufruct* rights, which are hinged on the nature of the relationship obtaining between them and men either as husbands, fathers, brothers or other male relatives. Such access can be denied as it is dependent on the whims of such male benefactors. This situation does not only place women in a precarious position in terms of their survival and livelihoods but stifles their effective role and contribution to national development.

Men and women's interaction with the environment reflects the gender division of labour and absence of other economic opportunities. Women's struggles to access land and property rights are part of the ordering of the ownership of means of production in capitalist settings.[176] It is within this context that one must isolate women's rights within marginalized communities such as the Ogiek. Women members of minority and indigenous communities are particularly and frequently marginalized.[177]

Women's rights and the law in Kenya

Law can be used to reinforce or give permanence to certain social injustices leading to the marginalization of particular groups of people. In the

---

[175] Report of the United Nations Commission on the Status of Women (1980). See also United Nations Development Fund for Women (2002).

[176] See Shiva (1995).

[177] See Banda and Chinkin (2004).

realm of women's rights, legal rules may give rise to or emphasize gender inequality. Legal systems can also become obstacles when change is required in legal rules, procedures and institutions to remove the inequality of the oppressed. This necessitates an inquiry into what injustices are intertwined within the legal systems and the extent of their operation. One often finds that the *de jure* position which may provide for gender neutrality cannot be achieved in practice due to the numerous existing obstacles which make the law powerless. For instance, there are certain legal rules and principles in our statute books which legitimize the subordination of women. The structure and administration of laws can also subordinate women to men and the socio-economic realities in Kenya and many African countries coupled with a patriarchal ideology (where political, economic, legal and social standards are set by and fixed in the interests of men) pervading society prevents the translation of abstract rights into substantive rights for women.

Women have been systematically removed from fully participating in the development process despite their active participation in the production processes alongside men. Even where women's legal rights have been provided for, ignorance of such rights exacerbated by illiteracy ensures that they do not benefit. The effectiveness of laws in according women equal opportunities to men depends largely on society's willingness and ability to enforce such laws. It is here that one gets caught up in the dichotomies and conflicts of statute law, customary law and law in practice which many woman find themselves wrapped up in.

To understand the role of law in women's lives, one needs to understand not only the intention and rationale behind the law but also the consequences of law for individuals. In Kenya, despite the gender neutrality of our legal provisions, equal rights and privileges cannot be assumed to be guaranteed and realized. Gender neutral laws have, in many instances, resulted in *de facto* discrimination. As Tove Stang Dahl (1987) aptly points out:

> 'As long as we live in a society where women and men follow different paths in life and have different living conditions, with different needs and potentials, rules of law will necessarily affect men and women differently. The gender-neutral legal machinery ... meets the gender-specific reality...'

The ratification and domestication of CEDAW has been identified as an important first step to removing obstacles in this area. Revision of national laws is perceived as crucial to the endeavour. Laws have a part to play in the process of eliminating barriers to women's advancement. The test of effectiveness of such laws, however, lies largely in their implementation. It is consequently imperative that implementation mechanisms are engrained into the specific pieces of legislation if they are to benefit Kenyan women. Another crucial area of concern is women's awareness of their rights. A right whose content is not known by the holder is at best a paper right. Legal awareness should be part of the task of achieving change in the legal status of women. Education of women on the content of their rights and modes of exercising those rights is a must if law reform is to achieve its stated objectives.

The legal framework

Land

Land in Kenya is owned by four entities: individuals, the state, local authorities and communities. Land held by local authorities is designated as trust land. Trust land consists of areas that were occupied by the natives during the colonial period and which have not been consolidated, adjudicated and registered in individuals or groups' names and native land that has not been taken over by the government.[178] It is governed by the Trust Lands Act and is vested in local authorities designated as councils.[179] State ownership of land is governed by the Government Lands Act chapter 280 of the Laws of Kenya while individual ownership is regulated under the Registered Land Act, chapter 300 of the Laws of Kenya and the Transfer of Property Act. Not surprisingly, state and individual ownership have been given prominence. Community ownership is regulated through the Land (Group Representatives) Act chapter 287 of the Laws of Kenya. This law was introduced to provide for the incorporation of representatives of groups who are recorded as owners of land under the Lands Act. It applies mainly to pastoralist areas. The process of getting groups together and leadership of such groups is influenced by patriarchal norms. The significance of the ordering of land ownership is that women are left out of ownership and control of land. Less than 1 per cent of women have title deeds to land.

The Registered Land Act chapter 300 is the statute under which excised land in Mau forest complex was issued. Section 147 of the Act, provides that first registrations, even if by fraudulent means, will not be challenged. Sections 27 and 28 confirm that registration of the title shall be proof of ownership of the land. For a person holding a title in the settlement scheme within Mau complex therefore, it does not matter whether you belong to the Ogiek community or not, your ownership is protected by law.

---

[178] See §115 of the Constitution of Kenya (1983).
[179] See § 114 of the Constitution of Kenya (1983) and Chapter 288 of the Laws of Kenya.

This means for women that where land has been registered in the husbands' names they have no control over the land no matter how much work they put into it. Section 27 and 28 allow the husband to dispose of the land any time he wishes to without her consent, hence the feelings expressed by the women that land may either be registered in their names or jointly with their husbands. The Act does not expressly recognize a holding in trust for the unregistered parties.

The constitution on the other hand provides for equality of the sexes and a right to own property but the usual rider that allows for discrimination in matters of personal law comes in. In the Ogiek community where women are regarded as property, it will not be easy for 'property to own property' hence efforts should be made to encourage ownership of property by women in the community.

Article 13 of CEDAW gives women the right to obtain family benefits and bank loans and financial credit so this would mean that women should be allowed to own property and giving them land would be a positive step towards this. Yet this instrument like many others has not been domesticated and is rarely relied upon even in court decisions. There is the issue of land being given to other communities without regard to Ogiek women's need for land or a specific programme to ensure the women at least have access to the land being allocated.

Articles 13 and 14 of CEDAW have placed a responsibility on state parties to ensure rural women have equal access to social and economic growth and participate in planning and implementation of programmes aimed at improving their economic and social welfare. Ogiek women do not benefit from the forest in terms of hunting as a natural resource or logging by big companies, neither is their interest taken into account when policies for environmental preservation leading to economic growth are taken into account.

Forests

The Forests Act chapter 385 of the Laws of Kenya provides the legal framework for the conservation of forests. It governs the conservation, management and use of forests and forest products but has no provisions with direct bearing on conserving and managing wildlife and its relation with surrounding communities. The forest legislation, like other environment-related legislation, emphasizes maximizing short-term gains through exploitative practices. Under the Forests Act, the minister responsible for natural resources is empowered to declare any forest area a nature reserve to preserve its natural amenities, flora and fauna. Killing wild animals in a nature reserve is prohibited. Vesting monopoly rights in the government is explained as based on the grounds that forests serve important functions that transcend the scope of immediate individual preoccupation and a system of public control is therefore imperative to assert the overriding public interest. Secondly, the management and conservation of forest resources entail the outlay of human, financial and technical resources beyond the capabilities of an individual. Lastly, state control is essential since it ensures an effective and sustainable framework for long-term planning and policy implementation.

The current practice of excluding other forms of land-use from gazetted forest areas may, however, not be sustainable since it does not allow for integration of farmers into forest areas. With increases in population, political pressure to convert portions of such areas for agriculture and settlement purposes has been mounting. While the Forests Act allows the minister discretion to excise forest areas, and this has been done to chunks of forest areas to satisfy the demands of adjacent populations, there have also been several instances of illegal conversions by populations bordering forest areas. The excisions of forest land by the government for grants to powerful politicians also impact negatively on forest conservation and management since they lead to perceptions of forests as open access areas amenable to appropriation.

The Forests Bill 2004 requires that an inventory is taken to determine the true nature of the forest. The inventory will include all resources in the forest and will determine the conditions upon which a management agreement is entered into between the Forests Service or local authorities and other parties. The Bill also allows for the formation of community forest associations to participate in the conservation and management of a state forest or local authority forest and may be the basis for involvement of the Ogiek in the management of the Mau forest.

The rights of indigenous peoples

The rights of indigenous peoples have been the subject of discussion for a number of years at the international level. While there is consensus that these rights ought to be recognized and protected, action at the national levels has been slow. In Kenya, the debate continues as to whether there are any indigenous peoples whose rights ought to be protected apart from other communities. There are concerns that recognizing the rights of indigenous communities would amount to introducing differentiated protection of rights for different communities. It is within this context that the Ogiek claim to rights to the land and resources in the Mau forest complex must be analyzed.

Land, environmental resources and feminism:
Making the connections

A feminist is a person who holds that women suffer discrimination because of their sex, that they have specific needs which remain negated and unsatisfied and that the satisfaction of these needs would require a radical change (or revolution) in the social, economic and political order. Feminist theories explore the incidence of oppression of women from different angles and proffer solutions to the problem as they see it. Ecofeminism stresses 'the depth to which human realities are embedded in ecological realities' and the connections represented therein (Cuomo, 2001). Ecofeminists reject the Marxist assertion that dominance is based primarily on class and money (Spretnak, 1990). They underscore the link between women and nature and link women's oppression to the degradation of the environment. This link is more pronounced among communities such as the Ogiek whose livelihoods are wholly based on the resources. The division of labour along gender lines and patriarchal notions also nuance the connections between people and environmental resources (Shiva, 1994).

In Kenya, land and resource tenure laws and policies have contributed to the removal of women from access, control and ownership of land. The marginalization of women has had negative impacts on the implementation of environmental management policies generally (Kanogo, 1992).[180] As providers of food for their families, women interact very closely with the environment.[181] In pre-colonial Kenya, for instance, women used their knowledge to maintain a workable balance between drawing sustenance from land and allowing for the regeneration of that land within the limits of their defined rights of access and use. The creation of reserves and the migration of male members of native communities to plantations and urban areas to seek paid employment, while redefining the mode of production, deeply entrenched the role of women as managers of the local environment. However, after the processes of consolidation, adjudication and registration, women lost control over the resources that they looked after and depended upon to sustain their families. Furthermore, individualizing property rights in land and vesting them in men alienated women, as managers, from the ownership of the managed property.

The role of women as tenders of the environment however, continued undisturbed notwithstanding that their claims to the land which they managed became more precarious and tenuous.[182] With subsequent in-

---

[180] In the process of consolidation, adjudication and registration, the major targets were heads of households (invariably male) who got absolute rights to the land in total disregard of the rights enjoyed by other members of the population. Some of the environmental management projects that women are involved in include reforestation, afforestation, and soil and water conservation.

[181] See, for example, Chiuri and Nzioki (1992). See also Agarwal (1995) on the effects of the diminution of fuelwood on women's performance of their tasks in India.

[182] See, for example, Thomas-Slayter and Rocheleau (1995).

troduction of cash crop farming for Africans and the controls put in place to ensure the adherence to good rules of farming, the workload of women increased without a concomitant enhancement of their de jure management and decision-making role.

Today women perform many tasks associated with environmental management and play a major role in the agricultural sector, which forms the economic mainstay of the country (Boserup, 1970). They provide the bulk of the labour required for day to day management of farms, including planting, weeding, harvesting and processing agricultural produce (Kanogo, 1992). Many women are also de facto heads of their households since their husbands have moved into the cities to seek or take up jobs. In times of drought, it is incumbent upon the women to provide food for their families.[183] They are also responsible for saving seeds for the planting season. Biotechnology innovations leading to production of seeds for planting and the undermining of local varieties further removes women from the tools they need to perform their multiple tasks of production and reproduction.[184] Further, women's groups continue to form the major drive behind environmental management initiatives at the grassroots level.[185] Women are involved in reforestation programmes and soil conservation projects.[186] Any attempt to address the issue of sustainable management of any aspect of the environment thus needs to take into account the roles played by women. It is however not unusual to see overseeing environmental resource management put in the hands of men with no regard for the need for women's representation.

4 Analysis of the Ogiek cases from a gender perspective

In this section, we look at the experiences of the Ogiek in their quest for control of their land and resources. As pointed out, land rights in forest areas are vested in the state. Additionally, customary rights and community tenure are not yet recognized legally. Couching the Ogiek issue as a community one can yield tensions when some members of the community are in conflict with others, for example when women feel that the

---

[183] See, for example, Thomas (1988) and Thomas-Slayter (1989).

[184] Women have traditionally been charged with the responsibility of preserving seeds for planting and the monoculturing of seeds through biotechnological innovations removes them from this role. See Juma (1989) and Shiva (1993) for a discussion on monoculturing of seed varieties. See also Shiva (1994) documenting how the green revolution and mechanization marginalized women in the production process.

[185] See generally, Thomas-Slayter and Rocheleau (1995). See also Chiuri and Nzioki (1992), Khasiani (1992) and Wangari *et al.* (1996).

[186] See generally Khasiani (1992) for examples on the diversity of environmental projects that women are involved in.

quest for community, cultural and land rights are not necessarily to their advantage (Banda and Chinkin, 2004). We will therefore look at the Ogiek search for justice through the judicial mechanisms and the gender dimensions in this quest. In analyzing the cases filed by the Ogiek, we seek to find out firstly whether the rights affecting women or their views have informed the quest for justice. Secondly, we seek to underscore the importance of including a women's law approach to courts' canvassing and deliberations on women's rights.

Indigenous claims and cultural identity

In one of the publications of the Ogiek newsletter,[187] when describing the men who represented the community in presenting the Ogiek views to the Constitution of Kenya Review Commission, the *Oasis* team wrote:

> 'There were four Ogiek sons. Assembly member Mr Charles Sena, a soft-spoken man in his early thirties who has unmatched hunting qualities besides being a shy honey eater, Dr Johnson Chengeiyo, in his early forties, also soft-spoken, a serious honey eater besides being a professional hunter, Kimaiyo Towett an outspoken gentleman in his early thirties, a shy honey eater and a firm believer in the integrity of creation and finally David Mpoiko Kobeil, a professional and a serious believer in Ogiek empowerment.'

The Ogiek believe that their lifestyle is distinct and that they fall under the category of indigenous communities similar to the San people of South Africa, Maori of New Zealand or Aborigine of Australia. The Kenyan constitution does not recognize indigenous people. The draft constitution has also not made provisions for them. Dr Smokin Wanjala,[188] a lecturer in the Faculty of Law at the University of Nairobi, summarized the position as follows:

> 'The characteristics of the Ogiek do not strictly qualify them as indigenous. This argument is a mixture of activism – all tribes belong to Kenya at least after colonialism no tribe can claim a better ownership than the other.'

John Mutakha, one of the constitution review commissioners, shared that view and opined that although the constitution needs to recognize certain group rights, one has to be careful to avoid a situation where some groups are singled out as having better claims to land and resources than others. He says that many other groups, including the Maasai, presented that opinion but this would result in discrimination at a time when Kenya needed a constitution to promote national unity. Liz, a programme

---

[187] *The Oasis*, Issue No. 3 October 2003.
[188] Interviewed 16 October 2003.

officer with Kenya Forest Working Group, however, pointed out that:

'When they (Ogiek) go to international forums, or when we invite them in our meetings, they are treated as indigenous people.'[189]

The Ogiek consider their connection to the forest as spiritual and most of their ceremonies, like initiation, birth, death and marriage, are linked to the forest. The use of herbs for spiritual purposes and ceremonies is pertinent here. They pray with the sunrise and the sunset and believe in a superpower. Both girls and boys undergo initiation ceremonies. Female genital mutilation is still practised in the community. The rites of passage into adulthood are emphasized because one is considered an adult thereafter. This happens between the age of 15 and 16 years for both girls and boys. Some of the implications of these rites of passage, such as boys getting out of control as they define their masculinity, need shifting by the community in their claim to a right to culture so that culture is not viewed negatively.

Labour is divided along gender lines. Men hunted and kept bees for honey and women gathered by collecting herbs as well as roots and carrying the hunted animals and honey harvested by the men. Medicine was collected by both men and women who had the knowledge. The women also worked on the skins to make clothing or ornaments, gathered firewood, cooked and generally waited for the return of their men. Men would hunt for long hours or days in the forest. They adhered strictly to traditional birth control.

A man was trained to be respectful; he kept away from his wife particularly if she had a small child. He lived separately from his wife. When the wife was ready for another child, she would send the elder child with a gourd of honey to the man; the man would know that the woman was inviting him to her house.[190]

Children were born about five years apart and so a couple had between four and five children. Under Ogiek culture women were perpetual minors:

'Women in the community are children, what can children discuss with me? I do not see why we should bother them with issues of importance like land.'[191]

Despite this, some women have tried their hand at politics. For instance, Helen Tieptoo Kiptiony was brave enough to take on seven men in the contest for councillorship in the 2002 election. Amongst the hurdles she had to face were: the community's perception of women as property; the

---

perception of a proper dress code for women which regarded trousers as taboo; the belief that it is disrespectful for a woman to stand in front of men to address them; the belief that a young woman (she was 28 years old) should not greet an older person; lack of adequate financial resources to run an election campaign, since she did not own any property; the fact that she professed to be a born again Christian and was told politics was a dirty game and strictly for men. In her words:

> 'It was a very difficult time in my life. I got encouragement from fellow women and I tried to overcome the taboos by always starting my speeches by apologizing to the men, particularly the elders, and asking for permission to address them, as for dressing, I forgot about the trousers' (*Oasis*, October, 2003).

She was motivated to join politics by her mother who taught her to be responsible and stand up for herself. She also wanted to use her position to assist the community to access resources, particularly education. While Helen did not win the election, she made the point that a woman can run for election and she hopes to try again in the future. She believes women in the community should be encouraged to overcome the cultural stigma that keeps them sidelined.

Life has changed for the Ogiek and their relationship with the forest needs to be reassessed in the light of changed times. While men continue to argue that they can manage the forest in the way they did before, women are emphatic that the old lifestyle cannot work. The men continue to talk about the forest while the women, who have become engaged in farming, consider it a better form of land use to hunting and gathering because now they do not have to wait for men for days to bring home food in the form of the spoils from hunting expeditions. In this respect, the women appeared generally more in touch with reality than the men who were holding onto their romantic idea of their life in the past. This is not to dismiss culture and the right to preserve it. This argument is based on the women's viewpoint which was the dominant voice. While men were willing to concede to the need for change and modernity, they still clung to the past. This illustrates how strongly men view their cultural identity. While the community is entitled to this claim, certain dynamics need to be looked into as they bring out the gender nuances of the claim to cultural identity which can result in discrimination against women.

The concept of ancestral land ownership
The issue of land ownership continues to be a sensitive issue in Kenya. This sensitivity is discernible among the Ogiek *Daily Nation* (5 October 2004). Significantly, five of the women interviewed had titles to land in

their own names, eight had joint titles with their husbands but the rest had none. Given that women appear to have adapted to the new lifestyle of farming and are mainly interested in putting up homes, their hard work is at risk of being appropriated by land owners if they cannot get title to the land. The issue of land allocation is not well understood among the Ogiek. They wonder what the purpose of excising and subdividing land into parcels to give to the Ogiek is. They compare such allocations to stealing a motor vehicle from someone and then giving them the log-book instead of the motor vehicle. They are of the view that the land belongs to them in the first instance and there is really no need to allocate it to them.[192] This position is diametrically opposed to the modern notion of tenure where the state grants and guarantees title to land.[193]

Male respondents interviewed believed that women should not be given title. One elder said that women who had title would leave their marriage or marry other men from outside the community. They believed that titles should be in men's names. Others advanced the view that land should be communally owned and not vested in individuals through parcelling out and granting title deeds. The women's view was that if the land is registered in the man's name only, they could be reckless and may sell the land any time, giving the family no security in ownership, use and access. Women wanted direct control over the land and assurance that their farming efforts were not in vain but would contribute to uplift their economic status and that of their families.

At Nessuit, women had formed groups tilling a common group farm where they planted maize and vegetables and they helped each other to till their own land. The Ogiek Welfare Council has been instrumental in women's progress in the Ogiek community, particularly in East Mau. Programmes on the ground include: forming men and women's groups and encouraging those already existing to continue; improving socio-economic activities, like farming for women and keeping beehives using modern technologies. Planting of trees is also encouraged, particularly in the women's groups that prepare and maintain tree nurseries. As one of the programme officers says:

> 'We carry out environmental programmes and in addition we have realized women are keener on doing farming so we encourage them to grow maize and vegetables to boost their income, we are introducing new movable combs as opposed to the old ones and some women have shown interest in them.'[194]

The men view activities along gender lines and believe they should con-

---

centrate on forest activities and leave farming to women since they consider it part of domestic work. Women are of the view that:

> 'Farming is better although we may not know the best ways but it is better than relying on a man to bring food which is not forthcoming; the hunting they talk about even in old days – men would go hunting for days and you waited for them, you either ate leaves or slept hungry. With farming, we can rely on ourselves.[195]

The women identified their current problems as: lack of modern farming knowledge or training; lack of title to land; lack of finances, education or markets; lack of health facilities and essential services; and absence of support from their spouses. In terms of land ownership, single women heading households appeared to have an advantage over those living within the marriage as they had freedom to make more decisions.

The international instruments

Article 15 of the International Covenant on Economic, Social and Cultural Rights refers to the right of everyone to take part in cultural life, enjoy the benefits of scientific progress and its application and to enjoy the protection of literary or artistic works. Article 22 of the African Charter on Human and Peoples' Rights provides for rights to develop a cultural identity. Article 27 of the covenant talks of rights of a person belonging to ethnic, religious or linguistic minorities to enjoy their own culture, to profess and practise their own religion or use their own language in community with other members of their group. In 1992 the United Nations made a declaration on the rights of persons belonging to national or ethnic religious and linguistic minorities.[196]

The Ogiek have identified themselves as an indigenous people, as defined in article 1(b) of International Labour Organization Convention No. 169 and the United Nations and the African Charter have recognized them as such members (Minority Rights Group International, 2003). Convention No. 169 stipulates that indigenous people shall have the right to retain their own customs and institutions where these are not incompatible with fundamental rights defined by the national legal systems and with internationally recognized human rights.

Rodolfo Stavenhagen has argued that cultural rights, particularly those pertaining to the preservation of cultural heritage, the cultural identity of a specific people and cultural development, are in certain circumstances considered 'peoples' rights' (UNESCO, 1998). The states have obligations to ensure the respect, protection and fulfilment of each of

---

[195] Mrs Regina Kipkemoi says of their decision to engage actively in farming, interviewed 4 December 2003.

[196] General Assembly Resolution 47/135 of 18 December 1992.

these rights and these should be spelt out in the case of cultural rights and their various interpretations.

It would appear that cultural rights, by their nature, cannot be exercised individually, only jointly with others in the community. It equally appears that these rights, if understood in the African concept, create more duties than rights. One appears to constantly relate one's behaviour to the expectations or demands of the society.

Fighting for cultural rights and recognition in terms of rights intertwined with the forest places the duty upon the Ogiek to practise these rights to justify their continued claims over the forest. In a community whose culture considers a woman a child or property and in which female genital mutilation is practised, discrimination of the sexes is created. The issue of de jure equality as opposed to de facto equality comes into this claim to cultural rights. Article 5 of CEDAW, however, provides for member states to modify culture to avoid discrimination against women based on stereotyping of gender roles.

Article 2 of the African Charter provides for the enactment of legislation that prohibits harmful practices that endanger the health and general wellbeing of women. This right is supported by the Protocol on Women's Rights in Africa which to date has not been ratified by Kenya. This in particular would apply to the female genital mutilation performed on Ogiek girls.

Environmental concerns: How have women participated?
In East Mau, the rate of forest excision can be shown by statistics of forest cover over the years. The forest cover was 89 per cent in 1986; 81 per cent in 1990; 80 per cent in 1995; 50 per cent in 2000 and 47 per cent in 2003.[197] As noted above, in addition to excising the forestland for settlement, the government has also licensed big logging companies and small saw millers to carry out activities within the forest complex. These enterprises are largely owned and run by non-Ogiek.[198]

It is interesting that though women interact very closely with environmental resources, including forests, very few are forest officers. The de facto role of women as environmental managers is not matched by the de jure institution of forest management officers. At the Nessuit for-

---

[197] Source: Swiss National Centre of Competence in Research North-South.

[198] Asked whether the Ogiek are part of the saw milling business, Mr Towett says: 'Never, the Ogiek are culturally trained not to fell trees, besides they are too poor to engage in such business. The one woman who had owned a sawmill was a non-Ogiek woman called Njeri. Her sawmill, Njeri Sawmill, was located near the town around the research sawmill and had been closed down. In most of the sawmills around the area, the employees are male because the work involves carrying huge logs and operating splitting machines, and they (the men) are non-Ogiek.

est office, for instance, a list of names of previous forest officers since 28 February 1950 posted on a notice board included only men. There was also not a single woman forest guard or forest officer in the area of research.

In terms of destruction of environmental resources, information from a forest officer in the area of research indicated that both men and women destroy the forest. Women collect firewood but men fell logs and burn charcoal. There is no planting of trees going on because of the settlement process and there are no particular programmes that target women.

The Ogiek feel that they are good forest managers so forest officers and their guards should not harass them because they are unlikely to destroy the forest. They view forest officers as uncooperative due to their insistence on following the law instead of dealing with issues as they are on the ground. Concerns for the environment through law have not underscored the role of women as environmental managers. Programmes on sound environmental management in the Mau forest complex are aimed at all members of the community. The Kenya Forest Working Group, for instance, conducts many workshops to sensitize the community in forest management, including areas in the Mau forest. They mainly target community-based organizations, government officers, opinion leaders and women's groups. There is the view that though attempts are made to include women as participants in such workshops, women do not attend in large numbers either because of community beliefs about the place of women or due to too much work. The working group has, however, had greater success with women's participation in areas where they have been sensitized, especially where the Green Belt movement is operational. The main limitation of the working group, however, is its lack of direct access to the community as it has to work through forest officers. The failure of the Forests Bill 2004 to become law has also meant that the operational policies are outdated and have not taken on new issues such as community involvement in forest management.

The Environment Management and Coordination Act 2000 provides mechanisms for public complaints in instances of environmental degradation. The Public Complaints Committee, set up under section 31 of the Act, is concerned with investigating complaints relating to environmental damage and degradation generally. They have received many complaints related to Mau forest on logging and excision which have not yet been processed. These have been brought mainly by groups that are not disaggregated along gender lines. The mandate of the Public Complaints Committee is very wide and other than ensuring that complaints are attended to, gender representation is not a concern that they have given much attention. Local groups such as the Ogiek Welfare

Council which work on the ground in the target areas have endeavoured to incorporate women in their programmes on keeping tree nurseries and learning new methods of farming.

It is apt to say that the use of the environment to preserve cultural and customary rights and natural resources for the protection of women is still a grey area in Kenya. The idea that women are good environmental managers is yet to be acknowledged and the obligation on the state to preserve the environment for them is not given priority. This is surprising given that Kenya has ratified multilateral environmental agreements, like the Convention on Biological Diversity, that underscore the roles that women play in environmental management and exhort states parties to put in place mechanisms for facilitating women in the performance of these roles.[199] The convention also requires state parties to respect, preserve and maintain knowledge, innovation and practices of indigenous people embodying traditional lifestyles relevant for the sustainable use of environmental biodiversity (article 8). Articles 21 and 24 of the African Charter provide for the rights of people to the use and enjoyment of their natural resources.[200]

The Protocol to the African Charter on Human and People's Rights on the Rights of Women has explicit provisions on the right of women to a healthy and sustainable environment at article 18. States parties are required to ensure greater participation of women in planning, managing and preserving the environment and in the sustainable use of natural resources at all levels and to protect and enable the development of women's indigenous knowledge systems. Article 19 further provides that women shall have the right to full enjoyment of their right to sustainable development. In this connection, states parties are required to: introduce a gender perspective in national development planning procedures; ensure participation of women at all levels in the conceptualization, decision-making, implementation and evaluation of development policies and programmes; and promote women's access to and control over productive resources, such as land, and guarantee their right to property.[201]

---

[199] See 'Preamble to the United Nations Conference on Environment and Development: Convention on Biological Diversity', Rio de Janeiro, 5 June 1992, which states: 'Recognizing also the vital role that women play in the conservation and sustainable use of biological diversity and affirming the need for the full participation of women at all levels of policy-making and implementation for biological diversity conservation.'

[200] African Charter on Human and Peoples' Rights, adopted by the 18th Assembly of Heads of State and Government, 27 June 1981 – Nairobi, Kenya, OAU Doc. CAB/LEG/67/3 rev. 5; 21 I.L.M. 58 (1982), entered into force 21 October 1986.

[201] Optional Protocol to the African Charter on Human and Peoples' Rights of Women in Africa, July 2003.

These provisions provide a basis for linking women's rights to the quest for the Mau forest complex by the Ogiek. This link is critical because the clearing of the forest has general as well as gendered impacts on the members of the Ogiek community. These include rivers flowing from the escarpment having less water and some drying up which, for women, means: water scarcity and more work in terms of accessing water; loss of plant and animal species and the concomitant substitution of indigenous trees with exotic varieties; loss of species used for medicinal purposes, a pertinent issue for women given that health facilities are inadequate and there is no maternal health care in the area; and the loss of indigenous medicinal knowledge associated with the lost indigenous plant species.

The law is unable to deal with these issues adequately. For instance, the Forest Act neither provides for the rights of the local community nor guarantees their rights to use the forest and its products. The Act has not only vested the ownership of the forest in the state but has made provision for supervision so as to exclude communities by designating certain forms of access to the forest as unauthorized and illegal. It has excluded the community and women particularly from participating in forest management since the forest managers are all male and furthermore they are government employees, not community members.

Equally, the Environment Management and Coordination Act, which came into effect in 2000, has not sufficiently addressed the issue of indigenous and women's rights. Since the operative constitution does not recognize indigenous rights, when the Ogiek fight for conservation of the forest they do so as any other interested party rather than as a people defending a resource vital for their existence and livelihood.

The legal framework described above places a responsibility on the government to preserve the forests and the environment and to engage the communities that live in them to practise proper use. However, lack of policies that include indigenous people and women and the failure to tap the Ogiek knowledge on conservation, are examples of policies that remain only on paper.

5   Conclusion, recommendations and way forward

Concluding remarks

Land and resource tenure laws and policies have marginalized the Ogiek, impacting on the livelihood of this forest-dwelling community. The dominant paradigms of state and individual ownership have had difficulty conceding to rights of communities. Moreover, the conception of resource conservation as removed from communities and carried out through state agency has pre-empted the enlistment of the Ogiek community in the conservation and management of the Mau forest.

State ownership of the forest occupied by the Ogiek and government replacing indigenous trees with exotic varieties with no medicinal value, hamper beekeeping activities from which they earn their living. Destruction of the forest has also destroyed their legacy and denial of land ownership lends credence to the Ogiek complaints against the state.

Constant evictions are not genuine if the government excises the forest to allocate it to individuals who are not members of the community without giving them first priority or recognizing their customary rights of ownership. The eviction has also exposed them to what they term human rights abuses because it has denied them the right to peace, property, culture and education or any development programmes.

This research looked at the Ogiek claims from a gender perspective, particularly from a women's law perspective, and data collected was done with a view to finding the women's voices. We have seen that part of the claim for the forest is so that the community lifestyle of hunting and beekeeping is continued and preserved but women in the community do not hunt or keep honeycombs nor is there any intention to incorporate them into these activities.

In the search for cultural identity and recognition, communities are rallied together against a common enemy, in this case, the state. Issues of intra-community inequities are put aside as all attention is focused on eliminating a common enemy. The Ogiek as a polity seek to preserve the forest as an embodiment of their culture but some current cultural practices are detrimental to the wellbeing of women and the negative practices need to be discarded while positive ones are promoted. This however is not seen as an immediate concern in most communities fighting a single enemy. It is not unusual to have rites that impact negatively on a particular group being promoted in the quest for ethnic identity in the face of threats from agents external to the ethnic polity. For instance, the initiation into adulthood for girls is a mutilation of the body which is life threatening and breaches a girl's right to life. Her belonging to the society is predicated on her going through the rite and failure to abide to the expectation could result in her being ostracized. Yet Ogiek ethnic identity is premised on the maintenance of cultural practices such as this and the concept of women as minors or as property which leads to discrimination on the grounds of sex and the dominance of sexes. The claim for cultural rights in this scenario then becomes purely a restatement of patriarchy and entrenchment of patriarchal norms.

A claim for land is a noble claim but how will women benefit if they are regarded as minors and property in the community? We have seen that women are ready to embrace modernity and learn new farming methods. All they need now is encouragement and access to resources in terms of land, skills and finance. Women find that engaging in farming gives them a better economic position where they can take care of the family. In a way, gender roles have changed and most women have become the family providers.

This chapter illustrates that in terms of marginalization of the community, the women fully supported the complaints but the problem is the emphasis on the public utilities required. Health, for example, was seen by men in terms of putting up a dispensary but they did not think of adequate maternity health care. It may not be enough to put up schools, for example, if the community is not ready to give the girl child the freedom to learn.

Recommendations

The excavation of women's rights in a traditional community such as the Ogiek community requires more than legal interventions. The dominant paradigm is that of male dominance over women and unless this is debunked, reforms will remain cosmetic. For instance, there are women among the Ogiek who have moved out of traditional domains and ventured into territories perceived as primarily male preserves. Narratives on these women should be used to begin a process of social engineering. In challenging dominant paradigms, law can be used to promote narratives that provide space for indigenous people and women among such people to enjoy their rights and free themselves from the shackles of discrimination. The constitution is useful in this regard and it should expressly provide for indigenous and group rights but with a rider adopting the Protocol of the African Charter on Women (article 17) to promote positive cultural practices and discard the negative ones, and to include the right to own property.

Domestication of international instruments would amplify and further buttress constitutional provisions by reinforcing the state's duty to recognize and protect these rights. In particular the protocol is a useful instrument that should be given full effect within our laws. Local legislation on land should equally be aligned with provisions of equality contained in international conventions.

To ensure that the rights provided for are enjoyed, mechanisms for community participation should be instituted. Incentives should be put in place for the community to participate in conservation measures through benefit-sharing schemes and access and use rights. Management committees should include women as a matter of course. In carrying out community management programmes, the government should tap the indigenous knowledge of the people in preserving forests. Government projects should target areas with no development projects to ensure, as much as possible, equality and equity amongst all citizens.

This can be done in formulating policies with affirmative action. In the allocation of land to the Ogiek, the government should involve only *bona fide* members of the community and ensure gender balance in title issuance. Community spokespersons should include men and women.

Access to justice is critical to the realization of rights to land and resources. In this regard, the Ogiek have several cases pending before the court. Priority should be given to the expeditious and judicious finalization of these cases.

The government has no development programmes in most areas occupied by the Ogiek. Nessuit is one of the forests forming part of Eastern Mau complex and there is in place a fully-fledged forest station complete with forest guards. This is surprisingly the only presence of an organized government infrastructure in the area. According to the elders in the group discussion, in their many years of living in that area, the only government programme they have seen is the destruction of the forest and allocation of land to 'foreigners'. To build positive relationships between the government and the Ogiek, the following should be done:

Recognition of the Ogiek as a tribe
The Ogiek claim that the government has not recognized them and, according to the Chief Rotich:[202]

> 'Official Kenyan tribes have for a long time been 42 and each has a code number. The Ogiek are not amongst them. We are now fighting to be included. The number should be 43 or more, this is being sidelined.'

Article 25 of the draft United Nations Declaration on the Rights of Indigenous Peoples states:

> 'Indigenous peoples have a right to maintain and strengthen their distinctive spiritual and material relationship with the lands, territories, waters and coastal seas and other resources whether they have traditionally owned or otherwise occupied or used them and to uphold their responsibilities to future generations.'

Article 6 of the same draft requires that the government include indigenous people's participation at all levels and seek their opinions while dealing with natural resources considered belonging to them. The government should recognize the Ogiek as a tribe and accord them rights as indigenous people.

---

[202] Interview, 24 October 2003.

Education

The level of illiteracy in the community is high and this relates to the government's constant threats of eviction and closure of schools. At independence few Ogiek were going to school but the number of schools in Mau forest increased, mostly put up by the Catholic Church. In 1987 the government closed several schools in the area and it was only towards 1992 in the dawn of multiparty politics that the schools were reopened. No secondary schools serve the community and the primary schools are scattered at distances of about 12kms.

Measures should be put in place to assure the Ogiek of education, especially in light of the free education programme. This should be coupled with provision of more schools and ensuring that children remain in school by stemming early marriages. The lack of schools is not the only issue hampering the education of Ogiek children. Part of the problem is cultural practices like initiation ceremonies that place emphasis on adulthood. Young boys who are still school-going age begin to take up adult responsibilities and girls are often pressurized to marry. The high level of poverty makes most parents get their daughters betrothed at an early age, some as early as 10 years. This hinders the progress of women in areas that require education.[203]

Article 26 of the Universal Declaration of Human Rights and article 13 and 17(1) of the covenant gives the state an obligation to provide for education for its citizens. Article 10 of CEDAW and article 28 of Convention on the Rights of the Child specifically make that provision for education of both women and children. At the local level, the Children's Act makes it mandatory for the government if the immediate family is unable, to ensure a child's education. Clearly, this obligation both at international and local level has not been met.

In terms of legal awareness, Regina (42 years) said she was not aware of any women's rights or child maintenance. Others agreed. They take their cases to the chief and go back home with them as they claim the chief is biased against women. There have been no groups sensitizing women about their rights and many have no idea what type of family cases they can take to court or whether there is such a thing as court fees or legal expenses. There is clearly need for sensitization on rights.

Employment opportunities

According to the chief, the Ogiek are part of Nakuru district, which has many other tribes who have either come for employment or left their

---

[203] Mzee Koros, an elder, interviewed 9 December 2003. He believed that though the Ogiek life is changing, special consideration should be given to them by the state in terms of education for their children, loans, training, employment and development projects.

own ancestral homes to settle there. When issues like employment opportunities arise and there is a quota for each district, the other tribes tend to gain both in Nakuru district and their home districts. The Ogiek, whose only homes are within Mau, are outnumbered and stand no chance of getting into the district quotas.

The highest politicians from the Ogiek community are two councillors who are men. It is clear that the marginalization of the Ogiek in politics has direct implications on women's discrimination. Few women are recognized as community representatives. Access to employment opportunities for the Ogiek generally and women in particular is critical to advancement of the Ogiek agenda and quest for their land rights.

Health

Article 12 of CEDAW specifically requires that states parties provide adequate health facilities for women but, as stated, the Ogiek occupied area lacks health facilities and women depend mainly on herbal medication. There is, for example, no maternity facility within Nessuit area and, according to Jane Machani, the Ogiek Welfare Council gender representative, women rely on traditional birth attendants. The inherent health risks and the need to address these cannot be overemphasized.

5 Right to freedom from harassment and discrimination

Evictions and constant harassment clearly violate Ogiek human dignity and right to life. Articles 1 and 2 of the Universal Declaration of Human Rights, articles 2 and 4 of the African Charter and articles 2 and 6 and 9 of the covenant are relevant here. They provide for freedom from discrimination, equal treatment and freedom to life and human dignity. The evictions have also interfered with the women's right to form and found a family because of constant disturbance. These need to cease.

At the root

One of the weaknesses of the Ogiek community in terms of fighting against marginalization, as the chief says, is that community development has been difficult because they are a small group, yet scattered. Lack of exposure has not seen them unite. Groups like the Ogiek Welfare Council may be making progress but the community looks at them as a source of employment and financial assistance rather than as groups that need their grassroots support.

While the women shared the men's view that they were marginalized, they felt that their men were partly to blame because:

> 'Most of our men are uncooperative, they have refused to adapt to the new lifestyle after the forest has been destroyed, they spend most of the day doing nothing, they have refused to farm and so the children

do not go to school because of lack of support from the husbands, how do you expect to progress if you have no education?' [204]

According to the women, the men are burying their heads in the sand thinking about hunting and keeping bees while these have become impossible. They are not facing reality and have refused to learn farming methods, leaving the full burden on the women. Another weakness on the part of the men is the failure to include women in the fight for their rights. To quote Sembene Ousmane a renowned Senegalese novelist and film maker:

'Women are the future of Africa. Yet too often they are ignored.'

Often the silent person may hold the solution to a problem. Women make good agents of sensitization in the community. Including them may open certain paths, even if these may come in the form of outside assistance to the women, the whole community stands to gain. It is imperative that their voices are heard in the Ogiek quest for justice.

Bibliography

Agarwal B. (1995) *Gender, environment and poverty interlinks in rural India: Regional variations and temporal shifts, 1971-1991*, UNRISD, Geneva.

Banda F. and C. Chinkin (2004) *Gender minorities and indigenous peoples*, report of the Minority Rights Group International, London.

Bentzon A. W. *et al.* (1998) *Pursuing grounded theory in law*, Tano-Aschehoug/ Mond Books, Oslo and Harare.

Biebuyck D. (ed) (1963) *African agrarian systems*, Oxford University Press, London.

Blackburn R. H. (1974) 'The Ogiek and their history', in *Azania* Vol. 9, 150.

Boserup E. (1989) *Women's role in economic development* (revised edition), Earthscan, London.

Chanock M. (1991) 'Paradigms, policies and property: A review of the customary law of land tenure', in R. Roberts and K. Mann (eds) *Law in colonial Africa*, Heinemann, Portsmouth.

Central Intelligence Agency (2006) *The world factbook*, available at http://www.cia.gov/cia/publications/factbook/

Chiuri W. and A. Nzioki (1992) 'Women: Invisible managers of natural resources', in S. R. Khasiani (ed) *Groundwork: African women as environmental managers*, African Centre for Technology Studies Press, Nairobi.

---

[204] Regina Kipkemoi, interviewed 9 December 2003.

Cuomo C. (2001) 'On ecofeminist philosophy', in *Ethics and the Environment*, Vol. 7, No 2.

Daily Nation (5 October 2004) 'Ogiek families were "robbed" of their land', Nairobi.

Falk Moore S. (1991) 'From giving and lending to selling: Property transactions reflecting historical changes on Kilimanjaro', in R. Roberts and K. Mann (eds) *Law in colonial Africa*, Heinemann, Portsmouth.

Fox-Genovese E. (1991) *Feminism without illusions: A critique of individualism*, University of North Carolina Press, Chapel Hill, North Carolina.

Juma C. (1989) *The gene hunters: Biotechnology and the scramble for seeds*, African Centre for Technology Studies Research Series, No. 1, Princeton University Press, Princeton.

Kamau J. (2000) 'The Ogiek. The history of the forgotten tribe', chapter 1 in *The Ogiek: The ongoing destruction of a minority tribe in Kenya*, Rights Features Service, accessed at http:www.ogiek.org.

Kanogo T. (1992) 'Women and environment in history', in S. R. Khasiani (ed) *Groundwork: African women as environmental managers*, African Centre for Technology Studies Press, Nairobi.

Kanogo T. (1992) 'Women and environment in history', in S. R. Khasiani (ed) *Groundwork: African women as environmental managers*, African Centre for Technology Studies Press, Nairobi.

Kenyatta J. (1938) *Facing Mount Kenya*, Secker and Warburg, London.

Leo C. (1984) *Land and class in Kenya*, University of Toronto Press, Toronto.

MacArthur J. D. (1961) 'Land tenure reform and economic research into African farming in Kenya', in *East African Economic Review* 82.

Minority Rights Group International (October 2003) *Kenya's castaways: The Ogiek and national development processes*, micro-study report available at http://minrights.org.dev.Kenya/mrg-pf.htm.October 2003.

Oduor J. A. (2004) 'Following God's constitution: The gender dimensions in the Ogiek claim to Mau forest complex', thesis written in partial fulfilment of the requirements for a Masters' in Women's Law, University of Zimbabwe, Harare.

Ogiek Welfare Council (October 2003) *The Oasis*, a quarterly newsletter of Ogiek news, Issue Nos. 3 & 5, Ogiek Welfare Council with support from Ford Foundation, Nairobi.

Okoth-Ogendo H. W. O. (1991) *Tenants of the crown : Evolution of agrarian law and institutions in Kenya*, African Centre for Technology Studies Press, Nairobi.

Osolo-Nasubo N. (1977) *A socio-economic study of the Kenya Highlands from 1900–1970: A case study of the Uhuru government,* University Press of America, Washington.

Shiva V. (1993) *Monocultures of the mind: Perspectives on biodiversity and biotechnology,* Zed Books, London.
– (1993) 'The seed and the earth: Biotechnology and the colonization of regeneration', in V. Shiva (ed) *Close to home : Women reconnect ecology, health and development,* New Society Publisher, Gabriola Island.
– (1994) 'The seed and the earth : Biotechnology and the colonization of regeneration', in V. Shiva (ed) *Close to home : Women reconnect ecology, health and development,* New Society Publisher, Gabriola Island.
– (1995) 'Biotechnological development and the conservation of biodiversity', in V. Shiva and I. Moser (eds) *Biopolitics: A feminist and ecological reader,* Zed Books, London.

Slayter B. T. and D. Rocheleau (1995) 'Gender, resources, and local institutions: New Identities for Kenya's rural women', in B. P. Thomas-Slayter and D. Rocheleau (eds) *Gender, environment and development in Kenya – A grassroots perspective,* Lynne Rienner, Boulder.

Sorrenson M. P .K. (1967) *Land reform in the Kikuyu country: A study in government policy,* Oxford University Press, Nairobi.

Spretnak C. (1990) 'Ecofeminism: Our roots and flowering', in I. Diamond and G. F. Orenstein, *Reweaving the web: The emergence of ecofeminism,* Sierra Club Books, San Francisco.

Stang Dahl T. (1987) *Women's law: An introduction to feminist jurisprudence,* Norwegian University Press, Oslo.

Stavanhagen R. (1998) 'Cultural rights: A social science perspective' in *Cultural rights and wrongs,* a collection of essays in commemoration of the 50th anniversary of the Universal Declaration of Human Rights, UNESCO.
– (1998) 'Cultural rights: A social science perspective', in Institute of Art and Law, *Cultural rights and wrongs,* UNESCO, Paris.

Swynnerton R. J. M. (1954) *A plan to intensify the development of African agriculture in Kenya,* Government printers, Nairobi.

Thomas B. P. (1988) 'Household strategies for adaptation and change in Kenyan rural women's associations' in *Africa* 58(4).

Thomas-Slayter B. (1989) *Politics, class and gender in African resource management: Examining the connections in rural Kenya,* African Studies Centre, University of Boston, Boston.

Thomas-Slayter B. P. and D. Rocheleau (eds) (1995) *Gender, environment and development in Kenya – A grassroots perspective,* Lynne Rienner, Boulder.

Towett J. (2002) *Mau forest complex in the spotlight*, Ogiek Welfare Council with support from Ford Foundation, Nairobi.

United Nations Development Fund for Women (UNIFEM) (2002) *Progress of the world's women 2002: Gender equality and the Millennium Development Goals*, UNIFEM, New York.

United Nations Commission on the Status of Women (1980) report, United Nations, New York.

Wangari E. *et al.* (1996) 'Gendered visions for survival: semi-arid regions in Kenya', pages 127–154 in D. Rocheleau, B. Thomas-Slayter and E. Wangari (eds), *Feminist political ecology: Global issues and local experiences*, Routledge, London.

Wanjala S. (ed) (2000) *Essays on land law: The reform debate in Kenya*, University of Nairobi, Faculty of Law, Nairobi.

Wong B. (September 2002) 'Racism and administration of justice, Kenya indigenous group faces October 1 court case', in *World Rainforest Movement journal* at <http://www.wrm.org.uy/bulletin/62/Kenya.html .

World Commission on Environment and Development (1987) *Our common future*, report of the commission (also known as the Brundtland Commission Report), United Nations, New York.

World Rainforest Movement (November 2000) 'Kenya: Local peoples' land rights ignored', in *World Rainforest Movement Bulletin* No. 40, at http://www.wrm.org.uy/bulletin/40/Kenya.html.

List of cases

Joseph Letuya & Others v the Attorney General & Others (Nairobi HCCC No.635 of 1997)

Joseph Letuya & 21 Others v the Minister for Environment & Natural Resources (Nairobi HCCC NO.2280/0I)

Francis Kemei & 91 Others v Attorney General & three Others (Nairobi HCCC No. 238 of 1999)

Simon Kiwape &19 Others v Muneria Naimodu & two Others (Civil Case No.19/97)

Narok and Representatives v Ministry of Environment & Ministry of Lands (Nairobi HCCC No.421/02)

Obiero v Opiyo (1972) East African Law Reports 227

Mwangi Muguthu v Maina Muguthu (Civil Case No. 377 of 1968) (Unreported)

Esiroyo v Esiroyo (1973) East African Law Reports 388

List of legislation

Laws of Kenya

African Courts (Suspension of Land Suits) Ordinance 1957

Children's Act 2001

Constitution of Kenya 1983

Crown Lands Ordinances of 1902 and 1905

Environment Management and Coordination Act 2000

Forest Act 1989

Government Lands Act, Chapter 280 of 1915

Land (Group Representatives) Act, Chapter 287 of 1968

Lands Act

Magistrates' Courts Jurisdiction Act, Chapter 10 of 1984

Native Lands Registration Ordinance No. 27 of 1959 (Colony and Protectorate of Kenya)

Native Land Tenure Rules of 1956

Registered Land Act, Chapter 300 of 1963

Transfer of Property Act 1882

Trust Land Act 1939

Regional and international

Organization of African Unity

African Charter on Human and Peoples' Rights 1981

Optional Protocol to the African Charter on Human and Peoples' Rights of
Women in Africa 2003

United Nations

Convention on Biological Diversity 1992 (Rio de Janeiro, United Nations
Conference on Environment and Development)

8

Rural women's access to landed property
Unearthing the realities within an East African setting[205]

Rie Odgaard and Agnete Weis Bentzon

This chapter challenges the often-held assumption that customary laws and traditions block African women from owning land, and argues that such a position often emerges if customs and 'traditions' are seen as static and if women are denied 'agency'. From the perspective of dynamic response to historical changes, the gendered analysis shows that many women in East Africa exercise land rights in their own right, although not uncontested. Also, men and women's struggles for land do not reflect conflicting interests between men and women but conflicting interests between a specific group of women (often supported by their fathers) and specific groups of men, especially women's brothers. Furthermore, the chapter argues that the family level cannot be seen as the only forum for conflict resolution because other levels of normative regulation, and conflicts of laws between these levels, indirectly influence the situation at the family level. Empirical evidence provided is from south western Tanzania, with reference to experiences from other African countries.

1 Introduction

In this chapter we show why and in which way many women in East Africa have access to land and other property in communities organized largely according to patrilineal principles. We deal with gender as well as generational aspects of access to land and land conflict. The empirical examples illustrate that men and women's struggles for access to land do not necessarily reflect conflicting interests between men and women generally but rather between specific groups of women (often sided by their fathers) and specific groups of men, especially women's brothers. It is shown that women's access to land in these societies in practice fares better today, and fared better previously, than the narrow general discourse about the issue would suggest, in spite of some obvious gender imbalances. Rosemary Okello's article (2003) about wom-

---

en's lack of land rights in East Africa in which she suggests that customary laws and traditions often block women from owning landed property is an example of this view. This chapter demonstrates how false conclusions can emerge when, firstly, customary laws and traditions are seen as static instead of dynamic and, secondly, when women are denied agency and considered unable to fight for their interests and oppose domination and discrimination.

In most African countries, including Tanzania, access to land for most rural people, and especially rural women, is in practice regulated in accordance with customary rules and norms of a different nature. In this chapter we are therefore concerned with this level of normative regulation, although the national and international levels of regulation also have an impact on customary rules and norms. Regulation of rights to land at the family level in Africa, at least in the rural areas, usually included, and still includes, lineage or clan authorities, local level dispute resolution mechanisms, village elders, village government leaders, and so on. Regulation of land rights at the family level also draws on different sources of law, including local customary rules and norms, national legislation and international regulations, and may be termed 'local law'.[206] With this background it is difficult to distinguish sharply between the family and the wider context of which it is a part in relation to questions, disputes and conflicts about property. It is thus difficult to talk about the family (in its narrow sense) as the only forum for conflict resolution, even though formal forums at higher levels[207] are generally not used in the cases we deal with.[208]

The empirical evidence provided in this chapter draws on data collected mainly by Rie Odgaard[209] in two communities in south-western Tanzania, namely the Hehe community in Iringa rural district and the Sangu community in Mbarali district.[210] Reference is also made to the

---

[206] The concept 'local law' is discussed in, for example, Hellum (1998 and 2000) where it is defined as a mixed product and a hybrid form of law that has evolved in colonial and post-colonial countries in Africa. See also le Roy (1985).

[207] For further elaboration on various levels see, for example, Odgaard and Bentzon (2002).

[208] This point is further discussed in the section about conflict resolution in the last part of the chapter.

[209] Most of the information presented here was collected by Rie Odgaard during fieldwork between 1985 and 1994 in Usangu Plains (Mbarali district) and as part of her involvement in subproject 3 under the research programme: 'Sustainable agriculture in semi-arid Africa' (SASA) from 1995 to 2000. The SASA fieldwork was carried out in Ismani and Mazombe divisions, Iringa rural district, and in close collaboration with Jannik Boesen and Faustin P. Maganga. All the research was financed by the Danish Council for Development Research.

[210] The nature of customary rules and norms differs from one part of Tanzania to the other depending on local interpretation and practices and on the status of the land

situation in patrilineal communities in other African countries. The chapter illustrates how general changes in the society and in gender relations have influenced the way rights to property were perceived and articulated in practice among the Hehe and Sangu peoples at various periods of time in history. It also provides examples of emerging conflicts of interest between various groups of family members and illustrates how such conflicts are currently dealt with in the local context.

2   Discourse about women's land rights in East Africa

The discourse about women's access to land in East Africa often rests on a number of assumptions, the most important of which are as follows:

Customary laws are oppressive to women; women's situation can be improved by legal intervention
Even though a number of recent studies[211] show that women's access to resources in East Africa may not be as restricted today as portrayed in some literature, it is still a common assumption among politicians and some researchers dealing with women's issues[212] that customary laws in general, and especially in patrilineal societies, are oppressive to women's rights. This attitude recurs in the international documents concerned with women's human rights[213] and is based on the understanding of customary law as static and composed of old customs and traditions. At the same time it has been a conviction within women's movements that legislation should be used as an important means to improve women's position in society.

This chapter is based on the understanding of customary law as dynamic and contingent on time and space.[214] Therefore the question of its oppressive or non-oppressive character is empirical and the structure of the article reflects that. By incorporating an historical dimension in our analysis, we show dynamic changes over time in the context in which

---

[210 contd] in terms of land use: grazing areas, public lands, cultivated land, forest and woodlands, and so on. See for example URT/NAI (1994). See also the various contributions in Benjaminsen and Lund (2003).

[211] Mackenzie (1989), Smith Oboler (1994), Lastarria-Cornhiel (1997), among others.

[212] See Ncube and Stewart (1995), Meinzen-Dick *et al.* (1997), Rwebangira (1996), Kapinga (1997) and Mukangara and Koda (1997), among many others.

[213] For example Beijing Platform for Action (1995) and reaffirmed in SADC Gender and Development Declaration.

[214] This position has been convincingly defended by many Africanists for some time, for example, Martin Chanock (1998), Terence Ranger (1993), Sally Falk Moore (1978) and Sara Berry (1989 and 1993), to mention a few.

customary law operates as well as how this ever-changing context has implied changes in rules and norms – that is changes in customary law itself. Our data also illustrate that legislation which supports women's position does not suffice to alter oppressive customs but may have an impact on the processes of change producing local law.

Customary law is an obstacle to progress
This is a common assumption among economists. The same line of thought is behind Göran Hydén's use of the concepts of 'economy of affection' and 'the peasant mode of production' in his book, *No shortcuts to progress*, which is based on studies from Tanzania. It refers to the economic importance of kinship and customary norms of reciprocal obligations of support, which are seen as hindrances to investment in new agricultural technology. His two concepts obviously imply ideas of a more or less undisturbed continuity in lifestyle and affiliated values.

The examples presented in this analysis clearly demonstrate that the societies in question have undergone fundamental changes, to a very large extent related to the interplay between these societies and the colonial powers and to the integration of these societies into a market economy. This has implied changes in customary rules and norms and in the way such rules and norms are interpreted and applied in practice at various times in history.

Conceptual tools in analyzing access to property from a gender perspective
A number of concepts and theories inspired our analysis. To analyze customary rules and their transformation into local law in the context of a complex society, the concept of 'semi-autonomous social fields' as defined by Sally Falk Moore proved useful. According to Moore, a semi-autonomous social field is defined by the fact that it has:

> '... rule-making capacities and the means to induce or coerce compliance; but it is simultaneously set in a larger social matrix which can, and does, affect and invade it, sometimes at the invitation of persons inside it, sometimes at its own instance' (Moore, 1978: 55).

If applied to the context of land rights among the Hehe and Sangu, an arena where groups like fathers, daughters and sons (see later) interact in relation to the question of land rights, this may, in accordance with Moore's definition, be seen as a semi-autonomous social field. But each of these groups may also by themselves constitute a semi-autonomous social field depending on their respective capacities for generating and enforcing rules. The important point here is that a social field is semi-autonomous not only because it can be affected by the direction of outside forces impinging upon it but because persons inside the social field can mobilize those outside forces, or threaten to do so, in their bargaining with one another (Moore, 1978: 64). As shown in the analysis presented here, the groups consisting of fathers, daughters and sons are engaged in a process in which each of them strives to become both rule or norm generating and enforcing. They are constantly involved in processes of negotiation about their respective rights and obligations in relation to their status in the family and the local community.[215]

The question of whether one is considered indigenous to an area or not is important in relation to the type of land rights one is endowed with in accordance with customary rules. The extent to which an individual is able to exercise such rights is a different question. In order to distinguish between ideal rights and rights which are exercised in practice, the terms endowments and entitlements in the meaning adopted by Leach *et al.* (1997) is useful. According to their analysis, endowments refer to the rights and resources that people have, for example, land, labour, skills, and so on. Entitlements on the other hand refer to legitimate effective command over such resources and the benefits which can be derived from them (Leach *et al.*, 1997: 8–9).[216]

In relation to land rights, endowments are the rights which each individual and groups of individuals may have in Tanzania in two different ways: firstly, as a member of an ethnic group and or family in accordance with indigenous and customary rules and, secondly, as a citizen of Tanzania in accordance with policies issued during the socialist era granting each individual resident of a village – irrespective of sex – a right to be allocated a piece of land (Fimbo, 1992). It seems that there were no legislative provisions for this previously[217] but with the new Land Acts the rights of both men and women to apply for and be allocated land by the village authorities are clearly specified.[218] Our data show that villagers – at least as far as male villagers are concerned – previously have been and still are able to exercise this right in practice to quite a large extent in villages where land is available for allocation.

In accordance with the interpretation of customary rules and norms in practice the type of endowments differ for different groups and individuals in the society, not only according to age, status and gender but

---

[215] In line with, for example, Sara Berry (1997), we look at land rights from the perspective of social relationships and processes of negotiation. For further illustration of this see Odgaard (2002).

[216] The jurist's usage of the two terms is slightly different. Entitlement is a legal right. Endowment is a gift, donated or congenital. An interesting discussion of entitlement is found in Manji (2000).

[217] Rwebangira (1996) and Sundet (1997), for example.

[218] See URT (1999a and 1999b) and Wily (2003).

also depending on whether you are *mwenyeji* (indigenous) or *mgeni* (a guest).[219]

For example *wawenyeji* (plural of indigenous) in a certain area have in principle two types of land endowments: indigenous rights and rights in accordance with the socialist land policies. So in principle Hehe and Sangu men and women are endowed with two types of land rights in their respective home areas. The *wageni* (guests) in the two districts, however, have land endowments in their home area but endowments in the immigration area only in accordance with the socialist land policy and only if accepted as members of the community by the village government.

The extent to which *wawenyeji* and *wageni,* respectively, as groups or individuals, are able to derive the potential benefits from their land endowments, that is to have legitimate effective command or entitlement over such benefits (what can be produced from the land – food crops, cash from sales, and so on), depends on a number of factors, one of which is the important question of access to power and bargaining power.

The nature of the existing inequalities in the *de facto* landholding structure in the two districts, both in terms of gender inequalities and social inequality in general, reflects that some individuals and groups have been able to exercise more bargaining power in their struggle for access to land than others.[220] The ever-increasing pressure on land due to natural population increases and immigration into the two districts and the general socio-economic development in the area mean that it has become more and more difficult to make land claims and be granted land rights, especially for groups of people like women and many of the immigrants[221] whose land rights are disputed. Paradoxically, the development referred to above composes the major reason why more and more women today find themselves in situations where they need to claim their land rights.

3   The Hehe and Sangu ethnic groups in Iringa and Mbarali districts

What are currently referred to administratively as the Iringa and Mbarali districts form part of the core home area for the Hehe and Sangu peoples

---

[219] It also depends on the nature of land use pattern (for example, pastoralism or cultivation). This is further elaborated in Odgaard (2005).

[220] This is being dealt with in detail in Boesen, Maganga and Odgaard (work in progress).

[221] See for example Odgaard (1987 and 1994), Odgaard and Maganga (1994) and Odgaard (2005).

who derive their main livelihood from agriculture and livestock rearing. Even though the populations in the two districts are now very mixed ethnically due to heavy immigration from other parts of Tanzania,[222] our focus is especially on the way rights to land have been interpreted and practised at different times in history by these two peoples. The justification for choosing this ethnic focus is that research has shown (Odgaard, 1987, 1994, 1997) that whether one is indigenous or considered a guest in an area is important in relation to land rights.

To distinguish between different ethnic groups in an African context is problematic, however, and needs some explanation. Many scholars have rightly shown[223] that the division of the African population into distinct tribes or ethnic groups is a colonial construct rather than inherent in traditional African society. Historical accounts show that what have been referred to as the Hehe and Sangu tribes or ethnic groups since colonial times, are in reality conglomerates of peoples who were previously carriers of different cultural identities (Iliffe, 1979; Redmayne, 1968). It is also well known that population movements and amalgamations of different peoples have taken place in Africa since time immemorial (Mamdani, 1996). Tanzania is no exception.

When we refer to the Hehe or Sangu, therefore, we are not talking about tribes in the colonial sense of the word but about people who identify themselves and who are identified by others as belonging to these specific groups. Moreover, as part of their self-identification, each of these groups refers to specific norm sets and customary rules as forming part of their culture. But as will emerge, the norm sets and customary rules on which the Hehe and Sangu base their self-identification and which are used to define rights of individuals to land and other property, are continuously being invented and or reinvented – through the interaction between developments taking place at the local, national and global levels of society.

The scramble for women's access to property
Interviews during the fieldwork with Sangu and Hehe people revealed different accounts of the rights of women and men to property, especially to landed property. As will be shown, the distinction between land as property and other types of property (like cattle) is intrinsically a fairly recent phenomenon in the communities in question. Thus it was argued by most of the Hehe and Sangu women of all ages interviewed that by custom (according to *mila na desturi* in Swahili) women have

---

[222] McCall (1982), Population censuses (URT, 1978 and 1988), Odgaard (1987, 1994), Odgaard and Maganga (1994).

[223] Lema (1993), Mamdani (1996), Ranger and Hobsbawn (1983), Ranger (1993), Chanock (1998), to mention a few.

the right to access to land in their paternal home area and to inherit such land from their fathers. Some of the women stressed, however, that they only have such rights in principle because in practice it can be very difficult to exercise such rights.

However, apart from most of the old men among the interviewees, a large number of the men, especially women's brothers, claimed that women in their own right have no rights whatsoever to land in their natal home area. According to these men, women's rights to land are as follows: they have the right to use their husband's land and only if a woman gets into trouble – for example, in case of divorce or if she is widowed and her children or her deceased husband's family do not allow her to stay in the husband's home area – can she be allowed to borrow a piece of land from her father or a brother. However, according to these men, land assigned to her in such cases cannot be considered her property and her children are not entitled to inherit it.

The version given by the women was, however, confirmed by most of the elderly men – those belonging to the generation of fathers of the interviewed women. As it appears, these views do not reflect a conflict between men on the one side and women on the other but rather conflicts between a specific group of women sided by their fathers and specific groups of men, especially women's brothers.

A number of questions arise from the different accounts given by the interviewees: Why did the different groups have different perceptions about their rights? Why did many fathers support their daughters' views and especially brothers oppose them? What type of changes over time, if any, could explain this controversy?

To pursue some answers to these questions, in-depth interviews were conducted with a large number of villagers (men and women) of different ages and socio-economic groups and with village authorities (formal and traditional leaders), councils of elders, and so on.[224] In addition, historical records and archival sources from the areas, as well as literature and field data collected during previous fieldwork periods[225] were consulted. This revealed that a substantial number of women in the two areas have been assigned or have inherited land in their natal home area

---

[224] Village leaders are often from the same circles as the councils of elders, referred to by villagers as very important in relation to the interpretation of customary rules and norms and in conflict resolution. It appears from information collected by Boesen, Maganga and Odgaard in Iringa and Mbarali districts that a large majority of villagers, including women, prefer to solve conflicts at the local level and by involving local conflict resolution councils (in Swahili *Baraza la wazee*) and village leaders at the level closest to the arena of the conflict instead of taking their cases to court.

[225] Rie Odgaard previously carried out field work in Mbarali district during the period 1985–1994.

(Odgaard, 1999) and they claim to have effective command over the land and the benefits derived from it, even though this may be shared with a husband and or other family members.

4   Rights to property – especially landed property

As in most other African countries there is legal pluralism in Tanzania, implying that rights to landed property are regulated by both customary and modern laws.[226] This is also reflected in the two new Land Acts passed by parliament in May 1999 and in the new land policy.[227] In addition there is legal pluralism in the sense that the formal, general and customary laws interact with local norms and practices, the so-called living law.

However, as mentioned, most rural people in Tanzania hold land (and property in general) in accordance with what may be termed customary rules and norms, so we focus on these and changes within them over time. But as stressed above, the larger framework which such rules and norms are part of cannot be left out. The various normative orders existing in Tanzania impinge upon each other and have done so throughout history. In the analysis below, therefore, the interface between customary rules and norms and formal legislation,[228] national policies and international conventions is reflected.

During the whole law reform process, many parties in Tanzania argued that the new Land Acts were not gender sensitive and they regarded this as a serious problem for women, especially those whose land rights had generally been negatively affected by previous developments.[229]

However, in the Village Land Act part II (URT, 1999), one of the general principles of the land policy is spelled out as follows:

> 'The right of every woman to acquire, hold, use and deal with land shall to the same extent and subject to the same restriction be treated as the right of any man' (URT, 1999: 26).

---

[226] United Republic of Tanzania (URT) (1983 and 1994), Fimbo (1992), James and Fimbo (1973). We should stress here that we are not dealing with rules and norms derived from religious laws, for example Islamic law which plays an important role in some parts of Tanzania and in many other African countries. Although there are many Muslims among the Hehe and Sangu in the area, Islamic law does not seem to have had much impact on the rules and norms regulating access to property for these two peoples.

[227] For further elaboration see later and the Land Act and Village Land Act 1999

[228] Some scholars, for example, Ben Cousins (1997), distinguish between informal and formal institutions.

[229] See for example Mbilinyi (1991), Koda (1998), Swantz (1998) or Odgaard (1997).

This gender equality principle is further reflected in provisions relating to land applications, for example (URT, 1999: 107), and in assignment of customary rights by villagers (URT, 1999: 141).[230]

In the Village Land Act, part IV: Village lands, section A, Management and administration, law applicable to customary right of occupancy, the following provision exists:

'(2) Any rule of customary law and any decision taken in respect of land held under customary tenure, whether in respect of land held individually or communally, shall have regard to the customs, traditions, and practices of the community concerned to the extent that they are in accordance with fundamental principles of the national land policy and of any other written law and subject to the foregoing provisions of this subsection, that the rule of customary law or any such decision in respect of land held under customary tenure shall be void and inoperative and shall not be given effect to by any village council or village assembly of any person or body of persons exercising any authority over village land or in respect of any court or other body, to the extent to which it denies women, children or persons with disability lawful access to ownership, occupation or use of any such land' (URT, 1999: 95–96).

Although it is not easy to extract the message from the quotation above, in our interpretation it provides significant support for the safeguarding of the customary rights which men and women are exercising and or are entitled to. At the same time it says that if women are discriminated against under customary laws, such laws are not to be applied.

In accordance with current policies and legislation people in Tanzania can also access land through purchase and through allocation by the village authorities. The involvement of local authorities in land allocation has always been an integral part of both the Hehe and Sangu so-called traditional land distribution system. In the colonial period, during which the Hehe and Sangu lived largely in fairly small and scattered settlements, chiefs and headmen were still in charge of land distribution for the African population living in the areas under the jurisdiction of so-called native authorities. Native authorities were of course subordinated to the colonial government and their colonial land policies and land legislation. The present role of village authorities in land allocation in Tanzania is greatly influenced by policies introduced during the socialist era,[231] especially the *ujamaa* villagization policies and land poli-

---

[230] For a clear and brief overview of specific provisions protecting women's land rights in the 1999 Land Acts see Wily (2003: 47-48).

[231] See later and URT (1983), Fimbo (1992), James and Fimbo (1973), URT (1994).

cies. During and after colonial times the Hehe and Sangu gradually became more settled in village communities.[232]

In the new Village Land Act, village authorities are still assigned a crucial role in land allocation.[233] Like men, women are entitled in principle[234] to be allocated land from the village government if they ask for it, but both male and female respondents generally confirmed that it is difficult for women, especially if married, to apply for land, unless the husband gives his consent. Generally, the way women's land rights are perceived in many circles in present day Tanzania is heavily influenced by paternalistic ideologies. Such ideologies have developed over time in Tanzania with the result that gender differences in relation to the regulation of rights and obligations for men and women have developed into gender imbalances with women often at the losing end.[235] However, gender biased ideologies are opposed in Tanzania and the scramble for women's rights to landed property in Iringa and Mbarali districts is one example of this.

In spite of many experiences revealing that village authorities do not desist from or are not immune to dubious transactions in relation to land – including some of our own from the study of the two districts (Boesen, Maganga and Odgaard, work in progress) – many observers agree that the village government is generally a democratic and sound institution. The village chairperson is democratically elected from among the villagers. The village government is composed of a number of committees whose members are also elected from among the villagers. There are various conflict resolution mechanisms at the local level and at public meetings villagers are involved in discussing rules or by-laws and sanctions against rule breakers (both in principle and to some extent in practice). The village authorities are therefore seen by many observers as best suited at present to safeguard rural people's rights to land and other natural resources.[236]

Contrary to what has often been thought, landed property has for a long time and is increasingly changing hands across family and clan divisions, and a land market, albeit different from the commercialized and liberalized ones developing at present in Tanzania and other African countries, has existed for a long time.[237] In principle women, like men,

---

[232] The next section deals with changes in settlement pattern and land distribution in the Hehe and Sangu societies.

[233] The Village Land Act 1999.

[234] Now confirmed in the new land legislation. See also Wily (2003).

[235] Mbilinyi (1991), Shivji (1997), Koda (1998), Swantz (1998), Odgaard (1986, 1997 and 2002), Falk Moore (1999), to mention a few documenting this.

[236] See for example URT/NAI (1994), Wily (1995).

[237] See for example Iliffe (1979), Maliyamkono and Bagachwa (1990), Bryceson (1993), Falk Moore (1999), Odgaard (1987 and 2002).

can buy land but according to information obtained in the area very few women in the two districts seem to have been able to do that.

Although most rural people in Iringa and Mbarali districts, as mentioned, hold landed property according to customary rules, all other forms of tenure identified above are also found in the area. There has always been – and still is – a dynamic interplay between the various types of rules regulating land acquisition and ownership. The way this interplay is articulated in practice is influenced by the large increase in the area's population, largely due to immigrants from other parts of Tanzania who have different customary rules and norms. But customary rules and norms are also influenced by the policies and legislation introduced in colonial and post-colonial times, as well as by Tanzania's position in the international community. This complex interplay has given rise to new norms that may be seen as reflecting local law.

Changes over time in Hehe and Sangu women's rights to property
Interviews as well as written sources show that land for cultivation has played different roles at different times in history in the two districts under study. The historical sources and information from elders interviewed seem to agree on at least the following points in relation to the pre-colonial situation in the areas:

- Land did not have any value as such, because there was plenty of it and more than enough to satisfy the needs of the people;
- Land did not constitute individual property and land users were not attached to any specific pieces of land;
- The role of livestock keeping was as important, if not more important, than cultivation for the livelihoods of the Hehe and Sangu peoples;
- In both communities major cultivation activities were undertaken by women.

One of the problems of tracing the history of the customary rules of the Hehe and Sangu societies is that the written sources we have, with only a few exceptions,[238] are produced by explorers and colonial officers. Thus it is their interpretation of the oral information they received from local people – mainly elderly people from the chiefly families with whom Europeans generally interacted – which is available in writing. So to rely on either written sources or interviews alone is problematic. To obtain a fair picture of the situation we have combined these sources of information with existing literature.

---

[238] Among the few exceptions are the writings by Alison Redmeyne. Her unpublished DPhil thesis 'The Wahehe people of Tanganyika' from 1964 (Oxford) seems to be one of the most coherent analyses of the Hehe community but unfortunately it has not been possible for us to access this work.

It is in the writings of Richard Francis Burton who travelled through the area in 1857 that we found the first mention of a people referred to as Hehe. Burton mentions that they 'have large flocks and herds' (Burton, 1860: 240). This is confirmed by Joseph Thomson (1881) who travelled through what was referred to by these explorers as Uhehe in 1879. According to Thomson, the Hehe 'depend to a great extent upon their cattle'. (Thomson, 1881: Vol. I, 122). He refers to very large grazing areas and plenty of cattle, and emphasizes that:

> 'As a purely pastoral race they depend almost entirely on their cattle
> for food, ...'. (Thomson, 1881: Vol. I, 215)

According to some of these observers there have been severe reductions in the herds of the Hehe due to rinderpest and other diseases, warfare and so on, at various points in history (Fülleborn, 1906). This implies that the extent to which the Hehe have, in practice, based their livelihoods on livestock keeping, has varied over time. The establishment of the German colonial authorities around the turn of the century led to a gradual change in the importance of livestock keeping and cultivation respectively.

The historical sources confirm that cultivation took place in the pre-colonial Hehe community but it seems to have been of minor importance. Thomson observes in Uhehe that:

> 'Very little ground is cultivated, producing two species of millet and
> Indian corn, and here and there sweet potatoes' (Thomson, 1881: Vol.
> I, 122).

He also mentions that there was little grain to be found in Uhehe and that cultivation is reduced to only 'small garden-like plots from which a poor crop of melons and *ulezi*[239] is raised' (Thomson, 1881: Vol. I, 215). According to Thomson, cultivation was almost exclusively done by the women. He mentions that 'the men never condescend to work in the field' (Thomson, 1881: Vol. I, 235). This is confirmed by Nigmann (1908: 59) and, as will emerge later, this is important in relation to the question of what constituted property at various times in history. The sources are not clear as to the role of women in relation to livestock but it appears from a later source (Brown and Hutt, 1935) that even though women were owners of cattle – albeit much fewer cattle than men – the responsibility for the care of cattle exclusively rested with the men or boys.

It also appears clearly in the historical accounts of the Sangu that they based their livelihood largely on livestock. Burton refers to them as a semi-pastoral tribe (1860: Vol. 2, 272). Bagshawe *et al.* (1929) talks about the Sangu as mainly cattle owners, rich in cattle and not enthusi-

---

[239] Swahili word for millet.

astic about agriculture. Moffett sees the Sangu as primarily pastoralists (1958, 240).

From some historical sources it appears that agricultural production has been of some importance, although most sources refer to the Sangu as being rich in cattle. Thus Elton (1879) talks about irrigated gardens and Heese (1913) gives a detailed description of the gender division of labour in relation to the cultivation activities from which it appears that the women were the major producers of agricultural products.

Considering that the Hehe and Sangu peoples are mainly seen as pastoralists, it is not surprising that land as a natural resource is not specifically dealt with in the early accounts of rules in relation to the regulation of property for men and women respectively. The most important type of property was then livestock.

Nigmann's description of Hehe inheritance rules is the earliest account concerning access to material resources that we have been able to identify (1908: 62-63). Land is not mentioned at all and property is mainly considered in terms of livestock. According to Nigmann, women had the right to inherit livestock in their own right from their fathers as well as from their brothers and sisters. This is also confirmed in later sources (Brown and Hutt, 1935).

The legal customs of the Hehe are also described in various files in the Tanzania National Archives and the following is based on secretariat files numbers 7794 and 7794/3, 1925. In spite of the file from 1925 containing a detailed description of Hehe legal customs, it is interesting to note that there is no specific mention of land as property. Land is only talked about as the territory held by the chief for the benefit of his people.[240] Apart from livestock, property is talked about in general terms and only such property as farm implements – axes and especially hoes which were valued and were an important means of payment in relation to fines and bride-wealth (TNA, 1925: 18).

Agricultural produce is also defined as property belonging to the persons producing it – and highly valued. This is indicated by theft from fields being considered a grave offence and, for example, the punishment given for stealing one basket of fruit could be a fine of anything from 2–3 goats up to a head of cattle (TNA, 1925: 12). This is interesting in the light of women being the major producers of crops and of the highly valued locally brewed beer produced from some of these crops.

The inheritance rules are described as follows in the file:

'The eldest grown-up son always inherits the major portion. However, by law a minimum share was always provided for for all other

---

[240] This is a simplification in relation to the Hehe as it was actually the headman who was responsible for land distribution. See for example Brown and Hutt (1935).

full, step and adopted children and full brothers and sisters of the deceased. All male ... heirs always received larger shares than the others.
All female and minor heirs received less. ... In the event of there being
no children, the legacy passes to the deceased's own brothers and sisters and grandchildren ...' (TNA, 1925: 20-21).

It is emphasized in the file that the reason why the eldest son should
receive the major share is that he has the obligation to take over the main
responsibility of caring for the old, the sick and young children. Thus it
appears that emphasis is on succession and not on individual exclusive
rights to inherit property.[241]

Specific rules related to disinheritance are also contained in the file:

'Disinheritance: ... was the result of any unfilial action as, for example, maltreatment of one's parents, failing to make provisions for them
and similar cases... Partial disinheritance very often happened i.e. the
person entitled to receive the chief share of the legacy was passed
over to ... a younger person' (TNA, 1925: 20).

There were, however, other ways than through inheritance for Hehe
women to acquire property (Brown, 1932). According to Brown, Hehe
mothers were given one third of the bride-wealth (*mafungu*) paid for
their daughters and the fathers kept two thirds. Brown mentions that:

'The mother keeps her share of the money, and the stock (cattle, sheep
and goats) she puts in the charge of her husband or brother, more often
than not the latter' (Brown, 1932: 147).

Thus, like a man, a woman could acquire property both through inheritance from her father, mother, sisters and brothers, and through the bride-
wealth paid for her daughters.

The question about land rights is dealt with more directly in later
accounts of Hehe customs but they are described in a general way. It
appears clearly that access to sufficient land was not seen as a problem
until much later in history.

The way the land allocation system worked was, according to the
author of the notes in the file, satisfactory as long as there were no permanent improvements made to the land. The author foresees though that
if such improvements were made, which was clearly the policy of the
colonial authorities, it would necessitate making new rules.

As we understand it, the developments since then reflect that the
rules have been made and written down to respond to a different concept
of land as property from the previous one.[242] But before continuing with

---

[241] For a distinction between the concepts 'inheritance' and 'succession' see Ncube
and Stewart (1995).
[242] This is reflected in a number of works on land laws, land tenure and land policy in
Tanzania, among others, James (1971), James and Fimbo (1973) and Fimbo (1992).

this discussion we will look into the records about the Sangu.

From one of the oldest published sources about the Sangu (Heese, 1913), it appears that women were able to hold property in their own right and acquire additional property either by working for others or by selling produce from the fields they were cultivating (Heese, 1913: 137). Heese emphasizes that man and wife manage their property independently of each other. According to Heese, a woman's inherited property would go back to her relatives, while property she herself had acquired would be inherited only by her children. Husband and wife did not have any joint property – both of them having property only jointly with their own consanguineous relatives.

It also appears from Heese (1913) that daughters usually, like sons, got their share of their fathers' property on his death. A woman also had the right to receive a piece of land from her husband on marriage. Mumford also stresses that Sangu women, like Hehe women, hold property of all and any kind in their own right and take their share in the inheritance of their father's property (Mumford, 1934: 207).

Concerning Sangu women's land rights there are no more details in the archival sources. But during interviews in 1991[243] Rie Odgaard obtained more information on that. While confirming the details described by the authors referred to above, elderly men and women added the following further details:

> Both sons and daughters inherit property from their fathers. If a man dies his wives will continue to cultivate the fields they have been given at marriage. The children – both girls and boys – will inherit the rest. If a girl gets married and the couple settle in the home village of the girl, her husband may be able to use her land together with her but would never be able to access her land on his own. She, however, can continue to cultivate it and keep it. If she is divorced and not living in her paternal village, she can return home and cultivate her land again. Daughters also inherit livestock. Thus a woman can be in possession of livestock when she gets married and her livestock remains her property.

When interviewing a group of elderly men in 1996, almost all of them argued that there were now some changes in relation to the question of women's rights to land. They said that there is now a tendency for younger men to try to monopolize land. According to the men, this is the reason why many fathers now distribute land to all their children while they are still alive to make sure that daughters get their share.

---

[243] Field notes recorded by Odgaard, 1991.

The relevance of the past to the present situation in the Hehe and Sangu societies

Discussing historical interpretations of customary rules raises the question of their current relevance. This seems clear: the women, some of the young and middle-aged men and most elderly men interviewed in Iringa and Mbarali districts still adhere to similar interpretations with the important difference, however, that land is now included in the definition of what constitutes property. But while fathers and daughters look at land as forming part of a father's property to be inherited by all his heirs, sons and brothers look at land as a special type of property to be passed on to only the male line. This shows the flexibility in the interpretation of customary rules under changing circumstances but, as will emerge below, flexibility can be manipulated in such a way that the relation between rights and obligations in customary law can be subject to different interpretations.

Changes in the socio-economic circumstances in Tanzania are well documented. From being a plentiful resource, land has become relatively scarce and access to it is crucial for the next generations. The causes behind this development are also well documented but it is not possible to deal with this in detail here so we shall confine ourselves to a few points.

There has been a continuous and increasing emphasis on cultivation activities in the areas concerned which started early in the colonial era. It was in the interests of the colonial powers to make productive use of the land and large areas were alienated and given to private companies, used for government purposes, made into conservation areas, forest reserves and national parks, and given to settlers.[244] Post-colonial government policies also emphasized agricultural production and many African farmers throughout the ages have invested in new crops and improved technologies, and accumulated large landholdings.[245]

Since colonial times, local people have become more involved in agriculture in order to produce a surplus to pay taxes and school fees, for example. Concurrently there has been a massive increase in population in the areas in question: due both to natural increases among the Sangu and Hehe themselves and to the large numbers of immigrants who, due to land shortages in other areas, have found their way to various parts of the Ruaha river basin, including the villages in which data were collected.[246] There is now increased competition for land, both for cultiva-

---

[244] See for example Bagshawe *et al.* (1929), James (1971), James and Fimbo (1973) and Mbilinyi (1991).

[245] See for example Raikes (1986), Odgaard (1986 and 1997), Bryceson (1993), Spear (1996).

[246] This appears clearly from the population censuses from 1978 and 1988.

tion and for pastures and therefore, naturally enough, increased focus on land rights.

The above-mentioned developments combined with increased influences of paternalistic and male-dominated ideologies, and changes in norms and values have meant that women now, more often than previously, find themselves in situations where they need to make use of their rights to claim land and property from their own clan. Many are divorced or are single mothers, either by choice (Odgaard, 1997) or because they do not have contact with the fathers of their children. Many men in the case study area complained that their sisters were increasingly coming home and trying to gain access to the land in their natal villages. In the opinion of many of the men, sisters or daughters can only be granted rights to use part of a brother or father's land – they are not entitled to acquire it as their property.

Furthermore, increased pressure on land means that there are cases where widows, instead of being allowed to continue cultivating in their husband's village, are driven away so they have to go back to their natal villages. Manipulation and reinterpretation of customary rules on the basis of male-dominated ideologies are confirmed by the interpretation of these rules adopted by many brothers in the study areas. While arguing that their sisters do not have land endowments in their natal village, at the same time they claim that wives are only allowed to use their husband's land during the course of marriage. In case of divorce or widowhood the women will, according to them, have to return to their own natal family or village.

The obvious contradiction here illustrates that these men, in order to protect their own interests and while still referring to customary rules, try to eliminate the connection between rights and obligations which is embedded in customary rules. According to customary rules and norms, the execution of a right cannot be seen independently from the fulfilment of obligations. The fact that the eldest son is entitled to larger shares of a father's estate than younger sons and daughters is, for example, related to his primary responsibility to take care of the old, the sick and other family members in trouble.[247] Sons or brothers' interpretations also reflect that, like their sisters and fathers, they reinterpret customary rules in accordance with changing circumstances (increasing land pressure) with the important difference, however, that fundamental guiding principles of customary rules are not adhered to.

The men taking the position referred to above see land as a part of property but, unlike the other group of men and the women, they distinguish land as special and distinct from other property, and stress that a

---

[247] See also section later dealing with disinheritance.

father's landed property can only be inherited through the male line. Moreover, instead of being concerned with succession, like the fathers who emphasize the connection between rights and obligations (also reflected in customary rules), the sons emphasize their exclusive right (in the modern sense of the word) to inherit property.

The following two examples show that not all the women who claim their rights are successful:

Example 1

An old Hehe woman in one of the fieldwork villages was asked about her rights to land. She responded without hesitating that a Hehe woman has the right to inherit land from her father. She explained that she lived in her husband's village but she had land in her natal home area which was being used by her brothers. She said that she could claim the land as her property if she needed to return to her home area, either because of divorce or widowhood. Under a tree not far from the place where we were talking (the old lady and Rie Odgaard) there was a group of young and middle-aged men sitting chatting. When they heard what the woman was explaining they interfered quite aggressively and corrected the old woman. According to them, Hehe women have no rights to land as property but are only entitled to be assigned a piece of land by their brothers as a help in case they are divorced, widowed, and so on. After a long patronizing lecture the woman retracted her original explanation.

Example 2

Another example is about a divorced woman who after her divorce had returned to her natal village and claimed her share of the land inherited from her father. However, one of her brothers (the youngest) refused to let her have her share. The other brothers who were very old and, as she put it, very weak, had not been able to convince the younger brother that she was entitled to her share and had not been able to insist that she got it either. The brother who was against giving the sister her share was said to be continuously harassing her and on one occasion he had attacked her with a panga (a big knife used for cultivation purposes) – and she showed a scar on her forehead.

One of the older brothers was present during the interview[248] and agreed with the sister that she had the right to inherit even though, as he said, this left less land for the brothers. For him this had actually been a

---

[248] Interview undertaken by Rie Odgaard.

problem since he had three wives, each of whom had a right to be assigned a piece of land to use as long as the marriage lasts. The land he had inherited from his father was not enough for that and he had then acquired land from the village government for the third wife. Until this time the divorced sister had not been given her share, even though they had tried to involve some of the village leaders. She had been able to mobilize some money in various ways and had bought a small piece of land from other relatives in the village. But she maintained that her right to her father's land had been violated and that a woman only had land rights (in her own right) in her paternal village and not in her husband's home area where she only has usufruct rights as long as the marriage lasts.

In spite of such examples and the fact that it is hard to deny that more sons than daughters manage in practice to get their share of fathers' land in both Iringa and Mbarali districts and in most other places in Tanzania,[249] our research uncovered numerous examples of daughters who had inherited land from their fathers in the two districts.

It appeared during interviews with both women and elderly male respondents, including elderly members of village governments and councils of elders, that fathers actively support their daughters' land claims if they are brought forward. This shows that the interpretation of the rules by brothers is in many cases challenged by the women and the fathers.

The information obtained in the area also highlights that the tendency for women to inherit land in their natal villages is increasing. This is no doubt related to changes in fathers' practices in relation to distribution of land among their children. Many fathers also said that nowadays they wanted to divide their land between all the children before their death to avoid conflicts from arising between them, and a number of them had already done so.

But why are fathers so keen on the issue? When asked directly, they argued that daughters are generally more caring towards their parents than sons, many of whom, due to education and or employment, live away from their home areas. Daughters are increasingly taking on the obligations of caring for the parents during sickness and old age. So the rights should go with the obligations, regardless of sex.

When the issue of sizes of shares of fathers' property sons and daughters, respectively, were entitled to was discussed, the answers varied a lot, even among respondents who recognized the women's rights of in-

---

[249] URT/NAI, 1994; *Change* Vol. 5, first quarter 1997; Koda (1998); Maganga (work in progress); Odgaard (2002).

heritance. A substantial number of both female and male respondents said that sons and daughters get equal shares.

Going back to the historical accounts, it appears here that in general male heirs were entitled to the largest shares, and especially the eldest son. However, it also appears from the accounts that the right to inherit was tied to obligations to care for parents, young children and sick members of the family. Many respondents argued, however, that today some people (especially men) can get away with acquiring the largest shares of a father's property without living up to obligations, thus giving rise to many conflicts.

In practice, a father's strategy when distributing his wealth among his children reflects his concern for ensured support during old age. As daughters have proved to be important in relation to this, fathers want to make sure that the daughters have a livelihood. Fathers, therefore, indirectly make use of rules of disinheritance for those children who would otherwise be entitled to the largest shares. They are concerned with the question of succession and if sons are unlikely to fulfil the responsibilities accompanying rights to property, and daughters are, they devise a strategy accordingly.

Again, we see the flexibility of customary rules to adapt to changing circumstances. And as the changing circumstances in a country like Tanzania have not resulted in the creation of a welfare system where the needs of the old, the sick and those unable to work are taken care of by the state, it is vital that the fundamental principle of a direct connection between rights and obligations in customary rules is adhered to.[250]

The present development policies, however, which promote liberalization and privatization and which, to a large extent, are imposed on Tanzania from outside, facilitate a process in which it becomes possible for strong enterprising individuals to pursue private interests and to dismiss fundamental principles of mutual responsibilities. Hence many conflicts arise between various groups of people when they fight to gain access to or to keep rights to resources.

---

[250] In comparison it can be noted that in the Nordic countries children have no duty to support their parents during old age. That children sometimes take care of their elderly parents cannot form the basis for a legal presumption in this respect with preclusion of social welfare entitlements. But nevertheless that is what some authorities do with regard to home help service (Ketscher, 1993). However, immigration authorities do not show much understanding when immigrants want their old father or mother to be allowed to stay with them.

5 Forum for conflict resolution

As is evident from Wily (2003), there are formal as well as more informal (although formally recognized) conflict resolution mechanisms at all levels of society in Tanzania – from state level down to village level.

In practice, however, a lot of conflicts are solved at levels lower than village level. The data clearly show that the preferred forum for resolution of disputes and conflicts related to land is the one as close to the 'arena' of the conflict as possible – that is first and foremost the family level – but very often with the help of clan leaders, sub-village chairpersons or members of the council of elders at the sub-village level. In cases where no solution is found in these forums a case may be taken to the village government and involve the village chairman, the village land committee and or the council of elders at the village level.

When asked directly about the preferred forum for resolution of conflicts, almost all female respondents in the areas in question as well as most male respondents answered that they preferred the lowest possible level. When reasons for this were discussed, reference was made to a number of factors: fear of damaging family ties and losing social networks; fear of not being well understood outside the village; lack of confidence in the higher levels (they made reference to corruption); fear that people from outside, due to lack of knowledge about the local conditions, norms and customs, would not understand all the details of the case; fear that norms, rules and laws with which the parties were unfamiliar might be used against them; and fear that the formal court setting would make them too shy and nervous. Finally, but no less importantly, people referred to the costs incurred by taking a case above the village level. For the majority of interviewees the costs were prohibitive in terms of: the money required – for transport, lawyers, meals and possibly accommodation, and so on; and the time required – time on a case outside the village would mean time away from responsibilities like child care and productive activities at home.

During the years when the data were collected we learned about only two cases where women in the field study area had taken cases to any level above the village level. One case was between a widow and her late husband's son. The son (who was not the biological son of the woman) claimed all the father's property after his death on the grounds that he was the only child of the family and that his father's wife, according to customary laws, was not entitled to inherit any property from her husband. This was disputed by the woman who insisted, among other

---

[251] This case has been described in Odgaard and Bentzon (2002).

things, that she personally had been allocated a large piece of land by the village authorities which she was cultivating, and that she had also contributed to the construction of a modern house and other properties acquired by the couple during the marriage. The case was resolved at the district level and the property divided between the two.[251]

The second case was a conflict related to a divorce where the husband claimed all the land and houses belonging to the family. It was solved at the ward tribunal and a compromise was arrived at: the wife was assigned part of the land and one of the two houses in the possession of the family. It should be mentioned here that both of these women belonged to more well-to-do rural households, and that the woman who took the case all the way to the district court was also well-educated.

It is interesting to note that while many women activists, including some in Tanzania, regard customary rules and norms as discriminating against women and call for formal legislation to abolish them, the only way most women can access land, at least in the areas where we have worked, are through customary rules and norms. As shown, there are areas where it is not uncommon that women exercise such land rights in their own right. Our data also showed that women are most confident of having their land rights administered and protected or defended and land conflicts resolved through local settings and in accordance with existing local rules and norms.

Fortunately, customary rules and norms, as mentioned, are not abolished in the new Land Acts in Tanzania and land administration and conflict resolution is still anchored at the local level. The important aspect of the new Land Acts for rural women in Tanzania is the provision that if certain parts of customary law discriminate against women, it is illegal to use them. However, not much is known about the new Land Acts in the villages where fieldwork was carried out nor in many other villages in Tanzania.[252] While it would be helpful for rural women to be more aware of the specific provisions against discrimination of women's land rights in the new Land Acts,[253] we are convinced that they stand a better chance of improving their land rights through a pragmatic, everyday approach within the changing local customary context where they live, rather than by trying to understand the formal land legislation and

---

[252] In recent years Rie Odgaard has carried out studies in several other parts of Tanzania.

[253] Based on recent information obtained by Rie Odgaard in northern Tanzania some non-governmental organizations are trying to provide information for rural people about the new Land Acts. However, this information has focused on inheritance rights to land of formally married women, that is the more modern part of the laws. As most women in the rural areas have customary marriages it would seem more relevant to inform them of rights particularly related to that situation, namely, for example, the provisions against discrimination of women in customary laws.

pushing for its implementation – a situation which is unlikely to occur anyway in the foreseeable future.

There are analyses from other parts of Tanzania which arrive at a similar conclusion. Englert (2003), for example, concludes on the basis of a case study from the Uluguru mountains in Morogoro region:

'In the light of the slow progress of implementation of the new land rights legislation in general and the difficulties to enforce it, women might be better advised to change their situation by exploiting the flexible and changing nature of customary systems than to lobby the government to do so. To have pro-women legislation is of no use when women are not conscious about their legal rights or lack the means to enforce them' (Englert, 2003:9).

6 Final remarks

The extent to which women are able to exercise customary land rights in their own right in patrilineal communities in Tanzania in general is difficult to assess and more research is needed to establish this but, as discussed, it is not uncommon in Iringa and Mbarali districts. That there may be more cases in Tanzania is indicated by the number of male and female interviewees belonging to the patrilineal Bena ethnic group in neighbouring Njombe and living as immigrants in Iringa and Mbarali who argue that the Bena have similar rules and norms to those of the Sangu and the Hehe. A few Bena women living in Iringa district who have inherited land from their fathers were identified during the fieldwork. Historical material also supports the view that Bena women have land rights similar to those of the Hehe and Sangu women.[254]

Recent literature from a number of patrilineal communities in other African countries also shows that in practice women exercise some fundamental rights to property (including land). Thus Rocheleau and Edmunds comment that:

'Ugandan national legislation, upheld by local communities, has defended the rights of widows against the land inheritance claims of their sons in many communities. In a more locally-based initiative, fathers in one community in Machakos district, Kenya, have begun to allocate land to single daughters who have had children, in a break with long-standing local practice ... This change has been sanctioned, even encouraged, by local elders in an effort to make place in the world for women and children who have been rendered "homeless" and "illegitimate" in terms of their own culture' (Rocheleau and Edmunds, 1997: 1355).

---

[254] See for example Mumford (1934) and Culwick and Culwick (1934).

Another example is analyzed by Jacinta K. Muteshi (1997) who shows that Kipsigi women in Kenya have established claims to cattle. A study by Fiona Mackenzie (1989) shows that processes set in motion through the intersection of a traditional land tenure system (*n'gundu*) and efforts to establish a system of freehold individual land tenure in Muranga district in Kenya has created an area within which women (and men) are able to contest rights to land.

As demonstrated in the empirical data from Tanzania, conflicts frequently occur between brothers and sisters about the right to inherit land or about a woman's right to an allotment of her father's land when returning to her own family after the dissolution of her marriage. On this basis (and on other data) we conclude that there is no agreement as to the legal regulation of women's access to and ownership of land and other kinds of property. The question is whether it can be considered a development of new customs and whether there is consensus between lawyers and in conflict-handling forums – formal as well as informal – with respect to women's rights in this area.

The data cannot establish the extent of valid rules with respect to women's land rights but we gain an insight into the dynamics through which norms adjust to new social conditions. In Sally Falk Moore's terms – by the processes of regularization and of situational adjustment (Falk Moore, 1978: 48f) – actors in the related conflicts are fathers, sons and daughters. All three parties support their claim with reference to existing norms but of different content. In our data there are no clear arguments referring to the legislation but that does not necessarily imply that it has no effect in individual cases or on the general sense of equity.

The fathers' arguments are interesting. They refer to norms but also to situational circumstances. They do not deny the rights of the sons but there are duties that go with these rights – duties to take care of the needs of close relatives. If these duties are neglected, the norms allow for disinheritance and the situation on the ground may point to those who deserve to inherit. When in the actual situation the daughter not the son takes care of the relatives, she should have her part of the land. In this way the fathers refer to situations where it is practical and sensible to modify the traditional prescripts. The findings in Odgaard's data have a certain general spread but without data from formal legal forums it is uncertain whether the formal court system will support the fathers or the sons' view on law and justice.

In WLSA's study on inheritance laws, customs and practice, there are findings of a similar development (WLSA Lesotho, 1994). In the formal court system sons seem to elicit greater attention to their arguments. Lawyers' customary law does not always take into account changes in norms and customs but the picture of inheritance rules and norms is far from unambiguous. This means that conflicts, regardless of the forums where they are treated, will be subject to negotiations and the power relations between the parties will be crucial. But regrettably parties involved in conflicts do not always have equal strength and, as mentioned, many women are typically in a weaker position than men in terms of access to power. But in relation to the type of conflicts dealt with here – namely conflicts within the family concerning the rights of individuals to resources and the obligations tied to such rights – the claims of the female party may under certain circumstances, like the ones we have described, be supported by male relatives like fathers.

The important message here is that the question as to which of the existing levels of conflict resolution provides the best opportunity for women (and for men) to gain access to justice depends on the nature of the conflict and the context within which it occurs. This and many other studies confirm that men and women prefer to seek the lowest level of conflict resolution when conflicts arise and in relation to land conflicts our empirical findings suggest that women will gain by seeking conflict handling in local forums – that is within the family and or by involving the local authorities. In the small local community the importance of women's efforts in daily life are known and appreciated and the model for conflict handling is forward looking and consequence oriented. At this level there is also a general interest in finding peaceful solutions to conflicts and a means of moving forward.

There are certainly many circumstances that limit women's choice between the various levels of conflict resolution. First of all, for poor rural women the distance to the formal forums and the formalities and procedures adopted by these institutions as well as the necessity to use advocates, compose huge constraints. Secondly, there is also the problem of finding one's way in the jungle of rules and norms, the delays in handling the cases, and the often considerable expenses involved.

In the conventional legal model for conflict handling in the forums within the formal legal system, the judges are interested in the conflict itself: what happened, where to place the conflict within the legal system – and what the sanctions are. The judge is rule oriented and looks backwards.

However, the extensive changes in conditions of life and human relations in the wake of globalization have also influenced the legislation of the nation state and at the same time the role of the judge in the formal court system. The formal legislation must take the form of standards which state objectives and instruct on means by which to reach the objectives. That makes room for interpretation and filling in and for taking changing customs into consideration.

But how can the informal system of norms and rule making and conflict handling be acknowledged by judges in the formal system? It is necessary for judges to understand what is going on in practice in society in order to be able to make decisions within the provided frameworks. The problem is that judges are generally not well informed about this. An interesting exception from this general picture is found in Mozambique where we took part in an evaluation of Danish support to human rights and democratization in 1999. We interviewed two judges from the Supreme Court in the country. They acknowledged that around 80 per cent of the population had access to justice only at the lowest level of conflict resolution which is below the hierarchy of formal courts in Mozambique. The two judges found it problematic that the formal system of justice was almost uninformed about the practices adopted by the population in the resolution of local conflicts. Unfortunately the 1992 reform of the Mozambican system of justice excluded the lowest level of conflict resolution from the formal systems.

Because a breach was created between the formal system and the widespread local practices of conflict resolution, the judges argued for more collaboration between the different levels of conflict resolution. They maintained that research of practices at the lower levels could generate knowledge for the courts which would ensure judges were kept informed about the continuous changes taking place in norms and customs in the different parts of the country. They emphasized the need for collaboration between judges and other scholars – and for the opening up of a dialogue with researchers.

As a step in that direction a team composed of Supreme Court judges, lawyers and social scientists has been involved in a large research project on administration of justice in Mozambique, including the role of traditional legal structures.[255] In order to ensure that research results inform the work of judges, researchers on their part have to be able to communicate their results in such a way that they can be made available for the law administrators and judges, and the necessary funds have to be provided. But until now researchers have not paid enough attention to the issue of their findings reaching potential target groups.

In Tanzania the present land legislation implies collaboration between the formal system of justice and the local systems because it prescribes that customary rules shall be taken into account in the formal courts unless, as mentioned above, such rules are discriminating against women. However, only by systematic and continuous research is it possible to understand how local systems function in practice at any given time. As demonstrated, a lot of this research still needs to be carried out in Tanzania and in communities throughout Africa.

---

[255] For further information about this see for example DANIDA (2000).

Bibliography

Bagshawe F. J., H. Wolfe, C. J. McGregor and M. F. Bell (1929) *Tanganyika territory land development survey first report 1928–1929: Iringa Province*, Crown Agents for the Colonies, London.

Benjaminsen T. A. with C. Lund (eds) (2003) *Securing land rights in Africa*, Frank Cass, London.

Bentzon A. W. (1994) 'Negotiated law', in H. C. Marcussen with C. Lund (eds), *Access, control and management of natural resources in sub-Saharan Africa*, Occasional papers No. 13, International Development Studies, Roskilde University, Rosklilde.

Bentzon A. W. with R. Odgaard (1997) 'Sædvaner og Udvikling', in *Den Ny Verden* 30(4): 5–12.
– (1997) 'Afrikanske sædvaner i historisk perspektiv', in *Den Ny Verden* 30(4): 13–30.

Bentzon A. W. with A. Hellum, J. Stewart, W. Ncube and T. Agersnap (1998) *Pursuing grounded theory in law: South/north experiences in developing women's law*, Tano Aschehoug and Mond Books, Oslo and Harare.

Berry S. (1989) 'Social institutions and access to resources', in *Africa* 59(1): 41–55.
– (1993) *No condition is permanent: The social dynamics of agrarian change in sub-Saharan Africa*, University of Wisconsin Press, Madison.

Boesen J. with F. P. Maganga and R. Odgaard (1999) 'Rules, norms, organizations and actual practices – Land and water management in the Ruaha river basin', in T. Granfelt (ed) *Managing the globalized environment*, Intermediate Technology Publications Ltd, London.
– (work in progress) *Managing natural resources: The role of rules, norms, policies and people's practices in south-western Tanzania* (working title).

Brown G. (1932) 'Bride-wealth among the Hehe', in *Journal of the International Institute of African Languages and Cultures* 5(2): 145-157.

Brown G. with A. M. B. Hutt (1935) *Anthropology in action: An experiment in the Iringa district of the Iringa province, Tanganyika Territory*, Oxford University Press for the International Institute of African Languages and Cultures, Oxford.

Bryceson D. F. (1993) *Liberalizing Tanzania's food trade*, UNRISD, London.

Burton F. (1860) *The lake regions of Central Africa, Vol. I and II*, Longmans, London.

Chanock M. (1998) *Law, custom and social order: The colonial experience in Malawi and Zambia*, Heinemann, Portsmouth.

Cousins B. (1997) 'How do rights become real? – Formal and informal institutions in South Africa's land reform' in *IDS Bulletin* 28(4): 59–68.

Culwick A. T. with G. M. Culwick (1934) 'The functions of bride-wealth in Ubena of the Rivers', in *Africa* 7(2): 140-159.

DANIDA (2000) *Evaluation of Danish support to promotion of human rights and democratization 1990–1998: Mozambique, Vol. 8*, Ministry of Foreign Affairs/ Danida, Copenhagen.

Elton J. F. *(1879) Travels and researches among the lakes and mountains of Eastern and Central Africa*, Frank Cass Publishers, London.

Englert B. (2003) 'From a gender perspective: Notions of land tenure security in the Uluguru mountains, Tanzania', in *Journal für Entwicklungspolitik (Austrian Journal of Development Studies)*, 19(1): 75-90.

Falk Moore S. (1978) *Law as process: An anthropological approach*, Routledge and Kegan Paul, London.
– (1999) 'Changing African land tenure: Reflections on the incapacities of the state', in C. Lund (ed), *Development and rights: Negotiating justice in changing societies*, Frank Cass, London.

Fimbo G. M. (1992) *Essays in land law*, University of Dar es Salaam, Dar es Salaam.

Fülleborn F. (1906) *Das Deutche Njassa und Ruvuma Gebiet, land und leute*, Dietrich Reimer, Berlin.

Heese (1913) *Sitte und Brauch der Sangu*, Archiv für Anthropologie, Neue Folge – Band XII, Braunschweig.

Hellum A. (2000) 'How to improve the doctrinal analysis of legal pluralism', in *Retfærd 89, Nordisk Juridisk Tidsskrift* 23(2): 40–63.

Hydén G. (1983) *No shortcut to progress. African development in perspective*, Heinemann, London.
Iliffe J. (1979) *A modern history of Tanganyika*, African Studies Series 25, Cambridge University Press, Cambridge.

James, R. W. (1971) *Land tenure and policy in Tanzania*, East African Literature Bureau, Dar es Salaam, Nairobi and Kampala.

James R. W. with G. M. Fimbo (1973) *Customary land law of Tanzania: A source book*, East African Literature Bureau, Nairobi.

Kapinga W. B. L. (1997) 'Some reflections on the Presidential Commission Report and the National Land Policy', in *Change* 5(1): 9–17.

Ketscher K. (1993) 'When invisible work becomes visible', in P. Blume with D. Tamm and V. Vindeløv (eds), *Suum cuique*, Jurist- og Økonomforbundets Forlag, Copenhagen.

Kiwasila H. with R. Odgaard (1992) *Socio-cultural aspects of natural forest management in the Udzungwa*, report prepared for Danida, Centre for Development Research, Copenhagen.

Koda B. (1998) 'Changing land tenure systems in the contemporary matrilineal social system: The gendered dimension', in P. Seppälä, with B. Koda (eds) *The making of a periphery*, seminar proceedings No 32, Nordic Africa Institute, Uppsala.

Lastarria-Cornhiel S. (1997) 'Impact of privatization on gender and property rights in Africa', in *World Development* 25(8): 1317–1334.

Leach M. with R. Mearns and I. Scoones (1997) *Environmental entitlements: A framework for understanding the institutional dynamics of environmental change*, IDS Discussion Paper 359, University of Sussex, Brighton.

Lema A. (1993) *Africa divided: The creation of ethnic groups*, Lund dissertations in sociology 6, Lund University Press, Lund.

le Roy E. (1985) 'Local law in black Africa: Contemporary experiences of folk law facing state and capital in Senegal and some other countries', in A. Allot with G. R. Woodman (eds.) P*eople's law and state law*, Bellagio Papers, Dordrecht.

Lund C. (1995) 'Law, power and politics in Niger', PhD dissertation, Roskilde University, Denmark.

Mackenzie F. (1989) 'Land and territory: The interface between two systems of land tenure, Murang'a district, Kenya', in *Africa* 59(1): 91–109.

Maganga F. (Work in progress) 'Resource conflicts and conflict management: Some insights from Iringa and Mbarali districts', in M. Boesen with R. Odgaard, *Managing natural resources*.

Maliyamkono T. L. with M. S. D. Bagachwa (1990) *The second economy in Tanzania*, James Currey, London.

Mamdani M. (1996) *Citizen and subject: Contemporary Africa and the legacy of late colonialism*, Princeton University Press, New Jersey.

Manji A. (1998) 'Gender and the politics of the land tenure reform process in Tanzania', in *Journal of Modern African Studies* 36(4): 645–667.
– (1999) 'The AIDS epidemic and women's land rights in Tanzania', in Recht in *Afrika* 1999/1: 31–49.
– (2000) 'Her name is Kamundage: Rethinking women and property among the Haya of Tanzania', in *Africa* 70(3): 482–500.

Mbilinyi M. (1986) 'Agribusiness and casual labour in Tanzania', in *African Economic History* 16: 107–141.
– (1989) 'Women's resistance in customary marriage: Tanzania's runaway wives', in A. Zegeye with S. Ishemo (eds) *Forced labour and migration patterns of movement within Africa*, Hans Zell Publishers, London.
– (1991) *Big slavery*, Dar es Salaam University Press, Dar es Salaam.
– (1997) 'The land issues', in *Gender Platform* (*Ulingo wa Jinsia*) 2(2):1, 3.

McCall M. K. (1982) *The population pressure on natural resources in Mbeya region and potential solutions*, RIDEP, Mbeya, Tanzania.

Meinzen-Dick R. S. with L. R. Brown, H. S. Feldstein and A. R. Quisumbing (1997) 'Gender, property rights and natural resources', in *World Development* 25(8): 1303–1316.

Moffett J. P. (ed) (1958) *Handbook of Tanganyika*, Government Printer, Dar es Salaam.

Mukangara F. with B. Koda (1997) *Beyond inequalities: Women in Tanzania,* Southern African Research and Documentation Centre, Dar es Salaam.

Mumford W. B. (1934) 'The Hehe, Bena and Sangu peoples of East Africa', in *American Anthropologist* 36(29): 203–222.

Mustafa K. (1997) *Eviction of pastoralists from Mkomazi game reserve in Tanzania: An historical review*, International Institute for Environment and Development, London.

Muteshi J. K. (1997) 'A refusal to argue with inconvenient evidence: Women, proprietorship and Kenyan law', in *Dialectical Anthropology* 23(1): 55–81.

Ncube W. with J. Stewart (eds) (1995) *Widowhood, inheritance laws, customs and practices in Southern Africa*, Women and Law in Southern Africa Research Project (WLSA), Harare.

Nigmann E. (1908) 'Die Wahehe, ihre gesichte, kultur, rechts, kriegs-und jagd', *Gebräuche*, Ernst Siegfried Mittler und Sohn, Berlin.

Nyerere J. (1969) *Socialism in Tanzania*, Nordiska Afrikainstitutet, Uppsala.

Odgaard R. (1986) 'Tea – does it do the peasant women in Rungwe any good?', in J. Boesen with J. Koponen, R. Odgaard and K. J. Havnevik (eds), *Tanzania – Crisis and struggle for survival*, Scandinavian Institute of African Studies, Uppsala.
– (1987) 'De tog til Usangu! – Bondemigration i det sydvestlige Højland', in *Den Ny Verden* 20(3): 69–90.
– (1989) *Hvad får Afrikanske Kvinder ud af Frivillig bistanden?*, Mellemfolkeligt Samvirke, Copenhagen.
– (1991) Field notes, interview with Wasee of Ruiwa, Usangu Plains, 10 October.
– (1994) 'Jordbesidddelsesformer og bæredygtig ressourceudnyttelse – eksemplet Tanzania', in *Den Ny Verden* 27(2): 50–68.
– (1997) 'The gender dimension of Nyakyusa rural-rural migration in Mbeya region', in S. Ngware with R. Odgaard, R. Shayo and F. Wilson (eds), *Gender and agrarian change in Tanzania – with a Kenyan case study*, Dar es Salaam University Press, Dar es Salaam.
– (2002) 'Scrambling for land in Tanzania: Processes of formalization and legitimization of land rights', in *European Journal of Development Research* 14(2): 71–88.

– (work in progress) 'Land above all! Continuity and change in the articulation of land rights in south-western Tanzania', in J. Boesen with F. Maganga and R. Odgaard (eds) *Managing natural resources: The role of rules, norms, policies and people's practices in south-western Tanzania* (working title).
– (2005) 'The struggle for land rights in the context of multiple normative orders in Tanzania', pages 243–264 in S. Ewers, M. Spierenburg and H. Wels (eds) *Competing jurisdictions; Settling land claims in Africa*, Afrika Studiecentrum Series, Brill Publishers, Leiden and Boston.

Odgaard R. with A. Weis Bentzon (1998 and 1999) 'The interplay between collective rights and obligations and individual rights, with examples from Greenland and Africa', in *European Journal of Development Research* 10(2): 105–116. Also printed in C. Lund (ed.) *Development and rights – Negotiating justice in changing societies*, Frank Cass, London.

Odgaard R. with F. P. Maganga (1995) *Local informal land and water management systems in Ruaha river basin*, Centre for Development Research, Copenhagen.

Okello R. (2003) 'Men's property: Why East African women have no land rights', *East African* 3–9 March, available at: http://www.caledonia.org.uk/land/okello.htm.

Raikes P. (1986) 'Eating the carrot and wielding the stick: The agricultural sector in Tanzania', in J. Boesen with K. J. Havnevik, J. Koponen and R. Odgaard (eds), *Tanzania: Crisis and struggle for survival*, Scandinavian Institute of African Studies, Uppsala.
– (1997) 'Traditionelle jordrettigheder – en kolonial konstruktion', in *Den Ny Verden* 30(4): 101–122.

Ranger T. with E. Hobsbawn (eds) (1983) *The invention of tradition*, Cambridge University Press, Cambridge.

Ranger T. (1993) 'The invention of tradition revisited: The case of colonial Africa', in T. Ranger, with O. Vaughan (eds), *Legitimacy and the state in twentieth century Africa*, Macmillan Press, London.

Redmayne A. (1968) 'The Hehe', in A. Roberts (ed.) *Tanzania before 1900*, East African Publishing House, Nairobi.

Rocheleau D. with D. Edmunds (1997) 'Women, men and trees: Gender, power and property in forest and agrarian landscapes', in *World Development* 25(8): 1351–1371.

Rwebangira M. (1996) *The legal status of women and poverty in Tanzania*, Research report No. 100, Nordic Africa Institute, Uppsala.

Shivji I. G. (1997) 'Land: The terrain of democratic struggles', in *Change* (Dar es Salaam) 5(1): 4–8.
– (1997) 'Grounding the debate on land: The National Land Policy and its implications', in *Change* 5(1): 37–47.

– (1997) 'Reflections on the woman question and land: Some debating points', in *Change* 5(1): 64–71.

Shivji I. G. with W. B. L. Kapinga (1997) 'Implications of the Draft Bill for The Land Act', in *Change* 5(1): 48–63.

Smith Oboler R. (1994) 'the house-property complex in African social organization', in *The Journal of the International African Institute* 64:352–358.

Spear T. (1996) 'Struggles for land', in G. H. Maddox, with J. L. Giblin and I. N. Kimambo (eds), *Custodians of the land: Ecology and culture in the history of Tanzania*, James Currey, London.

Sundet G. (1997) 'The politics of land in Tanzania', unpublished PhD dissertation, University of Oxford, Oxford.

Swantz M. L. (1985) *Women in development. A creative role denied?*, St. Martin's Press, New York.

– (1998) 'Notes on research on women and their strategies for sustained livelihood in southern Tanzania', in P. Seppälä, with B. Koda (eds), *The making of a periphery*, The Nordic Africa Institute, Uppsala.

Talle A. (1988) *Women at a loss: Changes in Maasai pastoralism and their effects on gender relations*, University of Stockholm, Stockholm.

Tibaijuka A. with F. Kaijage (1995) 'Land policy in Tanzania: Issues for policy consideration', paper prepared for the National Conference on Land Policy, Ministry of Lands, Housing and Urban Development (January).

Thomson J. (1881) *To the Central African lakes and back*, Vol. I. Sampson Low & Co., London.

Tanzania National Archives (TNA) (1925) Secretariat files nos: 7794 and 7794/3.
– (1938) Accession No. 157, file No. 6/42.

United Republic of Tanzania (URT) (1978) Population Census.
– (1983) *Agricultural policy of Tanzania*, Government printer, Dar es Salaam.
– (1988) *Population census*.
– (1994) *Report of the Presidential Commission of Inquiry into Land Matters. Vol. I: Land policy and land tenure structure*, published in cooperation with the Nordic Africa Institute, Uppsala.

Vuorela U. (1987) *The women's question and the modes of human reproduction: An analysis of a Tanzanian village*, Finnish Society for Development Studies/ Finnish Anthropological Society, Uppsala.

Wily L. (1995) 'The villager and the village in Tanzanian law', unpublished consultancy report, Orgut Consulting, Dar es Salaam.

– (2003) *Community-based land tenure management: Questions and answers about Tanzania's new Village Land Act 1999*, Issue paper No. 120, IIED, London.

Wilson M. (1958) 'The peoples of the Nyassa Tanganyika Corridor', unpublished paper, University of Cape Town, Cape Town.

Women and Law in Southern Africa Zimbabwe (WLSA) (1994) *Inheritance in Zimbabwe law, customs and practices*, WLSA, Harare.

Women and Law in Southern Africa Lesotho (WLSA) (1994) *Who inherits? The case of inheritance in Lesotho*, WLSA Lesotho, Lesotho.

Woodman G. R. (1988) 'How state courts created customary law in Ghana and Nigeria', in B. W. Morse with G. R. Woodman (eds), *Indigenous law and the state*, Foris Publications, Dordrecht.

Website
www.od.org/womenwatch/daw

List of legislation
Tanzania
Land Act 1999

Village Land Act 1999

Regional and international
Beijing Platform for Action 1995

Southern African Development Community (SADC) Gender and Development Declaration 1997

9
Women's work, perceived contribution and access to land in India

Reena Patel

This chapter explores the gender-bias in constructing women's work in society and the very real discrimination which follows. It explores the construction of women's claim to land through analysis of their lived realities as workers and contributors to production and income-generation. Focusing on women's roles and contribution in the case of agriculture, it argues that existing ownership rights of women may be problematized by the existence of gender-biased ideologies and resultant normative practices that undermine the social and cultural legitimacy of women's entitlement to land ownership. Although women in India have a right to inherit, acquire and own property independently, very few women actually own land. Despite numerous legal rights, women's access to land and other forms of property and inheritance are severely constrained by social and cultural attitudes and practices. This has particular significance in a country where the primary occupation of women is agriculture[256] within small, family-owned farms and where land ownership becomes a critical factor in maintaining even subsistence levels of agricultural production and averting a reliance upon wage work as the means of subsistence.

1   Introduction

This chapter explores the ways in which perceptions of women's work shape the social legitimacy of women's land rights in India. Based upon field research conducted among female marginal peasants and landless labourers in three districts of western Orissa during 1996–1997,[257] it draws upon their own analysis of work: the structural and ideological constraints within which their work is perceived and valued (or undervalued). Discussions held with women in Sundargarh and Sambalpur districts on the links between land rights and labour contribution formed an integral part of this research and I rely upon discussant's responses in making this chapter's argument.

---

[256] Over 90 per cent of women workers are in the informal sector, particularly in subsistence agriculture: http://www.undp.org.in/report/position/CCA.htm.

[257] See further, Patel (1999).

The underlying argument in drawing out the linkages between gender-biased perceptions of women's work and their (dis)entitlement to land ownership is one of equal treatment. Highlighting existing gender bias in the recognition and valuation of women's work through a systematic analysis, it seeks to add to the debate on equal treatment of women and contribute to the search for ways forward in establishing equality. Today, where there is concerted effort to realize and implement internationally agreed norms of equality within numerous bodies and initiatives, it assumes pertinence in highlighting the factors shaping inequality and grounding the contours that inequality may take.

Since the adoption of the United Nations Convention on the Elimination of all forms of Discrimination Against Women (CEDAW) in 1979, international law of the human rights of women has become entrenched.[258] CEDAW defines discrimination against women comprehensively to include any distinction made on the basis of sex which impairs women's equal human rights in any sphere ('...political, economic, social, cultural, civil or any other', article 1). Read in conjunction with other provisions[259] CEDAW provides a clear mandate to states parties to ensure equality in the field of employment. This includes the right to equal treatment in respect of work of equal value, as well as equality of treatment in the evaluation of the quality of work (article 11.1d).

However, as the United Nations acknowledges, although government action is essential for the implementation of the above and other international human rights treaties, it is necessary to examine the potential for using international human rights law at the domestic level (UN, 2000: 3). In the context of work and work-related rights of women, Krisztina Morvai notes that:

> '...the main obstacle for the application of international women's human rights law...is that there is very limited theory and systematically compiled applicable knowledge collected in different fields' (Morvai, 2000: 85).

She further goes on to argue:

> 'In order to be able to use women's international human rights law and its instruments competently...theoretical scholarship and theoretical as well as applied jurisprudence need to be developed and compiled in all the specific fields of women's human rights...' (Morvai, 2000: 85).

The report of the United Nations Secretary General on the implementa-

---

[258] For a further discussion of the development of CEDAW within international human rights law, see Ali (2001).

[259] Articles 2 (d), 5 (a) and 11. 1 (d)

tion of the Beijing Platform for Action further highlights:

> '…the need for country comparison and in-depth research on informal sector work, unpaid work, occupational segregation and wage difference by sex … Research on these issues should help to reveal women's…subsistence labour as well as further our knowledge of gender inequality in the world.' (UN, 2001: 131–132).

This chapter is an attempt to contribute to this felt need in the area of rural women's work, in the context of women peasants in Orissa, India. It examines and evaluates the cultural context of women's work, from which economic and legal consequences of inequality may be argued to follow. Gender is implicated in perceptions of value which in turn have implications for the norm of equality and entitlements. Through a discussion of women's work, this paper attempts to draw linkages between culturally and ideologically driven perceptions of women's work and constructions of their entitlement to land ownership within law. It will argue that the gulf between legal rights and socially constructed entitlements to land reflects the non-recognition of women as significant actors in agricultural production within the wider society, state and its laws. Following from this, I highlight the significant role that women play as peasants within the household and overall agricultural production, to emphasize that this role needs to be an important determinant in defining them as the subjects of ownership rights within law.

Towards this, the second part of this chapter describes rural women's work in the context of women peasants in Orissa, India. The third section brings out the close correlation between gender-biased ideology and the low value placed on women's work, often rendering it invisible. Furthermore, this ideological underpinning, dealt with in the fourth part, is crucial in factoring out women's work and its resultant contribution from official documentation, analysis and policy. Following upon this, the fifth section seeks to highlight the particular issues in evaluating women's work in agriculture and looks at the conceptualization of 'work' itself both by women and others, leading on to the facts and issues that need to be recognized and addressed in measuring women's work within agricultural production. The sixth section sets the discussion within the framework of women's human rights. Drawing upon particular provisions of CEDAW, it highlights the legal obligations which may be argued to follow directly from these and which are therefore obligatory on states parties to fulfil. The brief discussion of CEDAW, drawing out the legal obligations inherent upon the states, then leads on to an analysis of legitimacy which may be argued to influence claims at the individual level. The attempt is to show that, taken together, these perspectives provide a compelling argument for positive steps to be taken in ensuring women's claim to land. The concluding section highlights the argument that women must be recognized and addressed as workers, both in law and policy and at all levels of society, in order to strengthen the social, and ultimately the legal, legitimacy of their claim to land ownership.

2 Women's work in rice cultivation in Orissa

As part of my field research during 1996/97 I had discussions with 42 women from three villages in western Orissa – Sahaspur, Karamdihi and Ekatali. Drawn from land-owning castes and labourers with predominantly small and marginal landholdings, participants included both married and unmarried women aged between 20 and 66 years. It was important to draw participants from this wider group towards exploring the link, if any, between the legitimacy of women's claim and their work contribution in cultivation. This contribution is generally most significant among marginal landholding households because the landholdings are generally not large enough to require hired labour and the family income of such households is not large enough to pay for hired labour.

Ranging around the key issues for consideration, the discussions were held with participants in groups and based upon reflexive interviewing, using mainly non-directive questions and a few directive questions. This was a productive method for eliciting participants' views and opinions to the maximum possible extent. Relevant issues which were discussed included:

- The enumeration of 'work' by women;
- Women's evaluation of their own work in comparison with that of male family members;
- Others' evaluation of their work, as perceived by the women themselves;
- Entitlements or privileges, if any, resulting from work roles and contribution; and
- The link, if any, between legitimate property rights and work contribution.

As the discussions brought out and any pertinent literature on the subject reiterates, women are involved in a wide range of productive (and reproductive) tasks in all seasons every day throughout the year. It is also obvious that there is a clearly understood demarcation of tasks along gender lines. It is generally true that operations carried out using machines or animals are done by men and most work which requires direct manual labour is done by women. There are few tasks performed by both men and women in the same way.

Men are responsible for preparing the field by ploughing and then levelling it. They are also responsible for digging wells and the small irrigation canals that run between the fields and making the bunds around the fields. Women help with this by putting the mud from the canals on the bunds or removing stones and other debris from the fields. Men irrigate the fields before and after transplantation by drawing water from the wells using animals or with the help of a simple lever system using a long bamboo shaft, usually with a tin container attached at the end.

Women have to fertilize the fields with cow and buffalo dung before the actual planting of the seeds. This is done manually as they also clear the seed beds of stones. When the rice plants have grown to their required height, they are transplanted. This process requires that each individual sapling is handled separately and is the most labour-intensive part of rice cultivation. Weeding is also done exclusively by women and, like transplantation, involves no tools but is completely manual. The work in transplanting and weeding is particularly strenuous as it involves bending down to do the work for the entire time.

Though harvesting is done by both men and women, men do the threshing by driving animals over the rice, while women do the winnowing by fanning the grain to remove the husks. The drying, cleaning and processing of the grain is also done by women. This includes parboiling and drying the paddy rice and responsibility for storage and preparation for the next year's planting. They also prepare rice as storables in the form of puffed and flattened rice consumed throughout the year. In addition, women perform supportive tasks such as taking meals to the fields for other family members and the preparation of meals for hired labour.

In their own evaluation, women in the group asserted that they were the primary workers in their families. They were very clear that on the whole, taking into account field work and housework, there was no doubt that they worked more than the men of the household.

> 'As far as work is concerned, women work more because they not only work on the fields but also in the house and look after the family in general.'

In fact, according to them, it is the women who work more, even on the fields, in the various stages of cultivation throughout the year until the crop is finally sold or ready for consumption.

However, the issue that was problematic for women was the recognition of their work by others – their families and the society. Although in their own estimation their position was the same as their husbands and sons' in terms of the work put in for the family, they felt that this was not how it was perceived by their husbands and sons. This led to the feeling that their work was not recognized and was considered to be useless in the society, even though they thought otherwise:

'Even if I work for eight days a week it is nothing and if they (the men) do a little bit of work it is a lot. The way things are, I cannot say we should do this or that with the land, they are the ones who decide, and the women are supposed to be working as labourers as long as they have husbands and sons. As long as we have husbands and sons, we can only work for *them*…Even if we work, it is not considered to be work' (emphasis in original).

'Another factor is that men in peasant households start believing that they have power over the work done by the women because they are the owners of the land and the women are working for them. So they will never acknowledge or recognize the women's work, or give them any freedom or right in recognition for the work done by them. Women therefore cannot decide on any issues relating to the work done on the land or otherwise for the sustenance of the family; at best they may only make suggestions which may or may not be accepted by the men.'

Notwithstanding this large and varied amount of work done by women, the idea that it is men who do the 'harder' jobs remains. Ploughing, irrigation and work involving physical strength is considered more difficult in this division and, consequently, men are understood to do the more valued work.[260] Again, women's work is undervalued because it is considered to be part of their obligatory role in the marital household.

'The work we did at home (before marriage) was of our own free will, because we wanted to. After marriage, there is no choice, we have to work whether we want to or not. It is our duty … In our cases at least, though, women work much more than men; men enjoy a better position because they are men. They have a higher position because they are men and we have an inferior position because we are women. No matter how much we work, we will always be in this position once we are married. This is the reality, this is in our culture and tradition.'

3 Negotiating legal and social legitimacy – women's work and claims to land

In linking the global norm of human rights to the state, the critical element as the subject of rights is the individual woman. Further, it is the individual who embodies the principles, practices and effects of discrimination, and, as the right-holder, experiences its derogation. This chapter attempts to ground the project of equal rights for women through the perspectives offered by the bargaining approach.[261] The bargaining

---

[260] See further Mies (1986) and Patel (1999).

[261] See further, Sen (1983, 1987, 1990, 1999) and Agarwal (1985, 1994, 1995) in the South Asian context.

approach provides a framework for the analysis of women's claim to land as impacted both by ideological factors affecting perceptions of self-interest and material factors, particularly perceptions of their contributions. It enables us to expand the construction of women's property rights to include perceptions of women's work and contribution as a factor affecting legitimate claims to resources, in addition to explicit religious, political or cultural ideologies as the basis of gender equality protected by law. In conceptualizing women's effective access to land as an outcome of negotiating and bargaining, I analyze the extent to which the legal framework takes account of women's contributions to production from land.

In concrete terms, I argue that women's work and contribution to production provide the explicit basis for women's equal rights to land. As Sen (1987) has argued, individuals' access to resources is directly affected by perceptions of legitimacy. Further, what is perceived to be legitimately 'deserved' by a person is closely linked to what is perceived by *others* as that person's contribution. The impact of such perceived contribution may have been associated with acquiring food from outside and the fact that the sexual division of labour allocates tasks based upon social constructions of gender. These constructions typically allow males to do the work of 'acquiring' food while females are involved in other activities but this may not weaken the *perception of special importance of bringing the food home* (emphasis added; Sen, 1987).

This seems to have been supported by Boserup's observation that women fare relatively better in societies where they play a major role in bringing food from outside (Boserup, 1970). Again, studies of women's roles in the paid labour force, particularly in agriculture, have been based on the understanding that a woman's role in providing for the family from external means, and not from work within her own household, has increased visibility and therefore had greater impact on her status as provider (Bardhan, 1985). The underlying assumption is that since women have an income, they have control over certain economic resources which they may then manipulate in negotiating their socio-economic status within the household. This assumption has been summed up thus:

> 'Whether one views the increase in female agricultural labourers as an indicator of growing rural poverty or as a positive sign that more agricultural work is available for women, its effect in terms of our third criterion (decision making) should be examined separately. Evidence suggests that the increased paid employment outside the home may actually improve the women's bargaining position within the family' (Bennett, 1989 cited in Bagchi and Raju, 1993: 180).

The conditions of subsistence and overwhelming dependence on land as the means of livelihood that is pertinent to households with small and medium size farms have to be kept in mind. The evidence from a vast number of studies in India shows that families live in near poverty and land is the resource that provides the maximum security against absolute poverty. In this context, ownership of the scarce resource that is land is fraught with contestations and the social legitimacy of a claim is related to cultural norms as well as economic realities. In one instance I was told:

> 'When there is barely enough for the family's needs, how can we think of our own share? As it is, there is so little. There is one plough, a tiny bit of land. My brothers have to survive on that.[262] How can I think of a share in that as mine, and still expect to be cared for by them?'

Whereas women's equal ownership rights may have relevance within the family, in most cases[263] their work in the context of subsistence farming is predicated on the household as the basic unit of analysis.[264] In this respect, distinguishing between the family and household as the unit, where women as ownership rights holders are located, may appear unnecessary for the legitimacy and enforcement of their rights. Nevertheless, in evaluating the social legitimacy of their rights, which is in turn affected by perceptions of contributions, the distinction in the ordering principles of the family and the household as the locus of subsistence production must be recognized. Whereas gender ideology biased against the female can operate pervasively across both, the operation of gender ideology in subsistence production is predicated, in addition to culturally-defined gender relations, upon relations of production.

Although the relations of production at the subsistence level within a capitalist framework have implications for the value assigned to such production for export (Beneria, 1982; Mies, 1980; Sharma, 1985; Omvedt, 1994; Elson and Pearson, 1981) and, in the case of India par-

---

[262] What is being referred to here is that most inheritance rights guaranteeing females a share are seen as in competition with the other male heirs who traditionally would provide support in times of distress.

[263] This is on account of women's exclusion from property being traditionally and predominantly sanctioned under customary and religious rules relating to inheritance and succession. A corollary to such rules, based on gender, was that they operated to exclude independent ownership through other means as well, such as inter-personal transfers (sale or gift). As such, the focus of laws seeking to establish gender equality in ownership rights has been upon rules regarding *intergenerational* transfers of property through inheritance and succession. Thus, it is the family as a unit within which women's rights become located and which is relevant for such transfers.

[264] See further Deere (1995) for a fuller discussion of the relevance of the family farm and household as the basic unit of production within the fields of peasant studies as well as women and development.

ticularly for home-based workers (Mies, 1982) and landless labourers in agriculture, what is relevant to note is the separation of the family from productive processes, as a separate, private sphere, as opposed to the public sphere. Further, the sexual division of labour within most societies predicates that women are located within this 'domestic' sphere while men go out of it to do 'productive work' (Harris, 1981: 50). In the particular case of women in household or home-based production, the issue becomes more difficult due to location of the productive sphere as well as the family within the same physical space, leading to a submersion of women's productive role within their role as the nurturer. This exacerbates the non-visibility of women's role in income creation or contribution to the family's survival and sustenance:

> 'We are doing something for the family…we think that we work for the welfare of the entire family and not in terms of our personal efforts and rewards…whatever we earn belongs to everyone in the family.'[265]

Where the issue of land ownership is sought to be determined by law on the basis of gender, the legitimacy of such a law must not only be based on cultural norms and values but also on relations of production. The social legitimacy of a claim must be based on both these aspects in order to improve a person's bargaining position. On this issue, the framework provided by Sen to take account of women's role in production and the need to enhance perceptions of their contribution to production or income, provides a strategy that may be developed through appropriate policy. However, in this regard Agarwal (1994) argues that increased awareness of women's contributions may not necessarily bring about greater access to resources for women if, for example, another criterion for justifying particular shares such as needs, is taken. Allocation of resources may in fact be gender-biased against women where culturally-defined notions of needs may also be gender-biased.

Although this is a valid point, particularly in societies such as India where culturally-defined gender identities may be deep rooted among most people, it does not lessen the significance of the role that perceptions of contributions play in ascribing legitimacy. Further, Agarwal's argument is perhaps also relevant to a subsequent stage in policy analysis after perceptions of women's role in production have in fact been enhanced, since, as I shall bring out in the following sections, we do not yet have a policy focus on women's contribution with the aim of enhancing perceptions of the same.

The issue of land ownership and control has two different implications in the context of women in agriculture. First, the relationship to

---

[265] Response from field research.

land for those who do not own any land but work on it as wage labourers for others, is characterized by the absence of ownership over any land. Here the issue is one of redistribution or allocation of land through land reform policies establishing ownership and control for sections of the agricultural producers that hitherto had no land. Second, once land comes to be owned by an individual, ownership may then be transmitted to heirs including females, through succession. Women's work in agriculture may be classed according to the two contexts: women working as hired labourers primarily where they themselves do not have access to land for their own cultivation, or at least, not sufficient land, and women working as cultivators on their own land, or that owned by their husbands or fathers. My focus is the evaluation of women's work as cultivators, on land owned by themselves or their husbands or fathers.

Here the question of women having independent ownership and control over their lawful share becomes an issue of intra-household bargaining and negotiation, being affected by gender relations within the household and notions of legitimacy, including perceived contribution. My focus is on the issue of women's effective ownership and control over the land where they have a legal right to own the land; for instance where the land is owned by a member of the family, of which the woman is a member and on which land she works. It is for this category of women that problems regarding evaluation of their work, and therefore their role in agricultural production, is heightened. Firstly, the classification of their work becomes a problem as to whether it is domestic work, household work, leisure work or economically productive work in agriculture. Secondly the evaluation of their work is ambiguous, in so far as determining the necessity of their work to the level of agricultural productivity and income for the household. Thirdly, there is no specific remuneration that may provide an index of the cost or benefit to the family.

4   Cultural ideology and perceptions of women's contribution

Although research on working women, or women with access to an income, links employment to a higher status in terms of female welfare and autonomy, Ahmed-Ghosh argues to the contrary that gender hierarchy is so rigid within the household that mere wage labour of women does not guarantee a shift of balance in power relations between genders (Ahmed-Ghosh, 1993). Sharma's study of Punjab and Himachal Pradesh makes a similar point that the women's wage labour in itself is controlled by household members and not by the women themselves. She explains:

'In theory we might certainly expect to find that women who work for wages (and even women who work as family labourers) have a greater say in the household matters than women who perform their domestic work only, and this is an assumption that has often been made both by anthropologists and others. But the female labourer usually earns wages which are too small and sporadic to lend her any special leverage in household politics, and the work of the female family labourers does not give women any particular control over the products of their labour' (Sharma, 1989:196).

There is a dialectical link between women's work and the cultural context within which it exists (Agarwal, 1994; Mencher, 1993; Bardhan, 1985; Majumdar and Sharma, 1990; Gleason, 1991). Gender relations are so defined by the cultural ideology to construct women's subordinate position to the extent that their resources in terms of labour, time and productivity are controlled by males (Sharma, 1985; Bardhan, 1985). Cultural ideology determines not only the perception of others regarding women's work and contribution but also that of the women themselves (Agarwal, 1994). The effect of others' perceptions, based upon the prevailing cultural ideology, on the perceived legitimacy of a claim by women themselves is such that while women do have a conviction and perception of themselves as equal workers and contributors, this does not enhance the legitimacy of their individual claim. As I was told:

'As far as work is concerned, women work more…(Nevertheless) even if I work for eight days a week it is nothing…and I cannot say what should be done with the land…even if we work it is not considered to be work…it is the men who decide.'[266]

Women belonging to households at subsistence level do not distinguish between 'productive' labour and household work and claim that 'all the work that they do is for the family' (Ahmed-Ghosh, 1993: 192; Patel, 1999). However they do consider themselves to be workers equal to men in providing for the family. The asset base of the households at subsistence level is so small that most of the production is for household consumption. Bhattacharya maintains:

'Because total production work input of the household members will be much less in such [subsistence] households as compared to that in the households having larger asset bases, the contribution of women members of the households as participants in generating the non-marketed products can only be small in absolute size, however crucial it might be to the survival of the household. The separate identity of this marginal work, which in major cases is performed only intermittently

---

[266] See further, Patel (1999).

together with women's other work of housekeeping, is more often likely to be lost in reckoning. In effect the work becomes 'invisible' (Bhattacharya, 1985: 200).

The concept of hard work in the context of south Asian agriculture reflects the dialectical relationship between the material context of women's relationship to agriculture and the land on one hand, and gender ideology (here related to the valuation placed on what work they do in agriculture), on the other. Exploring women's involvement in rice cultivation in India, Mencher (1993) asks: how has it come about that women's work is regarded as easier than men's work, both by the workers themselves and by many social scientists who study them? Who is doing the defining and what are the criteria being used? She points out that for both males and females actual participation in manual field work has always culturally been considered degrading and withdrawal from fieldwork has always been associated with higher socio-economic class. Further, tasks in field work have always been segregated by gender in South Asia. For example, although, in addition to the many tasks they perform in rice cultivation, women may also plant vegetables and work the soil manually, they have rarely been considered worthy to plough the fields.

The belief that because ploughing has to be done with sanctity or by those who are sacred, only men can plough, as those who menstruate pollute the earth, is one factor in classifying a task as 'male'.[267] Nevertheless, while the definition of a task as male or female may change from place to place, what remains constant is the lower value placed on 'female' tasks, regardless of how the task becomes defined. For example, Mencher shows us that in many areas where transplanting was considered 'women's work', most men would not do this work even in the face of unemployment. On the task of pulling seedlings in Tamil Nadu and Kerala, she points out that pulling the seedlings for transplantation is considered to be 'hard work' where men do it in Tamil Nadu but 'easy work' in Kerala, where women do it (Mencher, 1993).

The above examples show that the value placed on women's work in agriculture, as well as other sectors, bears a relation to the visibility of such work that is mutually reinforcing. In its negative operation, as in the case of agricultural workers and cultivators in India, work that is not valued within the social framework remains invisible as it is not taken into account and its invisibility perpetuates underestimation and undervaluation (Beneria, 1988). Taken together, this has a direct effect on perceptions of women's contribution and the ultimate effect is one where

---

[267] In my own study, notwithstanding women's acknowledged role as workers of equivalent significance, the respondents justified men's primary position on the grounds that only they could plough which was 'most difficult work', 'too difficult for women', which 'women would never be able to do' (Patel, 1999).

the contribution made by women by virtue of their unrecognized and undervalued activities is also perceived to be low or non-existent.

5   Evaluating women's work in agriculture

The conceptualization of 'women's work' and its undervaluation, drawn from gender-biased ideological positions has resulted in the lack of identification and acknowledgement of the corresponding work participation, resulting further in the absence of women as independent providers or workers. This is further deepened by reinforced ideas of women as 'dependants' or supplementary to family subsistence requirements. Moreover, this cycle has led to women's own underestimation, as well as the gross underestimation and invisibility of women's work in official and other studies. The nature and extent of women's work participation in subsistence and agricultural labour documented in previous decades (Bardhan, 1985; Mies, 1986; Bagchi, 1993) remains true today.[268] To quote Mencher:

> '....women perform a very large part of the heavy manual work in rice cultivation in India. This is important to note because as compared to the African and South East Asian women in agriculture, the involvement of Indian women in the field has often been ignored (Mencher, 1993: 99).

That there still exists this gap in recognizing women's work for what it is may be brought out by how their work has been classified or understood in the policies and plans of the state. In this section I shall draw upon the issues around women's work in agriculture: what constitutes work as performed by women; the activities that have been documented as work done by women; and the process of statistical enumeration whereby women's 'work' comes to be defined.

Issues in conceptualizing and enumerating women's work
The population that has the ability and willingness to work constitutes the labour force. However, who is actually included in the work force depends on how 'work' is defined in such accounting. In evaluating work done by women in agricultural production, I will bring out some of the issues leading to how their work is presently enumerated and evaluated in official studies. This includes initially how women's work is conceptualized as predominantly 'domestic' and therefore unproductive, and then the translation of this limited understanding into under-enumeration and under representation of women's work in official statistics and

---

[268] In fact women's involvement in agricultural labour is increasing (Statistical profile of women's labour, 1993).

data collection through the exclusion of large areas of work that women undertake. The result is a logical exclusion of all activities outside the market mainstream as 'peripheral' and 'non-economic' (Beneria, 1988).

Since most of the pre-harvest and post-harvest operations in which women participate are carried out at home, a large number of self-employed women are excluded from the count. Allied agricultural activities such as dairy and poultry farming, along with the survival tasks of firewood or fodder collection and procurement of water are not considered work if they are for self-consumption. However, apart from cooking, cleaning, childcare and looking after the aged and the sick, which may fall within the 'pure' domestic sphere, Krishnaraj and Chanana (1989) has identified several categories of work which are predominantly performed by women in rural and urban India which clearly have components that are not pure domestic work. They are:

- Self-employment in cultivation for own consumption;
- Subsistence dairying and livestock rearing, fishing, hunting, and cultivation of fruit and vegetable gardens;
- Fetching fuel, fodder and water, repair of dwellings, making of cow dung cakes, and food preservation.

In addition, women's work in 'informal' health care is particularly invisible in official statistics.

The definition of 'work' determines who is counted as a 'worker' (Gleason, 1991; Agarwal, 1985). In the case of census data the example of definitional effects can be seen in the sharp decline of women's labour force participation in 1971 as compared to 1961. The reference period by which status as a worker was determined varied and in 1971 respondents were asked to identify their 'main activity'. This, given the nature of women's work, would often elicit the response of 'housewife' (Bagchi and Raju, 1993), resulting in the said decline in female participation rates in 1971 (Mathur, 1994).

The 1991 census continued to exclude from consideration the household work done by the women in its definition of 'work'. This 'statistical purdah' imposed by the existing methods of measuring labour force participation renders much of women's work invisible (World Bank, 1991) and the lack of precision in defining and measuring what is meant by 'subsistence or household production' and 'domestic' work has led to very different answers to the question of where Indian women are working. In the specific context of agricultural work this was highlighted decades earlier by the Report of the Committee on the Status of Women in India (1974: 162):

'While census data classifies agricultural workers into only two categories, namely, cultivators and labourers, this classification does not, in fact, reflect the realities of the agricultural community.'

Within the conventional labour force participation indices figures show that there is a far higher percentage of women (66 per cent compared to 37 per cent of men) who fall outside the labour force (World Bank, 1991). The figures from the 1991 census seems to suggest that the percentage of women who are working in the rural areas is only 27 per cent as compared to the men at 52.43 per cent.[269] However, if we extend the idea of work to include conventional domestic activity, then the picture changes and we find that almost 75 per cent of women are working as compared to 64 per cent of the men.[270]

Problems of under-enumeration, and inconsistent and inadequate measurement frameworks resulting in the invisibility of the true extent of women's work in the data are a reflection of prevailing societal perceptions. Female labour is perceived to be of secondary importance where the male is construed as the primary breadwinner, despite much evidence to the contrary (Gleason, 1991; Agarwal, 1985; Bagchi and Raju, 1993). Definitions of women's work tend to obscure the amount, the intensity and the productivity of female work (Mies, 1982). Although there are aspects of women's work which can come under conventional categorization, there is substantially more which does not that has a direct correlation with the agricultural productivity and total income of the household.

The various studies undertaken in the past three decades identifying and highlighting the whole range of tasks done by the women and the need to include that as 'productive work', has resulted in the growing sensitivity towards female contribution in non-wage activities. For example, the Indian census in 1991 has attached an explicit rider in the identification of workers to include 'unpaid work on the farm or in family enterprises'.

Notwithstanding policy change, women's work continues to 'vanish' in economic and policy analysis due to the ignorance and undervaluation that are prevalent (Ginwala *et al.*, 1990). Statistical exclusion leads to the undervaluation, through under-enumeration, while this process is reinforced by ignorance of the daily tasks and activities that women carry out. As Bardhan notes:

> 'The underestimation of peasant women's economically productive work is more than a statistical problem that concerns planners and policy makers. It reflects and legitimizes the devaluation of female labour in the household economy of peasants, helping the process of male-controlled accumulation' (Bardhan, 1985: 2214).

---

[269] See further, *Census of India* (1991), Paper 3 of 1991 – Workers and their distribution (Statement 3.1).

[270] See further, *World Bank Report of Gender and Poverty in India* (1991).

The next section highlights the range of women's tasks and the need to include these within women's 'work'.

What is women's work?
Traditionally, the definition of work is oriented towards capturing some form of remuneration or profit in return for labour and includes those engaged in wage and salaried employment, self-employment outside the household for profit and self-employment in cultivation and household industries for profit (Gleason, 1991; Benaria, 1988). Where a significant proportion of goods and services are produced for self-consumption through unpaid activity, the wide range of activities not geared towards exchange and market are excluded from the definition of 'work' (Bardhan, 1985; Beneria, 1988; Gleason, 1991; Bagchi and Raju, 1993; Mukhopadhyay, 1985). To counteract this the Indian census counts cultivation of crops as 'work' even if it is for self -consumption. However, the gulf between male and female participation rates continues because much of the related activity resulting in produce for self-consumption which is undertaken primarily by women is invisible and cannot be captured by the existing concept of work.

Suggestions to increase the consideration of 'work' to incorporate women's participation include the counting of all household work, such as cooking, cleaning, tailoring, child care and care of the elderly, as economic activities. This would be on the basis that these have a price in that they can be substituted for goods and services which would otherwise be paid for (Gleason, 1991; Bagchi 1993). However, while it would make the role of women in the economy visible:

> '...it (would) also cloud the real issues and a certain complacency may ensue because female labour would then no longer be invisible' (Bagchi, 1993: 5)

There is thus a continuing need to remove the ideological constructions upon which women's work is undervalued and thereby made invisible. Rendering greater visibility through correlation of the value of women's work and time expended therein, or through other methods, keeps open the underlying prejudices and gender-biased assumptions which must also be continually and independently addressed.

Measuring women's work
Even with the expanded concept of work it is unlikely that any large-scale survey could reflect the complex pattern of 'gainful activities' through which women and many men in poor families earn a livelihood and micro-level studies are most relevant in this context (Mies, 1986). Time allocation studies have been recognized as the most reliable means

of capturing women's work pattern since they do not depend on any prior definition of work (UNDP, 2000).[271] As such, data drawn from these studies determines the time involved in the expanded economic activities and conventional domestic activity and may reflect the actual participation of women in work.

Sen (1987) has argued that the perception of contribution has to be distinguished from the time actually spent. The correlation that more work is necessarily valuable work is often absent, and this disjuncture between perceptions and work done must be noted. Time allocation studies are useful to demonstrate precisely this issue: while facts show that women work longer hours than men, it is simply not accounted for as work. As has been found in various time use studies carried out in South Asia, women spend more time working than men.

Women's time allocation patterns in a study of two villages in Andhra Pradesh affirm this. Studying time allocation patterns for various activities such as crop production, animal husbandry, building and construction work, trading, marketing, transportation, domestic work, fuel gathering, food processing and all other social and religious obligations for each worker in the household, it was found that in all categories, women worked longer hours daily than men (Sudha *et al.*, 1993). Similarly, data on women cultivators and labourers in Kerala, Tamil Nadu and West Bengal show that the cultivators supervised work both within and outside the home. Apart from 'domestic' work, they worked with labourers in the field, looking after their employment and payment of wages in the absence of the husband. Those who had very little land worked on others' farms as wage labour in addition to this in order to supplement their income (Saradamoni, 1988). Further, there are various supplementary tasks that women perform towards the process of agricultural production. In preparing food for the workers, taking food for other family members who may be in the fields, recruiting labourers and negotiating their terms, women are directly involved in the entire process.

These studies bring out the underestimation of women's role in India's household-based, semi-subsistence agriculture. Expanding the narrower definition and using a simplified activity schedule instead of the standard 'yes' or 'no' questions, the labour force participation rates for the same sample of rural women in central India could be shown to vary from 3 per cent to 90 per cent (Anker *et al.*, 1993). This strongly suggests that there are few rural women in India who are not in some sense farmers, that is working as wage labourers, unpaid workers in the family farm enterprise, or some combination of the two.

---

[271] See further Hirway (2000) 'Tabulation and analysis of the Indian time use survey data for improving measurement of paid and unpaid work', ESA/STAT/AC.79/20, 17 October 2000.

6 Towards an internationally accepted norm with CEDAW?

That women's role in agricultural production is overlooked and under-valued in the legal framework is only a reflection of the situation in official and public accounts and policy. The necessity to detail the extent of women's work in this area and understand the major role that they play in agricultural production arises from the fact that most women do not actually control the land. The problem therefore is that the control over land by women must be increased so that they are considered in policy as major actors in agricultural production, not merely as 'supportive' ones. The secondary status of women with regard to land rights is a central factor in producing a two-fold outcome: reduced access to resources and livelihoods and reduced significance in policies for change in agrarian and land relations. In turn, these contribute directly to women's inequality and subordination in many societies.

As noted, women's human rights have assumed a central position in international as well as domestic legal frameworks since the adoption of CEDAW in 1979. The normative import of the principles embodied in CEDAW in today's world cannot be denied; even if its substantive force in various contexts may be arguable. Fundamental within CEDAW are two principles: firstly, the obligation of states to eliminate all discrimination against women and, secondly, the obligation of states to obtain full equality (both *de jure* and *de facto*) between men and women. Article 1 exhaustively defines 'discrimination' to cover *any* field, including the political, economic, social, cultural and civil. Articles 2 and 3 affirm the obligation of the state to take *all* appropriate measures to eliminate discrimination against women, including legislation. This clearly establishes the broad scope of state action possible. Thus, in addition to law-making, law-enforcement, education, administrative action, policy guidelines and any other action as may be necessary is within the scope of the state's obligation.

The breadth of means to overcome discrimination is in conjunction with an explicit recognition that discrimination may be the result of underlying social and cultural factors, and that states must necessarily undertake specific action ('all appropriate measures') against any such underlying causes (article 5). These articles, taken together, establish the basis for examining the existent inequality and discrimination that women suffer in the context of land rights. This chapter has argued that the inequality in access to land is 'propped up' by discriminatory practices in the value and recognition placed upon women's work on land. Social and cultural attitudes towards women's work are informed by notions of 'productivity', which in turn are drawn from opposing concepts of 'domestic' (read *non-productive*) and 'productive'. As such, there are two levels of inequality and discrimination; first in the undervaluation and non-recognition of women' work and, further, in this translating to women's lack of access to land.

Of significance is the focus on rural women within CEDAW (article 14). Read in conjunction with article 3 (the injunction to states parties to take all appropriate action in all fields, particularly the political, economic, social and cultural, to ensure women's equality), article 14 provides the basis for critically assessing rural women's contribution to family survival and their role in the non-monetized (or informal) sector. Article 14.2(g) further refers to equal treatment in land and agrarian reforms. Together with the ILO Equal Remuneration Convention of 1951,[272] the provisions of CEDAW arguably establish the principle of equality in the context of women's work as an internally recognized norm.

Taking all these provisions together, it is clear that the obligation placed upon states requires us to first critically examine these inequalities so as to argue effectively for appropriate state action. Specifically, in its General Recommendation No. 16 (Tenth session, 1991) the committee recommended the collection of data on unpaid women workers in rural and urban family enterprises and the inclusion of such data in states' reports. Additionally, CEDAW General Recommendation No. 17 (Tenth session, 1991) addresses the need to undertake specific studies to measure and value the unremunerated domestic activities of women (paragraph a). It further recommends that states parties quantify such unremunerated domestic activities and include this in the calculation of their national product as well as report these to the committee (paragraphs b and c).

An adequate and full accounting of women's work in the rural sector, particularly in family-owned farms, needs to be undertaken as the foundation for achieving women's equal land rights. Adequate accounting is necessary for the proper recognition and valuation of women's work, which could then be the basis for equal rights in land. In the context of India, the current constitutional regime for women's land rights through inheritance is ostensibly non-discriminatory. However, a closer examination reveals that they are based on welfare rather than equality.[273] An examination of women's property rights in Indian law, more widely, reveals the same bias in the absence of a matrimonial property

---

[272] This came into effect in 1953.

[273] For a fuller discussion on, for example, the legal regime pertinent to Hindu women in India, see Patel 'Gender, production and access to land: The case for female peasants in India' in Parpart, Rai and Staudt (2002).

law regime. At present, the allocation of property upon divorce is within the discretion of the judge. Although the concept of joint ownership of matrimonial property was proposed in 1986 and 1988, it is not incorporated in law.[274] This welfarist approach is echoed in the CEDAW committee's concern in its comments on India's report that its actions post-Beijing adopt a welfare approach and that its proposed gender empowerment policy should integrate a rights-based approach.[275] Land reform policy and practice clearly show that women are absent as the target of desired goals and objectives. Despite official assurances that all leases and allocations under the land reform regulations presently were issued jointly to both spouses, men appear to continue as beneficiaries in greater numbers than women. As of the end of 1995, for example, only 11 women had been granted leases under the Orissa Land Settlement Act 1959 as opposed to 29 men in one Indian district. Similarly, 35 women as opposed to 72 men, were allocated land under the Orissa Land Reforms Act 1962 within the period 1990–1995.[276]

7 Conclusion

This chapter argues that a rights-based approach is vital to secure women's rights in land on the basis of equality and non-discrimination and, further, that this approach is vital to overcome the existing socio-cultural and legal hurdles. This right may be drawn from a full recognition of women's work, cognisant of its value for the family, society and economy. Finally, that such an aim and methodology would only be in furtherance of the state's obligations within CEDAW and, as such, that international human rights law demands its fulfilment.

It is apparent from various studies that there is gross underestimation of women's work participation, especially in agriculture, where they play a significant role. This is especially true of wage labourers, generally the poorest section of society, who are often the mainstay of their family's welfare and of small and marginal peasant women whose work is particularly difficult to evaluate in terms of the contribution to family

---

[274] See further, Agnes (2000).

[275] In its concluding comment, the committee noted, under principal subjects of concern as follows:

'The committee notes that the Convention and the Beijing Platform for Action have not been integrated into policy planning and programmes. While there have been several national plans in the pre and post Beijing period, the committee notes that these adopt a welfare approach towards women.

'The Committee recommends that the proposed gender empowerment policy integrate the Convention and the Beijing Platform for Action and a rights-based approach' (CEDAW/C/IND/1 paras 54 and 55).

[276] Official communication received from Tehsildar of Sundargarh district.

income and resources. In the case of landless labourers, women's income is a major contribution to household income – essential for survival – even where wage rates for women are lower than for men.[277] This cannot be overemphasized because conventional development theory often assumes that even when Indian women work in agriculture, their income is largely supplementary to that of the males in the households (Mencher, 1993).

Nonetheless, numerous studies also point out that women lack any control over the inputs to agricultural production such as land, institutional credit, education and training in farming methods. The first step is to recognize that women are significant contributors in agricultural production. Enhancing and supporting women in this role will allow for better access to the necessary inputs for growth. This in turn will provide the basis for women to negotiate control of the primary resource, land. The increased recognition of women's contribution will increase the legitimacy of their demands and give them decision-making power over allocation of resources within their families. In addition to considering important issues regarding forms and modes of access to land and the wider social, institutional and organizational support that is needed for new prospects for women's land rights to become viable, such as propounded by Agarwal (2003), land rights for women can and must be linked more strongly with their unquestionable contribution to agriculture. As Agarwal says of daughters-in-law and daughters resident in a particular location, '…land access could be linked formally with residence and working on the land…' (2003: 216)

It has also been argued (Basu, 1990) that in order to analyze the agrarian structure and its role in development, it is necessary to take into

---

[277] The disparity in wages between men and women remains despite the Equal Remuneration Act 1976 which prohibits discrimination on the basis of gender. There have been numerous requests on this matter by the ILO committee to the government of India which have yet to be addressed satisfactorily. In its observation (CEACR 2002/73rd Session): '…The committee notes that, aside from indicating that no complaints have been received on the matter, the government's report contains virtually no reply to its previous comment on the observations of the National Front of Indian Trade Unions (NFITU), which alleged that the principle of equal remuneration for men and women workers for work of equal value is not respected in the informal and unorganized sectors. It further notes the comments of the ICFTU claiming widespread contraventions of the principle of the convention. In spite of the existence of the Equal Remuneration Act 1976, the ICFTU points out that wage gaps between men and women persist across all sectors. The ICFTU further maintains that, although the government has included policies and programmes to achieve the empowerment of women in its ninth plan, these have been criticized as superficial: much room for further action remains, particularly in traditional industries.' http://webfusion.ilo.org/public/db/standards/normes/appl/index.cfm?lang=EN.

account other non-economic factors such as interpersonal beliefs that prevail in the community, the nature of land tenure and the structure of property rights. On the role of interpersonal esteem in society, Basu points out that how hard people work and whether they try to innovate must be understood in terms of the social status accorded to those activities in a particular society.

The invisibility of home-based work is tied to a general neglect of the household economy and a narrow definition of work which precludes its inclusion in official statistics. Considerable overlap may exist between the household and extra-household work, the former expanding to use up extra-household work time during special or crisis occasions, and the latter expanding to encroach upon household work time during peak agricultural periods. The household work sphere also expands whenever needed to include extra-household work that is income substitution, referred to as 'status production work' (Sharma and Singh, 1993). Recognition of women's work as inclusive of the range of women's tasks is therefore central to the dominant conception of 'work', gender roles within the society and the cultural ideology which determine such roles.

In the case of women and ownership of land within the agrarian sector, a gendered access to land requires law to create a basis of legitimacy on two counts: legal and social. A gender equitable land reform policy could endow hitherto landless female agricultural labourers with ownership of land but land reforms policy in India illustrates the process highlighted in this chapter. The consideration of who constitute the subject group of 'farmers' or 'tillers' or 'tenants' within the law is premised upon the male as the active worker or producer, upon ignorance of the nature and extent of women's work and, lastly, of their contributions to the family's survival as a result of such work. Further, where women are taken into account, they are again treated mainly as 'dependants' or non-contributors to family income (Agarwal, 1994, 1995, 2003).

The perceptions of legitimacy, based on perceptions of women working in agriculture and their contribution, by both women and society at large, are crucial in two aspects. Firstly, recognition of the work and contribution of women in agriculture, and as producers in their own right, not merely as dependants or in supportive roles, would have the direct effect of greater gender equality within land reforms. Secondly, such recognition, in the policy framework of the state in its developmental policies generally and the legal framework in particular, can lead to greater effectiveness of the law in its effort to create new values and ideas. The effect of gender-equal land ownership is dependent in part on the creation of a new basis of legitimacy through recognition of women's contribution to and role in agriculture.

Bibliography

Agarwal B. (1988) 'Who sows? Who reaps? Women and land rights in India', in *Journal of Peasant Studies*, Vol. 15, No. 4, pages 531–581.

– (1985) 'Work participation of rural women in the third world: Some data and conceptual biases', in *Economic and Political Weekly,* Vol. 20, Nos. 51 and 52, December 21–28, pages A-155-164.

– (1992) 'Rural women, poverty and natural resources: Sustenance, sustainability and struggle for change', in B. Harriss, S. Guhan and R. H. Cassen (eds) *Poverty in India: Research and policy*, Oxford University Press, Bombay.

– (1994) *A field of one's own : Gender and land rights in South Asia'*, Cambridge University Press, Cambridge.

– (1995) 'Gender and legal rights in agricultural land in India', in *Economic and Political Weekly*, 25 March, pages A-39–56.

– (2003) 'Gender and land rights revisited: Exploring new prospects via the state, family and market', in *Journal of Agrarian Change*, Vol. 3 Nos. 1 and 2, January and April 2003 pages 184–224.

Agnes F. (2000) *Law and gender inequality: The politics of women's rights in India,* Oxford University Press, Delhi.

Ahmed-Ghosh, H. (1993) 'Agricultural development and work patterns of women in a north India village' in D. Bagchi and S. Raju (eds) *Women and work in South Asia: Regional patterns and perspectives*, Routledge, London.

Ali S. S. (2001) 'Women's rights, CEDAW and international human rights debates', in J. L. Parpart, S. M. Rai and K. Staudt (eds) *Rethinking empowerment: Gender and development in a global/local world,* Routledge, London and New York.

Anker R. *et al.* (1993) 'Methodological issues in collecting time used data for female labour force' in A. Sharma and S. Singh (eds) *Women and work: Changing scenario in India*, Indian Society of Labour Economics, Patna and B. R. Publishing Corporation, Delhi.

Bagchi D. (1993) 'The household and extra-household work of rural women in a changing resource environment in Madhya Pradesh, India' in D. Bagchi, and S. Raju (eds) *Women and work in South Asia: Regional patterns and perspectives*, Routledge, London.

Bagchi D. and S. Raju (1993) 'In sum and looking beyond: Suggestions for future research' in D. Bagchi and S. Raju (eds) *Women and work in South Asia: Regional patterns and perspectives*, Routledge, London.

Bardhan K. (1985) 'Women's work, welfare and status: Forces of tradition and change in India', in *Economic and Political Weekly*, Vol. 20, No. 50, 14 December, pages 2207–2269.

Basu K. (1990) *Agrarian structure and economic underdevelopment,* Harwood Academic Publishers, London.

Beneria L. (ed) (1982) *Women and development: The sexual division of labour in rural societies,* ILO, Geneva.
– (1988) 'Conceptualizing the labour force: The underestimation of women's economic activities', in R. E. Pahl (ed) *On work: Historical, comparative and theoretical approaches*, Basil Blackwell, Oxford.

Bhattacharya S. (1985) 'On the issue of under-enumeration of women's work in the Indian data collection system' in D. Jain and N. Bannerji (eds) *Tyranny of the household: Investigative essays on women's work*, Shakti Books, Delhi.

Boserup E. (1970) *Women's role in economic development,* Allen and Unwin, London.

Census of India (1991) *Provisional population totals: Workers and their distribution*, Paper 3 of 1991, Registrar General of India, Delhi.

Deere C. D. (1995) 'What difference does gender make? Rethinking peasant studies', in *Feminist Economics* Vol. 1.1: 53–72, Spring 1995.

Dreze J. and A. Sen (1999) *India: Economic development and social opportunity*, Oxford University Press, New Delhi.

Elson D. and R. Pearson (1981) 'The subordination of women and the internationalization of factory production' in K. Young, C. Wolkowitz and R. McCullaugh (eds) *Of marriage and the market: Women's subordination in international perspective*, CSE Books, London.

Ginwala F., M. Mackintosh and D. Massey (1990) 'Gender and economic policy in a democratic South Africa', discussion paper for 'Women, Colonialism and Commonwealth', Postgraduate Seminar, Institute of Commonwealth Studies, University of London, 16 November.

Gleason S. E. (1991) 'Gender bias in estimating female labour force participation', in J. G. Scoville (ed) *Status influences in third world labour markets: Caste, gender and custom*, de Gruyter Studies in Organization, Berlin.

Government of India (1974) *Towards equality: Report of the Committee on the Status of Women in India*, Department of Social Welfare, Government of India, New Delhi.
– (1993) *Statistical profile on women labour (fourth issue)*, Labour Bureau, Ministry of Labour, New Delhi.

Harris O. (1981) 'Households as natural units' in K. Young, C. Wolkowitz and R. McCullaugh (eds) *Of marriage and the market: Women's subordination in international perspective*, CSE Books, London.

Hirway J. (2000) 'Tabulation and analysis of the Indian time use survey data for improving measurement of paid and unpaid work', ESA/STAT/AC.79/20, 17 October 2000, United Nations, New York.

Krishnaraj M. and K. Chanana (eds) (1989) *Gender and household domain: Social and cultural dimensions*, Sage Publications, New Delhi/Newbury Park, London.

Mathur A. (1994) 'Work participation, gender and economic development: A quantitative anatomy of the Indian scenario', in *Journal of Development Studies*, Vol. 30, No. 2, pages 466–504.

Majumdar V. and K. Sharma (1990) 'Sexual division of labour and the subordination of women: A reappraisal from India' in I. Tinker (ed) *Persistent inequalities: Women and world development*, Oxford University Press, New York.

Mencher J. P. (1989) 'Women agricultural labourers and land owners in Kerala and Tamil Nadu: Some questions about gender and autonomy in the household' in M. Krishnaraj and K. Chanana (eds) *Gender and the household domain: Social and cultural dimensions*, Sage Publications, New Delhi/ Newbury Park, London.
– (1993) 'Women, agriculture and the sexual division of labour' in D. Bagchi and S. Raju (eds) *Women and work in South Asia: Regional patterns and perspectives*, Routledge, London.

Mies M. (1980) *Indian women and patriarchy*, Concept Publishing Company, New Delhi.
– (1982) *The lace makers of Narsapur: Indian housewives produce for the world market*, Zed Books, London.
– (1986) *Indian women in subsistence and agricultural labour*, Women, Work and Development: 12, International Labour Organization, Geneva.
– (1988) *Women: The last colony*, Zed Books, London.

Morvai K. (2000) 'Work and work-related rights of women and girls' in United Nations, *Bringing international human rights law home*, New York.

Mukhopadhyay M. (1985) *Silver shackles: Women and development in India*, Oxfam, Oxford.

Omvedt G. (1994) 'Dependency theory, peasants and third world crisis', in *Economic and Political Weekly*, January 22, pages 169–176.

Patel R. (1999) 'Labour and land rights of Hindu women in rural India – with particular reference to Western Orissa', PhD Thesis, University of Warwick, United Kingdom.
– (2002) 'Gender, production and access to land: The case for female peasants in India' in J. L. Parpart, S. M. Rai and K. Staudt (eds) *Rethinking empowerment in a global/local world: Gendered perspectives*, Routledge, London.

Sardamoni K. (1988) 'Women labourers, women cultivators and contribution to agriculture', in T. M. Dak (ed) *Women and work in Indian society*, Discovery Publishing House, Delhi.

Sen A. (1983) 'Economics and the family', in *Asian Development Review*, 1 (2): pages 14–26.
– (1987) 'Gender and cooperative conflicts', WIDER Working Papers, WP 18, July, UN University.

– (1990) 'Gender and cooperative conflicts' in I. Tinker (ed) *Persistent inequalities: Women and world development*, Oxford University Press, New York.

Sharma A. N. and S. Singh (eds) (1993) *Women and work: Changing scenario in India*, Indian Society of Labour Economics, Patna and B. R. Publishing House, Delhi.

Sharma M. (1985) 'Caste, class and gender: Production and reproduction in North India', in *The Journal of Peasant Studies*, Vol. 12, No. 4, pages 57–88.

Sharma U. (1989) 'Women, work and property in North-West India', in H. Alavi and J. Harris (eds) *Sociology of 'developing societies': South Asia*, Macmillan, London.
– (1984) 'Dowry in North India: Its consequences for women', in R. Hirschon (ed) *Women and property – women as property*, Croom Helm, London, Cranberra and St. Martin's Press, New York.
– (1994) 'Dowry in North India: Its consequences for women' in P. Uberoi (ed) *Family, kinship and marriage in India*, Oxford University Press, Delhi.

United Nations (2000) *Bringing international human rights law home*, United Nations, New York.
– (2001) *From Beijing to Beijing + 5: Review and appraisal of the Beijing Platform for Action*, United Nations, New York.

World Bank (1991) *Report of gender and poverty in India*.

Websites

http://www.undp.org.in/report/position/CCA.htm

http://webfusion.ilo.org/public/db/standards/normes/appl/index.cfm?lang=EN

List of legislation
India
Orissa Land Settlement Act 1959

Orissa Land Reforms Act 1962

Equal Remuneration Act 1976

International
Beijing Platform for Action 1995

Convention on the Elimination of all forms of Discrimination Against Women (CEDAW) 1979

International Labour Organization (ILO) Equal Remuneration Convention of 1951

10

Engendering the human rights protection of property rights:

Women's local land use in Tanzania[278]

Ingunn Ikdahl

This chapter discusses the human right protection of property rights in the light of women's local land uses in Tanzania. It is argued that the conventional interpretation of the concept of 'property rights' fails to take women's needs, experiences and contributions into consideration. This is illustrated through analysis of Tanzania's new land legislation and its implications for the situation of rural married women. In order to strengthen the human right protection of women's local land use, a stronger emphasis on the right to livelihood, integrity and non-discrimination is suggested as the way forward. The human rights arguments, as developed in this chapter, provide a legal backdrop for further recognition of rural women's quest for tenure security, not only as individuals but as providers of livelihood and food security for the children and elderly in the family.

1   Introduction

Land is essential for the livelihoods of the majority of the population in sub-Saharan Africa. It is the source of food and income, the home and a symbol of identity and belonging. Loss of land may lead to impoverishment, homelessness and hunger for women, men and children. Nevertheless, women and men often face different problems in obtaining, maintaining and protecting their access to land. In sub-Saharan Africa, access to land is linked to social relations. Land rights are socially embedded, complex, intermingled and overlapping. Gender stereotypes often underlie the way in which men and women's different relations to land are constructed. Men are often perceived as the heads of household and therefore the main decision makers. Women's access to land often de-

---

[278] The chapter is based on the author's Masters thesis. It was written as part of the research programme 'Women's law competence in development cooperation' at the Institute of Women's Law, University of Oslo, funded by the Norwegian Ministry of Foreign Affairs. The thesis is published in full (Ikdahl, 2001). An additional programme publication concerning the land reform in Tanzania is Lindstrøm (2001).

rives from the position as wife, sister, daughter, sister-in-law or mother – that is, through the relationship to a man. Although varying, the relations many women rely on have in common that the obtained access to land is seen as a right subsidiary to the man's right or not even as a right at all, just an accepted use.

Land reforms have for the last decade been undertaken in most countries in sub-Saharan Africa, as in other parts of the world (Toulmin and Quan, 2000). Due to the importance of land, changes in the legal framework may have massive impact on people's living conditions. The reforms have different characteristics, objectives and priorities. Nevertheless, a common feature of the different national reforms in recent years is the trend towards formalization of rights. Individualization, titling and registration of land rights may be an objective in itself or be part of establishing an official market for land rights. There is also an increasing recognition of the potential of customary land tenure systems, their existing rights, principles and institutions (Whitehead and Tsikata, 2003).

The new land laws are most often gender neutral. Nevertheless, the different bases for women and men's access to land can be to the effect that the laws fail to protect women (Ikdahl, Hellum, Kårhus and Benjaminsen, 2005). Formalization of existing rights combined with facilitating an official market in land rights calls for careful gender and class analysis. As new land laws have increased the opportunity for selling land, it has been claimed that a major demand for land, combined with the possibility of small profits and a potential economic crisis will lead to the already poor selling land to the richer (Raikes, 1997: 112).

Men's typically custom-based access to land leads to recognition and registration more often than it does for women. The importance of protecting married women in such situations is illustrated by the following quote from Kenya, where a process of registration of land rights has taken place:

> 'In a meeting with a group of churchwomen in Kenya, the commission was told that their greatest curse had been the titling system (ITR). Now with these pieces of paper their men would sell off the land in strips leaving them destitute. Even the traditional clan constraints on selling off land had begun to break down' (Shivji, 1998: 88).[279]

International human rights law creates legally binding obligations for states. In the following, I will develop human rights arguments that have a bearing on the protection of rural livelihoods in terms of women's land

---

[279] Several authors have documented the negative impact of registration on Kenyan women's land rights, see for example, Davison (1988), Shipton (1988), Nzioki (2002). Further analysis of the relationship between formalization and custom in Kenya can be found in Whitehead and Tsikata (2003) and Nyamu-Musembi (2002).

use. To demonstrate how land reform, women's rights and poverty prevention are linked I use the newly enacted land legislation of Tanzania as a starting point. My aim is to illustrate the gendered relationships that often underlie seemingly neutral law reform. The aim is to contribute to a wider human rights perspective, with emphasis on issues of livelihood, integrity and non-discrimination against women.

In the second section I deal with land as a human rights issue. The third section gives an overview of the situation in Tanzania including the legal system, land reform and its implications for the status of rural women's land use. Differences between men and women's access to and control of land are described. The fourth section provides a theoretical understanding of the different functions underlying the concept of property rights. These are the static function related to a person's integrity, the dynamic function providing space for markets and finally the livelihood dimension. In the final section the human right protection of rural married women's land use is further analyzed in the light of these three functions.

2   Land as a human rights issue

The human rights conventions do not provide a right to access land. Nevertheless, land is closely linked to a multitude of rights that are essential for life and therefore clearly a human rights issue.

Realization of the right to an adequate living standard,[280] including the right to housing and the right to food, often depends upon access to and right to land. The state is obliged to respect these rights and to take steps to fulfil them. Land issues may also be influenced by cultural rights, as many cultures are closely linked to a way of living interwoven with land.[281] The right to privacy[282] and the protection of property rights[283] are other examples of rights that have an influence on questions regarding land rights.

I will focus on the human right 'protection of property rights' and discuss what it has to offer women who use land on an informal basis. To examine what this right offers women with custom-based use of land, it is necessary to introduce the content of the right.

---

[280] The International Covenant on Economic, Social and Cultural Rights article 11 and Universal Declaration on Human Rights article 25. See also the African Protocol on the Rights of Women articles 15 (food) and 16 (housing).

[281] The International Covenant on Civil and Political Rights, article 27.

[282] International Covenant on Civil and Political Rights, article 17, Universal Declaration on Human Rights, article 12.

[283] Universal Declaration on Human Rights, article 17.

Characteristic for property rights is that they cannot be classified as exclusively civil or political or as merely a social right (Krause, 1995: 143–156). Seeing property rights as a negative right, protecting the right-holder against interference, western scholarship has seen it as a civil or political right. Yet the social and economic implications of property rights draw attention to their characteristics of a positive right. Property is from this perspective seen as a condition for a life in dignity. The right to a life in dignity puts an obligation on the state to ensure that every individual enjoys a certain minimum of resources. Emphasizing the social function of property, human rights scholars have in recent years turned their attention to the balance between property rights as individual civil rights and as social, economic and cultural rights (Krause, 1995: 144).

These two sides of property rights are both interrelated and conflicting, and the dual nature of the right created problems in the drafting of the international human rights instruments. Krause and Alfredsson have described the debates during the drafting of the International Covenant on Economic, Social and Cultural Rights and the International Covenant on Civil and Political Rights:

'There was disagreement on practically every aspect of the topic …, including such issues as the scope of property, conformity with state laws, expropriation and other allowable limitations, due process of law, compensation and indeed the very inclusion of the right' (Krause and Alfredsson, 1999: 365).

The protection of property rights was left out of these covenants but it is embedded in the Universal Declaration of Human Rights (article 17), the African Charter (article 14), the American Convention (article 21) and the Protocol to the European Convention (article 1). It is also found in certain conventions protecting the interests of vulnerable groups, for example, workers and refugees (Krause and Alfredsson, 1999: 373). The core of the human right 'protection of property rights' is that it imposes a substantial obligation upon states. As a starting point, they are not allowed to encroach upon certain existing property rights but must respect and protect them.[284]

This raises several questions regarding the scope of the term 'property right'. What exactly does it mean from a human rights perspective? A property right is not a physical object, it is a legal term describing a relationship between a person and a piece of property, for example, land. So what is protected is that specific relationship. Considering how the formal content of the term 'property' varies in different national sys-

---

[284] Derogations from this principle, such as the possibility of expropriating land for public purposes under certain circumstances, will not be dealt with here.

tems,[285] it can hardly be surprising that the international conventions do not include a definition of property rights.[286] The variations in the nationally defined legal concepts of property rights has resulted in criticism of the protection of property rights clause, as it makes the right vague and difficult to use (Krause, 1993: 73).

It is clear that the term 'property right' includes more than ownership. Rights related to land may be of several sorts: rights to sell or veto a sale, rights to establish a mortgage, holding security interests, rights to administer, rights to collect wood, grazing rights, and so on. Nevertheless, the emphasis has traditionally been on the formal owner, based on the assumption that you can find one sole owner to property, and that other rights-holders are of less relevance. This leads to focusing on the formal acquisition of rights in the nationally-defined legal system, without relating it to the real-life functions of property rights. This may work well in a European context, where a strong state defines and registers rights of ownership to land. This understanding of the concept of 'property right' has been seen as less suitable in an African socio-cultural context.[287] Rights to a piece of land are often multiple and overlapping, common and concurrent. As will be shown, in Tanzania concepts of ownership and land rights are more pluralistic and complex, based upon different kinds of use and different individual or collective bonds to land. Formal and more informal rights coexist and are intertwined. Thus, one essential question is how the protection of property rights can deal with this diversity of rights. Which of these rights, if not all, can claim human right protection?

A related question in the African context is whether customary law is capable of creating 'rights' in the human rights sense of the concept. While much academic energy has been used on customary law's relationship to and position in national law (for example in Bentzon *et al.*, 1998: 30–46), less attention has been given to the relationship between customary law and human rights law. If customary law is accepted as a basis of rights that can claim human right protection, this raises further

---

[285] This can be exemplified by comparing the Tanzanian concepts of property rights in relation to land, as described in section 3, to European legal tradition in this field.

[286] Protocol to the European Convention, article 1, uses the term 'possession' instead of 'property' but the supervisory organs have clarified that this right in substance guarantees the right of property. The difference in terms is therefore not decisive for the interpretations.

[287] Other articles in this volume exemplify how different circumstances and considerations influence rights to land. See Bentzon and Odgaard (1997) as regards the relationship between obligations to care for family members and rights to land in Tanzania, and Patel (1999) concerning the recognition of the value of women's work as a way to obtain support for women's land claims in India.

questions: Who should decide upon the substantial content of customary law and how should this be done?

In addition to the practical problem of dealing with diversity, non-discrimination is a pressing issue. The non-discrimination principle entails a demand for equal treatment of different groups in society in all matters related to human rights. In the African context access to and use of land is highly gendered. How should the protection of property rights be interpreted to be non-discriminatory in a context characterized by diversity and complexity?

3 Tanzania

Background

Tanzania is mainly an agricultural society.[288] Land is a main source of livelihood (for farmers and pastoralists) but it has also a vital symbolic function as it defines a person's home and status, and is seen as a part of the clan's relations to its ancestors (Moore, 1999: 46).

The legal concept of property rights regarding land in Tanzania differs from the typical European one. Traditionally, land has not been seen as something you own but as something you can use. There is no statutory definition of ownership, and the rights are more complex (Shivji, 1998: 84–85, James and Fimbo, 1973: 6–7; Ikdahl, 2001: 9–10). There may be several holders of different rights to the same piece of land and the rights often have collective aspects. The clan holds the land together and customary law regulates the allocation of land rights between the members of the clan. Sometimes the rights will also be linked to the needs and actual use of the holder: if a right is not used, it may be passed on to someone who needs it more (James and Fimbo, 1973: 28 and 303).

As regards women, statutory law allows them to enter into contracts on equal terms with men. Hence, they are allowed to buy land rights when such rights are for sale. Still, for most women this option is not available, as they are marginalized in the economy and have little or no commodities that can be used as security for loans.[289]

Most rural women base their access to land upon different family or marital relations. These may take multiple forms. As daughters and sis-

---

[288] Approximately 80 per cent of the economically active population works in agriculture (Africa, 2000:1086).

[289] This is at least partly due to the fact that women and men do different forms of work. Women produce food for the family while men grow cash crops, see for example, http://www.fao.org/gender/en/lab-e.htm and http://www.fao.org/sd/Wpdirect/Wpre0010.htm (December 2004); Ikdahl (2001:30–31); Shinyanga Report (1998:23–25).

ters, they are allowed to use the land of their natal family (Rwebangira, 1999; Odgaard, 1999). As wives, they move to land belonging to their husbands' clan and receive a plot there, mainly for cultivating food for the family. Such relationships to land are custom-based and (relatively) informal and it is debated whether they entail a secure right or just an actual but insecure access (Migiro, 1988: 78; Manji, 1999: 17). The status of these different ways of gaining access to land is debated in the family, in customary law and in statutory law. In addition, custom is continually changing and in development.[290]

Land is a classic example of legal pluralism where different formal and informal sets of norms interact. Customary law and statutory law have existed side-by-side since colonization and the land legislation from 1999 takes this further by explicitly referring to customary law. This is in line with what seems to be a general trend in direction of recognizing customary tenure in statutory land laws and policies (Whitehead and Tsikata, 2003).

The new Land Acts
In 1991 the government appointed a Presidential Commission of Inquiry into Land Matters.[291] The report from the commission, submitted in 1992, was marked by the wish to investigate the concerns of the land users from below and the major objective of its recommendations was to solve problems related to double-allocation and insecurity of tenure for small-scale farmers.[292] Village lands should generally be inalienable to outsiders – non-villagers (Shivji Commission, 1992: 158; Shivji, 1998: 52) and customary law should continue to be the main source of law in the villages (Shivji, 1997: 2–3).

Professor Shivji, who chaired the commission, later stated that the commission did not respond to the government's desire for a policy that 'would rationalize and legitimate the impending liberalization of land in line with the policy diktat of the international financial institutions' (Shivji, 1997: 2–3). As opposed to the normal procedure, the government refused to issue a White Paper in response to the commission's

---

[290] See the article by Bentzon and Odgaard elsewhere in this volume for a more detailed analysis.

[291] Hereinafter referred to as the (Shivji) commission, after its chair Issa G. Shivji, Professor of Law at the University of Dar es Salaam. For more extensive discussions of different aspects of the land reform, see Benschop (2002), Izumi (1998), Lindstrøm (2001) and Sundet (1997).

[292] Manji (1998). This was necessary after decades of confusion caused by villagization (the state policy in the 1970s, initiating large-scale forced moving of villages), double-allocation and a generally chaotic administration concerning rights to land (Shivji Commission, 1992:30, 43-63).

report. Instead, a British consultant was hired to draft a Land Bill.[293] The Bill went further in the direction of commercialization by suggesting a legal framework that enhanced the possibilities for a market for land rights. The legislators wanted to facilitate the use of land rights as collateral and thereby facilitate a market for land rights.[294] The rights had to be clear and secure to attract investors and thereby improve the country's economy.

Hence, solving problems related to insecurity of tenure for the existing right-holders and establishing a market for land rights became two overall objectives of the land reform. The tension between these two can create conflicts between different rules that aim at the one or the other objective (Lindstrøm, 2001: 82–83).

The draft Bill served as a basis for the two Land Acts enacted in 1999, namely the Land Act and the Village Land Act.[295] To ensure that land rights are secure and easily transferable, the new Acts established a process of individualization, titling and registration of land rights (ITR).[296] Rights were to be registered locally and these registers would be recognized by the state.[297] Customary law is one of the relevant factors when deciding which rights can be registered under the new Village Land Act (see article 23(2)e).

In addition to serving as a basis for registration, customary law is given a more general role. This is clear from article 20.1 in the Village Land Act:

> 'Subject to the provisions of this Act, any matter concerning the rights and obligations of a person, a group of persons ...or on another matter affecting land held under a customary right of occupancy ... shall, where the matter is not otherwise provided for under this Act or any other enactment, be determined in accordance with customary law.'

---

[293] Professor Peter MacAuslan from the University of London, sponsored by the British Overseas Development Agency.

[294] This was due to pressure partly from the inside (Moore, 1999) and partly from the outside – international financial institutions such as the International Monetary Fund and the World Bank (Manji, 1998).

[295] Some parts of the country are declared village land and are ruled by the Village Land Act ('generally land registered as village land or which the villagers have been regularly occupying and using during the last 12 years', the Village Land Act, article 7). The remaining land is governed by the Land Act. I will mainly focus upon the Village Land Act.

[296] The ITR process is governed by the Village Land Act, articles 7.7, 21.1 and 22 (Shivji, 1998: 96); Lindstrøm (2001: 83–85); Ikdahl (2001: 26–27).

[297] This can be seen as part of the general trend Cousins describes as currently taking place in Africa, where the registering of rights at a local level, accepted by the state, is one of the ways of performing land reforms (Cousins, 2002).

Hence, statutory law explicitly refers to customary law to solve matters that the Village Land Act does not regulate. This will typically be family matters where the state, both in the colonial and post-colonial era, has been more reluctant to interfere (Bentzon *et al.*, 1998:32; Shivji, 1998: 88–90; Lindstrøm, 2001:100–102). Statutory law mostly deals with questions of state regulations, for example use of land and transactions in a market. Transfer of land rights within the family (for example by inheritance or through gifts within the clan) is still governed by customary law (James and Fimbo, 1973: 302). But the private and the public are closely related in this context as the private sphere serves as a basis for the rights in the public sphere. The land reform process of Tanzania has been criticized because it did not sufficiently examine questions concerning women's land rights in the private sphere and instead mainly let existing practices continue. It has been pointed out how this may lead to an exclusion of women from the public sphere, as their rights and use of land become invisible in the national laws (Lindstrøm, 2001: 97–126).

The legal situation for married rural women's access to land:
Customary and statutory law
In this section, the consequences of the new land legislation for women will be highlighted by a closer look at the situation of married rural women. If a woman moves to the land of her husband's family after marriage, her bonds to the land of her natal family are often weakened. As regards the land she moves to, her relationship to it is seen as subordinate to that of her husband (Manji, 1998: 83–85). It is expected that the new legislation in most cases will mean that the husband becomes registered as the right-holder to the land they both live on.[298] As the new Acts have increased the opportunity for selling land rights, it is crucial to be registered as a right-holder. During two relatively short visits to Tanzania in 1999 and 2004, a recurrent concern of women's non-governmental organizations and women lawyers I met was how to ensure secure tenure for married women. There was a fear that men would mortgage or sell the family property without the wife's consent. Security for the wife's existing use may come into conflict with the husband's wish to gain from the established market for land. When transfer of land rights is made easier, the situation of users whose rights are not registered becomes less secure. The two overall objectives of the land reform may thus be at odds where overlapping rights are individualized.

The Village Land Act (article 3) contains general principles that must be taken into consideration when interpreting the other provisions of the

---

[298] The registration process in Kenya has resulted in a very low percentage of women registered as landowners (Shipton, 1988; Davison, 1988; Nzioki, 2002).

Act and is therefore important in the examination of women's position in this situation.

> 'Article 3 (1) The fundamental principles of National Land Policy which are the objectives of the Land Act, 1999, to which all persons exercising powers under, applying or interpreting this Act are to have regard to are …
>
> (c) to ensure that existing rights in and recognized long-standing occupation or use of land are clarified and secured by the law;
>
> (d) to facilitate an equitable distribution of and access to land by all citizens; …
>
> (f) to pay full, fair and prompt compensation to any person whose right of occupancy or recognized long-standing occupation or customary use of land is revoked or otherwise interfered with to their detriment by the state …
>
> (k) to facilitate the operation of a market in land'.

Article 3(1)c and f specifically protect existing rights and uses. If married women's use of land falls within the scope of these provisions, their situation must be taken into consideration when interpreting other provisions of the Act, for example, rules related to their husbands' right to sell. Due to the recognition of the different customary laws of different groups in Tanzania, the Act does not provide a definition of what, exactly, is meant by an 'existing right' or 'recognized use'. Due to lack of conceptual clarity the status of women's custom-based use is also unclear. The answer will depend on whether those who have the power to decide find the use to be a *right* or just an insecure *access* to land (Manji, 1999: 14–15). This question can only be answered after a thorough examination of the actual practices and conceptions in different parts of Tanzania, so only a few formal starting points will be mentioned here.

How to find and define the content of customary law is the subject of ongoing academic discussion (Stewart, 1998; Bentzon *et al.*, 1998; Hellum, 2000; Bentzon and Odgaard, 1997). If the starting point is customary law as interpreted and used by the state courts, one often reaches an understanding that is to the disfavour of women. This is related to the case law from the colonial courts which still carries weight. Recent research has demonstrated how the 'state court customary law' often differs remarkably from the living customary law as it is practised and conceived by the people affected by it (WLSA, Zimbabwe, 1994; Hellum, 1999: 385–397; Woodman, 1988). This is especially the case for the higher courts. It has also been shown that the living customary law may be more favourable to women than often predicted.[299]

---

[299] The article by Bentzon and Odgaard elsewhere in this volume describes fathers' support of daughters' right to inherit land.

A related discussion is to what extent one should consider both trouble-cases and trouble-less cases when examining the content of customary law. The legal anthropologist J. F. Hollemann points out that to find the 'whole story' of customary law, one should take into consideration both cases where conflicts occur and the everyday problems that are solved without conflicts. He specifically mentions questions regarding land rights as an area where an approach based solely upon trouble-cases can be misleading (Holleman, 1973: 592–594).

In line with this, it is important to examine how the situation of married women is perceived in the local society when situations are dealt with smoothly, as well as when conflict arises. Is it taken for granted that a woman should be allowed to use land belonging to her husband or his family? An analysis from a living customary law, trouble-less case point of view may lead to the conclusion that her use is seen as a right rather than just insecure access to use of land (Odgaard, 1999; Odgaard and Bentzon, 2005).

But the state courts have in many instances been reluctant to accept this dynamic and fluid understanding of customary law (Stewart, 1998; Stewart and Tsanga, 2005; Hellum, 2000).[300] It is thus a danger that married women's use of land derived from their husbands' family will not be accepted as a customary right by the higher courts. Their application of a more formal approach will thus reinforce existing unequal property relations.

If the interpretation of the customary law leads to a negative result for women, it may be found to '[deny] women … lawful access to ownership, occupation or use of any such land' and therefore be deemed void and inoperative according to the Village Land Act, article 20.2. But this provision does not address the question of which rules shall replace discriminatory custom when adjudicating such cases. Some guidance can be found in provisions specifically dealing with transferral of rights. Article 30(4)b demands that the village councils disallow assignments which 'would be likely to operate to defeat the right of any women to occupy land under a customary right of occupancy, a derivative right or as a successor in title to the assignor'. Article 33(1)d states that the village council, in approving a disposition of a customary right of occupancy, is bound, *inter alia*, to ensure that the special needs of women for land are adequately met and article 36 states that in case of a husband exercising his customary right of surrendered occupancy, first priority for offer of the land must go to his wife or wives. Hopefully, the implementation of this at the local level will be facilitated by the requirement

---

[300] An infamous example of this is the *Magaya v Magaya* inheritance case from Zimbabwe's Supreme Court 16 February 1999.

in the Village Land Act, article 60.2 that the village land council, which serves as the manager of the village area and as the first instance for dispute settlement, shall have at least three female members out of a total of seven.

The case of married women's use of land in Tanzania highlights several important points. Firstly, that the concept of 'land rights' encompasses a wide variety of relationships between individuals, groups and land. This is made even more complex by legal pluralism and the dynamics of customs and practices. Secondly, it illustrates that land rights is a highly gendered issue: men and women are differently situated. Thirdly, it provides a window to the importance of considering the interests and realities of different groups in times of change. The process of individualization and registration of rights in a market-based land tenure system increases the vulnerability for those whose use of land is not registered as a right. This, especially in the situation where a husband wants to sell land he has registered rights to, illustrates a tension between the role of land as a commodity that may be transferred for money and land as a resource used to sustain a person's livelihood.

4 Understanding the concept of property rights

As shown above, there is an ongoing discussion about the content and scope of the concept of 'land rights' in Tanzania, both at national and local level. There is lack of clarity regarding the distinction between the actual access, uses and the legal rights. This has a parallel in the uncertainty about the protection of property rights at the international level.

The complexity of property rights is closely related to the fact that the right is not an issue of the object itself but a recognition of a relationship between a person and an object. Therefore, rights to land are not necessarily exclusive but made up of a bundle of different relationships that may or may not be in the same hands. And the recognition of such relationships as 'rights' may take place at different levels and by different institutions.

In this complex situation, what is the content of the states' human rights obligations to respect and protect property rights? Does the concept of property rights have a cross-cultural meaning, despite the differences pertaining to national terminology and rules?

The lack of precise concepts makes it difficult to undertake a detailed analysis of the elements of property rights. I therefore suggest using the normative structure of property rights as a tool to analyze the underlying values in the rules protecting property rights in different fields of law. This approach was developed by Swedish law professor, Anna Christensen, for analyzing the changing nature of property rights in the

Swedish context, where she identified three basic functions of property rights: the protection of integrity, the market-economic function and the social function whereby property rights provide means for livelihood (Christensen, 1994: 1–7 and 355–389).

I have adopted her approach as a way of deconstructing the terms and reaching for the realities in the protection of property rights.

The first and most basic function of property rights is, according to Christensen, to ensure that the holder can keep his or her existing use of and relationship to the object. This is a *static function* and it is strongest concerning objects in the close private sphere of the person concerned, for example a person's clothes and home. This function serves to *protect the integrity* of the right-holder. The significance of this aspect is demonstrated in relation to the human right to housing, where legal security of tenure is one of the seven basic requirements for housing to be 'adequate' (United Nations, 1991: paragraph 8a).

The second function of property rights emerged as, in a changing world, the protection of integrity was no longer the only role played by property rights. The need to change the way property was used increased as the industrial revolution and the market economy changed society. Farmers used some of their land to build a sawmill or a factory, or they sold it to other farmers to take up paid employment. Populations grew, and there was a growing need for a functioning market for land. The second function of property rights is the *dynamic* one, the possibility of selling or at least changing the mode of use. This is sometimes referred to as the *market-economic* function of property rights. Today, this function is often emphasized by proponents of registration and titling as a means of giving a value to the property of the poor. The overall concern is the role land can play as security for obtaining credit (De Soto, 2000).

These two functions may be held in the same hands – the owner of a house can choose whether he wants to live in it or sell it – or they can be split between different right-holders: a landlord can sell a flat but he cannot use it as long as the tenant lives there, while the tenant can live there but not sell it. A scale shows the balancing of these two functions:

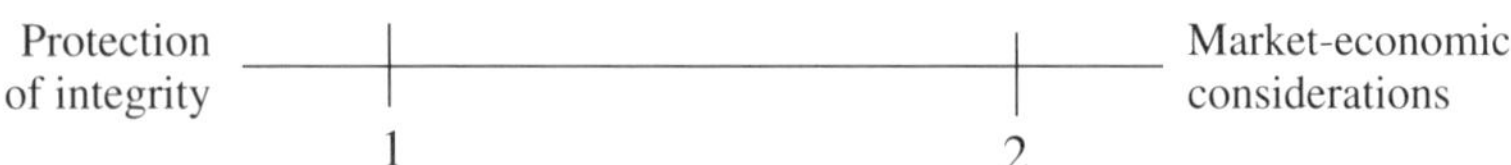

The interest of the tenant will be somewhere near 1, while the landlord's position is that of 2. If the state changes the laws in favour of the landlord, this may be described as a movement of the law towards the right side of this scale.

A third function of property rights is securing people's *livelihood.*

This is related to property rights as social and economic rights, not the protection of existing rights. It can demand change and redistribution rather than protection of the integrity of the right-holders, and is therefore not a static, conservative function. Neither is it based on market-economic arguments. It should therefore be placed as the third corner of a triangle defining the different aspects of property rights.

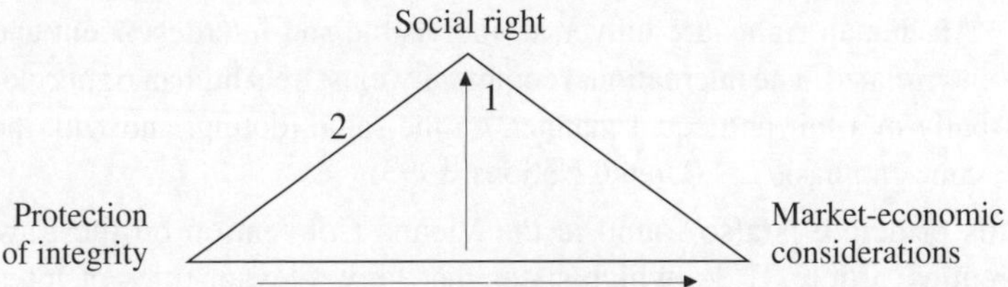

The concept of normative structure facilitates analysis and comparison across legal systems by making it possible to transcend the differing terminologies. The land reform in Tanzania can roughly be described as a movement to the right (1), as it aims to facilitate a land market and therefore increases the weight of the dynamic aspects of the property rights involved. The redistributive part of the land reform in South Africa is an example of a movement upwards (2), as it seeks to even out the distribution of land between rich and poor (Cousins, 2002; Hvidsten, 2000).

In the case of Tanzania these concepts can also be used to elucidate the above-mentioned sales situation and provide a different way of posing the question of the Tanzanian state's human right obligations when changing the administration of land from family-based to market-based. The mentioned situation exemplifies the double function of land rights, as both a right providing security and integrity for the wife, and a commodity with a monetary value on a market for the husband holding the registered right. How freely can the state promote the dynamic functions of property rights for some holders of rights if that means reducing the static, integrity-protecting function for others?

5   The human right protection of property rights: a norm in change?

Protecting integrity
The discussion of the normative structure of property rights shows the different values that are protected by property rights through its three functions. This provides a framework for the further discussion of which property rights are protected by the human rights. Should the market-economic interests have the highest priority or should the emphasis be

on protection of integrity? How should these different values be balanced?

The integrity of every person is one of the main concerns of the human rights. Guidelines to the more precise content of this can be drawn from other human rights. When interpreting human rights law, one is obliged to see each right in the context of other rights. This is clearly stated in the Vienna Declaration of 1993, article 5.1:

> 'All human rights are universal, indivisible and interdependent and interrelated. The international community must treat human rights globally in a fair and equal manner, on the same footing, and with the same emphasis ...' (United Nations, 1993).

This principle is also found in the Vienna Convention on the Law of Treaties, article 31.3c, which states that 'any relevant rules of international law applicable in the relations between the parties' is a relevant source when interpreting a convention.

As mentioned in section 2 above, there are several other rights that are closely related to the issue of land.

The right to an adequate standard of living, as found in the International Covenant on Economic, Social and Cultural Rights, article 11, adds a social and economic aspect to the interpretation of property rights. In rural communities, land is important both for food and for adequate shelter, important elements for the standard of living (United Nations, 1996: articles 1, 8, 9 and 11).[301] The states have an obligation to take steps to achieve realization of this right. According to the United Nations Committee on Economic, Social and Cultural Rights, security of tenure is one of the core factors for the right to housing to be realized (United Nations, 1991). Additionally, the interpretation of the right of minorities to enjoy their own culture has increasingly emphasized the role of land to realize this right (United Nations, 1994: paragraph 7). These provisions highlight the role of land use for the fulfilment of human rights. Land has a role due to its integrity-preserving, static functions, rather than the market-economic functions. Its relation to the market is indirect, through the products that may be grown on it, not direct as a commodity in itself.

The case of married women's land use in Tanzania illustrates this. If the land a woman is using is transferred from her husband to someone

---

[301] The African Protocol on the Rights of Women, article 15, links land to women's right to food and requires that states take 'appropriate measures' to 'provide women with access to clean drinking water, sources of domestic fuel, land and the means of producing nutritious food'. Also the Food and Agriculture Organization has emphasized the relationship between land rights and economic and social development in their work for land reforms and rural development.

else, she loses the resources she has previously gained from growing food and cash crops there and may even lose her home. And as rural Tanzania lacks social security apart from what family can offer, the woman's ability to obtain food will be weakened. If the process of individualization, titling and registration of rights weakens the protection of women's existing land use in Tanzania, this will make it more difficult for them to obtain and keep an adequate standard of living. Such a step in the wrong direction is problematic in the light of the state's human rights obligations. Thus it can be argued that use rights are more important for the fulfilment of these other human rights and should therefore enjoy a stronger human rights protection than land rights that mainly interact with the market-economic functions of property.

This argument is further strengthened by the fact that national laws in many cases let the protection of integrity of the user override the interests of the formal owner. The laws of different countries concerning protection of property rights illustrate problems that may appear, as well as the states' ideas of how those problems should be solved. Insofar as common general principles are identified, they can have weight as sources of law according to the Statute of the International Court of Justice, article 3.8.1(c):

'The court, whose function is to decide in accordance with international law such disputes as are submitted to it, shall apply: ...
(c) the general principles of law recognized by civilized nations;...'

Furthermore, the states' laws regarding property rights can be seen as implementation of their international obligations. As the protection of property rights is also treaty-based, state practice is given further weight by the Vienna Convention on the Law of Treaties, article 31.3(b), which states as a relevant factor of interpretation:

'...any subsequent practice in the application of the treaty which establishes the agreement of the parties regarding its interpretation.'

One example from national laws is how one often finds regulations limiting the landlord's ability to terminate the contract (Christensen, 1994). Thereby, the tenant's interest in continuing the use of the flat or house prevails over the owner's wish to sell or otherwise change the use of the property. It has been argued from a human rights approach that housing rights may require rent control measures that restrict the owner's property rights (Krause, 1995: 156).

Another example is the rules concerning acquisitive prescription. Since the period of Roman law, it has been common to have an arrangement where land being used over a long time and in good faith is given status as a right, even when it was not founded on rights from the start (Eriksen, 1993). The consideration behind this is the important role such rights may have for the person as a security for his or her home, work, economy and way of life. This is closely linked to the static function of property rights, the protection of integrity. The right given is of the same scope and extent as the use that has taken place. Even if these rules do not apply to a spouse, they show values that the states consider worthy of protection.

Although not directly relevant for the described situation in Tanzania, these different examples show situations where there exist two conflicting interests to the same landed property. They have in common that the states let considerations for the integrity of the user prevail over the market-economic interest of the owner. Thereby, they implicitly illustrate criteria the states rely on when prioritizing between different rights to the same object. This is very much the case if the use has been long term and has resulted in a perception of having a right – extra strong if the object at question is a person's home. These factors are all related to whether losing the right would amount to intrusion of the user's integrity.

Non-discrimination

The protection of property rights has been controversial and has been accused of being too conservative in regard to the distribution of resources. The focus upon the sole owner has been criticized for reinforcing existing social and economic inequalities between users and (formal) owners. It is argued that by protecting the owners on behalf of the poor, it hinders development and poverty alleviation and maintains the existing unequal distribution amongst groups, based on, for example, ethnicity, class and gender. Therefore it also hinders the fulfilment of social and economic human rights. Even if one agrees with this argument, it must be recognized that the protection of property rights is included in several human rights documents and accepted as customary international law, and thereby binding for all states (Krause, 1993; 45). Attempting to reinterpret the right thus seems a more productive way forward than simply condemning it.

Women are, in large parts of the world, working the land but hardly ever own it. As shown in the case of Tanzania, a gender-neutral law is no guarantee for non-discriminatory practice. People's lives form the basis for acquisition of rights and these lives are affected by culturally, religiously and locally determined gender roles. The reality of people's lives must be considered when deciding upon the interpretation of property rights if one wants to achieve a non-discriminatory result. Considering the fundamental role of property rights in ensuring the realization of several human rights, it is essential that the protection of property rights is carried out in a non-discriminatory manner. Recognition of the diversity of property rights related to land and ways to obtain it can open up a space for a non-discriminatory understanding of the state's obligation to respect and protect property rights while keeping in mind local and national variations.

The prohibition of discrimination based on sex is found in several human rights conventions and recognized as international customary law. It is especially clearly dealt with in CEDAW, which has the following definition in article 1:

> 'For the purposes of the present convention, the term 'discrimination against women' shall mean any distinction, exclusion or restriction made on the basis of sex which has the effect or purpose of impairing or nullifying the recognition, enjoyment or exercise by women, irrespective of their marital status, on a basis of equality of men and women, of human rights and fundamental freedoms in the political, economic, social, cultural, civil or any other field.'

A similar prohibition of discrimination against women can be found in the African Protocol on the Rights of Women, article 1(f). It is important to note that the prohibition of discrimination based on sex does not only cover formal discrimination; both *de jure* and *de facto* discrimination is covered. As long as the reality is gendered, a gender-neutral interpretation of the rights may lead to discriminatory results. One example is how the formally gender-neutral law in Tanzania can lead to inequalities as to who will be registered as holders of land rights. In the context of property rights, a definition of which rights should be protected cannot contain only the rights typical for men. It can be seen as a recognition of the gendered nature of property rights, and the need for special attention to the situation of women, when article 19(c) in the African Protocol on the Rights of Women obliges the state to 'promote women's access to and control over productive resources such as land and guarantee their right to property'.

If women shall have *de facto* possibilities to gain and keep land rights, the typically female way of *obtaining rights* (based on the marital relationship) must be considered worthy of protection on equal footing with the male way (based on a natal family relationship). Differential treatment of men's and women's ways of acquiring access to land will lead to continued and reinforced disadvantages for women.

Furthermore, women and men's roles in agricultural production often differ, including the kinds of work that they carry out. Often, men are in control of cash crops while women produce food for subsistence through vegetable gardens. The products grown in the gardens are used both for consumption and sale to provide cash for medicine, school fees, clothes and food (Hellum, in this volume). A strict distinction between domestic and productive uses or contributions in terms of cash, work or in kind, in relation to acquisition of property rights may thus have a discriminatory effect. In its general recommendations, the CEDAW committee emphasized the importance of recognition of women's unpaid and domestic work (CEDAW, 1991a and b). The consequences this will have for the concept of property can be seen in the committee's recommendation regarding article 16(1)(h) of CEDAW. Article 16 states:

'1. States parties shall take all appropriate measures to eliminate discrimination against women in all matters relating to marriage and family relations and in particular shall ensure, on a basis of equality of men and women: ...

(h) The same rights for both spouses in respect of ownership, acquisition, management, administration, enjoyment and disposition of property, whether free of charge or for a valuable consideration.'[302]

In General Recommendation No. 21 (CEDAW, 1994), it is clearly stated that financial and non-financial contributions to property 'should be accorded the same weight' (paragraph 32) and the woman should be consulted when property owned by the parties is disposed of (paragraph 31). It is also emphasized how rights to property are critical for the woman's 'ability to earn a livelihood and provide adequate housing and nutrition for herself and for her family' (paragraph 26). In addition, CEDAW, article 14, deals specifically with the problems faced by rural women, and requires *inter alia* equal treatment in land and agrarian reform (article 14.2g). Article 13(h) in the African Protocol on the Rights of Women obliges the states to 'take the necessary measures to recognize the economic value of the work of women in the home'.

At the national level, the development regarding matrimonial property shows how gender roles affect the acquisition of property rights, as well as how this can be dealt with to minimize discriminatory effects. During the last decades, both legislation and Supreme Court practice in several countries has shown a movement towards giving wives co-ownership in property acquired by the husband, especially in case of divorce (Ncube, 1989). The reasoning behind this seems to be based on both equity and economic arguments. The economic point of view focuses on the housewife's contribution, as her work at home gives her husband the possibility to spend his time making money, which is later used for acquiring property. The more equity-based argument is related to the fact that a marriage means an intermingling of work and responsibility, and that the wife has the same need for and feelings of ownership to the

---

[302] See also the similar provision in the African Protocol on the Rights of Women, article 6(j).

property, for example, their house (Sverdrup, 1997 and 1999). These rules and judgments are most often related to their home. It seems like the solutions chosen at national level to a large extent are in accordance with the requirements and recommendations of CEDAW and its committee. In the African Protocol on the Rights of Women, article 7(d) gives both women and men the rights to an 'equitable sharing of the joint property deriving from the marriage' in case of divorce and article 21.1 states that widows shall not only have rights to 'an equitable share' in the inheritance of the husband's property, she also has a right to 'continue to live in the matrimonial house'.

Another example of these new directions in the human right protection of property rights is the recognition of the land rights of indigenous and tribal peoples. The International Labour Organization has made two conventions on this issue (ILO, 1957 and 1989a). It is also dealt with in the International Covenant on Civil and Political Rights article 27, and a draft declaration on the rights of indigenous peoples is currently being prepared in the United Nations system.[303]

The development is especially clear when comparing the old and the newer International Labour Organization conventions. In the 1989 convention, article 14.1 defines the protection of the peoples' land rights:

> 'The rights of ownership and possession of the peoples concerned over the lands which they traditionally occupy shall be recognized. In addition, measures shall be taken in appropriate cases to safeguard the right of peoples concerned to use lands not exclusively occupied by them, but to which they have traditionally had access for their subsistence and traditional activities. Particular attention shall be paid to the situation of nomadic peoples and shifting cultivators in this respect.'

In the first sentence, the peoples' rights to the land which they have occupied are given a protection more or less like that of a right of ownership. 'Occupy' means that the use must be somehow similar to that of total ownership, with an exclusive, permanent and extensive use (NOU, 1997: 34). But the second sentence, which was new in the 1989 convention, makes it clear that the protection is not limited to lands which they 'traditionally occupy': it also applies to land they have not 'exclusively occupied' but to which they have 'traditionally had access for their subsistence and traditional activities'. This is of great importance for nomadic peoples who otherwise would often have no protection at all. A nomad does not 'occupy' the land and will therefore encounter problems in becoming owner in the traditional legal sense of the word. Nev-

---

[303] The draft declaration is contained in the 1994 sub-commission annual report: doc. E/CN.4/Sub.2/1994/56. It is annexed to resolution No. 45.

ertheless, his right to let his animals graze the land some months of the year is still fundamental for his life. The third sentence of the provision must be seen as an approval of this (NOU, 1997: 34).

The comparison of these documents shows a shift away from a protection adapted only to the needs of one group (the permanent residents) to a concept of property rights based upon different groups' cultures, their traditional relationship to the land, and the importance of land as both a means for subsistence, and as a way of life. ILO has pointed out that their conventions have a functional, not a formal concept of property rights (ILO, 1989b: 34–36). This should be seen as a development towards a more pluralistic view on law, leading to inclusion of a wider spectrum of rights in the protection. When customary law emphasizes integrity and use rather than market-economic arguments when defining and granting rights, the same will be the case in relation to the protection given by the convention.

The same trend is seen in national law in several countries. In Norway, a recent Supreme Court judgement let Saami customary law prevail over the national law on acquisition of land rights.[304] This happened after both legal theory (Jebens, 1999; Bull, 1998) and a commission appointed by the government to examine questions of land rights in the northern (saami) parts of the country (NOU, 1997) argued in favour of a more pluralistic view, including acknowledging the importance of saami customary law for peoples' lived realities. In a Danish High Court judgement of 1999, the Inuits of Greenland were rewarded compensation for the loss of their traditional areas in Thule.[305] Local customary law gave the population extensive rights to live, travel and hunt in the areas concerned. Even though these custom-based user-rights were not covered by the constitutional protection of property rights, they were of such importance for the lives of the Inuit population that they must be seen as protected in the same manner as the traditional Danish property rights. Denmark's international obligations were considered a relevant argument in favour of this.

The situation of indigenous peoples, especially the nomadic, has some similarities to that of the married women in Tanzania. Because of traditions, they do not fit into the pattern that is the foundation for the national laws regulating property rights. A woman's place of living is to a large extent decided by the different social relationships she is in: first as a daughter, then as a wife. She is a 'nomad' in that when she moves away from the land she has been living on with her family, this dilutes

---

[304] Judgement by Høyesterett (the Norwegian Supreme Court) 5 October 2001, published: Retstidende, 2001/1229.

[305] Judgement by Østre Landsret (a Danish High Court) August 1999: 488–497.

her relation to this land. Nevertheless, she is not seen as having a full and equal right to the land coming from her husband's natal family.

The national laws are often built upon the facts and needs of the typical lives of the lawmakers. This often means men, and more often farmers or paid labourers than pastoralists and nomads. In relation to indigenous peoples, the state has an obligation to ensure that their different way of life does not lead to a lack of protection for their use of land. Similar arguments can be used concerning women's situation.

Gender, ethnicity and culture are amongst factors that may lead to a way of life different from the one that is the standard for the laws. This may impede obtaining the formal ownership to land, for example when the wife works unpaid at home, while her husband has paid employment. To avoid discriminatory results, it must be considered whether use which does not extend to ownership is nevertheless covered by the human right protection and thus may even prevail over the formal rules about acquisition of rights.

6 Conclusion

The case of married women's use of land in rural Tanzania provides valuable insights into the reality of protection of property. It demonstrates the need to recognize the diversity and complexity of land rights, both in terms of its formal basis and the gendered character of a person's relationship to land. In addition, it shows the role of land rights in the fulfilment of a number of other human rights, such as the right to livelihood and the protection of a person's integrity as a whole.

In international law, the debate about property rights in general and land rights in particular is moving towards greater recognition of the ways in which both indigenous peoples and rural women relate to land. The definition of 'property rights' is gradually taking both indigenous peoples and women's realities into consideration. At the level of national law in Tanzania, there is certainly a positive potential for greater recognition of women's engagement with land, as mentioned in section 3.3. Research into the local recognition of women's land use is, however, needed to assess the impact of new law. The human right arguments, as developed in this chapter, provides a legal backdrop for further recognition of rural women's quest for tenure security not only as individuals but as providers of livelihood and food security for children and elderly in the family.

Bibliography

Africa (2000) *Africa South of the Sahara 2000*, 29th edition, Europa Publications, London.

Benschop M. (2002) *Rights and reality. Are women's equal right to land, housing and property implemented in East Africa?*, UN-HABITAT, Nairobi.

Bentzon A.W. with A. Hellum, J. Stewart, W. Ncube and T. Agersnap (1998) *Pursuing grounded theory in law: South–north experiences in developing women's law*, Tano Aschehoug and Mond Books, Oslo and Harare.

Bentzon A.W. with R. Odgaard (eds) (1997) 'Sædvaner eller uvaner. Hindrer sædvaneret udvikling i Afrika?', in *Den ny verden,* issue 4, pages 13–34.

Blume P. with K. Ketscher (eds) (1998) *Ret og skønsomhed i en overgangstid*, Akademisk Forlag, København.

Bull K. S. (1998) 'Norsk rett og samiske rettigheter', in *Lov og rett,* No. 6: 321–322.

Christensen A. (1994) *Hemrätt i hyreshuset. En rättsvitenskaplig studie av bostadshyresgästens besittningsskydd,* Juristforlaget, Stockholm.

Cousins B. (2002) 'Legislating negotiability: Tenure reform in post-apartheid South Africa', in K. Juul with C. Lund (eds) (2002) *Negotiating property in Africa*, Heinemann, Portsmouth, New Hampshire.

Davison J. (1988) 'Who owns what? Land registration and tensions in gender relations of production', pages 157–176 in J. Davison (ed) *Agriculture, women and land. The African experience*, Westview Press, Boulder and London.

De Soto H. (2000) *The mystery of capital: Why capitalism triumphs in the west and fails everywhere else*, Basic Books, New York.

Economic Commission for Africa (ECA) (2003) *Land tenure systems and sustainable development in Southern Africa*, Southern Africa Office, ECA/SA/EGM.Land/2003/2.

Eide A. with C. Krause and A. Rosas (eds) (1995 and 2001) *Economic, social and cultural rights: A textbook*, second revised edition, Martinus Nijhoff Publishers, Dordrecht/Boston/London.

Eriksen G. K. (1993) *Alders tids bruk. En analyse av teori og rettspraksis*, Universitetsforlaget, Oslo.

Hellum A. (1998) 'Women's human rights and African customary laws: Between universalism and relativism – individualism and communitarianism', in *European Journal of Development Research,* Vol. 10 No. 2.
– (1999) *Women's human rights and legal pluralism in Africa*, Tano Aschehoug and Mond Books, Oslo and Harare.

– (2000) 'How to improve the doctrinal analysis of legal pluralism: A comparison of the legal doctrine about custom and local law in Zimbabwe and Norway', in *Retfærd,* No. 2: 40–62.

Holleman J. F. (1973) 'Trouble-cases and trouble-less cases in the study of customary law and legal reform' in *Law and Society Review,* Vol. 7: 585–609.

Hvidsten G. S. (2000) 'Menneskerettigheter og kvinners landrettigheter. Kvinners rett til land i det nye Sør-Afrika', *Institutt for offentlig retts skriftserie nr. 4/2000, Kvinnerettslige studier nr. 42,* University of Oslo.

Ikdahl I. (2001) 'Menneskerettighetsvernet for kvinners bruk av jord. Noen utviklingstrekk ved eiendomsrettsbegrepet belyst gjennom Tanzanias jordreform', *Institutt for offentlig retts skriftserie nr. 5/2001, Kvinnerettslige studier nr. 45,* University of Oslo

Ikdahl I. with A. Hellum, R. Kårhus and T. A. Benjaminsen (2005) *Human rights, formalization and women's land rights in southern and eastern Africa,* Studies in Women's Law No. 57, Institute of Women's Law, University of Oslo.

ILO (1989b) *International Labour Conference*, 76th session, 1989, Report IV (2A).

Izumi K. (1998) *Economic liberalization and the land question in Tanzania*, PhD dissertation, Roskilde University, Roskilde.

James R. W. with G. M. Fimbo (1973) *Customary land law of Tanzania. A source book*, East African Literature Bureau, Nairobi/ Kampala/ Dar es Salaam.

Jebens O. (1999) *Om eiendomsretten til grunnen i Indre Finnmark*, Cappelen Akademiske Forlag, Oslo.

Krause, C. (1993) *Rätten till egendom som en mänsklig rättighet*, Åbo Akademi, Åbo.
– (1995) 'The right to property', pages 143–158 in A. Eide with C. Krause and A. Rosas (eds) (1995) *Economic, social and cultural rights: A textbook*, Martinus Nijhoff Publishers, Dordrecht/ Boston/ London.

Krause C. with G. Alfredsson (1999) 'Article 17', pages 359–378 in G. Alfredsson with A. Eide (eds) *The Universal Declaration of Human Rights. A common standard of achievement*, Martinus Nijhoff Publishers, the Hague/ Boston/ London.

Lindström E. (2001) 'Human rights and rural women's land rights: An analysis of the land tenure system and the land reform in Tanzania', in *Institutt for offentlig retts skriftserie nr. 4/2001, Studies in Women's Law No. 44,* University of Oslo.

Manji A. (1998) 'Gender and the politics of the land tenure reform process in Tanzania', in *Journal of Modern African Studies*, Vol. 36, No. 4: 645–667.

– (1999) 'Who's afraid of land rights? Women, AIDS and land reform in Tanzania', *Gender and the land question,* Working Papers in Women's Law No. 49, University of Oslo.

Migiro R. (1988) 'Women's rights to inheritance', *Guest lectures on women and law in Zimbabwe, Mozambique and Tanzania,* Working Papers in Women's Law No. 20, University of Oslo.

Moore S. F. (1999) 'Changing African land tenure: Reflections on the incapacities of the state', pages 33–49 in C. Lund (ed) *Development and rights. Negotiating justice in changing societies,* Frank Cass, London.

Ncube W. (1989) 'Comparative matrimonial property systems: The search of an equitable system for reallocation of matrimonial property', *Institutt for privatretts stensilserie No. 127,* University of Oslo.

NOU (1997) 'Urfolks landrettigheter etter folkerett og utenlandsk rett', *Norges Offentlige Utredninger No. 1997:5,* Statens trykning, Oslo.

Nyamu-Musembi C. (2002) 'Are local norms and practices fences or pathways? The example of women's property rights', pages 126–150 in A. A. An-Na'im (ed) (2002) *Cultural transformation and human rights in Africa,* Zed Books, London/New York.

Nzioki A. (2002) 'The effects of land tenure on women's access and control of land in Kenya', pages 218–260 in A. A. An-Na'im (ed) *Cultural transformation and human rights in Africa,* Zed Books, London/New York.

Odgaard R. (1999) 'Fathers and daughters in the scramble for women's land rights. The case of the Hehe and Sangu peoples in South Western Tanzania', paper presented at SASA International Conference, Copenhagen.

Odgaard R. and A. W. Bentzon (2007) (in this volume).

Patel R. (1999) 'Labour and land rights of Hindu women in rural India – with particular reference to Western Orissa', PhD Thesis, University of Warwick, United Kingdom.
Raikes P. (1997) 'Traditionelle jordrettigheter – en kolonial konstruktion', pages 101–122 in Bentzon and Odgaard (eds) (1997) 'Sædvaner eller uvaner. Hindrer sædvaneret udvikling i Afrika?', *Den ny verden,* issue 4.

Rwebangira M. K. (1999) *'Debating land on the threshold of a new tenure reform from a gender perspective',* paper presented for the Parliamentary Committee of Finance in Tanzania.

Shinyanga Report (1998) 'Human development report, Shinyanga region, Tanzania December 1998', unpublished material prepared by the Regional Government of Shinyanga, with technical assistance by the Institute of Development Studies and funded by UNDP.

Shivji I. G. (1997) 'Guest editor's introduction: Not yet uhuru', in *Change,* No. 5/1997, Dar es Salaam.

– (1998) *Not yet democracy: Reforming land tenure in Tanzania,* IIED, Hakiardhi and Faculty of Law, University of Dar es Salaam, Dar es Salaam.

Shivji Commission (1992, 1994): *Report of the Presidential Commission of Inquiry into Land Matters,* report delivered to the United Republic of Tanzania, reprint, Scandinavian Institute for African Studies, Uppsala.

Shipton P. (1988) 'The Kenyan land tenure reform: Misunderstandings in the public creation of private property', pages 91–135 in R. E. Downs with S. P. Reyna (eds) *Land and society in contemporary Africa,* University Press of New England, Hanover and London.

Stewart J. (1998) 'Why I can't teach customary law', in J. Eekelar and T. Nhlapo (eds) *The changing family, Family forms and family law,* Hart Publishing, Oxford.

Stewart J. and A. Tsanga (2007) (in this volume)

Sundet G. (1997) *The politics of land in Tanzania,* PhD dissertation, University of Oxford, Oxford.

Sverdrup T. (1997) *Stiftelse av sameie i ekteskap og ugift samliv,* Universitetsforlaget, Oslo.
– (1999) 'Ekteskapet – arbeidsfellesskap eller livsfellesskap?', *Tidsskrift for Velferdsforskning,* No. 2: 102–115.

Toulmin C. with J. Quan (eds) (2000) *Evolving land rights, policy and tenure in Africa,* DFID/IIED/NRI, London.

United Nations Committee on CEDAW
– (1991a) *Unpaid women workers in rural and urban family enterprises,* General Recommendation No. 16, reference A/46/38.
– (1991b) *Measurement and quantification of the unremunerated domestic activities of women and their recognition in the gross national product,* General Recommendation No. 17, reference A/46/38.
– (1994) *Equality in marriage and family relations,* General Recommendation No. 21, reference A/49/38.

United Nations Committee on Economic, Social and Cultural Rights (1992) *The right to adequate housing,* General Comment No. 4, reference: E/1992/23.

United Nations Human Rights Committee (1994) *The rights of minorities,* General Comment No. 23, reference: A/49/40.

Whitehead A. and D. Tsikata (2003) 'Policy discourses on women's land rights in sub-Saharan Africa: The implications of the re-turn to the customary', in *Journal of Agrarian Change* Vol. 3, issue 1-2: 67-112.

WLSA Zimbabwe (1994) *Inheritance in Zimbabwe: Law, customs and practices,* Women and Law in Southern Africa Research Project, Harare.

Woodman G. R. (1988) 'How state courts created customary law in Ghana and Nigeria', in B. W. Morse, with G. R. Woodman (eds) (1988) *Indigenous law and the state*, Foris Publications, Dordrecht.

List of legislation

Tanzania

Land Act 1999

Village Land Act 1999

Regional and international

African Charter on Human and Peoples' Rights 1981

Protocol to the African Charter on Human and People's Rights on the Rights of Women in Africa 2003

American Convention on Human Rights 1969

Convention concerning the Protection and Integration of Indigenous and Other Tribal and Semi-Tribal Populations in Independent Countries, ILO Convention No. 107 of 1957

Convention concerning Indigenous and Tribal Peoples in Independent Countries, ILO Convention No. 169 of 1989

Convention on the Elimination of All forms of Discrimination Against Women (CEDAW) 1979

Habitat II Declaration (Habitat II), United Nations Conference on Human Settlements 1996

International Covenant on Civil and Political Rights 1966

International Covenant on Economic, Social and Cultural Rights 1966

Protocol to the European Convention: the First Optional Protocol to the European Convention for the Protection of Human Rights and Fundamental Freedoms 1952

Statute of the International Court of Justice 1945

Universal Declaration on Human Rights 1948

Vienna Convention on the Law of Treaties 1969

Vienna Declaration and Programme of Action 1993

Part III

The legal and political accommodation of women and girls' bodies

11

I can't go to school today

Julie Stewart

This chapter postulates that there is a need to focus on a number of ancillary rights if girls' rights to education are to be fully and fruitfully realized. Management of menstruation and sanitation at selected primary and secondary schools in Zimbabwe is profiled. The need to provide pupils (both male and female), teachers and parents with timely and appropriate information on sexual maturation is discussed. The chapter seeks to link the grounded realities in relation to sexual maturation, menstruation and sanitation in schools and school administrations to broader national and international human rights obligations to provide a suitable and supportive environment for girls to fully benefit from educational opportunities.

1   Introduction

> 'When girls first come to school at the age of five or six they are very bright and do very well. But when they get to 11 or 12 they seem to lose their brains' – male head teacher, rural area in Zimbabwe (WLSA research interview).[306]

There is no substance to the observation that girls lose their brains at 11 or 12 years of age. When the WLSA[307] researchers probed the headmaster's comment he revealed that some girls at the school were missing four to five days of school each month. After a few months, if this persisted, the girls started coming to school even more infrequently until, eventually, some of them dropped out altogether. When asked what the cause of the problem was he responded:

> 'Well, the lady teachers know all about why. As far as I can see it is just one of those things. Girls just get less intelligent.'

The suggestion was made to the head teacher that possible explanations

---

[306] The interview was part of WLSA's research into women's access to resources in Zimbabwe, we had been discussing girls' attendance at school as part of our attempt to understand women's access to resources – we considered access to education as a key resource for women (Ncube and Stewart *et al.*, 1997).

[307] Women and Law in Southern Africa Research and Education Trust (WLSA), a collective research organization in seven southern African countries.

for this phenomenon were that the girls started menstruating, had inadequate sanitary protection and, as they reached puberty, more and more household chores and child-caring responsibilities were given to them. Perhaps the onset of puberty, coupled with menstruation and difficulties of its management in the school environment, for some girls started the slide out of school. He conceded that such factors were probably the cause but was at a loss as to how to deal with them.

Needless to say we were concerned about the issue but time passed, the research findings on the family in Zimbabwe had to be written up and although the matter of girls' menstruation and school did not fade from our memories it was not prominent among our immediate concerns. Then the issue resurfaced in the form of a request for me to head up a country exploratory research exercise launched by the Rockefeller Foundation into two education-related issues – the first researching and promoting the teaching of life skills in primary schools and the second exploring the management of sexual maturation and menstruation in primary and secondary schools in Zimbabwe. There were to be two other parallel studies, one in Kenya and one in Uganda. I barely paused for breath in accepting the role of Zimbabwe coordinator. My appetite was whetted by the prospect of addressing in-depth and from a legal perspective, issues of education for the girl child and the problems she faces in achieving an educational level commensurate with her abilities.[308] This was also an opportunity to explore the consequences of the realities of the physiological elements of sex as they intersect with the quest for gender equality and equity for girls and women.

---

[308] The research and research methodology – six exploratory case studies were undertaken following a broad design devised by Dr Katherine Namuddu of the Rockefeller Foundation, Kenya, and two consultants, Dr Carla Sutherland and the late Ben Makau. Dr Sutherland devised the outlines for the sexual maturation, menstruation and sanitation studies while Ben Makau devised the basic frameworks for the life skills studies. All six studies are reported on in Stewart (2004). There were parallel studies in Uganda and Kenya although these did not have a legal bias (see Mutunga, 2003 and Kirumira, 2003).

This chapter focuses on the sexual maturation, menstruation and sanitation studies and their aftermath. In Zimbabwe we decided to research at the upper levels of primary schools and the first two years of secondary school because girls usually experience puberty in these years, having started school in the year they turn six. In the other two countries only primary schools were researched as pupils commence school later.

The research methodology was similar to women's law methodology and, on reflection, I undoubtedly appropriated the studies to the discipline and imbued them with women's law perspectives. The in-depth approach was appropriate as the research focused on personal experience and tales of coping or opting out strategies. Males and females of all ages were interviewed, predicated on the basis that everyone experiences biological sex and its consequences and that male under-

The problem no-one speaks about – a consequence of being female

Education is a key resource for personal and national development, thus anything that impedes access to education or the capacity to benefit from education requires investigation and analysis. The barriers or limiters to educational retention or progress need to be identified and steps taken to remedy or alleviate the problem or problems that are produced. It is evident from the FEMED research that one of the problems that girls in school face is managing menstruation within the school environment. The problems may be their own sensitivity or lack of experience in managing menstruation; it may be that the school is unaware of the need to manage menstruation. The problem may be the responses or lack thereof by pupils, teachers, school management and parents to girls' physiological and psychological needs. Pupils' responses recorded by Kebokile Dengu-Zvobgo during the research graphically portray the experiences and the impact of menstrual experiences on girls:

> 'If you are laughed at, you become shy and have problems coming out of the toilet and facing others even after you have cleaned up. Some girls end up almost crying in class' (Dengu-Zvobgo, 2004: 209).

Preoccupation with spoiling one's uniform is a hindrance to full concentration. According to one young respondent:

> 'If you have spoiled your uniform you will be embarrassed to stand up and participate in class' (Dengu-Zvobgo, 2004: 214).

On the ignorance of male schoolmates:

---

standing or misunderstanding of female experiences is an important practical and emotional component of managing burgeoning sexuality and its consequences.

The research design was to be qualitative, the voices of the pupils, teachers and parents were sought on their experiences and understanding of the sexual maturation process and its management within the selected schools. The sexual maturation and sanitation research studies were carried out in urban and rural areas of the Midlands province while the management of menstruation research was focused on the capital city of Harare and a nearby rural area, Seke. The three studies were distinct research entities but each team kept an eye out for aspects of interest to the other studies. Thus, all three teams inspected sanitation and ablution facilities, looked at textbooks and materials at the schools and inevitably asked about protection materials because there were crosscutting concerns and linkages (Moyo *et al.*, Dengu-Zvobgo, Samkange in Stewart, 2004).

Suffice it to say that, in contextualizing and addressing the overall research findings, a women's law analytical perspective of contrasting formal legal requirements, perceptions about implementation and the reality experienced by women (in this case, girls) on the ground was used. There was also an implicit activist stance – identifying the problems would not be enough, a remedial action whether at the local, practical level or at national legislative and policy levels would be identified.

'Boys should stop teasing us and know that it (menstruation) is an unavoidable natural process' (Dengu-Zvobgo, 2004: 233).

On managing the process in school and staying at school while menstruating:

'Build changing rooms so that girls can clean up and go back to class instead of having to go home and miss school' (Dengu-Zvobgo, 2004: 232).

'Teach girls how to dispose of their used materials; place a tin of water and soap in the toilets' (Dengu-Zvobgo, 2004: 232).

On the insensitivity of a male teacher or perhaps male lack of appreciation of what menstrual pain is like:

'If a girl can walk all that distance to school she cannot be in pain!' (Dengu-Zvobgo, 2004: 213).

If this is what girls face, it is possible to see how some seem to 'lose their brains' at puberty. It is not their brains that are lost but self confidence, the capacity to confidently manage the inevitable, messy, often painful, unpredictable physiological consequences of being female. The emotional pain of exposure may deter girls from attending school if they are menstruating and do not have adequate means or facilities to manage the process. Lack of facilities and appropriate sanitary protection materials may combine with cultural constraints and restrictions on activities during menstruation to deter a girl from attending school.

This chapter draws heavily on the research findings made by the FEMED Zimbabwe team on the impact of sexual maturation, menstruation and its management on school girls and, to a lesser extent, on school boys in selected urban and rural secondary schools in Zimbabwe. The initial research did not emphasize the human rights or legal implications of these elements in the schooling process; however I sought to inject them into the research and analysis frameworks that were devised and designed by the external consultants and the individual researchers.[309]

Why I should be at school today: The human rights perspective
The irony in the comments from girls who were interviewed in the FEMED research is that there are multiple human rights instruments as well as domestic legislation and educational policies in most countries that address the importance of interventions to promote girls' attendance at school. International conventions exhort states parties to ensure that all necessary measures are taken to provide education for all and to remove impediments to accessing education but there is a profound si-

---

[309] See Gumbo (2004); Moyo *et al.* (2004); Stewart (2004).

lence around menstruation and its attendant management which affects some girls' ability to function adequately in school.

The Convention against Discrimination in Education (UNESCO, 1960), addresses the problem of sex discrimination which has the effect of depriving any person or group of persons from access to education of any type at any level. Further, article 4 enjoins states parties to take such measures as are necessary to ensure equality of opportunity in education and in article 4(a) to make primary education free and compulsory. Article 10 of the Convention on the Elimination of all forms of Discrimination Against Women (CEDAW) requires states parties to take all appropriate measures to eliminate discrimination against women in order to ensure them equal rights with men in the field of education: in particular to ensure, on the basis of equality between men and women, the same conditions for access to studies and for the achievement of diplomas in educational establishments of all categories in both rural and urban areas. Article 10(f) exhorts states parties to ensure that measures are taken to ensure the reduction of female drop-out rates and the organization of programmes for girls and women who have left school prematurely.

CEDAW in article 10(c) requires states parties to take all necessary measures to ensure the elimination of any stereotyped concepts of the roles of men and women at all levels and in all forms of education by encouraging co-education and other types of education which will help to achieve that aim. Indications are that there is a need to question the wisdom of such an exhortation in the light of the FEMED research if there are not programmes in place that specifically address issues of and menstruation and how they should be handled in the school environment. Being in a school environment which exposes girls to the jeers and uninformed mirth of boys when their menstrual protection fails probably negates some of the value to be obtained from co-education. Put differently, co-education is based on the premise that it will aid in gender parity and gendered understanding between the sexes but this must be premised on sex-sensitive and gender-sensitive education programmes and management regimes.

The Convention on the Rights of the Child requires in article 28 that states parties recognize the right of the child to education and that, albeit on a progressive basis, primary education is made compulsory, is available free to all and that measures are taken to encourage regular attendance at schools and the reduction of drop-out rates.

The African Charter on the Rights and Welfare of the Child quite explicitly spells out the obligations of the state and the rights of the individual in relation to access to education for all. Article 11 provides that every child has a right to education, and article 11(3)(d) requires states parties to take measures to encourage regular attendance at school.

Article 11(3)(e) also requires special measures to be taken in respect of female, gifted and disadvantaged children. More recently, being cognisant of the discrimination against girls and women in accessing education in the African context, African Heads of State in July 2003 adopted the Protocol to the African Charter on Human and Peoples' Rights on the Rights of Women in Africa (African Union Protocol on Women). The protocol[310] specifically addresses girls and women's marginalization in education; and further in article 12(2)(c) provides that:

'States parties shall take specific positive action to... promote the enrolment and retention of girls in schools.'

There is clear recognition in all these instruments that if girls or boys are not in school they are losing out on one of the most basic components of their future development and national development education. Schemes designed to provide incentives to encourage families to send girls to school and to keep them in school until they reach their maximum educational capacity must be supported and expanded. There is no doubt that measures to curb teenage pregnancies and programmes that deal with reproductive rights are required and need continuing support. Such initiatives are critical.

Yet the FEMED research points to the need to also focus at a very fundamental physiological level on what it means to be female and the implications of managing one's sexed body. The headmaster's words raise the distinct possibility that girls may be losing out, in the sense of dropping out or dropping out in school[311] (underachieving) because there is lack of official appreciation of what it is to be female. Thus, whereas there might be vigorous efforts to stimulate girls' attendance at school by providing parents with incentives if their daughters attend, the problem may be relatively simple, albeit hidden – the lack of adequate knowledge about and management of menstruation in the school environment.

The rest of this chapter will focus on the need to be explicit about managing sexual maturation, managing menstruation and providing appropriate and adequate sanitation facilities for girls in school, regardless of where the school is situated. The concluding section examines ways to draw attention to the needs of the girl child in this area of life and, frankly, women in general, through reporting mechanisms that are set up at international and national levels on issues related to compliance with various international instruments.

---

[310] Signed but at the time of writing not yet ratified by Zimbabwe. The Protocol on the Rights of Women in Africa came into force on 25 November 2005.

[311] During the FEMED research the term 'dropping out in school' was used to describe pupils who were just marking time in the education system until they met a barrier examination which would exclude them.

One might surmise that one of the reasons for the failure to recognize the management and educational needs in these areas is that educational administrators have until relatively recently been mainly male, yet conversely it might be that women in educational management and policy making have not felt enabled or emboldened to speak out on the issue. Whatever the reason for the silence and inaction, it cannot be denied that managing menstruation in the school environment needs to be taken seriously, so that the promise to the girl child and the promise to the nation, whichever nation it is, that the girl child is entitled to an education, can be fulfilled on an equal basis to boys.

Keeping things in perspective: What the research didn't find
At no time during the research was there any suggestion that menstruation and its management or mismanagement in the context of schooling in Zimbabwe was the sole or even a major reason why girls dropped out of school or, despite remaining in school, seemed to be underachieving but it became clear that it was a possible contributory factor to both these 'events'. Although the field research did not establish that many girls dropped out of school because of difficulties in managing menstruation, it clearly established that a number of girls found menstruation, sexual maturation and provision of sanitation at school a problem, particularly in rural areas.

Thus it was an issue that needed to be carefully investigated and measures to ameliorate, as far as possible, its adverse impact on girls in school explored so that the necessary changes – legal, physical or educational – could be undertaken. Measures to counteract the adverse experiences that girls had with sexual maturation and menstruation in school, it was postulated, did not need to be complex, expensive or difficult to put in place. Rather, it seemed to be a case of finding ways to highlight the issues and eliminating the 'taboo' of discussing such issues publicly, albeit discreetly, and stimulating local practical solutions to problems (Stewart *et al.*, 2004).

What needs to be highlighted is the silence, almost a vacuum, that exists between the exhortations to provide education to girls and correct the gender imbalances, and the provisions on the ground to address girls' sex-specific needs if they are to attend school with comfort, confidence and dignity. It is important to realize that the silence is profound, it is a silence of embarrassment, ignorance and constructed social and cultural restraints that inhibit frank speaking about an ordinary, normal physiological process. Lack of articulation of the problems masked by the silence leads to lack of action or attention to management needs.

One striking observation throughout the FEMED research in Zimbabwe was that once the problems surrounding menstruation for girls in school were drawn to the attention of ministry and school officials there was great readiness to intervene (Stewart, 2004: 287 ff).

Sex or gender? Does it matter?
One of the catchphrases of the 'current age' in relation to development paradigms is 'gender mainstreaming', however, to effect gender mainstreaming in real terms, sex-based needs and the overt consequences of that difference have to be provided for. The consequences of difference and the failure to explain and sensitively manage that difference lead to uncomfortable and emotionally bruising experiences for many girls and for some these experiences begin the slide out of or away from school. The main thrust of the argument in this chapter is that recognizing the problems of menstruation is a vital part of the management framework required to ensure that girls can access and use educational opportunities in a manner that equates to that of boys.

Taking a gender perspective that focuses on socialization and cultural elements alone seems to miss a critical step in dealing with the underpinnings of girls' problems with the schooling process. A gender-only perspective maintains the silence around the physiological realities of being female and fails to address the needs she has in managing her body and its products in a public space. Nowhere in any of the international instruments is there any direct reference to putting the basic educational, environmental and sanitation measures in place for the girl child once she reaches puberty to enjoy school, to feel confident about her sex and the management of the natural consequences of being female.[312]

The fundamental tenet of this chapter is that physiological sex does

---

[312] I defy any grown woman, unless they have never menstruated, not to be able to recall some embarrassing incident at school, in employment or elsewhere when her femaleness and the fact that she was menstruating became publicly obvious. I remember vividly when a female colleague grabbed my arm after a Faculty meeting, saying, 'Don't leave, stay seated'. I sat puzzled but she said nothing until everyone had left, especially the men who had lingered talking. When no one else was in earshot, she said, 'I have started'. Words that women understand. And she had, her pale-coloured skirt was red right across the back. Fortunately there was a toilet close by, I sort of frogmarched behind her providing cover and in she went. Then the hunt for sanitary-pads and cover-up measures began. Pads were found, but what could she wear? We solved it with an academic gown, clutched at the front and she drove home for more effective repairs. Girls at school facing this situation need similar help and assistance as a matter of course, not as something special but just plain management. But spare uniforms are rarely available; some school uniforms are in light, pretty, girl-flattering but not girl-friendly colours. Discussions with postgraduate and undergraduate classes of law students reveals that all the women ensure that they wear dark clothes, at least on their bottom halves, when they are expecting to menstruate or are menstruating, but it can creep up on you and is not always as regular as suggested in the textbooks.

matter in the quest for equality; its consequences for females have to be managed in the public arena so that as 'level a playing field' as possible can be created, so the quest for equality between men and women is not diverted by lack of consideration of essential but manageable differences between the sexes. However, as the FEMED research shows, inadequate attention has been paid to physiological sex and its consequences in the provision of education.

The 2004 UNESCO Education for all report (125) refers to the findings from the three FEMED country studies. It flags the problems in relation to menstruation noting that:

'Recent series of studies[313] about management of puberty in primary schools in Uganda, Kenya and Zimbabwe concluded that the current management of sexual maturation within the primary system fails to meet the needs of children, but especially those of girls.'

The report continues:

'The studies document the ways in which poor management of sexual maturation has had[314] a detrimental impact on children's acquisition of basic learning competencies, and how girls who experience menstruation without adequate preparation or facilities, were regularly absent or even dropped out of primary school.'

But the report is silent on the further unpacking of the issues and on possible solutions to the problems identified.

2   Identifying the problems

Sexual maturation: Speaking about the unspeakable?
In her exploration of the teaching that was taking place in schools around sexual maturation and the experiences that flowed from the ignorance of both boys and girls, Faith Samkange, a member of the FEMED team, found that this was a very stressful time for adolescents. It emerged that girls in rural areas had a much more difficult time coping with sexual maturation and its consequences than girls in urban areas. Comparing

---

[313] The studies referred to are the FEMED studies that form the basis of this chapter, thus I know what was being alluded to, I describe the findings in Zimbabwe below, suffice it to say that the findings in Kenya and Uganda on these issues were fundamentally the same, except that perhaps Zimbabwe performed better in the toilet stakes but as you will see even that leaves a great deal to be desired. All the studies when written up were very explicit about the problems of menstruation and their potential effect on the education of girls.

[314] The FEMED studies were not that definitive about the issue, rather it was found that there may have been an adverse impact on girls and boys' educational experiences, with girls facing the more difficult problems of adjusting to and managing their changing bodies.

the experiences of pupils in urban and rural areas revealed significant differences in knowledge and capacity to publicly manage puberty.

Pupils in the urban setting were able to articulate the biological, physical and psychological changes associated with the onset of sexual maturation. While the discussion largely emphasized menstruation, reference was made to sexuality, reproductive health, contraception, dating and boy-girl relationships.

Pupils in urban schools have multiple sources of information and are likely to be less subject to cultural constraints about discussing menstruation than pupils in rural schools who, according to Samkange:

'...demonstrated limited knowledge on sexual maturation issues as evidenced by the fact that they could only identify a few basic biological and physical changes associated with the onset of the sexual maturation process. Their discussion on sexual maturation was limited to menstruation. Of significance is that children in the urban areas were more knowledgeable and more articulate than their rural counterparts. The quality of discussions in the urban setting was characterized by a lot of confidence, enthusiasm and, above all, free interaction' (Samkange, 2004: 162).

It's someone else's responsibility!

Although both teachers and parents seemed aware that children required information on sexual maturation, there was confusion as to who ought to provide this information and in what form. Parents thought that teachers ought to be more involved while teachers felt that they were inadequately equipped as the available texts were unsatisfactory and the educational system did not emphasize the topic in the curriculum.

One might conclude that this is how it has always been; girls as they ventured into the public realm had to learn to cope with the problems related to their sex, namely menstruation, their burgeoning sexuality and the ever-present risk of pregnancy. However, this situation should not continue as the quest for equality of opportunity for all invokes the need to manage sex-based difference and its consequences so that its adverse impact is minimized.

Another dimension to the problem is that sex in the physiological sense and its consequences are treated as synonymous with sexuality. This chapter argues that just as there is a need to desegregate sex and gender there is a further need to desegregate, for management purposes, the sex of the body from sexuality.[315]

---

[315] The more profound implications of this are not explored in this chapter, it does however require specific attention and targeted theorizing. It is a topic to which I hope to return.

If education is to serve as a key tool in development it is not enough to teach the so-called 'three Rs' and assume that children's needs have been met, the whole child must be catered for, and catered for as a female or male according to sex-based needs. But for many, and arguably the most vulnerable, silence reigns; someone else needs to deal with it!

If that isn't already bad enough: Sanitary protection

Forget the promises of menstrual confidence peddled by marketers of female sanitary products – forget the blue ink that suffuses pads and tampons as a 'euphemism' for female menstrual fluid on television advertisements – welcome to the reality of the young girl and her sanitary protection options. Welcome to the world of poor families struggling to feed themselves and young girls making do with a variety of largely inadequate and even potentially health-threatening protection measures. At the time this research was conducted there was a move in Zimbabwe by women's groups to have import duties reduced on sanitary napkins and tampons or their imported components. These items were classified as 'luxuries' whereas every woman knows they are basic requirements. Eventually the reduction was effected but no amount of reduction would make them accessible for most of the girls in the study.[316]

The nature and form of sanitary protection that schoolgirls are able to access is varied and largely dependent on family resources. According to Dengu-Zvobgo (2004):

> 'Almost half of the menstruating girls interviewed use [ordinary] cotton wool for menstrual protection. The schools and teachers often give girls this form of protection [if it exists at the school]; they argue that it is the best material but some medical doctors say the way the cotton wool is used is unhygienic and could cause infection. Additionally, the distraction of a pile of cotton wool between the legs that has to be kept there by complex "leg work", presents a problem for girls when walking or standing up in class as the material may change position and result in the spoiling of one's uniform. In rural areas where some girls lack underpants, the inability to maintain the wad in place may force some girls to absent themselves from school.'

Only two out of 20 menstruating rural secondary school girls could access commercial disposable sanitary pads which are recommended as the most suitable form of protection.

---

[316] Coincident with this study I was asked to conduct a seminar for judges on gender issues and I raised the problem of girls' need for sanitary protection when menstruating. One concerned elderly, black judge said, 'But you just go out and buy them or give your daughter money.' I responded, 'In the village?' There was a very audible 'Oh' – I rested my case.

Besides being the most expensive product on the market, tampons are not recommended by both girls and their mothers because of their alleged effect on the hymen.[317]

Six brave girls in a rural primary school admitted using rags as menstrual protection material, thus exposing their poverty. Cloth irritates the skin because the girls do not change at school. They need at least two so one can dry at home whilst they are at school and the other dries at night.

During the study one rural-based nurse indicated that in reality far more girls probably used rags and other unsatisfactory and unsanitary 'materials' than actually admitted it:

> 'The protection materials common in this community are tissues and old rags, it is rare for girls to use cotton wool; they present with dirty rags just like their mothers.'

These unsanitary methods lead to chaffing and other skin irritation and at times infections. The nurse noted that the girls do not as a rule come to the clinic with these problems because they are shy:

> 'I guess the idea of having their private parts inspected is intimidating to them and they also fear they may be reprimanded for having such a problem. I think more health education is needed.'[318]

Kebokile Dengu-Zvobgo, who had been involved in a study on women's sanitary protection needs in urban high density areas[319] some years earlier observed that not much has changed over the years in terms of what girls and women are able to access in the way of sanitary protection and it is fair to conclude that the declining economic situation in Zimbabwe has made such access even more difficult:

> 'The Jacaranda Project over ten years ago established that women in both urban and rural areas use sanitary protection materials ranging from bark, leaves and toilet tissue paper through to cotton wool and commercial sanitary protection products. However, the latter were not affordable for most women. This study looking at a younger school-going sample has found similar unhygienic practices of using rags, newspapers, tissue paper and cotton wool' (Dengu-Zvobgo, 2004)

Coupled with the lack of material or financial capacity to provide for adequate sanitary measures during menstruation, this situation may con-

---

[317] That of breaking the hymen and creating the impression that the girl is no longer a virgin – however this is an unlikely consequence of tampon use.

[318] If girls are using such sanitary protection measures, the chaffing could be intense, if they are not able to counteract the pain and discomfort it is easy to see how they might be reluctant to attend school or be distracted in class. Walking or sitting can be very uncomfortable when the genital area is infected, irritated or inflamed.

[319] These are low-income suburban areas, where financial resources are often scarce.

tribute to some girls eventually 'dropping out' of school or doing less well than their previous record would indicate they are capable of – all this begs the question: *What is to be done?*

A private space to address a private problem?
Zimbabwe has regulations in place that specify the minimum standards for sanitation in schools. These regulations, at least in terms of numbers of toilets, recognize the different needs of girls and boys for adequate and appropriate toilet facilities. However, the only way in which the needs of girls in relation to menstruation is adverted to is through the increased number of squat holes in long drop toilets and the increased number of pedestal toilets for girls over boys. Statutory Instrument 367 of 1998 stipulates that there should be one toilet for every 15 girls and one for every 20 boys at a school.

What emerged from the FEMED research was, firstly, many schools fell below this standard requirement, for example at one primary school visited there should have been five times more toilets to meet government standards. At one urban secondary school there were 119 girls per toilet, way over the prescribed figures.

Secondly, even if there was compliance with the regulations there were problems in terms of comfortably using the toilet and the 'toilet space' to deal with the consequences of menstruation. In rural schools there might be compliance with the requirement of one squat hole or toilet for every 20 girls but the squat holes were literally in lines within the toilet, with no walls between them, no place, literally, to hide. No place to hide the embarrassment of menstruating, the embarrassment of soiled clothes, the embarrassment of your inadequate 'patch and make do' sanitary protection. No place within the toilet block to clean yourself up before emerging into the public gaze, a public gaze that is itself embarrassed and uninformed on how to respond to a menstrual accident and the pain of the girl child. Perhaps it is the embarrassment that produces the cruel and raucous comments; perhaps it is the embarrassment of male teachers who do not know how to respond that produces their ill-informed and seemingly insensitive responses.

For many girls in the rural areas faced with menstrual accidents, the nearest source of water would be a tap in the school grounds or water literally carried in plastic bottles to school by the children themselves. In many schools the water that is carried to school, usually by girls, is reserved for the use of teachers. If there are small 'communal' water tanks for pupils' use it is in a prominent open space. Every women, as suggested earlier, can recall, and if still menstruating knows, the emotional and physical discomfort of garments stained with menstrual fluid, difficult enough to deal with as an adult with adequate facilities to clean up and change, but even public access toilets for women in the first world context require the dash to the basin, the hope that no one finds you frantically scrubbing at your clothes and sloshing water everywhere.[320] The regulations call for a tap next to the toilet but this is a paper requirement which is not translated into reality. Even if there was a tap next to the toilet it would be an external, 'exposed' tap, so the problem of lack of privacy remains.

Coping with the same problem as a young girl, perhaps for the first time, without adequate facilities and no water at hand must be profoundly disturbing. Emerging into the school grounds would be a difficult decision. Better to do it when everyone else was back in class or to opt to go home or just hide out for the rest of the day.

One of the consequences of the teasing discussed above is that menstruating girls, especially those who lack adequate sanitary protection resources, often retreat from the classroom. Girls who have such experiences may choose not come to school if they are menstruating; they stay at home. Thus, they may well miss up to four or five days of schooling per month, if this is the case then there is a real possibility of cumulative lack of basic educational background.

In the schools researched the most usual responses to menstrual accidents or to girls with period pains were to send them home[321] – sending the message that menstruation is abnormal and akin to being ill. A word of caution, some women and girls suffer from acute dysmenorrhoea – painful, sometimes almost disabling pain when they menstruate. Such pain cannot be dismissed; it needs proper and effective treatment. Although some girls may need to spend time resting or even remain at home for a day or so due to the severity of their pain, it has to be recognized that they also have to learn how to cope and everyone has to help them cope with the pain so that they are not dislocated from the educational process. If everyone 'pussyfoots' around it and no one understands or seeks to understand then that is another form of disabling silence.

Getting rid of the evidence: Where is the bin?

Both socially and culturally, evidence of menstruation needs to be discreetly and safely disposed of. Many schools lacked appropriate sites to dispose of soiled sanitary products. Some schools had disposal sites but

---

[320] As illustrated in footnote 310.

[321] There was one school which kept spare uniforms and sanitary pads which girls could use if they had a menstrual accident. The same school also had analgesics and a room where girls could lie down until they felt ready to return to class. It was an all girls' school.

they were public. Males cleaned toilets and emptied bins. Girls often carried soiled commercial sanitary products home and disposed of them there. Seemingly there is an expectation on the part of the Ministry of Education, Sport and Culture that disposal facilities should be provided in toilets, however there is no formal legal requirement for provision of such facilities. Absence of suitable bins for disposal where there were flush toilets inevitably led to blocked toilets as pads were flushed down them. In rural long drop facilities, disposal was easier but again the possibility of someone seeing the item, especially a male cleaner, caused distress to some girls (Moyo *et al.,* 2004: 259 ff).

I should go to school today

The FEMED research as it was carried out in Zimbabwe was activist research, problems required solutions, the solutions to the problems surrounding sexual maturation, managing menstruation and sanitation, at least at the practical level were, we postulated as a team, feasible and inexpensive.[322]

From an action perspective the findings gave a new twist on age old notions of what can be discussed, what can be done and especially on breaking through the barriers of silence and layers of seeming inaction.

So what? The human rights connection

Readers at this stage might be thinking that the human rights component has gone missing in this chapter. Let me take you back to it. The rights to education, the right to development, the right to a clean and healthy personal environment are all fundamental rights. The girl child, as the woman to be, needs to be able to access education. She needs to maximize the benefits of that access; this is her right. She needs information that explains her physical being, demystifies her life processes, makes it a management issue not an issue of sexuality. Boys and men need the same basic information, about themselves and about girls and women's experiences. Both sexes need to understand that sex is largely immutable, gender and gendered roles can and do mutate. Distinguishing be-

---

[322] At one inter-country data analysis seminar, the Zimbabwe team recommended that there was a need to raise the issues publicly and look for solutions. The other two countries looked askance and said more research was needed. We went ahead, teams led by activist women's lawyers plunge in where others fear to tread. We theorized that even if it turned out later that large numbers of girls did not drop out for these reasons, the fact that girls suffered discomfort, were distracted in class and were socially humiliated by the boys clearly indicated that at the very least their right to dignity was infringed. Also they had a right to a clean and healthy environment and information about their own bodies and its management.

tween the two is the first stage in the process of actualizing women's comfortable involvement in public arenas.

What is needed to support girls and women accessing their right has so far, in terms of educational discourse, been conceptualized largely in terms of reversing gender discrimination. I have argued in this chapter that there is an important prior stage to this and that is ensuring that the girl child's physiological difference is recognized. That recognition involves providing different facilities and management regimes which differ from the male standard that usually informs planning and management strategies. It must be addressed as a broad-based management issue that underpins the girl child's engagement with the world at large – and that of the woman she is to become.

Clearly, based on our grounded engagement with the problems, simple local, implementable solutions were required. Low-cost accessible materials had to form the basis for putting appropriate facilities in place. Also, the research and the post-research action agenda, profoundly questioned the perception that it was taboo to discuss these subjects. Of course, discretion is required, but there is a space for the voice of the girl child on these issues and people are prepared to listen and respond.

The bigger agenda

Although solutions can be simple, inexpensive and local, there is a need to draw specific attention to the broader issues for universal, or more accurately, global attention. As the FEMED research revealed, although there may be adequate legislation in place, it is the execution of the obligations and the monitoring of implementation that is required. A powerful tool in raising human rights concerns is the process of reporting to institutionalized committees that has been created to track compliance with international conventions such as CEDAW and the Convention on the Rights of the Child. Not only do the committees track compliance, they also play an investigative role through the evolution of shadow reports by non-governmental organizations. The deliberations of the committees have stimulated the production of reporting guidelines that serve to interpret and embellish the bare directive bones of the conventions. It thus seems logical to recommend guidelines to be incorporated into the reporting processes by countries which specifically address the issues raised by the research.

The next section examines possible solutions to the problems identified during the research and seeks to link the solutions suggested to evaluation and monitoring guidelines to be included in the reporting requirements under international instruments.

3   Some simple solutions to complex problems

Sexual maturation: Just get talking

When the research commenced the team was reticent to openly discuss the very subject matter of the research. There were men on the team; I was the only non-black Zimbabwean involved. The taboos of discussing the topic seemed firmly in place. Euphemisms for menstruation and menstrual accidents abounded but the discussions took place. Somehow, almost imperceptibly, the team began sharing its understandings and experiences.[323] The men admitted that for the first time in their lives they began to understand what women and girls went through. Fathers discussed sexual maturation with their sons and daughters, team members began to feel more comfortable about conducting interviews and running group discussions that raised the so-called taboo issues.

These engagements with people through the empirical research process resulted in the realization that pupils, teachers and parents craved knowledge and information and, most importantly, discussion was possible.[324] As a direct result of the research findings on the need for simple straightforward literature on sexual maturation, a pamphlet was prepared for distribution to schools and schoolchildren.[325] At report-back sessions to schools and communities the pamphlets were distributed. Information and the right to information about one's burgeoning sexuality were recognized and purpose-specific information was made available.

Raising these issues with head teachers at national education conferences generated even more interest and an earnest desire for practical information and feasible interventions. The silence had been broken and it was far less difficult to achieve this than expected.

Both boys and girls responded positively to information which was provided during the exploratory research on menstruation. Boys even

---

[323] Dengu-Zvobgo brought samples of sanitary pads and tampons to one workshop; the men were fascinated, at first they tentatively explored the items and then became interested in their construction. Questions flowed and interest, real interest in the problems followed.

[324] I realized that the barriers had been truly broken down when the team was chatting together at the airport before departing for a meeting of the national teams. The toilet facilities at the airport had been scrutinized by both sexes and disposal facilities and washing facilities were being openly and loudly discussed with no inhibitions. Other passengers were looking at us in amazement as a mixed race and sex group loudly explored sanitation issues related to menstruation.

[325] Copies of the pamphlet are available from the Women's Law Centre, Harare; it can be reproduced and improved without any copyright restrictions. If improvements to the pamphlet are made or more adolescent friendly information is uncovered please let us know so that we can make the information as widely available as possible (stewart@law.uz.ac.zw).

apologized publicly for their teasing and disrespect to girls. Talking, raising issues was a simple solution; making space to address sex-based realities produced positive results.

Going further: Institutionalizing the concerns

Reporting guidelines under CEDAW for states parties in relation to article 10(f)(g) and (h) should require responses that directly focus on the generation and dissemination of information about sexual maturation and menstruation. Although menstruation could be subsumed under article 12(1),[326] raising the issue of information about menstruation and treating it as an aspect of school management de-medicalizes it, making it a matter for administrative attention and planning – in other words, a normal process since women and girls are not normally sick when they menstruate. If menstruation is treated as a health issue its management may be shuffled off to the Ministry of Health. Whereas it needs to be mainstreamed as a basic management issue. It is not just a concern in relation to education but needs to be factored into all spheres of public life as part of management priorities.

Similar considerations to those in CEDAW arise in reporting in terms of article 26 (implementation) of the African Union Protocol on Women under article 12 which covers the right to education and training and requires that states parties take all appropriate measures to eliminate all forms of discrimination against women and guarantee equal opportunity and access in the sphere of education and training. The FEMED research established that access to education is affected by inadequate knowledge on sexual maturation and menstruation on the part of girls and boys, as well as men and women. Article 12(1)(c) addresses the need to protect girl children from sexual harassment, arguably part of the problem that girls face is from boys and men who do not understand menstruation and the processes of sexual maturation. Article 12(1)(e) raises the need to integrate gender sensitization at all levels of education, including teacher training, thus it is a necessary interpretative strategy to include sensitization on sex and the physiological aspects of sex difference throughout the education system. Article 12(2)(c) requires states parties to take specific positive action to promote the enrolment and retention of girls in schools.

Thus, some of the questions to be answered when reporting should direct states parties to take measures to ensure the following:
- Provision of appropriate and adequate information in a sex-specific framework about sexual maturation processes in girls and boys and, more specifically, on menstruation so that both boys and girls un-

---

[326] Article 12 deals with health care for women.

derstand menstruation as a normal physiological process;

- Development and implementation of teacher training college, university and in-service training programmes as part of teacher education, preparing teachers to conduct awareness sessions and discussions with pupils at both primary and secondary school level on issues related to sexual maturation and menstruation;
- Appropriate focus and emphasis in the school curricula and examination processes, on all pupils, regardless of sex, having adequate information on sexual maturation and menstruation;
- Dissemination of knowledge and promotion of understanding of sexual maturation and menstruation amongst the wider public, especially to help parents and communities understand the needs of the sexually maturing adolescent and, in particular, to dispel cultural myths and physiological misunderstanding of menstruation.

The Convention on the Rights of the Child reporting guidelines on these issues in terms of article 45 would relate to the article 17 guidelines which address the use of the mass media for the purpose, inter alia, of disseminating and making information in 'sex and age friendly' form accessible to all children on the processes of sexual maturation and their physical and psychological implications. Likewise, information on menstruation and sanitary protection measures, especially forms of safe and hygienic menstrual protection products, both commercial and home-made, should be disseminated widely. Article 17(a) of the convention seems especially pertinent in this regard as it urges states parties to encourage the mass media to disseminate information and material of social and cultural benefit to the child in accordance with the spirit of article 29. Article 29 records that states parties agree that the education of the child shall be directed to 'the development of the child's personality, talents and mental and physical abilities to their fullest potential.

As the FEMED research indicates, failure to provide appropriate and adequate information about sexual maturation and menstruation can inhibit children from developing to their full potential. It is also important to use the mass media to reach those children not in school and the parents or carers who may regard sexual maturation and menstruation as reasons for withdrawing girls from school. In this context dissemination of information also becomes critical in terms of article 28(1)(e) in that states parties are urged to 'take measures to encourage regular attendance at schools and the reduction of drop-out rates'. Article 28(3) refers to the obligation imposed on states parties to cooperate at international levels 'in matters relating to education, in particular with a view to eliminating ignorance and illiteracy throughout the world and facilitating access to scientific and technical knowledge...'. Receiving, generating and disseminating new information and approaches to sexual maturation and menstruation to and from a wider international audience would seem to fall into this category.

In this regard reporting guidelines to the convention should help states parties interrogate themselves on whether, as parties to the convention, they have:

- Taken measures to minimize school attendance problems that may develop or be influenced by inadequate information about sexual maturation and menstruation;
- Recognized the impact of lack of information on male and female children's needs in relation to sexual maturation, menstruation and its management;
- Taken steps to ensure that information on sexual maturation and menstruation is readily available to children to help dispel the sometimes disabling myths and taboos that surround these normal physiological processes.

Managing menstruation in schools: We didn't know!

Managing menstruation in schools was another arena where ignorance was bliss – in most schools the girls just struggled along and teachers didn't see the problem, especially male teachers. Teachers, including some female teachers,[327] were surprised by the suggestion that providing a mild pain killer and somewhere to lie down was an effective way to deal with menstrual pain and cramps. Girls were not sick; most of them just needed support and simple remedies. If they could rest, perhaps change their uniform, they could return to class. Thus the negative impact of being sent home could be avoided.

But one problem persisted – the absence of cheap, hygienic and effective sanitary protection measures for schoolgirls whose families could not afford to purchase commercial sanitary protection measures.

The solution – develop a reusable, home-made or school-made sanitary pad that was recyclable. Fortunately a project undertaken some years earlier had already developed a prototype towelling pad that could be washed. Even more fortunately the patent on the pad had lapsed so the FEMED research team plunged into designing and sewing. Faith Samkange, one of the researchers, was by initial training a domestic science teacher and she produced a wide variety of possible pads, using simple patterns, including ones with double liners, plastic inserts and

---

[327] One must remember that the experience of menstruation varies from one female to another, so lack of understanding of other women and girls' problems may be located in one's own menstrual experiences or denial of them. Also the silence around menstruation and its management may cause women to suppress their experiences so that they can be seen to cope in the public arena.

other innovations. But how to get it to girls in school?

We didn't market the pad, rather the national domestic science teachers' association was contacted and the pad was 'marketed' as a possible school sewing project. It fell to me to demonstrate, with my clothes on, how the pad would be used. The response was overwhelming. We had raised the unexpressed, we had provided a solution. The pamphlet with the pad design, care and washing instructions was snapped up.

The demonstration of how to use it had a remarkable sequel. A national primary school head teachers' conference invited someone from the team to address them. As luck would have it, and it was luck, the only person available to attend was a man. Undeterred he went ahead and demonstrated, over his own clothes, how the pad was used. He was a hit! Unknowingly we had a formula for getting the message across, especially to men. After his presentation many men in the audience admitted that if he had not been there they would have retired to the 'pub' and let the women get on with women's business. They stayed on to see how he would cope. Again the ice was broken, men in charge of schools, men who had to manage the school environment, were alerted to the problem. Almost counter-intuitively the men seemed more concerned than the women; the issue had prominence and hopefully would be addressed at individual schools.

Male head teachers went off bearing pamphlets on sexual maturation and managing menstruation; they could instigate the making of sanitary pads in class. In some schools there were even competitions on pad designs. Breaking the silence, taking the daring leap produced results.[328]

If schools and schools curricula, teacher education and educational policy makers take the production of sanitary towels seriously, if governments treat women and girls' sanitary wear and the imported components for their manufacture as essential non-dutiable items, then many of the problems that girls face in school in managing menstruation may be resolved. However, as suggested in relation to access to information, reporting guidelines to CEDAW and the Convention on the Rights of the Child are needed that focus on states parties' compliance on taking measures that address the following:

- Developing school curricula that address the practical management of menstruation, such as making sanitary pads and care of one's body as a young female in relation to menstruation;

---

[328] A copy of the pamphlet on the making of the Femshuleni sanitary napkin is available from the Women's Law Centre. We did not take action to patent any of the additional design advances that had been made to the napkin – use the pattern freely – the only caveat is that we would like to know of any design improvements. See also Stewart (2004, 287 ff).

- Special needs and constraints that may be experienced by girls coping with menstruation in rural schools;
- Provision of low-cost sanitary wear and reduction or preferably abolition of sales tax, import duties and other revenue charges on sanitary wear for girls and women;
- Educational planning and policy acknowledging the need for appropriate uniforms, including sports uniforms,[329] for girls which reduce the risk of embarrassment if there are menstrual accidents.

Toilets: I never thought about that!

Toilets and toilet facilities at schools, private space to address menstruation and cleaning oneself up if necessary were needed. Somewhere to confidently dispose of used pads was also required. Fortunately we were able to engage the advice of a world leader in rural sanitary provision, Dr Peter Morgan. He was one of the team that designed the internationally acclaimed Zimbabwean Blair toilet – a long-drop toilet with special features to eliminate odours and exclude flies. In his work, he focuses on local materials, simple construction and recyclable materials. When we raised the problem with him, we received almost the same response as we had received on the other issues – 'I never thought of that'. Instant concern, instant feverish design of possible ways to provide privacy and water in toilets for girls. All simple, locally do-able, even as part of building classes at school. Using an inverted plastic water bottle with a stopper and slightly enlarging the toilet, gave girls space to clean up.

Even where there are long lines of squat holes, a few strategic walls made out of local sun dried bricks can work wonders. Solutions, especially in rural areas, needed to be simple; the Education Act has turned the responsibility for school development over to schools and local authorities to manage and improve (which is rare) the infrastructures themselves. Sun-dried bricks, local materials and local construction teams or using pupils in building and carpentry classes, are ways to provide new or adapted sanitation and disposal facilities.

Covered disposal bins and small, locally-built incinerators seemed to be the solution to the disposal problem. Of course if the pads were recyclable and could be taken home in a special bag, then disposal was not a problem.

The additional human rights elements involved in this process, be-

---

[329] Dengu-Zvobgo found that in some schools the sports uniform for girls was white shorts even though the regular uniform was of a suitable dark colour. Thus girls might be reluctant to take part in sports lest there be yet another situation that exposes her femaleness.

yond those already discussed, which would merit attention at the level of states parties reporting are article 14(2)(h) of CEDAW which requires measures to ensure that rural women enjoy adequate sanitation and water supply and article 18 of the African Protocol on Women which provides that women have a right to live in a healthy environment. The protocol further provides in article 18(2)(c) that states parties shall take all appropriate measures to regulate the management, processing, storage and disposal of domestic waste. Arguably, the by-products of menstruation produced in schools are tantamount to domestic waste. Thus in terms of CEDAW and the protocol, states parties in the African context have a clear obligation to provide a healthy and clean environment and to deal with issues of sanitation. Given that there is an antecedent obligation to keep girls in schools, lack of facilities should not lead to school closures but compliance with the obligation to ensure that facilities are in place. The remedies suggested are do-able and relatively inexpensive. However, states parties have to be kept on their toes – they should not be able to shuffle out of such obligations on the pretext that they have devolved the responsibilities to local government and communities when there is clear evidence that such entities are deeply impoverished, often as a result of macro-economic mismanagement on the part of the state.

Reporting guidelines would need to focus on whether measures have been put in place by states parties to ensure:

- Planning for and provision of adequate sanitary facilities at all schools and, in particular, facilities that address the special needs of menstruating girls;
- Adequate budgets to cover the construction, upgrading and maintenance of school sanitary facilities, including disposal facilities;
- Provision of water at all schools for use in toilets, with particular emphasis on the provision of water for the use of girls who are menstruating;
- Regular inspections and reporting on the state of school toilets and the general cleanliness and health environment at schools;
- That all the above requirements are met, albeit in a simple form.

Conclusion

I have argued that sexual maturation, menstruation and sanitary measures for the adolescent girl child are important components influencing, in some cases, the frequency of her attendance and retention in school. Attending to these issues provides a sex-based foundation that should positively affect the efficacy of initiatives to promote girls' rights to education and, eventually, to gender equality or at the very least gender equity. None of the solutions that have been suggested need expensive interventions; they do however require commitment, vision and dedication. Hopefully, they will help to retain girls in school and help them to perform to their full potential.

A word of caution is required. This is only part of the solution to getting the girl child to school and keeping her there, other issues also affect her attendance and retention. Nevertheless the issues raised in this chapter need to be attended to for the overall wellbeing of every child in school, especially the girl child.

This chapter has also demonstrated that human rights are local and global. They are attainable. They are often about the simplest things in life; about the unspoken and the unarticulated.

Bibliography

Dengu-Zvobgo K. C. (2004) 'The impact of school management on menstruation', in J. E. Stewart (ed) *Life skills, sexual maturation and sanitation: What's (not) happening in our schools – An exploratory study from Zimbabwe*, Weaver Press and Women's Law Centre, UZ, Harare.

Gumbo S. (2004) 'Life skills in primary Schools: A review. Curriculum development, implementation and assessment', in J. E. Stewart (ed) *Life skills, sexual maturation and sanitation: What's (not) happening in our schools – An exploratory study from Zimbabwe*, Weaver Press and Women's Law Centre, UZ, Harare.

Kirumira E. (ed) (2003) *Life skills, sexual maturation and sanitation: What's (not) happening in our schools – An exploratory study from Uganda*, Weaver Press and Women's Law Centre, UZ Harare.

Moyo S. *et al.* (2004) 'An evaluation of national sanitation policy, with an emphasis on the sexual maturation needs of girls vis-a-vis menstruation', in J. E. Stewart (ed) *Life skills, sexual maturation and sanitation: What's (not) happening in our schools – An exploratory study from Zimbabwe*, Weaver Press and Women's Law Centre, UZ, Harare.

Mutunga P. (ed) (2003) *Life skills, sexual maturation and sanitation: What's (not) happening in our schools – An exploratory study from Kenya*, page 198, Weaver Press and Women's Law Centre, UZ, Harare.

Ncube W. and J. E. Stewart with K. Dengu-Zvobgo, B. Donzwa, E. Gwaunza, J. Kazembe (1997) *Paradigms of exclusion: Women's access to resources in Zimbabwe*, page 156, WLSA, Harare.

Samkange F. (2004) 'Sexual maturation and education processes: the exploration', in J. E. Stewart (ed) *Life skills, sexual maturation and sanitation: What's (not) happening in our schools – An exploratory study from Zimbabwe*, Weaver Press and Women's Law Centre, UZ, Harare.

Stewart J. E. (2004) 'What happens next? in J. E. Stewart (ed) *Life skills, sexual maturation and sanitation: What's (not) happening in our schools – An exploratory study from Zimbabwe*, Weaver Press and Women's Law Centre, UZ, Harare.

UNESCO (2004) *Education for all: EFA monitoring report*, UNESCO Publishing, Paris.

List of legislation
Zimbabwe
Education Act, Chapter 24.04, 1987

Statutory Instrument 367 of 1998 Education (non-government schools) Regulations

Regional and international
African Charter on the Rights and Welfare of the Child

Protocol to the African Charter on Human and Peoples' Rights on the Rights of Women in Africa 2003

Convention against Discrimination in Education 1960, UNESCO

Convention on the Elimination of All Discrimination against Women (CEDAW) 1979

Convention on the Rights of the Child 1989

12

Where is the toilet? Getting down to basics in accessing women's rights

Shaheen Sardar Ali

This chapter seeks to highlight the institutional embeddedness of unequal gender relations in the public and private sphere of life and its implications for effective enjoyment of women's human rights. Using access to a toilet at health facilities in the North West Frontier province of Pakistan as an example, it aims to share some thoughts and experiences on women's real capacity to access health facilities and its linkages with the overall status of women in Pakistan.[330] The chapter argues that in a society where the female form is barely visible, women's perception of their own bodies and how they are perceived in the social context makes it difficult for them to operate in and engage in the public sphere. Since health and wellbeing entails interaction in a desegregated public space (in hospitals, dispensaries, health centres), women's right to health is compromised as a result of this constraint, in particular where special needs of women (such as a separate toilet or just a toilet) are not taken into account. Women's failure to access health facilities may be attributable to entrenched gender roles that transcend social class and permeate public policy, legislative enactments and implementation mechanisms.

Operationalizing and actualizing human rights clearly requires something more than statements of intent, policy formulation and legal documents, especially in a plural legal setting where unwritten norms often are more powerful than the black letter law. It calls for that extra mile in

---

[330] Pakistan is a South-Asian country with a population of 144,971,000 according to the 2001 census. It was carved out of the Indian subcontinent in 1947 when British colonial rule came to an end and India became two independent countries, India and Pakistan. Annual population growth between 1991 and 2001 was 2.6 per cent, total fertility rate in 2001 stood at 5.2 as opposed to 5.9 in 1991. Child mortality (probability of dying under five years) per 1000 in males is 105 and females 115. Total expenditure on health as a percentage of gross domestic product in 2000 was 4.1. Some national estimates of antenatal care, deliveries in health facilities and deliveries with skilled attendants are as follows: Ante natal care is available to 27 per cent of women, while 13 per cent of deliveries are done in health facilities, and only in 18 per cent of cases are skilled birth attendants present (Source: http://www.who.int/country/pak/en/ visited on 27 March 2003).

the human rights walk to try to capture what may be considered too mundane a subject for academic discourse. The importance of a toilet and facilities in public spaces is one such mundane yet crucial element in our endeavour to make women's human rights a reality. The purpose of this chapter is to argue that a seemingly ancillary service (in this case availability of a toilet for women) to the provision of health, needs to be canvassed in the discourse on women's access to a range of rights due to engagement with the public space. The chapter attempts to demonstrate that despite the presence and availability of health services, the absence or inadequacy of facilities such as toilets for women can hugely restrain their access to health services, both as users and service providers.

1   The toilet as an indicator of access to rights: Unravelling some 'uncomfortable' realities.

This chapter is, for the most part, experiential in nature and based on my term in office as the Minister for Health, Population Welfare and Women's Development in the North West Frontier province of Pakistan.[331] In my endeavour to institutionalize a system of monitoring of health facilities, I undertook to travel throughout the province and appear at a facility when the health personnel least expected it. These were known as 'surprise' visits and the cause of discomfort to employees as they tended to expose all sorts of undesirable practices, including unscheduled absences of service providers, dirty premises and poor quality service delivery.

I start by sharing an incident that has left an indelible mark on my conceptualizaton of women's human rights. It encapsulates the dilemma of accommodation of women's bodies in the public sphere of life, impinging on their ability to access their rights and entitlements, whether in a hospital, school or a government office.

On one of my numerous 'surprise' visits to a hospital, I heard sudden shouting and screaming. To my horror, I turned to see *chawkidars*[332] 'shooing' women patients and their families away from the further end of the corridor saying:

> 'You dirty people this is not a toilet, why can't you go to the toilet before coming to dirty this hospital. Can't you see, my superior will be here soon and how will I explain all this dirt?'

To which came the heroic response from a woman:

> 'We are human beings, where do you expect me to go when there is no

---

[331] November 1999–August 2001
[332] Porters or caretakers as they would be called in English-speaking countries.

toilet here for us? We are ill and come to see the doctor from far away. Going to the toilet is a natural requirement. Men can go anywhere they want to; where should we women go. My body is my honour, how can I expose it before the world, we need some privacy so we come here …'

On and on the tirade continued until the *chawkidar* and woman disappeared down the corridor duly encouraged in their disappearance by some hospital staff who had been alerted to my presence on the premises.

This episode came at the end of a chain of incidents brought to my attention where lack of access to a toilet had resulted in problems for women in the public sphere. In sexually segregated societies such as Pakistan, women's bodies are considered 'private', 'invisible' repositories of male honour and it is with reluctance and extreme circumspection that women venture outside the home. Women thus operate in the public sphere in self-implementing and self-perpetuating suppression of their bodies, learning to cope as best they can in an environment that demands their invisible presence. Lack of access to a toilet in a public place for a woman acquires significance considering that exposing her body is tantamount to breaking societal norms more strictly enforced than the strictest of black letter laws. The poignant words of the indignant female patient demanding 'privacy' says it all. Whether it is a court building, a school or public office, the 'toilet factor' looms large when determining how women's rights (to health, education, employment and participation in public life in general) can be delivered in an enabling environment by allowing them adequate and appropriate space in the public sphere (see also Stewart, chapter 11 in this volume).

Equally important is the availability of facilities for female service providers because their presence is linked to whether women will be allowed by male family members (and feel comfortable themselves) to access a health facility. Thus when women personnel are denied access to sanitary facilities, it is not simply a case of inhibiting women from employment. It has an adverse affect on women as users of the facility – they may not be allowed to seek help from a male doctor or health worker.

The notion of sexual segregation is a mechanism for ensuring that women (symbolizing male honour) remain invisible and 'out of view' in the (predominantly) male public sphere. Analyzing the practice one may argue that, at one level, it denotes protection of women on the assumption that the home is safer than the public space. But the more pronounced reason for sexual segregation is that for centuries men have been cast in a proprietary role vis-a-vis women; hence the self-acquired male prerogative for regulating women's lives. In the North West Frontier province, in particular, this regulation of women's mobility is considered a test of how strong and in command of his women a Pukhtun male is.[333] If any untoward incident were to happen outside the home involving a woman, it would cast aspersions on the male capability to protect the women in his domain, even if the woman had gone to access health services, to attend school or to her workplace. Reluctance of women to access basic facilities and services in desegregated environments must be understood in the light of this social stigma.[334] This understanding however does not and cannot go unchallenged because withholding women from accessing these services is a denial of their human rights and entitlements and reflects the lower value placed on women's lives.

This linkage between poor maternal health care and women's human rights on a basis of non-discrimination and equality is stated in the following excerpt from a recent editorial of a leading daily newspaper of Pakistan, *The News* (4 September 2005):

> 'The abysmal figures. . . . for the number of women dying of pregnancy-related causes should come as no surprise . . . . While it is true that maternal health care is closely linked to the overall health system, it is also important to note that *the characteristic neglect of women and their welfare has much to do with the poor care they receive* [emphasis mine].. . . There can be no substitute for better health outreach for these women and for the presence of trained birth attendants in villages and remote areas. *But it is equally necessary to eliminate the gender bias that exists in society if we are to make it to the ranks of nations that have a population of healthy mothers and children'* [emphasis mine].

Denial of women's human rights thus occurs at multiple levels: at the level of the family that does not value them sufficiently to facilitate access to health facilities; at the level of society that frowns upon women's presence in the public sphere and finally at the level of government that

---

[333] There is a growing literature on Pukhtuns, the ethnic group inhabiting the North West Frontier province in Pakistan, especially in relation to the position of women within these communities. Some of these include: O. K. Caroe (1958, repr. 1965), *The Pathans, 550 B.C.–A.D. 1957* ; J. W. Spain (1963) *People of the Khyber* , (1963) *The Pathan borderland* and (2nd ed. 1973) The *way of the Pathans* ; A. S. Ahmed (1976) *Millennium and charisma among Pathans. A critical essay in social anthropology*; A. S. Ahmed and Z. Ahmed (1981) 'Tor and Mor: binary and opposing models of Pukhtun womanhood' in Epstein and Watts (eds) *The endless day: Rural women. Asian case-studies. The Riwajnama Malakand Agency* (1964) is an interesting compilation of customary practices of that particular area of the NWFP and provides a rare insight into how custom undermines women's position making the male family member her virtual proprietor. For an overview of customary practices of various ethnic groups in Pakistan, see Ali and Rehman (2001).

[334] An oft-quoted saying of the Pushto language (spoken in North West Frontier province) sums up the confinement of women to the private sphere thus: *Khaza da kor dya the gor* meaning 'a woman belongs either to the home or the grave'!

imbibes the worldview of family and society by failing to open up spaces for women's full and equal enjoyment of rights and entitlements. Is it any wonder that one woman dies during pregnancy or in childbirth every minute? (Obaid, 2003). The Family Care International and Safe Motherhood Inter-agency Group report (2002) sums it up aptly by stating that:

> 'For a woman to die in pregnancy and childbirth is a result of social injustice. Such deaths are rooted in women's powerlessness and unequal access to employment, finances, education, basic health care and other resources.'

The above discussion clearly poses the question of what the contours of human rights are and how these might be actualized in plural normative settings. Taking the example of the right to health, it has been defined as '. . . a state of complete physical, mental and social wellbeing and not merely the absence of disease or infirmity' (WHO, 1948: 100).[335] By its very definition therefore, being healthy is not a right or entitlement that is enjoyed in isolation. In common with other economic, social, cultural, civil and political rights, it is inextricably linked to a wider range of supporting rights.[336] This is especially true in the case of women's right to health as articulated by Bharati Sadasivam:

> 'Health advocates and human rights scholars have argued that health is a socially produced good that needs a combination of civil and political rights (the right to decide the number and spacing of children) and economic and social rights (the availability of contraceptives and safe and affordable health services) to attain the highest standard of sexual and reproductive health' (Sadasivam, 1997: 314)

The re-orientation of human rights discourse thus calls for recognition that rights are like cascading waves of a waterfall, each reinforcing the other and unable to flow in isolation. Women's right to health demands rights to equal access to a range of related rights within the overarching framework of non-discrimination and equality and cutting across civil and political, and economic, social and cultural rights (see chapter 14 in this volume).

Access to women's human rights calls for deconstruction of pluralistic regulatory norms. In the context of Pakistan, fundamental rights

---

[335] Preamble to the constitution of the World Health Organization adopted by the International Health Conference held in New York 19–22 June 1946, signed on 22 July 1946 by the representatives of 61 states (official records of WHO, No. 2, page 100) and entered into force on 7 April 1948. The definition has not been amended since 1946.

[336] The indivisibility of civil and political rights and economic, social and cultural rights is a much debated thematic in human rights and development discourse. For various approaches on the indivisibility of rights, see Toebes (1999) and Evans (2002).

and principles of policy in the constitution of Pakistan compete with principles of Islamic law[337] and customary practices.[338] The emerging conceptual framework of rights remains dependent upon an interplay between these plural legal norms. Lack of access to a toilet for women in public spaces exemplifies this interface. Custom in Pakistan requires women to be confined to the home and to try their best not to engage with the public (male) space whereas formal legislation and government policies extend her equal access to health facilities. Since custom informs implementation of law and policy and is 'unprepared' for women's public presence, her genuine needs, like toilet facilities, are not catered for.

At the international level, various human rights instruments as well as policy declarations shape women's right to health and provide an example of essential prerequisites for actualizing a range of rights and entitlements. The right to health is embedded in article 12 of the International Covenant on Economic, Social and Cultural Rights and calls for the right to the highest attainable standard of physical and mental health. Conscious of the importance of giving content to this formal provision, the covenant committee, in its General Comment No. 14[339] presents a useful elaboration on women's health rights jurisprudence. The committee notes:

> 'To eliminate discrimination against women, there is need to develop a comprehensive national strategy for promoting women's rights to health throughout their life span. . . . The realization of women's right to health requires the removal of all barriers interfering with access to health services, education and information. . .'[340]

This is further developed and strengthened in article 12 of the Convention on the Elimination of All Forms of Elimination Against Women (CEDAW) which calls for states parties:

> '...to take all appropriate measures to eliminate discrimination against

---

[337] As indicated in an earlier section of this chapter, confinement of women to the home has its source in custom. Islam does not prohibit women from engaging with the public sphere; at the same time it has to be said that it discourages social interaction between men and women in a desegregated social environment.

[338] The Constitution of Pakistan 1973 has a chapter on fundamental rights, including article 25, which calls for equality before the law and equal protection of the law. It also provides for special measures to favour women and other vulnerable groups, including children and minorities. The chapter on principles of policy calls for the state to extend to its citizens, by all possible means at its disposal and keeping in mind the resources available, a range of economic, social and cultural rights.

[339] The right to the highest attainable standard of health (Article 12) General Comment No. 14 (11/08/00) (E/C.12/200/4).

[340] General Comment of International Covenant on Economic, Social and Cultural Rights Committee on article 12, paragraph 21.

women in the field of health care in order to ensure, on a basis of equality of men and women, access to health care services, including those related to family planning.'

Thus access to services is considered an essential component of the right to health, making it an obligation on the part of national governments to undertake measures ensuring access. What constitutes 'access' will vary in different jurisdictions and in different parts of a single jurisdiction and the onus for proving that these geographic and societal variations have been addressed will be on the government itself.

One clear, strong articulation of women's right to health as a bundle of interconnected entitlements is in General Recommendation No. 24 of the CEDAW committee which asks states parties to do the following, inter alia:

'28). When reporting on measures taken to comply with article 12, states parties are urged to recognize its interconnection with other articles in the convention that have a bearing on women's health. Those articles include: article 5(b) which requires states parties to ensure that family education includes a proper understanding of maternity as a social function; article 10 which requires states parties to ensure equal access to education, thus enabling women to access health care more readily and reducing female student drop-out rates which are often a result of premature pregnancy; article 10(h) which requires that states parties provide women and girls with access to specific educational information to ensure the health and wellbeing of families, including information and advice on family planning; article 11 which is concerned, in part, with the protection of women's health and safety in working conditions, including safeguarding the reproductive function, special protection from harmful types of work during pregnancy and with the provision of paid maternity leave; article 14, paragraph 2(b) which requires states parties to ensure access for rural women to adequate health-care facilities, including information, counselling and services in family planning and 2(h) which obliges states parties to take all appropriate measures to ensure adequate living conditions, particularly housing, sanitation, electricity and water supply, transport and communications, all of which are critical for the prevention of disease and the promotion of good health care; and article 16, paragraph 1(e) which requires states parties to ensure that women have the same rights as men to decide freely and responsibly on the number and spacing of their children and to have access to the information, education and means to enable them to exercise those rights. Article 16, paragraph 2, proscribes the betrothal and marriage of children, an important factor in preventing the physical and emotional harm which arise from early childbirth.'

Further, article 11 (elimination of discrimination in the field of employment) also elaborates the notion of equality as moving beyond 'sameness' and inclusive of the special needs of women employees.

In summing up the example of the right to health on a basis of equality and non-discrimination, it is evident that formal equality alone, without supporting entitlements, is neither adequate nor acceptable in contemporary human rights interpretation. It is acknowledged that what breathes life into the various human rights provisions outlined above is the structure, management and implementation of mostly procedural mechanisms at national and local levels. Without this element, any right, including the right to health, becomes a lifeless and meaningless aspiration. The reality is that since 'action' is at country level, the sum total of women's rights needs to be translated into policies, legislation, management and monitoring on the ground at national and local levels. More crucial than incorporating the norms of women's rights into national laws is internalizing them and ascertaining what factors prevent women from attaining the highest possible standards of health despite governmental commitment and resource allocations.

2   Accommodating women's bodies in gendered public spheres: The 'effects' of non-discrimination and equality

This section emphasizes how apparently neutral and non-gendered environments can and do ignore the needs of women and end up being oppressive for them both as employees and as clients. A safe, relaxed work environment is linked to effective service provision for women by women. Therefore implementing rights on the principle of non-discrimination and equality implies that, if women's access to services in the public sphere is to be ensured, the presence of women service providers is as important as the facility itself. This in turn means that women service providers must feel safe and confident in their work environment to be present and effective.

During my term as Minister for Health in the North West Frontier province I became convinced that to bring human rights home to women something more than an equal rights clause was required in the law. I arrived at this conclusion due to innumerable incidents exposing women-unfriendly work environments in public and private institutions, some of which I share below.

I particularly recall being confronted with a letter written to me by a woman secretary[341] who worked in an all-male government department

---

[341] Known as clerks in the Pakistan office system.

where she was the only female employee and one of the lowest paid. Her letter was the result of an initiative where I set up a government/non-governmental organization coordination committee on gender issues and asked all government line departments to send one representative to committee meetings to raise issues affecting women employees in their departments and in relation to their work as service providers. This news soon spread to women employees within government and the following letter[342] appeared to be a consequence of that initiative. It is an example of the gap between theoretical perspectives on human rights to health and employment and its translation into the realities of peoples' lives:

'Dear Madam Minister,

I am writing to you because you are in a decision-making position but more so because you are a woman. I have not met you but people have said that you do read all the letters sent to your office and you also try to do something about problems raised in them. I am a single woman working as a junior clerk in *XYZ*[343] department of the government and come from a poor family and have to work to support the family. But the working conditions in the workplace are terrible and have made me ill. I cannot confide in anyone at work because they are all men and I feel embarrassed to talk to them about what is a very personal matter. There is no toilet for women on the premises and I cannot use the one for male employees. I come to work by public transport and leave home very early in the morning. I reach home around three o'clock in the afternoon after finishing work. Please tell me how is it humanly possible for me to keep myself from going to the toilet for more than nine hours, six days of the week?[344] This condition becomes worse when I get my monthly period when I need the toilet more frequently. Moreover there is no place where I can sit and have a cup of tea or my lunch and I have either to go hungry or gobble it all down when my male colleagues are not in the room. I feel uncomfortable but no one seems to bother about the needs of a poor woman and an insignificant employee like me.'

---

[342] I have translated and edited this letter from Urdu which is the national language of Pakistan.

[343] I am withholding the name of the department to protect the privacy of the employee.

[344] Pakistan has a six-day working week. Fridays are half-days where offices close at around noon for Friday prayers.

I was filled with shame and disbelief. Here I was with an office with en suite toilet which I could not imagine being without for nine hours at a stretch. I tried to reassure myself by putting the letter down to the invisible hierarchy in bureaucracies rather than any overt disregard for the needs women employees. This secretary was on the lowest rung on the ladder of officialdom; hence her feeling of alienation and lack of respect for or sensitivity to her needs. The situation would be appropriately addressed by making sure that one toilet was made available for her.[345] In my naivety I assumed that women officers in higher positions would have better conditions at work. I must have tempted fate with my optimism because the phone rang and I was informed that a fairly senior woman officer wanted to meet me, and that it was urgent.

The officer sat on the edge of the chair, visibly agitated, not knowing where to begin. When I prompted her by asking how she was doing in her new position, she replied that while the job was challenging, with just three or so women in an office complex of more than 200 male colleagues, life was uncomfortable. There was no toilet for women and since one of the women officers had an office with an en suite toilet, the women decided to make that into the 'women's toilet'. But today as she was about to enter the toilet, a male officer emerged, giving her a defiant look. She was embarrassed and reminded him that this particular toilet was for women only. The man shrugged and retorted that she could not stop men from using it. 'Madam,' she said to me, 'I don't know what got into me, but I immediately took out a lock and key and locked the toilet. Here is the key!' (She held up a key). I congratulated her but she said her momentary courage had ebbed and she had rushed to my office to express her anxiety at how this would be received by a predominantly male workforce. Her junior colleague had insisted they should come and, if I was unable to provide them access to a women-only toilet, they should request a transfer out of that office.

The story of the senior women officers indicates how vulnerable women workers feel in a male-dominated work environment. It also shows that a sense of security has little to do with the level at which a woman is employed since it is her sex that actually places her at an inherent disadvantage. Adopting a gender-neutral approach does not alleviate the acute sense of unease that women experience in the public sphere in most societies. After all, some of the women officers referred

---

[345] The matter of the lone female secretary was resolved by a telephone call from the ministerial office. It would be interesting to know, however, whether that trend of providing women employees with toilet facilities continues or was considered a one-off favour to the sensitivities of a fussy, toilet-obsessed woman health minister!

to were in senior managerial positions, came from affluent backgrounds, were bright, confident, committed professionals; they had travelled and studied abroad and so had had exposure to the wider world. Nevertheless, despite being in their own country and place of work, they were unable to deal with access to a toilet. As a consequence of the blindness towards the special needs of women employees, the province, the health department and the men and women of the country, might well be deprived of their experiences and service – all due to lack of a toilet. What could be more ludicrous? Yet, denying access to a toilet in reality meant denying women access to a range of facilities in the public sphere, impacting upon their access to the 'public' space and their ability to negotiate the public sphere of life with confidence.[346]

The letter from the junior secretary and the senior women officers meeting echoed my own discomfort at being unable to articulate my need for the toilet when surrounded by hundreds of men. My thoughts go back to the initial days in public office when I felt too embarrassed to ask for the toilet and the courage it took to convince myself that going to the toilet in the presence of men was not exactly sacrilege. An interesting (read embarrassing) situation arose when I was inducted into the otherwise all-male cabinet meetings which were held in the governor's house, Peshawar. There did not appear to be a women's toilet and after the first few meetings, I committed my most 'courageous' act – asking His Excellency the Governor of the North West Frontier province of Pakistan bluntly, in the presence of my male colleagues, where the ladies' toilet was! The gallant general looked duly apologetic and a toilet in one of the guest rooms, usually kept locked, was designated as the women's toilet. Alas! despite standing orders to unlock it when Cabinet was meeting, I often found myself standing in front of a locked room, fumbling for the words to have the door unlocked while important matters of state were being discussed and decisions held up in the next room! The gurus of 'mainstreaming' gender into the development process would get a rude shock were they to discover that the toilet or, more accurately, the lack of one, could lead to women's marginalization, both as service providers and as clients, and jeopardize mainstreaming altogether.

In present-day Pakistan there is no legislation with mandatory provisions for government or individuals to construct toilets as part of a

---

[346] A friend who works in rejuvenating communities in the education sector told me this story: Her organization initiates 'adopt a school' programmes with the help of friends and communities. She was shocked when on visiting at least half a dozen girls' schools, she found no toilets. Further investigation led her to link this with teenage girls and younger girls dropping out due to no access to a toilet. When she placed construction of a toilet as the top priority, people could not understand why it was so important and why they could not leave that to the end, seeing it as a luxury, not a necessity.

building (a house, school, hospital, and so on) thus many schools have no toilets. Neither do government-owned service delivery outlets, such as hospitals and offices, make it a priority to construct toilets, adequately built and serviced for personnel and the public. Municipal bylaws, however, encourage the building of public toilets but since implementation is not mandatory, the service is uneven. Some municipal authorities tend to construct toilets to generate some income (charging per user); others simply ignore the recommendation. In the 1990s, under the World Bank Social Action Programme, 'model' toilets were built in schools as well as in 2 to 3 per cent of homes in the community. The idea was to encourage people in the community to build their own toilets with the technical assistance of these model toilets. The evaluation of this initiative was not positive and the idea did not take off as anticipated due to resource constraints of the target population.[347]

Insensitivity to basic needs when constructing public buildings is not confined to office complexes and schools. Even large hospitals operating in towns and cities are sometimes designed without public toilets. One example was the large, sprawling headquarters hospital at Kohat in the North West Frontier province of Pakistan. The building was impressive and well built and when I took office as the health minister it stood more than two thirds built but needed a small cash injection to finish it off. I was taken through the plans as well as given a tour around the premises. My first question was: *Where are the public toilets?* The officers could not believe they had heard me correctly. I repeated the question explaining that since we expected hundreds of people from far and wide to visit this facility on a daily basis, I wanted to know where they were expected to go to use a toilet. This was not a question they were anticipating and there was an uncomfortable silence and blank looks on the faces of all present. There was also some impatience in their response, as if to say, 'Don't you have anything more important to ask us?' I refused to commission the hospital unless we had constructed public toilets on the premises and I had seen them working. This 'policy' decision was met with sullen, resigned nods but not once did I see or hear any person seconding my thoughts. The link between lack of access to a toilet in a hospital and the fact that this might act as a disincentive to visit such a facility or work in one, was lost on these planners and implementers of public policy.

Similarly, during my numerous visits to basic health units and rural health centres in the province, the first move would be to ask for the

---

[347] I am grateful for this information and insight to Sardar Ali Khan who worked on the initiative as the executive engineer and subsequently superintending engineer, Public Health Engineering Department, Government of the North West Frontier province, Pakistan.

toilet. To my dismay I found dozens of units using toilets as storage rooms or simply leaving them locked up. Health sector personnel completely failed to comprehend why I was annoyed that the toilet was non-functional. Their dismay was apparent to me but mine unfortunately did not seem to register. I received messages from well-meaning colleagues that I was being overly fussy about this 'toilet business' and that I was well advised to turn my attention to more pressing matters of the health sector.[348]

In attempting to recall causes inhibiting women's use of health facilities, I have to admit that their strongest concerns were linked to the presence of women health professionals in these facilities and their ability to provide services. For the ailing women, by and large, not having access to a toilet was subsumed in the gigantic effort to reach a health facility and be seen by a health professional, preferably a female doctor. But that does not detract from the importance of facilities such as a toilet, clean drinking water and transport to and from the hospital to ensure minimum comfort levels for women not ordinarily seen outside the home and to encourage access to medical treatment.

Why is the toilet (or lack of it) not considered a facilitatory, essential requirement for optimal use of public services? Is it because a large percentage of the population in Pakistan do not have access to a toilet anyway (many people in rural areas 'go to the toilet' in a wide open field at the crack of dawn and that is the only toilet they know about)? Often when I have asked why a toilet in a public place is locked and out of bounds, the response is that: 'These people do not know how to use one, they will only make a mess of things!' So, to what extent do class and social hierarchies come into play in framing basic needs by people and for people? The professional middle classes are aware of the importance of the toilet as a basic facility, both in the home and workplace, and would be expected to raise demand for one. Yet, to the best of my knowledge the demand has not been framed as an essential prerequisite to the right to access a health facility. The underprivileged poor, on the other hand, neither in possession of a toilet nor made aware of it as a basic entitlement in the private or public sphere, do not articulate it as part of the right to health.

The question however remains: *How do women as clients in public*

---

[348] Simultaneously, it came to my knowledge that when medical superintendents of hospitals or other senior doctors in charge of health facilities compared notes about what preparations would be required when the Minister for Health was inspecting a facility, the prompt response was: 'Forget everything else, just make sure the toilets are clean, and working!'. Admittedly the importance and role of a toilet in service delivery and widening access for users was lost on most people I came across.

sector facilities offering health care services cope with the basic need for a toilet? If one were to follow the argument that most women are not used to a toilet in their own homes so why should they expect one in a health facility, we overlook an important step in the logical progression of events. Male users of public space also arguably require a toilet and are not used to having an 'indoor' facility at home, so why fuss over women's needs? The basic difference lies in their biological make up and the acceptable public space available to them – men can 'go to the toilet' behind a bush with relative ease, compared to women. The principle of equity, equality and non-discrimination, therefore, takes on an entirely new dimension in its scope and meaning if the sameness argument is to be applied in such situations. The argument that lack of a toilet affects both men and women does not hold true where women's needs require different treatment. In societies where women are the 'symbol' of male honour, their bodies acquire a place and position that transcends the equal treatment discourse and makes it virtually redundant. 'Female' space within the public domain, including an all-women toilet in health facilities thus assumes crucial significance in order to widen access for women to their right to health.

While the above narratives are not exhaustive of various aspects of the discussion, they highlight how a neutral and non-gendered environment, supposedly extending 'equal' access to health facilities, on a basis of non-discrimination, can ignore the needs of women and be oppressive for them.

3 Contextualizing women's right to health in a local-global world: Searching for missing links?

This chapter makes the case that for meaningful enjoyment of women's human rights, whether in the field of health, education, employment or access to justice, a number of simple yet concrete steps are imperative. Ensuring accessible, functional toilets for women service providers as well as clients in health facilities, schools, offices and court buildings, is one example of creating an enabling environment. The stories in this chapter also accentuate what many have said before – that the principles of non-discrimination and gender mainstreaming, magical as they appear, need to be grounded in the realities of women's lives (Stewart, 2004; Dahl, 1989). The transition from these theoretical concepts to practical application, demands deep sensitivity to the special needs of women as a group.

The chapter also demonstrates the need for practical mechanisms in translating normative human rights into government policy guidelines, and legislative and planning regimes, by making relevant linkages between rights and obligations. Human rights mainstreaming may thus be achieved through provision of toilets, accessible and affordable public transport and gender-sensitive measures to make women feel protected, safe and acceptable in the public sphere. In fact, the toilet might be considered an ancillary service that facilitates an enabling environment for implementing women's human rights to health, education, employment, and so on. Various government departments (and private organizations and institutions) should be required to provide detailed and specific guidelines and protocols regarding the number and placing of toilets, minimum acceptable standards of cleanliness and measures ensuring women's privacy.

At the international level, reports to human rights bodies, such as the CEDAW committee, might include the above information as well as the number of women professionals employed in various government departments and the levels at which they are employed. Quantitative and qualitative data must be generated and analyzed. Thus, in analyzing implementation of women's right to health on the touchstone of CEDAW, the question of how best to arrive at substantive equality must be raised and addressed. Various provisions of CEDAW and other human rights instruments must 'speak to each other' in a common language to create space for women's needs. For instance, article 5 of CEDAW calls for states parties to take all appropriate measures to:

> '(a) modify the social and cultural patterns of conduct of men and women, with a view to achieving the elimination of prejudices and customary and all practices which are based on an idea of the inferiority or superiority of either of the sexes or on stereotyped roles of men and women.'

Does this mean that women, who by virtue of their existing cultural patterns or by choice, feel more comfortable in a segregated environment and demand separate toilet facilities or to be seen by female service providers, should be denied such service in view of obligations imposed by CEDAW? Or, should article 5 of CEDAW be read in the light of article 12 of the same convention that provides for women's right to health, bearing in mind their special needs? How do we achieve that fine balance between opening up the public space for women who see themselves as able and willing to negotiate such space whilst addressing the needs of others who feel more comfortable and confident to operate in a sheltered environment?

A balance may be achieved by going beyond a mechanical reading of equal rights for women in international human rights law, assessing critically the evolutionary journey of the concept of 'equality' and 'non-discrimination' since its initial introduction into international human rights documents. In the initial stages of application, equality and non-discrimination were generally interpreted in formal legalistic terms on the premise that by making that statement in law, equality and non-discrimination would follow in practice. This interpretation and manifestation of the concept was flawed on a number of counts. Equality was perceived and defined as being like a man, as Catherine Mackinnon writes, 'Man has become the measure of all things'. Over the decades and with inputs from human rights scholars, activists, human rights treaty bodies and domestic courts, the non-discrimination norm and equality have achieved a more nuanced and sophisticated position. It now includes within its meaning the interconnectedness of various human rights to give it substantive content. Equal rights to health, employment and education may imply different and unequal measures – in order to arrive at equal access for all. Where the norm remains to be developed and tightened up is in the area of allocation of both human and material resources. Most importantly, measures such as gender budgeting need to be introduced as an integral component of any planning, monitoring and evaluation aspects of government projects. This aspect of the norm of non-discrimination and equality has also been articulated in General Recommendation No. 24 of the CEDAW committee as follows:

'(30) States parties should allocate adequate budgetary, human and administrative resources to ensure that women's health receives a share of the overall health budget comparable with that for men's health, taking into account their different health needs.

(31) States parties should also, in particular:

(a) Place a gender perspective at the centre of all policies and programmes affecting women's health and should involve women in the planning, implementation and monitoring of such policies and programmes and in the provision of health services to women;' (General Recommendation No. 24, CEDAW committee).

Men and women start the race for equal rights from totally different points as illustrated by the discussion in this chapter. It highlighted the inter-connectivity and inter-relational nature of civil and political rights (the issue of non-discrimination and equal access) with economic social and cultural rights (access to a toilet). Unequal access to a toilet in a health facility thus brought to the fore the structural inequality which has a spill-over effect into the right to health and a range of women's human rights. The legal and equal right to health borders on the farcical where hospitals are located so far away that women are unable to access them either for themselves or for their ailing children. Further, if those within reach do not have female staff, women's right to access all-male facilities is significantly diminished. Women's disadvantages are often based on structural injustices; rethinking human rights through innovative mechanisms, such as ensuring toilets for women in the public arena, may be some of the opportunities to address those injustices and make women's human rights a reality.

Bibliography

Ahmed A. S. (1976) *Millennium and charisma among Pathans. A critical essay in social anthropology,* Routledge and Keegan Paul, London.

Ahmed A. S. and Z. Ahmed (1981) 'Tor and Mor: Binary and opposing models of Pukhtun womanhood' in T. S. Epstein and R. A. Watts (eds) *The endless day: Some case material on Asian rural women*, Pergamon Press, New York.

Ali S. S. (2000) *Gender and human rights in Islam and International law: Equal before Allah, unequal before man?* Kluwer Law International, the Hague.
– (ed) (2001) *Reforming the health sector in the North West Frontier province: An overview,* page 83, co-authored and edited government policy document, Government of NWFP.
– (2002a) 'Reforming the health sector in NWFP: A nostalgic view from (?) afar', in 2002 (1) *Law, Social Justice & Global Development Journal (LGD)* at http://elj.warwick.ac.uk/global/02-1/ali1.html.
– (2002b) 'The "brass tacks" of institution-based practice: Myths and reality', in 2002(1) *Law, Social Justice & Global Development Journal (LGD)* at http://elj.warwick.ac.uk/global/02-1/ali2.html
– (2002c) 'Who writes the budget: A close-up of the politics of development projects: Implications for health care delivery, democracy and good governance. Towards a human rights development approach', in 2002 (1) *Law, Social Justice & Global Development Journal (LGD)* at http://elj.warwick.ac.uk/global/02-1/ali3.html

Ali S. S. and J. Rehman (2001) *Indigenous peoples and ethnic minorities of Pakistan: Constitutional and legal perspectives,* Nordic Institute of Asian Studies Press/Curzon Press, Copenhagen and Richmond.

Bogecho D. (2004) 'Putting it to good use: The International Covenant on Civil and Political Rights and women's reproductive right to health', *Law, Social Justice & Global Development Journal (LGD)* at http://www2.warwick.ac.uk/fac/soc/law/elj/lgd/2004_1/bogecho/

Caroe O. K. (1958) *The Pathans, 550 B.C.– A.D. 1957*, St Martin's Press, New York.

Cook R. (ed) (1994) *Human rights of women: National and international perspectives*, University of Pennsylvania Press, Philadelphia.

Dahl T. S. (1989) 'Taking women as a starting point: Building women's law', working papers in Women's Law No. 4, Institute of International and Public Law, Department of Women's Law, University of Oslo.

Evans T. (2002) 'A human right to health?', *Third World Quarterly* 23, 197–215.

Government of NWFP, Pakistan (1964) *The Riwajnama Malakand Agency* compiled by Zafar Ali Khan, Political Agent, Malakand.

Kadaga R. (2003) 'The dilemmas of an African woman politician at the crossroads; Law, reality and patriarchy', long essay submitted in partial fulfilment of Master's in Women's Law, Women's Law Centre, University of Zimbabwe, available at www.uz.ac.zw/law/women/long%20essays/women%20in%20parliament.pdf.

Obaid T. (2003) 'Saving women's lives', Smith College lecture, available at http://www.unfpa.org/news/news,cfm?ID=271.

Rehman J. (2003) *International human rights law: A practical approach*, Pearson Education Ltd, Harlow.

Sadasivam B. (1997) 'The impact of structural adjustment on women: A governance and human rights agenda', *Human Rights Quarterly* 19(3):630–665.

Spain J. W. (1963) *People of the Khyber*: The Pathans of Pakistan, Frederick A. Praeger, New York.
– (1963) *The Pathan borderland*, Mouton & Co, the Hague.
– (1972) *The way of the Pathans*, Oxford University Press, New York.

Stewart J. E. (2004) 'Sex? Gender? So what? Mainstreaming gender concerns', in Welpe, Thege, Henderson and Welpe (eds) *The gender perspective: Innovations in economy, organizations and health within the South African Development Community* (SADC), Peter Lang, Frankfurt.

Toebes B. (1999) 'Towards an improved understanding of the international human right to health', *Human Rights Quarterly* 21, 661–679.

United Nations (2002) *Family Care International and Safe Motherhood Interagency Group report*, United Nations, New York.
– Committee on Economic, Social and Cultural Rights (2000) *The right to the highest attainable standard of health (article 12 of the International Covenant on Economic, Social and Cultural Rights)*, paragraph 21, General Comment No. 14, reference: 11/08/00; E/C.12/200/4.
– Committee on CEDAW (1999) *General Recommendation No. 24, article 12, Women and health*.

World Health Organization (1948) 'Preamble to the WHO constitution', WHO, New York

List of legislation
Pakistan

Constitution of Pakistan 1973

International

Convention on the Elimination of All Forms of Elimination Against Women (CEDAW) 1979

International Covenant on Economic, Social and Cultural Rights 1966

13

From human development to human rights
A southern African perspective on women and teenage girls' right to reproductive choice[349]

Anne Hellum and Anne Lene Staib Knudsen

The human rights based approach to development has in recent years made its mark on international and national development policies. This chapter explores how human development is considered in the evolving body of human rights law. Focusing on the practice of human rights treaty bodies it addresses the interdependence between women and girls' human development, their right to reproductive choice and the right to life, health, education, participation and work. The relationship between the right to reproductive choice and economic and religious constraints is given particular attention. To what extent can state obligations embedded in human rights instruments be exempted on the basis of resource constraints? How does the policy of mainstreaming social, cultural and religious factors for advancing development goals affect the fulfilment of human rights? Are there rights which are more fundamental than others and, if so, which ones and on what basis?

1 Teenage pregnancies, human development and the indivisibility of rights

Women and girls' right to reproductive and sexual health demonstrates the close link between gender, human rights and development. The right to health includes a bundle of rights ranging from life, survival, liberty, integrity, security and reproductive self-determination (Cook *et al.*, 2003; Banda, 2005). This chapter focuses on the interdependence between women and girls' right to reproductive self-determination – in terms of

---

[349] This chapter is based on Anne Lene Staib's work 'Women's human rights and reproductive autonomy' which was funded by the programme Bistandsrelevant kvinnerett (Staib, 2003) and Anne Hellum's paper 'Women's and girl's reproductive rights: a site of legal and religious contestation' which was presented at the CROSSROADS Conference in Oslo, June 2005 (published in *Forum for Development Studies* No. 1 of 2006). We would like to thank Johanne Sundby, Julie Stewart and Shaheen Sardar Ali for useful comments. We are also grateful to the diploma and master students at the Southern and Eastern African Regional Centre of Women's Law at the University of Zimbabwe (SEARCWL) who have addressed these important issues in their research.

the right to information, education and services – and the rights to life, education, participation and work. These mutually constitutive rights are embedded in the Convention on the Rights of the Child, the Convention on the Elimination of All Forms of Discrimination against Women (CEDAW), the International Covenant on Economic, Social and Cultural Rights and the Protocol to the African Charter on Human and Peoples' Rights on the Rights of Women in Africa.

The reality of women and teenage girls' lives is a far cry from the ideals and principles embedded in these instruments. Half of all new HIV infections (over 6,000 daily) occur among people of 15 to 24 years of age (UNFPA, 2003). More adolescent girls die from pregnancy-related complications than from any other cause. Girls aged between 15 and 19 are twice as likely to die in childbirth as older women. Five million girls undergo unsafe abortions every year. In many African countries HIV/AIDS prevalence among 15 to 24 year-olds is often twice as high and sometimes up to six times higher for women than for men (Human Development Report, 2003: 97). Due to unequal power relations, women and adolescent girls are often unable to refuse sex or insist on safe and responsible sexual practices. A series of converging factors ranging from biology, poverty and illiteracy to cultural and religious beliefs make teenage girls particularly vulnerable.[350] On the one hand, lack of protection from unwanted pregnancies and HIV affects teenage girls' ability to exercise other human rights, most importantly, the rights to life, health, education and work. On the other hand, non-fulfilment of human rights reinforces the economic, social and culturally-embedded inequalities that constrain women and teenage girls' reproductive choice.

In theory, human rights constitute a non-hierarchic and indivisible whole. Yet the reality, as demonstrated by the case of women and teenage girls, is radically different. In spite of seemingly gender-neutral laws and policies, women and girls are often denied equal enjoyment of their human rights by virtue of lesser status ascribed to them by religion or custom. While the nation state is the main duty bearer under international or state law, in practice it is not the sole regulatory mechanism. How state law interacts and intersects with local religious and cultural norms for the better or to the detriment of women is well documented through the vast literature on legal pluralism (Moore, 1978; Bentzon *et al.*, 1998; Hellum, 1999; Merry, 2005). Women and girls' right to reproductive choice is often a site of contestation between international hu-

---

[350] Committee on Economic, Social and Cultural Rights, General Comment 14, paragraph 4; Committee on Convention on the Rights of the Child, General Comment 3 paragraph 11; CEDAW Concluding observations on the second and third periodic report of Burkina Faso, paragraph 265.

man rights law and co-existing social, cultural and religious norms. As a means of changing attitudes, behaviours and laws, international agencies dealing with gender relations and reproductive health rights such as the United Nations Population Fund have adopted a culturally-sensitive approach (UNFPA, 2004). The culturally-sensitive approach constitutes the following:

> '…creating a positive negotiating environment with partners and stakeholders, acknowledging that patience and transparency are necessary when programming for behaviour change, respecting people's culture and its expressions, honouring commitments to agreements and promoting universally-recognized human rights in ways that enable communities to own these rights' (UNFPA, 2004: 39).

In line with this policy a plethora of non-governmental organizations, including faith-based organizations, religious and traditional leaders have been called upon in the response to the HIV/AIDS pandemic.[351] A major challenge for the human rights based development approach is to work out ways of ensuring that women and girls' rights are not jeopardized in the process in which rights, and cultural and religious values are negotiated.

The need to monitor the culturally-sensitive approach within a human rights framework is demonstrated by the following incident:

> A couple of years ago I visited a home for single mothers run by a local Catholic organization on the outskirts of Harare.[352] Young pregnant girls who had been abandoned by their families were given a place to live before and after giving birth. While staying there they were taught childcare, embroidery and cookery. The people in the organization made contact with their families and tried to reconcile them so as to make it possible for the girls to return to their parents' home. The project was funded by the Norwegian Agency for Development Cooperation (NORAD). The girls were not given any information on sexuality, reproduction or contraception. No attention was paid to the circumstances under which they had fallen pregnant although a number of them may have been raped and would have had a right to abortion.

This case demonstrates the contentious relationship between religious doctrine – where sexuality is not for enjoyment but linked to childbearing and marriage – and girls' right to reproductive and sexual information. It also shows how the human rights of women and girls may be transformed through economic and legal transactions between states

---

[351] Convention on the Rights of the Child, General Comment 3, paragraph 42.
[352] Visit to Shelter Trust with Professor Julie Stewart, University of Zimbabwe, August 2003.

parties, international development agencies and private service providers. In this instance the right to reproductive choice, ratified by two states parties in development cooperation – the Zimbabwean and Norwegian states – was overruled by religious norms linking sexuality to marriage.[353]

To close the gap between theory and practice in how states, international donors and non-governmental organizations deal with these issues, poses a challenge for a human rights based approach to development. To make reproductive choice real we suggest an interdisciplinary and contextual approach that acknowledges the mutual interdependence of a broad spectrum of human rights. To strike a balance between conflicting economic and religious concerns we turn the attention to the indivisibility of human rights in fulfilling core obligations, such as the right to health and education. Towards this end international legal sources – ranging from conventions to the deliberations of human rights treaty bodies, resolutions, declarations and statements – are explored.

The questions that such an approach postulates are: How can recognition of the reality-based interconnectedness of human rights contribute to the commitment to reproductive health in the midst of crumbling health and education systems? What relationships exist between human rights ratified by states on the one hand, and health and education policies informed by neo-liberal economic and political doctrines on the other? To what extent can state obligations embedded in human rights instruments be exempted on the basis of resource constraints possibly due to duties to implement structural adjustment programmes? To what extent can states relinquish their obligations as they transfer health functions to the private sector?[354] What is the implication of the human rights based development approach for the policy of mainstreaming social, cultural and religious factors to advance development goals and human rights? Are there rights which are more fundamental than others and, if so, which ones and on what basis?

Part 2 of this chapter deals with human rights and development in general and women and girls' right to reproductive choice and human development in particular. Three converging policy frameworks and discourses – the millennium development goals, the capabilities approach to human development and the human rights based approach to development – are addressed. Part 3 sets out a dynamic framework linking human rights discourse to the political, ethical and legal considerations underlying conventions, case law, deliberations of human rights treaty

---

[353] In its concluding observation to Zimbabwe's first report the CEDAW committee urged the government to 'provide sex education and practical family planning to both youth and adults.' Concluding observations of the CEDAW committee: Zimbabwe: 14/05/98. A/53/38, paragraphs 120–166.

[354] CEDAW General Comment 24, paragraph 17.

bodies, resolutions, declarations and statements. Part 4 defines the right to a reproductive choice, which spans a combination of rights, ranging from the right to life, the right to health and the right to education without discrimination. Part 5 presents a framework addressing economic, cultural and religious constraints to reproductive choice. Part 6 discusses the right to reproductive and sex education in school. Part 7 deals with the obligations of states parties, international donors and private service providers. Drawing the different sources together the final part demonstrates how the ethical, political and legal concern for human development is making its mark on women and girls' right to reproductive choice.

2 Human rights and human development – gaps and convergence

The strong link between gender, human rights and human development has figured prominently in the United Nations for more than half a century. The United Nations Development Report (2003) sees the millennium development goals,[355] human development and human rights as mutually constitutive (UNDP, 2003). As articulated in the Millennium Declaration (UN, 2000) the millennium development goals are benchmarks for a vision of development, peace and human rights guided by fundamental values, including freedom, equality, solidarity, tolerance, respect for nature and shared responsibility. Women and girls' capabilities and right to equality are defined as key to achieving these goals.

The case of women and girls' right to reproductive choice illustrates both gaps and convergence between these closely related frameworks. Within the millennium development goals, the elimination of gender disparity in primary and secondary education is the only overall official target to assess progress towards the gender equality goal (UNDP, 2003: 86). Consequently the goals are limited compared to the human capabilities and human rights based development frameworks. The latter emphasize the interconnectedness of the right to equality, self determination, reproductive and sexual information, and education.

The human capabilities approach sees the right to reproductive choice as part of human development. Fundamental to developing human choices is building up human capabilities: the range of things that people can be.[356] The most basic capabilities for human development are living a

---

[355] The United Nations General Assembly adopted the millennium development goals which included the commitment to making the right to development a reality for everyone and to freeing 'the entire human race from want' on 8 September 2000, General Assembly Resolution 55/2.

[356] The capabilities approach was championed by Professor in Economics and winner of the Nobel Prize in Economics, Amartya Sen. According to Sen, substantive

long and healthy life, being educated, having a decent standard of living and enjoying political and civil freedom (UNDP, 2003: 28; Nussbaum, 2000). Lack of protection from unwanted pregnancies and HIV has a profound impact on a teenage girl's ability to exercise other human rights, particularly the right to education, work and participation. Scholars, such as the American philosopher Martha Nussbaum, the economist Amartya Sen and the human rights professor, Henry Steiner, all hold that reproductive autonomy is a fundamental freedom particularly important to women's empowerment, individual development and status in society (Steiner, 1998; Sen, 1994: 11; Nussbaum, 2000).

Women and teenagers' right to reproductive choice has been substantially addressed as a human development issue at several international conferences, such as the 1993 International World Conference on Human Rights held in Vienna, the 1994 International Conference on Population and Development held in Cairo and the 1995 Fourth World Conference on Women held in Beijing. These declarations provide platforms for action in the field of reproductive health, through which the potential of teenage girls as future contributors to and beneficiaries of development is particularly emphasized. The realization of women and girls' right to a reproductive choice is in all these statements seen as an effective means of promoting their freedom and development in general and is considered a core element in the process of economic, social and cultural development. The Beijing Platform for Action was confirmed by the Commission on the Status of Women in 2000 and 2005. A major concern stated in a series of United Nations declarations and platforms of action is the wider impact on women and girl's human development and the development of the nation.[357] Improved status in society is seen as closely linked to full decision-making capacity in the area of sexuality and reproduction.[358] How the consequences of unwanted pregnancies and HIV/AIDS affect women and girls as mothers and their contribution to the economic support of their families is a major concern.[359] A closely-related concern is how lack of reproductive choice undermines their right to education and work and, as such, not only their human development but also the development of the nation.

The human rights based approach to development constitutes a normative framework premised on the assumption that a fair and just distribution of basic resources such as health services, education, housing

---

[356contd]freedoms are constituent components of development, but also instruments of development (Sen, 1999: 568; Nussbaum, 2000).

[357] CEDAW General recommendation 21, paragraphs 21, 23, 36 and 37; Beijing Declaration, paragraphs 93, 97 and 268.

[358] Cairo Declaration, paragraph 4.1.

[359] Beijing Declaration, paragraph 88.

and work is vital for development and poverty elimination. It overlaps and supplements other development theories and policies seeking to balance liberalist and welfarist values and concerns in the quest for pro-poor and gender-equal development (Sen, 1992 and 1999; Nussbaum, 2000). Unlike development theories focusing on needs or capabilities, it provides a legally-binding framework based on the indivisibility of people's civil, political, social and economic human rights (Nowak, 2005; Hauserman, 1998; Frankovits, 2005). The human rights based approach sets out binding legal standards that oblige the states parties, and indirectly international and private actors, to respect, protect and fulfil the bundle of rights that make up women and girls' right to reproductive choice. It constitutes an international legal framework that is instrumental in putting the Beijing and Cairo declarations, the capabilities approach and the millennium development goals into practice.

3   Gender and development in human rights: a complementary approach

It is generally agreed that measures taken for development enhance the realization of values of freedom and justice as the overall goal and purpose of human rights protection. Equally important is how human development is considered in determining the scope and outreach of human rights and how conflicting human rights principles are balanced. A related question is whether and to what extent international law provides a method that responds to the needs of the poor and marginalized in a rapidly changing world.

To enhance development is an overall goal of the human rights system. The United Nations charter commits the United Nations to promoting these:

> '…with a view to the creation of conditions of stability and wellbeing which are necessary for peaceful and friendly relations among nations based on respect for the principle of equal rights and self-determination of peoples' (article 55).

The preamble to the United Nations Convention on the Elimination of All Forms of Discrimination against Women (CEDAW), adopted in 1989, links gender, law and development stating that:

> '…the full and complete development of a country, the welfare of the world and the course of peace require maximum participation of women on equal terms with men in all fields.'

Similar concerns are reiterated in article 14 of the International Covenant on Economic, Social and Cultural Rights and articles 6 and 18 of the Convention on the Rights of the Child.

In principle, the wording of international treaties is to be in accordance with 'the ordinary meaning of the wording in their context and in the light of its object and purpose.'[360] Despite the neutral wording of international treaties, a too strict interpretation is likely to fail in its object and purpose in a gendered and classed reality (Cook, 1995: 986-987; Hendriks, 1995: 2). In response to current challenges and developments, the existing human rights treaty bodies have adopted a dynamic interpretation of international law (Nowak, 2002: 106). The wording of human rights treaties is not seen as exhaustive but is interpreted in view of changing circumstances.

In principle, human rights constitute a non-hierarchic and indivisible whole. Yet the emphasis on the mutual dependency and interrelatedness of human rights in ensuring basic living conditions and poverty prevention begs the question of whether there are rights which are more fundamental than others and, if so, which ones and on what basis. The system constitutes an indivisible whole that in its application in a diverse and changing world calls for careful balancing of different principles such as the right to equality and freedom of religion. A human rights principle is not to be interpreted in such a way that it stands in the way of another principle. The emphasis on indivisibility, interrelatedness and mutual interdependence, however, implies certain rights may be facilitated by simultaneous fulfilment of other rights. In human rights theory it is argued that setting targets and committing resources to fulfilment of rights that are basic for human development, which in turn involve priority setting, may be justified under the circumstances. The principles set out in various human rights instruments and the deliberations of various treaty bodies, however, impose limitations (Osmani, 2003: 5-6). Three limiting principles are the non-discrimination principle, the principle of indivisibility and the principle of non-retrogression of rights.

The non-discrimination principle implies that in setting priorities governments will have to pay attention to those who are excluded from sharing. In relation to resource distribution governments are under an immediate obligation to prohibit and cease discriminatory laws and practices. They must also ensure immediate fulfilment of minimum targets with respect to food, health and education – identified as 'core obligations'. The principle of the indivisibility of human rights implies that no human right can be regarded as inferior to another. If a certain right is to be given priority over another it must be considered whether a certain right has been more under-realized than others or whether it is likely to

---

[360] Vienna Convention on the Law of Treaties, article 3 (1); Limburg Principles, paragraph 4; UN Doc.A/CONF.39/27.

act as a catalyst towards the fulfilment of others. The principle of non-retrogression of rights implies that if more resources have been allocated to certain rights, care must be taken to ensure that other rights maintain at least their initial level of realization.

4　The right to reproductive choice – religious and economic constraints

Women and girls are more vulnerable to HIV than other groups in society. This makes it vital that their actual situation and significance in development processes are considered in determining the scope and outreach of states' obligation to respect, protect and fulfil their right to reproductive choice. The following section focuses on the right to reproductive choice as a health right and its resilience in the face of economic, religious and cultural constraints.

The right to choice
The right to reproductive choice is an integral part of women and adolescent girls' international human rights. Article 12(1) of the International Covenant on Economic, Social and Cultural Rights recognizes 'the right of everyone to the enjoyment of the highest attainable standard of physical and mental health'. The right to health is also embedded in article 16 of the African Charter on Human and Peoples' Rights, article 14 of the Protocol to the African Charter on Human and Peoples' Rights on the Rights of Women in Africa, article 24 of the Convention on the Rights of the Child and article 12 of CEDAW.[361]

According to article 12(2)(c) of the covenant, the rights to health 'include the right to control one's health and body, including sexual and reproductive freedom …'.[362] The right to procreative freedom falls within the scope of article 12 and article 16(1)(e) of CEDAW, which entitles women, on a basis of equality of men, to:

> '…the same rights to decide freely and responsibly on the number and spacing of their children and to have access to the information, education and means to enable them to exercise these rights.'

According to article 14 of the protocol:

> 'States parties shall ensure that the right to health of women, including sexual and reproductive health, is respected and promoted. This

---

[361] CEDAW General recommendation 24, paragraph 2.
[362] Committee on Economic, Social and Cultural Rights General Comment 14, paragraph 8.

includes: a) the right to control their fertility; b) the right to decide whether to have children, the number of children and the spacing of children; c) the right to choose any method of contraception; d) the right to self protection and to be protected against sexually transmitted infections, including HIV.'

Article 24(e) and (f) of the Convention on the Rights of the Child extend these rights to children by providing a right to access to health information, education and services necessary to make responsible reproductive choices. The convention defines a child as a person below the age of 18. In striking a balance between the rights of the child and the duties of the parents, article 14(2) points to 'the evolving capacities of the child'. Applying this principle, courts do not generally permit parents to veto mature adolescent children's access to information and education solely on the grounds of minor age (Cook *et al.*, 2003: 204). Another implication of the evolving capacity principle is that laws, policies and practices that set age limits are in violation of the convention (Cook and Dickens, 2000: 12–13).

The right to choice constitutes a negative and a positive right. The state is obliged to respect the right by refraining from interference through legislation, policy or practice and to take active steps to promote and fulfil the right to choice. The CEDAW committee has stated that the convention gives women a positive right to access to health information, education and services necessary to make responsible reproductive choices:

> 'In order to make an informed decision about safe and reliable contraceptive measures, women must have information about contraceptive measures and their use, guaranteed access to sex education and family planning services, as provided in article 10(h) of CEDAW.'[363]

In a similar vein, the Economic, Social and Cultural Rights committee has held that states are obliged to take all necessary steps to provide a variety of facilities, goods, services and conditions in order for women and teenage girls to realize their highest attainable standard of health.[364] This implies an obligation to 'provide education and access to information concerning the main health problems in the community'[365] and to establish 'prevention and education programmes for behaviour-related health concerns such as sexually transmitted diseases, in particular HIV/

---

[363] CEDAW General recommendation 21, paragraph 22. According to article 10(h) of the women's convention.

[364] Committee on Economic, Social and Cultural Rights General Comment 14, paragraphs 9, 11, 12 (b) and 53.

[365] Committee on Economic, Social and Cultural Rights General Comment 14, paragraph 44 (b).

AIDS, and those adversely affecting sexual and reproductive health' as well as access to related information.[366]

Resource constraints

Due to resource constraints, all human rights cannot be implemented effectively without some consideration of economic priorities. States parties frequently argue that due to duties to implement structural adjustment programmes, resource constraints exempt them from being in breach of their human rights obligations. For instance, when presenting their report to CEDAW, representatives from Zambia insisted that the country was forced to breach article 13 of CEDAW due to the economic measures imposed upon the country by structural adjustment programmes with devastating effects on women.

In setting priorities, human rights treaty bodies consistently urge international actors, such as the International Monetary Fund, the World Bank and the World Trade Organization, to consider basic human rights, such as the right to health, education and livelihood, in their lending programmes. In the same vein they emphasize that states parties have a duty to ensure that basic human rights are not jeopardized by economic programmes.

That priority should be given to rights that are essential for the right to life, such as primary health care and education, is supported by the Economic, Social and Cultural Rights committee which requires that states budget to realize minimum core obligations.[367] To ensure the right of access to health facilities, goods and services on a non-discriminatory basis, especially for vulnerable and marginalized groups, is seen by the committee as a core obligation for the satisfaction of minimum essential levels.[368] According to the committee, states should in all actions, including in allocating resources, give the highest possible priority to children and 'under-served members of the society'.[369] Insufficient expenditure or misallocation of public resources violates the obligation to fulfil the right to health and deprives individuals or groups, particularly the vulnerable and marginalized, of their right to health.[370] In many parts of the world

---

[366] CEDAW, article 12; the International Covenant on Economic, Social and Cultural Rights, article 12 paragraph (2) (a) (b) and (c); Committee on Economic, Social and Cultural Rights General Comment 14, paragraphs 14, 16, 17 and 36. See also CEDAW General recommendation 24, paragraphs 29 and 31 (b); Cairo Declaration, paragraph 7.38.

[367] Committee on Economic, Social and Cultural Rights General Comment 14, paragraph 47.

[368] General Comment 14, paragraph 43a.

[369] Guiding Principle 11, Cairo, paragraphs 3.19 and 6.8.

[370] General Comment 14, paragraph 52.

teenage girls are considered among the most vulnerable members of society with regard to education, health and reproductive choices.[371] Article 6(1) of the Convention on the Rights of the Child applies to protection against HIV which is particularly threatening to their life and development. In accordance with this provision, the right to life and development of the child are to be ensured to the maximum extent possible. In considering states' reports, the convention committee has emphasized that the right to life extends to health and education issues.[372]

The CEDAW committee holds that lack of resources due to structural adjustment programmes does not 'absolve the state party of its obligations to provide social protection to the most vulnerable groups; namely women, the poor and the disabled.'[373] The CEDAW committee emphasizes that 'women's issues should always remain at centre stage even in times of economic distress.'[374] Similarly, the Economic, Social and Cultural Rights committee emphasizes the interconnection between liberalizing Kenya's economy and finances through structural adjustment programmes and the need to accompany the process by 'targeted programmes specifically designed to protect the vulnerable members of society'.[375] It indicates that additional positive obligations exist upon governments. This is in line with the view of the CEDAW committee which recommends that:

> 'Special measures should be taken to reduce the adverse effects of structural adjustment policies that generally affect women.'[376]

States need to prioritize financial resources to implement minimum core obligations when facing resource constraints. Although the implementation of one human right should not impede the implementation of another[377] – all human rights being of equal status – human rights bodies recognize that priority setting cannot be avoided. One right may be given priority over another if that right has been less realized than others or because it is likely to act as a catalyst towards the fulfilment of other rights. How the realization of certain rights may be facilitated by simultaneous fulfilment of other rights – particularly minimum core obliga-

---

[371] CEDAW General recommendation 24, paragraph 6

[372] Convention on the Rights of the Child committee's concluding observations on the initial report of Burundi, paragraph 30.

[373] CEDAW committee's concluding observations on the second periodic report of Senegal, paragraph 724.

[374] United Nations doc. A/49/38/, paragraphs 318–368, paragraph 366

[375] See, for instance, Committee on Economic, Social and Cultural Rights' concluding observations on the initial report of Senegal, paragraph 14.

[376] See, for instance, CEDAW committee's concluding observations on the second periodic report of Senegal, paragraph 727.

[377] A fundamental principle of human rights law.

tions, such as the right to life, the right to health and the right to education – is an important consideration. The independent expert on the right to development identifies three specific human rights 'closely related to the right to life – the most basic of all human rights' that should be prioritized in realizing the right to development, namely, the rights to food, primary health services and primary education.[378]

The indivisibility of human rights, arising from the fact that the realization of women and girl children's right to reproductive and sexual information and education is essential for fulfilment of other minimum core obligations such as the right to life, education and work, may under the circumstances justify that these rights be given priority in certain situations. The mutually-reinforcing features of women and teenage girls' right to reproductive choice and their potential for human development should thus be carefully considered in states' budgetary priorities.

Religious constraints

The right to reproductive and sexual information and education must, like the whole range of social and economic human rights, be provided without discrimination. The right to gender equality and non-discrimination is embedded in article 1 and 5 of the Women's' Convention, articles 2 and 3 of the Covenant on Economic, Social and Cultural Rights, article 2 of the Children's Convention and article 2 of Protocol to the African Charter on Human and Peoples' Rights on the Rights of Women in Africa. Article 1 of CEDAW implies that differential treatment of women on the basis of marital status constitutes sex discrimination.

In practice women and girl children are often denied equal enjoyment of their human rights by virtue of the lower status ascribed to them by religion or custom. Underlying all the monotheistic religions, Judaism, Christianity and Islam, are different constructions of gender, sexuality, procreativity and family that come into conflict with the principle of freedom and equality embedded in the human rights system.[379] These differences often result in religious or political resistance to women and

---

[378] United Nations doc. E/CN.4/1999/WG.18/2, paragraphs 34 and 69–71; see also the Maastrict guidelines, paragraph 30.

[379] The interpretative statements and reservations made to the Declaration and Programme of Action of the International Conference on Population of 1994 (The Cairo Declaration) are illustrative of the religious resistance to unmarried women's reproductive rights. The Holy See did not join the consensus and: 'expresses a reservation on paragraphs 232 (f) with its reference on a right of women to control sexuality'. This ambiguous term could be understood as endorsing sexual relationships outside heterosexual marriage. A number of Catholic and Islamic states followed suit. The Islamic Republic of Iran stated that it: '…upholds the principle that safe and responsible sexual relationships between men and women can only be legitimized within the framework of marriage.'

girls' reproductive rights that manifest themselves in reservations to United Nations declarations and conventions.[380] The interpretative statements and reservations made to the Cairo Platform Declaration of 1994 and the Declaration and Platform of Action of the Beijing Conference in 1995 are illustrative. Pioneering the resistance at the Cairo and Beijing conferences, the Holy See, in line with the Vatican's doctrine of sexual abstinence, stated that it '… in no way endorses contraception or the use of condoms, either as a family planning measure or in HIV prevention programmes.' In relation to the Cairo Declaration and Platform of Action, the Holy See, in line with its religious doctrine, made a reservation on paragraphs 232(f) with its reference to a right of women to control sexuality. This ambiguous term could be understood as endorsing sexual relationships outside heterosexual marriage.

In spite of the growing political or religious resistance, an unequivocal affirmation of the Beijing Platform of Action was reached in 2005 after the United States delegation withdrew their suggested modification that it 'does not create any new international human rights and does not include the right to abortion'.[381] Yet international policies related to development, population and gender have undergone significant changes since the election of George Bush as United States president. The United States has withdrawn all funding to international organizations like the International Planned Parenthood Federation and the United Nations Population Fund that play a vital role in implementing the Beijing Platform of Action. The emphasis on sexual abstinence and scepticism towards condom use in HIV/AIDS programmes has also hampered international reproductive health work (Cohen, 2004).

In practice women and girls' right to reproductive choice is resisted by a number of states that have signed and ratified these conventions and declarations without reservations. It is important to those monitoring human rights progress to be aware of the different religious attitudes that influence the implementation of reproductive rights. In 2001, the Zambian government, a signatory to CEDAW, the Convention on the Rights of the Child and the Cairo and Beijing Declaration, without reservations, suspended a television advertisement campaign promoting the use of condoms as a protection against HIV, particularly among young people (Kanyengo, 2004: 49). In doing so it responded to the Zambian Catholic Bishops Conference in 2001 stating: 'the adverts are offensive and in bad taste. They suggest to children and youth that sex is some-

---

[380] None of the countries in the Southern African region have taken reservations to provisions in CEDAW that entail the right to reproductive choice.
[381] Commission on the Status of Women, report on the 49th session. E/CN.6/2005/9.

thing nice to have provided it is done with a condom.'[382] The government's decision was also in breach of Zambia's national family planning policy that was put in place in 1997.[383] The policy recognizes that young people not only need but have a right to reproductive health information and services. In principle the policy abolishes parental consent, makes teenagers eligible for services and authorizes community-based distributors of contraceptives.

The tension between religion, culture and women and teenagers' reproductive rights has been explicitly and implicitly addressed by a series of human rights treaty bodies in their interpretation of the scope and outreach of the right to reproductive choice. Commenting on the right to reproductive choice without discrimination, the CEDAW committee, in General recommendation 24, page 14, states that:

> 'States should not restrict women's access to health services or to the clinics that provide those services on the grounds that women do not have the authorization of husbands, partners, parents or health authorities because they are unmarried or because they are women.'

In a similar vein the Economic, Social and Cultural Rights in its interpretation of the right to health embedded in article 12 of the convention states that the right to equality embedded in article 3 is to the effect that:

> 'The realization of women's right to health requires removal of all barriers interfering with access to health services, education and information, including the area of sexual and reproductive health. It is also important to undertake preventive, promotive and remedial action to shield women from the impact of harmful traditional cultural practices and norms that deny them their full reproductive rights'.[384]

The case of adolescents' access to sexual and reproductive information is a site of contestation. In striking a balance between the girl child's right to equality and non-discrimination on the one hand and the right to religion and culture on the other, the Economic, Social and Cultural Rights committee has recommended that:

> 'States should provide a supportive environment for adolescents, that ensures the opportunity to participate in decisions affecting their health, to build life-skills, to acquire appropriate information, to receive counselling and to negotiate health-behaviour choices. The realization of the right to health for adolescents is dependent on youth friendly health

---

[382] Statement by the Zambian Bishop's Conference spokesperson on the basis of the Bishop's pastoral letter, 2001.

[383] *Zambia family planning policy, Guidelines, standards and strategies* (1997).

[384] Committee on Economic, Social and Cultural Rights General Comment 14, paragraph 21.

care which respects confidentiality and privacy and includes appropriate sexual and reproductive health services.'[385]

The Child Rights committee has, in two recent general comments, come up with an interpretation of the relevant provisions in the Convention on the Rights of the Child. As regards children and adolescents' right to non-discrimination, under article 2 in the convention the committee states that:

'Of particular concern is gender-based discrimination combined with taboos or negative or judgmental attitudes to sexual activity of girls, often limiting their access to preventive measures and other services. In the design of HIV/AIDS strategies and in keeping with their obligations under the convention, states must give careful consideration to prescribed gender norms within their societies with a view to eliminating gender-based discrimination as these norms impact on the vulnerability of both girls and boys.'[386]

As regards children and adolescents' right to information, skills development, counselling and health services, the Child Rights committee states that:

'In light of articles 3, 17 and 24 of the convention, states parties should provide adolescents with access to sexual and reproductive information, including information about family planning and contraceptives, the dangers of early pregnancies, the prevention of HIV/AIDS and the prevention and treatment of sexually transmitted diseases (STDs). In addition, states parties should ensure that they have access to appropriate information, regardless of their marital status and whether or not their parents or guardians consent. It is essential to find proper means and methods of providing information that is adequate and sensitive to the particularities and specific rights of adolescent girls and boys.'[387]

The state obligation to take 'appropriate means' to eliminate discrimination is a standard that provides for the need to take social, cultural and economic circumstances into consideration (Hellum, 1999). The non-discrimination principle, however, limits the discretion of states parties. In its analysis of article 2, the CEDAW committee concludes that:

'The convention allows for the interpretation and application in the most appropriate ways to the social and cultural structure of each state

---

[385] Committee on Economic, Social and Cultural Rights General Comment 14, paragraph 23.
[386] Convention on the Rights of the Child General Comment 3, paragraph 8
[387] Convention on the Rights of the Child General Comment 4, paragraph 28

but with the premise that the states parties will follow the principle of non-discrimination on the basis of sex.'[388]

As demonstrated, the committees of the Human Rights Convention, the Economic, Social and Cultural Rights Covenant, the Convention on the Rights of the Child and CEDAW unanimously hold that the interdependence between the right to life, health and education calls for modification of religious doctrinal constraints.[389] The human right protection of religious freedom is not extended to beliefs and practices that inhibit the realization of rights, such as the right to life, health and education of teenage girls, that are essential for the human development of vulnerable groups. This constitutes a limitation to the culturally-sensitive approach to reproductive rights. Governments are under an immediate obligation to prohibit and cease all discriminatory practices that inhibit the right to reproductive choice. If they are caused by deep-rooted beliefs and traditions among the population, they must adopt and enforce laws prohibiting any discrimination by states and private actors alike.

5   Obligations to provide sex education in school?

A girl's capacity to protect herself from unwanted pregnancies and HIV is closely connected to the right to education. There is established evidence that comprehensive sex education delays the onset of sexual activity and provides the life skills needed for responsible and safe sexual behaviour (Aggleton and Warwick, 2002). Whether and to what extent states are obliged to include sex education in school curricula is a critical issue. Article 13(1) of the Covenant on Economic, Social and Cultural Rights states that:

> 'The states parties to the present covenant recognize the right of everyone to education. They agree that education shall be directed to the full development of the human personality and the sense of its dignity, and shall strengthen the respect for human rights and fundamental freedoms. They further agree that education shall enable all persons to participate effectively in a free society.'

In this section the content of the right to education is interpreted in the light of the girl child's right to life and health embedded in the Convention on the Rights of the Child, the Covenant on Economic, Social and Cultural Rights and CEDAW.

Setting the scene
The literacy rate of women in developing countries is 60 per cent com-

---

[388] CEDAW C/1995/4, paragraph 105.
[389] On priority setting and the complementarity of human rights, see Osmani (2003).

pared to 80 per cent for men. The difference is linked to unwanted pregnancies and vulnerability to HIV. Lack of protection from unwanted pregnancies and HIV has a profound impact on a teenage girl's ability to exercise other human rights, particularly the right to education, work and participation, her access to human development and the socio-economic development of her country.

Teenage girls' right to reproductive and sexual information in southern Africa leaves a lot to be desired. The research findings of Teemba, Moyo and Kanyengo, post-doctoral graduates from the University of Zimbabwe, show, for instance, that teenagers in Tanzania, Zimbabwe and Zambia enjoy limited or no access to the knowledge necessary to protect themselves from pregnancies and sexually transmitted infections. Information is not freely available from parents, schools or health services (Teemba, 1995; Moyo, 1996; Kanyengo, 2004).

Many teenagers feel that neither their need for privacy nor their need for information are met by existing health facilities. The information provided is often moralistic or insufficient:

> 'I want to see that one is taught more on how our bodies function. So that I know what is right and wrong for me. Not, don't do this, don't do that. We need to know as teenagers what is best for our bodies' (Kanyengo, 2004: 51).

In practice there are often great inconsistencies between international and national policies, laws and practices. In spite of Zambia's adoption of a family planning policy in line with the Cairo Declaration, the Zambian Minister of Education has recently banned the distribution of condoms in Zambian schools by non-governmental organizations (Kanyengo, 2004: 51). He was supported by the Minister of Health who stated:

> 'We are not teaching the young ones the morality that is required. Children have no business to engage in sex, they have to wait until they are married.'[390]

Even when youths are provided with sex education in school, they are not necessarily given sufficient information. For instance, 77.5 per cent of the youth interviewed by Teemba in Tanzania had a scant knowledge of contraception (Teemba, 1995: 4.9). The Ministry of Education in Tanzania introduced family life education in 1987. By 1995, it was no longer established as a single subject but integrated with other relevant carrier subjects. This, according to Teemba, resulted in no sex education being offered in practice. As parents have handed over their educational duties to teachers, Teemba concluded that girls would continue to be victims

---

[390] Comment from the Minister of Education, www. post.co.zm.

until family life education was taught as a separate subject in school (Teemba, 1995: 5.8).

In practice many teenagers learn from their friends whose information at times is not correct as this teenager from Misis Compound in Zambia experienced:

> 'I thought I was smart and knew how to prevent pregnancy. My friends had told me that you could not get pregnant if you drink 10 aspirin tablets before or immediately after you have sex. The method was said to be "not human" and referred to as *chigayo,* meaning 'hammer mill'. Before long I noticed there was a big lump in my stomach, I thought I was diseased and asked my mother. She took a good look at me and she started crying fearing what my father would do to me' (Kanyengo, 2004: 46).

Many teenagers believe that women will be punished by being unable to give birth to children if using certain contraceptives. One girl believed that:

> '(…) pills cause cancer, a disease that has no cure just like HIV/AIDS.' (Kanyengo, 2004: 48).

'Education for full development'

These brief insights demonstrate the need for improved education on sexual and reproductive matters in primary and secondary school. According to the wording of article 13(1) of the Economic, Social and Cultural Rights Covenant, education shall be directed to the full development of the human personality, the sense of its dignity and shall strengthen the respect for human rights and fundamental freedom.[391] The Economic, Social and Cultural Rights committee holds education as an empowerment right, the primary vehicle through which economically and socially marginalized children can 'obtain the means to participate in their society'.[392] The committee considers directing curricula to 'the full development of the human personality' to be the most fundamental objective of education.[393] A key concept in this context is the obligation to provide 'timely access to preventive health education' which is embedded in the Economic, Social and Cultural Rights Covenant and CEDAW.[394] The significance of reproductive education in girls' human development is substantiated by the Convention on the Rights of the

---

[391] Universal Declaration on Human Rights, article 26 (2); International Covenant on Economic, Social and Cultural Rights, article 13 (1); Convention on the Rights of the Child, article 29 (1) (a); Cairo Declaration, Guiding principle 10.

[392] Ibid., paragraph 1

[393] Ibid., paragraph 4

[394] Under article 12 and 12 (2) (d) respectively.

Child committee which emphasizes, in particular, that 'adequate measures to address HIV/AIDS can be provided to children and adolescents only if their rights are fully respected'.[395] According to the committee, the most relevant rights in this regard are the rights to preventive health care, sex education and family planning education and services, the right to health and the right to education. The CEDAW committee suggests directly that family life education should be part of the school curricula.[396] This view is in accordance with the Cairo and Beijing Declarations which recommend that in order for sex education to be most effective, it should be provided to teenagers through formal education and school curricula.

The rights to education and health are intimately interwoven. In determining the content of the right to education one should bear in mind that although the issue of children and HIV/AIDS is perceived as mainly a health issue, it impacts so heavily on the lives of children that it affects all their rights – civil, political, economic, social and cultural.[397] This speaks to the inclusive nature of the right to a reproductive choice.[398] A crosscutting concern expressed by different human rights treaty bodies is the obligation to provide education for full development and timely access to preventive health education. All these normative fragments indicate a duty for states parties to ensure that reproductive and sexual education is included in primary and secondary education.

There is established evidence that the skills achieved through sexual and reproductive education are highly dependent on the education methods. While short-term interventions may not have the desired effect there is evidence that interactive and well-targeted education programmes may make a difference.[399] This implies that states parties must take measures to improve the quality of sex and reproductive health education. States must ensure that sufficient economic resources are allocated to research, curriculum development and training of school teachers.

Education versus religious conviction

In practice, adolescents' right to sex and reproductive health education often comes into conflict with religious beliefs. Due to the perception of the role of virginity in many religious communities, it is shameful to indulge in sexual relations before marriage. Parents and teachers of dif-

---

[395] Children's convention committee, General Comment 3 paragraph 4

[396] United Nations doc. A/50/38, paragraphs 278-344, paragraph 343.

[397] Children's convention committee, General Comment 3 paragraph 3.

[398] Committee on Economic, Social and Cultural Rights General Comment 14, paragraph 11; CEDAW General recommendation 24, paragraphs 5, 7 and 28; Cairo Declaration, paragraph 73 and Beijing Declaration, paragraph 95.

[399] For an overview of the record of a wide range of school-based education programmes, see Sundby (2006).

ferent religions often oppose sex education for teenagers, arguing that such information promotes promiscuity among teenagers creating conflict in the context of family values.[400] Accordingly, many governments have upheld legislation that works as an obstacle to teenage girls' access to information. For instance, states parties, parents and teachers argue that sexual relations are criminal below a certain age, they set a high minimum age of eligibility for family planning services or they require marital status in their quest to prevent teenagers having sex education in school.

A number of human rights treaty bodies have responded to these restrictive practices. The CEDAW committee has in its comments to states reports stressed its concern about laws, religions and social practices that are incompatible with human rights obligations.[401] Article 13(3) of the International Covenant on Economic, Social and Cultural Rights obliges states 'to respect parents' liberty and right to ensure guidance in accordance with their own beliefs, religion and morals'. Where compulsory sex education in schools has been challenged on religious and moral grounds, courts have tended to favour access to educational opportunities (Cook *et al.*, 2003: 212). The European Court of Human Rights has addressed the human rights dimension of sex education being taught in school. The court held that compulsory sex education 'conveyed in an objective, critical and pluralistic manner' does not violate the right of parents to ensure education of their children in conformity with their religious beliefs.[402] To let parents' morals prevail over adolescents' interest in sex education thus amounts to a violation of their right to reproductive freedom, as HIV/AIDS is potentially devastating to their health and human development. The increased risk to teenagers' health posed by HIV/AIDS suggests that parents' rights under article 13(3) of the International Covenant on Economic, Social and Cultural Rights must not override teenagers' right to sex education as long as it is conveyed in an objective, critical and pluralistic manner.

The human right protection of religious freedom, as demonstrated by the practice of human rights courts and treaty bodies, is not seen as extending to beliefs and practices that inhibit education that is crucial for girl children's capacity to achieve health, education and work.

---

[400] United Nations doc. Convention on the Rights of the Child/C/80, paragraph 230.

[401] See, for instance, CEDAW concluding observations on the combined initial, second and third periodic report of Ethiopia, paragraph 139.

[402] *Kjeldsen, Busk Madsen and Pedersen v. Denmark*, 1976 EHHRR 711 paragraph 53.

6 The state obligation and beyond

The state is the main duty bearer under human rights law. Health and education systems are crumbling in many countries as a consequence of neo-liberal privatization. There is growing evidence that states are relinquishing their obligations as they transfer health functions to the private sector.[403] To counter the negative consequences for the poor, international policy makers have called for social service provision by non-governmental organizations (UNDP, 2003). Yet the wide range of non-governmental organizations that act as service providers in the health sector are not fully aware of women and girls' right to reproductive choice.

It is clear that states parties cannot absolve themselves of responsibility in these areas by delegating or transferring these powers to private sector agencies. States parties have an obligation to ensure that third parties do not limit people's access to health information and services. They have an obligation to monitor and regulate the conduct of non-state actors to ensure that they do not violate the equal rights of women and men to enjoy economic, social and cultural rights. This applies in cases where public services have been privatized or to health services run by donor-funded non-governmental organizations or religious organizations.[404]

Most discrimination against women – in the health sector as elsewhere – rests not on the law but on legally-tolerated religious and customary norms, so the state obligation under article 2 of CEDAW encompasses 'any person, organization and enterprise'.[405] The state has a duty to ensure that both public and private health education policies and programmes take cognizance of people's rights to equality and non-discrimination, which are among the most fundamental tenets of international human rights law. This implies a duty for states parties to ensure that health and education programmes and projects run by religious organizations respect, protect and fulfil teenage girls' right to sex and reproductive health education and information without discrimination.

Under international law and specific human rights covenants, states may be held responsible for private acts if they fail to act with due diligence to prevent violations of rights. Furthermore, there is an obligation on states parties, acting as parties in bilateral and multilateral development cooperation, to ensure that human rights inform the aims, means and expected outcomes of any health-related project. Finally, states parties' obligations to respect, protect and fulfil the right to health encom-

---

[403] CEDAW General Comment 24, paragraph 17.

[404] Committee on Economic, Social and Cultural Rights 16, paragraph 20.

[405] CEDAW, article 2e.

pass their actions as members of international organizations.[406] As members of the International Monetary Fund, the World Bank and regional development banks, they must pay attention to how the right to health is influenced by lending policies. While this implies an indirect responsibility of non-state actors in development, an overall challenge for human rights is to confront today's reality of transnational economic and religious 'lawmaking'.[407]

7   Towards a right to human development

Recognizing the interrelationship between the rights to life, health, and reproductive information and education in women and teenage girls' human development, the human rights based approach to development sets binding legal standards that are instrumental in putting the Beijing and Cairo platforms of action and the millennium development goals into practice. To make the rights real the human rights treaty bodies address the whole chain of international, national and local actors that are part of the implementation process.

By taking a crosscut through the freedom and equality rights underlying women and teenage girls' right to sex education and reproductive health information, we have shown in this chapter how the human development argument is making its mark on international human rights law. The Human Rights, Economic, Social and Cultural Rights, the Rights of the Child and the CEDAW committees have all developed a dynamic interpretation of international health law, taking a wide range of social and economic factors influencing the right to health into consideration.[408] In their interpretation of the right to health and the right to education all these treaty bodies emphasize the close connection between the right to reproductive choice and the right to human development. Considering the strong emphasis on the indivisibility of human rights cutting across

---

[406] Committee on Economic, Social and Cultural Rights 14, paragraph 39.

[407] Human rights, structural adjustment and economic globalization has been addressed by Skogly (2001), Shelton (2000), Likosky (2005) and De Feyter (2005).

[408] 'Since the adoption of the two international covenants in 1966 the world health situation has changed dramatically and the notion of health has undergone substantial changes and widened its scope. More determinants of health are being taken into consideration, such as resource distribution and gender differences. A wider definition of health also takes into account such socially-related concerns as violence and armed conflicts. Moreover, formerly unknown diseases, such as HIV/AIDS, and others that have become more widespread, such as cancer, as well as the rapid growth of the population, have created new obstacles to the realization of the right to health which need to be taken into account when interpreting article 12 of the Committee on Economic, Social and Cultural Rights' General Comment 14, paragraph 10.

these sources we conclude that women and teenagers' access to sex education and reproductive health information in given situations should be given priority when faced with economic or religious constraints.

This legal development shows how human rights discourse is responding to the quest for human development by expanding principles of freedom and justice beyond the public/private, individual/collective and national/international divide. Most importantly the case of women and teenage girls' right to reproductive choice shows how an individual right to human development is gradually emerging as a result of concerted ethical, political and legal efforts by a wide range of international, national and local actors.

Bibliography

Aggleton P. and I. Warwick (2002) 'Education and HIV/AIDS prevention among young people', in *AIDS Educ Prev*, 14: 2263–267.

Banda F. (2005) *Women, law and human rights: An African perspective*, Hart Publishing, Oxford.

Bentzon A. W., A. Hellum, J. Stewart, W. Ncube and T. Agersnap (1998) *Pursuing grounded theory in law: South-North experiences in developing women's law*, Mond Books and Tano Aschehoug, Harare and Oslo.

Børresen K. (2004) 'Religion confronting women's human rights: The case of Roman Catholicism', in T. Lindholm *et al.* (eds) *Facilitating freedom of religion. A deskbook*, Martinus Nijhoff Publishers, Dordrecht.

Byrnes A. (2002) 'The Convention on the Elimination of All Forms of Discrimination against Women', in W. Benedek *et al.* (eds) *Human rights of women: International instruments and African experiences*, Zed Books, London/New York.

Cohen S. A. (2004) 'US global reproductive health policy: Isolationist approach in an interdependent world', in *The Guttmacher Report on Public Policy*, 7(3): 1-6.

Cook R. J. and B. Dickens (2000) 'Recognizing adolescents' 'evolving capacities' to exercise choice in reproductive healthcare', *International Journal of Gynaecology and Obstetrics*, Vol. 70:13–21.

Cook R., B. Dickens and M. Fathalla (2003) *Reproductive health and human rights*, Clarendon Press, Oxford.

Cook R. (ed) (1994) *Human rights of women: National and international perspectives*, University of Pennsylvania Press, Philadelphia.
– (1995) 'Human rights and reproductive self-determination (excerpt)', in the *American University Law Review*, 44: 975.

Coomaraswamy R. (1997) 'Reinventing international law: Women's rights as human rights in the international community', Human Rights Programme, Harvard Law School, Cambridge, MA.

De Feyter K. (2005) *Human rights: Social justice in the age of the market*, Zed Books, London/New York.

Frankovits A. (2005) 'Introduction', pages 1–14 in M Scheinin and M. Suksi (eds), *Empowerment, participation, accountability and non-discrimination: Operationalizing a human rights-based approach to development: Human Rights in Development Yearbook 2002*, Martinus Nijhoff/ Nordic Human Rights Publications, Dordrecht.

Hauserman J. (1998) *A human rights approach to development: Rights and humanity*, Department for International Development, London.

Hellum A. (1999) *Women's human rights and legal pluralism in Africa: Mixed norms and identities in infertility management in Zimbabwe*, Tano Aschehoug and Mond Books, Oslo and Harare.

Hendriks A. (1995) 'The right to health promotion and protection of women's right to sexual and reproductive health under international law: The economic covenant and the women's convention', in *American University Law Review*, 4: 1123–1134.

Hox M. (2002) 'Women, sex and the Pope: The Roman Catholic church and women's reproductive rights', Masters thesis, Norwegian Institute of Human Rights, Faculty of Law, University of Oslo.

Kanyengo K. B. (2004) 'A study of sexually active teenagers and their access to contraceptive services in Lusaka (urban) and Sesheke (rural) Zambia', thesis in fulfilment of the Masters in Women's Law, Southern and Eastern African Regional Centre for Women's Law, University of Zimbabwe, Harare.

Lai S., Y. Lai and R. E. Ralph (1995) 'Sexual autonomy and human rights', in *Harvard Human Rights Journal*.

Likosky M.. B. (2005) *Privatizing development; Transnational law, infrastructure and human rights*, Martinus Nijhoff Publishers, Leiden/Boston.

Lubinda M. (2004) 'An investigation into married women's reproductive rights in Lusaka, Zambia with particular focus on the right to decide freely and when to have children', dissertation submitted for the Postgraduate Diploma in Women's Law, University of Zimbabwe, Harare.

Merry S. E. (2005) *Human rights and gender violence: Translating international law into local justice*, University of Chicago Press, Chicago.

Moore S. F. (1978) *Law as process*, Routledge & Kegan Paul, London.

Moyo S. (1996) 'Social, educational and legal attempts at the management of teenage sexuality and pregnancy: A Gweru-based study', dissertation submitted in partial fulfilment of the Postgraduate Diploma in Women's Law, University of Zimbabwe, Harare.

Mullally S. (2005) 'Debating reproductive rights in Ireland', in *Human Rights Quarterly*, 27, 1: 78-104.

Ngewena C. (2003) 'Aids in schools: A human rights perspective on parameters for sexuality education', in *Acta Acadmica*, Vol. 35, No. 2:184–204.

Nowak M. (2002) 'The prohibition of gender-specific discrimination under the International Covenant on Civil and Political Rights', in W. Benedek *et al.* (eds) *Human rights of women: International instruments and African experiences*, Zed Books, London/New York.
– (2005) 'A human rights approach to poverty', pages 15–36 in M. Scheinin and M. Suksi (eds), *Empowerment, participation, accountability and non-discrimination: Operationalizing a human rights-based approach to development: Human Rights in Development Yearbook 2002*, Martinus Nijhoff/ Nordic Human Rights Publications, Dordrecht.

Nussbaum M. (2000) *Women and human development: The capabilities approach*, the Press Syndicate of the University of Cambridge, Cambridge.

Osmani S. (2003) 'An essay on the human rights approach to development', paper delivered at the Nobel Symposium organized in Oslo from 13 September –1 October 2003, Norwegian Centre for Human Rights, Oslo.

Packer C. A. A. (1996) *The right to a reproductive choice*, Institute for Human Rights, Åbo Akademi University, Helsinki.

Rosas A. (2001) 'The right to development', in A. Eide, C. Krause and A. Rosas (eds) *Economic, social and cultural rights*, Martinus Nijhoff Publishers, Dortrecht.

Sen A. (1999) *Development as freedom*, Alfred A. Knopf, Inc., New York.

Sen, G. and A. Germain and L. Chen (1994) 'Reconsidering population policies: Ethics, development and strategies for change', in G. Sen, A. Germain and L. C. Chen (eds) *Population policies reconsidered*, Harvard University Press, Harvard.

Shelton D. (2000) *Commitment and compliance: The role of non-binding norms in the international legal system*, Oxford University Press, Oxford.

Skogly S. (2001) *The human rights obligations of the World Bank and the International Monetary Fund*, Cavendish, London.

Steiner H. J. (1998) 'Social rights and economic development: Converging discourses?', in *Buffalo Human Rights Law Review*, 4: 25–42.

Sundby J. (2006) 'Young people's sexual and reproductive health rights', in *Best Practice and Research: Clinical Obstetrics and Gynaecology*, Elsevier.

Teemba R. A. (1995) 'Access to contraceptive information and services for teenagers in Tanzania: A case study of girls aged 13–19 years in Dar es Salaam', dissertation submitted in partial fulfilment of the Postgraduate Diploma in Women's Law, University of Zimbabwe, Harare.

Tomasevski K. (2001) 'Health rights', in A. Eide with C. Krause and A. Rosas (eds) *Economic, social and cultural rights*, Martinus Nijhoff Publishers, Dortrecht.

UNDP (2003) *Human development report*, Oxford University Press, New York.

UNESCO, (2004) *Education for All: EFA monitoring report*, UNESCO Publishing, Paris.

UNFPA (2003) *Imagine, the largest generation of adolescents in history*, New York.

UNFPA (2003) *Working from within. Culturally sensitive approaches in UNFPA programming*, New York.

United Nations Commission on Human Rights (2002) *Resolution 2002/69 on the right to development.*

United Nations Committee on CEDAW (1999) *Article 12 Women and health*, General Recommendation No. 24.
– (1994) *Equality in marriage and family relations*, General Recommendation No. 21.
– (1996) *Concluding observations: Initial report of Zimbabwe*, reference: 14/05/98. A/53/38, paras. 120-166.
– (2001) *Concluding observations: Guyana*, paragraph 92.
– (1996) *Concluding observations: The combined initial, second and third periodic report of Ethiopia*, paragraph 139.
– (1994) Concluding observations: The second periodic report of Senegal, paragraph 724.

United Nations Human Rights Committee (2002) *Equality of rights between men and women* (article 3), General Comment No. 28, reference: CCPR/C/21/Rev.1/add. 10.
United Nations Committee on Economic, Social and Cultural Rights (2000) *The right to the highest attainable standard of health*, General Comment No. 14, reference: E/C.12/2000/4.
– (2005) *Article 3: The equal right of men and women to the enjoyment of all economic, social and cultural rights*, General Comment No. 16, reference: E/.12/2005/3.
– (2001) *Statement on poverty and the International Covenant on Economic, Social and Cultural Rights.*

United Nations Committee on the Rights of the Child (2003) *HIV/AIDS and the rights of the child*, General Comment No. 3, reference: Convention on the Rights of the Child/G/2003/3.
– (2003) *Adolescent health and development in the context of the Convention on the Rights of the Child*, General Comment No. 4, reference: Convention on the Rights of the Child/CG/2003/4.
– (2000) *Concluding observations: The initial report of Burundi*, paragraph 30, reference: CRC/C/15/Add.133 (2000).

van Dijk P. and G. J. H. van Hoff (eds) (1998) *Theory and practice of the European Convention on Human Rights*, Kluwer Law International, New York.

List of cases

Kjeldsen, Busk Madsen and Pedersen v. Denmark, 1976 EHHRR 711 paragraph 53.

List of legislation

Regional and international

African Charter on the Rights and Welfare of the Child 1990

Protocol to the African Charter on Human and Peoples' Rights on the Rights of Women in Africa 2003

African Charter on Human and Peoples' Rights 1981

Beijing Platform for Action 1995

Convention against Discrimination in Education (UNESCO) 1960

Convention on the Elimination of All Discrimination against Women (CEDAW) 1979

Convention on the Rights of the Child 1989

Declaration and Programme of Action of the International Conference on Population and Development, 1994

Declaration on the Right to Development 1986

International Covenant on Civil and Political Rights 1966

Millennium Development Goals 2000, General Assembly Resolution 55/2. 8 September 2000

Vienna Declaration and Programme of Action 1993

14

New fellow citizens –
challenges and possibilities
Implementing human rights among immigrants,
the case of female circumcision in Norway

Gro Hillestad Thune

State obligations under international human rights law include having effective measures in place to stop female genital mutilation. This chapter deals with the measures taken by Norwegian state authorities to provide girls at risk with better protection. On paper, the official policy documents hold great promise of dialogue and cooperation and identify immigrant communities as key to the solution. This chapter discusses the adequacy and efficacy of the methods and measures that have been adopted in practice, from the perspective of the immigrant women concerned. The author, who has given human rights assistance to a centre for immigrant women in Oslo, shows how the authorities' work suffers from lack of inclusion, dialogue and cooperation with immigrant women's organizations. Rather than being respected and protected, immigrant women are left without a voice in a one-sided and top-down process.

1 Introduction

My interest was awakened in the controversies surrounding female circumcision while working as an advisor to Somali organizations in Norway.[409] I was invited as a Norwegian expert on human rights to assist at a centre[410] for immigrant women in Oslo, the PMV. This centre provides an opportunity for immigrant women to give practical assistance to other women, particularly those of the same national background. The centre felt a need for more knowledge about international human rights in order to be able to apply these rights in their daily activities. This appeared particularly relevant when female genital mutilation emerged as a matter of concern. In this context my main challenge was to find out whether and to what extent human rights could be useful, not only in theory but

---

[409] According to 2005 statistics available at http://www.ssb.no/english/subjects/00/minifakta_en/en/index.html, Somalis constituted 16,765 (over 38 per cent) of the 43,794 immigrants from Africa in Norway in 2005.

[410] Primærmedisinsk Verksted, Senter for Helse Dialog og Utvikling (Centre for Health, Dialogue and Development), Sverres gt 4, 0652 Oslo.

also in practice. The experience gave me fascinating insights into a world totally unknown to most Norwegians. In addition, I was able to learn a good deal about Norwegian society as seen through the eyes of immigrants. This knowledge is worth sharing with lawmakers, policy-makers, administrators and non-governmental organizations.

As a human rights lawyer this experience was a useful reminder of the importance of the human dimension in promoting human rights. The content of both national and international law is important but equally important is interpreting and applying the legal provisions in compliance with basic ethical standards as well as common sense. My experience through the years is that the quality of scholarly work in the field of human rights should not be measured solely in terms of knowledge of formal rules and legal doctrine. There must also be a focus on the situation of the individual. If society is to support and respect human rights, these rights must be seen as relevant, not only by the authorities, but also by those individuals who experience injustice and violations. With the influx of new citizens from cultures and societies different from the Norwegian norm, situations arise that challenge human rights at the practical level.

With immigration and increasing globalization come opportunities but also conflicts. While new cultures and traditions represent a positive and enriching contribution to society, we must also recognize that some of the traditions that immigrants bring with them may conflict with our own values. Some may be seen as so harmful as to represent a human rights dilemma – as is the case with genital mutilation, also known as female circumcision.

In this chapter, I focus on the challenges facing state authorities in terms of implementing human rights laws among immigrant groups in such cases. I ask whether the methods normally applied in the west are appropriate in such cases – particularly in a situation involving a practice deeply rooted in the age-old traditions of a group of recent immigrants to Norway. To shed some light on that question, I will show how, in recent years, the Norwegian authorities have approached the problem of female circumcision with the clear intention of protecting young girls living in Norway. Immigration from some of the countries where this tradition is still practised has imported the issue to our part of the world. This represents a challenge on many levels which we are not necessarily well-equipped to tackle. Part of the reason for this is our reactions of shock and horror when confronted with actions that, in effect, involve severe physical measures taken against defenceless children. From our perspective, it seems unbelievable that such a practice can continue.

Through my work at the PMV and as advisor to the Somali Women's Association, I have been able to follow developments at close hand as I was involved in discussions in various forums and attended meetings with a range of groups and agencies as a 'participatory observer'. I have witnessed the complexity involved in working with human rights in a case like this. I have also become aware of the need for new thinking in trying to change well-established attitudes in an alien culture. It is my hope that by presenting these experiences from Norway concerning a practice which international society finds abhorrent, I may also have some influence beyond the borders of my own country,

The second part of this chapter deals with female genital mutilation as a human rights problem, the third part relates particularly to the United Nations Convention on the Rights of the Child. The subsequent parts explain various aspects of the Norwegian policy aimed at putting an end to this practice. The last part of this chapter explains the specific legal initiatives taken, how immigrant women have argued against these proposals and how the politicians deliberately chose to ignore this advice.

2   Genital mutilation as a human rights problem

Genital mutilation or the circumcision of girls is a tradition dating back several thousands years. It is still practised in more than 28 countries in Africa. The Norwegian anthropologist, Aud Talle, terms it a 'cultural practice', referring to it as socially accepted and widespread throughout the societies in which it occurs, as well as being deeply rooted in local power structures, moral rules and cultural ideas of what constitutes a good life. Within the relevant cultures, female circumcision is seen by many as something positive that every woman must undergo in order to live a worthwhile and good life, get married and become the mother of healthy children; usually, there is no alternative to circumcision. Conducting anthropological studies on the topic has proved difficult, not least because, in societies where it is practised, female circumcision is seen as a part of life, something that people *do* – not a topic to be deliberated and discussed openly. Knowledge about female circumcision remains a form of silent knowledge, more apparent in culture than in words (Talle, 2003).

Defining genital mutilation is not necessary for the purpose of this chapter. It exists in a range of forms – some more and some less comprehensive or extreme, with varying degrees of consequences, in terms of health and other aspects. In all cases, however, it is a far more drastic procedure than male circumcision. There is wide variation as to the age at which female circumcision is carried out – from infants a few months old, to fully-grown women. According to World Health Organization estimates, some two million women each year are in the danger zone.

The terms 'genital mutilation' and 'female circumcision' are often used interchangeably, as is the case in this chapter. The recent trend, at international as well as national level, is to use the term 'female genital mutilation' but, in accordance with the preference within the Somali population in Norway, I tend to refer to the practice as 'female circumcision'.

It is difficult to give an exact description of the problem as this is a practice which is generally kept secret in Norway, even within the immigrant circles concerned. The largest group of immigrants practising female circumcision are Somalis and discussions of circumcision in Norway have tended to focus on them. When asked, Somalis themselves say that they do not know how widespread the problem is. They also explain that when girls living in Norway are circumcised, they are taken out of the country – to places like Syria, Djibouti, Ethiopia and London.

Genital mutilation is serious physical abuse which the international community has long recognized as a human rights problem. Several regulations in the major international conventions are applicable; additionally, both the United Nations Convention on the Elimination of All Forms of Discrimination Against Women (CEDAW) and the United Nations Convention on the Rights of the Child have specific regulations dealing with such practices. In 1991 the United Nations appointed a Special Rapporteur on Violence against Women, and in 1994 the United Nations Subcommission on the Promotion and Protection of Human Rights adopted a plan of action aimed at eliminating traditions harmful to the health of women and children (E/CN.4/Sub.2/1994/10/Add.1). The problem has also been discussed among various human rights organizations and agencies.

Initially, female circumcision was seen as a health issue but gradually a greater awareness has developed that it represents a serious violation of the physical and mental integrity of girls and women. At the international level the focus has been on preventive measures to enable national authorities to deal with the problem. While it is unreasonable to expect that there will be many individual appeals under the European Convention on Human Rights or the United Nations Covenant on Civil and Political Rights, the issue has repeatedly been raised in connection with CEDAW. In 1999, the CEDAW committee issued its General Recommendation No. 24 to states, requesting them to ensure effective application of laws prohibiting genital mutilation.

3   On the Convention on the Rights of the Child

The issue of circumcision arose during the preparation and later implementation of the United Nations Convention on the Rights of the Child. In Norway this has been a particularly important legal source after the

Convention on the Rights of the Child became Norwegian law on 1 October 2003, taking precedence over national legislation.[411]

Many of the articles in the convention are applicable to genital mutilation. According to article 24, 'States parties recognize the right of the child to the enjoyment of the highest attainable standard of health'. Article 24.3 emphasizes the duty of states to 'take all effective and appropriate measures with a view to abolishing traditional practices prejudicial to the health of children'. This should be seen in connection with article 19, which requires that children be protected against 'all forms of physical or mental violence, injury or abuse, neglect or negligent treatment, maltreatment or exploitation, including sexual abuse', and article 2 which prohibits discriminatory treatment against children.

From the preparatory work done for the Convention on the Rights of the Child, it is clear that female circumcision was considered a serious abuse against young girls and putting an end to it as soon as possible was an important goal. It was specifically proposed that the convention text should contain direct references to the genital mutilation of girls and young women. This was not adopted because, among other reasons, several delegates preferred the term 'traditional practices', pointing out that it would also cover other types of abuse against children and young girls that should be prohibited. In order to underline the gravity of the issue, it was decided that work against this particular tradition should be given priority, as this practice 'continues to threaten the health of an estimated 75 million women and children' throughout the world.

The Committee on the Rights of the Child, established to monitor implementation of the convention, has evaluated the situation facing many western countries when citizens take children abroad in order to have them circumcised. In its report to the Netherlands, the committee wrote:

> 'The Committee welcomes the efforts made and understands the difficulties faced by the state party in protecting girls within its jurisdiction from female genital mutilation carried out outside its territory. Nevertheless, the Committee urges the state party to undertake strong and effective targeted information campaigns to combat this phenomenon, and to consider adopting legislation with extra-territorial reach which could improve the protection of children within its jurisdiction from such harmful traditional practices.'[412]

---

[411] Menneskerettighetsloven av 21 mai 1999, med tilføyelse vedtatt 1 august 2003. §3 (Act of 21 May 1999 No. 30 Relating to the Strengthening of the Status of Human Rights in Norwegian Law (the Human Rights Act). with additions adopted as of 1 August 2003, §3).

[412] Netherlands IRCO (1999) Add. 114, para.18.

From this it follows that the state has a duty to implement effective measures to protect young girls from genital mutilation, wherever this might take place. But which kinds of measures are effective? In connection with our discussion, have the Norwegian authorities fulfilled their obligations to sufficiently protect young immigrant girls living in Norway?

4   Norway: measures against female circumcision

In 1995, a special law against genital mutilation was adopted in Norway. It consists of only one regulation which declares that carrying out genital mutilation or aiding and abetting such practice is punishable by law. The penalty may be as much as eight years' imprisonment in cases with particularly serious consequences.

Both during the preparatory work and later, the question was raised as to why this was not included in the general penal code instead. The main reason given was that both Sweden and England have enacted similar special acts; administration considerations were also cited, as well as the special need for professional health expertise in any future court cases. The following quote from the remarks made by the Standing Committee of the Norwegian Parliament (Storting) that dealt with the issue in 1995/96, may indicate what seemed to be the main concern of the authorities:

> 'Enacting a special law under the Penal Code means actively employing the force of the law to show disapproval of such mistreatment of women.'[413]

In the commentary, the committee stressed the importance of informing immigrant communities, in clear and understandable language, that genital mutilation was now forbidden in Norway and would be punishable by imprisonment. The government was urged to inform and train health workers. To date, no charges have been brought against any person for breaking this law.

During the first years of its existence the law was generally little known among immigrants from Somalia and other countries where female circumcision is practised. No special measures were taken to ensure that information was provided to immigrants on arrival in Norway or later. Moreover, at that time, the law was not translated into the relevant languages, even though the Storting had specifically urged that this be done.

---

[413] Innst.O.nr 9 (1995-1996) Innstilling fra Sosialkomiteen om Lov om forbud mot kjønnslemlestelse (omskjæring av kvinner) (Recommendation no. 9, 1995–1996 to the Odelsting, from the Standing Committee on Social Affairs, on the prohibition against genital mutilation).

The first official measure of a more comprehensive character was the preparation of guidelines for health personnel, completed in October 2000 (Norwegian Board of Health, 2000).

5 Circumcision becomes a hot topic

Genital mutilation was not a subject of open debate until autumn 2000, when Kadra, a young Somali woman, appeared on a television programme and criticised her community in Norway for continuing to practise circumcision. Her statements were greeted with shock and horror. At once, circumcision became a hot topic and a political challenge. The media insisted on political action which led to a series of proposals and ideas – some serious, others not – being presented in public, including those from politicians with scant insight into or contact with the immigrant communities in question. The spotlight fell on the law against female circumcision: the time for implementation had come. Most proposals involved various forms of control, such as a more active stance from the police and the child welfare authorities, as well as more health checks and stricter border controls.

The television programme had literally altered the situation overnight. It marked the beginning of a period of lively and noisy public debate about circumcision among various politicians who appeared to be competing for the limelight.

The immigrant community was unprepared for these extreme responses and reacted with shock. This was particularly true within the Somali community where some women had already begun working on the issue. They had received some financial support from the authorities but not sufficient for their efforts to be effective against circumcision in their own circles. The day before the television programme was transmitted, a representative of the Ministry of Children and Family Affairs informed me that the last application for financial support from the Somali Women's Association was most likely to be rejected. Immediately after the programme, the situation changed. Government ministers paid a visit to the women at the PMV and declared themselves willing to support their work with money this time, as well as promises.

6 Government initiatives

A few months later, the Norwegian government put forward a plan of action (Ministry of Children and Family Affairs, undated) and pledged that work against circumcision among female immigrants in Norway was to have political priority. The plan contained 16 specific points, one of which was to have the law translated into the languages of the communities in question. Also in the plan of action were proposals to implement various information activities directed at young girls, relevant immigrant groups, Norwegian health and social workers, teachers, the police force and other professional groups.

It should be emphasized that one of the four principal aims set out in the action plan was to work together with organizations and individuals in the relevant immigrant communities. The government pointed out that this was in line with the international practice of choosing a cooperative approach rather than drawing up lines of confrontation on the issue of genital mutilation. They intended to follow this approach in working against circumcision in Norway. The government stressed the importance of building up trust and confidence between immigrants and the authorities: Members of the communities in question would have considerable influence and greater potential for working against this practice than representatives of mainstream society.

A central issue here is the principle of developing relationships and fostering two-way communication. The various information and communication activities need to be prepared in close liaison with the target groups.

The demands for political action continued. A few years later, the Norwegian government presented a new list of measures, entitled 'The government's work against genital mutilation 2002'. Among the 33 measures presented were the following:
– Obligatory information to be given to new immigrants on arrival;
– A signed declaration that they received and understood the information to be required;
– Information to be requested on whether any children or young people in the family had been circumcised;
– An information campaign to be implemented at Oslo International Airport Gardermoen and at schools with a high enrolment of pupils from minority backgrounds;
– Information measures to be communicated through the immigrants' own media, such as Somali Radio;
– A website network to be developed;
– Brochures aimed at immigrants, written in their own languages, to be published and distributed;
– Information to be provided for public agencies, institutions and professional groups.

The introduction to this 33-point document stressed the importance of bringing about a change in attitudes. The government reiterated that it would encourage involvement from the minority communities in question because members of these communities were better situated to tackle such a culturally-anchored tradition than representatives of mainstream Norwegian society. Considerable funding was allocated to implement the various measures.

7   Intervention – a legal obligation?

Among the specific steps to stop immigrants living in Norway from circumcising their children was a draft law making it a legal duty, enforceable by punishment, for members of specific professions to prevent circumcision, overriding their professional oath of confidentiality. On the face of it, this may have seemed a good idea, since nobody would want professional confidentiality to prevent someone from saving a girl from circumcision.

This draft Bill, proposing the following new paragraph to be added to the law on genital mutilation, was circulated for public hearing:

> Any individual who, through his or her profession or work, receives information that genital mutilation as mentioned in §1 is being planned, is to attempt to prevent this from taking place, by reporting the case or by other means. This is to apply without reference to the professional oath of confidentiality. Failure to do so is punishable by fines or by up to one year's imprisonment (unofficial translation).

In general, reactions were positive and the regulation did not seem particularly problematic in legal terms. However, there were negative reactions among the organizations that commented on the proposal. It is worth noting that the organizations which most strongly expressed their opposition were those with practical experience through health work with immigrant women. The harshest criticism was directed at the punishment aspect. Also, the part of the proposal which included the possibility of setting aside the right to professional confidentiality was heavily criticised among religious leaders. Furthermore, it was seen as discriminatory to establish rules concerning circumcision in a special law instead of in the ordinary legislation covering professional conduct in general. It was further argued in the comments that the situations addressed through this proposal were already sufficiently covered by existing legislation.

The Ministry of Justice and the Police warned that such a provision would be difficult to enforce. They also pointed out that the proposal involved singling out one specific kind of abuse against children, among the many other types of physical violence and neglect. Also the Directorate for Health and Social Affairs was sceptical, noting in particular that threats of punishment are not an appropriate means of persuading people to abandon practices that they consider their own established traditions. The Union of Education, Norway, which represents schoolteachers and kindergarten personnel, was worried that its members might find themselves in situations where they risked punishment because they either lacked sufficient information on such practices or did not know how to go about preventing them from taking place. The County Governor of Oslo and Akershus believed that placing greater punishable responsibility on specific groups of personnel was sidetracking the main issue. If the aim is to change behaviour, one should not raise the level of fear by introducing punishment.

The Norwegian Nurses Association eventually became deeply engaged against the law. They pointed out that such a penal regulation could work contrary to intent by making it more difficult to establish relations of trust between young girls and health or social workers. The association further noted that by introducing different regulations for different groups of children and young persons exposed to welfare neglect, the proposal could have a stigmatizing effect.

The women at the PMV where I was working, were unanimous in condemning the law. They were concerned that people in the communities where circumcision is practised would see this as a kind of 'tattletale clause' and that they themselves, as well as others working actively against circumcision within the community, would be branded as the long arm of the law. The likelihood of having face-to-face talks would vanish because people would no longer dare to say what they felt. That would mean a major step backwards in a situation where the women had just begun to break down some of the taboos surrounding the issue and where people were at last starting to speak of circumcision as being a problem. Once again, they feared, things would 'go underground'.

The message to the Norwegian authorities from these women was clear: do not adopt the proposal.

> 'Such a law would mean that we will lose confidence and trust among members of the communities in question, we will lose the possibilities of saving many girls and lose the opportunity of getting people to change their attitudes to the tradition of circumcision. If this law is passed, we will lose everything we have achieved through many years of working against circumcision. If one case is reported, that could mean saving one girl – but we would lose ten.'

These viewpoints were based on many years' experience of work directed precisely at altering attitudes towards circumcision among immigrants in Norway. The women had worked actively against circumcision even before Kadra made her television appearance. Their work had been strongly supported by the Norwegian authorities who had established that positive results had been obtained. The working method included discussions in groups of women and young people where the participants analyzed both advantages and disadvantages of circumcision in depth. It became clear that when participants felt safe and confident, they were prepared to talk about such a sensitive issue. Even within the family, circumcision is not normally a topic that is discussed. The experience from such group work has been that many of those involved in the discussions have changed their views on circumcision. Some have even become motivated to start working within their own circles to convince others that the tradition is harmful and should not continue. Gradually the women began to argue that more men should be included in this work as well.

The work at the PMV is being led by what in the Norwegian context are referred to as 'natural helpers' or 'cultural assistants' who have managed to build confidence and trust within the communities, and ensure the active involvement of local resource persons. These are individuals with the unique opportunity to create the atmosphere of confidence that enables people to speak about health problems, sex and personal relations, marriage, childbirth, menstrual problems and urinary infections. These are sensitive subjects that many Norwegian women also hesitate to discuss with representatives of the public health service or the school system. It must be acknowledged that civil servants working in public health, childcare or schools do not have the same opportunity to persuade immigrant women that circumcision is a harmful practice and is not necessary to ensure young girls a good life.

To return to the question of the law on circumcision, in the further process of the Bill, some changes were made and the following text was unanimously adopted by the Storting for inclusion in the law against genital mutilation:

> 'Professionals and those working in kindergartens, the child welfare services, the health and social services, schools, after-school arrangements and religious groups can be punished with fines or with up to one year's imprisonment if they deliberately neglect, by not reporting or otherwise, to attempt to prevent instances of genital mutilation, cfr § 1. This applies to religious leaders and heads of congregation as well. Moreover, it applies above and beyond the professional oath of confidentiality for these groups. Such negligence is not punishable if the act of genital mutilation is not carried out.'[414]

---

[414] Put forth in Ot.prp.nr. 21 (2003–2004) (Proposition no. 21 to the Odelsting). The proposal was unanimously adopted by the Storting in spring 2005, despite strong protests from the Norwegian Nurses Association, the Somali Women's Organization and PMV/the Church City Mission.

No one could doubt the good intentions underlying this regulation. All the same, several questions remain. First of all, why should the authorities rely to such a large extent on the performance of people who are peripheral when it comes to solving the problem of female genital mutilation among immigrants in Norway? It seems unlikely that charges would be pressed against relatives or guardians. To date, the prohibition against female circumcision has not been applied in any court case in Norway. Experience from France, where some cases have been taken to court, have revealed the complexity and the dilemmas involved in dealing out punishment when the action was carried out with the clear intention of ensuring a good life for the girl in question.[415] For a mother, a prison sentence means that the court is sanctioning a new offence against her daughter – depriving her of her mother – this time committed by mainstream society and aimed at protecting her. Incidentally, a similar line of reasoning could also be applied to cases where the child welfare authorities assume legal guardianship of a young girl and provide placement outside the family home.

Another question concerns the approach taken by the standing committee of the Storting that dealt with the Bill. The committee invited organizations and groups to attend an oral hearing. However, when the women at the PMV contacted the Storting for the first time in order to protest against the Bill, they were told that it was too late. The legislative process had gone too far and they should have approached the Storting earlier. The politicians did not seem concerned that immigrants would not necessarily be familiar with the normal legislative process in Norway.

The draft Bill was adopted by the Storting as proposed by the government. The women at the PMV and at other relevant organizations had protested through written as well as oral submissions to the government. A number of organizations also met before the standing committee to confirm their views. One is left with the impression that the need for the authorities and many individual politicians to demonstrate their disgust at female genital mutilation outweighed the real arguments against the adoption of this particular provision. What other explanation could there have been for not listening to the women who repeatedly said the law would make their work against female genital mutilation more difficult?

---

[415] For an interesting presentation of experiences from France, see M. Dembour (2001) 'Following the movement of a pendulum: between universalism and relativism', chapter 3 in Cowan, Dembour and Wilson.

8 What are the 'lessons learned'?

Since autumn 2000 the Norwegian authorities have spent vast sums on what is often referred to as 'our' or the government's work against genital mutilation. The matter has received considerable publicity and efforts have been made on many fronts. All this should indicate that young girls are now less at risk of being sent abroad to be circumcised. Whether this is the case, we do not know. What we do know is that many people within precisely those groups and organizations most qualified to determine the best way to achieve the goal have been ignored, bypassed and belittled by the authorities, despite the many promises of dialogue and cooperation.

In May 2002 a group of Somali women and mothers wrote a letter to the Norwegian Prime Minister and three cabinet ministers. The women began by stating their clear support for the government's involvement and praising many of the specific measures that have been implemented. However, they also expressed deep concern about how the work against circumcision was being implemented and presented to the public. Here they referred to reports in the mass media but even more to politicians and members of the government who, in their opinion, had engaged themselves in a process which neither served the cause nor took into consideration the various minority groups in Norway.

> 'As we see it, what you say as ministers is one thing, but through the choices you make you send out very different signals. You say that you want dialogue with the groups concerned, including the Somalis. And yet you choose to work together with groups that stand for the exact opposite ... In writing this letter, we do not wish to get involved in personal attacks on anyone but we do feel that it is time that we told you what we feel and how we experience the way circumcision and the communities involved have been presented. We can agree on the goal: circumcision represents a brutal and unacceptable offence against innocent children and is against the basic principles of human rights. No girls should have to experience this, whether in Norway or elsewhere. On the other hand, it is hardly necessary to have deep psychological insight to understand that a minority group which is already heavily stigmatized, discriminated against and surrounded by myths and misperceptions – as is the case with Somalis in Norway – will react by closing ranks rather than opening up, when we feel ourselves publicly trampled and spat upon and when solutions are forced on us without explanation. As a group we may not be so good at languages and public speaking as to make a big impression in populistic television debates – but in our opinion this is not where the main debate

should take place anyhow. In this struggle, let us take part on our own premises and in a form that has room for cultural codes and perspectives. Only in that way can the message be spread to as many as possible. The majority has been speaking in a negative, judgemental and stigmatizing way but that is of no use. We realize that the Norwegian authorities have no patience where it concerns offences against children but at the same time we ask you to understand that this is a fight that will take time. And yet, we believe that our methods will get results more quickly than the aggressive and one-sided approach that the government seems to be supporting. Our information and discussion project, which the government has supported, has managed to gain trust and legitimacy among Somali women, but if it comes to be associated with forces that are seen as aggressive and uncompromising, we fear the project will be weakened. If the ministers should wish it, we would be glad to meet you to talk about these matters. We have no desire for publicity. All we want is the chance to be heard by you, who have the power to do something.'

It should be noted that this letter was never answered.

9   Conclusion

Implementing human rights is a challenge, especially when it comes to preventing abuse among private citizens. The authorities charged with this responsibility do not always have a broad range of tools at hand which makes it all the more important to make use of the resources that do exist. In the case presented here, the Norwegian authorities repeatedly stressed that work to change attitudes deeply rooted in the culture of a people cannot be based solely on threats of punishment, sanctions or information campaigns. It is important to rely on dialogue and cooperation with people who enjoy respect and thus have influence in the communities. Because female circumcision is a tradition maintained largely by women, it is vital to build up relations of trust and confidence with those working for change. The government's own information and discussion project among the women concerned has been based on precisely this approach – and has achieved results. Other countries seem to have had similar experiences.

The Norwegian authorities have indicated that they recognize this but they have been unable to follow up in practical policy and action. Instead, they have succumbed to the temptation to rely on measures and methods that alienate the immigrant communities who view these efforts as expressions of disgust and revulsion rather than as attempts to build relationships and establish two-way communication. Looking at what the women of these immigrant communities have sought to communicate, we cannot but be struck by the absence of dialogue. While they are told how important their views are, they experience the opposite when it comes to concrete action and involvement. The result is a feeling of mistrust and lack of respect for their expressed intention to work hard against female genital mutilation. Massive publicity, media exposure and sharp words of condemnation – including from leading politicians – have led to fear and insecurity. Girls from countries where circumcision is common feel ostracized and condemned. No one should be surprised to hear that responsible, resourceful women now fear that, after all their efforts at getting members of their communities to speak about it openly, circumcision will once again become a taboo subject.

In our Norwegian society we still overlook and marginalize immigrant women, instead of seeing them as the resource that they are. At the international level, those involved in development and assistance work have long recognized the strong role of women, not least in Africa. And yet, when these women come to Norway, the authorities are quick to assign to them the 'victim' role – from which they intend to save them. In this process we make ourselves great and powerful while the immigrants concerned are made small and insignificant.

How the Norwegian authorities have approached the issue of genital mutilation is illustrative. In various ways, they have tried to ignore the realities on the ground: that this is a difficult problem that cannot be solved quickly and effectively by means of simple, demonstrative measures. It is a paradox that government has refused the outstretched hand offered by groups of women – Somalis and others – while the same government clearly supported their earlier efforts. On the other hand, perhaps this experience serves a purpose: there are lessons learned that will prove useful in other situations where the national authorities have to deal with any forms of abuse within the immigrant community.

In order to put an end to problems like forced marriage, domestic violence, the sequestration of women, trafficking and trade in women, and female circumcision, it is necessary to establish good relations with women from the communities in question. They can provide the key to solving such problems – if solutions exist. Women know their own culture and they often have experience in dealing with conflict. If the national authorities are to fulfil their human rights responsibilities to prevent such abuses, they will have to establish ways of working with strong and resourceful women from the communities in question, involving them in the work and giving them responsibility. The way to achieve this is not by imposing action plans and packages on them, willy-nilly. Nor is anything achieved by information, meetings and documents that stress the aim to build mutual confidence – and then result in nothing. The way to start is by establishing arenas for dialogue, where people speak *with* and not *to* one another. Representatives of the authorities should take the time to listen to what the women have to say.

This may sound trite but resolving the issues simply depends on giving real content to words like 'trust' and 'respect'.

Bibliography

Dembour M. (2001) 'Following the movement of a pendulum: Between universalism and relativism', chapter 3 in J. K. Cowan, M. Dembour and R. A. Wilson (eds) *Culture and rights: Anthropological perspectives,* Cambridge University Press, Cambridge.

Government of Norway, Ministry of Children and Family Affairs (undated) 'Governmental action plan against female genital mutilation', Order number: Q-1012E, Oslo.

Norwegian Board of Health (2000) *Veileder for helsepersonell i Norge om kvinnelig omskjæring* (Guidelines for health personnel in Norway concerning female circumcision), Statens Helsetilsyn, Oslo.

Talle A. (2003) *Om kvinnelig omskjæring* (On female circumcision), Det norske Samlaget, Oslo.

United Nations Committee on the Rights of the Child (1999) *Concluding observations of the Committee on the Rights of the Child: Netherlands,* Add. 114, para.18, IRCO Netherlands.

List of legislation

Norway

Menneskerettighetsloven av 21 mai 1999, med tilføyelse vedtatt 1 august 2003. §3 (Act of 21 May 1999 No. 30 Relating to the Strengthening of the Status of Human Rights in Norwegian Law with additions adopted as of 1 August 2003, §3)

Ot.prp.nr. 21 (2003–2004) (Proposition no. 21 to the Odelsting)

Innst.O.nr 9 (1995-1996) Innstilling fra Sosialkomiteen om Lov om forbud mot kjønnslemlestelse (omskjæring av kvinner) (Recommendation no. 9, 1995–1996 to the Odelsting, from the Standing Committee on Social Affairs, on the prohibition against genital mutilation).

Regional and international

Convention on the Elimination of All Forms of Discrimination Against Women (CEDAW) 1979

Convention on the Rights of the Child 1989

European Convention on Human Rights

International Covenant on Civil and Political Rights 1966

Part IV

At the crossroads between human rights, constitutions, laws, culture and religion

15

Interpretative strategies for women's human rights in a plural legal framework
Exploring judicial and state responses to Hudood laws in Pakistan

Shaheen Sardar Ali

The last quarter of the twentieth century witnessed a burgeoning international interest in Islamic law in general and Islamic criminal law in particular. Codification of the religious text in Islam relating to crime and punishment, and its application in some Muslim jurisdictions raised a number of controversies including its adverse impact on women and minority communities residing within these countries. Islamic criminal law of Hudood on extra-marital sexual relations (zina) acquired prominence with the cases of, amongst others, Safia Bibi (Pakistan),[416] Amina Lawal (Nigeria)[417] and the most recent case of Zafran Bibi (Pakistan)[418] as well as some cases in Afghanistan under the Taliban. The purpose of this chapter is to contribute to this discourse and debate by highlighting the complexities of transforming religious text into contemporary legal formulation using the example of the Hudood laws of Pakistan.

1   Introduction

In plural legal systems such as in Pakistan, laws derived from religious text operate alongside constitutional provisions, secular civil and criminal law, customary practices and, more recently, international human rights law. A review of selected case law reveals this legal pluralism at play within judicial forums; judges are increasingly 'making law' by drawing upon principles across the range of legal systems using a combination of Islamic law, constitutional and statutory law, human rights instruments and customary practices. This chapter is a commentary on this emerging jurisprudence and attempts to explore the extent to which a dynamic, women-friendly, trend, using a rights-based approach is discernible.

---

[416] *Safia Bibi v The State* PLD 1985 FSC 120, *Safia Bibi v The State* PLD 1986 SC 132.

[417] *Amina Lawal Bakori v The State* KTS/SCA/FT/86/2002

[418] *Mst. Zafran Bibi v The State* PLD 2002 FSC 1.

Internationalizing Islamic criminal law: The cases of Safia Bibi, Amina Lawal, Zafran Bibi

Safia Bibi was a poor 18 year old near-blind girl who alleged rape by her employer and his son. As a result she became pregnant and a child was born who later died. Safia's father registered a 'first information report' for rape after the death of the baby. The alleged rapists were acquitted due to lack of evidence while Safia was found guilty of illegal sexual relations (zina) on account of her pregnancy which was considered a 'confession'. She was sentenced to three years imprisonment, 15 lashes and a fine of 1000 rupees. A huge public outrage ensued resulting in the Federal Shariat Court taking suo moto[419] notice of the case, directing the subordinate court to transfer it to the Federal Shariat Court for review. Safia Bibi's conviction and sentence was set aside.

Amina Lawal, a Nigerian woman, was sentenced to death by stoning by the Shariat Court of Bakori (Nigeria) while the man she was alleged to have committed unlawful sexual intercourse and begotten a child with, was acquitted for lack of evidence. The Upper Shariat Court upheld the sentence but this was quashed by the Sharia Court of Appeal.

Zafran Bibi was convicted of zina on the basis of her pregnancy and sentenced to stoning to death. Her husband had been imprisoned for nine years in a murder case; hence the pregnancy was considered a 'confession' of adultery. She alleged rape but due to contradictions in her statement, the accused was acquitted while she was found guilty. On appeal the Federal Shariat Court set aside the conviction.

Safia Bibi, Amina Lawal and Zafran Bibi are only the tip of the iceberg in the vast array of cases that came to the fore after promulgation of the Hudood laws in Muslim jurisdictions, most of which resulted in conviction and imprisonment of women and even children. In Pakistan the number of women in prison increased manifold after the Hudood laws were set in motion in 1979 under General Zia ul Haq. In contrast to the figure of 70 women convicts in the whole of Pakistan in 1982, the figure rose to 7,000 in 2002/2003. The National Commission on the Status of Women report states that 88 per cent of women prisoners in Pakistan were charged under the law relating to zina. At the same time, more than 90 per cent of persons charged with zina are acquitted on appeal. There is a problem here. How does one account for the large numbers of zina cases? If it is assumed that the prosecution has a case,

---

[419] Refers to an initiative by a court (or other competent institution) to investigate an event or situation believing itself bound to intervene in the interest of justice. Courts in Pakistan have a constitutional prerogative to take up such cases (Government of Pakistan, 1973). For many countries of Africa and South Asia where access to courts is limited due to financial and other constraints, suo moto notice by a court is a valuable mechanism for protection of human rights.

how does one explain conviction at trial court and the almost complete reversal on appeal? In order to address these questions it is important to present the substantive and procedural content of Islamic criminal justice, its scope and purpose and requisites of application.

2 Introducing Islamic criminal law: Hadd, Qisas and Tazir punishments

A critical analysis of Islamic criminal law necessitates a brief overview of the sources and accompanying juristic techniques of the Islamic legal tradition, namely, the Quran and Hadith as primary sources and Ijma, Qiyas and Ijtihad as subsidiary sources, complementing the former. The Quran,[420] believed by Muslims to be the word of God, is the first and definitive source of Islamic law, followed by the Hadith which is custom or usage of the Prophet Mohammad, known as sunna (his words and deeds).[421] Hadith collections were not compiled under state supervision and have more than one chain of narrators. Hadith literature is surrounded by controversies, in particular over the question of their authenticity (Mernissi, 1991: 46).[422] Ijma or consensus of opinion is defined as agreement among Muslim jurists in a particular age on a question of law (Rahim, 1995: 97).[423] Qiyas, translated as analogical deduction, is the fourth source of Islamic law and comes into operation in matters which have not been covered by a clear text of the Quran or Hadith nor determined by ijma (Rahim, 1995: 117). The law thus arrived at is based upon a rule laid down in the other three sources of law (Quran, Hadith and Ijma). Qiyas evolved as a jurisprudential method during the early Abbasid period,[424] gradually replacing the principle of

---

[420] The Quran which is in the Arabic language was revealed piecemeal to the Prophet Muhammad over a period of 22 years, 2 months and 22 days. It has 6666 verses divided into 114 chapters and 30 sections.

[421] Technically speaking, a hadith consists of two essential parts: the text or matn of the tradition (hadith) and the chain of transmitters or isnad 'over whose lips it (hadith) had passed'. But hadith literature is surrounded by controversies in particular due to questions of their authenticity.

[422] It is an historical fact that numerous Ahadith were generated to reinforce societal norms and on the basis of political expediency.

[423] Ijma as a source of law draws its validity from the Quran and Hadith. Quranic verses supporting ijma include: *Today we have completed your religion; Obey God and obey the Prophet and those amongst you who have authority; If you yourself do not know, then question those who do.* Hadith favouring ijma include: *My followers will never agree upon what is wrong; It is incumbent upon you to follow the most numerous body.*

[424] The Abbasids came into power in 750 AD and soon became a powerful Muslim empire. Their capital city was Kufa where the Hanafi school of Islamic jurisprudence was based and flourished.

arbitrary (independent) opinion known as ra-ay. Its objective was to develop systematic reasoning in the interest of consistency and coherence. Simultaneously, it opened up spaces for interpretations of the religious text that would be more relevant and applicable in contemporary societies (Coulson, 1964: 39–41).[425]

Two other concepts need some explanation here: Sharia and fiqh. Sharia stems from the Arabic root word *shar* which means 'the road to the watering place, the clear road to be followed, as a technical term, the canon law of Islam' (Schacht, 1961: 524). It follows from these definitions that Sharia, or the principles of Islamic law, has an inbuilt dynamism and mobility in its very meaning and is an evolving and responsive process. Fiqh is the science of jurisprudence based on the Sharia and evolved over centuries by Muslim jurists of the various schools of thought (Ali, 2000: 23–24).

Islamic law and positions adopted by various schools of juristic thought are not uniform; this lack of a unified position on the interpretation and application of injunctions of the Quran and Hadith, as well as of the secondary sources, account for the difficulty that modern-day legislators confront. One such example is the codification of Islamic criminal law in some Muslim jurisdictions.

Principles of Islamic criminal justice draw support from and are based on the sources of law described above. Offences are categorized according to the punishments for each offence which are, broadly speaking, three in number: (1) hadd, (2) qisas and (3) tazir. Hadd (plural Hudood) offences are considered offences against God or against the interests of society as a whole. Punishments for hadd offences are mandatory in accordance with clear injunctions laid down in the Quran and Sunna (Hussein, 2003: 37; Zahur-ud-din, 2003: 5–11; Rahim, 1995: 304–306).[426] Offences attracting hadd punishments include: theft, dacoity or highway robbery; sexual intercourse outside marriage, known as zina (adultery and fornication); consumption of alcohol; and apostasy (Hussein, 2003; Rahim, 1995).[427] Punishments prescribed for hadd offences, being

---

[425] Coulson describes an early example of analogical deduction whereby the minimum amount of dower payable to the wife by a husband was determined as ten dirhams in Kufa and three dirhams in Medina. A parallel had been drawn between the loss of virginity at marriage and amputation of the hand as the penalty for theft. The sums of ten and three dirhams was the minimum value of stolen goods for which the penalty of theft could be imposed in Kufa and Medina respectively.

[426] Hussein adds: 'Hudood crimes once proven before the judge, are not and cannot be subject to forgiveness or pardon; punishment must be imposed upon criminals who are committing such crimes.'

[427] Hussein presents the following as Hudood offences: adultery, launching a false charge against a chaste person, drinking alcohol, theft, hiraba, unjustified and violent disobedience to the Muslim ruler in the Islamic state and turning back from the Muslim faith (apostasy). Rahim includes whoredom, theft, highway rob

very serious in nature, have a level of proof that far exceeds ordinary evidentiary requirements (see discussion below). In qisas (retaliation) the next of kin can demand life for life whereas in diyat (compensation) form of punishment, the next-of-kin of the deceased may demand and accept blood-money.[428] Tazir punishments are applied to offences for which no fixed punishments are prescribed and lie at the discretion of the judge. Offences attracting tazir punishments include charging interest, slander, bribery, adulteration of food products, false testimony, breach of public trust, and so on (Sherif, 2003: 6). Where evidence falls short of a hadd offence, tazir may be applied. Punishment ranges from 'a disapproving look' to admonition, reprimand, threat, boycott, public disclosures, fines and seizure of property (Schacht, 1964: 175; El-Awa, 1993: 101–106).

This chapter focuses on one of the Hudood offences, sexual intercourse outside marriage (zina) which includes fornication and adultery.

3   The historical (con)text of the offence and punishment for zina: The Quranic text[429]

I begin with the genesis of Islamic criminal law on extra-marital sexual relationships (zina), its definition, evidentiary rule and punishment. The term zina denotes unlawful sexual intercourse between a man and a woman outside marriage, regardless of their marital status. The Quran criminalizes extra-marital sexual relations, starting from declaring it a transgression and punishable as tazir to making it a hadd offence (El-Awa, 1993: 15). Verse 17:32 prescribes thus:

> 'And do not go near fornication (zina) as it is immoral and an evil way.'

No particular punishment is prescribed at this stage.

Chapter four of the Quran, entitled *An-Nisa* (Women) declares:

> 'If any of your women Are guilty of lewdness,[430] Take the evidence of

---

[427 contd] -bery, drunkenness and slander imputing unchastity as offences liable to hadd punishments.

[428] Incorporation of qisas and diyat into the penal laws of Pakistan has meant that where women are killed in the name of honour by their male relatives (who are also their next-of-kin), these laws are invariably used as a way of evading punishment. Theoretically, the court has the authority to punish the offender, even though, at a private level, she or he has been forgiven and the case settled because these do fall under tazir punishments. In practice, it is not common for courts to do so.

[429] I use the English translation of the Quran by Abdullah Yousaf Ali. Capital letters appearing in the middle of a sentence signify the beginning of a new line.

[430] In the Quranic verses cited on sexual intercourse outside of marriage and hence illegal under Islamic criminal justice, clear reference to heterosexual relationship is made. 'Lewdness' or 'lewd' behaviour is being employed in these verses to indicate sexual impropriety amongst women.

four (Reliable) witnesses from amongst you Against them; and if they testify, Confine them to houses until Death do claim them, Or Allah ordain them Some (other) way (The Quran 4:15).

If two men among you Are guilty of lewdness, Punish them both. If they repent and amend, Leave them alone; for Allah Is Oft-Returning, Most Merciful (The Quran 4:16).

Some writers on Islamic criminal law have read the above verses as applicable to zina (illegal sexual intercourse between a man and a woman) and as a precursor to the more strict hadd punishment. Abdullah Yusaf Ali, in his commentary on the Quran, however, makes the point that verses 4:15 and 4:16 address homosexuality and not zina. While I tend to agree with this view, as the verses appear to refer to women as a group ('your women") and men as a group ('If two men among you'), there is a difference in the two statements. While the first statement refers to women, the acts of lewdness are not identified specifically as a lesbian relationship, while the second statement refers to 'two men' and clearly denotes a homosexual relationship. Punishment for both acts is imprisonment but, as in other verses of the Quran, there is space for atonement and forgiveness.[431]

Chapter 24 of the Quran goes on to create the hadd offence of zina and prescribes punishment as follows:

'The woman and the man Guilty of adultery or fornication, Flog each of them With a hundred stripes; Let not compassion move you In their case, in a matter Prescribed by Allah and the Last Day: And let a party Of the Believers Witness their punishment (The Quran 24:2).

'Let no man guilty of Adultery or fornication marry Any but a woman Similarly guilty, or an Unbeliever, Nor let any but such a man Or an unbeliever Marry such a woman: To the Believers such a thing Is forbidden' (The Quran 24:3).

Contrary to the punishment of stoning to death presently on the statute books of Pakistan, Saudi Arabia, Iran, Nigeria (only some states) and Sudan (and enforced by the Taliban in Afghanistan), flogging is the Quranic punishment for the offence of zina. Stoning to death is said to be prescribed under the sunna. This extremely harsh penalty[432] is subject to equally stringent and, it is submitted, virtually impossible evidentiary rules for establishing the offence of zina and inflicting the above pun-

---

[431] Lewdness implies improper behaviour short of sexual intercourse.

[432] Another penalty, stated in the sunna (and not the Quran) is exiling the offender for a year. If the person guilty of sexual intercourse outside of marriage is himself or herself married then the punishment is stoning to death under sunna (Hussein, 2003:38).

ishment. The establishment of guilt must be proved beyond *any* doubt (not simply *reasonable* doubt).[433] Four male, adult, trustworthy Muslim witnesses must testify that they saw the two persons committing the act of adultery and that the man's organ was inside the woman. Nothing less than committing a public act of sexual intercourse where four men are standing close enough to confirm the actual act, would constitute the offence of zina and attract the penalty mentioned above (El Fadl, 2003: 111–113).[434]

A further important sequence of producing evidence to substantiate the offence of zina is the hadd offence of qadfh or wrongful allegation or testimony implicating a person for zina. The next verse of the Quran, 24:4–5 states:

'And those who launch A charge against chaste women, And produce not four witnesses, (To support their allegation), Flog them with eighty stripes; And reject their evidence Ever after: for such men Are wicked transgressors; Unless they repent thereafter And mend (their conduct): For Allah is Oft- Forgiving, Most Merciful.'

'Those who slander chaste, indiscreet but believing women, are cursed in this life and in the hereafter: For them is grievous penalty. On the Day when their tongues, their hands, and their feet will bear witness against them as to their actions, on that day God will pay them back (all) their just dues, and they will realize that God is the (very) Truth, that makes all things manifest' (The Quran 24:23–25).

A contextual analysis of the Quranic text raises the question of what brought about the harsh statement towards extra-marital sexual activity and more so to allegations and insinuations thereof? The above verses were revealed following the famous 'Affair of the necklace', in which the Prophet Mohammad's wife, Aisha, was inadvertently left behind by a caravan in the desert as she went searching for her necklace that had gone missing. She was spotted by one of the young, single men in the Prophet's entourage and brought back to Medina leading to widespread rumours about her time alone with this man. The subsequent weeks turned

---

[433] Guilt of the offence of zina is also established if the accused makes a confession, willingly and without coercion in the presence of a judge.

[434] El Fadl cites an important seventh century case of alleged zina against the Governor of Basra, Al-Mughirah bin Shubah, presided over by the Caliph, Umar ibn al Khitaab. Abu Bakrah an influential Basran accused the governor of adultery stating that he along with his three half brothers had witnessed the actual act. During the trial, however, one of the witnesses, Ziyad, testified that while one could extrapolate it from the actions and situation of the accused persons, he could not state under oath that what he had actually observed was, indeed, the act of sexual intercourse. The witnesses therefore were declared guilty of qadfh (wrongful accusation of zina) and sentenced.

into a nightmare for Aisha as her honour and dignity had come under question and she was being suspected of inappropriate behaviour. The verse, therefore, in no uncertain language and tone, silenced rumours against not only Aisha but for future generations of women and proceeded to prescribe a very harsh punishment for a person or persons who attempt to slander a woman's good name.[435]

Commenting on the context of implementation of this law, Hussein (2003:38) states:

> 'The presentation of this form of proof has not once occurred in the history of the application of the Sharia.'

The standard of proof for all Hudood offences under Islamic law is very arduous and the crime must be proved beyond any atom of doubt. This is based upon the tradition of the Prophet Mohammad which stated:

> 'Avert the Hudood punishment in case of doubt . . . for error in clemency is better than error in imposing punishment' (Baderin, 2003: 80).

Baderin also cites the Islamic scholar Shalabi who pointed out that:

> '…the proof required makes the punishment for zina applicable only to those who committed the offence openly without any consideration for public morality at all, and in a manner that is almost impossible and intolerable in any civilised society' (Baderin, 2003).

Rahim (1995: 305), while stating some of the important limitations and conditions under which Islamic law permits infliction of hadd punishment, emphasizes that 'any doubt would be sufficient to prevent the imposition of hadd'. He further explains that in cases of zina:

> 'Some jurists go so far as to recommend to a man who has seen it committed not to give information or evidence. . . I may mention that the policy of law in connection with this offence is to punish only those offenders who defy public decency and openly flaunt their vices.'[436]

Kusha echoes similar views:

---

[435] See the Quran 24:13-19: 'Why did they not bring Four witnesses to prove it? When they have not brought The witnesses, such men, In sight of Allah, (Stand forth) themselves as liars! Were it not for the grace And mercy of Allah on you, In this world and the Hereafter, A grievous penalty would have Seized you in that ye rushed Glibly into this affair. Behold, ye received it On your tongues, And said out your mouths Things of which he had No knowledge; and ye thought It to be a light matter, While it was most serious In the sight of Allah. And why did ye not, When ye heard it, say – "It is not right of us To speak of this: Glory to Allah! This is A most serious slander!" Those who love (to see) Scandal published broadcast Among the Believers, will have A grievous Penalty in this life And in Hereafter: Allah Knows, and ye know not.'

[436] It is also pertinent to mention here that Rahim employs the term 'whoredom' and not adultery or fornication as a hadd offence.

'The Quran is absolutely against surveillance for the detection of un-lawful activities in which one may engage in one's private residence (drinking, illicit sex or use of drugs). In fact the Quran advises believ-ers, including spouses, to safeguard each other's secrets' (Kusha, 2002: 160).

As well as stringent evidentiary rules, enforcement of Hudood punish-ments is also subject to the prerequisite that an ideal Islamic society exists. If the defence can make a case that the offender was a product of sociological problems of society, Hudood punishment may be mitigated. Therefore, despite the rigid and unquestionable prescription of Hudood punishment, its application by the state is subject to sociological factors existing within the state (Baderin, 2003: 83).

Read together and in light of the context in which the verses were revealed, it is evident that the focus of the pronouncements was to safe-guard women's reputation and good name and not flag up in the public gaze, people's extra-marital relationships. The Quranic advice is to walk away from a place where rumour-mongering or impropriety (of behav-iour) is rife.[437]

Few writers on Islamic criminal justice have made the crucial con-nections described above. They 'read' the Quranic verses declaring zina as an offence and its punishment as one autonomous concept, as in the case of the Pakistan Hudood laws, and false accusation of zina (qadfh) and punishment for this falsehood, as a separate offence. Their indi-vidual worldview of crime and punishment, victim and wrongdoer, in-forms 'reading' of the Quranic text on zina. In other words, the 'written word' of the Quran has over the centuries become 'overwritten' by inter-pretations informed by plural legal systems and varied perspectives.[438] In contemporary state practice of Muslim jurisdictions, this has led to serious consequences due to attempts to codify the Quranic text through literalist transformation of the divine word into statutory formulation.

---

[437] The Quran Verse 24:16-17 'It is not for us to speak'.

[438] I am indebted to my colleague Professor Upendra Baxi who kindly agreed to my using what he describes as 'the world of three Cs'. Attending his seminars on constitutional law and theory in the third world provided the inspiration for ex-ploring legal pluralism in Pakistan through the lens of the three Cs. In his own words: 'C1 stands for the word as the world, the site of initially formulated his-toric constitutional texts. C2 represents constitutional hermeneutics, the site of what is understood in the dominant discourse as constitutional interpretation or constitutional law. C3 signifies 'constitutionalism', a set of ideological sites that provide justification/mystification for constitutional theory and practice.' See U. Baxi (2000) 'Constitutionalism as a site of state formative practices', Vol. 21 *Cardozo Law Review* 1183-1210 at 1188; U. Baxi, 'Outline of a "theory of prac-tice" of Indian constitutionalism', a paper presented to an international seminar on the philosophy of Indian constitution (Goa, 7–9 September 2001).

Saudi Arabia, Sudan, Iran, Nigeria and Pakistan are some of the Muslim countries that have codified elements of the Islamic criminal justice system and met with extreme criticism due to the lack of contextual thought and effort into the rationale and objective of the Quranic pronouncements on the subject. For instance, in 1979, General Zia ul Haq promulgated a set of 'Islamic' laws and in the preamble stated the objective of these legislative pronouncements was to bring existing laws into 'conformity with the injunctions of Islam as set out in the Holy Quran and Sunna'.[439] But in so doing, he introduced a law devoid of context and spirit attempting to codify essentially uncodifiable religious text, the Quran, which in addition to punishments also contains injunctions of justice, equity, morality, ethics, mercy and goodwill as alternative and complementary concepts. This juxtaposition of the religious text, its interpretation and transformation into legal text by General Zia reflects the dangers of the transformative processes of law as process and outcome, particularly when laws are transplanted from one normative 'soil', in this case, religious text, to a totally different 'terrain' – a secular, post-colonial legislative framework, interpreted through the patriarchal lens of customary norms.

The next section addresses the codification of the Pakistan Hudood law on zina.

4 Transcribing Quranic text to black letter law in contemporary Muslim jurisdictions: Codifying the uncodifiable?

The Offence of Zina (Enforcement of Hudood) Ordinance 1979 of Pakistan criminalizes zina or sexual relations outside of marriage. It consists of a preamble and 22 sections and defines zina as follows:

'A man and a woman are said to commit 'zina' if they wilfully have sexual intercourse without being validly married to each other.'[440]

Section 5 of the ordinance states that:

'1 Zina is liable to hadd punishment if –

(a) it is committed by a man who is an adult and is not insane with a woman to whom he is not, and does not suspect himself to be married, or

(b) it is committed by a woman who is an adult and is not

---

[439] The Offences Against Property (Enforcement of Hudood) Ordinance 1979; The Offence of Zina (Enforcement of Hudood) Ordinance 1979; The Offence of Qadfh (Enforcement of Hadd) Ordinance 1979; The Prohibition (Enforcement of Hadd) Order 1979.

[440] Section 4, The Offence of Zina (Enforcement of Hudood) Ordinance 1979.

insane with a man to whom she is not, and does not
suspect herself to be married.

2 Whoever is guilty of zina liable to hadd shall, subject to the
provisions of this ordinance:
    (a) if he or she is a muhsan,[441] be stoned to death at a public
    place; or
    (b) if he or she is not a muhsan, be punished, at a public
    place with whipping numbering one hundred stripes.'

The zina ordinance also incorporates under section 6, the offence of
rape translated as 'zina-bil-jabr':

'1 A person is said to commit zina-bil-jabr if he or she has sexual
intercourse with a woman or man, as the case may be, to whom
he or she is not validly married, in any of the following circumstances, namely:
    (a) against the will of the victim;
    (b) without the consent of the victim;
    (c) with the consent of the victim, when the consent has
    been obtained by putting the victim in fear of death or of
    hurt; or
    (d) with the consent of the victim, when the offender knows
    that the offender is not validly married to the victim and
    that the consent is given because the victim believes that
    the offender is another person to whom the victim is or
    believes herself to be validly married.

2 Zina-bil-jabr is zina-bil-jabr liable to hadd if it is committed in
the circumstances specified in sub-section (2) of section 5.

3 Whoever is guilty of zina-bil-jabr liable to hadd shall, subject to
the provisions of this ordinance —
    (a) if he or she is not muhsan, be stoned to death at a public
    place; or
    (b) if he or she is not muhsan, be punished with whipping
    numbering one hundred, at a public place, and with such
    punishment including the sentence of death, as the court
    may deem fit having regard to the circumstances of the
    case.'

The Quranic verse outlining rules of evidence in case of zina is translated and applied to both the offence of zina and zina-bil-jabr thus:

'Proof of zina or zina-bil-jabr liable to hadd shall be in one of the
following forms, namely:
        (a) the accused makes before a court of competent jurisdic-
        tion a confession of the commission of the offence; or

---

[441] Muhsan means a married person.

> (b) at least four Muslim adult male witnesses, about whom the court is satisfied, having regard to the requirements of tazkiah-al-shuhood,[442] that they are truthful persons and abstain from major sins giving evidence as eyewitnesses of the act of penetration necessary to the offence;
>
> (c) provided that, if the accused is a non-Muslim, the eyewitnesses may be non-Muslims.'

This translation of the Quranic text into contemporary legislation immediately raises a number of issues. First and foremost, the law on zina fails to incorporate a warning against false accusations and the dire consequences of allegations of zina against women. This, it is submitted, detracts from the very objective of the Quranic verses that are directed at protecting women, not leaving them vulnerable to conviction. The high evidentiary limits are meant to deter frivolous allegations.

Secondly, the Quranic verses on zina do not mention the offence or punishment for rape, neither does the evidentiary rule apply. Yet by placing the same evidentiary ceiling as for consensual sexual relations, a violated woman finds herself vulnerable to be accused as soon as she fails to produce the requisite witnesses. Provisions of section 6 of the ordinance is a cut and paste job of the provisions on rape in the colonial Indian Penal Code, later known as the Pakistan Penal Code.

Criminal culpability for parties accused of zina starts at puberty, which for women could be as young as eight or nine whereas for a man it is likely to be much older.

The Islamic legal tradition lays emphasis on protecting the good name of women and in this regard the law on paternity provides that a child born within six months of marriage is ascribed to the father as well as a child born up to two years after the death of the father or dissolution of marriage of the parents (Pearl and Menski, 1998: 399–401).[443]

El-Fadl (2003) in his incisive treatise makes a highly pertinent observation in this regard and highlights the difficulty of taking on the task of transforming the divine text into human legislation:

> 'One characteristic of the Islamic legal experience is its irrepressible pluralism. In the first centuries of Islam, there was a proliferation of legal schools of thought, each one named after its symbolic founder. By the fourth/tenth century, for reasons that are not entirely clear, a large number of these schools became extinct leaving less than ten in the Sunni sect and less than five in the Shii sect. Nonetheless there continued to be a remarkable diversity in legal opinions and trends,

---

[442] The term means mode of inquiry adopted by the court to satisfy itself as to credibility of a witness.

[443] In some schools of thought it is a longer period.

even within each of the surviving schools. The broad range of diversity was such that it was fairly difficult to ascertain the predominant view within a particular legal guild, let alone being able to establish a predominant view in Islamic juristic thought as a whole.'

As stated in the preceding section, the Quranic verses on zina must be read together with the verses on qadfh and not as separate laws. Asifa Qureshi is one of the very few writers who 'see' the connection in her 'reading' (interpretation) of the Quranic text on zina. She believes that zina and qadfh verses of the Quran cannot be read but as a composite whole; hence a legal formulation that separates the two sets of verses into two different statutes is unacceptable and a corruption of the religious text. She states that the main purpose of the Quranic verses on zina and its punishment are to protect the privacy of people and public morality. Secondly, that this is linked with the strict evidentiary threshold as well as protecting women's honour. But Hussein (2003) and Baderin (2003) do not appear to include or read this interpretation in their reflections on the Quranic text on zina.

An-Naim's interpretation of Islamic criminal law as advanced in his *Towards an Islamic reformation* (1990) displays a clear confidence in the Islamic tradition as a system capable of delivering justice in the contemporary world. He believes that any project of introducing Islamic law must take into account 'westernized' legal systems operating in contemporary Muslim jurisdictions and international human rights law. If we take Pakistan as an example of a Muslim jurisdiction where 'westernized' legal systems operate, it is evident that (western) colonization placed a common law legal system in place resulting in codification of law, the court system and institutions of governance akin to a 'western' jurisdiction. Two major consequences (among others) emerged. Firstly, despite serious efforts, the colonial project of codifying religious law, mostly in the field of family law, failed. (At the time, legal pluralism was neither fashionable nor acknowledged.) Secondly, the irreversible governmental and court structures as well as post-colonial constitutional documents, the tenor of which is clearly 'western', became a reality.[444]

---

[444] A number of factors may be cited as evidence of this position. For instance, the Iranian revolution, despite its massive shift to a theocratic state, maintained the legislative, executive and judicial triumvirate of state structure. Likewise, the Muttahida Majlis Amal, an alliance of religious parties who are now in government in the North West Frontier province of Pakistan, have continued with all governmental structures, institutions and procedures. They are engaging with all international organizations and enthusiastically invite collaboration with the United Nations agencies, World Bank, Asian Development Bank and others, to advance their governmental and political agenda. At an international level, acceptance and accession of Muslim states to the plethora of treaties is further evidence that those espousing an Islamic form of government are amenable to the existing post-

Any project of Islamization therefore is akin to planting a religious text in a secular soil.[445] Confronting the gigantic and hugely complex task of converting the Quranic text into contemporary criminal legislation is imminent in view of the increasing number of Muslim countries adopting Islamic criminal law as part of their legal systems.[446]

As indicated in the discussion above, to what extent can statutory formulation be a faithful representation of the 'original' text? Further, and more importantly for our present discussion, how have courts in Pakistan responded to the challenge of this interpretation, with particular reference to the Hudood laws on zina? What are the dominant themes and trends emerging from a review of decisions in Hudood cases where zina has been alleged?

Application of Islamic criminal law in Pakistan: lessons from the field
Since the promulgation of the Hudood ordinances in Pakistan in 1979, a number of studies have referred to the indiscriminate use of this law for implicating women and men and confining them to long prison sentences as well as lifelong social stigma (Jehangir and Jilani, 1990; Mehdi, 1994; Government of Pakistan, 1997; National Commission on the Status of Women, 2003). These studies have highlighted personal vengeance, socio-economic compulsions or simply social control of women as reasons for increased cases under the zina laws. Patriarchal and misogynistic trends reflected in the judgements, too, have been the subject of discussion. What was lacking in this discourse was a review of Hudood cases where an interpretative strategy had been employed by the court using a combination of constitutional rights, Islamic law and international human rights with a view to advancing women's rights.

The present research collected judgements of the superior[447] judiciary in zina cases between 1980 to 2003. Of these, the sample was narrowed down to those cases where the court had used its interpretation of plural legal norms to challenge a monolithic and narrow reading of the religious text in Islam as well as the zina laws adopted in the name of

---

[444contd]Westphalian formulation srf nation states. Finally, looking at the Charter of the Organization of Islamic Conference (OIC), an organization of 57 Muslim countries, makes reference to the United Nations and has registered it under article 102 of the United Nations Charter on 1 February 1974. For details on the OIC see www.oic-oci.org.

[445] The criminal laws of the Indo-Pakistan subcontinent during colonial rule were secular in formulation and not based on religious doctrine.

[446] Pakistan, Sudan, Iran, Saudi Arabia and Nigeria (some states only) are some examples of Muslim jurisdictions where Islamic criminal law applies.

[447] Including High Courts of Peshawar, Lahore, Sindh, Baluchistan and Azad Jammu and Kashmir, Supreme Court of Pakistan, Federal Shariat Court and its Appellate Bench.

religion. A further factor in the choice of sample was cases where judges had applied human rights law (including the United Nations Charter, Universal Declaration of Human Rights and the United Nations Convention on the Elimination of All Forms of Discrimination Against Women – CEDAW).[448]

Exploiting the 'sublime' for the vindictive? Islamic criminal law of Hudood as an instrument of personal vengeance

The single most startling 'revelation' of this research has been that the vast majority of cases registered under Hudood laws of zina and zina bil jabr are based on the personal and ulterior motives of near relatives. First investigation reports are usually fabricated and meant to achieve personal objectives. In most cases, evidence is doctored and constructed, in collaboration with investigation agencies (in this case, invariably local police). These cases are indicative of laws' violence in the hands of individuals and groups who appropriate and employ them in playing out 'battles' of often 'localized' power relations. Case law is reflective of how the religious text is abused and misused without any qualms of conscience. The distinction between employing 'secular' laws and religious law is completely blurred. Some examples of this approach are presented below.

Mst. Humaira Mehmood v The State (PLD 1999 Lah 494) is a case of alleged zina and abduction registered by a father against the husband of his daughter as she had married a man of her own choice. The father knew, at the time of his complaint, that his daughter and the accused were lawfully married but went ahead and filed a case of zina implicating his daughter and her husband as a result of which they had to flee their home to avoid being arrested. Details are as follows: Humaira, a 30 year old woman married Mehmood Butt, against the wishes of her parents. Her father was a sitting member of the provincial legislature. The couple, apprehensive of their lives and safety, fled to Karachi and sought refuge in Edhi Centre.[449] The brother followed them to Karachi and filed a first information report to the effect that his sister had had a row with her mother and left home and he may be given her 'possession'.[450] There

---

[448] Forty sample judgements became the subject of this review.

[449] The Edhi Trust is a national welfare organization. Abdus Sattar Edhi established his first welfare centre and then the Edhi Trust with a mere Rs5000 (less than 50 pounds sterling). What started as a one-man show operating from a single room in Karachi is now the Edhi Foundation, the largest welfare organization in Pakistan. The foundation has over 300 centres across the country, in big cities, small towns and remote rural areas, providing medical aid, family planning and emergency assistance. They own air ambulances, providing quick access to far-flung areas.

[450] This term is in itself indicative of the view that women require to be in the 'possession' (protection, guardianship) of a male member of their family.

was no mention of Humaira's existing marriage to another man or her alleged abduction by her husband, Mehmood. The family, on 'recovering' Humaira went through a 'false' marriage ceremony which they documented on video film and later produced in court as testimony of a prior marriage to a person of the family's choice. The case, through the support of human rights activists, made it to the High Court of Lahore invoking the writ jurisdiction under the Constitution of Pakistan (Article 199). The judgment by Honourable Justice Jillani is a landmark decision and important in more ways than one. It draws strength from a combination of Islamic law, the Constitution of Pakistan and international human rights instruments emanating both from the United Nations human rights regime and comparable documents from Islamic forums. What is also crucial in developing a women-friendly and human-friendly interpretative strategy for securing human rights is the complementary manner in which these three different legal frameworks are used. (Pages 512–13 of the judgement sum up this argument and approach rather well.)

Justice Jillani emphasized the duty of state institutions in respecting, protecting and promoting fundamental rights of everyone:

> 'Coming to the role of the state functionaries in this case I find that the police officials who handled this case passed orders and acted in a manner which betrayed total disregard of law and the land and mandate of their calling. Articles 4 and 25 of the Constitution of the Islamic Republic of Pakistan guarantees that everybody shall be treated strictly in accordance with law. Article 35 of the constitution provides that the state shall protect the marriage, the family, the mother and the child. As a member of the international comity of nations we must respect the international instruments of human rights to which we are a party.'

Justice Jillani reminded the parties that Pakistan is a member of United Nations and is signatory to CEDAW. He especially drew attention to article 16 which enjoins all member states to respect rights of women to family life on a basis of equality with men. He also refers to article 5 of the Cairo Declaration on Human Rights in Islam to reinforce his argument of women's human rights within an Islamic framework. He condemned in no uncertain language the 'alliance' of state, society and family to undermine women's human rights:

> 'The police officials are guardians of the lives, liberties and the honour of the citizens. They owe their place in society to the taxes which are paid by citizens. If these guards become poachers then no society and no state can have even a semblance of human rights and rule of law.'

Likewise, in *Rashid Ahmad v The State*, the father of a girl registered a case of zina-bil-jabr and abduction against the accused. This was done primarily to hide the 'shame' of the family as the girl had wilfully left home with one of the accused and subsequently returned. Similar cases were lodged by fathers against daughters who had married of their own volition in *Mst. Bakhtawar Mai v SHO PS Khairpur Saadat, Distt. Muzaffargarh and others* (PCrLJ 2001 Lah 188) and *M Sharif and 8 others v The State* (1997 SCMR 30).

Personal vengeance against a real or perceived wrongdoing also motivated plaintiffs to use the religious law of Hudood and bring disrepute to the adversary. *Asghar Ali v The State,*[451] *Lala v The State,*[452] *Muzammil Khan v Fateh Khan and others*[453] and *Abdul Majeed v Ghulam Yaseen*[454] are some examples of this approach.

Mst. Zafran Bibi v The State (PLD 2002 FSC 1) is another landmark case where the Federal Shariat Court took suo moto notice of a stoning to death sentence of a married woman Mst Zafran Bibi. During the course of examination of the convicted woman (who was originally a complainant) and her husband, it transpired that she had been pressurised to accuse a person of zina bil jabr to protect the younger brother of her husband (who according to her statement used to commit zina bil jabr with her). Zafran Bibi, who was sentenced to stoning to death by the trial court, was acquitted by Federal Shariat Court for erroneous reasoning of the trail judge. This case, which initiated in the Kohat region of the North West Frontier province of Pakistan, hit the headlines when Zafran Bibi was sentenced by the court of first instance. The public outrage and wide support for her resulted in the superior courts hearing the appeal and acquitting her of the offence of zina.

---

[451] In this case the defence pleaded that the complainant registered a case against the accused and his (complainant's) wife (since divorced), as he wanted to settle old scores with the accused. Some time before, the accused was also one of the prosecution witnesses against the complainant in an electricity theft case.

[452] The complainant registered a case of zina against the accused and his (complainant's) wife. During the trial, however, the accused pleaded that the complainant was only avenging his 'honour' as he (complainant) was not given the hand of a sister of the accused.

[453] In this case the accused claimed that a false case of zina was registered against him on the behest of a police officer in whose father's murder case he appeared as a defence witness. He claimed that the police officer was avenging this by registering a false and fabricated zina case against him.

[454] In this zina case, the accused claimed that he had an enmity with the complainant, as the complainant had snatched some belongings from him some time ago. The village panchayat, deciding the dispute and ordering return of snatched goods, imposed a fine on the complainant, from which he had defaulted. The accused claimed that he was implicated in a false zina case because of that incident.

Divergence between trial court decisions and appellate or superior courts: Substantive or procedural conflict?

Another finding from a review of the sample revealed that there appeared to be a huge divergence between the approach, reasoning and decisions of the subordinate courts and the superior judiciary in Hudood cases. Registration of cases under Hudood offences, especially zina and zina bil jabr, subsequent investigation and trial in subordinate courts, appears to be conducted arbitrarily. The cursory manner in which legal and Islamic law knowledge is applied is painfully apparent in almost all such cases. This results in acquittals and quashing of conviction orders of subordinate courts by the superior judiciary. But what is most unsatisfactory is that despite the consistent pattern of reversals and admonishment by the appellate courts, the trend continues unabated as does the human suffering it entails. Complete disregard for basic human rights and social implications for the accused is the repetitive trend emerging from this research.[455] The constant stream of appeal cases where women's reputations are tarnished forever for being implicated in zina is made all the more stark where the male co-accused is acquitted for want of evidence while the woman is convicted for her pregnancy. In the case of Zafran Bibi cited above, the additional sessions judge sentenced Zafran Bibi to be stoned to death. She was a married woman who had accused a person of zina bil jabr. She was found to be pregnant, and despite her pregnancy antedating the alleged offence, the trial court found her pregnancy a conclusive proof of her guilt (her husband was in jail at the time of occurrence). The accused was, however, acquitted for want of evidence. Upon appeal, the Federal Shariat Court found the reasoning of the trial judge erroneous and held that pregnancy of a complainant cannot be proof of her guilt, especially so in this case where it was antedated and legitimacy of child was accepted by her husband. Zafran Bibi was acquitted by the Federal Shariat Court.

Two judgments however stand out from the sample reviewed. In *Lubna and others v Government of Punjab* (PLD 1997 Lah 180) and *Qaiser Mehmood v M Shafi and another* (PLD 1998 Lah 72), the Lahore High Court refused to quash a first information report which was registered against the (allegedly) legally wedded husband and wife. The girl had left home with a person and then married him. The court held that such runaway couples are not entitled to a relief either in equity or

---

[455] *Rashid Ahmed v The State* 1996 PCrLJ 612; *Asghar Ali v The State* 1996 PCrLJ 1687; *Lala v The State* PLD 1987 SC 414 (Shariat Appellate Bench); *Abdul Majeed v Ghulam Yaseen* 1997 PCrLJ 896 (Federal Shariat Court); *Ayoob and 8 Others v The State* 1996 PCrLJ 642 (Federal Shariat Court); *Major Nasir Mehmood and another vs State and 9 Others* 2002 PCrLJ Lah 408.

in extraordinary writ jurisdiction of the court. The court advised them to seek other official or administrative remedies for quashment of the first information report and rejected the petition.

'Unholy' alliance between the religious and secular: The role of prosecution and investigative institutions

As a crosscutting issue and following on from the cases cited above, a further common element in judgments of superior courts was the specific reference to substantive and procedural inadequacies and the partisan nature of investigation officers and incompetence of trial judges. It is pertinent that despite these almost persistent lapses in the cases reviewed, it was only in one instance that a superior court specifically took to task 'delinquent' investigation officers. In *Muhammad Siddique v The State* (PLD 2002 Lah 444), the court notes that the police and subordinate courts did not act in a lawful and timely manner that may have prevented a triple-murder in the name of honour (PLD 2002 Lah 444: 457a). Likewise, in *Abdul Zahir and other v The State* (2000 SCMR 406), the court found that records were tampered with and false succession documents were prepared by the accused to obstruct rights of a woman (wife of deceased), even by her close relatives (page 97d). In the Zafran Bibi case, the court observed:

> 'The controversy around the applicability of Hudood laws in Pakistan is related more to the erroneous application of these laws in the country, rather than the laws per se' (PLD 2002 Federal Shariat Court 1 at page 12 bc)

Zarina Bibi v The State (1997 PCrLJ 313, Federal Shariat Court), however, presents an instance of one of the strongest judicial comments on misapplication of Hudood laws by investigation officers and lower courts. The court finds that the application of Hudood is, by and large, arbitrary and that the lower courts seem to be every-ready to convict, which their Lordships declared to be against Islamic principles (page 319c). The court criticises the conduct of the trial judge as he failed to perform his obligations (page 318c). In the same case the court was critical of the police which considers 'the poor and the minorities their fief' (page 316c) and that the collection of evidence and investigation was partisan and arbitrary (pages 316-317).

Shift in position of judicial forums re: killings in the name of honour

Historically, sections of the Pakistan Penal Code have been employed to evolve a case for 'mitigating circumstances' where an accused has murdered under 'grave and sudden provocation'. These cases included (but not exclusively) instances where a woman and or her spouse were killed as a result of their defiance of 'custom' and marrying of their own choice.

The defence would convince the court of the need for a lighter sentence since the accused was supposedly acting impulsively to protect his 'honour'; a line that was quite commonly accepted by courts, both subordinate and superior. The law was thus manipulated and advanced the sanctity of male honour and legitimizing control over women.

This perception of superior courts vis-a-vis honour killings of women by their male relatives (brothers, fathers, uncles or husbands) has changed somewhat in recent years. In most judgments under review, judges make it a point to distance themselves from condoning killing in the name of honour and admonish such social trends. Superior courts are now increasingly rejecting the old excuse of being 'provoked by sight of a female relative in compromising position' for murders. In certain cases, courts have refused to give any benefit whatsoever to the accused of honour killing on the pretext of his 'ghairat' (honour).[456] In *Muhammad Siddique v The State* (PLD 2002 Lah 444) the court upheld the conviction of a father who had murdered his daughter, her husband and their infant child to teach his daughter a lesson for marrying of her own free choice. The court severely criticises such tendencies and social trends. Justice Jilani in his judgment stated:

> 'These killings are carried out in an evangelistic spirit. Little do these zealots know that there is nothing religious about it and nothing honourable either. It is male chauvinism and gender bias at their worst. These prejudices are not country specific, region specific or people specific. The roots are rather old and violence against women has been a recurrent phenomenon in human history… Notwithstanding the Quranic commandments and the penal law of the land, the incidents of violence against women remain unabated… This is a typical example of misuse and misapplication of the Hudood laws in the country. . . A murder in the name of honour is not merely the physical elimination of a man or woman. It is, at a social-political plane, a blow to the concept of a free dynamic and egalitarian society. In a great majority of cases, behind at play is a certain mental outlook, and a creed which seeks to deprive equal rights to women, in other words, inter alia, the right to marry or the right to divorce which are recognized not only by our religion but have been protected in law and enshrined in our constitution' (pages 447–448).

In *Pehlwan and other v The State* (PLD 2001 Quetta 88) and *Abdul Zahir and other v The State* (2000 SCMR 406), the court refused to accept the notion of honour killing. The judge traces at length the history of op-

---

[456] Further investigation and analysis needs to be undertaken to see whether this is in a chronological order, to find out whether this 'change' in mindset of judiciary is a progress narrative or not.

pressive treatment meted out to women from pre-Islamic to modern times and bases its conclusion on Quranic prescription in Surah Noor (Justice Jilani: 95c-96c). The court calls for jihad[457] against honour killing (98a). Further, it is interesting to observe that whereas in pre-Islamic times, female infanticides and honour killings were matters of routine, we do not find any incident of honour killing of women in the early years of Islamic caliphate.

The courts have also taken the view that customary practices supporting honour killings are unacceptable. In *Rasool Bux v The State* (2000 SCMR 731), the court specifically refuses to 'condone a murder 'on the 'ground of siahkari' and holds that such murder is to be punished with death. In *M Akram Khan v The State* (PLD 2001 SC96; page 100), the court adopted a stern position on the issue of honour killing and declares it to be a violation of fundamental rights as guaranteed in the constitution. The court, thus, refuses to mitigate the circumstances and maintains that the death penalty be awarded in a case of honour killing.

5 Introduction of international human rights discourse by national courts

The review of case law, as illustrated above, reflects that contemporary international discourse on human rights is being increasingly adopted, accepted and acknowledged by the superior courts. The superior judiciary does not determine questions of human rights in isolation and, at times, is seen invoking international human rights law in conjunction with constitutional rights and rights accorded to women in the Islamic legal tradition. It is important to make the point, though, that despite an introduction to and use of international human rights law by the superior judiciary in Pakistan, there is no uniformity of approach in this regard and there is a wide range of judicial reasoning in the reviewed judgments. A clear-cut judicial consensus or approach is yet to develop and is only discernible in its rudimentary or fledgling form.

---

[457] The term 'jihad' comes from the Arab verb 'jahada', meaning to struggle or exert. The Prophet Muhammad is believed to have stated that the exertion of force in battle is a minor jihad, while 'self-exertion in peaceful and personal compliance with the dictates of Islam (constitutes) the major or superior jihad'. The Prophet is also reported to have said that the 'best form of jihad is to speak the truth in the face of an oppressive ruler'. Jihad has also been defined as 'exertion of one's power to the utmost of one's capacity'. Al-Kasaniy presents a particularly succinct definition of jihad wide enough to include all aspects of the doctrine, stating thus: 'Jihad in the technology of law is used for expending ability and power in fighting in the path of God by means of *life, property, tongue and other* (emphasis added) than these'.

Redefinition of social role by the judiciary

This review suggests that the superior judiciary in Pakistan is in the process of redefining its social role and even transforming the classic Anglo-Saxon conception of judicial activism. In some cases, judges[458] proclaim that their role is one of a mujtahid and that therefore they are entitled to deduce new Islamic law by logical induction from Quran and Sunna, which previously was considered a prerogative only of theological figures like fuqaha,[459] aaima[460] and muftis.[461] Superior courts, and especially the Federal Shariat Court, are engaging in a serious discourse to bring centuries old Islamic jurisprudence into conformity with modern social reality. In some cases, interpretative strategies employed by superior judiciary are an amalgam of traditional, Islamic, modern and Anglo-Saxon trends.[462] The work of female Muslim scholars needs mention here, especially for their role in evolving interpretative strategies on the basis of the Quran and other sources of Islamic law.[463] These, in turn, are providing a basis for Muslim women to argue for rights and entitlements from within their religious tradition which men and governments find difficult to denounce. Discomfort of the self-appointed 'clergy'[464] at seeing an increasing number of women engaged in scholarly research and interpretation of the religious text is apparent as the power of religious discourse appears to be slipping out of their domain.[465] At the same time, the voices of some 'enlightened' male clergy are being heard joining the debate on women's rights within the Islamic tradition.[466]

---

[458] In *Hafiz Abdul Waheed v Mrs. Asma Jehangir and another* PLD 1997 Lah 301.

[459] Legal scholar, jurist. The singular is faqih.

[460] Plural, meaning leader. Singular imam.

[461] Plural, meaning a legal scholar competent to deliver fatawa (edict).

[462] *Muhammad Siddique v The State* PLD Lah. 444.

[463] F. Mernissi, Z. Mir Husseini, H. Afshar, A. Al-Hibri, L. Ahmed, M. Yamani, N. Hamadeh, S. Haeri, R. Hassan, S. S. Ali, A. Wadud, to name a few.

[464] Islam has no clergy in the sense that other religious traditions subscribe to. Two clear avenues are offered to Muslims in the fulfilment of their religious obligations: either endeavour to arrive at an independent position and adopt that particular path or, if one does not feel confident to do so, follow the opinion of a learned person. This following of a learned person's opinion is called *taqlid*.

[465] On a number of occasions, I have personally experienced this discomfort where the 'clergy' took issue with the fact that I was speaking the language of religion and therefore challenging them on what they considered their home turf. This has happened both in Pakistan and the United Kingdom in seminars, conferences and public lectures.

[466] Dr Javaid Ghamdi and Dr Muhammad Farooq are such scholars whose position on women's human rights is equivocal and an example of the potential of interpretative strategies in evolving women-friendly jurisprudence based on the religious text in Islam.

Element of qadfh has been ignored

Our review invoking Islamic criminal laws on Hudood, on zina and zina bil jabr, suggests that courts have failed to take the Quranic law to its logical conclusion – they have failed to implement the law on qadfh which requires persons giving false evidence and bringing false cases implicating women of illegal sexual relations, to be whipped and their evidence forever disregarded. There could be two possible ways to ensure effective enforcement of qadfh law: through suo moto powers of courts – the Federal Shariat Court believes that legislature must amend the qadfh ordinance so as to empower courts to take people to task for falsely implicating people in offences of zina and similar cases. This, the court holds, would undermine the tendencies to achieve personal ends and fulfil ulterior motives through false cases of Hudood against enemies or 'runaway' females of family.[467] It is suggested that the superior judiciary might wish to consider circulating clearly worded instructions to the subordinate judiciary in this regard. Meanwhile, since qadfh proceedings can only be initiated when a complaint is made by the one who was alleged to have committed zina, an active campaign for awareness of the legal profession and members of the public at large is imperative. Courts can be more proactive by making victims of such 'motivated' trials aware of their rights and procedures for initiating qadfh proceedings.[468]

Last, but not least, this review also indicates that while the country is still debating changes in the Hudood laws, some simple but crucial procedural modifications would be useful to consider. It is evident that criteria for registration of Hudood offences has to be different from other offences. From this review, it seems that, in most of the cases, routine application of the criminal procedure code for registration of Hudood offences results in injustice and undue duress to the victims (accused). This is evident from the fact that most of the cases registered under the Hudood (especially zina) have an ulterior motive, are fabricated and fallacious and end up in acquittals. Victims, the vast majority of whom are women, even after acquittals, are left with a lifelong social stigma.

---

[467] *Zarina Bibi v The State* 1997 PCrLJ 313 Federal Shariat Court at page 320c.

[468] Further research at the grassroots level must be undertaken to understand the 'living' custom, ethos and value system of society. All too often customary practices and societal values are considered a fossilized, static concept. In the subject under research – zina and its punishment in the name of religion – it is imperative to unearth the mindset of people on the ground in this regard. Has custom taken a turn where shaming people publicly for exercising their choice of marriage partners is an acceptable course of action? Does settling scores include allegations of zina against one's foe? Is abuse of law adopted in the name of religion legitimized by society? And finally, is there place for some basic minimum standards of human rights in this discourse of crime and punishment?

Courts have also found faults with application of Hudood laws. Thus, criminal procedure designed for common law crimes should not be mutatis mutandis used for initiation, investigation and trials of Hudood laws and special filtering procedures must be put in place to screen out the frivolous and malafide allegations.

Is the Hudood law on zina essentially a faulty piece of legislation and the 'positive' inclinations of the appeal courts a damage-containment exercise? Or have judges of the superior courts had more exposure to progressive, liberal interpretation of law and religion and also become more aware of international human rights laws and become more willing to use them in their judgments? Is it a faithful reflection of the Divine Will as expressed in the Quran? If not, why has it found such ready acceptance in its use? Why and how does one explain the disparity between the judgments of the trial and superior courts?

This research was based on an analysis of over 40 judgements of the superior judiciary in Pakistan where zina offences have been at issue. It advances the argument that absence of a contextual, grounded and holistic approach to Quranic verses and other sources of Islamic law, has resulted in a fractured and incomplete reflection of its substantive provisions. It also highlights some important policy implications for the judiciary in Pakistan. The country has judicial academies – national and in four provincial high courts. Findings of research such as these may be used to develop sessions of continuing professional development for members of the subordinate judiciary, members of the Bar and government planners, policy makers and implementers as well as academics, researchers and non-governmental organizations. Workshops, seminars and conferences with a hands-on component may be organized where participants are provided with information and access to using human rights treaties as well as domestic law and religious text from a rights-based perspective.

Bibliography

Ali S. S. and J. Rehman (2001) *Indigenous peoples and ethnic minorities of Pakistan*, Curzon Press, Richmond.

Ali S. S. (2000) *Gender and human rights in Islam and international law. Equal before Allah, unequal before man?*, Kluwer Law International, the Hague.

An-Naim A. (1990) Towards *an Islamic reformation*, Syracuse University Press, Syracuse.

Baderin M. A. (2003) *International human rights and Islamic law*, Oxford University Press, Oxford.

Baxi U. (2000) 'Constitutionalism as a site of state formative practices', Vol. 21 *Cardozo Law Review* 1183-1210 at 1188.
– (2001) 'Outline of a "theory of practice" of Indian constitutionalism', a paper presented to an international seminar on the philosophy of Indian constitution, Goa, 7–9 September 2001.

Coulson N. J. (1964) *A history of Islamic law*, Edinburgh University Press, Edinburgh.

El-Awa M. S. (1993) *Punishment in Islamic law*, American Trust Publications, Indianapolis.

El-Fadl K. A. (2003) *Speaking in God's name. Islamic law, authority and women*, Oneworld Publication, Oxford.

Government of Pakistan (1997) *Report of the Commission of Inquiry for Women*, Government of Pakistan Printing Press, Islamabad.
– (1973) *The Constitution of the Islamic Republic of Pakistan 1973*, Government of Pakistan Printing Press, Karachi.

Hussein G. M. (2003) 'Basic guarantees in the Islamic criminal justice system' in M. Abdel Haleem, A. O. Sherif and K. Daniels (eds) *Criminal justice in Islam: Judicial procedure in the Sharia*, I B Tauris, London.

Jehangir A. and H. Jilani (1990) *The Hudood Ordinances: A divine sanction?*, Rohtas Books, Lahore.

Kusha H. R. (2002) *The sacred law of Islam. A case study of women's treatment in the Islamic Republic of Iran's criminal justice system*, Ashgate, Aldershot.

Mehdi R. (1994) *The Islamization of the law in Pakistan*, Curzon, Richmond.

Mernissi F. (1991) *Women and Islam,* translated by M. J. Lakeland, Basil Blackwell, Oxford.

Pearl D. and W. Menski (1998) *Muslim family law*, Sweet & Maxwell, London.

Rahim A. (1995) *Mohammadan jurisprudence*, Mansoor Book House, Lahore.

Schacht J. (1961) 'Sharia' in H. A. R. Gibb and J. H. Kramers (eds) *The shorter encyclopedia of Islam*, Cornell University Press, Ithaca.
– (1964) *An introduction to Islamic law*, Clarendon Press, Oxford.

Sherif O. A. (2003) 'Generalities on criminal procedure under Islamic Shari'a' in M. Abdel Haleem, A. O. Sherif and K. Daniels (eds) *Criminal justice in Islam: Judicial procedure in the Sharia*, I B Tauris, London.

Zahur-ud-din M. (2003) *New Islamic laws (Hudood) 1979,* Mansoor Book House, Lahore.

List of cases

Abdul Majeed v Ghulam Yaseen 1997 PCrLJ 896 (Federal Shariat Court)

Abdul Zahir and other v The State 2000 SCMR 406

Asghar Ali v The State 1996 PCrLJ 1687

Ayoob and 8 Others v The State 1996 PCrLJ 642 (Federal Shariat Court)

Hafiz Abdul Waheed v Mrs. Asma Jehangir and another PLD 1997 Lah 301

Lala v The State PLD 1987 SC 414 (Shariat Appellate Bench)

Lubna and others v Government of Punjab PLD 1997 Lah 180) and

Major Nasir Mehmood and another v State and 9 Others 2002 PCrLJ Lah 408

M Akram Khan v The State PLD 2001 SC96

M Sharif and 8 others v The State 1997 SCMR 30

Mst. Bakhtawar Mai v SHO PS Khairpur Saadat, Distt. Muzaffargarh and others PCrLJ 2001 Lah 188

Mst. Humaira Mehmood v The State PLD 1999 Lah 494

Mst. Zafran Bibi v The State PLD 2002 FSC 1.

Muzammil Khan v Fateh Khan and others

Pehlwan and other v The State (PLD 2001 Quetta 88)

Qaiser Mehmood v M Shafi and another PLD 1998 Lah 72

Rashid Ahmed v The State 1996 PCrLJ 612

Rasool Bux v The State 2000 SCMR 731

List of legislation

Pakistan

Offences Against Property (Enforcement of Hudood) Ordinance 1979

The Offence of Zina (Enforcement of Hudood) Ordinance 1979 of Pakistan

The Offence of Qadfh (Enforcement of Hadd) Ordinance 1979

The Prohibition (Enforcement of Hadd) Order 1979

Regional and international

Convention on the Elimination of All Forms of Discrimination Against Women (CEDAW) 1979

United Nations Charter 1945

Universal Declaration of Human Rights 1948

16

The widows' and female child's portion
The twisted path to partial equality for widows and daughters under customary law in Zimbabwe

Julie Stewart and Amy Tsanga

In this chapter we explore the twisted processes of the distortion of the customary law of inheritance as it intersected with imported common law norms and colonial statutory interventions. We outline the legal processes which led, as we argue, to the obscuring of women's and the girl child's rights and entitlements under customary law regimes in Zimbabwe. The interventions that were made both through the courts and statutorily over the years to ameliorate the position of women and the girl child in relation to inheriting from a male family member in an intestate succession are discussed and evaluated. We discuss the importance of women who are prepared to take up the challenge of pursuing their rights through the courts and illustrate the significance of their actions even if at times they fail. Special emphasis is laid on the importance of thoroughly grounded research into general law, customary law and local customs and practices before law reform measures are attempted which will significantly reform official versions of customary law where male vested interests in the current formal legal position are challenged. The value of having tools, theoretically and methodologically, to conduct an informed dialogue with politicians, legal drafters, chiefs and other perceived 'stakeholders' is highlighted. The chapter also explores using human rights standards which are set globally and regionally to measure progress in women and girls' attainment of equality with their male counterparts and the further legal and social interventions needed to attain true equality with their male counterparts.

1 Introduction

Death of a spouse or parent raises a host of legal, social and economic questions and problems. These are difficult enough to resolve when there is only one regulatory regime in place but they become nightmarish when there are competing legal, normative and social regimes metaphorically battling over the property that is needed to sustain the family into an unknown future. The difficulties that women in particular face in accessing resources from deceased estates are clearly recognized at the international level. Women's rights to equality and equity in inheritance are called for in international instruments.

The Convention on the Elimination of All Forms of Discrimination against Women (CEDAW) in article 2 condemns discrimination against women in all its forms and requires in article 2(f) states parties:[469]

> 'To take all appropriate measures, including legislation, to modify or abolish existing laws, regulations, customs and practices, which constitute discrimination against women.'

Article 16(h) demands that states parties ensure, on a basis of equality of men and women:

> 'The same rights for both spouses in respect of ownership, acquisition, management, administration, enjoyment and disposition of property ...'

The Protocol to the African Charter on Human and Peoples' Rights on the Rights of Women in Africa (the women's protocol) in article 21 expressly addresses the right to inheritance by widows and daughters in the estates of husbands and parents:

> '1. A widow shall have the right to an equitable share in the inheritance of the property of her husband. A widow shall have the right to continue to live in the matrimonial house. In case of remarriage, she shall retain this right if the house belongs to her or she has inherited it.
>
> 2. Women and men shall have the right to inherit, in equitable shares, their parents' properties.'

Attaining such equitable shares is multifaceted. Firstly, there is need for a legal framework giving women rights to inherit from their spouses and parents and giving widows the right to use the matrimonial home after the death of a spouse. Secondly, women have to be prepared to fight for their rights if they exist and if they do not exist, they need to be pursued either through creative judicial interpretations or through legislative intervention. The quest for women to have equitable, let alone equal inheritance rights in the African context is frequently highly contested. There are conceptual clashes as to the form and content of customary law, coupled with clashes over which is dominant, received law over

---

[469] Zimbabwe only became a signatory to CEDAW in 1991. It has also ratified the convention without reservations. Interestingly, as this chapter will show, at the judicial level the most innovative interpretative methods took place before the signing of CEDAW. Thereafter a form of defence of assumed patriarchal value systems took place. Given its composition, one might have expected parliament to have been more conservative but parliament embraced the need for clear, unequivocal intervention to secure inheritance rights for women, which were cast as an attempt to reassert customary values, in a new social and economic light. But read on, for the rest of the tale.

customary law, all under a pall that assumes that patrilineal male-based patterns of succession should and do dominate.

Engaging with reform of inheritance laws and practices, and looking for opportunities to channel research results into grounded customs and practices back into the law's engagement and mediation of inheritance, may be bedevilled by a seemingly unresponsive constitutional framework under which the national law operates. Some national constitutions in the African context, as with section 23 of the Zimbabwean constitution, continue to give protected status to customary law, dispensing with the need for it to comply with the equality and non-discrimination provisions in the constitution. In one sense, the protection given to customary law is a 'colonial hangover' but customary law may have an iconic status in national representations of identity. Thus the representational values perceived in customary law may be vigorously protected against legal interventions that are questioning the nature and form of customary inheritance practices and, even more problematically, the way in which men and women are treated under customary law.

The customary law debate and the question as to whether it is oppressive to women or values women and women's lives and contributions, is ongoing and persistently interrogates various models for the most effective ways of meeting the international imperatives for the improvements in the rights and entitlements of women in whatever legal area is being targeted. The legal interventionist[470] or law reform strategies that are used at any point in time are a product of the depth of understanding of 'legal opportunities' and the politics or perceived politics[471] that might affect the implementation or efficacy of law-based action initiatives.

This chapter maps the twisted path from women's entitlements to support under customary inheritance regimes in Zimbabwe. During this period they were dispossessed and colonial legislative interventions and judicial interpretations prevented them from benefiting, except in an extremely tenuous and indirect fashion, from men, namely husbands, fathers and brothers. It then examines the attempts that were made to use the provisions of the Legal Age of Majority Act to establish or re-establish women's rights under customary law to benefit from the estates of deceased males. The failure of this interpretative intervention is exam-

---

[470] We distinguish in this chapter between legal interventions, such as test case litigation, creative use of legal options in the administration of estates, administrative reform that falls short of law reform and active law reform initiatives that lead to new legislation and or the amendment of existing acts or regulations.

[471] We use the term *perceived*, as will be shown in this chapter, because often there is an historical or context-based assumption that reform cannot be undertaken when in reality launching reform initiatives may be far less problematic than expected.

ined and analyzed. The potential efficacy of using an alternative path, that of ascertaining the principles underlying customary inheritance practices to determine women's actual rights under customary law is assessed, and the strategies employed in that process analyzed.

An assessment is made of how close the provisions of the Administration of Estates Amendment Act 6/1997 come to meeting international and African continental standards for the protection of widows and other dependants of deceased persons whose rights would otherwise fall to be determined under customary law. This Act gives spouses and children, irrespective of their sex, the right to inherit from the intestate estate of their deceased relative,

Finally, we briefly examine the significance of the nationwide 'Wills and inheritance campaign' which sought to advertise and boost use of the new law introduced on 1 November 1997.

As Professor Anne Hellum[472] commented, this is a tale not just about the law but also a tale about the women and men who strategized, sometimes effectively, sometimes unsuccessfully (or even counterproductively) to find the most effective way at any point in the legal timeframe of inheritance entitlements and rights, to secure inheritance rights for women and children in customary estates of deceased males. Thus we examine and analyze, in a parallel process to the reforms and initiatives, the strategies that were used by lawyers, law-based non-governmental organizations and the interventions of women themselves, to exploit changes in the law and the political climate to attain equity in the distribution of the estates of males.

2 The terrain of the path: An overview of customary inheritance regimes in Zimbabwe

Inheritance of property, especially for women in so-called customary regimes in the African context, has been largely characterized by exclusion, deprivation and profound inequities that are arguably more problematic when there are mixed social and legal regimes in which families

---

[472] In pointing out to us the importance of revealing and discussing the initiatives that were taken, we had to examine our own roles, motivations and stratagems, we had to get out of the third person mode and unpack our own involvement and strategizing, perhaps not least of this being that between us throughout the period from the early 1970s to 2002 at least one of us at any one time had been involved in teaching, researching, information dissemination or law reform initiatives in relation to inheritance matters in Zimbabwe. We overcame our reluctance to 'advertise' our role and conceded that a review of what took place and what stimulated it was important for legal activists who might want to use some of the same strategies and avoid the pitfalls we found.

are embedded. A husband and wife or husband and wives, may exercise or hold rights to communal land, own land and a house in an urban area, they may be employed in the urban area, farm the communal land, and provide financial or material support to a variety of relatives. There may also be complex intra-family support obligations, which create expectations for recompense in one form or another among potential beneficiaries. Older brothers or sisters of the parties to the marriage or marriages may have assisted with the costs of education of the husband or wife or there may be other forms of hidden investment and death marks a point where 'pay back' may be sought.

There are multiple sets of interests that impinge on the relationships between husband and wife or wives, each one mediated by a different set of social and legal considerations. During life there are complex networks that underpin family survival strategies (WLSA, 1997a and 1997b). Death exposes these networks and the implicit demands that are made upon them but the general law's solutions to the complexities of these support interactions are simplistic allowing little room for manoeuvre in cases of special need or for the evolution of creative approaches to solving inheritance problems.

We should also stress that there are many potential initiatives for change and that in this quest the activist or law reformer needs to be alive to the reality that the problem is not necessarily customary law or, more accurately, 'customs and practices', but their ossification through the judicial process (WLSA, 1995; Stewart, 1998).[473] Developing within and used by families and communities, customary law has responded, as will be shown later, to changing social and economic circumstances. The lower courts picked up these 'vibes' in the early 1990s and whereas the higher courts have from time to time responded negatively to women's burgeoning rights and entitlements under local customs and practices, many magistrates have been ready to reconceptualize customary law and its jurisprudential underpinnings.[474]

---

[473] Nor should the reader make the assumption that customary law is automatically adequate for modern purposes. The point we make is that customary law has the capacity to respond to new circumstances and further that a thorough understanding of customary law and its underlying jurisprudence makes it much easier to undertake law reform which is likely to be taken up by the community – even if the very least you use it for is to establish the entry points for dialogue about the need for change and how the change will benefit families. We discuss this issue more deeply in our chapter on advertising the law.

[474] For a further and much fuller discussion of this process see Stewart (1998), Himonga (1995) and WLSA (1995). To be fair there have been times when the higher courts were prepared to consider reconceptualizing customary law or at least to investigate which version to apply as in *Matambo v Matambo* 1969 (2) RLR 154 and *Masango v Masango* SC-66-86 (unreported), but this has not characterized the Supreme Court in recent years.

Walking alone or with others?

Customary regimes do not vest real rights in specific individuals but are reflected in group survival strategies. Yet a concomitant of group survival is the welfare of the individual, thus there are critical individual entitlements to use and enjoy which carry group support obligations. Wider rights of support and care are enforceable against the family group care obligations rather than exercised against land or property in a direct legal sense (Stewart, 1998). A widow or children of a deceased male should be able to look to their natal family (the widow's marital family) for their continued support and livelihood. The WLSA Zimbabwe inheritance research[475] established that among the Ndebele, one of the ethnic groups in the country included in part of the research, a widow would be left to continue farming, grazing cattle and managing her life while her youngest son moved in next to her to provide logistical support and help with farming activities. He did not control her life or unilaterally control her land or cattle; it was a support relationship. On her death, the cattle and farming implements would devolve upon him as his full and half blood brothers would have been previously allocated land and cattle in their own right, perhaps by their father at earlier points in time when they married or sought to move out on their own.[476] His sisters might not have benefited directly, having married into other families, but, as WLSA research in Zimbabwe established, women had what might be styled a right of return to their natal families and a concomitant right to support from the family (WLSA, Zimbabwe, 1995, 1997a and 1997b). Women were also able to benefit from inheritance processes, depending on family circumstances and situations (WLSA, 1995).

The deceased male's eldest son, as determined by the family of the deceased, would have inherited his father's name, symbols of power and authority and his duties in relation to propitiating the family spirits, conducting family rituals, presiding over family disputes and negotiating marriages and so-called bride-wealth (WLSA Zimbabwe, 1995). He did not inherit his father's estate as the sole heir. His role was at best custodial in relation to the family as a whole and the property that he inherited was to be used for the benefit of the family; it was not his to

---

[475] The Women and Law in Southern Africa Research and Education Trust (WLSA) undertook research into inheritance issues in six southern African countries (Botswana, Lesotho, Mozambique, Swaziland, Zambia and Zimbabwe). It is this research base that provided initiatives and strategies from the mid-1990s through to the present on reforming inheritance law and addressing the adverse impact of inheritance practices in the Southern African region.

[476] Although entitlement to land to farm as an individual male would normally only arise at the time of a man's marriage, thus it can be argued that a man's land rights in these customary settings are in a sense joint rights to be exercised with a spouse.

dispose of as and how he saw fit. In fact it was impossible to dispose of immovable property, as it was incapable of alienation outside the family or ethnic group. As heir he had onerous duties and responsibilities, not a role that could be lightly or capriciously carried out without reference to the wider family group (WLSA Zimbabwe, 1995).

Similar patterns existed among the Shona, the major ethnic group in Zimbabwe, among whose sub-groups the WLSA research on inheritance was also carried out. As Chief Mangwende[477] put it during the debates on what was to become the Administration of Estates Amendment Act, 6/97:

'There is no estate until the surviving spouse dies.[478] In the case of a widow she remains, or ought to remain on the land and farm as she had done or she and her co-wives had done previously.'

Many estates are never formally administered. In other estates, only those assets, which cannot be accessed or used without formal administration processes being invoked, come to be dealt with through the Master's Office or magistrate's courts. Thus even when the judicial pronounce-

---

[477] At that time, President of the Council of Chiefs in Zimbabwe. It was probably this response that paved the way for the acceptance of what was seen, especially by the Ministry of Justice, Legal and Parliamentary Affairs, as the radical notion that women could inherit from a male in estates that were previously regulated by customary law. This was critical to the acceptance in the drafting of the Administration of Estates Amendment Act 6/97 that widows should be full beneficiaries in their husband's estates. It should also be revealed that asking the question was a calculated risk, it could have backfired horribly. I (Julie Stewart) asked the question during a meeting between the Chiefs, Ministry of Justice, Legal and Parliamentary Affairs and women's organizations, things had not been going well from the women's perspective with Ministry officials pushing the patrilineal and primo geniture line, thus preferring males. The women, some of them my former students, were mouthing at me to 'do something'; a white female challenging the primogeniture argument seemed somewhat counterproductive – so I took the daring step, my hair literally standing on end and my heart pounding, of asking Chief Mangwende the question "What are the underlying principles of customary inheritance laws?'. I knew it was a make or break point. But it was a calculated risk; the WLSA research had confirmed that customs and practices on the ground were far more amenable to women than the superior court's version of the law. The reader cannot even begin to imagine my relief when the answer came back – the wind went out of the Ministry's sails and the rest of the meeting, in so far as I can recall it, was on how to legislate for the change. It should also be noted that there were twelve other chiefs in the room who all supported the version given by Chief Mangwende. (To this day even writing about what took place, causes my hair to stand on end and shivers to go up and down my spine.)

[478] This would also be the case in polygynous unions. It is not uncommon to find widows of a man coexisting on a piece of land long after his death. In fact looking back on the WLSA Inheritance research this was quite a prevalent situation among widows on agricultural land but at the time we did not interpret it in quite this form.

ments were denying women's rights to inherit from male relatives, families were recognizing these rights, often by doing nothing – leaving the widow alone.

One powerful expression of 'nothing' was articulated in a planning meeting which was part of the design process for the nationwide wills and inheritance campaign sponsored by DFID.[479] When the planning group, composed of media and non-governmental organization personnel, the majority of whom were black Zimbabweans, was asked to draw on their own experiences as to what happens to the property he held when a man dies in a rural (communal) area, the answer which received the affirmation of the group was 'nothing'. 'Nothing' was then interrogated, and it was finally unpacked as – the widow or the widows and the children are left to go on farming. Support ought to come from the deceased's natal family but the reality is probably nothing comes from them. In other words, life goes on as it had, the women continue to farm as they would have done previously but not always without a price. Depending on age and status, a widow would have been expected to enter into a levirate marriage[480] and continue to bear children for her husband's lineage and to provide subsistence support to her children from her farming activities.

This process of doing nothing or changing little by leaving the family alone ought not to be romanticized.[481] Widows were not immune to deprivation of access rights to land. In some cases, attempts, successful or unsuccessful, to drive away the widow, widows or a specific widow in a polygynous set-up, would be made.[482] Childless widows found that

---

[479] This campaign is briefly discussed in the final part of this chapter.

[480] Marriage to a younger brother of the deceased or to some other male relative is seen as a way of reaffirming the bond to and entitlements from the marital family. This can be problematic for widows but is reputedly dying out under the impact of AIDS and with the increasing financial independence of widows. Levirate marriages are not always contrary to the widows needs and interests. On at least one occasion during the WLSA research we came across a widow who was eager to marry one of her brothers in law and had negotiated the union, unfortunately he died before the marriage took place. It is an offence in terms of section 14 of the Customary Marriages Act Chapter 5:07 (formerly the African Marriages Act) to compel a woman to marry against her consent, although enforced levirate marriages may be unregistered unions thereby escaping the provisions of the Act. Customarily the widow has a choice as to whether or not she wants to enter into levirate marriage. The difficulty is that if she refuses, there is the possibility of not being allowed to remain on the family homestead.

[481] Doing nothing and providing no active support to widows, declining to use the land as collateral may be a way of ensuring the widows are not actively assisted but it may conversely be the best way to support them when there are few resources available.

[482] Not all members of the deceased's family would support such actions and widows often benefited from alliances with their deceased husband's relatives. In modern

they lacked the basis on which to assert their right to remain, that of having contributed labour and reproductive value in the form of children to their husband's family. Older widows with a greater stake and support structure in their marital families, through the existence of senior sons, might be able to drive out younger widows with lesser status and fewer 'credits' within the family. However, the evidence indicates that survival and continuance of the family was paramount and that dispossessed widows could and did return to their natal families for support. Widows who were sent away were, it seems, often made to leave their children behind with their marital families, especially if the children were over seven years of age.[483]

Widows were not entirely powerless in these situations. Widows in rural areas who were interviewed in the WLSA inheritance research, asserted their rights by remaining and sitting, not passive sitting but sitting in the sense that they were pressuring their marital families to respect their entitlement to support, care and access to resources. They were able to use accumulated status[484] to protect or enforce their perceived entitlements (WLSA, 1995).[485]

Although this may continue to be the case for some widows in rural areas, the impact of colonization, the monetary economy, rural urban migration, education and changing socio-economic patterns have created a far more complex interrelationship within families and heightened intra-family expectations of what individuals should receive on the death of a family member. When estates or parts of estates of deceased males, to whom customary law would have been applicable, came to be administered as intestate estates, the potential for some kind of equity (in the sense of the protection and support that the deceased's family provided to widows and children) was obscured, if not negated, in the conceptual clash between customary processes and the imposed laws that sought to regulate and control rights in property.

[482contd] urban settings widows continue to benefit from protective interventions from their deceased husband's families (WLSA Zimbabwe, 1992).

[483] One might also question how totally dislocating this might have been, given that before horse-drawn or mechanical transport most couples would have married from within a relatively small geographical compass. The present day dislocations of parents from children who are living with distant family members would not have been present in most families. It is our speculation that mothers in such situations probably continued to see their children.

[484] For a discussion of how women build up status in their natal families see WLSA (1997a).

[485] Effectively interpreting the strategy of 'sitting' requires, as WLSA found as a regional collective, a not inconsiderable amount of insight. One country group dismissed this kind of action as passive and submissive. When the practice was described to the larger group and analyzed it emerged that it was probably not a passive act but one that was socially assertive and effective (Bentzon *et al*, 1998).

The map is muddled: How did we get here?

At the commencement of the colonial process in what was to become Zimbabwe, the principle for the governance of the indigenous population was as far as possible in civil matters, especially those related to family matters, to apply the customs and practices of the people themselves. Thus the British South Africa Company Charter provided:

> 'In the administration of justice to the said peoples or inhabitants, careful regard shall always be had to the customs and laws of the class or tribe or nation to which the parties respectively belong, especially with respect to the holding, possession, transfer and disposition of land and goods and testate or intestate succession thereto ...'

After the purported conquest of the country in 1893, the Matabeleland Order in Council of 1894 which set up the civil jurisdiction and administration in the country provided that:

> 'In civil cases between natives the High Court and magistrates shall be guided by native law so far as that law is not repugnant[486] to natural justice or morality ...'

The result being that if the issue arose before a court of law, the administration of a deceased estate of a member of the indigenous population would fall to be decided by his or her so-called native law – what is now referred to as customary law. The formal legal position was tightened in 1906 by an amendment to the Administration of Estates Ordinance which in section 69[487] provided that:

> '1 If any native who has contracted a marriage according to African law or custom or who being unmarried, is the offspring of parents married according to African law or custom, dies intestate, his estate shall be administered and distributed according to the customs and usages of the tribe or people to which he belonged.
>
> '2 In case any controversies or questions shall arise among his relatives or reputed relatives, regarding the distribution of the property left by him, such controversies or questions shall be determined in the speediest and least expensive manner consist-

---

[486] The repugnancy clause has since disappeared, but there is always a sense that its influence remains in place – but that is another debate.

[487] In the consolidated Statute of Zimbabwe Volume 1 of 1996 this section became section 68 of the Administration of Estates Act Chapter 6:01 as opposed to section 69. For ease of reference the section will be referred to as section 68. It is this section that was amended in 1997 to produce the main provisions of the Administration of Estates Amendment Act which conferred direct rights of inheritance in intestate succession on surviving spouses and all children of deceased persons to whom customary law would have been otherwise applicable.

ent with real and substantial justice according to native usages
and customs by the magistrate of the district in which the
deceased ordinarily resided at the time of his death, who shall
call and summon the parties before him, and take and record
evidence of such native usages and customs, which evidence he
may supplement from his own knowledge.'

Where an African couple had married according to civil rites, usually in
the form of a marriage within a Christian denomination, the law to be
applied to the intestate estate of such person was initially general law,
namely the provisions of the Deceased Estates Succession Act, which
treated all legitimate children equally in the case of a male deceased and
all children equally in the case of a female deceased.[488] This was to be a
short-lived entitlement as in 1917 the Native Marriage Ordinance,[489] as it
was then entitled, excluded the operation of the general law in such intestate estates, so that for the next 70 years in terms of what was to be
referred to as the infamous section 13 of that ordinance:

'Notwithstanding the fact that any natives have contracted a marriage
in accordance with the terms and provisions of the Marriage Ordinance in Council 1838 … such forms of marriage shall not affect the

---

[488] The received law in Zimbabwe, normally referred to as the general law by way of
distinguishing it from customary law, is of mixed Roman Dutch and English origin, derived from the law in operation at the Colony of the Cape of Good Hope on
10 June 1891. At that date the laws of intestate succession that were applied, and
came to be applied in what is now Zimbabwe, divided property of an intestate,
male or female, equally between his surviving legitimate children or her surviving children in the case of a female, or in the event of the predecease of any
legitimate child his or her legitimate descendents, per stirpes (by family branch).
A surviving spouse was not an heir in such an estate, being entitled by virtue of
community of property, to an automatic half share of the joint estate of the spouses.
This entitlement of the surviving spouse to an automatic half share of the property
in community was abolished by the Married Persons Property Act, 10/1928 that
came into effect on 1 January 1929. From that date couples who married under
civil law did so out of community of property unless they entered into an antenup-
tial contract to the effect that the marriage was to be in community of property,
thereby creating separate estates for husband and wife and at that time, most importantly, excluding the vesting of the marital power in the husband. Express provision was thereafter made in the Deceased Estates Succession Act which came
into force on 21 June 1929, that a surviving spouse would inherit a child's share or
a minimum specified amount, whichever was the greater, from the deceased
spouse's estate where the couple were married out of community of property. The
legitimate children, if any, each received in the case of a male, a child's share
while in the case of a female all her children received a child's share. There was
no notion of primogeniture, male and female children shared equally in the deceased estate, subject only to the requirement of legitimacy in relation to sharing
from a deceased father's estate.

[489] Over the years this ordinance mutated, predominantly with changes of name into
the African Marriages Act and the Customary Marriages Act.

property of the spouses, which shall be held, may be disposed of, and unless disposed of by will, shall devolve according to native law and custom.

Such a provision was not of itself inimical to the rights of widows or to female children, the issue was, what were their rights at so-called 'native law' or in terms of customs and practices (customary law) and how was such law or were such customs and practices ascertained? Perhaps, more pertinently, how were entitlements that women had to support, protection and access to resources, including land to farm, going to be translated into concepts to be applied by the state courts? As it transpired, in the translation process women's entitlements ceased to be recognized, only rights conferred on males survived the transmutation into the rights-based framework of the colonizers' understanding of legal entitlements.

At this point it is critical to note that the general law which stipulated how intestate succession was to take place, in what we would now call customary regimes, made no reference to the sex of beneficiaries or to restrictions on the number of beneficiaries there could be in an estate. The nature and form of the regulatory norms had to be determined, so it seems, on a case by case basis according to the customs and practices of the deceased's tribe or people to which he belonged.[490] It must be appreciated that the legislation also allowed the presiding magistrate to supplement the evidence put before him[491] from his own knowledge; this allowed over a period of time for a self-informing process within the judiciary at all levels to begin (WLSA, 1992).

The gateway for the determination of the content of customary law was left open by the criteria set out in the Administration of Estates Act but it was soon to be hidden from view in the confusion created by section 7 of the African Wills Act 13/1933[492] which sought primarily to control the testamentary capacity of an African to dispose freely of immovable property by will. Section 7 provides for the devolution of immovable property in the intestate estate of a deceased African (male) as follows:

'The heir at African law of any deceased African shall succeed in his

---

[490] No one seems to have considered at that point in time that women might have something to inherit, so the reference to his estate is a reflection of that state of affairs.

[491] At the time of introduction of the law it was a 'he' who dealt with the issue – a male magistrate – it is now very common to find female magistrates, they are becoming the backbone of the magisterial system in Zimbabwe.

[492] This Act was part of the land apportionment exercise which divided the then Southern Rhodesia into racially segregated areas.

individual capacity to any immovable property[493] or any rights attaching thereto forming part of the estate of such deceased African and not devised by will.'

Section 7 required the ascertaining of the heir at so-called African customary law. However, as pointed out earlier, there was no such universal heir but nonetheless the law had to be satisfied and thus the eldest son of a deceased African male came to be identified as the sole and universal heir to his father.[494] Although technically this section was only applicable to commercial land, it seems to have pervaded the overall process of determining who inherited in such estates. Pragmatism was gone and one heir had to be identified. The entitlements of other beneficiaries or dependants of the deceased were subsumed in the rights of a universal heir, an entity that did not exist at customary law.[495] What became especially problematic was the way in which the open framework in section 69 (now section 68) of the Administration of Estates Act for ascertaining the heir to movable property was restricted to the eldest son of the deceased.

The path becomes twisted and overgrown
The scene was now set for the evolution of a judicially created, static or ossified version of customs and practices which were increasingly dislocated, with a few short-lived divergences, from the day to day realities or needs of the people it was supposed to benefit.

Widows and other children of the deceased were now dependent on the largesse of this heir, such an heir could with impunity dispose of

---

[493] This is a reference to immovable property other than communal land, that is land within the commercial sphere.

[494] In a precursor of a similar judicial event, that of determining rights in a case that arose prior to a major change in the law, that took place at the end of the century in the infamous Magaya case, the High Court determined in 1935 in *Komo and Leboho v Holmes* 1935 SR 86 after the passage of the African Wills Act, that commercial landholdings by an African devolved according to the general law of intestate succession in terms of the Deceased Estates Succession Act. This would mean that a widow or widower and children of the deceased would have been entitled to share in the inheritance of such property. However, although that was the case for that family, in intestate estates which came into being after the date of the operation of the African Wills Act in 1933, the search had to be undertaken for the heir at African law.

[495] In *Matambo v Matambo* 1969 (3) SA 717, Beadle CJ remitted the matter back to a magistrate to specify the basis for determining the heir under customary law, however that was a brief respite in the relentless march towards a single heir in the form of the deceased's eldest son. In his judgement, Beadle CJ refers to the important role that the sister of a deceased male (*tete* in Shona) plays in determining who should be the successor to the deceased in relation to the family. This was a role that was overlooked in subsequent judicial determinations.

immovable property and use the movable property, including monies, as he saw fit.

There were occasional attempts to rein in this unfettered discretion but they were largely unsuccessful or at best paper victories. In *Masango v Masango* SC 66/86 Beck J found that the heir at customary law had support obligations to the family of the deceased person.[496] However, this decision never had the potential impact – that of restricting the unfettered rights of the heir at African law to do as he chose with the property he had inherited.[497] Arguably, by the mid-1980s the understanding of the right to inherit under customary law had been restricted to the eldest son of the deceased; and in such a fashion that he could do with the estate as he pleased. There were forays into the courts to try to extract more for widows and dependants of a deceased but these fell woefully short of providing adequate remedies for widows or female children of deceased males.[498]

In the clash of conceptual frameworks that occurred, between the colonizer's versions of law and that of the colonized, women and children have been the most profoundly affected victims. The colonizers' laws that stressed the individual overrode those of the colonized that focused on the group and the needs of the family, to produce a regime that favoured the colonizers control over and regulation of property rights

---

[496] This was an early classic example of turning back to customary law as a source of regulatory measures to improve the rights of women. Certainly, in teaching the law of inheritance to students, this was sold to them as a breakthrough remedy and recommended as a possible strategy to pursue in the struggle to improve the rights of widows and children.

[497] A phenomenon well illustrated by the case of *Seva v Dudza* 1992 (2) ZLR 34 (S) where the eldest son of the deceased who had had no contact with the family for a protracted period of time was appointed heir and inherited the immovable property which had been contributed to by the surviving wives. He subsequently sold the property and the widows and their children were faced with an eviction order from the new owner. The Supreme Court confirmed that he had every right to sell as the heir. The remnant family, the dependants of the deceased, might have sued him for maintenance or for provision of alternative accommodation but like most such heirs he was long gone with the proceeds.

[498] At the level of the magistrate's courts the remedy of using a spoliation order (order for the return of property removed from one's possession even if title was in doubt at the time of removal) was used as a way of reasserting control over property by a widow while the inheritance rights were formally determined. Lecturers often wonder how much attention is paid to their suggestions but this suggestion came back to haunt me (Julie Stewart) during the inheritance campaign when one of my former students got into a savage argument with someone about how to recover property removed from deceased estates. She stated that you had to use a spoliation order and dismissed references to using section 10 of the Deceased Person's Family Maintenance Act which had come into effect after she had graduated and become a magistrate herself.

on a broad scale (WLSA, Zimbabwe, 1992). The readily identifiable rights of males as those who had ostensible control of land within family structures were conveniently adopted and the entitlements of women obscured. Sole male heirs were imposed on the loose fabric of support and overall management of family interests that characterized their role under local customs and practices (WLSA, Zimbabwe, 1992; Stewart, 1998a and 1998b).

A side path – but an obscure one
The Deceased Persons Family Maintenance Act Chapter 6:03 which came into effect in 1978 provides a right to a dependant of a deceased person to make a claim for a share of the deceased estate where they have been deliberately excluded from sharing in the estate, are inadequately provided for from the estate or in an intestate succession where the intestate portion is inadequate for the needs of the claimant. The principles underlying the Act were compatible with the support and care elements of customary law and the legislation was carefully framed to be applicable to polygamous unions. It refers to 'a spouse' which is a specific recognition of the possibility that widows in a polygynous union may require maintenance from their joint husband's estate. The Act created the potential for maintenance claims to be made against estates but was severely under-used.

3   Paths are made by walking:[499] A viable path? Problems of use

Given the persistent lack of access of women to the estates of their male relatives in intestate estates falling under customary law and the (albeit erroneous) impression that women did not have inheritance rights, only at best an entitlement to support from the estate, other methods – creative legal arguments – were brought into play in the quest to find the appropriate vehicle to effect change.

The Legal Age of Majority Act was passed in 1982 and was an evident demonstration of the post-independence government's determination to grant equal status to both sexes. It seemed at the time to provide a potential cut through a variety of legal barriers which had negative implications for the status of women in terms of customary law. As feminist legal activists we saw this Act, even without constitutional change to repeal section 23 of the constitution, as having the potential to ameliorate the adverse applications of laws to African women who were re-

---

[499] This is an old Shona proverb and is frequently used to encourage local populations, women especially, to take up new initiatives.

garded as minors at law regardless of their age.

The Act[500] which gave majority status to everyone at the age of 18, was greeted with as much controversy as jubilation by different circles, given the customary law position where women in particular, as well as some men depending on social hierarchy, are generally considered minors. Customarily, women, for whom marriage consideration is paid, were seen as falling under the guardianship of the father before marriage and under that of their husband thereafter. However, the Legal Age of Majority Act is worded as being applicable to customary law:

> 'On and after the 10th of December 1982, a person shall attain the age of majority on attaining 18 years of age.

> 'A person who immediately before the 10th December 1982, has not attained the legal age of majority shall on that date attain the legal age of majority if he or she has then already attained eighteen years of age.'

Most importantly the Act reads that:

> 'Subsection (1) and (2) shall apply for the purpose of any law including customary laws and in the absence of a definition or any indication of a contrary intention the construction of "full age", "major", "majority", "minor", "minority" and similar expressions, any enactment, whether passed or made before, on or after the 10th December 1982, any deed, will or other instrument of whatever nature made on or after that date.'

The Legal Age of Majority Act seemed to give women a legal framework through which to channel their claims. The potential of the Act was first tested in the celebrated case of *Katekwe v Muchabaiwa*[501] in 1984. The issue for determination was whether a father of an eighteen-year old woman could, in the light of the Act, still claim seduction damages on her behalf. The Supreme Court held that he could not, as such a woman was now a major and could claim damages in her own name under general law if she so desired. Besides articulating the implications of the Act for African women, the case of *Katekwe v Muchabaiwa* served as the barometer for a contemporary outlook on customary law for at least fifteen years before the Supreme Court gave a different interpretation of the Act in 1999.

The potential of the Legal Age of Majority Act as a way of widows and children accessing resources was apparent and litigation on deceased

---

[500] The Legal Age of Majority Act No. 15 of 1982 which reduced the age of majority from 21 to 18 is now section 15 of the General Laws Amendment Act Chapter 8:07.

[501] *Katekwe v Muchabaiwa* 1984 (2) ZLR138(S).

estates took place. We analyze four cases, all heard by the Supreme Court, which track the initial attempts to use the Legal Age of Majority Act to secure inheritance rights for daughters and widows and how those gains were ultimately reversed as the judicial climate changed. Each one of the cases needed someone to initiate the litigation, most especially, it needed a woman who felt aggrieved by the way an estate was being distributed and who turned to the law for a solution.

Women prepared to walk the path
There are multiple factors that explain why people act in the ways they do. A crucial reality is that while people may generally endeavour to tailor their acts to suit the dominant beliefs in their society, they do not always conform. They are also willing and able to introduce change, particularly where their own self-interest is concerned, even if this means going against accepted norms. The reality for most widows in today's society is that they carry the burden of looking after their families, not just in the emotional and social sense but financially as well. With their heavy dependence on a monetary economy, the reluctance to see others reap where they did not sow explains why widows and daughters in the cases analyzed below showed a willingness to channel their claims through the law. They were encouraged by the changes in the law and society but also risked social and economic ostracism because of their daring.[502]

There will always be 'movers and shakers', even if they do not realize it, who are willing to give voice to their individual identities instead of being subsumed under those of the group. The cases were not brought by middle or upper middle class women with resources to seek legal advice and engage lawyers. Ordinary women, often living in the high-density areas, brought many of the claims to the courts. This also demonstrates the changing dynamics that were taking place among ordinary people, especially women.

There were parallel developments taking place that would help to promote new initiatives. The opening up of the legal profession at independence meant a considerable increase in the number of lawyers as well as the establishment of numerous non-governmental organizations disseminating legal information. There were many efforts to disseminate legal information, there were greater chances of the ordinary person knowing someone who knew something about the law and this is an important stage in engaging with the legal system. In an African context

---

[502] They were also, probably, inspired by the information dissemination campaigns by non-governmental organizations that advertised the new law and its potential.

where relatives abound and where success of a clan member is expected to be put to the benefit of the extended family, this social context can often come in handy. In one of the cases, the celebrated Magaya case, the fact that Venia Magaya, the woman who laid her claim to inherit, was distantly related through marriage to a lawyer who owned a legal practice and was willing to help an extended family member with her case, was crucial in getting her matter before the courts in the initial instance.

Women were prepared to challenge a cross-section of men over inheritance rights. From a feminist and a human rights standpoint, this is a significant move, at least for some women, passivity and acceptance were eschewed. Challenges were made against a grandfather, a son, a brother-in-law, a full brother as well as a half brother.

While by no means uniform or unitary, a discernible trend from the four cases is the general willingness by the lower courts to take cognisance and give expression to changes in customary practices that are taking place on the ground. In so far as magistrate's courts are often staffed by magistrates who have studied law at a time when gender issues are an integral part of some law courses, this difference in perspective also points to the significance of exposure of the judiciary to grounded realities and human rights concepts if change and legal development is to take place through the courts (WLSA Zimbabwe, 1992).

Going round in circles: An analysis of the cases
The first inheritance case to come before the courts capitalizing on the Legal Age of Majority Act was that of *Chihowa v Mangwende*[503] in 1987. The deceased had no children with his surviving wife but had two daughters from a previous union. The dispute as to who should inherit was between the father of the deceased, Leonard Chihowa and the deceased's eldest surviving daughter, Auxillia Mangwende. A divorcee, Auxillia had gone back to live with her father and had helped him in his business. When it became apparent that her father's estate had been distributed without her involvement, she brought her case before the community court[504] to be appointed as heir. Her claim in the community court, with customary law jurisdiction, was successful in that the court appointed

---

[503] *Chihowa v Mangwende* 1987 (1) ZLR 228 SC.
[504] Community courts soon after independence were then responsible for matters involving customary law. They were presided over by presiding officers, whereas chiefs ran village courts. Community courts had jurisdiction in inheritance matters involving customary law. An appeal from the community court lay with the magistrate's court, acting as a district court, and from there directly to the Supreme Court. The courts were restructured by the Customary Law and Local Courts Act Chapter 7:05 of 1990. The present court hierarchy is that the headmen's courts

her as heir. The grandfather then appealed from the community court to the provincial magistrate's court. Like the community court, the provincial magistrate's court dismissed the appeal on the grounds that the Legal Age of Majority Act altered the previous incapacity of African women to be declared as heirs. Leonard Chihowa further appealed to the Supreme Court where his appeal was once again dismissed on the grounds that African women were now majors and that this capacity entitled them to be appointed intestate heiresses. However, the then Chief Justice, Enock Dumbutshena, emphasized in his judgement that, like the male heir, the eldest daughter inherits not only for herself but on behalf of the deceased dependants and consequently has the same duties and obligations towards them in accordance with African laws and customs.[505] More significantly, the court relied on the wording of the Legal Age of Majority Act that made it applicable for 'the purpose of any law including customary law....'.

His decision was also influenced by the acknowledgement that:

> '...traditional anchors and obligations of African society have broken down and are being intentionally abused by those who want to derive benefit from the old situation' (page 233 of the judgment).

In the Chihowa case, all three courts, the community court, the magistrate's court and the Supreme Court[506] were in agreement that times had changed and that there was no reason whatsoever to continue with a limited, narrow interpretation of customary law if customary practices on the ground and through legislative expression, were clearly contributing to its re-interpretation.

The increasing emphasis on women's human rights, supported by a progressive judiciary across the board, led to a decision that no doubt added voice and visibility to the changes that were inevitably taking place in people's lived realities, especially regarding the contributory roles that women play in today's society as far as the acquisition and

---

[504contd] are at the lowest level of the hierarchy followed by the chief's courts. They do not have any jurisdiction in inheritance matters and a range of family law issues such as dissolution of registered marriages, custody and guardianship, to mention a few.

[505] He was invoking the principles enunciated in *Masango v Masango*, already discussed. The learned Chief Justice also referred to articles that had been written on the Legal Age of Majority Act and it was the same team and advisors that formulated the arguments, this time for the plaintiff, who had developed the use of the Act in *Katekwe v Muchabaiwa*.

[506] Arguably section 69 of the Administration of Estates Act gave the courts the power to ascertain what the customs and practices of the deceased's 'tribal' group were at the time of his death, although the emphasis in these cases was on the opportunities presented by the Legal Age of Majority Act.

maintenance of family property is concerned. By allowing Auxillia Mangwende, a divorced woman who had gone back to her family, to be appointed as heir to her father's estate, there was a clear acknowledgement, at least from the court and from women such as Auxillia herself who had brought her claim, that women no longer needed to see their lot in marriage or regard themselves as transient within their own natal families.

Yet the inherent tensions and incipient resistance emanating from legislative changes that sought to alter inequitable accesses to resources, whether gender or race based, as evidenced by resistance and counterclaims, were lurking on the horizon ready to pounce on the unwitting. Following the Supreme Court's acknowledgement that girl children could be appointed as heirs, it was not long before cases, such as *Vareta v Vareta*[507] and *Antonio v Antonio,*[508] added the rejoinder that if there is a younger son in existence, even where a daughter is older, then the son should be preferred in the appointment as heir and that this aspect was not affected by the Legal Age of Majority Act.

In the second major inheritance case for analysis, that of *Murisa v Murisa,*[509] *the* issue was whether James, a son whom the deceased was purported to have had prior to his marriage and whom the widow only got to know about after the death of her husband,[510] was entitled to inherit. This was against a claim by the widow who had two sons from her marriage to the deceased during his lifetime. The deceased's brother represented the interests of James. The traditional cleansing ceremony carried out approximately a year after a deceased's death and not part of any court process, had appointed Lloyd, the widow's son, as the heir to his late father's estate.[511]

However, the community court had a few weeks earlier appointed James as the deceased's heir, and the deceased's brother as guardian. The widow appealed to the provincial magistrate's court against the community court's decision and succeeded not only in reversing the decision but also in being appointed heir to her late husband's estate. Presumably, unable to have her own son appointed by the court by virtue of his not being the eldest son, the alternative was to endeavour to be ap-

---

[507] *Vareta v Vareta & Ors* 1992 (2) ZLR 1 (H).

[508] *Antonio v Antonio* 1991 (2) ZLR 42 SC.

[509] *Murisa v Murisa* 1992 (1) ZLR 167 (S).

[510] Widows, appearing out of the proverbial woodwork, or, in the African context, the long grass, is a disturbingly common occurrence in Zimbabwean society and there is a good deal of strategizing that takes place using such widows and their children to secure inheritance entitlements. There is also the practice of 'keeping up appearances' on the part of men that they are in monogamous marriages.

[511] For a further discussion of the cleansing ceremony and its significance see WLSA (1992).

pointed heiress herself. In that way she could look after her children. At this level she succeeded.

An appeal was launched on the grounds that the provincial magistrate had misinterpreted the provisions of customary law regarding a widow's right to inherit. It was argued that the important role of the magistrate, to call the parties and summon evidence in determining the true position of customary law in cases where there are disputes involving who is heir under customary law, had not been performed.[512] While acknowledging the progressive reasoning in the Chihowa case regarding the effect of the Legal Age of Majority Act and its impact on women's status, Judge Ebrahim, who gave the main judgement in this case, found that the judgement did not go as far as to say that a widow could inherit from her husband's estate. He found that given the general perception that a widow is an outsider; the magistrate had misdirected herself in the appointment of the widow as heir. He found that the magistrate had largely focused on 'who would be suited to administer the estate on behalf of the deceased's children', rather than who was heir.[513]

It was argued that the contest for heirship was really between the deceased's son James from his prior union, and his other son Lloyd, whom he had during his marriage. The widow's entitlement to inherit was dismissed and the matter was referred back for a fuller determination of the status of the son, James. It was held that the Legal Age of Majority Act did not extend to according widows the right to inherit. The case ominously heralded and openly paved the way for other narrower interpretations of who qualifies as an heir, and continued to obscure the open framework for determining how an estate could be distributed in terms of section 68 of the Administration of Estates Act. It also starkly revealed that legislative innovation is one thing, legislative interpretation clearly another, but perhaps equally starkly, how the battle for control of resources can be interpreted in ways that continuously seek to exclude rather than to integrate.

---

[512] This role was in terms of the then operational Act governing administration of customary law estates, namely section 68(2) of the Administration of Estates Amendment Act Chapter 6:01 which has since been amended by the Administration of Estates Amendment Act No. 6 of 1997 for deaths which occurred after the 1 of November 1997.

[513] Arguably, looking for a responsible person to administer the estate would be consistent with the provisions of section 68 of the Administration of Estates Act and in accordance with the customs and practices of the people or tribe to whom the deceased belonged but the appeal was not argued on that basis. One might also take the view that this was a pragmatic approach from the female magistrate, who was taking a grounded approach and framing it within an ethic of care that is often associated with women.

Going backwards rapidly: *Mwazozo v Mwazozo*

If Zimbabwean women under customary law had turned a major corner with the decision in *Chihowa v Mangwende* and had then been steered into a somewhat narrower lane with the decision in the case of Murisa, the third case for analysis, *Mwazozo v Mwazozo,*[514] clearly heralded even more dangers ahead for women, in the sense that the road they were now on was not only constricted but dangerously bumpy as well. With an altered Supreme Court bench, it was becoming increasingly clear that there was no guarantee that women would remain on this path unswerved.

In Mwazozo's case, the two claimants to the intestate estate were both legitimate children of the deceased. The matter had been referred to the district court[515] from the community court because of a dispute in the appointment of an heir. The male child, Watson Mwazozo, argued that he should be appointed heir by virtue of being a son. Beauty Mwazozo, the female child and elder of the two, argued that she should be appointed as heir by virtue of the Legal Age of Majority Act which had emancipated women. The magistrate's court was in agreement with her claim on the basis that the spirit of the Act was to allow women to enjoy the full benefits of their majority status. The magistrate found that the case of *Vareta v Vareta* merely expressed a preference for the appointment of a male child rather than a hard and fast rule. Both children were acknowledged to be fit and proper persons to inherit in both a moral and physical sense. It was in this light that the magistrate appointed the girl child, as the eldest, heir to the estate and that the deceased's son, Watson, appealed to the Supreme Court.

Whereas in the seminal case of *Chihowa v Mangwende* the court gave precedence to the need to accord full effect to the intention of the legislature and also to give centre stage to the changing practices of the people and the need to equalize the playing field for women, the Supreme Court's approach in the Mwazozo case was to play the 'customary law as sacrosanct' card. This it did by emphasizing the historical origins and patrilineal nature of inheritance amongst the Shona tribe to which the deceased belonged. At the core of the court's reasoning was that under patrilineal systems such as those of the Shona, male children inherit and not female children. The respondent, Beauty, couched her argument on the basis that the Legal Age of Majority Act gave a new meaning to the status of women and opened new possibilities as a result of this new legal status, amongst which was the possibility to inherit.

---

[514] *Mwazozo v Mwazozo* S 121-94.

[515] During the period when community courts were responsible for the administration of such deceased estates, any dispute was referred under the provisions of section 69 of the Administration of Estates Act to the magistrate's court functioning as a district court.

Justice Muchechetere, who wrote the majority judgement, found that the Legal Age of Majority Act did not alter the customary law of succession since the exclusion of women had nothing to do with their minority status but with the fact that succession is traced through patrilineal lines. As such a man's property is supposed to benefit his lineage and while women perpetuate lineages by giving birth to children, they are not part of their husband's lineage. As Justice Muchechetere put it:

> '...to permit them to inherit would be tantamount to diverting patrilineal wealth to strangers, that is sons in law's families. ... in the circumstances to permit daughters to inherit their father's estates in preference to the male child would do violence to the patrilineal nature of society.'[516]

He found that the concepts of majority and minority were part of the common law and had no real meaning under customary law.[517] The remedy, as the judge saw it, was for parliament to enact legislation addressing the whole issue of succession and inheritance in Zimbabwe. It could be argued that while legislative change serves to make definitive pronouncements, if the expectation was that parliament would and should pass a law giving widows and girl children rights to inherit in the light of changed societal circumstances, there was nothing inherently wrong in the courts passing judgements which accorded existing legislation, such as the Legal Age of Majority Act, a positive interpretation which was in line with modern cultural development.[518] This was precisely what the lower courts had consistently sought to do. In Chihowa's case there was a positive interpretation of the Legal Age of Majority Act by both the lower courts and the higher court. In Murisa and Mwazozo at the level of the magistrate's court a progressive interpretation of customary law by recognizing women's claims to inherit was employed. But in both cases, the Supreme Court reversed these progressive, lower court level determinations.

---

[516] See pages 4 and 5 of the judgement.

[517] It was argued by the counsel for the respondent and by Professor Welshman Ncube who was requested to act as *amicus curiae* (friend of the court to deal with key issues) that local customs and practices now recognized women's rights to inherit, the submissions that were made were based on the WLSA research work and other investigations into customary practices. Muchechetere JA informing himself, we assume, in terms of section 68 of the Administration of Estates Act and indirectly informed no doubt by the provisions of the Customary Wills Act (as the African Wills Act had by then become), reverted to male primogeniture and a very constricted interpretation of customary inheritance practices.

[518] Ncube as *amicus curiae* raised the interpretative possibility of using international conventions such as CEDAW to deal with discriminatory laws; this was brushed aside, being given virtually no recognition.

Losing the path

The case which finally veered Zimbabwean women off their progressive path in their attempts at using the Legal Age of Majority Act to gain inheritance rights is the case of *Magaya v Magaya*.[519] The case came before the Supreme Court after the law introducing radical changes in favour of women and children in inheritance under customary law had already been passed.[520] However, the death leading to the dispute had occurred prior to the operative date of the new legislation which was the 1 November 1997, so the matter proceeded. There was a genuinely high hope that the re-visioning of customary law would hold the day or, at the very least, that the Zimbabwean obligation to implement CEDAW would be invoked. As activists we were to be profoundly disappointed (nay, shattered) at the outcome of the case. Our only solace was that the law had already been changed but the long-term implications on the stability of change to benefit women still stalks our work as there is still political resistance to any amendment of section 23 of the constitution.[521]

The dispute in *Magaya v Magaya* was between two half siblings and, as in *Mwazozo v Mwazozo*, centred on who had a better claim, the older female child or the younger male child. Judge Muchechetere, as in the Mwazozo case, rejected the female child's claim on virtually the same basis; namely the patrilineal nature of our society and the transient nature of girl children within their own families. The judge found that the Legal Age of Majority Act had been interpreted too widely and that it had been wrongly decided in previous cases in that it conferred a right on women that they could not have had under customary law. He particularly relied on the explicit protection accorded to customary law by the constitution in matters such as adoption, marriage, divorce, burial, devolution of property on death and other matters of customary law. Moreover, as he pointed out, the Legal Age of Majority Act explicitly stated that it was to be interpreted subject to any legislation in force impacting on customary law. The constitution was clearly one such piece of legislation. Also, although there was a new law in place, the case in point was not covered by the new law. This narrower interpretation given

---

[519] *Magaya v Magaya* 1999 (1) ZLR 100 (S).

[520] The case had previously been heard by a district court magistrate on appeal from the community court. In the district court the presiding judge found in favour of Venia as had the community court. Interestingly, the district court magistrate had been one of the first participants on the Diploma in Women's Law first mounted at the University of Oslo in 1988 (now run at the Southern and Eastern Regional Centre for Women's Law at the University of Zimbabwe and elevated to Masters level).

[521] However, there has been a constant process of government at least reviewing laws that affect women adversely but not the key section in the constitution which remains as a permanent threat to women's rights.

to the application of the Legal Age of Majority Act, as having no bearing on the content of customary law matters, had clearly set women back. What this case shows is that arguments, whether progressive or retrogressive, can be effectively clothed in legality and appear convincing either way. Given this reality that judges also make law and that change is constant, it would seem prudent for them to take a path that seeks to achieve social justice rather than that which actively seeks to hinder it. Certainly the decision created a major local and international furore. Venia Magaya became an overnight heroine of the women's movement in Zimbabwe.[522] The sting in the judgement at the wider level was alleviated by the existence of the Administration of Estates Amendment Act which recognized the right of widows and other females to inherit under customary succession regimes.[523]

4   Almost the end of the path: The new legislation

As we pointed out in the introduction to this chapter, the women's protocol is explicit in terms of the rights that it accords widows. A significant issue arising from this is to what extent the Administration of Estates Amendment Act of 1997, which introduced significant changes to the administration of property in intestate customary law estates, is in consonance in letter and spirit, with the human rights standards articulated in various international human rights instruments, including the Protocol to the African Charter.[524] Granted, the Administration of Estates Amendment Act predates the explicit provisions of the protocol. However, at the time that the legislation was formulated, Zimbabwe was already party to human rights instruments such as CEDAW[525] that also articulate the expected human rights standards in addressing women's inequality. As we pointed out, articles 2(f) and article 16 of CEDAW give

---

[522] For a detailed discussion of the case and its background see WLSA Zimbabwe (2001).

[523] What was especially disturbing was that the judge chose not to point out in the judgement that parliament had passed the Administration of Estates Amendment Act which gave women and girls the right to inherit from their male relatives and that it was already in operation. This failure, which we hope was an oversight, created confusion in the minds of the public when the case was reported in the media, as the impression was created that women had now lost their inheritance rights.

[524] The Act came into effect on 1 November 1997, my (Julie Stewart's) 50th birthday. I still vividly remember seeing the newspaper headlines that morning announcing that the new law was now in force. It was literally the best birthday present I had ever received it could only be bettered by further improvements in the rights of women and girls to inherit.

[525] Zimbabwe signed CEDAW in May 1991.

a clear indication of the need to do away with discriminatory legislation as well as the need to introduce equality in marriage and family life.

While the Act recognizes the right of the heir to inherit the deceased's name and traditional items that normally pass on to the heir in line with certain customs and practices,[526] it clearly introduces far-reaching provisions that have significant implications for the rights of widows and daughters to inherit. In terms of the Amendment Act, the primary beneficiaries to a deceased's estate are the surviving spouse or spouses and the children of the deceased, regardless of sex. While dependants are recognized in terms of their right to support or to inherit where the deceased has not left any immediate family, of significance is the priority accorded to the deceased's more immediate family.

As part of what might be regarded as an incremental approach to the introduction of change, the Act also makes provision for the drawing up of an inheritance plan by the executor, which states how the estate is to be distributed.[527] The Master is supposed to ensure that the plan has the consensus of beneficiaries and that it is basically equitable. What the use of the plan allows is greater flexibility in distribution beyond the general guidelines, set out below, should there be a need to do so.

The Act gives priority to the surviving spouse as executor of the estate and, as such, widows, at least theoretically, have some measure of control in drawing up the plan. Whether in practice such plans are being drawn up is an issue that would need to be researched. Another issue is whether the plans are being allowed to retain the fluidity that was envisaged by the Act or whether the guidelines that are stipulated as applicable in cases of dispute are being treated as a hard and fast rule.

The provisions that impact favourably on women and daughters are to be found in the Act's guidelines as to how the estate should ideally be distributed or the form of disposition that should take place if there is no consensus. In such instances, much depends on the nature of marriage that the deceased had during his lifetime. In a monogamous marriage or in instances where the deceased is survived by one wife and one or more children, the formulation for distributing the estate is fairly straightforward and generally mirrors the provisions that govern distribution under general law. The surviving spouse gets ownership or usufruct over the house in addition to all the household goods in that house. The surviving spouse also gets to share in the remainder of the state together with the children, in line with the stipulated legal proportions that govern intestate estates under general law.[528] To the extent that the Act makes these

---

[526] This is provided for in terms of section 68C of the Act.
[527] See section 68D of the Act.
[528] See section 68F(2)(d) of the Act.

provisions that are further bolstered by the potential use of the Deceased Persons Family Maintenance Act where necessary, it certainly introduces far-reaching measures of equality in monogamous marriages in line with human rights standards.

However, the complications as far as human rights standards of equality are concerned arise in relation to the continued recognition of polygamous marriages.[529] The Administration of Estates Amendment Act rightly recognizes the need for widows and children in such marriages to inherit from the deceased's estate. Thus in terms of the Act, where a man has left more than one wife, then each wife is expected to continue residing in the house she was living in during her marriage and she is also entitled to the household goods in that house. The inheritance of the house or at the very least the right to a lifetime usufruct over all or part of the house by the surviving spouse or spouses clearly makes a lot of difference to the lives of women who have the burden of looking after the family.

In the distribution of the remainder of the estate, the surviving spouses get to share a third of the estate in the proportion of two shares to the first or senior wife, and one share to the other wives.[530] Needless to say, this formulation can cause disputes especially where the younger wife or wives may feel that they contributed more to the estate than the first wife. But what really complicates the picture is that, in reality, a woman may only get to know of the deceased's other wife or wives after his death, even if his own family were privy to his additional marriage. In a bid to prevent hardship falling on the spouse and children in polygamous marriages, the Act recognizes and condones the mixing of monogamous and polygamous unions for purposes of inheritance. As such, a woman who all along may have thought she had a safe monogamous marriage may be surprised after her husband has died that he had contracted another customary marriage and that such a marriage is recognized for the purpose of inheritance. Even a registered monogamous marriage may be treated as a customary marriage for the purposes of inheritance if it is established that the deceased already had a customary law union, albeit unregistered, at the time of his civil marriage.[531]

---

[529] See the following chapter where Tsanga cites what transpired in the South African constitutional case of *Bhe and others v Magistrate, Khayelitsha and others* CCT 49/03 which sought to challenge the exclusionary nature of customary inheritance law.

[530] See Section 68F(b)(2) of the Act.

[531] One key observation from the WLSA Zimbabwe inheritance research was that without polygamy it would be much easier to reform the law of inheritance and provide at least paper equality to men and women and boys and girls in inheritance matters, but polygamy is still with us and we have to think creatively and daringly as to how to deal with the problems it creates.

It could be argued that fewer disputes would arise if the Act had taken a clear standpoint against polygamy but then that would have resulted in hardship for beneficiaries in such unions. At the same time, the continued recognition of polygamy pits women against each other in ways that often force them to engage in humiliating court battles in an effort to assert their rights and to pull together the pieces that result from a man's polygamous marriage, after he has safely departed from the scene. Often as a result of polygamy, there is also fractionalization of limited resources, generally leaving the family worse off, both in terms of material resources and through soured relations.

A clear indication of the unequal nature of polygamy is that where a man is the survivor in such a marriage, he is entitled to inherit a third from the estate of each wife who has predeceased him, the remainder of the estate going to the woman's children.[532] It could be argued that since the Act does not mention his inheriting the house, there is a measure of equity. However, the reality is often that immovable property is registered in the man's name and so he gets to keep what is his. As a result of polygamous marriages, we are at best talking of the Act having achieved partial, as opposed to real equality in relation to customary law based marriages and unions. The failure to meet human rights more fully is also complicated by the Amendment Act not applying to estates where the death occurred before the 1 November 1997. As illustrated with the Magaya case, this can cause hardship, especially where the old law in uncritically applied.

Advertising the law

Finally, we touch briefly on the activism that was put in place in terms of making the Act known after it was passed. In 2001 a concerted, nationwide campaign, sponsored by DFID and based on a multimedia and multi-disciplinary approach to information dissemination, was initiated. Use was made of radio, television, written materials as well as oral discussions to raise people's awareness of the law. The campaign also brought together community leaders, law enforcement agencies, lawyers, social scientists and media experts. It further drew on the research that had preceded the passing of the Act, as well as lessons from the film *Neria*. It is beyond the scope of this chapter to detail the lessons emerging from the campaign.[533] However, suffice it to say that one of the key emerging lessons is the significance of monitoring and evaluating law reform campaigns in terms of their efficacy and impact and keeping a

---

[532] See Section 68F (2)(e).

[533] The activism and the nationwide advertising campaign that took place to market the new law will be described and discussed in the next volume in this series.

close eye on the need for reform, whether in the form of amending the law or reforming administrative processes. The spirit and the messages from that campaign have been kept alive by the non-governmental organization community and the Master's Office. That is a story for the next book.

Conclusion

This was a long walk, and at times a difficult one, and it has not yet been completed. It required and it will require consistent activism and a determination to ensure that widows and children obtain the right to inherit from their male relatives. What is especially interesting for others who might want to follow the same route is the overwhelming importance of doing the background research that establishes what the customs and practices are on the ground – one should use every possible legal and political angle to make the case for the rights of women, even under customary law. Most importantly, it must be realized that the versions of the nature and form of customary law as recorded and decided by the superior courts should not be treated as definitive. Even when rebuffed by the courts, intellectual forces should be regrouped and the battle rejoined. If the opportunity were to arise again, in regard to an intestate testate where the deceased died before 1 November 1997, we would urge litigation that revisited the Magaya decision.[67]

Bibliography

Bentzon A. W., A. Hellum, J. Stewart, W. Ncube and T. Agersnap (1998) *Pursuing grounded theory in law: South-North experiences in developing women's law*, Mond Books and Tano Aschehoug, Harare and Oslo.

Dengu-Zvobgo K., W. Donzwa, E. Gwaunza, J. Kazembe, W. Ncube, J. Stewart (1994) *Inheritance in Zimbabwe: Law, customs and practice*, WLSA, Harare 1994, (second edition WLSA, 1995).

Himonga C. (1995) *Family and succession law in Zambia*, Harper Collins Canada, Westview.

Stewart J. E. (1998) 'Why I can't teach customary law', in J. Eekelaar and T. Nhlapo (eds) *The changing family: Family forms and family law*, Hart Publishing, Oxford, also (1997) in *Zimbabwe Law Review*, Vol. 14.
– (1998) 'Rights, rights, rights: Women's rights', in P. Blume, and K. Ketscher (eds) *Ret og skonsomhed i en overganstid*, Akademisk Forlag, Copenhagen.

WLSA (1997a) *Continuity and change: The family in Zimbabwe*, WLSA Harare>

WLSA (1997b) *Paradigms of exclusion: Women's access to resources in Zimbabwe*, WLSA, Harare.

List of cases

Antonio v Antonio 1991 (2) ZLR 42 (S)

Bhe and others v Magistrate, Khayelitsha and others CCT 49/03

Chihowa v Mangwende 1987 (1) ZLR 228 (S)

Katekwe v Muchabaiwa 1984 (2) ZLR 136 (S)

Komo and Leboho v Holmes 1935 SR 86

Magaya v Magaya 1999 (1) ZLR 100 (S)

Masango v Masango SC 66 -86 unreported

Matambo v Matambo 1969 (3) SA 717

Murisa v Murisa 1992 (1) ZLR 167 (S)

Mwazozo v Mwazozo SC 121-94 (unreported)

Seva v Dzuda 1992 (2) ZLR 34 (S)

Vareta v Vareta & Ors 1992 (2) ZLR 1 (H)

List of legislation

Zimbabwe

Administration of Estates Act Chapter 6:01

Administration of Estates Amendment Act No. 6 /1997

African Marriages Act

African Wills Act 13/1933

Amendment to the Administration of Estates Ordinance 1906

British South Africa Company Charter

Customary Marriages Act

Customary Law and Local Courts Act Chapter 7:05 of 1990

Customary Wills Act

Deceased Estates Succession Act

Deceased Persons Family Maintenance Act Chapter 6:03

General Laws Amendment Act Chapter 8:07

Legal Age of Majority Act No. 15 of 1982, now General Laws Amendment Act Chapter 8:07

Married Persons Property Act, 10/1928

Native Marriage Ordinance 1917

Regional and international

Convention on the Elimination of All Forms of Discrimination against Women (CEDAW) 1979

Protocol to the African Charter on Human and Peoples' Rights on the Rights of Women in Africa 2003

17

Reconceptualizing the role of legal information dissemination in the context of legal pluralism in African settings

Amy S. Tsanga

This chapter focuses on the challenges confronting those seeking to implement legal information dissemination programmes within plural legal settings. While cognisant of the multiplicity of interdependent factors that contribute to an effective communication strategy, for example, the nature of the communication framework as well as the ideological framework adopted by those disseminating information, the significance of gender and age dynamics, and the crucial role of the intermediaries used, this chapter regards legal pluralism as positing specific challenges that merit a more detailed analysis. This is particularly so at a time when, in spite of globalization and its contribution towards building interlocking bridges, non-western societies are engaged in a process of asserting their cultural identities as opposed to simply fashioning themselves to suit the cloth that other people may have cut with their own societal dimensions in mind.

1   Introduction

The focus of this chapter on reconceptualizing the role of legal information dissemination suggests that there are lessons to be learnt from ongoing practices. That is the case given that two or more decades have passed since the concept of popularizing the law to the masses became a serious focus of many African non-governmental organizations. Some were set up specifically for the purpose while other existing ones redefined their focus to take into account dominant concerns with making justice accessible to ordinary people.

Due to limited state initiatives in popularizing the law, the emphasis by non-governmental organizations has often been on training community-based people to disseminate different aspects of state law that are regarded as impacting on people's lives. A study[534] commissioned by the

---

[534] The study was conducted by Tsanga, Johnson and Sogo (1996). 20 countries were covered in the review, including Benin, Botswana, Burkina Faso, Cameroon, Ethiopia, Ghana, Kenya, Mall, Lesotho, Malawi, Mozambique, Namibia, Nigeria, Senegal, Swaziland, Tanzania, Togo, Uganda, Zambia and Zimbabwe.

International Commission of Jurists and the Legal Resources Foundation on organizations providing legal services unearthed three primary strategies that organizations often employ in providing legal services. These include training, community legal education and giving legal advice. The training targets community-based intermediaries who then carry out broad-based legal education campaigns in their communities. Legal advice is rendered through legal aid centres staffed by paralegals. The study also revealed a broad range of issues that non-governmental organizations generally focus on in their awareness campaigns and these include: family law matters such as maintenance, divorce, marriage, inheritance and custody; abuses such as gender violence and child abuse; property laws; the court structures and court processes; as well as constitutional and human rights matters. A considerable number of these non-governmental organizations therefore focus on various aspects of women's rights.

Of importance is the similarity in the contexts in which non-governmental organizations carry out their work. Most operate in a context of legal pluralism. Generally the three bodies of law that have shaped African legal systems most include western law as a direct result of colonial influence, customary law and Islamic law (Bryde, 1976). While the legal systems of some countries reflect the influence of all three systems, in some countries the competing mix is between western law and customary law and in others it is between Islamic law and western law. In a few instances in North Africa, Islamic law alone has become paramount due to perceptions that both western law and Christianity have been negative influences on Islam. The picture is complicated further where Africans, despite embracing Islam, remain strongly tied to their own traditional practices (Moyo, 2001: 299–329).

So the lack of familiarity with the state system, which is often the law of the land in former colonies, does not mean that people are not familiar with any justice system at all. Most countries have competing legal systems by incidence of history, the majority of the population – both men and women – are often not as aware of their legal rights under received law as they are of the system that is closest to their personal lives.

The received law as modified by statute and case law in most former colonies, particularly in sub-Saharan Africa, provides the overall backbone of the legal system. For some people the resultant pluralism presents competing values from which they can draw but in reality few people are as familiar with the received law as they are with their own indigenous justice systems. Local systems remain alive and well, particularly in rural areas, and in some cases continue to play a more significant role in people's lives than state law. Also, while rural–urban migration is a phenomenon of our times, people more often than not carry their values with them into the towns with the result that they are often caught between competing systems or freely straddle the two as a matter of choice and expediency. People may also be unaware of how state laws and state systems operate due to factors such as distance to courts or the sheer unavailability of state infrastructure in remote rural areas. It is also a reality that a considerable number of people, if not the majority, tend to solve their problems outside official court processes (Bidaguren and Estrella, 2002). There is also the crucial though controversial issue (from a gender perspective) of the role played by the family, particularly in resolving matrimonial disputes.

In Africa, besides the influence of Islamic laws, people draw from Christian values in solving disputes. Religious leaders often play a significant role in fostering social harmony and sometimes in preventing disputes from reaching the courts. As such their role should not be neglected in programmes that seek to disseminate information about possible solutions to disputes. In discussing the role of religion in Africa, Moyo notes that religious leaders in Africa also include spirit mediums and diviners (2001:307). The latter often communicate with the spirit world in times of calamity to seek possible solutions.

From my grounded experience in carrying out legal literacy,[535] I argue that, despite the phenomenal efforts at raising people's awareness of their rights in an effort to promote access to justice, the approach that has often been adopted by the dominant players has been short-sighted, if not flawed. They have focused largely on state law as a point of departure, both in terms of content and solutions within a context of legal pluralism.

I argue that the prevalent trend of engaging with the reality of legal pluralism from the periphery, in terms of content, solutions and vision for the future, has often generated resistance in the form of cultural protectionism. More significantly, as a result of cultural defensiveness, crucial issues stemming from gendered power relations as well as cultural and customary practices that no longer fit the dictates of modern societies, have tended to be clouded if not sacrificed at the altar of cultural protectionism.

I further argue that given that the reason behind communication is often to effect some behavioural change, desired outcomes cannot be

---

[535] I worked with a non-governmental organization, the Legal Resources Foundation from 1988–1993 before joining the university. My work experience there was the basis of carrying out a more detailed study on community legal education published as *Taking law to the people: Gender law reform and community legal education in Zimbabwe* (2003).

divorced from contextual realities. This means coming up with strategies that are alive to the potential that can be harnessed from making use of customary or religious laws as well as the limits of so doing.

In projecting these arguments, the chapter is divided into four main parts. This first part has outlined the broad background to the chapter. In the second part, accepting that knowledge of laws is a central aim of legal information dissemination campaigns, I address emerging challenges of disseminating information on gender-related topics from a 'know your rights' approach in a plural legal setting. This approach constituted the first wave in legal information dissemination programmes. I argue that while lessons have been learnt about the futility of a rights-only approach for empowering women within the context of pluralism, these lessons boil down to the need to engage more fully with feminist ideology and jurisprudence in its various forms in designing legal information dissemination programmes.

In the third part, I take the use of legal knowledge acquired as another central aim of legal information dissemination campaigns. I then illustrate how treating the reality of legal pluralism as secondary has all too often resulted in projecting remedies that may not be as effective as those which consciously seek to locate themselves within the context of pluralism.

In the fourth part, I address the issue of long-term behavioural change as a core aim of legal information dissemination programmes and how this makes it necessary for programmes to draw persuasive strength from ideological foundations as well as human struggles that are likely to strike a chord with the target group. I then make some concluding remarks in terms of long-term strategies in ensuring that we produce lawyers in particular who are able to work effectively within a context of legal pluralism.

2 Challenges in addressing women's rights in plural legal settings

A call for engagement with feminist ideology

How to engage in an effective and meaningful dialogue on women's rights in a pluralist legal setting is one of the central issues that needs to be reconceptualized by those implementing legal information dissemination programmes. Most of the non-governmental organizations engaged in legal information dissemination have tended to focus on women's rights because of the comparative disadvantages women face. Examples of such organizations include FIDA Uganda, FIDA Ghana, FIDA Kenya and the Zimbabwe Women Lawyer's Association, to mention a few. There are also other legal rights organizations that cover legal rights issues in general but include women in their mandate. Examples of these include Kituo Cha Sheria in Kenya, the Legal Resources Foundation in Zimbabwe, the Legal Resource Centre in Namibia and Ditshwanelo in Botswana, again to mention a few.

In analyzing the challenges of the late 1980s and early 1990s in creating legal awareness amongst women in Uganda, Butegwa (1990: 109–115) isolated four main categories of obstacles. She isolated what she called economic-based obstacles emanating from the fact that even if women are aware of their new-found rights, they might not be able to exercise them because of lack of resources. In the second category were cultural obstacles emanating from the perception that women have their place in society and woe befall those who dare to deviate from the norm. The third category of obstacles she pointed to were religious in that women may fear acting contrary to religious values that have been instilled in them, such as those regarding divorce as anathema. The fourth category was the challenge posed by the country's history of violence, corruption and general breakdown in law and order. As she pointed out, under such circumstances, it was not unheard of for men to think they could act with impunity. Because change is slow in coming and requires a lot of hard work, many of these obstacles remain in place today, as they were when these programmes were initiated.[536]

Similarly criticising the first wave of legal information dissemination in Ghana, when it was naively assumed that knowledge of rights was a panacea to women's problems, Kuenyehia (1990: 117–125) noted the dangers of lawyers perceiving women's problems from a purely legalistic standpoint. As she pointed out, engagement and dialogue with target groups was central if lawyers were to be effective, particularly given that women's problems often emanate from their socio-cultural and economic positioning.

In my study of community legal education in Zimbabwe, I unearthed similar limitations that emerged from confining legal information dissemination to the bare bones of the law, without engaging in the wider social context that the laws are supposed to operate within. The initiative I was examining more closely centred on using paralegals as community-based workers to disseminate legal information. For example, in discussing violence against women, the following remarks were made by men in community gatherings (Tsanga, 2003: 97-98):

'I know fighting is bad but what steps should I take if a woman misbehaves?'

'Does this law mean that there should be no head of the house?'

---

[536] For a background to some of the initiatives in Africa, see generally Schuler (1990).

'Some women have no manners and that is why they are beaten.'

'Women invite assault. Laziness is the cause.'

'If a woman takes your wages, she deserves to be beaten.'

'If a woman pokes you in the eye, you are not just going to stand there and do nothing.'

'Some women deserve to be beaten because they make the man the tortoise of the house.'

'Some women actually say that if you do not beat them, you do not love them.'

'Women should listen to their husbands because they have paid *roora*.[537] A man in the family is like a steam engine that pulls the train. If women want equality, then they too should pay *roora*.'

'Women should realize that what causes fighting in the home is the bossy and insubordinate attitude of some women. This is even against the bible. The man is the head and the woman is the neck. Just as you cannot have two heads on one neck, you cannot have two heads in one house.'

The above rationalizations are grounded in culture, customary practices and religion as well as in patriarchal justifications. Without engaging in how violence against women is a feminist issue and how violence is disproportionately directed against women, effecting behavioural change is unlikely to happen. These limitations from earlier programmes in legal literacy bring out the significance of the need for a holistic feminist approach to legal literacy that combines an understanding of the role of social, cultural, political and economic factors in women's lives. While the approach of many programmes is no longer as purely legalistic as it was when they were conceived, those carrying out legal information dissemination programmes need to have a firm feminist understanding of issues. This would provide a basis for the analytical tools which they draw from in engaging in discussions on the ways in which customary law and religious laws impact on women's lives.

The development and use of African feminist thought in particular is a key challenge. Whether our approach to African feminism is in finding and using women's voices as expressed in their lived realities or through understanding and building onto the ways that African women have used to negotiate around patriarchy, community legal education

---

[537] This is a word from the Shona language in Zimbabwe and is used here to mean bride price or the payment of money by the groom to the bride's family. A commonly used word in the southern African context is *lobola*.

that seeks to change women's lives is likely to have meaning by drawing strength from the continuous development of African feminist philosophies.

At another level, those carrying out legal literacy initiatives also need to be alive to the changes that are taking place on the ground, particularly relating to customary practices. As is fully discussed in the previous chapter, 'The widows' and female child's portion: The twisted path to partial equality for widows and daughters under customary law in Zimbabwe', jurisprudence emanating from the higher courts on customary law has often served to consolidate women's inferior position despite the fact that in reality people may be altering their behaviour to address the challenges of the times. An emerging lesson in carrying out legal information dissemination in plural legal settings is the need to draw imaginatively from living customary law in fashioning messages. For example, to the extent that organizations such as Women and Law in Southern Africa (WLSA) have shown through their research (Dengu-Zvobgo *et al.*, 1994) that customary law as practised on the ground, at least in the area of inheritance, is not as exclusionary or as discriminatory as the interpretations often placed on it by the higher courts suggest, these findings and developments also need to inform the content of the message that is disseminated in a plural legal context. Implementers pressing for change cannot afford to fail to engage with these dynamics. This is even more so where the legislature has taken the initiative to pass laws that accord women rights that appear to be at variance with stated customary law practices. If such legislation is to be accepted, it needs to be bolstered with concrete examples to illustrate that legislative changes may merely be giving effect to transformations already taking place on the ground. In that way, the changes may not be as radical as they seemed to be when people are confronted with examples of what is already taking place among communities that are no different from their own. The difficulty with changes that take place as living customary law is that they tend to be localized.

However, even in their seeming resistance, people concede to inevitable change and deviate from the norm, which provides crucial entry points in the reconceptualization of the approach to legal dissemination in a plural legal setting. If changes are inevitably taking place, then it is these that must find their way into the dialogue on gender in a manner that is convincing and sustained. Although changes are often localized they can nonetheless be used as examples of best practices. Even though people may be changing their practices in tune with the times, it is inevitable that there will be equally large pockets of people, if not those in the majority, who may, for various reasons to do with their own interests, continue to insist on old ways. It is such people who need to be persuaded that, in the long term, there are greater advantages to be gained from inclusion of others than from their exclusion. Also the changes in customary practices need to be examined from a feminist perspective. A key issue is whether the emerging practices are really working in the interests of women when put under careful scrutiny.

The strategy of locating dialogue within the context of ongoing changes to customary practices also calls for in-depth research before legal information campaigns are embarked upon. While the trend is to carry out some form of community survey and needs assessment before implementing legal literacy programmes, all too often the nature of these surveys does not translate into in-depth studies of prevailing customs and practices on the topics to be focused on.[538] A lot of persuasive energy could be saved if more time was spent on understanding the issues around which resistance is most likely to be encountered and framing strategies accordingly.

3   Locating remedies within plural legal settings

One of the key aims in disseminating legal information is that legal knowledge will translate into the use of legal remedies. Just as the content of legal messages must draw strength where applicable from the plurality of laws, so too must the remedies projected. The issue of locating remedies within a system that people are familiar with is one of the most critical challenges facing those engaged in legal information dissemination within a plural legal context. Far too often the remedies that are given centre stage are too alienated from people's realities to have any real impact in terms of use.

In crafting alternative conceptual frameworks in a post-independence era, western legal norms have more often than not continued to be regarded as a guiding light for developing countries. This is largely as a result of historical influence but also because legislators lacked serious innovativeness and were hesitant to adopt truly revolutionary African approaches which are informed by the social, economic and cultural realities of their people. Western legal norms are seen as embodying the elements of contemporary civilized legal systems with the result that customary law has tended to play a peripheral role as an element in the development process. When it comes to dispute resolution mechanisms

---

[538] An example of an in-depth campaign is the nationwide wills and inheritance campaign which was carried out in Zimbabwe by the Ministry of Justice following the amendment of intestate succession under customary law in 1997. See chapter 16 for the details of the legislative changes that took place.

the tendency is to see non-western systems as inferior within the justice system and, as such, occupying a lower level in the hierarchy of courts.

The argument for building onto existing cultural legal systems rests on the philosophical understanding among African scholars and activists alike, that the ideal context for growth and development on the continent is one that is grounded in the cultural identity and reality of the people (Hillard, 1997; Ogundipe-Leslie, 2001; Fanon, 1965). Access to justice by the bulk of the population and not just the few, is an area where, as Africans, we are truly at the crossroads in terms of how best to harness the potential that exists in our midst. The challenge confronting us is to build onto systems that are more in consonance with our rich cultural heritage and identity and that illustrate creativity in the way we address our problems. The official legal system is virtually meaningless for the bulk of the population as a result of Africans ourselves continuing to take a limited and imposed view of the meaning of cultural diversity.

The legal, educational and public health systems, to mention a few, represent some of the areas where Africans have experienced forms of cultural genocide. Clearly, the institutionalized adherence to received legal systems as the foundation stone for the law of the land has not worked to the benefit of the majority in Africa. Apart from being strange to the people, the laws are often founded on totally different value systems. It is ridiculous that women, for instance, often fail to access justice in maintenance cases using the formal system because the forms they are expected to use require them to understand and state their issue in the English language. They are alienated from the system not just by the nature of the system but because of language.

When I finished my legal training and started working with grassroots communities, I was deeply disturbed at just how divorced from ordinary people's realities my legal training had been. I found myself with profound questions as to who exactly the training I had received was meant to serve. Clearly not the bulk of the population whose lives I found to be divorced from the Roman-Dutch law that formed the basis of my legal training. While customary law had featured in the legal curriculum, it was to the extent of the few grains of pepper added to salt.

While the interdependence and interconnectedness of cultures is a given fact that few countries can escape, the problem of a predominantly western influence as the beacon for reforms is the neglect of more appropriate systems which may exist at the local level and also the real danger of curtailing the positive development of local justice systems that may speak more to the experiences of the people than the values embodied in received laws. This is even more so when it comes to processes of dispute resolution as opposed to the actual content of customary laws, which are largely fraught with controversy due the exclusionary and largely discriminatory manner in which they treat women.

Most efforts at raising awareness about legal rights tend to emphasize the use of state court structures although they may also allude to traditional forms of dispute settlement as part of the mix. Those who have travelled across rural Africa are aware of just how remote some places can be. Even where there are central places where government offices may be located, these are often a considerable distance away for most villagers. Yet despite this, non-governmental organizations working on popularizing rights often provide solutions which imply relative ease of access or which work on the expectation that the target group will drag themselves to the structures that dispense official justice, whatever the cost. If implementers of legal information dissemination programmes wish to encourage use of state systems, they have to burn as much activist energy in advocating for effective justice systems as they do in raising awareness.

In my detailed analysis of the experiences of the Legal Resources Foundation in taking law to the people (Tsanga, 2003), I found that many of the remedies that were offered to women in dealing with domestic violence, for example, were far too premised on the imagined ease of accessing the official justice system to be of any real use to women in rural areas. Phoning the police, going to the nearest police station to make a complaint and seeking divorce or judicial separation are all remedies that assume that the machinery and necessary assistance are all in place. In most cases, nothing could be further from the truth. In instances where the target group has no choice but to take the matter before official courts, then the challenge is ensuring that the state also channels its resources towards projects to ensure that justice is accessible. It is no use expecting people to take their cases to official courts when the courts are not available, are poorly staffed or funds are limited to assist those who may need legal assistance.

Besides issues of general lack of infrastructure, shortage of personnel and limited availability of legal aid, there are numerous other considerations at a personal level that women have to take into account before making a decision to report a violent husband. These can range from factors such as concern for the children, fear of divorce, fear of lack of support, reluctance to have the husband imprisoned or the simple hope that the man will change.

The reality in the rural areas is that chiefs still play an important role in dispute resolution and it is therefore necessary to have more than a peripheral understanding of the operation of their courts. Yet very rarely, if at all, are information dissemination campaigns informed first and foremost by the reality that most people still operate outside the official system in favour of localized and more easily accessible and understandable forms of justice or that they may opt to solve their disputes outside court processes altogether. The tendency has been to project the official system as embodying desired change. If traditional channels of dispute resolution are able to play an effective role in solving disputes then it is folly not to encourage them and support their use.

Armstrong (1998: 55–71), for instance, in her study of culture and choice in relation to domestic violence in Zimbabwe, unearthed how the family and the chiefs often play a central role in dealing with matters of domestic violence. She observed that in some cases chiefs and headmen took a much stronger stance against violence than the families of the victims. As she noted:

> '.... in the rural areas the process of bringing the husband before the chief or headman was so humiliating that it was often effective. The whole community heard about the transgressions of the abusive husband. The respected headmen and elders expressed their disapproval. However, the power of headmen and chiefs is limited. Some husbands simply refused to see the headman or attend the village meeting at which the case was being discussed' (Armstrong, 1998: 64).

It is in dealing with such eventualities where people refuse to cooperate, that knowledge of other options available is important. But even then, implementers of legal information dissemination programmes need to recognize that state systems are of use only if they are accessible and affordable.

One of the major challenges in reconceptualizing legal information dissemination in plural legal systems is ensuring that the solutions that are offered to women and men are informed by an in-depth knowledge of the dispute resolution means that they are likely to use. This does not mean that state-centred alternatives have no role to play. Choice is important. Also, in some cases due to jurisdictional constraints imposed on lower courts applying customary law in terms of the matters that they can hear, the centrality of state-based dispute resolution means is inevitable. The expectation is that people will go to the courts with the right jurisdiction to hear their matter.

African governments as well as women's organizations need to engage more fully with the role of traditional leaders in plural legal systems, especially given that large swathes of the rural population still rely on their services. For example, much to the chagrin of the people, in the early years of Zimbabwe's independence, the role of chiefs was severely curtailed in favour of appointed judicial officers in the lower courts. The following comments were made during legal information dissemination programmes:

> 'Why do young people sit in the village and community courts as presiding officers when they have limited knowledge of customary law? People should be chosen to preside in these courts on the basis of their knowledge of customary law and not because they can read or write. We would rather have chiefs, as they understand the basis of our customary laws' (Tsanga, 2003: 83).

From a feminist perspective, the problem is that traditional structures are often seen as bastions of male power too steeped in tradition to be given too much leeway in family-related matters where progress has been made through legislative changes. In their Zimbabwe study on justice delivery, WLSA researchers commented that they found traditional courts patriarchal and sexist although the actual manifestations of this behaviour are not detailed (Stewart *et al.*, 2000). It is for reasons of their perceived conservatism that in some countries their jurisdiction is often limited to exclude important areas of family law. For example, in Zimbabwe, in terms of section 16 of the Customary Law and Local Courts Act,[539] chiefs and headmen currently do not have any jurisdiction to hear matters relating to issues such as validity of wills, dissolution of marriages, custody and guardianship of minors, maintenance cases, and any matters relating to land and immovable property.[540] They can, however, adjudicate on marital relationships in customary law marriages which have not been solemnized before the law. They also have monetary limitations placed on their jurisdiction.

It could be argued that there may be more merit in forcing traditional courts to embrace new outlooks on gender as opposed to shutting them out from the process. Limiting their jurisdiction in the face of new legislation impacting on women could unwittingly be slowing down the process of change. The reality is also that despite their limited jurisdiction they nonetheless often hear matters over which they have no power. According to the WLSA study on justice delivery, they tend to ignore their jurisdictional limits and even hear criminal matters. They have always tended to ignore efforts to curtail their jurisdiction from the time when their powers to hear cases were taken away from them in 1981, only to be restored again in 1990.

Such realities would appear to necessitate doing away with the veneer of the chiefs' limited jurisdiction. They are a crucial part of the

---

[539] Customary Law and Local Courts Act Chapter 7:05.

[540] The Ministry of Justice has indicated that their powers may soon be expanded to allow them to dissolve marriages as part of the decentralization of services and making justice more accessible. Presently those with registered customary law marriages have to apply for divorce in the magistrate's courts.

chain in a plural legal context and the tendency to accord them a place at the bottom of the chain needs to be reconceptualized. It could be argued that if they are given jurisdiction to hear some of the matters they are currently not allowed to hear, it would be easier to introduce rigorous training on gender issues and to monitor them. Their defiance in all probability emanates from the fact that they regard it as an insult not to be granted jurisdiction in some matters that they have traditionally focused on. People also probably continue bringing their matters before them because of their own beliefs that chiefs should have jurisdiction in those matters. In a plural legal setting, the role of non-governmental organizations should certainly not be that of disseminating just 'the ABCs of the law' (Schuler, 1992: 44–93) but more appropriately should also be that of activist research on justice processes and using people's lived experiences as a basis for making recommendations for changing structures and building capacities.

A central issue therefore is how best to engage with traditional leaders in the development of customary law so that it is responsive to the dictates of changing societies. According to Busia (2003: 75) in Ghana, for instance, following reform of the constitution in 1992, the National House of Chiefs was tasked with 'studying, interpreting, and compiling customary law with a view to evolving a unified system of rules of customary law'. They were also tasked constitutionally with undertaking an evaluation of traditional customs and usages so as to eliminate those that are outmoded and socially harmful. While the merits of codifying customary law are debatable, since it is a key reason for its ossification, the process of engaging chiefs in identifying harmful customs and practices is a step in the right direction. At least if they play a part in defining and isolating what they consider to be harmful practices, then, given their key role in the community, it should be easier to persuade people to begin to change their attitudes. Non-governmental organizations need to work closely with chiefs by feeding into this process with crucial information from their experiential data.

We cannot, however, set too much store by the participation and full cooperation of chiefs, as reflected in the recent South African constitutional case of *Bhe and others v Magistrate, Khayelitsha and others* CCT 49/03, where the National House of Traditional Leaders was asked to make submissions regarding customary law of inheritance and omitted to do so, most likely because the case centred on challenging the exclusionary nature of the customary law of inheritance. Not all chiefs are conservative and there are indications that those who are progressive can be used to pave the path for change.

African scholars and activists accept that the area of culture calls for urgent attention in so far as transformation is concerned. The challenge, as Ogundipe-Leslie (2001) puts it, is deciding which aspects of culture need to be reformed and which need to stay. Central to this evaluation of culture is an understanding of continuity and change as inherent in virtually all cultures and African culture is no exception. The fact that some customary beliefs are prejudicial to women and that those who dispense justice are often caught in a web of patriarchal belief systems, should not result in throwing out the baby with the bath water, in the way we look at African legal systems. Formal courts introduced through colonial processes are not free from male dominance in both content and form either, yet in those countries where they have their cultural foundations, no one calls for the abandonment of the legal system or sidelining it in favour of foreign systems of dispute resolution. The challenge is transforming the players who dispense justice through continuing education. Approaches can and must be changed to take into account present-day realities. This is the angle from which we must approach African systems of dispute resolution. The foundation stone that we need to work on is the informal nature of African legal processes, as they are clearly more in tune with the cultural heritage of the people than any form of received system can ever hope to be.

Non-governmental organizations could also contribute towards the development of African legal systems through gathering data from the people and by working closely with structures at the lower levels so as to gain an understanding of how they operate and the challenges that they may encounter with a view to their improvement.

The important point is that if traditional structures are to have any teeth, they must be responsive to modern day challenges and realities instead of basing their appeal on tradition alone.[541] The reality is that we live in an era where relations between men and women have undergone significant changes. Modern existence has brought new meaning to forms of property, new roles, as well as a variety of opportunities for both men and women which no longer fit in with traditionally-assigned roles and duties. Customary laws that may have made sense in a different time no longer hold the same logic in today's society.

Because traditional structures have their own inherent appeal compared to received structures, ultimately the challenge is to build upon these structures so that they have their rightful developmental place in African legal systems. Their advantages in terms of the role they play in solving disputes at the community level, the fact that they are comparatively more accessible in terms of language and procedure, as well as

---

[541] For an interesting discussion on the resurgence of pre-colonial political institutions in Africa see Englebert (2002: 345-368).

being less bureaucratic, should not be overlooked. Their unique blend of law and morality is also a model to build upon (Bidaguren and Estrella, 2002). It is partly the task of those carrying out legal literacy programmes, with their underlying vision for community empowerment, to bring out the best in traditional practices and to lobby for these best practices to be incorporated within the legal system.

The potential for making effective headway by working within an accepted normative framework should not be underestimated. In addressing the specific challenges that confront lawyers working in Islamic contexts, Ali Ahmad from Nigeria (2004) makes some poignant observations about those challenges. Since non-governmental organization activist work is often centred on changing people's attitudes and values, an understanding of the system from which people draw their values is important. More significantly he gives an example of how Islamic law was finally effectively used in dealing with an environmental problem on Misali Island in Zanzibar where the majority of the people are Muslim. Concerned with unsustainable fishing methods being used on the island, rich with turtles and rare corals, he describes the initial approach of environmental non-governmental organizations such as World Life Foundation International to change the fishing habits of the islanders with no success. However, when the non-governmental organizations concerned engaged the Islamic Foundation for Ecology and Environmental Sciences which conducted training workshops for community leaders within the framework of an Islamic environmentalist perspective, not only were there discernible changes in people's practices but an increase in fishing reserves. What is important is that by operating within a framework that was familiar to the people and eliciting value systems from a source that they could identify with, the organizations concerned were able to make headway. According to Ali Ahmad, so spectacular was the success that the project was recognized by the World Wild Life Foundations as a Gift of Islam to global environmental management efforts.

4   Harnessing the human rights debate to women's advantage

Finding a framework for empowering people for change
At the heart of revisiting the approach to legal literacy in plural legal systems is the manner in which customary law and religious laws and their supportive institutions have often been marginalized. As illustrated above, the overall weakness of approach from past initiatives was that only the received law tended to provide the frame of reference, whether in terms of the content to customary law or the solutions in addressing

problems. In many situations where the people deemed received law alien, it presented problems of acceptability. Resistance to changes to customary laws also emanated from the inherent tendency of colonialism to look down on everything African. If legal information dissemination programmes are to be effective in Africa in promoting long-term behavioural change, they need to have firm African foundations from which to launch their call for change.

I note in my study of community legal education in Zimbabwe that legislative change that is seen as being rooted only in western cultural ideology and which sends the message that local culture is under siege, results in defensive reactions. I encountered many such reactions, particularly in discussing the Legal Age of Majority Act, which, among other things, had the effect of according majority status to everyone at the age of 18, a concept whose effects were deemed alien and western. The perception by the people was that their culture was being denigrated in favour of 'western ways of doing things'. The following comments are illustrative of these views (Tsanga, 2003: 65–66):

> 'Why are laws, which have no bearing on our reality, being imposed upon us? Marrying without parental consent is inviting trouble and is uncustomary. We should beware of losing our culture.'

> 'If a woman marries without parental consent then her parents can refuse to bury her because they will not have been consulted before the marriage.'

> 'We have our own culture, which we should be proud of, and we should not allow our children to marry like chickens or donkeys, which do not follow any culture.'

> 'Carry back the message to whoever made the law that we want to be left alone to live as we are used to and that this western culture does not go hand in hand with our tradition. This law destroys the relationship of respect between parents and children.'

> 'This pamphlet should be torn [up] and should not be seen by children.'

> 'Since you are the one who brought this law to us, go back and tell the government to sit down and discuss these laws with the people before passing them. It does not help to mix cultures especially where people have their own culture. This book should simply be removed from our sight.'

> 'African custom does not go hand in hand with this way of thinking. If those who make laws want to impose laws on us they should make a law stating that any man who makes a woman under 25 pregnant should

automatically be liable to pay damages. If they cannot do this then they should leave us to lead our lives as we are used to. Government has choked us with this law.'

It is the top-down approach that seems to rile most people, particularly any approach that suggests instant change because customary ways of doing things are inferior. Finding a strategy that transcends defensiveness and creates dialogue is a key challenge. The issue is whether there is such a framework or happy medium that those carrying out legal information dissemination programmes can draw from.

In view of the fact that the gender debate in plural legal contexts is increasingly influenced by the centrality that is being accorded to the human rights framework and to constitutionalism, it is worth analyzing the potential and limits that these frameworks hold for legal information dissemination programmes. A notable development since the time when the first wave of legal information dissemination took hold has been the dramatic rise in the number of African countries that have ratified international human rights instruments such as the Covenant on Civil and Political Rights, the Covenant on Economic, Social and Cultural Rights as well as conventions dealing with the rights of special groups such as the Convention on the Elimination of all Forms of Discrimination Against Women (CEDAW) and the Convention on the Rights of the Child. Human rights concepts have also increasingly found expression in constitutional reforms at the country level.

Countries such as Ghana, Uganda, Namibia, South Africa, Mozambique, Zambia, Malawi and Angola have introduced new constitutions that have significantly altered the standing of women and the place of customary law and cultural practices that discriminate against women within the constitution (SADC Parliamentary Forum, 2003). Key principles embodied in major human rights instruments have found expression in the Bill of Rights of some of these new constitutions. Even in countries where new constitutions have not yet come to fruition, the global human rights discourse has not failed to have an impact on the manner that women's entitlements and rights are increasingly conceptualized.[542] Most of these new constitutions have given primacy to issues of gender in a manner that has opened doors to women in social, private and public spaces that had hitherto been closed. For example, according to article 24 of the constitution of Malawi, women are given the same rights as men with regard to contracts, rights to acquire property, rights

---

[542] See, for instance, the case of Unity Dow in Botswana. Although Botswana still has an old constitution, the human rights framework has provided important parameters for the interpretation of the rights of marginalized groups.

to custody and guardianship as well as citizenship. According to article 24(2) the state is also enjoined to pass legislation to eliminate practices that discriminate against women, particularly with reference to practices such as sexual abuse, sexual harassment, domestic violence, and discrimination at work, in business and in public affairs. Among the many provisions granting women rights in the South African constitution is article 12(2) which recognizes women's rights to make decisions concerning reproduction control and security over their bodies.

Of interest are also those provisions in some of the new constitutions that now make the exercise of culture subject to the human rights provisions of the constitution. For example, while recognizing the right of everyone to enjoy, practise, maintain and promote any culture, language or religion of their choice, article 19 of the Namibian constitution makes it clear that the exercise of these rights is subject to the condition that they do not impinge on the rights of others or the national interest. The South African constitution accommodates customary law provided that it is not in conflict with the constitution.[543] Cultural diversity is also recognized. For example, section 30 recognizes the right of everyone to participate in the cultural life of his or her choice but not in a manner that is inconsistent with the constitution. Section 31 of the constitution also states that persons belonging to a cultural or linguistic community may not be denied the right with other members of that community, to enjoy their culture, practise their religion and use their language but, again, subject to the constitution. Institutions that are linked to customary law, such as traditional leadership, are also recognized as subject to the constitution.[544]

With these developments, the point of reference in legal information dissemination also needs to shift. If received western law is no longer the mirror which reflects the desired developments to customary law, clearly for those countries with new constitutions that place customary law under the purview of democratic principles, the frame of reference for any changes and advances in customary law should now be the constitution. The value of a progressive constitution is that it can be used as the basis for making arguments in favour of human dignity and equality and for the application of the concept of non-discrimination. The foundation stone in terms of vision and impetus for change has shifted from received laws to nationally-crafted constitutions.

An additional foundation stone has clearly become the language of human rights through the plethora of human rights instruments that we

---

[543] See section 39 of the South African constitution.
[544] See section 211 of the South African constitution.

have in our midst.[545] Of significance for women's rights in the African context is no doubt the Protocol on Women's Rights to the African Charter which was adopted by heads of states in 2003 and has the potential for creating dialogue on customary law that could change women's lives.[546] A significant number of the principles contained therein in theory do away with customary law practices that are at variance with modern day concepts of equality and dignity of all.

Article 2, for instance, clearly calls for the elimination of all discrimination against women and for states to include in their national constitutions provisions on equality between men and women. State parties are also urged to implement legislation curbing harmful practices that endanger the health and wellbeing of women. State parties also undertake to modify social and cultural practices that are based on stereotypical roles of men and women. Article 5 in particular is devoted to the elimination of harmful practices and singles out female genital mutilation, in its multiple forms, for eradication. Also of significance is article 6 on marriage which, among other things, encourages monogamy as the preferred form of marriage although it protects the rights of women and children in polygamous unions. The right to inheritance is recognized in article 21, including the right to have an equitable share in the inheritance of the property of the husband. Widows are also to be protected through legislation from inhuman and degrading treatment and to have the right to marry a person of their choice.

From a human rights and developmental perspective, these advancements in the legal and human rights arena have significant implications for the reconceptualization of both the content and methodology adopted by those engaged in legal information dissemination programmes. Most of the issues that are addressed by the protocol are extremely hot issues in terms of ongoing practices and values on the ground. It would be a mistake for implementers of legal awareness programmes to take the narrower liberalist approach, which tends to emphasize rights outside their social, historical and political context, in working with new concepts.

In plural legal systems the shift from received law as a frame of reference to human rights and constitutions as the dominant frameworks for revisiting customary law does not mean that people will automatically be receptive to the changes. The success or otherwise of introduc-

---

[545] The difficulty with international instruments is that they are often not automatically incorporated into national legislation unless explicitly stipulated by an Act of Parliament. Nonetheless the act of ratification by a country means that the state has undertaken to pursue progressive measures in implementing the international instrument in question.

[546] Fifteen countries were needed to ratify the protocol before it could come into force.

ing new values is affected by how deeply ingrained within the society a particular practice is that the new value in question seeks to alter. A lot also depends on the degree of participation that informed the making of constitutions as the highest law of the land. Even though a significant number of African countries have new constitutions, rural people, in particular, may not be as aware of the contents of these documents or of the content and effect of international instruments that may have been ratified. Although a constitution may contain progressive principles regarding women's lives, people may still feel distanced from its seemingly progressive provisions if they did not participate actively in formulating its principles. In such situations in may be unrealistic to expect that constitutional principles will result in the acceptance of wholesale inroads into customary law. There is the issue of general conservatism when it comes to change. Even though the constitution is the highest law of the land and customary laws may be made subject to it, its principles may be regarded as equally idealistic and foreign inspired as those from received law which provided the framework for change in the past.

Also, customary practices are unlikely to experience a rapid demise simply because an instrument by heads of states has sounded the death knell. At the risk of stating the obvious, human rights principles are not self-implementing and the great human rights lyrics in themselves do not result in behavioural change. Those implementing legal information dissemination programmes stand a far greater chance of success in effecting behavioural change if they work towards the acceptance of changes to customary law as their end goal as opposed to academic notions that statements in instruments alone have resulted in the death of customary law. From an empowerment and legal literacy perspective such emphasis may result in ill-thought out messages that create resistance and that may delay rather than expedite the desired goal of behavioural and normative change.

In plural legal settings, those raising human rights awareness will need to anticipate and be prepared to deal with the clash between the norms that they may be advocating and those that exist on the ground. Discovering major points of resistance as a programme unfolds is costly, not only in terms of resources spent producing materials which people reject but also in terms of the amount spent on damage control. They must also be equipped to deal with patriarchal responses to efforts to do away with practices such as polygamy[547] which fly in the face of women's equality and dignity. A key problem with customary laws is that

---

[547] For the nature of patriarchal responses that activists can expect on an issue such as polygamy, the article by Dlamini provides some insights. See Dlamini (1989). The essence of his argument is that the scriptures do not contain any clear verse

their core values have tended to be articulated from the standpoint of men.

Every society has some entry point that they can use to give best effect to key human rights values that we all wish could become a reality. In former colonies within Africa, it is despicable that men, in particular, are often quick to harp on the evils of colonialism and yet so often fail to appreciate just how critical the gender dimension is to the liberation of Africa if progress is to be made. Again it behoves those seeking to raise awareness in plural legal settings to find the most effective entry point for creating sustainable dialogue. The same arguments can be made about disseminating legal information where the context of pluralism emanates from a religious context. In analyzing the topical issue of gender and democracy in Islamic countries, Abdullahi An-Na'im (1995: 197–204) makes critical observations regarding the necessity to frame the gender debate using principles that are contained in the Quran. The gist of his argument is that as there are as many verses in the Quran giving women the same rights as men as there are those which appear to accord women a minority status. Women can use the Quran to their advantage. As he sees it, the apparent conflict is a result of the differing interpretations that have been given to the text over time which were no doubt influenced by dominant power relations pertaining at those times. In his view, for women governed by Islamic law, trying to find equality within the framework of the text is likely to be more effective than over reliance on principles that are seen as external. Engaging with human rights from a local perspective does not detract from the core universality of those principles. It should not be a shield for cultural relativity but instead should be a way of giving effect to core values by meaningfully engaging with local realities.

[547 contd] condemning polygamy and therefore its condemnation is more a result of western missionary zeal as opposed to anything biblical. He expends considerable energy on illustrating through biblical interpretations that God may indeed be an ally rather than an opponent of men when it comes to polygamy. In attacking the moral objections to polygamy he argues that equating polygamy with promiscuity is flawed as people in polygamous unions are often not promiscuous or no more promiscuous than from those where polygamy does not exist. While from a human rights perspective he concedes that polygamy certainly does not give women the same rights as men since only men are entitled to more than one spouse, he says that no woman is forced into a polygamous marriage. He also goes further to say that a practice that women favour and that they benefit from cannot be discriminatory. Such arguments reveal the significance of addressing cultural practices with feminist as opposed to culturally defensive lenses.

Conclusion and recommendations

The current emphasis on human rights in general and women's human rights instruments in particular, both globally and regionally, holds some potential for deepening the gender debate within plural contexts provided those who engage in awareness raising resist the all too familiar trap of remaining locked in a liberal human rights approach. Besides the human rights framework, Africa's liberation struggle, as one of the greatest quests by humanity for freedom and dignity, needs to be projected as a continuum, particularly when it comes to gender equality. It remains under-used by Africans ourselves in fashioning a grounded concept of empowerment.

The reconceptualization of legal information dissemination in plural legal settings also has implications for the way in which we train lawyers in law schools since increasingly lawyers within Africa find themselves playing a significant role in legal activism. While it is true that we cannot teach law students everything in law school and that there will inevitably be aspects which they pick up from practice, the first wave of information dissemination in Africa revealed that lawyers were ill-prepared to address the challenges of lawyering amongst their own people.

Given the role that lawyers play in the legal system, a key challenge is that of ensuring that the content that forms the subject matter of legal training embraces the realities of the bulk of the people within the context of the legal system that predominantly impacts on their lives. Legal training in pluralist legal settings should not leave lawyers strangers to their own people where they articulate largely foreign values that leave the bulk of the population at the margins of the system. Realistically the legal system as a whole in Africa needs to be revisited so that changes are crosscutting rather than piecemeal. There needs to be coordination in vision among legislators, academics and activists alike if real changes are to take place.

Bibliography

An-Na'im A. (1995) 'Which way Islam – democracy or oppression?' and 'Gender and democracy in the Islamic context: The current experience of Sudan', in Mia Melin (ed) *Democracy in Africa: On whose terms?*, Forum Syd, Stockholm.

Ahmad A. (2004) 'Educating lawyers for transnational challenges: The challenge of Islamic law', unpublished paper presented at a conference on educating lawyers for transnational challenges, 26–29 May, American Association of Law Schools, Hawaii.

Armstrong A. (1998) *Culture and choice: Lessons from survivors of gender violence in Zimbabwe,* Violence Against Women in Zimbabwe Research Project, Harare.

Bidaguren J. A. and D. N. Estrella (2002) 'Governability and forms of popular justice in the new South Africa and Mozambique', *Journal of Legal Pluralism* No 47.

Bryde B. O. (1976) *The politics and sociology of African legal development*, Alfred Metzner Verlag, Frankfurt/Main.

Busia N. K A., (2003) 'Competing visions of liberal democracy and socialism', in A. A. An-Na'im (ed) *Human rights under African constitutions: Realizing the promise for ourselves,* University of Pennsylvania Press, Philadelphia.

Butegwa F. (1990) 'Creating grassroots legal awareness in Uganda' in M. Schuler (ed) *Women, law and development in Africa: WILDAF origins and issues,* OEF International, Washington.

Dengu-Zvobgo K. *et al.* (1994) *Inheritance in Zimbabwe: Law, customs and practice,* WLSA/SAPES Trust, Harare.

Dlamini C. R. M. (1989) 'Should we legalize or abolish polygamy?', *pages 330–345* in *The Comparative and International Law Journal of South Africa Vol. XX11.*

Englebert P. (2002) 'Born again Buganda or the limits of traditional resurgence', pages 345–368 in *Africa Journal of Modern African Studies* 40,3.

Fanon F. (1965) *The wretched of the earth,* MacGibbon and Kee (reprinted by Penguin Books in 1990), London.

Hilliard A. G. (1997) *SBA: The awakening of the African mind,* Makare Publishing Company, Florida.

Kuenyehia A. (1990) 'Legal services and education in Ghana' in M. Schuler (ed) *Women, law and development in Africa: WILDAF origins and issues*, OEF International, Washington.

Moyo A. (2001) 'Religion in Africa', in A. Gordon and D. Gordon (eds) *Understanding contemporary Africa,* Lynne Reinner Publishers, Boulder, Colorado.

Ogundipe-Leslie M. (2001) 'Moving mountains, making the links', in K. Bhavnani (ed) *Feminism and race,* Oxford University Press, New York.

Schuler M. and S. Kadigamar-Rajasingham (eds) (1992) *Legal literacy: A tool for women's empowerment,* UNIFEM, New York.

Schuler M. (ed) (1990) *Women, law and development in Africa: WILDAF origins and issues*, OEF International, Washington.

Tsanga A., A. Johnson and M. Sogo (1996) *A directory of legal services programmes in Africa,* Legal Resources Foundation and the International Commission of Jurists, Harare and Geneva.

Tsanga A. S. (2003) *Taking law to the people: Gender law reform and community legal education in Zimbabwe* Weaver Press, Harare.

Stewart J. *et al.* (2000) *In the shadow of the law: Women and justice delivery in Zimbabwe,* WLSA Trust, Harare.

Southern African Development Community (SADC) (2003) *A guide to gender dimensions in SADC constitutions,* SADC Parliamentary Forum, Windhoek.

List of cases

Bhe and others v Magistrate, Khayelitsha and others CCT 49/03 – 2005 (1) SA 580 (CC)

Unity Dow v Attorney-General (Botswana) [June 1991].

List of legislation

Zimbabwe

Customary Law and Local Courts Act Chapter 7:05

Legal Age of Majority Act NO; 15 of 1982

Matabeleland Order in Council of 1894

South Africa

South African constitution

International legislation

Convention on the Elimination of all Forms of Discrimination Against Women (CEDAW) 1979

Convention on the Rights of the Child 1989

International Covenant on Civil and Political Rights 1966

International Covenant on Economic, Social and Cultural Rights 1966

Protocol on Women's Rights to the African Charter on Human and People's Rights 2003

List of Acts (by country)

Botswana
Marriage Act 1970 154, 163

Ethiopia
Constitution of the Federal Democratic
 Republic of Ethiopia 1994 126, 138

India
Equal Remuneration Act 1976 256
Orissa Land Reforms Act 1962 255
Orissa Land Settlement Act 1959 255

Kenya
African Courts (Suspension of Land
 Suits) Ordinance 1957 174
Children's Act 2001 201
Constitution of Kenya 1983 178, 201
Crown Lands Ordinances of 1902 and
 1905 172, 201
Environment Management and
 Coordination Act 2000 175,
 189, 201
Forest Act 1989 164, 166, 179, 201
Forests Bill 2004 180, 189
Government Lands Act, Chapter 280 of
 1915 178, 201
Land (Group Representatives) Act,
 Chapter 287 of 1968 178, 201
Lands Act 178, 201
Magistrates' Courts Jurisdiction Act,
 Chapter 10 of 1984 174, 201
Native Lands Registration Ordinance
 No. 27 of 1959 174, 175, 201
Native Land Tenure Rules of 1956 174,
 201
Registered Land Act, Chapter 300 of
 1963 174, 178, 201
Transfer of Property Act 1882 178, 201
Trust Land Act 1939 178, 201

Namibia
Namibian constitution 454
Water Resources Management Bill of
 2001 126, 138

Norway
Act of Allodial Privilege 1987 54, 58
Allodial or Freehold Law of 1821 34
Income Tax Act, §16.5, 1948 37, 58
Marriage Act 1991 38, 50, 58
Menneskerettighetsloven av 21 mai
1999, med tilføyelse vedtatt 1 august
2003.

§3 (Act of 21 May 1999 No.
30 Relating to the Strengthening of
the Status of Human Rights in
Norwegian Law with additions
adopted as of 1 August 2003, §3)
377

Ot.prp.nr. 21 (2003–2004) (Proposition
 no. 21 to the Odelsting)

Innst.O.nr 9 (1995-1996) Innstilling fra
 Sosialkomiteen om Lov om forbud
 mot kjønnslemlestelse (omskjæring
 av kvinner) (Recommendation no. 9,
 1995–1996 to the Odelsting, from
 the Standing Committee on Social
 Affairs, on the prohibition against
 genital mutilation) 377

Pakistan
Constitution of Pakistan 1973 333, 396
Offence of Qadfh (Enforcement of
 Hadd) Ordinance 19 390, 406
Offence of Zina (Enforcement of
 Hudood) Ordinance 390, 394
Offences Against Property (Enforce-
 ment of Hudood) 390, 406
Prohibition (Enforcement of Hadd)
 Order 1979 390, 406
The Offence of Zina (Enforcement of
 Hudood) Ordinance 1979 406

South Africa
Constitution of the Republic of South
 Africa 98, 101, 125, 132, 138, 454,
 460
Bill of Rights in section 27(1)(b) of the
 South African Constitution 125

Tanzania
Land Act 1999 206, 210, 224,
 235, 268, 269, 271, 288
Village Land Act 1999 210, 212, 235,
 269, 270, 272, 273, 288

Uganda
Children Act Chapter 59 2000 65,
 66, 69, 71, 75, 77
Children Statute 6 of 1996 65
Constitution of Uganda 1995 66, 77
Executive Committee (Judicial
 Powers) Act 76, 77
Local Government Act Chapter 243 76
Resistance Committee (Judicial
 Powers) Statute 1/1 76, 77

List of cases (alphabetical)

Index

PUBLICATIONS IN ARCHAEOLOGY

George J. Gumerman, General Editor

also in this series

The Star Lake Archaeological Project:
Anthropology of a Headwaters Area
of Chaco Wash, New Mexico
*edited by Walter K. Wait
and Ben A. Nelson*

Mobility and Adaptation:
The Anasazi of Black Mesa,
Arizona
by Shirley Powell

Center for Archaeological Investigations
Southern Illinois University at Carbondale

Papers on the Archaeology of Black Mesa, Arizona, Volume II

Edited by Stephen Plog and Shirley Powell

Southern Illinois University Press
Carbondale and Edwardsville

Library of Congress Cataloging in Publication Data
(Revised for volume 2)
Main entry under title:

Papers on the archaeology of Black Mesa, Arizona.

(Publications in archaeology)
Vol. 2 edited by Stephen Plog and Shirley Powell.
Vol. 1 not in series.
Includes bibliographies and indexes.
1. Indians of North America—Arizona—Black Mesa (Navajo County and Apache County, Ariz.)—Antiquities—Addresses, essays, lectures.   2. Black Mesa (Navajo County and Apache County, Ariz.)—Antiquities—Addresses, essays, lectures.   3. Pueblo Indians—Antiquities—Addresses, essays, lectures.   4. Arizona—Antiquities—Addresses, essays, lectures.
I. Gumerman, George J.   II. Euler, Robert C.   III. Plog, Stephen.
IV. Series: Publications in archaeology (Southern Illinois University at Carbondale. Center for Archaeological Investigations)
E78.A7.P27   979.1'35   75-32340
ISBN 0-8093-0734-0 (v. 1)
ISBN 0-8093-0735-9 (pbk. : v. 1)
ISBN 0-8093-1149-6 (v. 2)

Contents

Plates

Tables

Figures

Foreword

The studies produced by any long-term research endeavor change in scope and character over the history of the project. This has certainly been the case with the now 17-year-old Black Mesa Archaeological Project. Perusing the Black Mesa publications, one is struck by the diversity of questions that have been asked and the variety of methods we have used to answer them.

The first monographs were largely descriptive reports of surveys and excavations, with informed but somewhat speculative statements about what we thought had happened and why on northeastern Black Mesa. There was, in those initial years, little opportunity to test these broadly stated generalizations because the questions that were asked were usually too broad and the data too limited to address the questions adequately. Nevertheless, data continued to accumulate, and the initial generalizations became targets against which to focus more answerable questions.

During the middle years of the Black Mesa project, as in other multiyear research efforts, data continued to be collected, but greater consideration was given to how collections were made in order to make analytical results more comparable and to permit more appropriate statistical tests. Descriptive reports continued to be published. In addition, methodological papers were produced as it became necessary to devise ways to control the collection and evaluation of data. The large number of sites excavated and the manipulation of data on an unprecedented scale demanded that ways be found to collect and analyze the information in a more economical way.

The papers in this volume represent the maturing of a project and reflect methodological concerns and the testing of hypotheses related to more narrowly focused research questions. The bulk of these studies are essential building blocks that provide the kinds of information needed to answer larger questions, some of which are addressed by Plog and Powell in the last chapter of this volume. The studies reported on here share an important characteristic. They narrow the gap between data and hypotheses by ensuring that tests of hypotheses are operationalized correctly. Measuring behavior indirectly through the material residues of behavior has always been and will always remain a complex and difficult task. Although the focus of the level of investigations has narrowed, this does not mean the questions have been trivialized. It means that the questions are potentially more answerable and represent a foundation without which the broader hypotheses cannot be adquately tested.

In a number of instances these papers help support earlier published studies; sometimes they conflict with them. Often they present alternative explanations. This too is the nature of long-term projects. As more information becomes available and research methods are refined, it is possible to reject certain hypotheses and to develop new ones. Unfortunately, hypotheses seldom get verified, but instead become ranked—often as the fad of the period dictates. But, as Plog and Powell observe, that is how social science in general operates, and we should view it as a step in the process of understanding how and why human behavior on Black Mesa changed.

The only way to avoid the appearance of conflicting interpretations of a changing data base in a long-term project is not to publish anything except descriptive statements until the research effort has reached a conclusion. This we have not chosen to do. In this light, the published statements about Black Mesa prehistory form a chronological record of shifting method and theory—not only of Black Mesa studies but of Anasazi or even American archaeology as well. In short, they are reflections of reality, some more accurate than others.

The next and final step in the evolution of the project is to reconcile the conflicting interpretations of the larger questions or to eliminate those no longer tenable scenarios of how and why people behaved the way they did on Black Mesa. Work is in progress on this most vital stage of long-term research projects.

George J. Gumerman

Acknowledgments

The fieldwork on which this volume is based was made possible by several individuals and organizations. It was sponsored by the Peabody Coal Company and aided by several of their personnel including John Arnold, Kelly Nolan, John Gingrich, and Leonard Sawtelle. Permission to conduct the fieldwork was granted by the Navajo and Hopi Tribal Councils as well as by the United States Department of the Interior.

Analysis of much of the data discussed in the volume was done using the laboratories and computing facilities of Southern Illinois University at Carbondale, Arizona State University, and the University of Michigan. The Black Mesa project is administered through Southern Illinois University, but the other institutions also generously provided support such as analytical space and personnel.

The task of revising and editing the manuscripts was aided by several colleagues who read parts of the volume and provided comments. These individuals included David Braun, George Gumerman, Fred Plog, and Michael Schiffer, as well as two anonymous reviewers. Also assisting in aspects of the editorial process were Lee Hill, Veletta Canouts, Donna Butler, and Yvette Duncan. Kathy Zeh, Becky Bottlemy, Willow Ealy, Kathy Morgan, and Yvette Duncan typed portions of the manuscript. Plate 1 was photographed by John Richardson, and the figures were drafted by Rob Dunlavey (Figures 2–5, 7, 10, and 11), Tom Gatlin (Figures 6, 8, and 9), Carole Prowse (Figure 1), and Cindy Clabough of Scientific Illustration (Figures 12–19).

Contributors

KATHY BAGLEY-BAUMGARTNER, M.A., Southern Illinois University at Carbondale, 1979, worked on Black Mesa in 1976 and was a research assistant from 1976 to 1978. She was employed by New World Research, Inc., as an Associate Archaeologist from 1980 to 1982 and is currently retained by them as a consultant.

DAVID ECKLES, M.A., Southern Illinois University at Carbondale, 1979, is the Director of Contracting in the Office of the Wyoming State Archaeologist. His research interests include lithic technology, paleoenvironmental change, faunal analysis, Northwest Plains culture change, and historic sites archaeology. He was an assistant crew leader for the Black Mesa Archaeological Project in 1977 and served as a research assistant from 1976 to 1978.

KATHARINE W. FERNSTROM, M.A., Southern Illinois University at Carbondale, 1980, is a doctoral candidate at that institution. Her interests include economic anthropology, archaeological problems of material exchange, information processing, and social organization. She has done fieldwork in the Flagstaff area and on Black Mesa in Arizona, at Salmon Ruins in New Mexico, and at the Great Salt Springs site in southern Illinois.

RICHARD I. FORD is Professor of Anthropology at the University of Michigan, serves as Curator of Ethnobotany for the Museum of Anthropology at that university, and is also a former director of the museum. He has published extensively on the archaeology and ethnology of the Southwest, with particular emphasis on aspects of human ecology. Dr. Ford has directed paleoethnobotanical research on Black Mesa since 1975.

MARGERIE GREEN received her Ph.D. from Arizona State University in 1982. As a long-term participant in the Black Mesa Archaeological Project, her major contribution has been in the sourcing of chipped stone raw materials for the Black Mesa region. This research was reported in her dissertation, *Chipped stone raw materials and the study of interaction*. Her other interests are cultural resource management and Hohokam subsistence-settlement systems.

ANTHONY L. KLESERT, Ph.D., Anthropology, Southern Illinois University at Carbondale, 1980, is currently Tribal Archaeologist for the Navajo Nation, Window Rock, Arizona. His interests are southwestern archaeology, cultural resource management, sociopolitical evolution, and archaeological methods. He worked on Black Mesa from 1975 to 1979 and served as assistant director of the Black Mesa Archaeological Project from 1977 to 1979.

SHEREEN LERNER, M.A., Anthropology, Arizona State University, 1979, is a doctoral candidate at that institution. Her research interests include regional studies, ceramic analysis, and computer applications to archaeology. She has had extensive archaeological field experience throughout central and northern Arizona and was an assistant crew leader on Black Mesa in 1977.

STEPHEN PLOG is Assistant Professor of Anthropology at the University of Virginia and served as director of the Black Mesa Archaeological Project from 1975 to 1978. His research interests include exchange systems, stylistic analysis, method and theory, and cultural change in the American Southwest.

SHIRLEY POWELL is a senior archaeologist with the Center for Archaeological Investigations at Southern Illinois University at Carbondale and has been director of the Black Mesa Archaeological Project since 1978. Her research interests include ethnoarchaeology, prehistoric technology, and settlement systems. Her study of prehistoric settlement on Black Mesa, *Mobility and adaptation,* was published recently by Southern Illinois University Press.

MICHELE SEMÉ received an M.S. in biological sciences from the University of Texas at El Paso in 1980 and an M.A. in anthropology from Southern Illinois University at Carbondale in 1981 and is currently a doctoral candidate at Southern Illinois University at Carbondale. Her research interests include prehistoric hunting strategies and methods of analyzing faunal remains. She has directed analysis of the Black Mesa faunal remains since 1977.

ALAN T. SYNENKI, M.A., Anthropology, Southern Illinois University at Carbondale, 1977, is a doctoral candidate at that institution. He is employed by the Division of Cultural Resources in the North Atlantic Regional Office of the National Park Service. His present research interests include the structure of decision making and information flows, as they relate to organizational change among "tribal" societies, and the curation of archaeological collections in cultural resource management.

1

Archaeological Research on Black Mesa

Stephen Plog and Shirley Powell

In 1976, George Gumerman and Robert Euler (1976b) prefaced the volume entitled *Papers on the archaeology of Black Mesa, Arizona* with the statement that the volume consisted of a number of specialized reports of the type normally generated by long-term research projects. In the years since the publication of that book, continuing fieldwork and research have resulted in additional specialized reports, and we again have elected to publish a number of these research efforts in a single volume.

In the following sections of this chapter, we hope to provide the reader with some basic information on the Black Mesa area and on the archaeological research presented in this volume. We will first briefly describe the environment and cultural history of the research area. Next, we will summarize aspects of the research orientation of the project and of the development of that research in recent years. Finally, the individual papers included in the volume will be introduced.

Physical Environment

The project research area on Black Mesa has been determined by the boundaries of two coal lease areas negotiated with the Navajo and Hopi tribes by Peabody Coal Company of St. Louis, Missouri. These two areas (the western and eastern leases) are shown in Figure 1.

Black Mesa lies within the Colorado Plateau in northeastern Arizona (Plate 1). A general description of the physiography of the area is provided by Gumerman (1970:5):

> The cap and encircling walls of the mesa are composed of Mesa Verde sandstone. Black Mesa, with a diameter of some 75 miles and a circumference of 275 miles, has often been described as a hand with the palm being the highest point to the northeast. The hand dips to the southwest with the fingers forming the Hopi Mesas which are the southern extension of Black Mesa.

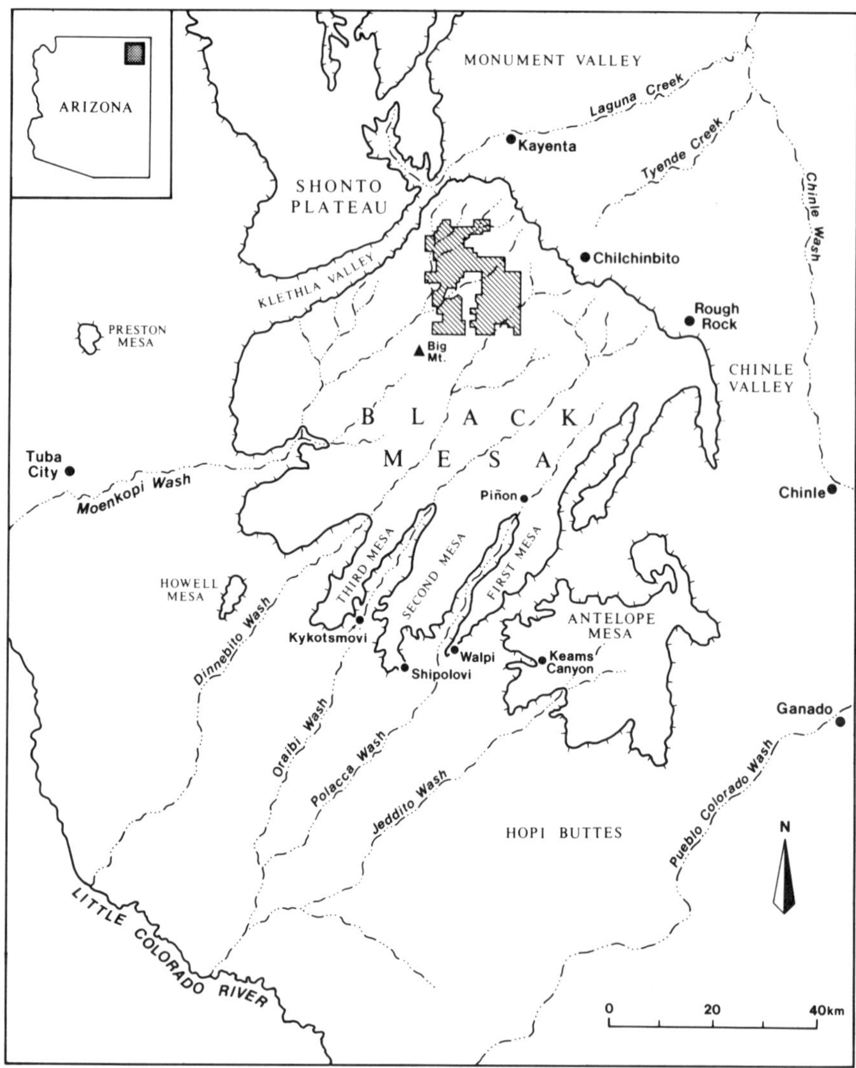

Figure 1. Black Mesa and vicinity showing area of survey and excavation.

Elevations range from 2,472 m at the northeastern edge of the mesa to 1,920 m at the southern edge. The mesa is composed of layers of sedimentary rock; the surface is dissected by numerous small washes, resulting in a landscape of rolling hills. The area is drained by the Tusayan washes—Moenkopi, Dinnebito, Oraibi, Polacca, and Jeddito—which carry water only intermittently after heavy rainstorms. However, standing water sometimes may be found in the wash bottoms or may be obtained by digging shallow

Plate 1. Northern scarp of Black Mesa. View is from the mesa top to the northeast overlooking Long House Valley and Marsh Pass.

wells. Seeps are found at the exposed junctures of the Mesa Verde sandstone and Mancos shale and are currently a major source of drinking water. Along the southern edge of the mesa, seeps are covered by sand dunes banked against the cliffs. These dunes inhibit evaporation of moisture (Hack 1942).

Annual rainfall varies from 25 to 40 cm, with greater amounts of rain falling at higher elevations. The major portion of the annual precipitation currently falls during the summer months. However, there is marked variability in rainfall and annual temperature patterns. The length of the frost-free growing season is 120–150 days (Hack 1942).

Vegetation varies with the rainfall, ranging from grasses and shrubs at lower elevations (Plate 2) to sage, pinyon and juniper, pine, Douglas fir, and aspen at the highest elevations (Plate 3). In general, vegetation can be characterized as belonging to the Upper Sonoran life zone, especially the pinyon and juniper woodland.

Data collected by the Black Mesa Archaeological Project over the past years suggest the presence of four primary plant associations (S. Plog 1977a): (1) pinyon and juniper with sage understory, (2) pinyon and juniper with a cliffrose understory, (3) sagebrush, and (4) sagebrush with dwarf pinyon. The vegetation on and around each site can be classified as belonging to one of these categories, although they rarely fit the exact description.

The physiographic distinction that has been emphasized most frequently in previous publications on Black Mesa is the upland/lowland dichot-

Plate 2. Upland pinyon and juniper environment in lease area.

Plate 3. Lowland sagebrush environment in lease area.

omy. Although this distinction has never been systematically described, the implication is that lowland areas are adjacent to major washes and their tributaries and that upland areas are located in the hilly dissected regions between these washes. Phillips (1972) feels that there is a different subsistence base associated with sites located in the two areas: occupants of lowland sites were able to engage in floodwater agriculture, while the upland peoples were limited to dry farming. Past cultural-historical reconstructions for northeastern Black Mesa have suggested that as population increased over time, groups were forced to emigrate from sites along the major washes and to occupy the "marginal" upland areas. Some researchers (Karlstrom et al. 1976) feel that this population spread was possible only because of climatic amelioration accompanying the population increase. Thus, upland areas are deemed less desirable than lowland areas for occupation by human populations with an agricultural subsistence base.

Cultural History

The prehistoric occupation of northern Black Mesa spans the period from at least 1200 B.C. to A.D. 1150. This span has been divided into seven phases for descriptive purposes and for comparisons with other areas in the plateau Southwest. The phases correspond roughly to stages in the Pecos System classification (Kidder 1927). Major processes in the Black Mesa cultural sequence include the introduction of ceramic technology in the Dot Klish phase; rapid population growth commencing in the Dinnebito phase; changes in technology, exchange networks, and social organization from the Dinnebito through Toreva phases; and abandonment at the end of the Toreva phase. Because several papers in this volume question early cultural reconstructions on methodological grounds, we prefer not to summarize the cultural history here in detail. To facilitate reading of the papers that follow, Table 1 lists Black Mesa phase names, their Pecos equivalents, and the major characteristics that have been suggested to distinguish each phase.

Research Orientation

The papers included in this book cover a variety of topics. This diversity reflects the philosophy of the Black Mesa Archaeological Project: in order to progress toward the goals of explaining cultural change on Black Mesa and contributing to the development of anthropological theory, research must focus on a variety of theoretical, methodological, and technical problems (Goodyear 1975; House and Schiffer 1975). Adequate testing of theoretical models, for example, demands efficient and representative data collection techniques and rigorously tested methods of measuring variables such as room function, diachronic change in faunal procurement, and variation in ceramic vessel function. The papers included in the volume focus primarily on methodological and technical problems, although theoretical questions

Table 1. Current Black Mesa Phase System and Pecos Classification Equivalents.

Phase	Date and Pecos Classification Equivalent	Settlement Pattern	Distinguishing Characteristics
Lolomai	Archaic and Basketmaker II 700 B.C.–A.D. 100	Floodplain pithouse villages; upland hunting-gathering camps	Pithouses; white-baked siltstone lithics; one-hand manos; no ceramics
Dot Klish	Basketmaker III A.D. 600–750	Floodplain pithouse villages; upland hunting-gathering camps; population decrease	Lino Gray and Lino Black-on-gray ceramics; one-hand manos; pithouses
Tallahogan	Basketmaker III–Pueblo I A.D. 750–875	Floodplain villages; upland hunting-gathering camps; population increase	Kana-a Gray and Kana-a Black-on-white ceramics; two-hand manos; slab-lined storage cists
Dinnebito	Pueblo I A.D. 875–975	Upland and lowland farming villages; rapid population increase	Kana-a Black-on-white, Wepo Black-on-white, Kana-a Gray, and Lino Gray ceramics; masonry rooms, jacals, and kivas
Wepo	Pueblo I–II A.D. 975–1050	Upland and lowland farming villages; continued population growth	Wepo Black-on-white, Black Mesa Black-on-white, and Kana-a Gray ceramics; masonry rooms, jacals, and kivas
Lamoki	Pueblo II A.D. 1050–1075	Upland and lowland farming villages; continued population growth	Black Mesa Black-on-white, Sosi Black-on-white, and Tusayan Corrugated ceramics; masonry rooms, jacals, kivas, mealing pithouses, and mealing bins
Toreva	Pueblo II–III A.D. 1075–1150	Upland and lowland farming villages; population decline	Sosi Black-on-white, Dogoszhi Black-on-white, and Tusayan Corrugated ceramics; masonry rooms, jacals, kivas, mealing pithouses, and mealing bins

are considered in a few. More detailed discussions of theoretical aspects of our research have been presented elsewhere (Braun and S. Plog 1982; Klesert 1980; S. Plog 1978, 1980a, 1980b) or will appear in future volumes (S. Plog 1983a).

A detailed discussion of the overall project research design will not be repeated here (see S. Plog 1978; Klesert 1979; Klesert and Layhe 1980).

We do feel it is important to note that many changes have occurred in recent years in the research conducted by the Black Mesa project, although the overall goals of the project have remained the same. These changes have affected several different aspects of our research. First, excavations were begun in 1976 in the eastern half of Peabody Coal Company's lease area. Previous excavations had concentrated exclusively on sites in the western half of the lease area, as shown in Figure 1. As a result, our overall research area has doubled in size and now includes about 256 km² (100 mi²). In addition, the eastern half of the research area differs from the western half in several environmental characteristics. For example, the former area includes portions of both of the major drainages on northern Black Mesa, the Moenkopi and the Dinnebito, whereas the western half primarily encompasses the Moenkopi and its tributaries. The eastern part of the study area is also somewhat higher in elevation, on the average, than the western area, and topographic relief is greater in parts of the western lease area. Finally, preliminary botanical research (Moore 1979) has noted vegetation differences between the two areas, such as more variable densities of pinyon trees in the eastern lease area, that could have affected procurement strategies. We thus have begun to be able to examine adaptive strategies over a wider range of environments, decreasing the extent to which our set of excavated sites is likely to be a biased sample of the research universe (Gumerman and Euler 1976a:163).

Second, the amount of fieldwork that has been done each season has increased considerably in the last five years. Whereas fewer than 10, and often fewer than five, sites were excavated during each season of work prior to 1976, 15 to 25 sites have usually been excavated in each of the succeeding seasons. While this growth in the amount of fieldwork has created some problems, such as ensuring that field information is recorded in an accurate and usable manner (see Bagley-Baumgartner, this volume), it has also increased the feasibility of some types of research. Gumerman and Euler (1976a:164) noted, for example, that a study of paleopathologies was unlikely because of the small number of burials that had been excavated and were likely to be excavated in future years. With the intensification of fieldwork, however, the available burial population has increased significantly, and a comprehensive study of the population is now being made by Debra Martin, George Armelagos, and Alan Swedlund of the University of Massachusetts at Amherst.

In addition to the increased intensity of fieldwork in recent years, more emphasis has been placed on the excavation of sites that are small and have few or no surface indications of structures. This is shown in Table 2. In the parts of the lease area where mitigation work was carried out from 1968 to 1970 (Gumerman 1970; Gumerman et al. 1972), 15 of the 19 (78.9 %) sites with surface indications of structures were excavated, but only one of 11 (9.1 %) sites without surface indications of structures was excavated. In contrast, during the years from 1976 to 1979, only 20 of the 41 (48.8 %) sites

Table 2. Numbers of Sites With and Without Surface Indications of Structures Which Were and Were Not Excavated During Mitigation Work from 1968 to 1970 and from 1976 to 1979.

	1968–1970		1976–1979	
	Excavated	Not Excavated	Excavated	Not Excavated
Surface Indications of Structures Present	15	4	20	21
No Surface Indications of Structures	4	10	29	28

with surface indications of structures were excavated, while a much larger sample of sites (29 of 57, or 50.9 %) without surface evidence of structures was investigated.

Along with this change in data collection strategy, probability sampling of all portions of sites that were not completely excavated and the sifting of all excavated deposits through quarter-inch mesh screening were initiated in 1975. These changes were made in an effort to obtain a more representative sample of prehistoric Black Mesa sites and of artifacts and structures within sites. Not surprisingly, it now appears that some previous conclusions concerning prehistoric Black Mesa sites are no longer valid. For example, Green (this volume) notes that chipped stone tools are not as rare on sites as previous excavations (Gumerman 1970:19) had suggested. In addition, it now appears that sites are not as standardized as earlier studies (Karlstrom et al. 1976:154; Gumerman and Euler 1976a:168) had suggested. As a result of the discovery of increased variation between sites, studies were initiated to describe the variation more thoroughly and to explain it (see the papers by Powell and by Eckles, this volume). Also, research was begun on the relationship between surface and subsurface remains in order to increase our ability to adequately use survey data for research topics such as demographic change and to maximize the information obtained from excavations. The papers in this volume by Synenki and by Klesert and Powell address such issues.

Another important research development has been the initiation of a major effort to recover plant remains from sites by means of flotation techniques. This work has been done by personnel of the Ethnobotanical Laboratory of the University of Michigan, under the direction of Richard I. Ford. Along with the continued research on faunal exploitation, the ethnobotanical research is significantly increasing our knowledge of prehistoric subsistence on Black Mesa. In conjunction with that work, studies have been made to improve our understanding of the Black Mesa environment (Moore 1979), a topic that could not be investigated adequately in previous years (Gumerman and Euler 1976a:163–164). Ultimately, we hope that this research will enable us to test thoroughly various models of cultural change in the American Southwest that have emphasized the importance of subsistence change (e.g., Schoenwetter and Dittert 1968; Glassow 1972, 1977) despite the lack of direct evidence on subsistence. Some initial analyses of the environmental and subsistence data are presented in the papers by Eckles, Semé, and Ford in this volume.

More effort has also been directed toward a study of the Navajo occupation of Black Mesa. This work has largely been supervised by Belinda Blomberg, Shirley Powell, Scott Russell, and Steven Sessions. The Navajo occupation is not only an important topic in and of itself, but it also provides an ethnographic and ethnoarchaeological data base that can aid in the interpretation of the prehistoric record. This is illustrated by Powell's paper on patterns of space utilization on Navajo sites.

Finally, as research on Black Mesa has progressed and as alternative models of cultural change have been generated, we have increasingly realized the necessity of expanding our research universe beyond the Peabody Coal Company lease area. Studies such as Klesert's (1980) investigation of the northern rim area and the survey for chipped stone raw material sources by Margerie Green (Green 1977b) and Phil Schafer of the U.S. Geological Survey have therefore been initiated. Use of data obtained during the latter survey is a critical component of the papers by Green and Fernstrom in this volume. The necessity for continued research outside the lease area is discussed in more detail in the volume's concluding paper by Plog and Powell.

The Individual Papers

The papers included in this volume are based on analyses of data collected during one or more of the field seasons from 1975 through 1980 and were written sometime during the period from 1976 to 1981. Thus, many of the papers use different data, and the later efforts have the benefit of information and ideas accumulated over a longer time period. The papers by Bagley-Baumgartner, Eckles, Fernstrom, and Synenki are condensed versions of masters theses submitted to the Department of Anthropology, Southern Illinois University at Carbondale. Virtually all of the remaining articles are revised versions of papers presented at the annual meetings of the Society for American Archaeology.

Descriptive reports on excavations conducted during the field seasons from 1975 to 1980 have been published (Layhe et al. 1976; S. Plog 1977d; Klesert 1978; Klesert and Powell 1979; Powell et al. 1980; Andrews et al. 1982). These reports discuss in detail the sites excavated, the excavation techniques used, and the data collected. For this reason, we feel it is unnecessary to repeat descriptions of data and techniques here. Each paper includes a short section on data collection techniques, which should suffice for most readers. The reader desiring more information is referred to the descriptive volumes cited above.

For the purpose of convenience, the papers have been grouped into four general categories: (1) the measurement of surface-subsurface relationships; (2) functional interpretations of material remains; (3) subsistence reconstructions; and (4) studies of chipped stone raw material procurement, use, and exchange.

The papers by Synenki and by Powell and Klesert focus on processes affecting the visibility and interpretation of surface remains. Synenki demonstrates that the relationship between surface and subsurface artifact frequencies is highly complex and variable at both the intrasite and intersite levels. Consequently, surface remains are predictive of subsurface remains only when various cultural and natural variables are recognized and their effects controlled. Synenki uses multiple regression analysis and partial correlation coefficients to measure the importance of each of the variables affecting the surface-subsurface relationship.

Powell and Klesert have tackled the problem of identifying subsurface structures on artifact scatters using only survey data. They note the importance of understanding variation in sites classified as artifact scatters and demonstrate that it is possible to discern variation within that category of site without resorting to excavation. Such scatters may represent the loci of activities that do not occur at larger habitation sites and thus are critical to understanding prehistoric subsistence-settlement systems. Furthermore, the ability to predict the nature of subsurface variation on artifact scatters prior to excavation greatly enhances the decision-making ability of the archaeologist working under contractual constraints.

The papers by Bagley-Baumgartner and by Lerner and the two papers by Powell investigate the relationship between categories of material culture and the functions they serve. Bagley-Baumgartner tests the hypothesis that room types (e.g., masonry, jacal, or pit structures) can be used to predict the activities that took place in the rooms. It has generally been assumed that masonry structures on Black Mesa were used for storage, and pithouses and jacal structures were used for habitation. Bagley-Baumgartner tests this assumption using artifactual and feature information as well as structure size measurements from excavated rooms. Although she finds that the assumptions noted above are a simplification of reality, her results suggest that masonry rooms generally were storage rooms, and jacal structures were in most instances habitation rooms. Pithouses appear to have been much more variable in function than previous analyses have suggested. While some were specialized mealing rooms, others have characteristics suggesting that they were multifunctional. Careful consideration of the characteristics of each room, however, is shown to be necessary before inferences concerning room function can be made. That is, information on room architecture alone is not sufficient for inferring the activities carried out in the structure. Bagley-

Baumgartner also found that room characteristics such as room size and the presence or absence of hearths, which are less affected by a variety of formation processes, show the strongest patterns of association and appear to be the best indicators of room function.

Lerner examines attributes of ceramic vessels that she suggests will vary with the use of the container. She notes, for example, that ceramic vessels used for different purposes such as food storage or cooking would require differing degrees of vessel access and containment security. Lerner devises and tests a classificatory system based on vessel form, presence/absence of decoration, vessel wall thickness, orifice diameter, and neck height. Functional interpretations are proposed for the statistically significant attribute associations. In addition, wall thickness and orifice diameter for both bowls and jars and neck height for jars are examined for temporal variation. The temporal patterns on Black Mesa are compared with the results of similar studies by Turner and Lofgren (1966) and by Beals et al. (1945). Explanations for some of the observed patterns of change are proposed.

Powell questions the proposal that a continuous relationship exists between the area a group occupies and the number of individuals in the group. She contends that the season in which a site is occupied will affect patterns of use of interior site space. Measures of interior and total site area for 34 seasonally occupied Navajo sites were used to test the proposition that summer-occupied sites have proportionally and absolutely less interior space on them than winter-occupied sites have. The propositions are validated statistically, and the implications of Powell's findings for studies of prehistoric population dynamics are considered.

In a second study, Powell considers the relationships among site size, seasonality, and site function. She notes that many interpretive studies use site size measures to infer both the function of a site and the season it was occupied. If large and small sites coexist in a region, for example, the large sites usually are inferred to be permanent habitation sites, and the small sites are assumed to be seasonal outliers of the large sites. This assumption implies a difference in the activities performed at the sites that, in turn, implies variation in the artifact inventories, features, and environmental settings of the sites. Powell statistically tests this implied variation and finds little variation among sites assigned to different size categories.

The papers by Ford, Semé, and Eckles evaluate data used to make subsistence reconstructions. Ford investigates the natural biomass of potentially edible plants that grow at elevations above 2,000 m. He notes that such plants typically are variable in yield, unpredictable in occurrence, and diverse in nutritional content. This ecological situation confronted Archaic gatherers and hunters who exploited these upper elevations. The introduction of cornfield agriculture in high-elevation settings was an ecological process that created new habitats for pioneer annual species such as chenopods, pigweed, purslane, and Indian ricegrass. Thus, in these anthropogenic plant communities, plant diversity was encouraged, yields were increased, and useful biomass became more predictable. Ford argues that although extensive areas were not disturbed, sufficient amounts of land were affected to encourage greater subsistence security and longer residence in one locality. He evaluates this model by examining charred plant remains from sites on northeastern Black Mesa dating between 600 B.C. and A.D. 200.

Semé also considers the effects of human alteration of the physical environment on plant and animal biomass. She notes that the introduction of cornfield agriculture created habitats for potentially exploitable animal as well as plant species. The artificial concentration of small rodents and other animals in anthropogenic field communities resulted in increased yields of a more predictable resource from garden hunting. Analysis of faunal remains from excavated sites suggests three faunal categories that coincide with structural diversity indexes. Only one site category has strong evidence for garden hunting, however, and the frequency of sites falling in this category varies over time.

Eckles evaluates the effect of two variables, site function and site location, on the types and diversity of faunal remains at different sites. He demonstrates that there is a significant relationship between faunal and structural diversity at the sites. This relationship appears to be the result of seasonal variation in resource procurement and of the priority of procuring plant resources as opposed to animal resources. Site location is found to have less impact on intersite variation in faunal remains.

The papers by Green and by Fernstrom investigate patterns in the use of chipped stone raw materials. Green tests proposals concerning prehistoric use of effort-minimization strategies in carrying out prehistoric activities. More specifically, she examines the hypothesis that the use and conservation of chipped stone raw materials are related to the distance of a site from the various raw material sources. Using information from two sites, several test implications are examined, and these generally confirm the employment of effort-minimization strategies. Differences between the two sites in the use of raw materials are also discussed.

Fernstrom views exchange networks as dynamic systems that are affected, in a predictable manner, by social systemic changes external to the network. She uses nonlocal lithic raw materials from excavated Black Mesa sites to measure fluctuations in the organization of local exchange networks. Fernstrom posits that during periods of subsistence stress, systemic reorganization will be reflected in a significant decrease in the frequency of nonlocal chipped stone materials found on the sites. Instead, less desirable local materials will be used because less energy is expended in their procurement. The observed patterns do not conform to her predictions, however, and Fernstrom concludes that population density and information-exchange may have been two additional variables affecting the configuration of the chipped stone procurement networks.

In the concluding paper, Plog and Powell discuss the implications of recent fieldwork and research for models of the spatial organization of procurement systems. They suggest that procurement systems were not static, as has been suggested previously, but changed between A.D. 800 and 1125 along with other aspects of the cultural system such as population density. These changes also required alterations in exchange systems and social networks, and hypotheses about the nature of these alterations are proposed. Finally, they argue that the primary environmental model of cultural change that has been developed for prehistoric Black Mesa cannot account for the pattern of change in procurement systems, exchange systems, and social networks.

Before presenting the individual research papers discussed above, we would like to note that the Black Mesa project has been especially fortunate in the longevity of the investigations and in the continuity of the personnel associated with the project. Those of us involved in the ongoing research have benefited from the continued accumulation of data and from the interpretive efforts of earlier researchers. However, this longevity has also led to some interpretive disagreements among the researchers working with Black Mesa project data. Continued fieldwork has produced data which conflict with some published accounts of Black Mesa and Anasazi prehistory or which, more often, fall outside the range of variation of the site, artifact, or adaptive patterns suggested by initial research. Many of the papers in this volume represent first attempts to understand the sources of the variation that confronted us as fieldwork continued. As such, they use early published accounts as springboards for reevaluation and elaboration. Reevaluation of earlier research is, thus, a result of the evolution of the project and should not be regarded as a criticism of the initial research. We expect that the coming years will also bring refinements and reinterpretations of the research presented here.

2

Understanding the Relationship Between Surface and Subsurface Remains: An Approach to Isolating Potential Sources of Variation

Alan T. Synenki

At one time or another, virtually all archaeologists have to rely to some extent on surface distributions of artifactual debris. Lack of time and money resulting from contractual demands and the lack of archaeological information about a given area contribute to this situation. Archaeologists who have worked on Black Mesa during the past 12 years have had to contend at times with both factors.

Archaeologists have utilized the spatial distribution of surface artifacts for a variety of purposes. For example, the distributional patterning and the density of artifact types have been used to infer the locale of specialized activities or to estimate duration and intensity of occupation at a particular site. In areas of the world where little or no archaeological work has been conducted, surface materials have been collected to obtain a representative sample of the artifactual inventory at a specific site and to make predictions about subsurface remains. For example, site boundaries are frequently delineated on the basis of the spatial distribution of surface remains. More commonly, surface debris densities have been employed to plan excavation strategies.

All of these uses of the surface distribution of artifactual remains are based on the assumption that a meaningful relationship exists between the surface and subsurface of an archaeological site. Although this assumption has not always been verified by empirical tests, it has been followed quite regularly as a rule of thumb (Hole and Heizer 1973:176). Consequently, there are both practical and methodologically sound reasons for studying the relationship between surface and subsurface remains. First, knowledge of this relationship will allow construction of an efficient, productive sampling strategy for a site. That is, strategically located excavation squares would more likely recover the particular data needed to answer specific research questions. Second, explicit knowledge of the relationship between surface and subsurface remains is important for regional surveys. A better understanding of this relationship will provide a firmer basis for interpreting temporal, functional, and demographic aspects of sites. Finally, precise knowledge of the relationship between surface and subsurface remains is particularly important in contractual archaeology, where time and budgetary constraints are of great concern. Since decisions must be made during mitigation as to which sites will be excavated and which ones will not, an understanding of surface-subsurface relationships could aid decisions concerning which sites to excavate and where to excavate within a given site.

Past Studies

As early as the first quarter of the twentieth century, a number of archaeologists began to question and assess the reliability of using surface artifacts to answer specific questions about subsurface remains. For instance, questions were raised about the validity of using surface materials to obtain a reliable intrasite chronology (Spier 1917; Ford and Willey 1949; Phillips et al. 1951; Ford 1951; Tolstoy 1958).

Recently, there has been a renewed interest in the relationship between surface and subsurface materials. Binford et al. (1970) evaluated traditional field methods for selecting intrasite locations for excavation at the Hatchery West site in Illinois. Specifically, they were interested in assessing the degree to which surface artifacts correlated with subsurface structures or features. The following summarized results were obtained: (1) the areas that had the highest density of surface ceramics overlay refuse areas; (2) the surface areas that had the lightest ceramic densities overlay house structures; (3) in areas of the site where preceramic occupation occurred, no ceramics were present on the surface, but a high density of other artifacts existed; and (4) the distributions of different gross artifact classes spatially varied independently of one another. They observed that a surface collection of artifacts from any one location at Hatchery West would not provide the investigator with a representative sample of all artifacts present. Furthermore, Binford et al. determined that surface artifact densities alone told them little about the internal structure of the site. Nevertheless, they did conclude that with a program of stratified sampling and/or prior knowledge of the cultural history of the site, surface artifact densities could serve as a useful guide for planning excavation strategy (1970:71).

In another recent study, Redman and Watson (1970) at Cayönü and Girik-i-Haciyan in southeastern Turkey carried out an intensive investigation of the relationship between surface and subsurface remains. The purpose of this study, not unlike that at Hatchery West, was to examine whether surface distribution of artifacts could be used to design efficient intrasite excavation strategies. In particular, Redman and Watson (1970:280) were interested in testing the hypothesis that surface and subsurface artifacts are interrelated to the extent that a description of the first would allow prediction of the second. The results of their study revealed that at both Cayönü and Girik-i-Haciyan the surface distribution of artifactual debris is significantly related to the sub-surface content of the sites. They also demonstrated a meaningful relationship between the different proportions and classes of artifactual materials both on and underneath the surface. Finally, Redman and Watson were able to establish that the first 50 cm of artifact deposition was almost identical to the surface distribution of artifactual debris.

Schiffer (Schiffer and Rathje 1973; Hanson and Schiffer 1975:81–84; Reid et al. 1975), using data from the Joint Site in east-central Arizona, also conducted a study of the relationship between surface and subsurface remains. He examined this relationship to assess the validity of using surface artifact distributions to plan a more productive excavation strategy. Schiffer's analysis indicated that in general the density of surface materials at this particular site proved to be a poor predictor of the density of subsurface artifactual materials. To account for these results, Schiffer examined the noncultural factors that were responsible in the formation of the archaeological record at the Joint Site. He concluded that erosion was the primary cause for low surface artifact densities in certain areas of the site, and he reasoned that aeolian sand deposition was another principal cause for low surface artifact densities in other areas of the Joint Site.

In another study, Tolstoy and Fish (1973, 1975), working in the Basin of Mexico, suggest that two important factors—the length of occupation and the quantity of overburden—account for a significant proportion of the variability in the configuration and density of surface artifacts on a site. From this they reasoned that in order to use surface artifactual debris to predict subsurface remains, an attempt should be made to control for the effects of these two factors. Surface artifact collection and test excavations at the Coapexco site confirmed Tolstoy and Fish's assertions. In particular, they discovered that not all surface concentrations represent the remains of contemporary occupations. Further, they found that although structures and features were located where surface concentrations generally indicated they would be, houses and features frequently appeared where one would not expect them. Excavations further confirmed Tolstoy and Fish's suspicions that the amount of surface artifacts is a function of how deeply buried the prehistoric occupation strata are from the present surface of a site. In particular, they found that few subsurface artifact concentrations below 25 cm could be located by surface indicators. Tolstoy and Fish used these findings to illustrate the importance of intersite variation in surface artifacts to make inferences about the population size of a prehistoric community in the Basin of Mexico.

Flannery (1976) also studied the relationship between surface and subsurface remains using the site of San Jose Mogote in Oaxaca, Mexico, as his test case. Assumptions and predictions were made about subsurface remains from particular classes of surface artifactual debris. His study yielded a large number of predictors for the early, middle, and late Formative periods at the site. Specifically, he discovered that different classes of surface artifact concentrations could predict such things as different residential patterns, the location of public versus residential structures, and the boundaries of the site at the aforementioned temporal periods. While Flannery (1976) expressed optimism in the use of surface materials to predict subsurface remains, he, like Tolstoy and Fish (1975), suggested that both natural and cultural disturbances need to be considered in future research in order to increase the precision and hence the confidence in their results.

Despite the valuable knowledge gained by these studies, two problem areas were neglected. First, with the exception of Schiffer (Schiffer and Rathje 1973; Hanson and Schiffer 1975:82–84; Reid et al. 1975:220–224) and Tolstoy and Fish (1975), all previous studies have been descriptive in nature—not explanatory. For example, although Binford et al. (1970) and Redman and Watson (1970) recognized that both cultural and noncultural factors affect the relationship between surface and subsurface remains, no attempt was made to isolate and measure them. As a result, neither study could adequately account for why some areas of the sites had an overall closer correspondence between surface and subsurface remains than other areas of the sites. Second, except for Redman and Watson, previous studies were conducted at only a single site, thereby neglecting variability in the relationship between surface and subsurface remains at the intersite level. Indeed, the study of intersite variability is crucial in isolating and measuring those critical variables that uniformly affect the relationship between surface and subsurface remains. Only through intersite analysis will it be possible to predict adequately and explain when there will or will not be a significant relationship between surface and subsurface remains. The research discussed below, which was conducted during 1976–1977 (Synenki 1977, 1978a), is an attempt to remedy the above deficiencies.

Explaining Variability in the Relationship Between Surface and Subsurface Remains

The major goal of this research was to construct an explanatory model for the relationship between surface and subsurface remains. Model, as used here, simply refers to a conceptual construct or "piece of machinery that relates observations to theoretical ideas" (Clarke 1972:1–2). The term relationship is used here as statisticians use it. That is, a relationship is a specified set of ordered pairs that can, in some instances such as multiple regression, include the property of conditionality (Kerlinger and Pedhazur 1973:11–12).

The construction of such a model is important because it will allow us to better understand several of the specific factors that account for variance in the relationship between surface and subsurface remains. This could ultimately permit researchers working on Black Mesa and in other areas of the southwestern United States to design more efficient and effective survey and excavation strategies.

Constructing such a model necessitates investigating natural and cultural formation processes (Schiffer 1972, 1976; Schiffer and Rathje 1973) to answer the important question of how the archaeological record was produced. Schiffer (1972, 1976) has argued that the structure of the archaeological record as we observe it is in many ways a distorted reflection of the structure of past human activities. As a result, the investigation of almost any archaeological problem requires that the archaeologist understand those factors responsible for this distortion. Indeed, this is particularly important in modeling the relationship between surface and subsurface remains. Thus, we must attempt to isolate and explain which natural and cultural factors could account for the variability we observe in the relationship between surface and subsurface remains. Several factors that may be important are discussed below, with emphasis on factors that may be important in the North American Southwest, where the research described below was conducted.

Two primary natural variables—density of vegetation and slope of the land—are believed to have a significant effect on the relationship between surface and subsurface remains. Vegetation affects the relationship between surface and subsurface remains in at least three ways.

The first and perhaps most important effect of vegetation density is on postdepositional erosional processes (Morgan 1969:239–240; Kirkby 1969b:215, 217, 225), especially in semiarid and arid regions of the world such as the Southwest (Kirkby 1969a:235). For example, dense surface vegetation increases the infiltration rate of water into soils by lessening the impact of rainfall on the surface. This reduces soil compaction, thereby preventing or at least minimizing erosion.

Second, root growth is believed to play an important role in surface and subsurface movement of material remains. Plants may serve as obstructions that stop the downslope movement of artifacts from erosion or other processes. Also, in many instances, as the density of surface vegetation increases, the associated root system beneath the ground also increases. This can affect the displacement of objects in several ways. First, a more compact root system may restrict the amount of displacement of an object by constraining its movement by various underground soil or fluvial processes. On the other hand, the very act of root growth itself can displace subsurface objects both vertically and horizontally. Obviously, variability in the amount of object displacement will be conditioned by such things as the type of vegetation, root size, and extent of root growth.

Third, vegetation also has an important effect on the visibility of surface artifactual debris. Thus, type and density of vegetation cover affect survey results. For example, at sites where pinyon trees predominate, needle cover will affect the quantity and type of artifactual materials visible on the surface. Density of individual plants also plays an influential role in surface artifact visibility. For instance, artifactual materials may be obscured on archaeological sites with dense sagebrush cover.

Slope is also believed to have an important effect on the relationship between surface and subsurface remains. Given a set of circumstances, a variety of processes can be responsible for both the rapid movement (e.g., earth flows, mud flows, and landslides) and slow movement (e.g., creep and solifluction) of materials downslope. In all likelihood, the predominant process associated with slope is erosion, but few controlled, quantitative studies have been conducted to measure its specific effects. However, the studies of Schumm (1964; 1967) and Eardley and Vivavant (1967) in the southwestern United States have successfully demonstrated that the rate of erosion is in most cases directly related to the slope gradient. A variety of factors—including water, gravity, air, plants, and animals—can trigger the process.

The movement of materials downslope through water erosion can be the result of either rain splash or flowing water. Careful measurements have demonstrated that in some areas of the United States, rain splash from a heavy rainstorm can move as much as 100 metric tons of material per acre (Leet and Judson 1954:207), while other studies have revealed that splash back following raindrop impact can move some stones as far as 40 cm (Kirkby 1969a:229). Downslope erosion occurs when the infiltration capacity of the soil is reached or when rainfall intensity exceeds the rate at which infiltration can occur. The latter process, referred to as the "Horton Overland Flow Model" (Horton 1945), occurs in semiarid and arid environments (Kirkby 1969b:217) where high-intensity summer rains dominate.

The movement of materials downslope through the force of gravity is also important (Leet and Judson 1954:189). The processes associated with this force have generally been termed graviturbation. According to Wood and Johnson (1978:346):

> Graviturbation is the mixing and movement of soil and rock debris downslope, including subsidence, principally under the influence of gravity, without the aid of the flowing medium of transport such as air, water or glacial ice.

Various graviturbation processes such as creep, subsidence, and solifluction are considered to be especially important to the movement of archaeological materials downslope.

The actual movement of materials downslope will occur when the inertia of an object is overcome. A variety of sources can initiate downslope movement: for example, certain human activities, animal burrowing (Reed 1957:386–389; Bourlière 1964; Gile 1975), and plant growth and decay (see Wood and Johnson [1978:328–333] for a review). On the other hand, various other processes such as frost weathering (Washburn 1973; Embleton and King 1968), thermal expansion and contraction of the soil (Peel 1966; Tricart and Cailleux 1962), and salt hydration (Evans 1970) occur regularly in arid and semiarid environments and therefore may provide the stimuli for movement. Furthermore, in arid and semiarid regions, underground fluvial processes such as "piping" (Kirkby 1969a) may be responsible for the initial movement of materials downslope. Once the movement of an object occurs, it will continue to move until it is stopped by an obstruction or it has dissipated its kinetic energy. The resulting distribution of artifacts based on differences in weight, density, and size is well illustrated by Rick's (1976) analysis of the downslope movement of artifacts at the site of Ccurimachay in Peru.

In closing the discussion of the natural variables that can affect the relationship between surface and subsurface remains, it is necessary to mention briefly a number of other subsidiary variables. However, none of these variables will be measured quantitatively and included in the tests discussed below.

It has been observed that in arid and semiarid areas throughout the world, wind action can be responsible for soil particle detachment, which in turn is closely related to hydraulic erosional processes (Morgan 1969:242). In reference to northeastern Arizona, Hack (1942:44) argued that wind action is more severe today than it was during early Puebloan times. Specifically, Hack sees the change in severity of wind action occurring during or slightly after Pueblo III times. Although strong winds may not move artifactual debris to any great degree, both deflation and deposition of soil as a result of wind action are viewed here as important variables affecting the relationship between surface and subsurface remains. Deflation exposes artifactual debris, but deposition buries materials.

The type and amount of precipitation could also be an important factor. In northeastern Arizona, for example, seasonal torrential rainstorms have been the pattern for a great many years (Sellers and Hill 1974:9). Arroyo cutting, along with the general erosional processes discussed above, has been considered one result of this type of rainfall pattern.

Soil composition and chemistry also play roles in the formation of an archaeological site. However, these variables are not viewed as critical factors affecting the relationship between surface and subsurface remains in the Black Mesa study area because of the homogeneity in soil type and chemistry (U.S. Department of the Interior 1964) at both the intra- and intersite levels. Nevertheless, aeolian deposition will be carefully considered for its effect on the archaeological sites under investigation.

The grazing of sheep and goats may also affect the relationship between surface and subsurface remains, not only by breaking and moving materials on the surface of a site but also by removing the vegetation that may then allow erosion to occur. Precise records of grazing have not been recorded for Black Mesa; however, Navajo sheep and goat herding has been a long-recognized tradition. Systematic studies of grazing in other areas of the Southwest (e.g., Cottam and Stewart 1940; Pickford 1932) have confirmed the general plant successional changes that have occurred over time. These studies indicate that as a result of heavy grazing, a serious depletion of the perennial grasses occurred, followed by an increase in the density of sagebrush and other perennial weeds. Furthermore, several other studies have confirmed that vegetational changes caused by overgrazing have greatly affected the rate of runoff (e.g., Forsling 1931).

In addition to the natural transformational processes discussed above, two types of cultural modifications of the natural landscape—structures and refuse areas—are considered to have a significant effect on the relationship between surface and subsurface remains. The presence and frequency of masonry, surface, and subterranean structures are believed to affect the relationship in different ways as a result of two primary factors.

First, different types of materials used to build structures will result in their differential preservation. This in turn will contribute to variability in the deposition of material remains. For example, surface structures such as jacal rooms, which are constructed of wood or wattle-and-daub, are subject to rapid destruction through burning, wood removal, or natural decay. On the other hand, masonry structures do not deteriorate as quickly. Although roof-fall from structures may initially cover material remains left on the floor, in most instances masonry wall-fall will ultimately be responsible for burying and anchoring items both within and adjacent to masonry structures. In other instances, portions of the stone walls of masonry structures will stand, allowing aeolian deposits to accumulate and hence to cover artifactual remains. At the Joint Site, Schiffer made special note of the above occurrence and concluded that, all other things being equal, the accumulation of aeolian soil should be proportional to the height of a standing wall (Schiffer and Rathje 1973:173). In subterranean structures, roof-fall and aeolian deposition will be primarily responsible for burying material remains. In some instances, subterranean structures no longer inhabited or used for ritual activities may be used as secondary refuse deposits. In either case, the depth of subterranean structures restricts the movement of items inside these structures. Because collapsed subterranean structures form depressions in the landscape, they tend to collect the material remains through time.

Second, the relationship between surface and subsurface remains will be affected by the specific activities performed in and around different structures. The important point here is that different activities that are associated with different kinds of structures will have a direct effect on the processes of refuse disposal. Schiffer (1976:161) suggests that variability in refuse disposal patterns is governed primarily by the ease of moving the activity as opposed to the ease of moving the trash. I suggest that other factors can also account for variability in refuse disposal patterns, such as the cost of procuring certain raw materials versus the cost of curating items manufactured out of scarce materials (see Green, this volume) or simply the desire to maintain sanitary conditions. Several examples illustrate this point.

With the possible exception of late Toreva phase sites, sites with abandoned grinding rooms on Black Mesa often contain large grinding stones or slabs that appear to still be usable. Similarly, on the floors of masonry storage rooms, unbroken large and small whiteware and grayware ceramic vessels have frequently been recovered. In both instances, we may infer with some confidence that the cost of curating these items was greater than the cost of leaving them behind at the abandoned site. In other instances, both within and adjacent to habitation units such as surface jacal structures on Black Mesa, relatively few artifacts have been recovered. It is suggested that a major reason for this occurrence may be periodic cleaning activities of the prehistoric inhabitants. Indeed, an ethnoarchaeological study by DeBoer and Lathrap (1979:127–134) indicates that one of the main reasons little refuse accumulates in and around habitation structures is the daily removal of refuse from these areas to secondary deposits located at the perimeter of the inhabited site. The essential point is that different activities, different structures, and different discard behaviors result in different assemblages.

In addition to the effect of structures, that of refuse areas is also considered in the tests below. A refuse area, as used here, refers to a centralized disposal location where unused or exhausted material items are purposely discarded (e.g., secondary refuse areas, in Schiffer's [1976:161] terms). The presence of refuse areas affects the relationship between surface and subsurface remains in the following ways. The accumulation of a trash mound often results in an artificially increased slope, thereby fostering the movement of artifacts downslope. The extent or rate of this movement is primarily affected by the height, depth, and extent of the refuse. A number of factors can be responsible for the configuration that a refuse deposit displays. For instance, the mode of disposal behavior exhibited by a specific prehistoric population is considered important here. By disposal behavior I am referring to the range of behavioral properties that select for the particular choice of disposal locations. In certain situations, for example, certain items or classes of items may be consistently disposed of in specific discard locations. In other instances, all items may be thrown together in a single location at the perimeter of the inhabited site.

Refuse production rates are also believed to be an important factor in the development of refuse deposit configuration. Refuse production rate generally refers to the frequency with which items are discarded and are regarded as a function of artifacts' use-lives (Schiffer 1972:158–160). An artifact use-life is related directly to its cost in terms of the energy required to procure, manufacture, and maintain it. This cost in turn affects the decision to transport the artifact to a different site or to discard it. Refuse production rates are significantly affected by the rates of recycling (e.g., reworking a projectile point into an end scraper) and lateral cycling (e.g., families passing ritual paraphernalia over the generations). For more lengthy discussions of recycling and lateral cycling, see Schiffer (1972:158–159, 1976:38–39).

Other important factors affecting the configuration of a refuse mound, as well as surface-subsurface relationships on the site as a whole, include the size of the community, the duration and intensity of occupation, and the site's primary function (e.g., special or limited activity versus multiple activities). The extent of prehistoric human and nonhuman scavenging may also be an important factor.

The above discussion is offered to render a better understanding of an admittedly complex reality. Considerable attention was devoted to both the cultural and natural processes that could alter the relationship between surface and subsurface remains. General as well as specific arguments were presented as to how each process could affect the spatial distribution of material items. Given these arguments, the following hypotheses have been generated; they will be tested using data from Black Mesa:

H_1: Given the direct relationship between the degree of slope and the amount of downslope movement of materials, as the slope of the land on sites increases, there will be a decreasing correspondence between the frequency of surface and subsurface artifacts on sites.

H_2: If vegetation is restraining artifact movement and if the visibility of surface artifacts is not impaired by vegetation, then as the density of vegetation increases on a site, there will be an increasing correspondence between the frequency of surface and subsurface artifacts on the site.

H_3: As the area encompassed by jacal, masonry, and subterranean structures increases at a site, there will be a decreasing correspondence between the frequency of surface and subsurface artifacts on the site due to the burial of materials upon collapse of the structures and to the increased aeolian deposition that may occur in or around structures. As noted above, these effects may be more significant for masonry structures than jacal structures.

H_4: As the size of refuse areas increases at a site, there will be a decreasing overall correspondence between the frequency of surface and subsurface artifacts on the site.

These hypotheses lead to somewhat different expectations for different types of sites. On the one hand, the last two hypotheses suggest that there will be a decreasing correlation between the frequencies of surface and subsurface artifacts whenever there are increases (1) in the density of site inhabitants, and probably structures, per square meter of occupation area; (2) in the number of structures, such as mealing rooms, built for specialized activities; and (3) in the duration of occupation. Thus, better correlations would be expected on special-activity sites than on habitation sites. On the other hand, special-activity sites on Black Mesa tend to be located in upland areas where vegetation density, particularly sagebrush density, is low and relief is high, while habitation sites tend to be found in areas with greater densities of sagebrush and lower relief (Catlin 1978). Given these tendencies, if the first two hypotheses are correct, better surface-subsurface correlations would be expected on habitation sites than on special-activity sites.

In order to evaluate these hypotheses, several different tests are carried out below. The Pearson product-moment correlation statistic is used to measure the relationship between the frequency of artifacts on the surface and subsurface at each site. This statistic will also be used to measure the relationship between surface and subsurface remains within each type of structure as well as in refuse areas. Analysis of variance is employed to discern whether one can predict the presence of refuse areas and different types of structures solely on the basis of surface artifact frequencies. Finally, a series of tests using the semipartial regression statistic measures the individual contribution and effect of each of the natural and cultural factors discussed above to the total variability in the relationship between surface and subsurface remains.

The Data

Sample Size

The data used to test the hypotheses consisted of 14 prehistoric Anasazi sites excavated in the summer of 1976 in the eastern lease area of northeastern Black Mesa (Table 3). There are two reasons why these sites were chosen for this analysis.

First, data are comparable at all 14 sites. That is, all sites were surface collected and then excavated in 2×2 m grid units. As a result of this procedure, comparison of surface and subsurface remains was accomplished with little difficulty. The excavation strategy that was followed at each of the sites varied somewhat, but a probability sample was excavated on all parts of each site where only partial excavation of the area was possible. In addition, dense concentrations of shrubs were removed prior to the surface collections in order to increase the visibility of artifacts on the surface (see S. Plog [1977b] for a detailed description of the specific sampling designs used).

Second, the attributes of the 14 sites vary. To adequately investigate any complex phenomenon, the researcher must have variance: "If variables do not vary, if they do not have variance, the scientist cannot do his work" (Kerlinger and Pedhazur 1973:3). For example, the occupation dates of these sites range from about A.D. 800 to 1150. Although some sites appear to have had a lengthy occupation, others were inhabited for only a short duration. In terms of functional variability, many were used as year-round habitation sites, but some sites excavated in the summer season of 1976 were considered nonhabitation sites. A nonhabitation site is defined as a temporary or seasonally occupied site where the range of activities was limited in scope (Plog and Hill 1971:8).

The sites also differ in other characteristics. For instance, variability exists in the number and types of structures at different sites. Similarly, at different sites the volume or density of debris in the refuse area also varies.

Furthermore, there are some similarities and some differences among the sites in vegetation cover and the slope of the terrain on which they are situated.

To study the relationship between surface and subsurface artifact frequency at an archaeological site, all ceramic, lithic, and groundstone artifacts were analyzed, and their frequencies were totaled for each 2 × 2 m square. These totals were used in the analyses discussed below. Although ceramics are by far the most frequent artifact type found on archaeological sites on Black Mesa, chipped stone and groundstone are considered important in this study for the following reason. At some sites, or in certain areas of some sites, different activities may have required the use or manufacture of groundstone and lithic artifacts as opposed to ceramics. For example, we might expect mealing rooms or tool-manufacturing areas to have a higher frequency of groundstone or chipped stone than ceramics. Therefore, analyzing ceramics alone could bias or skew the results considerably.

Variable Definition and Measurement

As previously noted, six variables were isolated, and their effects on the relationship between surface and subsurface remains were predicted by the model. The following variable definitions are offered to avoid possible confusion. The method by which each variable was measured is also discussed below.

Slope, as used in this study, simply refers to the vertical angle of the land on which a site is located. To measure the effect of slope on the relationship between surface and subsurface remains, the average slope angle (measured in degrees) was obtained for each of the 14 archaeological sites. The average slope angle on a site is considered an accurate measurement for this study because this research is concerned with assessing the general or overall effect of slope on the site as a whole. The slope angle for each site was calculated by the following procedure. First, the lowest elevational point was subtracted from the highest elevational point on each site map to derive the drop in elevation. Second, the distance between the planes of the lowest and highest elevational points was measured. Third, these two measurements were fit into the following equation for deriving the slope of an angle:

$$\text{Slope Angle} = \frac{\text{Vertical Distance Between Highest and Lowest Points}}{\text{Horizontal Distance Between Highest and Lowest Points}}$$

Density of vegetation is defined as the quantity of plants or shrubs per unit area on a site. To measure the effect of vegetation on the relationship between surface and subsurface remains, the density of vegetation per m^2 on each site was calculated. At each of the 14 archaeological sites, the density of vegetation was calculated from a single vegetation quadrat. Each quadrat is considered to be a representative sample of the vegetation present on the entire site. The size of the quadrat was either 50 × 20 m or 30 × 20 m.

Table 3. Summary Characteristics of the Sites Used in the Analysis.

Site	Phase	Site Type	Predominant Vegetation Cover	Surface Indications	Number of Structures
D:11:97	Early Toreva	Small habitation site	Sagebrush; small patches of grama grass	Light artifact scatter; circular depression; refuse area	2 surface jacals; 1 subterranean kiva; 1 semisubterranean grinding room
D:11:290S	Late Lamoki/ Early Toreva	Large habitation site	Sagebrush; scattered pinyon and juniper trees	Moderate artifact scatter	3 surface jacals; 3 masonry structures; 1 subterranean kiva; 1 subterranean grinding room; 1 subterranean pithouse
D:11:298	Late Toreva	Small seasonally occupied site	Sagebrush	Light artifact scatter	Several features, but no structures or refuse areas
D:11:324	Toreva	Small seasonally occupied site	Sagebrush; grama grass; a small number of pinyon seedlings	Light artifact scatter	4 surface jacals
D:11:348	Toreva	Small habitation site	Sagebrush	Large artifact scatter; circular depression; refuse area	1 surface jacal; 1 subterranean grinding room
D:11:352	Late Lamoki	Large habitation site	Sagebrush	High artifact density; rubble mound; circular depression; concentrated refuse area	2 surface jacals; 1 subterranean kiva; 1 subterranean pithouse; 2 masonry structures
D:11:354	Late Lamoki	Small limited-activity site	Sagebrush	Moderate artifact scatter	2 surface jacals

D:11:356	Toreva	Small habitation site	Sagebrush	Moderate artifact scatter; rubble mound; circular depression; concentrated refuse area	1 surface jacal; 1 masonry structure; 1 surface grinding room; 1 subterranean kiva; 2 semisubterranean pit structures
D:11:409	Lamoki	Small habitation site	Sagebrush; scattered pinyon and juniper trees	Light artifact scatter; circular depression; refuse area	4 surface jacals; 1 subterranean kiva; 1 subterranean grinding room
D:11:814	Wepo	Small habitation site	Snakeweed; scattered juniper trees	Light artifact scatter; circular depression	2 surface jacals; 1 subterranean pithouse
D:11:1081	Early Lamoki	Small seasonally occupied site	Sagebrush; scattered pinyon and juniper trees; small patches of grama grass	Light artifact scatter	2 surface jacals
D:11:1084	Wepo	Small seasonally occupied site	Cliffrose; scattered pinyon and juniper trees	Light artifact scatter	1 surface jacal; 1 large, deep storage structure
D:11:1153	Dinnebito	Small habitation site	Scattered pinyon and juniper trees; relict sage area	Extremely light artifact scatter; circular depression	3 subterranean pithouses
D:11:1170	Toreva	Small limited-activity, seasonally occupied site	Sagebrush; grama grass	Light artifact scatter	3 surface jacals

Within this quadrat, all trees, cacti, and shrubs were counted; however, counts for grass plants were not available. It should be pointed out that although trees and cacti were present at most sites, the number of shrubs appears to have the greatest effect on the vegetation density for each site. Fortunately, the lack of quantifiable information on grasses and herbaceous plants is not viewed as a problem to this study because at all of the 14 sites, little or no grass cover or herbaceous plants were present.

A masonry structure is defined as any four-sided, single- or multiple-room surface unit that is constructed either partially or totally of worked or unworked stone blocks. On Black Mesa, masonry structures are believed to have been used primarily for storage (Reed 1971; Bagley-Baumgartner, this volume). However, at some sites, masonry rooms appear to have been the location of a variety of activities (see discussion of D:7:19 in Synenki [1978b]).

Subterranean structure refers to any structure greater than 80 cm deep. Pithouses, kivas, and mealing rooms are included under this heading. The activities associated with subterranean structures vary greatly, ranging from daily maintenance activities (e.g., food processing and preparation, tool manufacture and repair, and storage) and general habitation (e.g., sleeping and eating) to ritual performances.

Surface structure refers to any structure (except masonry) less than 80 cm deep. Jacals, ramadas, and shallow pit structures are included under this heading. Surface structures also appear to have been the center of a variety of activities. However, surface units are believed to be more specialized than subterranean structures. General habitation or a "living room" function (Bagley-Baumgartner, this volume) seems to best characterize the surface structure.

Justification for combining structures under the headings of subterranean and surface structures is based on similar within-group and dissimilar between-group properties, each of which, as discussed previously, has distinct effects on the relationship between surface and subsurface remains. For example, because there is little to no difference in the size of the depression created by structures built 80 cm deep or deeper, the effect on the relationship between surface and subsurface remains will not be significantly different. This effect, however, contrasts sharply with the effect of structures that exhibit little or no depression as a result of being built less than 80 cm below the occupation ground surface. A depth of 80 cm was chosen as the dividing point between surface and subterranean structures because it was the midpoint between two modes discovered by constructing a histogram of structure depths.

To measure the effect a structure or refuse area should have for any one site or series of sites, the proportion of the total site area that a particular structure or refuse area encompasses was calculated. This was done by the following procedure. At each of the 14 archaeological sites, the number of 2 × 2 m excavation squares associated with a particular structure or refuse area was divided by the total number of 2 × 2 m squares used to calculate the frequency of artifacts above and below the surface.

Analysis and Results

To test the previously stated hypotheses, the following analytical methods were employed. First, it was necessary to describe the relationship between the frequency of artifacts on the surface and subsurface of each of the 14 sites. This was achieved by correlating the total frequency of all types of surface and subsurface artifacts in each of approximately 30 2 × 2 m squares at each site. Squares were selected from specific areas (e.g., structures and refuse areas) in proportion to the occurrence of those areas on the site. At some sites, however, the total site area was composed of fewer than 30 2 × 2 m excavation squares. In those instances, the total number of 2 × 2 m excavated squares was used.

As already discussed, the number of 2 × 2 m squares chosen from structure and refuse areas was based on how much area each of the above contributed to the overall area of a specific site. In addition, areas adjacent to or adjoining the structure or refuse areas were used; these areas will be referred to as outside areas. The reason for including outside areas in the analysis is that many sites are composed of large areas that contain neither structures nor refuse areas. In some instances, these site areas were the center of daily maintenance activities. In other instances, they represented occasional discard areas for broken or exhausted items. In any event, a complete understanding of the relationship between surface and subsurface areas at a particular site or series of sites must include these areas in the analysis. Like the structures and refuse areas, the number of 2 × 2 m squares chosen from outside areas was based on how much area they contributed to the total site area.

The overall relationship between surface and subsurface remains at each site was calculated using the Pearson product-moment correlation statistic (Nie et al. 1975:280–286). This statistic was chosen after data screening was performed as suggested by Speth and Johnson (1976). It should be noted that the correlation coefficient measures the extent to which there is a linear relationship between two variables. The results revealed that at the 0.05 level, eight of the 14 sites had a statistically significant relationship between the total frequency of artifacts on the surface and subsurface of the 2 × 2 m squares sampled. In fact, there is considerable variability in both the temporal and functional dimensions of the sites that had statistically significant correlation coefficients. It should be noted, however, that the significance tests are presented only for assessing the probability of a spurious correlation coefficient. As stated above, the primary objective was to obtain a general measure of the relationship between surface and subsurface remains. As such, this study emphasizes *relationships* rather than probabilities. To provide a better perspective on this relationship, the r^2-values for each site were also calculated (Table 4). The r^2-value is a measure of the amount of variance explained by the relationship. As Nie et al. (1975:279) have noted, r^2-values are more easily interpreted than r-values when one is interested in the strength of the relationship between two variables (see also Blalock 1972; McNeil et al. 1975; Roscoe 1975). However, values of r^2 can also be strongly affected by extreme values, or outliers. Interestingly, these figures reveal that the strength of the relationship between surface and subsurface remains is high (above 0.66) at only one site (D:11:356, see Table 4) and that only four values exceed 0.22.

The second step in the analysis was to examine more specifically the relationship between surface and subsurface remains at the intersite level. This was accomplished by comparing the frequency of surface and subsurface artifacts within masonry structures, other surface structures, subterranean structures, refuse areas, and outside areas. For example, all excavated squares within or adjacent to masonry structures on all 14 archaeological sites were used to measure the surface-subsurface relationship for masonry structures. The same method was then repeated for surface structures, subterranean structures, refuse areas, and outside areas.

With the exception of outside areas, all 2 × 2 m squares excavated on all 14 sites were used in order to achieve a large sample size. However, because of the extremely large population of excavation squares for outside areas, a random sample was chosen. A sample size of 50 was deemed sufficient, given the level of confidence and degree of accuracy chosen (see Blalock 1972:401–403; Dixon and Massey 1969:204).

The Pearson product-moment correlation was also used in this aspect of the analysis. The results revealed that at the 0.05 level, a significant rela-

Table 4. Intrasite Analysis of the Relationship Between Surface and Subsurface Remains.

Site	n^a	r	r^2
D:11:97	18	0.63*	0.40
D:11:290S	31	0.30*	0.09
D:11:298	30	0.69*	0.48
D:11:324	30	0.43*	0.18
D:11:348	30	0.25	0.06
D:11:352	23	0.28	0.08
D:11:354	30	0.47*	0.22
D:11:356	30	0.90*	0.81
D:11:409	30	0.40*	0.16
D:11:814	30	0.75*	0.56
D:11:1081	26	0.16	0.03
D:11:1084	30	0.16	0.03
D:11:1153	30	0.15	0.02
D:11:1170	29	−0.14	0.02

$^a n$ = sample size
*$p \leq 0.05$

tionship between surface and subsurface remains exists only within outside areas (Table 5). The calculated r^2-values also show that only within outside areas is there a very strong relationship between surface and subsurface remains. In contrast to the outside areas, there is not a statistically significant relationship between surface and subsurface remains within masonry structures, other surface structures, subterranean structures, or refuse areas.

Two reasons discussed previously are offered to explain the poor relationship within masonry structures. First, through time, masonry wall-fall tends to bury materials both within and surrounding these structures. Second, this wall-fall, as well as the standing masonry walls, acts as a barrier that allows aeolian deposition to accumulate and thus obscure artifactual remains associated with the structure. These suggestions are in agreement with those proposed by Schiffer for the Joint Site (Reid et al. 1975). The deposition of material in the physical depressions often associated with subterranean structures may also be a cause of the statistically insignificant correlation for that structure type.

Factors different from those above appear to be responsible for the poor relationship between surface and subsurface remains within nonmasonry surface structures. For example, the walls of jacals initially may have acted like masonry walls to obstruct the movement of artifacts. However, because jacal walls are constructed from organic materials and daub, they break down more rapidly than masonry walls. Thus, after abandonment, eventual disintegration of these structures occurs, thereby removing barriers to movement.

In refuse areas, it is apparent that the accumulation of trash most likely creates an artificial slope, thereby fostering the downslope movement of materials. But as previously noted, the particular configuration of a mound can be the result of many different factors.

The reasons why outside areas have the highest correlation between surface and subsurface artifact frequencies are not well understood. They may, however, result in part from the absence of factors such as walls or depressions, which would bury material or promote soil deposition. In addition, scatterplots suggest that the coefficient may be somewhat inflated as a

---

Table 5. Intersite Analysis of the Relationship Between Surface and Subsurface Remains.

	n[a]	r	r^2
Masonry structure	68	-0.24	0.06
Subterranean structure	14	0.41	0.17
Surface structure	41	0.14	0.02
Refuse area	18	0.22	0.05
Outside areas	50	0.98*	0.96

[a]n = sample size
*$p \leq 0.05$

result of a few extreme values. At this time, no other reasons are offered to explain the high correlation.

Given these results, the next question addressed was whether a distinction can be made between surface structures, subterranean structures, refuse areas, and outside areas solely on the basis of differences in the frequency of surface artifact distribution. This information could be extremely valuable, for example, in gathering certain kinds of data about such structures on archaeological sites in a region. A test was performed to determine whether there were any statistically significant differences between the mean frequency of artifacts on the surfaces above the three different types of structures, refuse areas, and outside areas. The same sample that was used in the above analysis was used here.

The analysis of variance statistic was utilized (Kim and Kohout 1975:398–432). This statistic was chosen after preliminary data screening. The results of this screening initially indicated that two of the three assumptions of this statistic, normality and independence of scores, were met. The Cochran C-test for homogeneity of variances, on the other hand, disclosed that the samples had unequal variances. Nevertheless, further examination of the data indicated that the F probability for the analysis of variance test was so low (less than 0.001) that a numerical adjustment for the violation of this assumption would not change the results of the statistical test or the probability statements (see Glass et al. 1972:273).

The results confirmed that at the 0.05 level, there were significantly different surface and subsurface artifact densities for the structures, refuse areas, and outside areas (Table 6). However, the post hoc Scheffé test (Scheffé 1959) revealed that the only significant pairwise difference was between refuse areas and all structures and outside areas. Unlike the Joint Site (Hanson and Schiffer 1975:81–84; Reid et al. 1975) but like Hatchery West (Binford et al. 1970), refuse areas were found to have a higher frequency of artifacts on the surface than structures or outside areas. The single most important aspect of the above results is that with the exception of refuse areas, one cannot distinguish among the different types of structures or outside areas of a site solely on the basis of differences in the frequency of surface artifact distribution.

Table 6. Data Used in the Analysis of Variance.

	n^a	$\bar{x}^b$
Masonry structure	14	7.14
Subterranean structure	18	1.22
Jacal structure	68	1.61
Refuse area	41	29.93
Outside areas	50	0.92

[a]n = sample size
[b]$\bar{x}$ = mean frequency of surface artifacts
$F \geq 2.37$, $p(F) \leq 0.05$

The final and most important component of this research was the examination of the individual effects of the natural (i.e., slope and vegetation) and cultural factors (i.e., structures and refuse area) on the overall relationship between surface and subsurface remains at the 14 archaeological sites under investigation. This analysis included two steps. First, those variables that accounted for or explained a considerable amount of the variability in the relationship between surface and subsurface remains were isolated. Second, each variable's specific effect on this relationship was measured and compared to the hypothesized expectations.

Regression analysis, the semipartial statistic (McNemar 1962:167–168; Nunnally 1967:155; Kerlinger and Pedhazur 1973:92–99), was used in the first step of the analysis. This statistic should not be confused with the similar partial correlation statistic. The semipartial statistic was chosen because it is ideally suited for providing the kind of information needed to answer adequately the research question stated above. That is, this statistic specifically measures how much of the total variation in a dependent variable can be explained by a particular independent variable while controlling for the effects of the other independent variables. As Kerlinger and Pedhazur (1973:97) have noted, the semipartial statistic is currently the best technique for estimating the relative contributions of a series of independent variables to variance in a dependent variable.

Before proceeding further, it should be noted that in the regression analysis the sample size is relatively small. Therefore, it is necessary to remember that we may be dealing with only a very small portion of the total variability. Further, the number of observations relative to the number of predictor variables is quite small. The potential effect is that spurious results may be produced by overfitting the data (McNeil et al. 1975:350). Overfitting simply means that the obtained sample r^2 may result in an overestimate of the actual population ρ^2. Although the effects of overfitting can be particularly acute in the full multiple regression equation, its effect on each semipartial regression coefficient is, in all probability, relatively small if any (John Mouw, personal communication). In presenting the results of the full multiple regression equation, the degree of overfit will be quantitatively assessed and its effects on the regression analysis discussed.

The independent variables in this analysis were the natural and cultural factors mentioned above. The dependent variable was the correlation coefficient computed by measuring the relationship between surface and subsurface artifact frequencies at each of the 14 sites (Table 4). Prior to the analysis, however, these coefficients were logarithmically transformed. This was done because correlation coefficients usually are not normally distributed (Minium 1970:318). Fischer's logarithmic transformation was used because it has been shown to cure the problem of nonnormally distributed correlation coefficients (Minium 1970:321). The transformed coefficients and other data used in the regression analysis are presented in Table 7.

The program DPLINEAR (McNeil et al. 1975) was selected to compute the semipartial statistic because it is a specialized multiple regression package

Table 7. Data Used in the Semipartial Regression Analysis.

Site	r Log	Slope of the Land	Density of Vegetation	Masonry Structures	Subterranean Structures	Surface Structures	Refuse Areas
D:11:97	0.74	2°50′	1.00	0	0	4	1
D:11:290S	0.30	3°10′	0.62	4	2	5	5
D:11:298	0.84	2°30′	0.27	0	0	0	0
D:11:324	0.46	2°50′	0.68	0	0	9	0
D:11:348	1.47	2°50′	0.53	0	0	1	5
D:11:352	0.28	2°20′	0.09	4	1	6	7
D:11:354	0.15	2°30′	0.89	0	0	6	0
D:11:356	1.47	2°10′	0.92	1	.2	0	1
D:11:409	0.42	1°30′	0.71	0	2	10	4
D:11:814	0.97	1°50′	0.39	0	1	5	0
D:11:1081	0.16	2°00′	0.30	0	0	4	0
D:11:1084	0.16	7°30′	0.27	0	1	2	0
D:11:1153	0.15	8°50′	0.33	0	4	1	4
D:11:1170	−0.14	7°10′	0.39	0	0	3	0

intentionally constructed to compute the kind of statistic desired in this analysis. Several advantages of the DPLINEAR package should be noted. First, the calculation of the semipartial statistic for each independent variable does not operate off the error of the previous variable that was entered into the regression equation. Second, the order of entry of the independent variables into the regression analysis will not change the magnitude of the regression coefficients. Lastly, this package has a demonstrated effect of being more sensitive for controlling Type 1 errors (McNeil et al. 1975).

The analysis revealed that slope, surface structures, subterranean structures, and refuse areas explain most of the variance in the relationship between surface and subsurface remains (Table 8). For example, 45 % of the variance in this relationship was accounted for by slope alone. Moreover, the semipartial correlation coefficient of the relationship of slope and the transformed coefficients shows a negative relationship ($r = -0.67$), thereby supporting the first hypothesis. That is, as the slope of the land increases on a site, the correspondence between the frequency of artifacts on its surface and subsurface decreases.

Explanation of these results is rather simple and straightforward and revolves specifically around earlier discussions about the movement of artifacts as a result of various natural processes. With respect to those sites with a relatively high correspondence between surface and subsurface remains

Table 8. Semipartial Regression Analysis Results.

	r	r^2	F-Ratio	p
Full regression equation	—	0.833	—	—
Slope of the land	−0.67	0.447	16.05	0.003
Density of vegetation	0.19	0.037	1.33	0.15
Masonry structures	−0.11	0.012	0.43	0.27
Subterranean structures	0.44	0.190	6.83	0.02
Surface structures	−0.43	0.182	6.55	0.02
Refuse area	−0.37	0.136	4.87	0.03

and a low slope angle (e.g., D:11:97, D:11:298, D:11:356, D:11:814), the movement of artifacts through time appears to have been minimal. This is true because in most cases, the inertia of the artifactual objects has not been overcome. A slope angle of one or two degrees will hardly be conducive to the movement of physical objects, whatever the forces (natural, human, or animal) providing the impetus to initiate movement.

On the other hand, the physical movement of artifacts downslope is apparent at sites that had relatively low correspondence between surface and subsurface remains and steep slope angles (D:11:1084, D:11:1153, D:11:1170). However, the processes that produced this pattern differ somewhat at each site. For example, the surfaces of both D:11:1084 and D:11:1153 were dissected by several moderately deep washes, indicating hydraulic erosional processes. Therefore, it is postulated that the downslope movement of artifacts on these two sites was due primarily to water action, the result of seasonal torrential rainstorms, and/or to a lesser degree, melting snow and ice. At D:11:1084, this proposition is supported further by the presence of a light gray soil at the bottom of the washes, presumably the result of water leaching (Klesert and McAllister 1977:121). Additionally, at D:11:1153, some of the movement of artifacts downslope may have been initiated by sheep and goats. The ethnobotanists noted in their vegetation quadrat sample of D:11:1153 that the site had been noticeably overgrazed.

In contrast to D:11:1084 and D:11:1153, portions of the ground surface of D:11:1170 were covered with grass and showed no sign of erosion. Moreover, D:11:1170 does not appear to exhibit many of the other natural processes such as thermal expansion and contraction that are responsible for the physical movement of objects downslope on other sites. Therefore, it is tentatively suggested that both human and animal activity may have initiated the movement of objects downslope. As with D:11:1153, this contention is supported by the fact that the surface of D:11:1170 exhibits evidence of extreme overgrazing.

In contrast to the degree of slope, the density of vegetation was not found to be a substantial contributor to the explanation of variation in surface and subsurface remains (H_2). In fact, only 4 % of the variance in the relationship between the frequency of artifacts on the surface and subsurface of the 14 archaeological sites was accounted for by the density of vegetation alone. Nevertheless, a positive relationship ($r = 0.19$) between the density of vegetation and the transformed coefficients indicates that as the density of vegetation increases on a site, the relationship between surface and subsurface remains will also increase and vice versa. As noted above, overall vegetation density on Black Mesa sites is primarily determined by the density of shrubs. This test result therefore supports the second hypothesis.

One would expect the density of vegetation to correlate negatively with the degree of slope. A site with a steep slope angle would be expected to have a low vegetation density, whereas a site with a low slope angle would be expected to have a high vegetation density. These expectations are based on well-accepted hydrological theory (Kirkby 1969a). A Pearson product-moment correlation statistic was calculated between slope and vegetation to test this assumption. Unexpectedly, the results revealed that there was not a very strong relationship ($r = -0.35$, $r^2 = 0.12$) between these two variables, although the coefficient is negative. Despite the fact that sites with steep slope angles consistently have low vegetation densities (e.g., D:11:1084, D:11:1153, D:11:1170), it is readily apparent that some sites with low slope angles will have high vegetation densities (e.g., D:11:97, D:11:354, D:11:356, D:11:409), and other sites with low slope angles will have low vegetation densities (e.g., D:11:298, D:11:352, D:11:1081). One plausible explanation for this occurrence could be depletion of vegetation through overgrazing. Unfortunately, the effects of overgrazing at each site were not studied in detail, and they cannot be quantitatively assessed.

In contrast to slope and vegetation density, the presence of surface structures on sites accounted for only 18 % of the variance in the relationship between surface and subsurface remains. In addition, a negative relationship ($r = -0.43$) between the presence of surface structures and the degree of correlation between surface and subsurface artifact densities was demonstrated, indicating that as the area encompassed by surface structures increases on a site, the correspondence between the frequency of artifacts on its surface and subsurface decreases. This result supports the third hypothesis but contrasts sharply with the study by Tolstoy and Fish (1975).

Similar to the results shown for surface structures, the presence of subterranean structures was found to account for 19 % of the variance in the relationship between the frequency of artifacts on the surface and subsurface remains at the 14 sites. A positive relationship ($r = 0.44$) exists between the presence of subterranean structures and the degree of correlation between surface and subsurface artifact frequencies. Thus, as the area encompassed by subterranean structures increases on sites, the correspondence between surface and subsurface frequencies will also increase. This result also conforms to the hypothesis.

The presence of masonry structures, on the other hand, accounted for only 1 % of the variance in the relationship between surface and subsurface remains. This result suggests that, like the density of vegetation, masonry structures do not appear to contribute substantially to the explanation of intersite variance in the correlation between surface-subsurface artifact frequencies in the study area. Nevertheless, analysis does indicate that on archaeological sites with masonry structures, as the area encompassed by these structures increases, the relationship between the frequency of artifacts on the surface and subsurface of a site decreases ($r = -0.11$). This result supports the hypothesized relationship (H_3).

Finally, the regression analysis revealed that the presence of refuse areas accounted for 14 % of the variance in the relationship between the frequency of artifacts on the surface and subsurface of the sites. Moreover, it supported the fourth hypothesis that as the size of refuse areas increased on a site, the relationship between surface and subsurface remains decreased ($r = -0.37$).

One final aspect of the analysis should be noted. The full regression equation (i.e., all independent variables together regressed against transformed r) was found to account for 83 % of the variance in the degree of correlation between surface and subsurface artifact totals. However, as indicated earlier, this figure may be somewhat inflated due to the effects of overfitting. Yet a calculated unbiased estimate of the population ρ^2 (Kerlinger and Pedhazur 1973:283) is 0.63, indicating that the relative shrinkage (0.20) and hence the degree of overfitting is relatively low. This suggests that although there is little reason to believe that the results obtained in this particular analysis are unreliable, the potential for inaccuracy still exists. Therefore, while quite exciting but not overly startling, the results of the full multiple regression equation indicate that much of the variability in this relationship is explainable when all variables are considered together.

In sum, the results of the above analysis indicate that the *effects* that surface structures, masonry structures, and refuse areas have on the relationship between surface and subsurface remains conform quite closely to the hypotheses. As previously argued, the effects that structures and refuse areas have on the relationship between surface and subsurface remains of sites result from two primary factors: (1) the type of physical alteration of the landscape that each feature represents; and (2) the kind, nature, and frequency of activities that were performed in and around each of these features. The implication of this aspect of the analysis is important because it suggests that consideration of the effects of these variables should promote more effective and efficient survey and excavation strategies.

Conclusion

This study is important in two ways. First, the results allow us to reconsider previous notions about the relationship between surface and subsurface remains. It demonstrates that the relationship is internally complex and highly variable at both the intrasite and intersite levels. This conclusion contrasts with most previous studies that found, often on the basis of a single site, that surface remains are a good predictor of subsurface remains in almost all instances. In fact, the results of the Pearson correlation coefficients indicate that the correspondence and strength of the relationship between surface and subsurface remains have a considerable range of values (e.g., $r^2 = 0.2$ to 0.81) even within a relatively small geographical area on Black Mesa. This suggests that archaeologists must not blindly rely on the assumption that a high frequency of surface artifacts will yield high frequencies of subsurface artifacts or, more importantly, the most intense areas of human activity.

The second significance of this study is the attempt to isolate, measure, and explain variability in the relationship between surface and subsurface remains. That is, the study ascertained the amount of variability as well as the specific effects that each variable accounted for in this relationship. These results are considered useful for archaeologists attempting to evaluate not only the natural or cultural factors producing distortion or noise in the archaeological record but also the precise effects that the distortion will have on the record. This information, in turn, could be employed to devise a more efficient excavation strategy.

Hence, one of the most significant contributions this study has made is its demonstration that it is to a certain extent unimportant whether there is a positive relationship between the frequency of artifacts on the surface and subsurface of an archaeological site. Rather, there may be predictable anomalies in this relationship. The strength of this study lies in its use of a method that, as discussed above, has substantial predictive abilities.

In conclusion, it is hoped that similar studies will be conducted in other areas of North America. Only then may be achieved what Schiffer and Rathje (1973:169) have noted as an efficient exploitation of the archaeological record.

Acknowledgments

This manuscript is a much revised version of my M.A. thesis and a paper presented at the 43rd annual meeting of the Society for American Archaeology, Tucson, Arizona, May 5, 1978 (Synenki 1978c). The research undertaken in this manuscript was conducted under the auspices of the Black Mesa Archaeological Project, then directed by Stephen Plog, under the sponsorship of Peabody Coal Company of St. Louis, Missouri. Computer time was provided by the Department of Anthropology, Southern Illinois University at Carbondale. Many individuals have assisted in the completion of this manuscript and deserve special thanks. I am grateful to Stephen Plog for his time, advice, and helpful criticism in all phases of this project. Reviewers Michael Schiffer and R. G. Matson are thanked for their criticism and much-needed suggestions concerning both the organization and substance of the manuscript. John Mouw, Ernie Lewis, and Paula Woehlke, statisticians in the Department of Guidance and Educational Psychology at Southern Illinois University, deserve special thanks for providing sound advice on all aspects of the statistical analysis.

3

A Method for Predicting the Presence of Buried Structures on Unexcavated Artifact Scatters

Shirley Powell and Anthony L. Klesert

One research topic investigated by the Black Mesa Archaeological Project has been the role of small artifact scatters within the overall subsistence-settlement system. Basic to the consideration of this problem is an understanding of the range of subsurface variability within this site type. Catlin (1978), investigating site types within a portion of the study area, has shown that modal site size is 16 m². Further, he found that 40 % of the sites in the study area were less than 100 m² in size and had no structures visible from the surface. Prior analyses of subsistence and settlement in the American Southwest have generally dismissed such sites or have simply assumed that they are all special- or limited-activity loci. However, recent studies have shown that small sites or "nonsites" are frequently the loci of activities that do not occur at larger sites (e.g., Thomas 1975:62–63). Thus, to dismiss small sites from consideration is to ignore a potentially important subset of the overall subsistence-settlement system.

Excavations during the past few years on Black Mesa have shown a great deal of variability in the subsurface configurations of small artifact scatters. For example, excavations have shown a range from sites with several pithouses, jacals, and/or extramural features to sites with no subsurface component at all. This in turn implies a great deal of variability in the nature of activities performed at artifact scatters (see Bagley-Baumgartner, this volume). This variability has not, in the past, been identified from survey information.

This paper, then, is an explicit attempt to discover patterns in subsurface site configurations that can be predicted solely from data recovered during survey. An earlier version (Powell and Klesert 1980) presented results of analyses performed with data collected from 21 sites excavated during the summers of 1976, 1977, and 1978. Because the sample was small, statistical results were quite tentative. This paper incorporates data from 13 additional sites excavated during the 1979 and 1980 field seasons. The larger data base produced slightly different statistical patterns; however, the strength of the interpretations is enhanced as a result of the increased sample size.

This continuing effort is important given the constraints under which all archaeologists must work. All archaeologists sample; all the data are never collected. Sampling decisions must frequently be made on the basis of survey data alone. For this reason, our analyses are purposely limited to those data that were collected from sites during past surveys and recorded on field survey forms. In addition, data manipulation should be relatively straightforward since many such field decisions must be made in the absence of elaborate or expensive technical aids. Thus, the statistical procedures employed in this paper are all bivariate and can be computed with the aid of a pocket calculator.

Data Base

The data base for this study includes 34 excavated sites that were all termed by the survey crews as artifact scatters, with no surface signs of structures. These sites were excavated by the Black Mesa Archaeological Project between 1976 and 1980. Excavations led to the discovery of structures on 21 of the 34 sites. These structures most commonly included jacal rooms and pithouses. Only one of the sites had a masonry room. Usually masonry rooms are visible from the surface, but in this case the site (D:7:222) had been covered by a thick layer of colluvium from the cliff that backed the site.

The following variables, derived from survey forms, simple field and laboratory tallies, and maps, were used in the analysis to predict the presence of structures: number of ceramic wares; presence/absence of whitewares, graywares, and red-/orangewares; presence/absence of lithic artifacts and groundstone; number of manos; number of metates; number of visible slab-lined features; number of surface stains; total ceramic density; lithic density; artifact variety; site elevation; site area; and on-site vegetation. Tsegi Orange-wares and San Juan Redwares were lumped into a single category since it is difficult to distinguish between the two without a microscope. With the exception of the density measures, each of these variables can easily be noted by a survey crew in the field. Density figures can be derived easily in the field laboratory.

Analysis

In keeping with the stated goal of finding the simplest means to predict the presence of structures on artifact scatters, we began our analysis by examining single categories. In our first analysis we used contingency tables (Table 9) to examine the presence or absence of single artifact categories across our two site categories (with and without structures). Chi-square tests were used to evaluate the possibility that associations occurred by chance. The chi-

Table 9. Chi-square Test Results Using the Presence/Absence of Single Categories to Predict the Presence of Rooms on Artifact Scatters.

Artifact Type	χ^2	p	ϕ^2
Tusayan Whitewares	8.20	0.004	0.56
Tusayan Graywares	0.06	0.801	—
Tsegi Orangewares and/or San Juan Redwares	9.11	0.002	0.58
Lithic artifacts	5.09	0.024	0.45
Groundstone	1.98	0.159	—
Slab-lined features	1.05	0.305	—
On-site vegetation	4.12	0.042	0.42

square values were corrected for continuity in order to adhere to constraints on the use of the statistic (Blalock 1972:285). In three cases the presence of a single artifact category predicted the presence of subsurface structures on sites. Sites that had Tusayan Whitewares, Tsegi Orangewares and/or San Juan Redwares, or lithic artifacts also had structures significantly more often than sites without these artifact classes. Phi-square, a strength of association measure, was calculated to assess the improvement in the ability to predict the presence of structures on sites when whitewares, red-/orangewares, or lithic artifacts are present on the site (Blalock 1972:295). The presence of Tsegi Orangewares and/or San Juan Redwares is the best single indicator of subsurface structures ($\phi^2 = 0.58$); the predictive capability of Tusayan Whitewares and lithic artifacts is slightly less ($\phi^2 = 0.56$ and 0.45, respectively). The remaining single artifact categories failed to predict the presence or absence of subsurface structures on sites.

In addition, we considered the predictive capability of on-site vegetation and site elevation. Site elevation did not predict the presence or absence of subsurface structures on artifact scatters. However, there is a pattern of association between the presence of structures and on-site vegetation. Sites with structures are located in sage flats, while sites with no structures are equally likely to be found in areas with or without sage ($\phi^2 = 0.42$) (Tables 9 and 14).

In the next set of analyses, artifact categories were grouped to see if combinations of pairs or threes were better predictors of the presence of subsurface structures than were single artifact categories (Tables 10 and 11). We found that redwares in combination with whitewares, graywares, or lithic artifacts occurred significantly more frequently on sites with subsurface structures than on sites without structures. When artifact categories were grouped in threes, combinations of redwares, graywares, whitewares, and lithic artifacts occurred significantly more often on sites with subsurface structures. However, combinations of artifact categories (either twos or threes) did not greatly increase the predictive capability of the single artifact category of redwares. This was because in most cases in which redwares were present

Table 10. Chi-square Test Results Using the Presence of Two Artifact Categories to Predict the Presence of Rooms on Artifact Scatters.

Artifact Type	χ^2	p	ϕ^2
Whitewares/graywares	10.54	0.001	0.625
Whitewares/redwares	9.11	0.002	0.581
Whitewares/lithic artifacts	9.60	0.002	0.592
Whitewares/groundstone	1.27	0.259	—
Graywares/redwares	9.11	0.002	0.581
Graywares/lithic artifacts	5.09	0.024	0.448
Graywares/groundstone	1.98	0.159	—
Redwares/lithic artifacts	6.63	0.01	0.508
Redwares/groundstone	0.16	0.691	—
Lithic artifacts/groundstone	0.65	0.421	—

Table 11. Chi-square Test Results Using the Presence of Three Artifact Categories to Predict the Presence of Rooms on Artifact Scatters.

Artifact Type	χ^2	p	ϕ^2
Whitewares/graywares/redwares	9.11	0.002	0.581
Whitewares/graywares/lithic artifacts	9.60	0.002	0.592
Whitewares/graywares/groundstone	1.27	0.259	—
Whitewares/redwares/lithic artifacts	6.63	0.01	0.508
Whitewares/redwares/groundstone	0.16	0.691	—
Redwares/lithic artifacts/groundstone	0.16	0.691	—
Whitewares/lithic artifacts/groundstone	0.65	0.421	—
Graywares/redwares/lithic artifacts	6.63	0.01	0.508
Graywares/redwares/groundstone	0.16	0.691	—
Graywares/lithic artifacts/groundstone	0.65	0.421	—

on a site, whitewares, graywares, or lithic artifacts were also present. Red-wares alone predict the presence of structures nearly as well as redwares in combination with other artifact categories ($\phi^2 = 0.56$ for redwares, but $\phi^2 = 0.58$ for redwares and graywares together). Whitewares and graywares in combination are the best indicator of subsurface structures ($\phi^2 = 0.625$).

Lerner's analysis (this volume) of ceramic function indicates covariation between vessel form and the presence of decoration. She notes that painted decoration occurs more frequently on whiteware vessels, presumably used for food service, than on grayware culinary jars (redwares are not considered). She further notes that painted jars (frequently whitewares) had characteristics that enhanced containment security. She infers that these jars were used for storage. If whiteware sherds are the remnants of storage vessels, by inference the sites on which they are found were the loci of storage activities. Storage concentrates resources in space and ensures their availability over time (Binford 1980:15). Thus, if the whiteware sherds are evidence for storage at the site, the artificial concentration of resources there would result in more intense use of the site area during the period in which the stored resources were consumed. Further, as more time was spent at the site, it would be increasingly more likely that a wider range of maintenance activities would also take place there—thus "explaining" the coexistence of whitewares with redwares, graywares, and lithic artifacts.

Subsequent analyses employed data coded at an ordinal or interval level. We anticipated that sites with structures would have a longer occupation span, be used by more people, and be used to stage a greater variety of activities than sites with no structures. The effect of such a set of behaviors would be to increase the variety and volume of the artifacts recovered at sites with structures. Thus, we expected sites with subsurface structures to have a higher density and a greater variety of artifacts than sites with no subsurface structures. We tested these expectations using the Wilcoxon two-sample test and Student's *t*-distribution (Tables 12–14).

We found that, in general, the above expectations were supported. Ceramic and lithic *densities* were significantly greater at sites with structures (Tables 12–14). Additionally, ceramic *variety* was greater at sites with structures (Table 14). That is, sites with structures had a greater variety of ceramic

Table 12. Wilcoxon Two-sample Test Comparing Ceramic Densities on Sites With and Without Structures.

With Structures			Without Structures		
Site	Density	Rank	Site	Density	Rank
D:7:222	1.81	28	D:7:424	3.81	32
D:7:1134	0.18	6	D:7:441	0.11	3
D:7:1135	0.41	11	D:7:723	0.57	16
D:7:3003	0.12	4	D:7:1104	0.63	18
D:7:3021	0.45	12.5	D:7:1109	0.73	19
D:7:3034	1.52	27	D:7:1115	0.19	7.5
D:7:3038	5.50	33	D:7:1118	0.19	7.5
D:7:3055	1.25	24	D:7:1119	0.13	5
D:11:324	1.27	25	D:7:1125	0.45	12.5
D:11:338	1.91	29	D:11:298	0.58	17
D:11:354	1.29	23	D:11:878	1.0	22
D:11:409	2.34	30	D:11:1096	0.56	15
D:11:879	1.4	26	D:11:1152	N/A	
D:11:1081	0.34	10			
D:11:1084	0.85	20			
D:11:1136	0.55	14			
D:11:1153	0.02	1			
D:11:1158	0.3	9			
D:11:1161	0.1	2			
D:11:1170	0.99	21			
D:11:1244	3.30	31			

$n_1 = 20$ $\mu_w = 357$ $Z = 1.104$
$n_2 = 12$ $\sigma_w = 26.72$ $p(Z) = 0.07$ (one-tailed)

Table 13. Wilcoxon Two-sample Test Comparing Lithic Densities on Sites With and Without Structures.

With Structures			Without Structures		
Site	Density	Rank	Site	Density	Rank
D:7:222	0.02	21.5	D:7:424	0	8.5
D:7:1134	0	8.5	D:7:441	0.01	18
D:7:1135	0.01	18	D:7:723	0	8.5
D:7:3003	0.55	33	D:7:1104	0	8.5
D:7:3021	0.02	21.5	D:7:1109	0.05	29
D:7:3034	0.04	26.5	D:7:1115	0	8.5
D:7:3038	0	8.5	D:7:1118	0	8.5
D:7:3055	0	8.5	D:7:1119	0	8.5
D:11:324	0	8.5	D:7:1125	0	8.5
D:11:338	0.02	21.5	D:11:298	0.01	18
D:11:354	0.02	21.5	D:11:878	0	8.5
D:11:409	0	8.5	D:11:1096	0	8.5
D:11:879	0.03	24.5	D:11:1152	0	8.5
D:11:1081	0.05	29			
D:11:1084	0.05	29			
D:11:1136	0.06	31			
D:11:1153	0.38	32			
D:11:1158	0.04	26.5			
D:11:1161	0.80	34			
D:11:1170	0	8.5			
D:11:1244	0.03	24.5			

$n_1 = 21$ $\mu_w = 367.5$ $Z = 2.746$

$n_2 = 13$ $\sigma_w = 28.22$ $p(Z) = 0.002$ (one-tailed)

wares in their surface artifact inventories and a significantly greater variety of all artifact types.

Conclusions

Most generally our results suggest that variation in surface attributes for sites with and without structures is due to increasing occupation span and greater functional variability at sites with structures. Artifactual variety and density patterns certainly support this conclusion, as does the coexistence of specific artifactual classes. Whiteware sherds (one of the best single indicators of subsurface structures) may be the remnants of storage facilities. One would expect greater occupational intensity (and more structures) at sites with storage facilities than at sites with none—an expectation that is supported by the cooccurrence of whitewares with redwares, graywares, and chipped stone.

To summarize, we have shown that it is possible to discern variation within the category of small artifact scatters without resorting to excavation. Portions of the artifact inventory can be used to determine the presence or absence of structures on sites that have no superficial indication of structures. Specifically, the greater the variety in the surface artifact inventory, the greater

Table 14. *T*-test Results—Density and Variety Measures on Sites With and Without Structures.

	t	*p(t)*
Whiteware density	−3.42	0.001
Grayware density	−1.97	0.026
Overall ceramic density	−1.22	0.116
Lithic density	−2.07	0.026
No. of different ceramic wares	−5.95	0.000
No. of different artifact types	−6.75	0.000
Site elevation	0.68	0.25

	With Structures		Without Structures	
Descriptive Statistics	$\bar{x}$	*s*	$\bar{x}$	*s*
Whiteware density	0.214	0.226	0.031	0.075
Grayware density	0.486	0.379	0.238	0.312
Overall ceramic density	1.20	1.298	0.688	0.982
Lithic density	0.101	0.211	0.0054	0.014
No. of different ceramic wares	2.57	0.598	1.38	0.506
No. of different artifact types	3.57	0.811	1.69	0.751
Site elevation	2072.1	42.7	2081.4	30.7

Note: All probabilities are for one-tailed tests.

the probability that structures will be present on a given site. In addition, the differential density of artifacts on scatters has a high capacity to predict the presence of structures: the greater the artifact density, the greater the chance that structures exist. Finally, it appears that the presence of redware ceramics on a Black Mesa site also has a certain predictive value in terms of the existence of structures. Knowledge of the presence of this artifact class on a site improves the prediction of the presence of structures by almost 60 %. More accurately, the *absence* of redwares correlates with the *absence* of structures. To reiterate, artifact density, artifact variety, and, to a lesser extent, the occurrence of redware ceramics, all aid in the determination of the presence of structures on artifact scatters.

In conclusion, archaeologists are faced with the basic constraints of conserving cultural resources whenever possible, while at the same time maximizing scientific benefits and fulfilling contractual obligations. All too often, these constraints work against each other, resulting either in a loss of information due to conservation or a loss of the resource due to information gathering. The above exercise can be seen as an attempt to live with both constraints. Being able to predict the subsurface configuration of a site without excavating it is of great service to a client, such as Peabody Coal Company, because it can reduce the expensive digging of so many of these sites. It can also be of direct benefit to the science of archaeology. For example, many questions concerning population dynamics and site function can be approached more accurately using the methods described here, even though the data base, as it so often does, consists solely of survey-derived data. Actual excavation of these sites to acquire the requisite data is most often prohibitively expensive as well as destructive to the resource base. All too often the direct result is that important questions are never addressed, since the required data are absent.

This study indicates that survey information can be used to assess variability within the class of sites called artifact scatters. In this sense, survey data can be used profitably to refine decision making prior to the costly and time-consuming process of excavation. The results of this study have important implications for cultural resource management decisions as well as for research utilizing survey data.

4

Toward a Functional Classification of Nonceremonial Structures on Black Mesa, Northeastern Arizona

Kathy Bagley-Baumgartner

This paper attempts a functional classification of nonceremonial structures on Black Mesa (see also Bagley 1979). These structures (jacal rooms, masonry rooms, and pithouses) are analyzed in relation to relevant internal attributes. These attributes include floor area, the presence or absence of hearths and storage pits, and the frequencies of grayware and whiteware ceramics, chipped stone, and groundstone. Chi-square analysis and analysis of variance are used to determine significant associations among these variables. The strength of these associations allows the inference of a functional classification of architectural types.

The functional classification of structures is important for making a variety of higher-order inferences concerning prehistoric cultural systems, as demonstrated by a number of different studies. For example, F. Plog (1975) considers dwelling units the best spatial criterion on which to base paleodemographic inferences. Swedlund and Sessions's (1976) estimation of population growth on Black Mesa also depended on identifying dwelling rooms and sites. Interpretations of settlement patterns are enhanced if there is an understanding of the functional variability of rooms on sites. In Trigger's (1968) early discussion of settlement pattern determinants, he designated the individual structure as the most basic of the three levels of settlement patterns. The second and third levels dealt respectively with community layout and zonal patterns. He suggested that the identification of individual structure function is necessary to understand the higher community- and zonal-level patterns. Although Wilcox (1975:131) did not directly analyze room function, he noted the importance of understanding space utilization for laying a firm basis for social organizational inferences. Hill (1970) based inferences of community organization at Broken K Pueblo, in part, on the analysis of room functions. Finally, in an analysis of house form variability, Hunter-Anderson (1977:295–296) recognized two possible lines of investigation. The line most commonly taken in the past emphasized "interfering environmental agencies" (1977:296). She argued, however, that the "nature of the housed contents" (bulk versus differentiated) may also affect house shape. The nature of the contents will be determined by the activities conducted in the structures. Thus, the identification of the functions of different structures is important in a number of ways.

The primary research question of this study is: How did jacal rooms, pithouses, and masonry structures on Black Mesa differ in function? This question is important for ongoing work on the study and explanation of prehistoric cultural change, a primary objective of Black Mesa research (S. Plog 1977d:4). Studying the functional groupings of structures may contribute information to this long-range goal by clarifying questions on other topics of interest such as village size, intercommunity specialization, and intracommunity differentiation (S. Plog 1977d:12). For example, establishing the functional nature of rooms is critical for questions dealing with intersite variation in activities on Black Mesa. Increased attention should be paid not just to the architectural types, which have been emphasized in previous discussions of Black Mesa structures, but to their functional comparability, both spatially and temporally. We need to make our assumptions about structure functions on Black Mesa both explicit and empirically testable. In the remainder of this paper, I first discuss alternative approaches to identifying room functions and then use one method to isolate room functions for a number of structures on Black Mesa.

Approaches to Room Function Identification

Generally, three procedures have been used to classify structural variability according to function: the architectural approach, the inventory approach, and the activity-oriented approach (Sullivan 1974:95). The architectural approach assigns a room a specific function on the basis of architectural features (Sullivan 1974:93). Smith (1952:154–165) used this approach in his attempt to determine the presence or absence of kivas in his excavations in the Big Hawk Valley, Arizona. Having examined a good deal of literature, Smith came to the conclusion that a reasonably accurate identification of a kiva could be made on the basis of the morphological features of the room and its location within the architectural unit. The second line of investigation, the inventory approach, utilizes the occurrence of particular artifacts and nonarchitectural features on past occupational surfaces to assign rooms to functional categories (Sullivan 1974:93). In their report on the excavations of Table Rock Pueblo, Arizona, Martin and Rinaldo (1960:171–173) basically relied on an inventory of interior artifacts and features (e.g., the presence/absence of fire pits, ventilators, groundstone, bowls, and jars) in assigning rooms to either a habitation or storage category. Finally, the activity-oriented approach assesses the relationships between material remains and their distributions on living surfaces in the examination of room space utilization (Sullivan 1974:93).

The use of these three approaches is hampered in those circumstances in which the appropriate interior artifacts, features, or architectural characteristics are missing. In addition to this drawback, Sullivan (1974:94) notes two contextual problems with the inventory- and activity-oriented approaches. These problems are referred to by Schiffer (1976:28–34) as representing types of cultural processes that transform materials from an ongoing behavioral system (systemic context) to their archaeological context. Specifically, they are normal and abandonment processes. Normal, or discard activities, may result in material thrown away at its use location (primary refuse) or material transported away to a dump (secondary refuse). Abandonment may result in usable materials being left where used when an area is deserted (de facto refuse).

Noncultural as well as cultural formation processes should not be ignored in studies of structure functions. On larger sites where differential abandonment may have occurred, early-abandoned room floors may contain secondary refuse (Schiffer 1976:34). The identification of different refuse types must be carried out during the actual excavation of the site and gathering of the data. Faced with the lack of such information, Schiffer dealt only with floor proveniences in his study of rooms at the Joint Site in Arizona. He thought the artifacts to be "possible primary and de facto refuse units" since they were resting on what was considered to be floor (1976:139). However, he acknowledged that these floors may have contained the first discards of secondary refuse from the fill. Just how much the existence of possible secondary refuse may skew one's interpretations when conducting an analysis in this manner cannot be known if there are no control data for comparison.

The strengths, weaknesses, and similarities with each of the three approaches to studying room functions—architectural, activity, and inventory—may be illustrated by a critique of four studies dealing specifically with the problem of room function. Freeman and Brown's (1964) study of Carter Ranch relied on a very specific type of inventory approach based on particular floor features and pottery types. Hill's (1970) work at Broken K Pueblo is a mixture of the inventory- and activity-oriented approaches. The inventory preceded the examination of the relationships between material remains and their distributions. Jorgensen (1975) also mixed these two approaches in an analysis of rooms at Table Rock Pueblo, but in a somewhat different manner. Finally, Sullivan's (1974) architectural approach at Grasshopper Ruin represents an alternative to the others.

Carter Ranch

The Carter Ranch site, located in east-central Arizona, was the source of the data used to perform one of the first statistical studies on pottery (Freeman and Brown 1964). Having established by means of chi-square tests that differences existed in the frequencies of pottery types within the Carter Ranch site, Freeman and Brown were interested in knowing if the variation in pottery types was due solely to their association with different types of structures and deposits. To answer their question, they established a preliminary set of four room types on the basis of the presence and kind of floor features. Each room type occurred in all areas of the site and crosscut contemporaneous roomblocks. Thus, Freeman and Brown hypothesized that the difference between pottery type frequencies might be partially due to the different functions of the room types.

The hypothesis that pottery types occurred nonrandomly in room types was tested by means of chi-square analysis. For this test, Freeman and Brown "made a preliminary grouping of pottery types whose 'behavior' with respect to other types was nearly identical" on the basis of correlations among the 14 pottery types from floor samples (1964:134–135). Results indicated that their four room types showed differences "greater than would be expected (with respect to pottery frequency) if they had only architectural validity, and were not functionally or temporally different as well" (1964:137). The authors considered the rooms in their study to be more than architectural types since they contained specific associated ceramic types and were scattered throughout the site. They concluded, on the basis of the presence and kind of floor features, that the four room types were "distinguishable in frequencies of pottery from their floors." On this basis, they suggested that different cultural activities occurred in each room type (1964:141).

There are several problems inherent in the study by Freeman and Brown. First, they never actually explain why they chose to base their room typology on only the presence and shape of features. Nor do they offer any suggestion as to what the features were (according to Martin's [1964:221] summary of the site, they were all fire pits).

The authors consider the rooms at Carter Ranch to be functional types on the basis of differentiation in the frequencies of specific ceramic types. However, they do not address the question of what this functional differentiation actually represents. They only conclude that different cultural activities existed; they do not provide an explanation of what those activities might have been.

Broken K Pueblo

Hill (1970) has produced a comprehensive work involving an examination of room types and their functions at Broken K Pueblo. Broken K Pueblo, located in east-central Arizona and dating ca. A.D. 1150–1399, is a one-story, rectangular surface masonry pueblo containing approximately 95 rooms. Hill's primary concern in the Broken K study was the examination of prehistoric social organization and activity structure, as well as how changes in this organization acted as adaptive responses to the shifting environment. To obtain the information needed for an understanding of the social organization of Broken K's past inhabitants, Hill found it necessary to classify all artifacts (including rooms) and nonarchitectural materials. Regarding the necessity for developing room types, he felt that preceding typologies were often lacking because of their heavy reliance on only one or two attributes. Hill therefore inventoried four attributes—floor area, mealing bins, fire pits, and ventilators—to determine room types. Later, using the activity-oriented approach, he utilized other attributes to verify the room types and to analyze their functions. Floor area was demonstrated to have a bimodal distribution, so rooms were divided into two groups, large (6.6–16 m^2) and small (2.5–6.5 m^2). Chi-square tests were then used to determine which attributes were associated with these size classes. Tests indicated that ventilators, fire pits, and mealing bins were all associated with large rooms, as well as with each other. At this stage in his analysis, Hill labeled all large rooms containing fire pits, mealing bins, and ventilators as habitation rooms. Small rooms, which were essentially characterized by their lack of artifacts or features, were labeled storage rooms. In addition to these two kinds of rooms, there existed a special category usually referred to as kiva. Hill was less concerned with developing a means for classifying the latter category of rooms since their function is usually recognized as ceremonial (1970:37–40).

It seemed evident to Hill that the variability in rooms was due to the functional nature of the room classes. Further, tests indicated that lithic waste, animal bone, and seeds were associated most strongly with large or habitation rooms. In contrast, pollen was more common on the floors of smaller storage rooms, which contained very little of anything else. A chi-square test demonstrated that there were more sherds in habitation rooms than in storage rooms. Hill obtained the same results using both ceramic frequencies and densities. In addition, each room type contained distinctive pottery types (1970:42–43).

Hill's interpretations of the functions of the basic room types were based on the distributions of features, artifacts, and nonartifactual materials. The functional meanings of these materials were derived from ethnographic and worldwide comparative evidence. Hill inferred the functions of habitation rooms to be preparation of food, eating, water storage and use, and manufacture of hunting tools. Other suggested functions with more insubstantial evidence included sleeping and the manufacture of pottery, ground and pecked implements, and ornamental items. Storage rooms functioned as repositories for both food and nonfood items. Palynological studies (1970:46–52) provided supportive evidence for the latter. Hill recognized that these functions were primary and most likely overlapped room types; that is, each room type actually was multifunctional.

Hill's study is noteworthy. He produced a systematic classification of rooms before proceeding to more complex questions regarding the organization of social groups (uxorilocal residence units), the population peak at

Broken K, the size of the residential groups, and the existence of an environmental shift (1970:75–77, 91).

Schiffer (1975) identifies two weaknesses in Hill's method for inferring room function when it is generalized to other, less appropriate sites. These are the recognition of cultural formation processes and variations in activity space partitioning (1975:104). Hill's test implications do not take into account how archaeological remains were produced, but rather are "simply statements about what is found in rooms of the same type occupied by the ethnographically-known Hopi and Zuni" (Schiffer 1975:105). Although Hill's method was successfully applied to Broken K material, because of the probable presence of sufficient primary and de facto refuse, he assumed that all artifacts had been discarded at their original use locations. That is, he did not take into account the possibility that some of his material might well have represented secondary refuse (1975:104). This is, however, a weakness of many studies of room function, including the Black Mesa analysis reported below.

Schiffer further notes that, ultimately, approaches to the understanding of space utilization should be free of specific sets of ethnographic data. He suggests that the archaeologist ask what kind of activities could be expected to have occurred on a site and then discover where they were performed. Schiffer presents an approach based on what he calls "behavioral chain analysis" (1975:104–105). This approach begins with a set of behavioral chains that incorporate the sequence of activities utilizing a particular element (he uses maize as his example) while being used in an ongoing cultural system. After outlining activities and their constituent elements, Schiffer thinks it feasible to examine any existent regularities in the data to see if they correspond to spatial-functional differentiation (1975:117).

An additional problem that I perceive with Hill's study is his failure to explain the existence of anomalous rooms. There were six rooms in his study that exhibited attributes of both his general categories. They were placed in the category to which they best corresponded (Hill 1970:39–40). Schiffer (1975:118) has noted that such exceptions to the rule may well "provide clues to meaningful variability in the activity structures that can serve as a basis for generating or testing further hypotheses about past organization." Such hypotheses might refer to aspects of organization such as "the location of different kinds of rooms with respect to each other, patterns of construction . . . , patterns of doorways and communication . . . , and design attributes of element classes" (Schiffer 1975:118).

Table Rock Pueblo

Jorgensen (1975) focused on the problem of room function at Table Rock Pueblo, Arizona (ca. A.D. 1300–1400). She extended Martin and Rinaldo's (1960) inventory approach to include the presence/absence of 39 artifactual (primarily tools) and architectural categories (room size, flagstone floors, niches, and platforms) for the 42 rooms in question. All artifacts were from room floors. She analyzed the artifact distributions using both factor analysis and implicational analysis. Only presence/presence relationships were examined in the implicational analysis.

Factor analysis was selected to calculate independent groupings of artifactual categories, which in turn were used to define room types. Jorgensen's test implications concerning room functions emphasized artifacts and features and were based on ethnographic information drawn from Hill's earlier work on the distinctions among habitation rooms, storage rooms, ceremonial rooms, and plazas (1975:158). Along with these test implications, she incorporated Woodbury's (1954) list of associations between stone artifacts and certain activities. Woodbury based his associations on wear patterns and ethnographic data from Awatovi (Jorgensen 1975:158). Jorgensen identified 12 factors equated with room types; however, interpretations were attempted for only four factors. Activities that she associated with these included ceremonies, cooking, weaving, and possibly storage. Jorgensen concluded that factor analysis was insufficient for distinguishing among habitation, ceremonial, and storage rooms, and she suggested that the inclusion of quantitative data and variables pertaining to ceramic and pollen distributions might have produced finer distinctions (1975:159–160).

Jorgensen used implicational analysis in addition to factor analysis. First, all variables were dichotomized and examined for relationships at a 0.15 probability level. These relationships were linked as implicational chains and then as digraphs. They contained relationships of inclusion indicated by unidirectional arrows. On the basis of the significant inclusive relationships, four major groupings (A, B, C, and D) of implicational relationships and two minor ones (E and F) were inferred. The major groups were broken down to represent manufacturing activities in either habitation or ceremonial rooms (A and B), artifactual contents of ceremonial rooms (C), and architectural features of ceremonial rooms (D) (1975:154–156).

Apparently, having formed all possible dichotomies of all variables, Jorgensen examined the frequency of occurrence of each pair across all 42 rooms. If a particular pair occurred 85 % of the time, it was considered significant. She does not explain her reason for selecting this criterion. She then further narrowed the number of variable pairs by looking only at relationships of inclusion (1:1 or presence/presence) over those of presence/absence (1:0 or 0:1) (1975:154). Significant inclusive relationships were formed into implicational chains.

The most basic flaw in the above procedure is Jorgensen's failure to explain how her various criteria were selected, whether arbitrarily or deductively. Also, implicational analysis fails to indicate the proportion of variance in each artifactual category accounted for in the digraphs of implicational chains. There also is no measure of the significance or strengths of relationships. These problems raise the question of whether implicational analysis is more meaningful functionally than factor analysis. Although Jorgensen seems to suggest that it does, her research does not demonstrate it adequately.

The results of the analysis give a pictorial model of all presence/presence occurrences that exceed an unexplained criterion. This is scarcely more information than is immediately evident in the original data matrix.

Grasshopper Ruin

Sullivan presents an interesting alternative to the above studies (1974). He explores the possibility of an association between room size and roofing tree species in the determination of original room function. He suggests that this might provide a tentative solution for estimating original room function when problems arise such as lack of artifacts, floor features, or architectural information. Sullivan believes it unlikely that the size of the room and its roof would have undergone alteration even if the function of the room had changed. Thus, he hypothesizes that it is possible "to estimate original room function by means of assessing the covariation between design features" (1974:94–95).

For his study, Sullivan chose a sample of 16 rooms at Grasshopper Ruin in Arizona. The selected rooms exhibited evidence of having been roofed and also had reliable artifactual arrays and stratigraphic information indicative of original room function. He chose such a sample because it was important to test his model with samples that were not characterized by any contextual problems.

Rooms were categorized by comparing the floor area of the sample room to the mean floor area of all excavated rooms from that roomblock. Hence, a given room was classified as large or small if its floor area was above or below the mean.

The roof was qualitatively defined by the tree species employed in its construction. Examination of the data revealed that large rooms tended to be roofed with ponderosa pine and small rooms with juniper. Sullivan then used a t-test to test the hypothesis that the mean floor area of those rooms roofed with ponderosa pine was greater than that of rooms roofed with juniper. This hypothesis was confirmed at a significance level of 0.05 (1974:95–96).

To explain the association between room size and roofing species, Sullivan investigated the difference between the two roofing materials. He found that ponderosa pine had a linear growth pattern and was readily available in the area but that it also decayed more rapidly than juniper. Thus, the former would have been well suited to the construction of large habitation rooms. Juniper, a denser wood possessing a specific decay-retarding chemical, was more suited to the construction of smaller storage rooms (1974:98).

Sullivan's method seems especially suitable when other indicators such as interior artifacts and features are absent or nonrepresentative and there is definite evidence of roofing materials. In essence, it is simply an indirect method for estimating room size, a characteristic that usually can be measured directly. In addition, this study offers more to those working on sites with better wood preservation than is found on Black Mesa, where roofing materials are rarely preserved. Other studies, such as the analysis by

Smith (1952) described above, have used a wider variety of architectural characteristics than Sullivan considered.

The Black Mesa Analysis

Although it has been the location of archaeological research since 1967, a study of structure function on Black Mesa has not been carried out in a systematic manner. It generally has been assumed that each architectural type—jacal, masonry, and pithouse—was primarily unifunctional. Only two studies, by Reed (1971) and Clemen (1976), have attempted to test that assumption.

Reed's (1971) study involved a graphic examination of specific attributes for both jacal and masonry rooms at 16 sites on Black Mesa. She drew her test expectations primarily from those developed by Hill (1968) in his study of Broken K Pueblo. She postulated that if jacal rooms were used for habitation and masonry rooms for storage, there should be a specific pattern of floor features, a differentiation between the two architectural types in frequencies of utilitarian artifacts, and differences in the percentages of decorated and utilitarian (corrugated and plain gray) ceramic wares. Jacal rooms were expected to contain more hearths, storage pits, and utilitarian artifacts (hammerstones, scrapers, bone awls, worked sherds, culinary jars, decorated bowls, and ladles) than were masonry rooms. Masonry rooms were expected to lack hearths and storage pits (since all floor space was utilized for storage), have few stone or bone artifacts, have more large decorated jars used for storage, and have a greater percentage of decorated wares than were jacals.

Bar graphs were constructed to show the differences between the two architectural types in the frequencies of floor features and artifacts and in ceramic ware percentages. These graphs indicated that floor features in the room types varied as expected. The artifactual data were too scanty to reveal any obvious patterns, and grayware ceramics were unexpectedly found to be more frequent (59 %) in masonry rooms than in jacal rooms (57 %). Reed concluded that the jacals functioned as habitations and the masonry rooms as storage structures. Her study focused primarily on the expected differential functions of masonry rooms and jacals and made no real allowance for possible functional overlap between the two types.

Clemen (1976) also dealt cursorily with the question of functional room types in his analysis of residential groups occupying a particular site on Black Mesa. He was interested primarily in evidence that might reflect how residential groups interacted in their common use of structures, particularly the kiva, the mealing room, and storage rooms. To test his hypotheses on the presence of matrilocal residence groups and their individual and/or common utilization of special-purpose areas, Clemen first determined the functions of the rooms pertinent to his study. Following Hill's (1968) proposal that plain utilitarian wares should occur more frequently in living than storage areas, Clemen determined the ratio of plain to decorated wares in masonry rooms, jacal structures, the mealing room, and the kiva of a Toreva phase site. Applying the chi-square statistic, masonry rooms showed significantly fewer plain wares, while jacals had a higher number of plain wares, a result that contradicts Reed's findings (1971). Unfortunately, Clemen failed to include other variables that might have been relevant to determining functional room types.

Given the lack of rigorous studies of room function on Black Mesa, the primary aim of this paper is to construct a valid and reliable functional classification reflecting variability and patterning in the data, in the hope that significant information about both room function and the functional relationships of artifacts will be provided. The method used here incorporates aspects of the architectural, inventory, and activity approaches. Structural attributes and the features and artifacts found in the rooms are used to develop and test the classification. However, an effort is made to interpret the attributes, and therefore the functional classes, behaviorally. Further, care is taken to ensure that the effects of postdepositional processes are minimized as much as possible.

Selection of the Variables

Since the success of this analysis depends rather heavily on the ability to associate specific activities with the variables, the variables selected must have definite and unambiguous functional meanings. The above survey of literature illustrates that there is an accepted set of variables for indicating room function in the Southwest. The variables employed in this study are of this set. They are floor area; number of hearths, storage pits, and mealing bins; and frequencies of chipped stone, groundstone, and different ceramic wares. Although other variables such as hammerstones, animal bone, worked sherds, seeds, and pollen are potential indicators, they have not been used here because of the lack of such data at the time of analysis.

Each variable is discussed separately below. Each discussion includes the variable's definition, the mode of measurement, the criteria for selection, the functional or behavioral meaning, and those inferences that may be derived from the presence or quantity of each variable.

Floor Area

Floor area is that space encompassed within a structure's boundaries. It is measured as a continuous variable in square meters. The floor areas of all structures in this study were measured with a Bruning Areagraph (Chart No. 488849). Floor area is a useful measure for understanding the function of a room, since that area limits the number of people who can simultaneously interact and carry out activities. In the Southwest, it has been demonstrated that generalized habitation rooms tend to be larger than those used for storage or specialized activities (Hill 1970:45; Sullivan 1974:98; Schiffer 1976:153). As already mentioned, Hill's cutoff between his two categories, habitation and storage, was 6.5 m². Schiffer's (1976:153) dividing point for the same two categories was 6.7 m². The fact that size limits for rooms of different functions cannot be absolutely defined does not affect the usefulness of room size as a *relative* criterion for establishing functional differences between structures. However, it has been suggested that an area less than 0.465 m² (5 ft²) would probably be too small to provide adequate interior space for comfortable habitation (Dean 1969:28). As a point of demarcation for a habitation structure, this is probably too low, and the size limit can most likely be placed somewhat higher than 0.465 m².

Hearths

Pits (i.e., storage pits and hearths) reflect activities such as storing, cooking, heating, and lighting. In this study, a hearth is defined as any pit that shows evidence of burned clay, fire-cracked rocks, or a heavy concentration of charcoal and oxidized soil. Hearth occurrence is measured only in terms of presence or absence.

A hearth is the most commonly used indicator of habitation activities in a room. Schiffer (1976:149–150) relied on the presence/absence of hearths to devise a rough room use classification for the Joint Site. He regarded the presence of a hearth as indicative of a habitation function and absence as indicative of a storage function. In their study of household size among the prehistoric western puebloan Indians, Turner and Lofgren (1966:117) used the presence of a "single fire-hearth" to define the existence of a household. They defined a household as "any persons who habitually ate of food prepared around and cooked on the hearth" (1966:117).

A hearth is assumed to indicate cooking, as well as activities not involving food preparation such as heat treatment of nonedible objects (e.g., projectile points). The range in hearth size and depth varies greatly among the sites under study here. This variability is considered significant since there are functional differences between a shallow cooking or heating pit and a deep roasting pit. However, this difference is unimportant for discriminating habitation from storage rooms. It is assumed that storage structures would contain flammable materials and therefore would not have hearths.

Storage Pits

This variable is defined as (1) a pit that is greater than or equal to the mean depth plus one standard deviation of all pits that do not exhibit the characteristics of hearths or ashpits or (2) a pit containing a vessel. This arbitrary method of discriminating storage pits from others is necessary because little analysis of storage pits has been done in the Southwest. The need for a detailed analysis of pits in the Southwest has already been pointed out by Martin and Plog (1973:232). Storage pits generally are considered to be greater in volume than hearths (Stewart 1975:24; Martin and Plog 1973:232), but how much larger seems to remain a subjective judgement. Storage pit frequency is also measured in terms of presence/absence.

It should be mentioned that Martin and Plog's (1973:258) discussion of portable containers noted that very large jars without handles were used for the storage of water or grains in the Southwest. Ethnographic studies also have noted that the Hopi and Zuni often stored food in large jars (Cushing 1920:208; Bunzel 1929:41). A quantitative comparative study of average storage jar size to storage pit size has not been attempted. This might have produced a better size criterion for how large an uncharred pit must be to be considered a storage feature. An analysis of soil samples for fossil pollen would further support interpretations of the functions of supposed storage pits and jars on Black Mesa. Although analyses of soil samples taken from these contexts have been conducted, they unfortunately were not complete at the time of this study.

Pottery

The general category, pottery, is subdivided into Tusayan Grayware (plain or textured) and Tusayan Whiteware (black-on-white or plain white polished) ceramics. Although in his study of Broken K, Hill (1970:25) grouped pottery types into sets and related them to certain vessel forms (e.g., jars and bowls), such classification is considered unnecessary here. The two categories, grayware and whiteware, are felt to be sufficient for a general understanding of vessel use (see Lerner, this volume).

Activities such as cooking, serving, and storing are frequently inferred from the presence of pottery fragments (Martin and Plog 1973:199, 201). Stephen (in Parsons 1936:1190) and Donaldson (in Hill 1968:117) both indicate that Hopi cooking containers lacked any type of slip or decoration. Plog (1980b:83–85) also has found this to be true for a number of Indian groups in the Southwest. Thus, on the basis of ethnographic evidence, plain and corrugated ceramics are designated as utilitarian (cooking) ware. Hill (1970:49–50) found that most of the utilitarian pottery at Broken K occurred in habitation rooms rather than in storage rooms. He also found that large, small-orificed decorated jars occurred primarily in habitation rooms. Stephen (in Parsons 1936:614) notes that large decorated pots were used by the Hopi to store water, although he does not note in what kinds of rooms these jars were placed. Decorated whiteware is generally associated with storage and food service functions (Martin and Plog 1973:199). As already noted, Clemen (1976:114) used the amount of utilitarian pottery as a test variable to determine whether rooms in a Toreva phase site on Black Mesa were used in different ways. The masonry rooms, which he had hypothesized to be storage areas, showed a lower relative percentage of plain ware than did the jacal rooms.

Lithic Artifacts

Lithic artifacts are simply defined as fine-grained stone materials that show evidence of human modification other than grinding. Accordingly, rocks used as grinding stones or architectural materials are not included. Although Hill (1970:50) gave no ethnographic data on the Hopi or Zuni with which to compare his results, he found lithic artifacts to be a useful variable in differentiating between habitation and storage rooms at Broken K. Overall, he found that chipped stone occurred more often on floors of habitation rooms than on those of storage rooms (1970:42).

Lithic artifacts represent a variable for which finer distinctions could be used to form subcategories. While the possibility of finer distinctions is recognized, they are unnecessary here. In a broader sense, lithic artifacts are considered as evidence of activities associated with maintenance, manufacturing, and food preparation and procurement (Read 1974:216). All such activities are likely to be more associated with habitation or specialized-activity rooms, such as workrooms, than with storage structures.

Groundstone and Mealing Bins

The groundstone category includes whole or fragmentary metates and manos, objects that reflect the specific activity of grinding corn into flour and/or refining plant materials for cooking and eating (Read 1974:216; Woodbury 1954:501). This interpretation is supported by ethnographic evidence (Mindeleff 1891:211–212). Groundstone also is a variable that may be more finely subdivided to reflect changes in a subsistence economy and the efficiency of grinding (Martin and Plog 1973:216). In this study, the term is used in a general sense to represent the function of food preparation.

Hill (1970:48) found most of the groundstone at Broken K to be located in what he had defined as habitation rooms. However, it is not uncommon to find special mealing rooms in the Southwest (Martin and Plog 1973:203; Dean 1969:33). These special rooms are more easily identified when mealing bins are present (Dean 1969:33). In his excavations at Awatovi in northeastern Arizona, Woodbury (1954:59) found that an architectural transition occurred at the same time as the transition from portable to nonportable implements for grinding foodstuffs. This is evident in the creation of the stationary mealing bin, a processing pit defined by ground slabs and used in conjunction with metates and manos in food preparation. He found that the pithouses used for mealing were special work areas. Even with metates leaned against the wall of the room, floor space would not have been adequate for sleeping (1954:61). In his study of Betatakin and Kiet Siel in northeastern Arizona, Dean (1969:33) found that mealing bins were present in both grinding rooms and living rooms. He determined the room type by the presence/absence of other features. As the above discussion indicates, groundstone, which specifically reflects the activity of food preparation, is most likely to be associated with habitation or specialized workrooms. Although the number of mealing bins was too low to include in this analysis, rooms containing them are noted.

The Data and Analysis

The data for this study are drawn from information on sites excavated during the 1975 and 1976 field seasons on Black Mesa. There are 16 sites ranging in time from A.D. 850 to 1150. The sites excavated during the summer of 1975 (D:11:73, D:7:134, and D:7:135) are located in the western portion of Peabody Coal Company's lease area; the remaining sites are located in the eastern area. Only those structures at the 16 sites that had no missing data were included in this study. The total number of structures analyzed was 85. At some of the sites, masonry rooms, jacal structures, and pithouses were all present, while at others only jacal structures or jacal structures and pithouses were present.

The data used were the artifacts in the zone 5 cm above and below the specified floor level and the contents of floor features. As mentioned previously, different refuse types ideally should be identified during excavation, but this was not done for the structures in question. Thus, the possibility exists that all artifacts may not be primary or de facto refuse, but may include some secondary refuse. The identification of the floor level presented the most difficulty in assembling the data. Because of ambiguities in the reporting of the data, it was often difficult to determine the actual depth of many floors. Recorded floor depths were ultimately obtained from a variety of sources, including architectural, feature, and ceramic forms; bag sheets recorded in the field; and the preliminary reports on the sites (Layhe et al. 1976; S. Plog 1977d). The data were analyzed using chi-square tests and one-way analysis of variance. Chi-square tests were used to test nonrandom associations between the architectural types and the other variables. The phi-coefficient (ϕ^2) or Cramer's V was used to indicate and compare strengths of any nonrandom relationships shown by the chi-square results. Yates continuity correction was also used on the 2 by 2 tables, although its use is somewhat controversial (Roscoe 1975:257).

Since the chi-square test is a nonparametric statistic that uses nominal data, the interval scale measurements for each variable were grouped into two nominal categories: presence or absence (used for hearths, storage pits, and groundstone) and/or frequencies above or below the median (used for floor area and whiteware, grayware, and chipped stone frequencies). This test was utilized for hearths, storage pits, and groundstone because of the low range of variation in the frequencies of the variables. For the other variables, the chi-square test was used in addition to the analysis of variance tests because of the significant effect that formation processes can have on artifact frequencies within a structure. It was felt that using both the median test and tests for presence/absence might indicate more accurately the regular occurrences of high or low frequencies of particular artifacts in certain room types. In addition, the median test is not as subject to bias by accidental occurrences as is the presence/absence measurement. The median was preferred over the mean since the mean may be affected by extreme scores that occur with several of the variables. This is not true for the median, and it is therefore a more appropriate measure of central tendency in cases where skewness occurs (Blalock 1972:69–70; Roscoe 1975:59).

Analysis of variance (ANOVA) was also employed to test for differences among the architectural types in the frequencies of all continuous variables. This helped mitigate the loss of information that occurs when continuous data are reduced into nominal or ordinal categories. It was felt that using both tests would minimize the effect of formation processes while possibly allowing more specific functional inferences. It should be emphasized that although ANOVA indicates whether group means are significantly different from each other, the test does not imply that every group mean differs significantly from every other group mean. Since sample size affects a group's contribution to a test of significance and the architectural categories are unequal in size, it cannot be assumed that the largest mean is significantly larger than the smallest mean (Roscoe 1975:309). The Scheffé test allows one to contrast pairs of group means when a null hypothesis of equal means has been rejected and unequal sample sizes exist, thereby indicating which group means do differ in a significant manner (Roscoe 1975:311).

Step 1

The notion of formation processes and the recognition of their importance has already been alluded to in a previous section. Since it can be logically argued that the values for floor area, hearths, and storage pits are not strongly affected by formation processes, as these characteristics are more stable spatially, Step 1 consisted of the calculation of tests involving these variables and architectural type. Several hypotheses were tested, and the results are presented in Table 15. The tables for all chi-square tests are given in the appendix.

The chi-square tests revealed significant relationships between the type of architecture and the presence/absence of hearths and the area of rooms. The analysis of variance test also indicated statistically significant differences between the architectural types in floor area. The greatest differences between the expected and observed frequencies in the chi-square tests occurred with masonry and jacal rooms. Sixteen of 18 of the masonry structures had floor areas less than the median (6.33 m^2), and 27 of 40 (67.5 %) of the jacal structures had floor areas above the median. The average floor area for each architectural type (shown in Table 16) and the histograms of room size for each architectural type (Figure 2) clearly illustrate the differences in the sizes of the rooms. In addition, Scheffé tests (Roscoe 1975:313–314) were calculated to supplement the analysis of variance results. These

Table 15. Chi-square Test for Independence and an Analysis of Variance Test for Architectural Types, Floor Area, the Presence/Absence of Hearths, and Storage Pits.

Variables	χ^2	ϕ^2	ANOVA
(1) All architectural types: Floor area above, below median	16.04*	0.43	$F = 12.26$*
(2) All architectural types: Presence/absence hearths	18.94*	0.47	—
(3) All architectural types: Presence/absence storage pits	2.07	0.16	—

*$p \leq 0.05$

Table 16. Mean and Standard Deviation of Floor Area (in m^2) for Each Architectural Type.

Architectural Type	$\bar{x}$	s
Masonry	4.57	2.50
Jacal	11.22	7.25
Pithouse	6.13	3.03

tests indicated that jacal rooms were significantly larger than both masonry structures and pithouses but that there was no statistically significant difference in the floor area of masonry rooms and pithouses.

Similarly, 16 of 18 (88.9 %) masonry rooms lacked hearths, and 29 of 40 (72.5 %) of the jacal rooms had hearths (Figure 3). Pithouses displayed no pattern with respect to the occurrence of hearths. Hearths were present/absent in approximately an equal number of cases. It is possible that pithouses were functionally more generalized than the other architectural types and, depending on their size and other factors, might have served as either habitation or storage areas or as both.

The test results also indicated that the presence or absence of storage units is not significantly associated with architectural type (Figure 3). In order to verify this, more specific pairwise comparisons of architectural types were made, and the results of these tests are presented in Table 17. Even though none of the chi-square tests are statistically significant, they do indicate that jacal rooms and pithouses differ most in the degree to which storage pits are present. Storage units are most common in pithouses and are least frequent in jacal rooms.

In another series of tests, floor area, hearths, and storage pits were cross-tabulated in pairs. The results of these tests are shown in Table 18. A strong association was found between the presence/absence of hearths and floor area above and below the median. This was in fact the largest chi-square value found for any test. The results show that hearths occur approximately three times more often in structures with large floor areas (greater than 6.33 m^2) than in smaller structures. This is expected since any structure containing a hearth probably served a habitation function, thus requiring a fairly large floor area. It may prove, on further examination of the data, that the combined presence of these two variables is a good indicator of a habitation function.

No statistically significant relationship was found between the presence/absence of storage pits and floor area or between the presence/absence of storage pits and hearths.

To summarize, these tests indicate a strong association between architectural type, floor area, and the presence/absence of hearths. This is particularly true for masonry and jacal structures. Hearths occur primarily in rooms with high floor areas and, hence, more often in jacal rooms. Hearths tend to be absent in small rooms, and 89 % of the masonry structures are below the

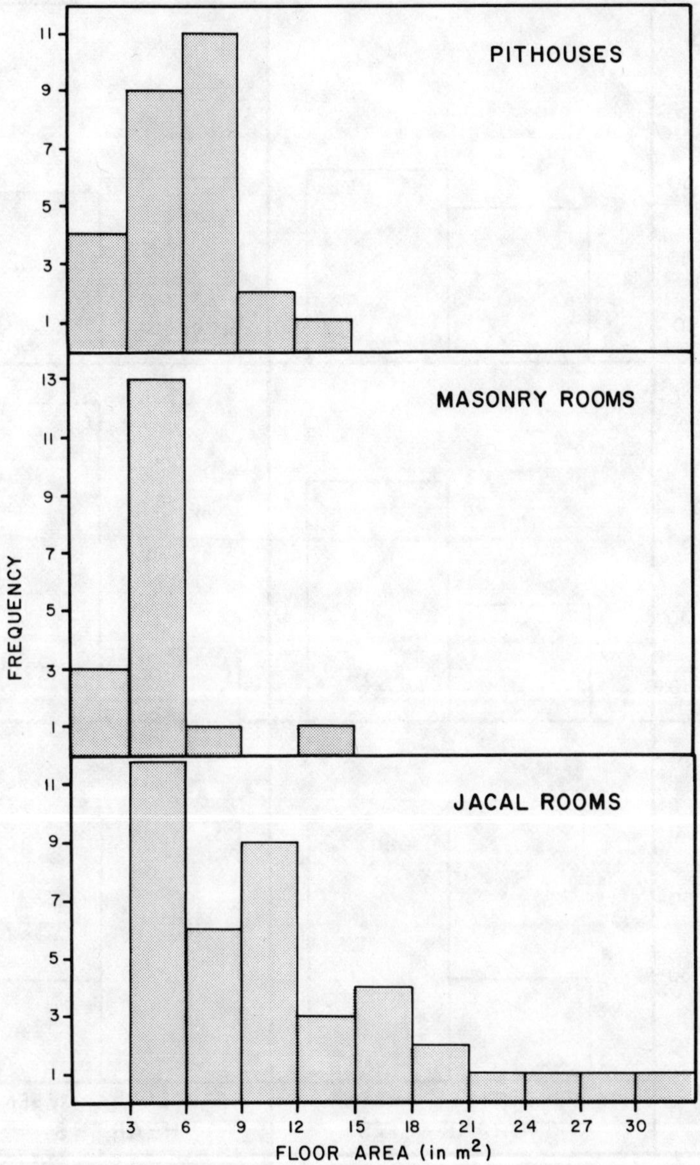

Figure 2. Histograms of room size for each architectural type.

median room size. The test results also indicate that presence/absence of storage units is not significantly associated with architectural type, floor area, or hearths. This may indicate that variation in the distribution of storage pits among architectural types is a sign of secondary differences in storage, per-

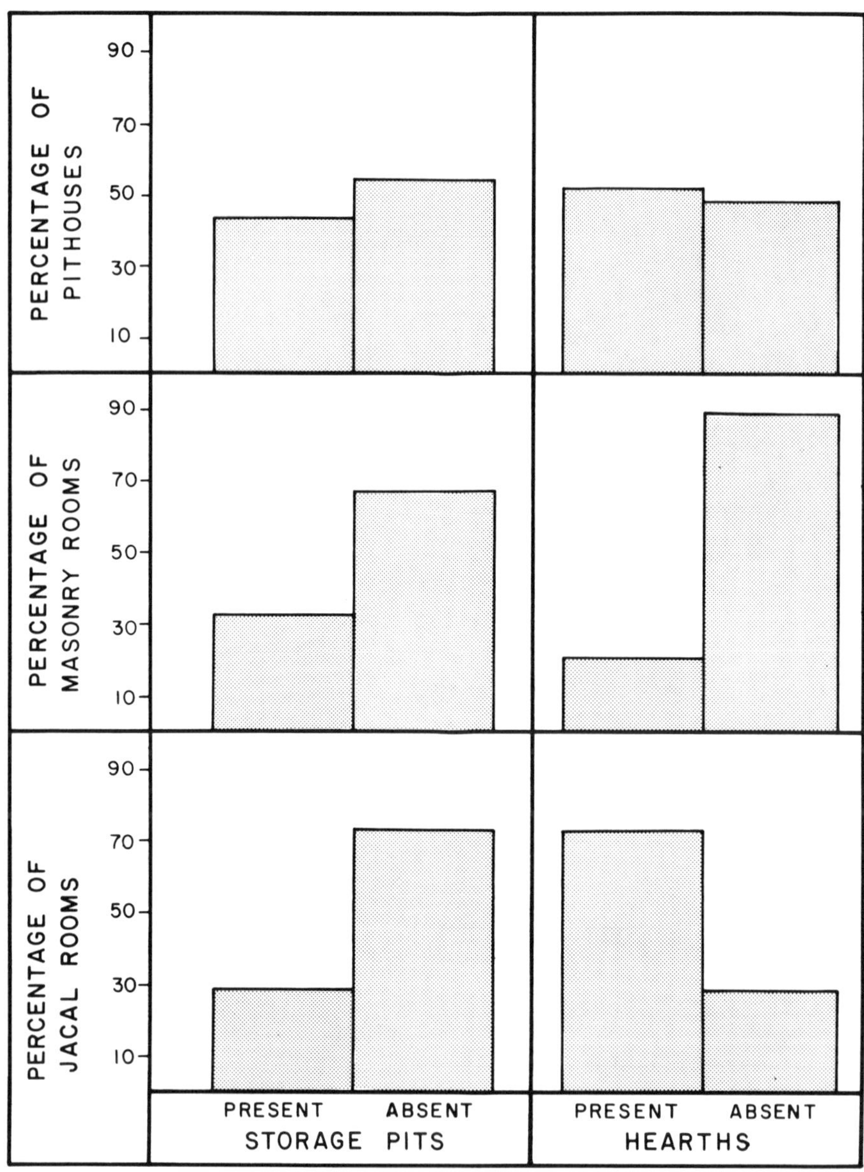

Figure 3. Histograms of the relative frequency of hearths and storage pits for each architectural type.

haps linked specifically to whatever was stored, how long it was to be stored, and the size of the population for which it was being stored. A study of the various types of pollen found in different room types might provide better information as to whether certain architectural types were preferred for stor-

Table 17. Chi-square Test for Independence Between Pairs of Architectural Types and the Presence/Absence of Storage Pits.

Variables	χ^2	ϕ^2
(1) Masonry, jacal rooms: Presence/absence storage pits	0.02	0.02
(2) Masonry, pithouses: Presence/absence storage pits	0.19	0.07
(3) Jacal rooms, pithouses: Presence/absence storage pits	1.37	0.14

Table 18. Chi-square Test for Independence Between the Presence/Absence of Hearths, Storage Pits, and Floor Area.

Variables	χ^2	ϕ^2
(1) Presence/absence hearths: Floor area above, below median	23.99*	0.53
(2) Presence/absence storage pits: Floor area above, below median	0.48	0.08
(3) Presence/absence hearths: Presence/absence storage pits	0.03	0.02

*$p \leq 0.05$

ing certain food materials. It is possible that, even aside from architectural composition, there may have been more than one type of storage room. One group of structures, while characterized by small floor area, might have been large enough to house storage units. Another group of structures may possibly have acted as total storage units in and of themselves. Such a dichotomy could be explained by the type of occupation (permanent or temporary) of a site and/or the type of contents being stored (bulk or nonbulk, preservable or nonpreservable, and even food or nonfood). If so, it is not surprising that a significant relationship is not manifested between the presence/absence of storage units and hearths, floor area, and architectural type.

Step 2

In order to examine further the differences between architectural types suggested by the above tests, additional tests were conducted to determine whether the architectural types differ in frequencies of white- and grayware ceramics, chipped stone, and groundstone. In addition to the use of analysis of variance, chi-square tests were also calculated using both presence/absence measurements and variable frequencies above and below the median, with the exception of groundstone frequency. For the latter variable, only a presence/absence measure was used because of the low median value of 0.88 pieces of groundstone per structure. The means and standard deviations of whiteware, grayware, and chipped stone frequency for each architectural type are presented in Table 19, and frequency distributions are illustrated in Figures 4 and 5. Test results are shown in Table 20. Contingency tables for the chi-square tests can be found in the appendix.

Table 19. Means and Standard Deviations of Whiteware, Grayware, and Chipped Stone Frequencies for Each Architectural Type.

Architectural Type	n	Whiteware		Grayware		Chipped Stone	
		$\bar{x}$	s	$\bar{x}$	s	$\bar{x}$	s
Masonry	18	4.17	9.05	23.11	30.10	2.78	6.78
Jacal	40	4.83	12.06	23.93	69.63	4.75	8.15
Pithouse	27	9.93	13.30	46.16	67.72	3.89	6.89
All structures	85	6.78	11.99	30.81	62.96	4.06	7.44

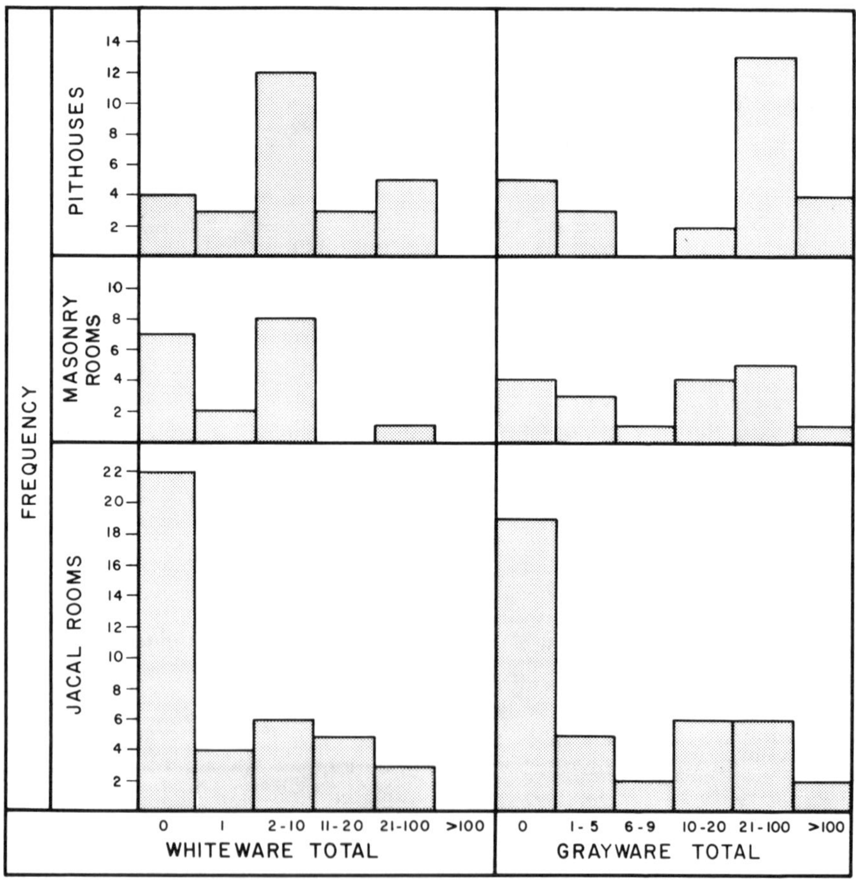

Figure 4. Histograms of the frequency of whiteware and grayware for each architectural type.

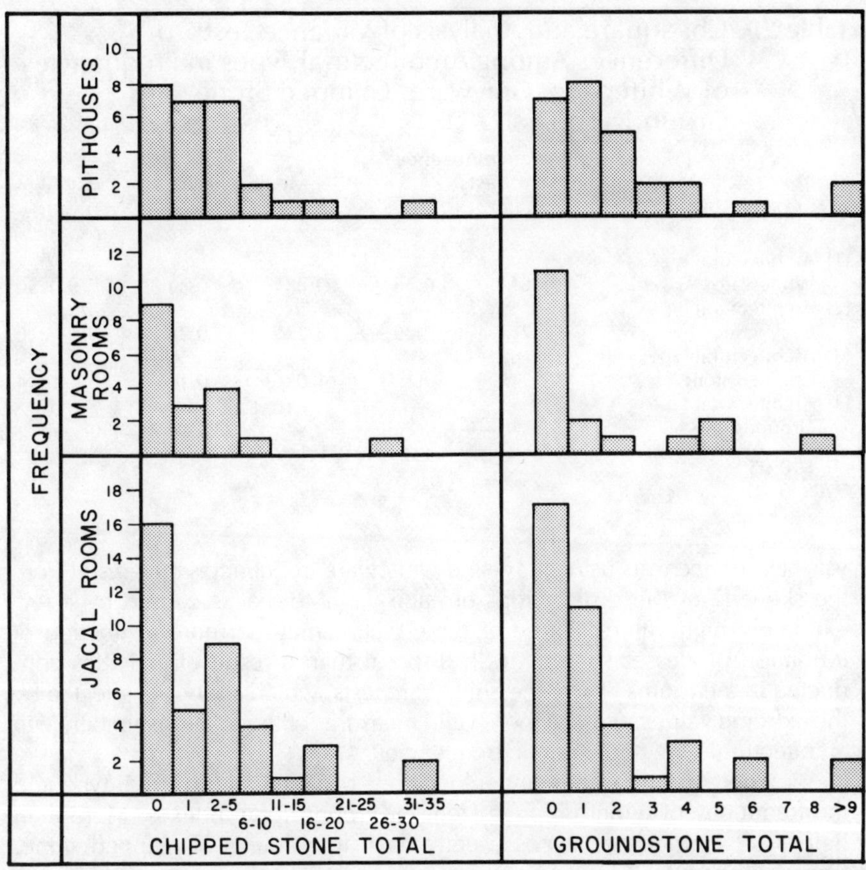

Figure 5. Histograms of the frequency of chipped stone and groundstone for each architectural type.

The chi-square tests demonstrate significant associations between architectural type and the frequencies of gray- and whiteware ceramics, although no statistically significant results were obtained with the analysis of variance tests. For the cross-tabulations involving whiteware frequencies, the greatest difference is between pithouses and other structures. Whitewares are present in a greater proportion of the pithouses and in higher frequencies. In masonry structures, whitewares are absent in 61.1 % of all cases, and frequencies tend to be lower than in the other structures. In contrast to the contingency table for whitewares, the tables for graywares suggest that the greatest difference is between jacal rooms and other structures. Graywares are absent from jacal rooms in a greater percentage of the cases (47.5 %) than for either masonry rooms (22.2 %) or pithouses (18.5 %), and they occur in lower frequencies in jacal rooms. The statistical insignificance of the anal-

Table 20. Chi-square and Analysis of Variance Tests for Differences Among Architectural Types in Frequencies of Whiteware, Grayware, Chipped Stone, and Groundstone.

Variables	Presence/Absence Tests		Median Tests		
	χ^2	ϕ^2	χ^2	ϕ^2	ANOVA
(1) Architectural type: Whiteware	10.96*	0.36	9.85*	0.34	$F = 1.50$
(2) Architectural type: Grayware	7.32*	0.29	8.29*	0.31	$F = 1.18$
(3) Architectural type: Chipped stone	1.93	0.15	1.03	0.11	$F = 0.44$
(4) Architectural type: Groundstone	5.57**	0.26	—	—	—

$*p \leq 0.05$
$**p \leq 0.10$

ysis of variance tests using gray- and whiteware frequencies may result from the skewing of the distributions of each variable that is caused by a few extremely high values. These extreme values may be more a function of formation processes such as trash disposal than a result of activities conducted in the rooms. Thus, the chi-square tests, which are not as affected by the extreme values, may be more valid measures of the relationship between architectural type and ceramic frequencies.

There are no significant associations between architectural type and the frequency of either chipped stone or groundstone indexes. More than half of all architectural types usually have low counts of chipped stone. Comparisons of cell frequencies show that the difference between masonry rooms and pithouses is the primary contributor to the chi-square value for groundstone. Pithouses tend to have groundstone present more often (74 %) than not, while only 39 % of the masonry structures have groundstone. Fifty-seven percent of the jacals contain some groundstone. The evidence suggests that work activities such as grinding and food processing and the manufacture of chipped stone were pursued in rooms regardless of their architectural type. However, grinding activities were more likely to have been conducted in pithouses. These activities may have been consigned to particular rooms or areas on the basis of room size, on the basis of certain characteristics such as hearths, or according to other unknown characteristics not included in this study. Such workrooms may not be apparent here if the activities were carried out in a range of different environments, including rooms of different architectural type. Even if they were primary, these activities would not have required a great deal of floor space. In some cases the activities could also have been secondary in larger rooms, since a larger floor area ought to provide space for a greater number of potential activities, both day-to-day and occasional.

On the basis of the above two steps and the results obtained, a few preliminary conclusions can be drawn for each architectural type. In general, masonry structures (Plate 4) appear to be characterized by small floor areas; almost no hearths or storage pits; and uniform, though small, amounts of both white- and graywares. Evidence in the form of pits or vessels for use of masonry rooms as repositories for storage is lacking. Only 33 % of the masonry structures contain storage pits. However, the presence of ceramics, noted above, may indicate that both grayware and whiteware vessels were used for storage purposes (although Lerner's analysis of ceramic container function [this volume] suggests that while painted whiteware jars were used for storage, grayware jars may have had a culinary function).

Masonry structures may represent the most specialized of all three groups in that an entire structure may have served a unifunctional storage purpose. Given the consistent absence in such rooms of the theoretically most important indicator of domestic use, hearths, one may infer that their purpose was storage. This does not negate the potential use of jacal structures and pithouses for storage. It is logical that masonry structures would be used most often for storage because of their more solid construction, which would provide greater protection from weather and rodent damage. As a group, masonry structures also show weak evidence for domestic functions such as specialized work activities. Approximately one-third of the structures contain

Plate 4. Excavated masonry structure.

groundstone. Chipped stone is present as frequently as it is absent, and only one-third of all masonry structures have more than one lithic artifact.

Jacal rooms (Plate 5) as a group are characterized by significantly larger floor areas (greater than 6.33 m^2), the presence of hearths, and low counts of whitewares (one sherd or less) and graywares (nine sherds or less). With regard to test results that were not statistically significant, evidence for presence of storage pits is scanty. Seventy-three percent of all jacal structures lacked such units. This would seem to point toward a general habitation function for jacal structures and is most strongly indicated by their larger floor areas and the more frequent presence of hearths.

The low counts of whitewares may indicate that jacal rooms only occasionally contained storage vessels. The low numbers of grayware sherds are somewhat surprising given the common occurrence of large floor area and hearths, and may indicate that most cooking activities took place outside structures. Groundstone and chipped stone, which may reflect food preparation and manufacturing tasks, further indicate (although not significantly) some occurrence of general habitation activities. Fifty-eight percent of jacals have groundstone present. Lithic artifacts are present more often than not.

On the whole, pithouses are distinguished by marginal tendencies toward low floor area (56 %), the absence of hearths (52 %), the absence of storage pits (56 %), and the absence of chipped stone (56 %). These tendencies do not appear as strong as those found for jacal rooms and masonry

Plate 5. Excavated jacal structure.

structures. Occurrences of whitewares (74 %) and graywares (70 %) were particularly high for pithouses. While not significantly associated with any architectural type, groundstone was present in 74 % of the pithouse structures. Thus, the major distinctive features of pithouses seem to be the frequent occurrences of ceramics and groundstone. Storage pits do not appear to have been a common feature; however, they do occur more often in pithouses than in either jacal rooms or masonry units.

These results imply a multifunctional purpose for pithouses, which appears to be more characteristic of pithouses than either jacal structures or masonry structures. Further evidence might show a habitation/storage differential for pithouses. The significantly higher counts of pottery sherds of both types tend to support this. Pithouses do not quite fit the habitation "ideal" in that a majority fall below the median floor area (6.33 m^2) for all structures, and they generally lack hearths. They do show evidence of habitation activities in the presence of larger numbers of grayware sherds and a larger number of groundstone tools. This tendency toward having more groundstone than the median value for all structures might also reflect a greater frequency of specialized mealing activities. In fact, four of the six structures that contain mealing bins are pithouses (Plate 6). At the same time, pithouses also do not fit neatly into a storage category. They are characterized more by the absence

Plate 6. Excavated mealing pithouse.

than the presence of storage pits; yet, contrary to this evidence, whiteware frequency is significantly higher than the median. From the test results, it can only be inferred that pithouses may have served a combination of habitation, storage, and food-processing functions.

Step 3

Two factors are apparent in the results of the foregoing steps: the associations of (1) hearths with architectural type and (2) hearths with floor area resulted in the two highest phi-coefficients, indicating the strongest relationships. This suggests that the presence of hearths might serve as a good attribute on which to base an initial division of all data into two groups as a means of further searching for significant patterns or associations in a manner somewhat similar to the analysis by Whallon (1972). A hearth is probably the strongest indicator that a room was occupied by people relatively frequently and/or for some period of time. It is also one of the few truly necessary discriminators between storage and nonstorage areas. However, although it is regarded as a necessary indicator for habitation, it is not a fully sufficient one.

Since all structures were divided on the basis of presence/absence of hearths, it was necessary to recalculate the medians for the two groups in order to carry out additional tests. These are given in Table 21. Chi-square values were calculated between architectural type and all variables within the two groups defined above. The chi-square statistic is an approximation of the multinominal probability distribution, and certain assumptions must be met if results are to have any meaningful validity in relation to this curve. In 2 by 2 tables with small sample size, where no a priori manipulation to establish equal expected cell frequencies is possible, chi-square tests may be overly liberal (Roscoe 1975). The Yates continuity correction factor is used in this study to help offset this tendency. Also, in keeping with the restrictions regarding sample size, a check was made of all the expected and average expected frequencies for the contingency tables in Step 3. The restrictions referred to include the following:

1. For a 2 by 2 table, one should have an average expected frequency of 7.5 or more, which is equivalent to a minimal sample of 30;
2. Expected frequencies in the cells of the contingency table should not be less than five in general, especially if there is strong departure from equality (Blalock 1972:285–286).

Structures with Hearths Absent

On examination of the test results in Table 22, it can be seen that all chi-square values are nonsignificant. Some values, with their measure of association, must be interpreted with caution, as certain cells within the tables had expected cell frequencies below five.

Table 21. Medians for All Variables, for All Structures, and for Structures With and Without Hearths.

Variables	All Structures	Structures With Hearths	Structures Without Hearths
Floor area	6.33	8.90	4.33
Whiteware	1.57	1.30	1.80
Grayware	9.60	10.00	7.00
Chipped stone	1.13	1.39	0.88
Groundstone	0.87	1.23	0.43
Storage pits	0.26	—	—
Hearths	0.55	—	—

Table 22. Chi-square Tests for Differences Among Architectural Types Without Hearths in Floor Area and in Frequencies of Chipped Stone, Grayware, Groundstone, Whiteware, and Storage Pits.

Variables	χ^2	ϕ^2
(1) Architectural type: Chipped stone (median test)	3.62[a]	0.30
(2) Architectural type: Grayware (median test)	3.40	0.29
(3) Architectural type: Floor area (median test)	3.37	0.29
(4) Architectural type: Groundstone (presence/absence)	3.28	0.28
(5) Architectural type: Whiteware (median test)	3.19	0.28
(6) Architectural type: Storage pits (presence/absence)	2.46[a]	0.25

[a]Some expected cell frequencies are lower than 5.

Since all results are nonsignificant and some violate an important assumption, the raw data, quickly summarized here, are presented in the contingency tables in the appendix. The majority of masonry structures (16 of 18) not containing hearths are small and tend to lack storage pits, chipped stone, and groundstone. Jacal rooms without hearths (11 of 40) are characterized by floor areas larger overall than those in masonry structures but smaller than the average for all 85 structures and by the presence of storage pits (55 %). The majority of them have low whiteware (64 %), grayware (73 %), and chipped stone (64 %) frequencies. Fifty-five percent contain no evidence of groundstone. Pithouses not containing hearths (14 of 27) are also small rooms, and few (36 %) have storage pits. In general, these pithouses tend to contain high ceramic counts in contrast to jacal rooms and masonry units. Pithouses without hearths are also characterized by the presence of groundstone (64 %) and chipped stone (71 %).

Structures with Hearths Present

The chi-square results shown in Table 23 were calculated using jacal rooms and pithouses, since only two masonry structures had hearths. Not much distinguishes these two masonry structures other than their hearths.

Table 23. Chi-square Tests for Differences Between Jacal and Pit Structures With Hearths in Floor Area, and in Frequencies of Grayware, Groundstone, Whiteware, and Storage Pits.

Variables	χ^2	ϕ^2
(1) Architectural type: Chipped stone (median test)	1.28	0.18
(2) Architectural type: Grayware (median test)	4.88*	0.34
(3) Architectural type: Floor area (median test)	6.09[a]*	0.38
(4) Architectural type: Groundstone (median test)	1.69	0.20
(5) Architectural type: Whiteware (median test)	4.88*	0.34
(6) Architectural type: Storage pits (presence/absence)	4.25*	0.32

[a]Some expected cell frequencies are less than 5.
*$p \leq 0.05$

One is large; both contain storage pits. Perhaps they were originally used for storage and were later converted to serve another function. The larger structure has a variety of artifacts with a high frequency of grayware ceramics. This, along with the presence of a hearth, may indicate a habitation use. The smaller structure contains a good deal of groundstone and chipped stone, which may indicate that it served as a special-activity area.

Significant chi-square values were obtained for the cross-tabulations between architectural type and floor area, whiteware, grayware, and storage. Given the presence of a hearth, jacals are significantly larger (greater than or equal to 8.9 m^2) than pithouses and lack storage units 83 % of the time. Pithouses, however, have significantly more whiteware and grayware sherds than do jacal structures. While there does not appear to be a statistically significant association between chipped stone or groundstone and architectural type, the raw data suggest that chipped stone occurs more often in jacal rooms. High amounts of groundstone appear more often in pithouses (62 %) than in jacal rooms (35 %).

The evidence suggests that pithouses with hearths fall rather neatly into a general habitation category. Although only 44 % tend to have floor areas larger than the grand median (8.9 m^2), 85 % of them have floor areas of 8.9 m^2 or less, the median for the group containing hearths. Evidence exists for a variety of day-to-day activities (e.g., eating, food preparation, and storage facilities) as indicated by counts greater than the medians for whitewares, graywares, storage pits, and groundstone. The presence of chipped stone, though not significantly different from values for jacal structures, may also point to some manufacturing or retouching of chipped stone. Pithouses seem to have been quite multifunctional, housing a range of activities. Jacal rooms, while not exhibiting as high a number of specific attributes, also appear to have a full range, although low frequencies of artifacts occur when hearths are present. Whitewares and graywares are significantly low, and 66 % have very low counts of groundstone (one or less). Storage pits are absent in the majority of jacal structures, so that they do not appear to have been used very often even as temporary storage facilities. High counts of chipped stone occur in 55 % of all jacal rooms with hearths, as opposed to 31 % of all pithouses with hearths.

Conclusions

The intention of this paper was to produce a functional classification of the structures under study. This of course is not meant to imply that there is only one classification of a data set or that the results lack interpretive problems. The development of a classification is not an end in itself; rather, it furnishes new information and facilitates more refined analyses of problems under consideration. The general results of the analysis are summarized below.

Masonry rooms without hearths were characterized by very small floor areas and a low probability of having storage pits. High counts of ceramics occurred at least 50 % of the time, suggesting that some storage may have occurred in ceramic vessels. Greater attention to the more common forms of pottery found in these rooms might be more revealing. Large-bodied vessels would be expected to occur more often than the wide-mouthed jars and shallow bowls used for cooking and eating (see Lerner, this volume). The lack of evidence for chipped stone and groundstone in any quantity discounts the inference of the use of these structures as specialized workrooms. In sum, masonry structures may represent a group in which, as a rule, the entire structure served a storage purpose. Evidence for large amounts of economic pollen would support this assumption. Further flotation analysis of soil samples from the interiors of masonry structures is recommended.

Only two masonry structures contained hearths. These two structures were discussed, and it was hypothesized that their function had changed over time from storage to habitation or special use.

Pithouses as a group displayed greater generality in the sense that they contained more frequent evidence for the occurrence of a wider range of activities. Although pithouses with hearths were characterized by a mean floor area approximately half that of jacal rooms with hearths, they show overall a greater abundance of artifacts, with the exception of chipped stone. This group appears to constitute a general category of structures with both habitation and storage functions. The larger numbers of sherds of both types support this inference. These structures then appear to have been used for many different habitation activities including not only cooking, eating, food-grinding and some lithic-knapping activities but also storage. Storage pits are present at least 50 % of the time.

Pithouses without hearths tend to lack storage pits, and the ceramic densities are almost twice as high as the densities for pithouses with hearths. This suggests a different use for these pithouses. It is likely that they served a more unifunctional role, perhaps as total storage units homologous to masonry structures. Further research is necessary to determine the activities carried out in this subgroup of structures.

Although not statistically significant, there is a consistent occurrence of groundstone within both groups of pithouses (74 % of all pithouses), indicating that when grinding activities took place inside structures, they did so more often in pithouses. This is further supported in that four out of six structures containing mealing bins are pithouses. Three of these lacked hearths, but they are characterized by unusually high counts of both white-wares and graywares, and chipped stone and groundstone. Only one of these had a storage feature. The fourth pithouse containing a mealing bin is characterized not only by large numbers of artifacts but also by the presence of a hearth and eight storage units. These characteristics leave little doubt that they were specialized rooms.

Jacal structures with hearths may also be considered habitation structures. However, they appear to be more specialized than the multifunctional pithouses. Although they have the highest mean floor area of all groups, they tend to contain fewer artifacts than any other group. High counts of chipped stone do occur at least 50 % of the time, so some lithic-related activities seem to have taken place in these rooms. Only 17 % of these jacals have a storage pit. Storage pits may be lacking in the large jacals because specialized masonry units almost completely assumed the storage function on the same sites. The lower numbers, density, and probability of occurrence of ceramics in jacals relative to pithouses may be related to food storage and food-processing activities in pithouses. This would further indicate the use of jacal rooms for a purer living room function.

Jacal rooms lacking hearths, while smaller in size, appear to have the same contents as their larger counterparts. When size is taken into account, densities suggest little difference in the average number of artifacts per square meter. The greatest differences appear with respect to the occurrence of groundstone and storage pits. There is a lower probability of occurrence of groundstone and a noticeable increase in the presence of storage pits in jacal structures without hearths. These structures may have served the same habitation function as did large jacal rooms, but on a seasonal basis (see Powell, Chapter 7 of this volume), perhaps with the hearths located outside the structures. They conceivably may represent temporary, summer constructions, assuming that jacals are less time-consuming to construct than pithouses or masonry units. Thus, a variety of functional possibilities exist for these smaller jacals and pithouses without hearths. It might be revealing to make a more intensive examination of a sample of these structures and contiguous features and a more in-depth analysis of the apparent pattern of interaction among floor area, the presence of storage pits, and architectural type.

In summary, the results support the inference of a functional polarization between jacal and masonry structures. The exact nature of this relationship is, of course, contingent on the assumption that masonry structures do indeed represent storage units; ideally, this hypothesis would be further supported by pollen analysis. Pithouses suggest a greater diversity of functions than do the other two types of structures. Given the possibility that pithouses represent an earlier form of structure, the developmental hypothesis of a functional polarization and structural specialization, through time, of habitation and storage activities in jacal and masonry units gains credence. However, given the temporal variability and the ambiguity of the patterns revealed, these inferences should not be applied automatically to all structures and sites without further intensive research.

Several topics can be suggested for future research. First, the lack of evidence for a strong relationship between whiteware and grayware frequencies and specific architectural types is not consistent with the notion that whitewares were used for storage and graywares for domestic functions. More information is really needed than just whiteware and grayware counts to interpret ceramics as an indication of specific functions. Data on specific vessel attributes may be more informative (see Lerner, this volume). In addition, the weight of all sherds from each structure may be a better measure than sherd count. The weight for 100 large sherds, for example, would be greater than the weight for a larger number of very small sherds and might give a better estimate of the number and size of whole vessels originally in the structure. Second, the results of pollen analyses for floor features and room floor samples is imperative. Third, the investigation of temporal trends in the construction and use of structures would be valuable. To conduct such a study, better temporal control is needed to date individual structures; a larger number of excavated sites more evenly distributed through time also would be necessary. Research on the above topics would contribute to the development of a functional classification of structures on Black Mesa. As noted above, such information on structure functions is extremely important in studies of population levels, demographic changes, and temporal change in organization. It is hoped that the results of this study have provided useful information as well as ideas for future Black Mesa research.

Appendix

Results of Step 1

	Floor Area		
	Lo[a] (< 6.33 m^2)	Hi[b] (> 6.33 m^2)	
Masonry	16	2	18
	(9.31)	(8.63)	
	89 %	11 %	
Jacal	13	27	40
	(20.70)	(19.29)	
	32.5 %	67.5 %	
Pithouse	15	12	27
	(13.98)	(13.02)	
	56 %	44 %	
	44	41	85

$\chi^2 = 16.04$, significant
$\phi^2 = 0.434$

Hearths

	Absent	Present	
Masonry	16 (8.68) 89 %	2 (9.31) 11 %	18
Jacal	11 (19.29) 27.5 %	29 (20.70) 72.5 %	40
Pithouse	14 (13.02) 52 %	13 (13.98) 48 %	27
	41	44	85

$\chi^2 = 18.94$, significant
$\phi^2 = 0.472$

Storage Pits

	Absent	Present	
Masonry	12 (11.86) 67 %	6 (6.14) 33 %	18
Jacal	29 (26.35) 72.5 %	11 (13.65) 27.5 %	40
Pithouse	15 (17.79) 56 %	12 (9.21) 44 %	27
	56	29	85

$\chi^2 = 2.07$, nonsignificant
$\phi^2 = 0.157$

Storage Pits

	Absent	Present	
Masonry	12 (12.72) 67 %	6 (5.27) 33 %	18
Jacal	29 (28.27) 72.5 %	11 (11.72) 27.5 %	40
	41	17	58

$\chi^2 = 0.02$, nonsignificant
$\phi^2 = 0.019$

Storage Pits

	Absent	Present	
Masonry	12	6	18
	(10.80)	(7.20)	
	67 %	33 %	
Pithouse	15	12	27
	(16.20)	(10.80)	
	56 %	44 %	
	27	18	45

$\chi^2 = 0.19$, nonsignificant
$\phi^2 = 0.065$

Storage Pits

	Absent	Present	
Jacal	29	11	40
	(26.27)	(13.73)	
	72.5 %	27.5 %	
Pithouse	15	12	27
	(17.73)	(9.27)	
	56 %	44 %	
	44	23	67

$\chi^2 = 1.37$, nonsignificant
$\phi^2 = 0.143$

Hearths

		Absent	Present	
	Lo[a]	33	11	44
	(< 6.33 m^2)	(21.22)	(22.78)	
Floor		75 %	25 %	
Area	Hi[b]	8	33	41
	(> 6.33 m^2)	(19.78)	(21.22)	
		19.5 %	80.5 %	
		41	44	85

$\chi^2 = 23.99$, significant
$\phi^2 = 0.531$

		Storage Pits		
		Absent	Present	
Floor Area	Lo[a] (< 6.33 m²)	31 (28.98) 70.5 %	13 (15.01) 29.5 %	44
	Hi[b] (> 6.33 m²)	25 (27.01) 61 %	16 (13.99) 39 %	41
		56	29	85

$\chi^2 = 0.48$, nonsignificant
$\phi^2 = 0.08$

		Storage Pits		
		Absent	Present	
Hearths	Absent	25 (25.88) 62.5 %	15 (14.12) 37.5 %	40
	Present	30 (29.12) 67 %	15 (15.88) 33 %	45
		55	30	85

$\chi^2 = 0.03$, nonsignificant
$\phi^2 = 0.019$

Results of Step 2

	Whiteware		
	Absent	Present	
Masonry	7 (6.99) 39 %	11 (11.01) 61 %	18
Jacal	22 (15.53) 15 %	18 (24.47) 45 %	40
Pithouse	4 (10.48) 15 %	23 (16.52) 85 %	27
	33	52	85

$\chi^2 = 10.96$, significant
$\phi^2 = 0.358$

Whiteware

	Lo[a] (< 1)	Hi[b] (> 1)	
Masonry	9 (8.89) 50 %	9 (9.11) 50 %	18
Jacal	26 (19.76) 65 %	14 (20.24) 35 %	40
Pithouse	7 (13.34) 26 %	20 (13.66) 74 %	27
	42	43	85

$\chi^2 = 9.85$, significant
$\phi^2 = 0.340$

Grayware

	Absent	Present	
Masonry	4 (5.93) 22 %	14 (12.07) 78 %	18
Jacal	19 (13.18) 47.5 %	21 (26.82) 52.5 %	40
Pithouse	5 (8.89) 18.5 %	22 (18.11) 81.5 %	27
	28	57	85

$\chi^2 = 7.32$, significant
$\phi^2 = 0.293$

Grayware

	Lo[a] (< 9)	Hi[b] (> 9)	
Masonry	8 (8.89) 44 %	10 (9.11) 56 %	18
Jacal	26 (19.76) 65 %	14 (20.24) 35 %	40
Pithouse	8 (13.34) 30 %	19 (13.66) 70 %	27
	42	43	85

$\chi^2 = 8.29$, significant
$\phi^2 = 0.312$

Chipped Stone

	Absent	Present	
Masonry	9 (6.99) 50 %	9 (11.01) 50 %	18
Jacal	16 (15.53) 40 %	24 (24.47) 60 %	40
Pithouse	8 (10.48) 30 %	19 (16.52) 70 %	27
	33	52	85

$\chi^2 = 1.93$, nonsignificant
$\phi^2 = 0.151$

Chipped Stone

	Lo[a] (< 1)	Hi[b] (> 1)	
Masonry	12 (10.16) 67 %	6 (7.84) 33 %	18
Jacal	21 (22.59) 52.5 %	19 (17.41) 47.5 %	40
Pithouse	15 (15.25) 56 %	12 (11.76) 44 %	27
	48	37	85

$\chi^2 = 1.03$, nonsignificant
$\phi^2 = 0.109$

Groundstone

	Absent	Present	
Masonry	11 (7.41) 61 %	7 (10.59) 39 %	18
Jacal	17 (16.47) 42.5 %	23 (23.53) 57.5 %	40
Pithouse	7 (11.12) 26 %	20 (15.89) 74 %	27
	35	50	85

$\chi^2 = 5.57$, nonsignificant
$\phi^2 = 0.256$

Results of Step 3—Hearths Absent

Floor Area

	Lo[a] (< 4.33 m^2)	Hi[b] (> 4.33 m^2)	
Masonry	10 (7.41) 62.5 %	6 (8.59) 37.5 %	16
Jacal	3 (5.10) 27 %	8 (5.90) 73 %	11
Pithouse	6 (6.49) 43 %	8 (7.51) 57 %	14
	19	22	41

$\chi^2 = 3.37$, nonsignificant
$\phi^2 = 0.287$

Storage Pits

	Absent	Present	
Masonry	12 (10.15) 75 %	4 (5.85) 25 %	16
Jacal	9 (6.97) 45.5 %	5 (4.02) 54.5 %	11
Pithouse	9 (8.88) 64 %	5 (5.12) 36 %	14
	26	15	41

$\chi^2 = 2.46$, nonsignificant
$\phi^2 = 0.245$

Whiteware

	Lo[a] (< 1)	Hi[b] (> 1)	
Masonry	8 (7.41) 50 %	8 (8.59) 50 %	16
Jacal	7 (5.09) 64 %	4 (5.90) 36 %	11
Pithouse	4 (6.49) 29 %	10 (7.51) 71 %	14
	19	22	41

$\chi^2 = 3.19$, nonsignificant
$\phi^2 = 0.279$

Grayware

	Lo[a] (< 7)	Hi[b] (> 7)	
Masonry	8 (8.20) 50 %	8 (7.80) 50 %	16
Jacal	8 (5.63) 73 %	3 (5.37) 27 %	11
Pithouse	5 (7.17) 36 %	9 (6.83) 64 %	14
	21	20	41

$\chi^2 = 3.40$, nonsignificant
$\phi^2 = 0.288$

Chipped Stone

	Absent	Present	
Masonry	9 (7.80) 56 %	7 (8.20) 44 %	16
Jacal	7 (5.37) 64 %	4 (5.63) 36 %	11
Pithouse	4 (6.83) 29 %	10 (7.17) 71 %	14
	20	21	41

$\chi^2 = 3.62$, nonsignificant
$\phi^2 = 0.297$

Groundstone

	Absent	Present	
Masonry	11 (8.59) 69 %	5 (7.41) 31 %	16
Jacal	6 (5.90) 54.5 %	5 (5.10) 45.5 %	11
Pithouse	5 (7.51) 36 %	9 (6.49) 64 %	14
	22	19	41

$\chi^2 = 3.28$, nonsignificant
$\phi^2 = 0.283$

Results of Step 3—Hearths Present

Floor Area

	Lo[a] (< 8.90 m^2)	Hi[b] (> 8.90 m^2)	
Jacal	11 (15.19) 40 %	18 (13.81) 61 %	29
Pithouse	11 (6.80) 85 %	2 (6.19) 15 %	13
	22	20	42

$\chi^2 = 6.09$, significant
$\phi^2 = 0.381$

Storage Pits

	Absent	Present	
Jacal	24 (20.71) 83 %	5 (8.29) 17 %	29
Pithouse	6 (9.29) 46 %	7 (3.71) 54 %	13
	30	12	42

$\chi^2 = 4.25$, significant
$\phi^2 = 0.318$

Whiteware

	Lo[a] (< 1)	Hi[b] (> 1)	
Jacal	19 (15.19) 65.5 %	10 (13.81) 34.5 %	29
Pithouse	3 (6.81) 23 %	10 (6.19) 77 %	13
	22	20	42

$\chi^2 = 4.88$, significant
$\phi^2 = 0.341$

Grayware

	Lo[a] (< 10)	Hi[b] (> 10)	
Jacal	19 (15.19) 65.5 %	10 (13.81) 34.5 %	29
Pithouse	3 (6.81) 23 %	10 (6.19) 77 %	13
	22	20	42

$\chi^2 = 4.88$, significant
$\phi^2 = 0.341$

Chipped Stone

	Lo[a] ($<$ 1)	Hi[b] ($>$ 1)	
Jacal	13 (15.19) 45 %	16 (13.81) 55 %	29
Pithouse	9 (6.81) 69 %	4 (6.19) 31 %	13
	22	20	42

$\chi^2 = 1.28$, nonsignificant
$\phi^2 = 0.175$

Groundstone

	Lo[a] ($<$ 1)	Hi[b] ($>$ 1)	
Jacal	19 (16.57) 65.5 %	10 (12.43) 34.5 %	29
Pithouse	5 (7.43) 38 %	8 (5.57) 62 %	13
	24	18	42

$\chi^2 = 1.69$, nonsignificant
$\phi^2 = 0.201$

---

[a]Lo = frequencies below median
[b]Hi = frequencies above median

5

Functional Interpretation of Black Mesa Ceramics

Shereen Lerner

The relationship between material culture and behavioral patterns is of critical interest to archaeologists (Binford 1968; Schiffer 1976). This study attempts to isolate functional classes of ceramics through the analysis of rim sherds collected from 21 prehistoric sites on Black Mesa in northeastern Arizona. Such research is important because information on the kinds of vessels used at a site may serve as the basis for inferences concerning the range of activities performed there (Braun 1980). A method derived from work by Braun (1980) and S. Plog (1977c) tests relationships between physical properties of ceramic containers and their primary functions. Regularities in the cooccurrence of ceramic morphological characteristics are interpreted by reference to ethnographic ceramic container functions. Intersite variation in ceramic inventories is then considered with particular emphasis on change in ceramic inventories over time.

Hypotheses

Two null hypotheses are tested. I will first outline these hypotheses and then discuss the specific morphological characteristics used in the tests.

H_1: There is no covariation among morphological characteristics in vessels.

Ethnographic evidence suggests several attributes that change with the function of a vessel and thus covary (ethnographically) in a predictable manner (Braun 1980; S. Plog 1977c). These patterns of covariation are tested for prehistoric ceramic collections from the Black Mesa area using the attributes described below.

H_2: There is no temporal pattern in the frequencies of morphological traits of vessels.

Temporal variability is examined with the expectation that ceramic vessels from different temporal phases have different attribute measurements, as suggested by the studies of Turner and Lofgren (1966) and Beals et al. (1945). Turner and Lofgren found changes in culinary vessel capacity through time while serving vessel capacity remained the same. They interpreted the changes as the result of variation through time in household size.

Beals et al. (1945:87–148) noted three general diachronic patterns in formal attributes of ceramic vessels. Because their study included ceramics from one site on Black Mesa and from several sites situated immediately to the north of the present study area, their generalizations are pertinent to this analysis. First, they noted a relationship between traditionally defined ceramic ware categories and vessel form: Tusayan Graywares tended to be jars, while Tusayan Whitewares were more commonly bowls. Second, orifice diameter for whiteware bowls decreased though time (1945:143). If whiteware bowls correspond to Turner and Lofgren's (1966) serving vessel category, this generalization contradicts the pattern of no variation in serving vessel capacity noted by Turner and Lofgren. Finally, early Pueblo I whiteware vessels tended to have thicker walls (almost 60 % were 4.5–5.0 mm thick) than Pueblo III vessels (only about 40 % were 4.5–5.0 mm thick) (Beals et al. 1945:143). However, early Pueblo II whitewares were thicker than either, averaging about 7 mm (1945:142). Each of these patterns is evaluated in subsequent sections of this paper.

Attributes

A number of studies have sought to determine the relationships between specific vessel properties and vessel functions (Beals et al. 1945; Binford 1965; Braun 1980; Ericson et al. 1971; Ericson and Stickel 1973; Fitting and Halsey 1966; S. Plog 1977c; Rogers 1936). These studies have focused on the concept of the ceramic vessel as a tool, or container, and the use of technological and morphological attributes as indicators of ceramic function. Summaries by Braun (1980) and S. Plog (1977c) of various ethnographic studies (e.g., Fontana et al. 1962; Thompson 1958; Tschopik 1941) have suggested formal regularities in vessels used for similar activities and in the raw materials used to manufacture different functional classes of vessels. Their research thus indicates that pottery is designed and manufactured with specific functions in mind.

Several different vessel attributes have been suggested to be indicative of the planned use of a vessel. On the basis of the previous research, five attributes were selected as relevant to isolating functionally distinct classes of vessels. These are listed and then discussed below.

1. Vessel form (bowl or jar).

2. Presence or absence of decoration (this basically corresponds to traditional distinctions between Tusayan Graywares and Tusayan Whitewares).

3. Wall thickness. Measurements were taken as near to the margin of the vessel orifice as possible to compute an "average" thickness (in milli-

meters) corresponding to various rims. A cautionary note, however, is that the vessel edge may be shaped, reinforced, and elaborated in many ways unrelated to function (Shepard 1974:248).

4. Neck height. Measurements were made in millimeters with a caliper and were taken where the vessel contour changes from concave to convex for jars.

5. Orifice diameter. The curvature of the rim provides a means for calculating orifice diameter (the size of the vessel opening). The measurements were made using a dial indicator, which is more accurate than measurements made with a graded series of concentric circles (S. Plog 1983a; Egloff 1973). Measurements were taken in millimeters.

These attributes were chosen because recent study has suggested that variation in these attributes may be determined by the planned function of the vessel. Vessel morphology and function have long been assumed to be related. Only recently, however, has this relationship been tested. Braun (1980) did one of the most comprehensive analyses of vessel form to date in an effort to determine whether variation in certain morphological traits was determined by vessel function. His analysis showed that among historic groups, including Yuman, Piman, and Puebloan populations, a vessel classification based on rim and neck measurements of bowls and jars was a viable means of deriving vessel function. Among other attributes, Braun measured orifice diameter, the presence or absence of a neck, and neck height (on jars with necks) (1980:172–173). He reasoned that necked vessels with small orifices had less spillage and thus provided greater containment security than open, nonrestricted vessel forms such as bowls. The size of the vessel orifice and its neck attributes also determine the ease of access to the contents (1980:172–173). The smaller the orifice, the more difficult is the access to the vessel contents. In addition, these measurements indicate the quantity of material able to pass through the mouth of the vessel. For example, a Papago water canteen is designed to carry water long distances, an operation for which containment security must be maximized.

Shepard's (1974:224–228) structural classes for vessels, which also emphasize neck height and orifice diameter, served as a model for Braun's classification. Shepard identifies three structural classes: unrestricted, simple restricted, and necked (Figure 6). Unrestricted vessels have a maximum vessel diameter at the orifice and are suited for all activities that require the use of hands inside the vessel or the display and/or drying of vessel contents. Simple restricted vessels retain their contents better than unrestricted vessels and have a maximum vessel diameter below the orifice. Necked vessels prevent spillage and facilitate pouring.

Another attribute that has been shown to be related to vessel function is the presence or absence of painted decoration (S. Plog 1977c). "A potter sees no need to decorate a pot that is going to be placed over an open fire and thus have its design obliterated by smudging" (Fontana et al. 1962:48). Stephen Plog's (1977c) survey of ethnographic literature showed that painted

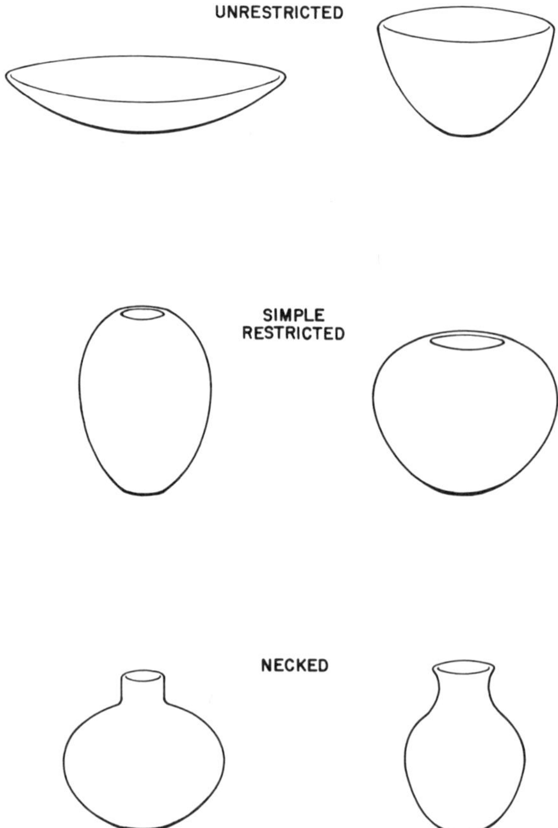

Figure 6. Structural vessel classes.

vessels were consistently used for noncooking activities, although there were some exceptions to this "rule" (e.g., when painted vessels were old or when nothing else was readily available for the task at hand [Fontana et al. 1962:94]).

A final attribute considered was wall thickness. Although neither S. Plog (1977c) nor Braun (1980) discusses this attribute, it was felt that wall thickness might be an indicator of tensile strength and/or thermal conductivity. Thicker vessels might have been used for cooking or long-term storage where breaking a pot is of concern. In addition, I wanted to retest the conclusion of Beals et al. (1945:143) concerning change in vessel thickness through time.

Other attributes such as tempering material and/or method of construction were not selected, since they do not display much variability in the ceramics from Black Mesa. Coil-and-scrape is the general construction method of most of the vessels; temper varies more in sand grain size than in materials used. Micrometric analysis would have been advantageous for determining the porosity of a vessel and thus refining definitions of vessel functions (S. Plog 1977c). However, time constraints did not permit such analyses to be carried out.

Data

The data used in this study are from the 1977 excavations conducted by the Black Mesa Archaeological Project. Twenty-one prehistoric sites (dating between A.D. 875 and 1150) were excavated or surface collected. A sample of 1,063 rim sherds was selected from these sites by a two-stage procedure. The number of sherds from each site is shown in Table 24. Because the samples from several sites are quite small (10 sites have fewer than 10 sherds each), all 21 sites are not used in all of the tests that follow.

At the time of this analysis, the total number of rim sherds available from each site was unknown. Thus, the decision was made to select a grab sample from each bag of sherds from every site, in order to sample a pro-

Table 24. Site Distribution Frequencies of Rim Sherds Analyzed.

Site	Absolute Frequency	Relative Frequency (%)
D:7:18	115	10.8
D:7:19	94	8.8
D:7:23	136	12.8
D:7:209	5	0.5
D:7:233	3	0.3
D:7:234	13	1.2
D:7:259	10	0.9
D:7:311	4	0.4
D:11:201	17	1.6
D:11:275	441	41.5
D:11:311	5	0.5
D:11:338	96	9.0
D:11:390	4	0.4
D:11:392	7	0.7
D:11:394	4	0.4
D:11:452	15	1.4
D:11:456	1	0.1
D:11:469	7	0.7
D:11:478	15	1.4
D:11:879	70	6.6
D:11:1158	1	0.1
Total	1,063	100.0

portionate number of sherds from each site. However, all rim sherds from structures and/or features were selected, since there appeared to be a small number of rim sherds found within these units. An original intent of the analysis was to examine the nature of the association between room function and ceramic vessel function. However, the small sample of rim sherds from these units precluded such an analysis.

Tests

The chi-square statistic was used to test for associations between attributes. It evaluates whether observed frequencies differ significantly from those expected under a certain set of theoretical assumptions (Blalock 1972:275). For the chi-square tests, neck height and orifice measurements were grouped into gross categories so that expected frequencies would be large enough to meet the requirements of the test statistic. These categories were derived on the basis of descriptive statistics such as mean, mode, and standard deviation. Neck height measurements were divided in approximately 10 % increments, with missing values excluded. Orifice measurements were grouped to approximate a normal distribution (see Table 25 for group breakdowns and for category labels). However, because of skewed measurements, small orifices were divided into two categories rather than grouped into one (21–80 mm = '1'; 81–104 mm = '2'). Labels for orifice diameter and neck height categories were taken from Shepard (1974) for the former attribute and from Braun (1980) for the latter.

Table 25. Recoded Attributes—Neck Height and Orifice Diameter.

Measurement (mm)	Code	Label	Percentage
Neck height			
0	1	None	51.6
3–13	2	Shallow	10.3
14–17	3	Restricted	14.4
18–22	4	Simple high	13.9
23–62	5	Unrestricted	9.8
Orifice diameter			
21–80	1	Very narrow	5.0
81–104	2	Narrow	5.6
105–155	3	Medium	18.3
156–206	4	Medium-wide	20.7
209–276	5	Wide	20.3
280–452	6	Very wide	16.9
476–4000	7	Extremely wide	12.6

Analysis

The first stage of the analysis involved determining the relationships among the morphological characteristics of the ceramic vessels. Four chi-square tests were performed for the following sets of attributes:

1. Vessel form: decoration.
2. Decoration: thickness.
3. Decoration: neck height (jars only).
4. Decoration: orifice diameter.

Tests 2–4 controlled for vessel form. For example, decorated bowls were contrasted with undecorated bowls, and decorated jars were contrasted with undecorated jars. The results of these tests are discussed individually below.

As noted above, Beals et al. (1945) found significant associations between vessel forms and ware classifications. On the basis of their findings and other studies (e.g., S. Plog 1977c), it was expected that the presence or absence of decoration would covary with different ceramic vessel forms. The result of the chi-square test indicated that a significant association exists between vessel form and decoration. Bowls were usually painted (62.5 %), while jars were predominantly unpainted (83.8 %) (Table 26). The observed pattern supported the expectation generated from Beals et al. (1945): the majority of the bowls were Tusayan Whitewares, and most jars were Tusayan Graywares.

As discussed earlier, vessel wall thickness may be a possible indicator of function because of its effect on tensile strength and/or resistance to thermal shock. It was expected that vessels used for culinary purposes (those without decoration) would be thicker to prevent breakage. The chi-square test proved significant for the cross-tabulation of thickness and bowl decoration ($\chi^2 = 17.11$). Decorated bowls tend to be thinner than undecorated bowls. However, the relationship between jar thickness and the presence or absence of decoration proved not to be statistically significant (Table 27).

It was predicted that the neck height would covary with vessel decoration; again, this prediction was based on the expectations about vessel

Table 26. Frequencies of Painted and Unpainted Bowls and Jars.

	Vessel Shape					
	Bowls		Jars		Total	
Black-on-white	344	(62.5 %)	83	(16.2 %)	427	(40.2 %)
Unpainted grayware	110	(20.0 %)	407	(79.3 %)	517	(48.6 %)
Unpainted whiteware	96	(17.5 %)	23	(4.5 %)	119	(11.2 %)
Total	550	(100.0 %)	513	(100.0 %)	1063	(100.0 %)

$\chi^2 = 468.53$, $df = 5$, $p = 0.001$

Table 27. Frequencies of Decorated and Undecorated Ceramics for Different Vessel Wall Thicknesses.

Recoded Thickness Measurements	Decorated		Undecorated		Total	
Jars						
2–3	7	(8.4 %)	48	(11.3 %)	55	(10.7 %)
4	31	(37.3 %)	140	(32.5 %)	171	(33.3 %)
5	30	(36.1 %)	148	(34.4 %)	178	(34.7 %)
6	15	(18.1 %)	70	(16.2 %)	85	(16.6 %)
7	0	(0.0 %)	18	(4.2 %)	18	(3.5 %)
8	0	(0.0 %)	6	(1.4 %)	6	(1.2 %)
Total	83	(100.0 %)	430	(100.0 %)	513	(100.0 %)

$\chi^2 = 5.88$, $df = 6$, $p > 0.10$

Recoded Thickness Measurements	Decorated		Undecorated		Total	
Bowls						
2–3	43	(12.5 %)	30	(14.5 %)	73	(13.2 %)
4	142	(41.6 %)	70	(34.1 %)	213	(38.7 %)
5	123	(35.8 %)	63	(31.0 %)	186	(33.8 %)
6	32	(9.3 %)	33	(16.0 %)	65	(11.8 %)
7–8	3	(0.9 %)	10	(4.4 %)	13	(2.4 %)
Total	344	(100.0 %)	205	(100.0 %)	550	(99.9 %)

$\chi^2 = 17.11$, $df = 4$, $p < 0.005$

function. However, the relationship between neck height and the presence or absence of decoration on jars proved to be insignificant (Table 28). Decorated jars were anticipated to have been used for storage, and thus to exhibit neck attributes indicative of greater containment security than undecorated jars. Yet decorated and undecorated jars were very similar in the distribution of neck height values.

As mentioned previously, Beals et al. (1945) noted relationships among orifice size, vessel ware classification, and form. Because of the statistically verified relationship between vessel form and the presence or absence of decoration, it was expected that the presence or absence of decoration on a vessel would covary with orifice size. Stephen Plog (1977c) has also noted that cooking vessels were predominantly unpainted widemouthed jars with short necks, whereas serving vessels were painted bowls with medium orifices designed for easy access. The chi-square test revealed a statistically significant relationship between the presence or absence of decoration and jar orifice size ($\chi^2 = 151.88$). Decorated jars tend to have smaller orifices than undecorated jars, a pattern expected if the decorated jars are being used for storage and the undecorated jars for food preparation. A significant association between the presence or absence of decoration and orifice size was also determined for bowls ($\chi^2 = 35.9$). In contrast to the pattern for jars, decorated bowls tend to have larger orifices than undecorated bowls (Table 29).

Table 28. Frequencies of Vessel Neck Height by Vessel Decoration (Jars Only).

Recoded Neck Measurements	Decorated		Undecorated		Total	
1	32	(38.6 %)	134	(31.3 %)	166	(32.5 %)
2	9	(10.8 %)	53	(12.4 %)	62	(12.1 %)
3	19	(22.9 %)	91	(21.3 %)	110	(21.5 %)
4	10	(12.0 %)	93	(21.7 %)	103	(20.2 %)
5	13	(15.7 %)	57	(13.3 %)	70	(13.7 %)
Total	83	(100.0 %)	428	(100.0 %)	511	(100.0 %)

$\chi^2 = 4.8$, $df = 4$, $0.20 \geq p \leq 0.30$

Table 29. Frequencies of Orifice Diameters for Decorated and Undecorated Vessels.

Recoded Orifice Measurements	Decorated		Undecorated		Total	
Jars						
1	11	(13.2 %)	9	(2.1 %)	20	(3.9 %)
2	18	(21.7 %)	11	(2.6 %)	29	(5.7 %)
3	34	(40.9 %)	45	(10.5 %)	79	(15.4 %)
4	13	(15.6 %)	81	(18.8 %)	94	(18.3 %)
5	6	(7.3 %)	100	(23.3 %)	106	(20.7 %)
6	0	(0.0 %)	107	(24.8 %)	107	(20.9 %)
7	1	(1.3 %)	77	(17.9 %)	78	(15.2 %)
Total	83	(100.0 %)	430	(100.0 %)	513	(100.1 %)

$\chi^2 = 151.88$, $df = 6$, $p = 0.001$

	Decorated		Undecorated		Total	
Bowls						
1	23	(6.7 %)	10	(4.9 %)	33	(6.0 %)
2	17	(4.9 %)	14	(6.8 %)	31	(5.6 %)
3	68	(19.8 %)	50	(24.3 %)	118	(21.4 %)
4	92	(26.7 %)	37	(18.0 %)	129	(23.4 %)
5	78	(22.8 %)	31	(15.0 %)	109	(19.8 %)
6	49	(14.2 %)	25	(12.1 %)	79	(13.5 %)
7	17	(4.9 %)	39	(18.9 %)	56	(10.2 %)
Total	344	(100.0 %)	206	(100.0 %)	550	(99.9 %)

$\chi^2 = 35.90$, $df = 6$, $p = 0.001$

Finally, one additional test was conducted to confirm the prediction discussed earlier, that vessel form and orifice diameter do indeed covary. The results of the chi-square test support the previous findings in that there is a tendency for jars to have wider openings than bowls (Table 30). Combined with the neck height patterns, the results suggest that undecorated jars are

Table 30. Frequencies of Vessel Forms by Different Orifice Diameter Measurements.

Recoded Orifice Measurements	Bowls		Jars		Total	
1	33	(6.0 %)	20	(4.0 %)	53	(5.0 %)
2	31	(6.0 %)	29	(6.0 %)	60	(5.6 %)
3	118	(21.5 %)	79	(15.0 %)	197	(18.5 %)
4	129	(23.4 %)	94	(18.3 %)	223	(21.0 %)
5	109	(19.8 %)	106	(19.8 %)	215	(20.2 %)
6	74	(13.4 %)	107	(20.8 %)	181	(17.0 %)
7	56	(10.1 %)	78	(15.2 %)	134	(12.6 %)
Total	550	(100.0 %)	513	(100.0 %)	1063	(99.9 %)

$\chi^2 = 27.64$, $df = 13$, $p = 0.01$

used in situations requiring relative accessibility of their contents as well as containment security.

A brief review of the statistical results of the analysis suggests the following conclusions:

1. Bowls are decorated more frequently than jars. Jars tend to be undecorated, with unpainted graywares and unpainted whitewares accounting for 83.8 % of the total jar inventory.

2. Decorated bowls tend to have thinner vessel walls than undecorated bowls. There is no apparent variation in wall thickness for decorated and undecorated jars.

3. Grayware jars exhibit wide to extremely wide orifices (66.5 %) rather than narrow orifices.

4. Decorated jars have narrow orifices (76.0 %), and plain whiteware jars exhibit a propensity toward wider orifices (66.0 %). This tendency of unpainted whiteware and grayware jars toward wide orifices suggests a need for frequent access, while decorated jars have smaller orifices, providing greater containment security.

5. The majority of bowls exhibit medium to wide orifice diameters.

As a result of these tests, two conclusions are drawn: (1) there is a significant association between the shape of a vessel and the presence or absence of decoration, and (2) orifice diameter measurements are related to the shape of a vessel.

Given the ethnographic model presented earlier, the results indicate that functional classes of vessels based on the association of morphological traits may exist. Functional correlates were assigned on the basis of the characteristics of these classes. Ethnographic data (Fontana et al. 1962; Rogers 1936), the results of this analysis, and previous archaeological studies (Braun 1980; Fitting and Halsey 1966; S. Plog 1977c; Whallon 1969) were utilized to define several functional classes.

Functional Classes

The strong correlation between vessel form and the presence or absence of decoration permits a primary subdivision of functional classes on the basis of vessel decoration. It is assumed here that the presence of decoration, or lack thereof, is a partial indicator of vessel function. For example, as stated earlier, decorated vessels were probably not used as cooking utensils, but more likely functioned as serving or storage activities. The consistently strong association between vessel form, vessel decoration, and orifice diameter also indicated the importance of orifice diameter in determining vessel function. These three variables were combined, as follows, to create four functional categories (shown below in italics).

Most *decorated jars* exhibit very narrow to medium orifices (75.8 %). These vessels were probably used to store material with the ultimate goal of restricting spillage (Plate 7). A subcategory, decorated jars with medium wide

Plate 7. Tusayan Corrugated jar.

to extremely wide orifices (24.2 %), provided relatively easy access to the material contained in the vessel, suggesting use for serving or short-term storage.

For the most part, *undecorated jars* have medium wide to extremely wide orifices (85.3 %). This tendency toward a wider orifice suggests frequent access to the material contained in the vessel. For example, cooking, pouring, and stirring activities require these wider openings (Plate 8).

Most *decorated bowls* exhibit medium to wide orifices (69.1 %), suggesting frequent access to the material contained in the vessel. Interestingly, 19.1 % of the decorated bowls exhibit very or extremely wide orifices. Vessels such as platters or large mixing bowls fall into this group in which there was little need for containment security.

As in the case of decorated bowls, very few *undecorated bowls* have very narrow or narrow orifices (11.6 % in both cases). Rather, the majority of the undecorated bowls exhibit medium to extremely wide orifices (88.4 %). These vessels were probably used for cooking activities in which ease of access was important.

Plate 8. Sosi Black-on-white jar.

The above vessel groupings with corresponding functions were established primarily on the basis of the results of tests that measured the associations among various physical properties of vessels. These inferences are based on the assumption that vessel shape and decoration are related to vessel function.

Temporal Variation

The final section of this paper examines temporal variation in the functional attributes. Unfortunately, it is impossible to use the functional classes just established for this endeavor. Attributes of a total of 1,063 rimsherds were recorded initially. These sherds could be divided into four groups, each consisting of 100 to 400 sherds, by assigning the sherds to the funtional categories just established. However, examination of temporal variation among these functional classes would require further subdivision of each category, resulting in insufficient sample sizes. With five time periods, each category could potentially be reduced to approximately 20 sherds per class. Any patterning seen from such a subdivision could be the result of random processes due to low sample sizes. Examination of attribute variation through time thus requires analysis of each attribute individually. The values for thickness, neck height, and orifice diameter are therefore compared among five sites with known dates (Table 31).

Analysis of variance was used to determine whether statistically significant differences exist among the means for the five sites. The three attributes were tested for bowls and jars separately. Further division into

Table 31. Change Over Time in Ceramic Attribute Measures.

Site	Tree-Ring Dates	Orifice Diameter (mm)	Thickness (mm)	Neck Height (mm)
Jars				
D:11:338	A.D. 925–975	168.2	3.9	17.75
D:7:23	A.D. 900–1000	226.55	3.8	22.6
D:7:18	A.D. 1050–1075	349.37	4.4	19.53
D:11:275	A.D. 1100–1125	323.96	4.9	18.1
D:7:19	A.D. 1117–1150	272.11	4.6	17.0
F ratio		4.067	20.932	18.845
p(F)		0.003	0.001	0.001
Bowls				
D:11:338	A.D. 925–975	260.98	4.0	
D:7:23	A.D. 900–1000	226.58	4.0	
D:7:18	A.D. 1050–1075	256.42	4.5	
D:11:275	A.D. 1100–1125	265.48	4.8	
D:7:19	A.D. 1117–1150	256.22	4.1	
F ratio		0.338	19.640	
p(F)		0.858	0.001	

decorated and undecorated vessel forms was not done because of the sample size problems noted above.

For jars, orifice diameter, vessel wall thickness, and neck height initially increase in size and then decrease through time. These trends suggests that jars increased in size until approximately A.D. 1100 when size began to decrease somewhat.

Bowl walls tend to increase and then decrease in thickness through time, a pattern that is similar to the findings of Beals et al. (1945, discussed earlier). In contrast to the pattern exhibited in jars, bowls reflected a slight increase in orifice size, following an initial decline. However, these changes were not of comparable magnitude to those found among jars over the same time span.

The behavioral implications of the results are not clear. It is possible that the vessels were used less frequently for high-volume storage after A.D. 1100 (as indicated by the decrease in jar capacity). This interpretation is supported by the pattern of increase in occurrence of alternative storage facilities, especially masonry rooms, on late Black Mesa sites. Since bowl attributes did not display much variation through time, the functions of these vessels also did not vary much.

A previous study (Turner and Lofgren 1966:118) found that the average size of individual serving bowls for the western Pueblos remained unchanged from A.D. 500 to 1600, while jars (with capacities less than 8,000 cc) increased slightly in capacity through time. Although the results of the present study found a similar pattern in vessel sizes for bowls (with only slight increase in size), contrary results were found for jars used after A.D. 1100. Turner and Lofgren infer that an increase in jar capacity indicates an increase in household size, necessitating the use of larger vessels for food preparation. Following a similar line of reasoning, the increase in the capacity of jars until ca. A.D. 1100 suggests an increase in household size on Black Mesa. The gradual decrease in size may indicate declining household size, reflected by the smaller capacity of later cooking and storage jars. Alternatively, however, the decrease in jar capacity could reflect the replacement of ceramic storage vessels by more permanent masonry storage facilities. Verification of these inferences would involve increasing the sample size and number of variables.

Summary and Conclusions

This study tested the validity of the hypothesis that morphological ceramic attributes could be used to infer the function of a vessel. Five attributes of vessels were analyzed: form, decoration, wall thickness, neck height (jars only), and orifice diameter. The study noted that vessel wall thickness and neck height did not covary significantly with the other attributes. Strong associations among the other traits enabled the following functional classes to be established:

1. Decorated jars with very narrow to medium orifices: *storage*. Sub-

category—decorated jars with medium wide to very wide orifices: *serving or short-term storage.*

2. Undecorated jars with medium wide to very wide orifices: *cooking, pouring, and food preparation.*

3. Decorated bowls with medium wide to very wide orifices: *mixing, serving, or eating.*

4. Undecorated bowls with medium to very wide orifices: *cooking.*

Variation in ceramic traits through time was tested with the expectation that variation would exist in attribute values in different temporal phases if the way in which vessels were used also varied. The results suggest an initial increase, then a decrease in jar capacity from early to late periods, but little variation in bowl volume. This pattern suggests changing functions for jars, resulting in a need for different morphological characteristics.

Certain problems encountered in this analysis merit discussion. Intrasite variation was not examined because of extremely small sample sizes. However, future research with larger samples of ceramics from within structures would permit testing the hypothesis that functional classes of ceramics covary with functional room types (Hill 1968; Bagley-Baumgartner, this volume). Secondly, the attributes chosen for this study may not have provided sufficient information for the evaluation of functional variability. As mentioned earlier, other attributes such as temper would be useful in determining the porosity and/or density of a vessel. This variable would be especially informative if much variety existed within temper types (e.g., sand grain size distinctions).

The technique described in this study, combined with ethnographic information, can be a useful tool for understanding prehistoric behavior. Valuable information concerning inter- and intrasite settlement variation could potentially be obtained through interpretations of functional classes of ceramics. The development of a functional typology, as described here, may permit closer examination of past behavior.

Acknowledgments

This paper was originally written in 1977 as part of a contractual agreement with the Black Mesa Archaeological Project. I would like to thank Shirley Powell for improving this paper considerably through her editorial advice. I am also indebted to Stephen Plog for providing valuable criticism and advice on all phases of the analysis and writing.

6

Artifact Inventories and Site Function on Black Mesa

Shirley Powell

One of the important research strategies used in determining the way pre-historic populations adapted to their natural and social environments has been the identification of subsistence-settlement systems. Such an approach requires the identification of different functional components of the system as well as the analysis of the distribution of those components through space. Identification of functionally different components in turn requires methods for isolating differences in the types or proportions of activities conducted at sites and the seasons during which sites were occupied.

Unfortunately, while many of the questions that have been asked about prehistoric cultural change on Black Mesa have emphasized the importance of understanding settlement systems, little research has been directed toward fundamental problems such as identifying functionally different components. This paper represents an initial step in that direction. In the sections below, I first review the primary methods that have been used by south-western archaeologists to identify functional components of settlement systems. Next, I evaluate the little research that has been directed toward this question on Black Mesa. Finally, I present a method for testing the utility of one frequently used index of site function, site size. Using data collected during the 1976 excavations on Black Mesa, I carried out several tests, the implications of which are discussed.

Past Inference of Site Function

Site size has traditionally been used in the American Southwest as a major criterion for determining the season of occupation and the function of archaeological sites. If a site is small, with few or no observable habitation units, it is often classified as a seasonal site. Depending on the location of the site (near or far from good agricultural lands or hunting and gathering areas) and to some degree on the nature of the artifact inventory at that site, it might be classified as a temporarily or seasonally occupied hunting and gathering camp or as an agricultural field house. The dichotomization of sites into seasonal and permanent categories is often reinforced when large and small sites coexist in an area contemporaneously. In such instances, the small sites are interpreted as seasonal or special-activity outliers of the larger sites, frequently on the basis of survey data alone (Doyel 1972:8; Shaffer 1972:142, 143). The historical precedents for such an interpretation are considered below.

During the period of initial archaeological research in the Southwest, it was assumed that there was one homogeneous culture in the Southwest that was broadly similar to that of ethnohistorical and modern Pueblos. Therefore, interpretation of prehistoric remains was through direct historical analogy. There was an interest in ethnographic patterns and oral tradition, especially migration myths. Archaeology was used as a tool to reconcile apparent inconsistencies in the myths (Longacre 1970). The assumption of a single southwestern culture was shown to be false by basic, preliminary fieldwork. Subsequently, a concern with chronology developed. Refinement of relative and absolute chronological measures was the focus of much archaeological research. There was virtually no concern with the reconstruction of Puebloan social organization between approximately 1910 and 1940. All effort was directed toward the goals of cultural-historical reconstruction and areal syntheses development.

A major means of implementation of these goals was cross-cultural comparison. Lists of important or defining traits that composed a phase were compared and contrasted. Ideally, the resultant classifications were monothetic, divisive systems, although in practice they were used as polythetic systems. Thus, early archaeological research was oriented toward getting as much information as possible about the attributes considered by the classificatory system.

For this reason, sites investigated during this time were generally quite large; they provided more of what was considered to be data (data being defined by a temporal-spatial research orientation). Using these data, a site type for a particular phase would be defined and all other roughly contemporaneous sites from the same region would be compared to this archetype. This inference in site function parallels developments in sociocultural anthropology in which inferences would be derived from an ethnographic community and applied to the entire ethnographic culture. This was, in large part, due to the effects of a normative anthropological theory. A major result of such an approach was to emphasize similarities within a group and differences between groups. In this manner, variability in site morphology within areas was minimized; essentially, it was assumed that one site was like any other site in an area during a specific time period. This sort of classificatory system and the data defined by the temporal-spatial research orientation frequently precluded the investigation of small sites.

Small sites were occasionally investigated if it was felt that they might provide information about earlier, "more primitive" times. For example, small sites were investigated in Chaco Canyon to see if they might indicate a developmental sequence leading to the large town sites on the north bank of Chaco Wash (Vivian 1970). However, in general, knowledge of the total regional site configuration and the range of variability of different types of sites was not considered necessary. Small sites were not, for the most part, noted or investigated unless they clarified the problem of a developmental sequence from small, primitive sites, to large, complex sites. Not until 1966 was the concept of an intensive areal survey with identification of all cultural remains, regardless of size, defended in a major professional archaeological journal (Ruppé 1966). Intensive surveys had been performed previously, but were neither a common nor a generally accepted procedure.

Current archaeological goals include the explanation of regularities and variability in the cultural record. Evolutionary theory and concern with part-whole community relationships have increased interest in the entire range of site variability. There is also a concern with empirical verification of previously assumed archaeological truths, one of which relates to the nature and function of small sites in the Southwest. As noted above, if they did not indicate development and elaboration over time, very small sites were assumed to be agricultural field houses occupied on a seasonal basis. This interpretation was derived from modern and ethnohistoric Pueblo analogues.

Although the seasonal interpretation of small sites continues to be invoked, there is increasing concern with the uncritical use of this interpretation. It has been noted that in many areas and time periods in the Southwest, small sites are the norm or that the total number of rooms on small sites is greater than the total number of rooms on large sites. In general, the number of rooms per site is less than 10 for most regions and time periods (McAllister and Plog 1978).

Two general approaches have been taken in the study of small site function. The first of these is a locational analysis approach. Through the use of several assumptions about small site or field house location, models have been generated for the expected relationship of small to large sites in a particular region, assuming an agricultural field house function for the smaller sites and a permanent habitation function for the larger sites. The actual site patterning then has been compared to the model for goodness of fit. For example, DeBloois and Green (1978) predicted that if a field house function were assumed for small sites, those sites would be located farther from large sites than they would be in a randomly generated model. The rationale for this assumption is that field houses were established to eliminate time-consuming travel between the habitation site and distant fields. They found that in southern Utah, small sites were located closer to habitation sites than in their randomly generated locational models. This finding does not support a field house interpretation for small site function.

The second approach to the study of small site function is the differential inventory approach. If large and small sites are assumed to be used for different functions, then it follows logically that different tools and features were necessary to perform these different functions. In the few studies employing this approach, the premise that site size alone is an indicator of tool inventory configurations on the sites has been tested with analysis of variance. The studies done to date have demonstrated that site size alone does not predict artifact or feature patterning at the sites in question. Site size defined by number of rooms on a site does not define site groupings with homogeneous artifact inventories (McAllister and Plog 1978). It appears, then, that common assumptions made about small site artifact assemblages and location are not necessarily true. The nature of site occupation and the interpretation of small site function is, as yet, ambiguous.

Site Function on Black Mesa

The determination of the nature of site occupation (seasonal or year-round) and of site function is also problematical on Black Mesa. The range of site size on Black Mesa is not as great as in other areas of the Southwest. Sites are generally quite small with only a few habitation rooms. However, there is some question as to the permanence and nature of occupation of Black Mesa sites. In his report on the 1968 field season, Gumerman (1970:118–119) offers the possibility that northeastern Black Mesa may have been occupied only seasonally. He gives as supporting evidence for this supposition the following characteristics: (1) sites are generally small; (2) sites are generally scattered; (3) there is little evidence of trade goods on the sites; and (4) there is also little evidence of luxury goods. Gumerman characterizes the typical settlement on Black Mesa as "an independent community consisting of a few extended families at the most, practicing subsistence agriculture with some reliance on hunting and gathering" (1970:118).

Phillips (1972) has also discussed the function of Black Mesa sites, suggesting that sites of the Toreva phase (A.D. 1075–1150) on Black Mesa can be characterized as primary or secondary. He defines primary sites as those that provide for habitation, storage, and preparation of food, as well as socioreligious activities. Secondary sites are those "capable of satisfying the immediate biological needs of the inhabitants, but lacking at least the important dimension of socioreligious facilities, i.e., a kiva" (1972:201). For purposes of his analysis, Phillips includes so-called special-activity sites with secondary sites. He defines special-activity sites as those with no habitation units. Phillips implies, then, that sites with habitation units serve a complete range of functions necessary to fulfill the biological needs of the occupants and are occupied on a year-round basis, regardless of size. However, he does not test this assumption, nor does he make clear his definition of habitation unit.

One problem with using the presence or absence of habitation units as a criterion for defining site types on Black Mesa is the variety of construction styles used there. Although it is generally accepted that on early sites pithouses are habitation units, at later sites masonry rooms, jacal units, and pithouses often occur on the same site. It has previously been assumed that masonry rooms, because they are small and generally lack interior hearths, served a storage function, whereas jacals served as dwellings (Gumerman et al. 1972:19). However, the interpretation of other structural types is not so clear. Recent work by Bagley-Baumgartner (this volume) has helped to clarify these issues.

In addition to determining the functions of structures, there is also the problem of determining during what part of the year a habitation unit was used. Swedlund and Sessions (1976:141) circumvent this problem by defining habitation units with a well-used exterior hearth as occupied for the summer season only. Conversely, units with a well-used interior hearth and storage features were considered to have been used year-round. However, Swedlund and Sessions do not address the question of how one determines whether a whole site was occupied seasonally or year-round.

There is, then, a real problem of distinguishing between seasonal and year-round occupation of a site and of determining whether there were full-range or only special-activity functions for a site on Black Mesa. The writers referenced above have based their interpretations of site function and seasonality on one or more aspects of the site feature or structure inventory. In contrast to that approach, in this paper I examine artifact inventories as well as features at sites excavated on Black Mesa. Without classifying the sites as to duration of occupation or function, I look for patterns in the relative frequency of artifact types and features at sites of different size.

The Hypothesis and the Tests

Many previous studies, because of their interpretation of large sites as having been occupied year-round and small sites or artifact scatters as having been seasonally occupied, implied a difference in site function and in the number and variety of artifacts present at the sites. That is, larger sites are expected to have larger and more varied artifact inventories, suggesting a broader range of activities and more intensive occupation than smaller sites. Smaller sites are expected to have smaller and less varied inventories that reflect the shorter occupation and the special-activity function of the sites. This hypothesis, that small and large sites are functionally different and therefore will have different artifact assemblages, is tested in this paper. In the analysis presented below, no attempt is made to predict the nature of artifact or feature patterns on the sites; only the implied variation among sites of different sizes is examined.

This implied variation will be examined using several variables. These variables, which include artifact types and nonarchitectural features, are described in the following section. If the variation in artifact inventories and features present at the sites is related to site size, the hypothesis will have been verified, and site size would appear to predict functional variability. If site size alone does not account for variability in tool inventory, other factors must be taken into consideration.

This hypothesis is tested using analysis of variance. Because of the small sample of 14 sites, the nonparametric Kruskal-Wallis *H*-test is employed. This is a simplified one-way analysis of variance that evaluates whether the *k* samples are derived from populations with the same distribution. The null hypothesis will be supported unless significant differences between artifact inventories and features present at sites of different sizes at the 0.10 level are discovered.

Collection of Data and Variables

Fourteen sites excavated by the Black Mesa Archaeological Project during the summer of 1976 were the source of data for this paper. The sites cover a temporal span from A.D. 800 to 1150. A short description of each variable considered in this study is listed below.

1. Site size. Site size was determined by counting the number of rooms on each site. Types of rooms included in this count are masonry units, jacals, ramadas, mealing pithouses, kivas, pithouses (other than mealing rooms or kivas), and storage rooms. Since it is likely that jacals are habitation rooms, a second determination of the site size variable will be made using the number of jacals on the site. In addition, sites were dichotomized on the basis of presence or absence of kivas, masonry rooms, and mealing pithouses for a third set of tests. That is, sites with kivas (mealing pithouses or masonry rooms) were contrasted with sites lacking this type of structure.

2. Features. Features were considered because of their assumed differential presence on permanent or seasonal sites (Swedlund and Sessions 1976). These include interior and exterior storage features and interior and exterior hearths.

3. Ceramic artifacts. Ceramic variability was examined by looking at relative proportions of Tusayan White- and Graywares and Tsegi Orange- and San Juan Redwares. Formal and functional variability is implied indirectly by these categories; Tusayan Whitewares primarily include painted types and are either bowl or jar in form, and Tusayan Graywares are generally unpainted jars (Lerner, this volume). Tsegi Orangewares and San Juan Redwares most commonly are painted and include bowl and jar forms. The white- and red- or orangewares were probably serving or storage vessels, while graywares were most likely cooking vessels (Lerner, this volume). In addition, the relative proportion of San Juan Redwares alone will be examined. At the time of this study, San Juan Redwares are the only ceramics found on Black Mesa that are known to be intrusive.

4. Lithic artifacts. Variability in the chipped stone tool inventory was characterized by dividing these tools into three broad categories: (1) tools that reflect manufacturing activities (cores, hammerstones, and unutilized

flakes); (2) tools that required little manufacturing time (utilized flakes); and (3) tools that required greater manufacturing time and most likely were curated (e.g., projectile points and drills).

5. Groundstone tools. Variability related to groundstone tools was measured primarily by the differential presence or absence of food-processing implements at the sites. Ethnographic data from the Colorado Plateau region indicate that groundstone tools associated with food processing are necessary household implements in permanently occupied habitation units (Bartlett 1933; Cushing 1967; Lange 1959; Underhill 1946). For this reason it has been assumed that (1) groundstone tools are necessary household implements and were present in permanently occupied dwellings; (2) they are too heavy and unwieldy to carry for seasonal movements; and (3) they are too valuable to abandon at sites occupied for only short periods each year. If this is the case, it can be expected that these tools will be present at permanently occupied sites and absent (or present in smaller quantities) at seasonally occupied or special-activity sites. Specifically, metates, one-hand manos, and two-hand manos were considered.

6. Temporal period. Because the relationships between site size and artifacts and features might vary over time, temporal period will be controlled. The ceramically defined Black Mesa phase system (Gumerman et al. 1972:24–28) will be used. Ideally, only sites from the same phase would be compared. However, exigencies of the sample, particularly its small size, make it necessary to dichotomize sites temporally. Sites from the early and late Toreva phase (A.D. 1075–1150) are considered as one group. Sites from phases prior to the Toreva phase (before A.D. 1075) make up the second group.

The Statistical Analysis

The Kruskal-Wallis test is a one-way analysis of variance. The test involves a comparison of the sums of the rankings for each of the categories of the nominal-scale variable. A statistic H is computed to measure the degree to which the various sums of ranks differ from what would be expected under the null hypothesis (Blalock 1972:349). The sampling distribution of H is approximately that of chi-square, if there are more than five cases in each class.

Several Kruskal-Wallis analyses of variance were run on these data. First, the sites were divided into two groups on the basis of size. Sites with one to three rooms compose one group, and sites with four to 25 rooms make up the other group. This breakdown of the site size variable was made for two reasons. First, in preliminary one-way analysis of variance tests, this breakdown resulted in slightly increased between-group variability. Second, this breakdown equalized the number of cases in each group ($n = 7$ for each group). Dependent variables used in the tests are listed in Table 32. The sites were further divided into early and late categories as noted above. Thus, the

Table 32. Dependent Variables Used in Statistical Tests.

Percentage of Tusayan Whitewares in the site ceramic inventory
Percentage of Tusayan Graywares in the site ceramic inventory
Percentage of Tsegi Orange- and San Juan Redwares in the site ceramic inventory
Percentage of San Juan Redwares in the site ceramic inventory
Percentage of interior hearths in the site feature inventory
Percentage of exterior hearths in the site feature inventory
Percentage of interior storage features in the site feature inventory
Percentage of exterior storage features in the site feature inventory
Percentage of metates in the site groundstone tool inventory
Percentage of one-hand manos in the site groundstone tool inventory
Percentage of two-hand manos in the site groundstone tool inventory
Percentage of lithic assemblage used in manufacturing activities in the site chipped stone
  tool inventory
Percentage of utilized flakes in the site chipped stone tool inventory
Percentage of formal tools in the site chipped stone tool inventory

Table 33. Kruskal-Wallis H Test Results.

Dependent Variables	H[a]	p (approximate)
Percentage of whitewares	3.2271	0.40
Percentage of graywares	4.7568	0.20
Percentage of red- & orangewares	0.8856	0.80
Percentage of San Juan Redwares	6.6574	0.10
Percentage of interior hearths	0.6729	0.90
Percentage of exterior hearths	6.4617	0.10
Percentage of interior storage features	2.1837	0.50
Percentage of exterior storage features	6.3480	0.10
Percentage of metates	3.3744	0.30
Percentage of one-hand manos	0.2847	0.95
Percentage of two-hand manos	2.0784	0.50
Percentage of lithic assemblage associated with manufacturing activities	1.3163	0.70
Percentage of utilized flakes	3.4282	0.30
Percentage of formal tools	0.2019	0.98

[a]H statistic is to be compared with a chi-square distribution with $df = 3$.

independent variables define four categories: small early sites ($n = 4$), small late sites ($n = 3$), large early sites ($n = 4$), and large late sites ($n = 3$). (It should be noted that group size is less than the minimum of five cases necessary if the distribution of H is to approximate that of chi-square. For this reason, results should be interpreted cautiously.)

Between-group variance for each dependent variable was considered separately. The results of these tests are shown in Table 33. (Tests such as these are not independent since the percentages are derived from closed arrays, i.e., the percentages of San Juan Redware, Tusayan Whiteware, and Tusayan Grayware add up to a fixed sum, 100 %.) The majority of these artifacts and features exhibit no patterns in their presence at either large or small sites. However, the *H* statistic for the San Juan Redwares indicates patterns in the presence of this ceramic ware at sites of different sizes, and the *H* statistics for exterior hearths and exterior storage features are nearly significant. Table 34 shows values for these three variables by site type. The largest proportions of San Juan Redwares occur on small early sites. The largest proportion of exterior hearths is also found on small early sites, which seems to substantiate the expectations of Swedlund and Sessions (1976). However, exterior hearths are also commonly found on large late sites. Exterior storage features occur in greatest proportion on small late sites. Nevertheless, sample sizes are so small that further investigation is warranted before placing any great credence in these results.

Additional calculations of the Kruskal-Wallis statistic were made to determine whether the breakdown of features, ceramics, and lithic artifacts into several subgroups masked any overall variability in the patterns of these items. Thus, the percentage of hearths and storage features (interior and exterior combined) out of the feature inventory was determined for each site. (Features of unknown function were not included in these calculations.) The percentage of sherds and chipped stone was also calculated (total number of sherds divided by the sum of sherds plus lithic artifacts) along with the percentage of manos out of all manos and metates combined. Again, it should

Table 34. San Juan Redware, Exterior Hearth, and Exterior Storage Feature Percentages by Site.

Sites	Percentage of San Juan Redwares	Percentage of Exterior Hearths	Percentage of Exterior Storage
Small early sites			
D:11:354	3	56	0
D:11:814	1	80	0
D:11:1081	2	17	0
D:11:1084	0	43	0
Small late sites			
D:11:298	0	0	13
D:11:348	0	24	44
D:11:1170	0	0	0
Large early sites			
D:11:290	1	4	6
D:11:352	0	12	6
D:11:409	0	19	4
D:11:1153	0	56	6
Large late sites			
D:11:97	0	86	0
D:11:324	0	24	8
D:11:356	3	56	0

Table 35. Kruskal-Wallis *H* Test Results for Recalculated
        Dependent Variables.

Dependent Variables	H^a	p (approximate)
Percentage of hearths	6.0185	0.10
Percentage of storage features	8.9598	0.05
Percentage of $\dfrac{\text{sherds}}{\text{sherds \& lithics}}$	7.6280	0.05
Percentage of $\dfrac{\text{manos}}{\text{manos \& metates}}$	1.8286	0.70

[a]*H* statistic is to be compared with a chi-square distribution with $df = 3$.

be noted that the first tests are not independent since the relative percentages are derived from a closed array. The *H* statistics and probabilities associated with those values are given in Table 35. The differential presence of hearths and storage features is more distinct when these features were not broken down into exterior and interior groups. The overall mean hearth-to-storage ratio (89/7 = 12.7) is greatest at small early sites. At large sites, whether early or late, the mean hearth-to-storage ratio favors hearths, but storage features are present at these sites in greater proportions than at small early sites (large early = 65/30, or 2.17; large late = 76/17, or 4.47). The ratio of the mean proportion of hearths to storage features at small late sites is almost unity (45/47 = 0.96). These findings suggest that large sites tend to have similar feature inventories regardless of temporal period. The shift in the hearth-to-storage ratio on small early and small late sites may indicate a change in small site function over time. There is also a significant between-group variability ($p = 0.05$) in the differential presence of sherds and chipped stone on sites of different sizes. Examination of the percentages of sherds and chipped stone on the sites (Table 36) shows that this variability may be due to temporal and/or site size factors. The relative percentage of sherds increases while the relative percentage of lithic artifacts decreases over time. This temporal trend has been noted for several areas in the Southwest, using the Southwestern Anthropological Research Group (SARG) data base (F. Plog et al. 1978). Of the four site categories, lithic artifacts appear to be most prevalent on small early sites.

These findings support conjectures about the changing adaptive strategies of the prehistoric occupants of the Colorado Plateau. It has been proposed that increasingly eclectic food procurement patterns, combined with increased use of storage facilities, is one response to subsistence stress. It has been shown (S. Plog 1978) that there was an increase in the use of gathered plant foods during the Toreva phase on Black Mesa just prior to abandonment. This period of increased variety in utilized plant foods corresponds to the increased use of storage facilities shown in this paper. These two trends, occurring as they do, support the interpretation that a subsistence disequilib-

Table 36. Hearth, Storage Feature, and Sherd Percentages by Site.

Sites	Percentage of Hearths	Percentage of Storage Features	Percentage of Sherds
Small early sites			
D:11:354	100	0	95
D:11:814	90	10	98
D:11:1081	100	0	94
D:11:1084	67	17	94
Group mean	89	7	95
Small late sites			
D:11:298	50	50	99
D:11:348	35	42	98
D:11:1170	55	50	100
Group mean	45	47	99
Large early sites			
D:11:290	56	44	97
D:11:352	50	36	98
D:11:409	80	15	98
D:11:1153	75	25	99
Group mean	65	30	98
Large late sites			
D:11:97	100	0	99
D:11:324	64	16	99
D:11:356	65	35	98
Group mean	76	17	99

rium preceded abandonment of northeastern Black Mesa at approximately A.D. 1150.

Additional tests were run using independent variable groups defined on the basis of number of jacal structures. This breakdown was used since it has been suggested that jacals were the habitation rooms on sites and therefore might be expected to be a more reliable predictor of the population that inhabited the site. The site size variable using jacals was broken down as follows: small sites had one or two jacal structures; large sites had three to nine jacal structures. The variable was controlled temporally by subdividing the groups into early (before A.D. 1075) and late (A.D. 1075–1150) groups. The sample sizes for the four categories were, then, small early sites ($n = 5$), small late sites ($n = 3$), large early sites ($n = 3$), and large late sites ($n = 3$).

The results of these tests (Tables 37 and 38) appear to substantiate the trends indicated by the previous tests. Small early sites again are distinct in that they have a higher ratio of hearths to storage features. Small late, large early, and large late sites are very similar to one another in that they have more storage features. Small early sites are also somewhat distinct because

Table 37. Kruskal-Wallis *H* Test Results Using Number of Jacals as the Independent Variable.

Dependent Variables	H^a	p (approximate)
Percentage of hearths	3.1339	0.05
Percentage of storage features	2.0436	0.20
Percentage of sherds	0.5410	0.50
Percentage of manos	0.1500	0.70

[a] *H* statistic is to be compared with a chi-square distribution with *df* = 3.

Table 38. Hearth, Storage Feature, and Sherd Percentages by Site (Independent Variable = Number of Jacals).

Sites	Percentage of Hearths	Percentage of Storage Features	Percentage of Sherds
Small early sites			
D:11:354	100	0	95
D:11:814	90	10	98
D:11:1081	100	0	94
D:11:1084	67	17	94
D:11:1153	75	25	99
Group mean	86.4	10.4	96.0
Small late sites			
D:11:97	100	0	99
D:11:298	50	50	99
D:11:348	35	42	98
Group mean	61.7	30.7	98.7
Large early sites			
D:11:290	56	44	97
D:11:352	50	36	98
D:11:409	80	15	98
Group mean	62.0	31.7	97.6
Large late sites			
D:11:324	64	16	99
D:11:356	65	35	98
D:11:1170	50	50	100
Group mean	59.7	59.7	33.6

they have relatively more lithic artifacts than other sites. However, there does appear to be some temporal patterning in the relative presence of these artifact types on the sites. Again, the shifts in the patterns of these features and two artifactual categories might be explained by reference to the subsistence changes over time on Black Mesa.

A third set of tests was carried out because it was felt that there might be a relationship between tool and feature inventories and the presence of

Table 39. Kruskal-Wallis *H* Test Results Using Structure Presence/Absence as Independent Variable.

Dependent Variables	H^a	p (approximate)
Presence/absence of masonry rooms		
Percentage of hearths	1.0568	0.30
Percentage of storage features	1.7749	0.20
Percentage of sherds	0.5268	0.50
Percentage of manos	2.1879	0.20
Presence/absence of kivas		
Percentage of hearths	0.2751	0.70
Percentage of storage features	0.2702	0.70
Percentage of sherds	0.0402	0.80
Percentage of manos	1.3500	0.30
Presence/absence of mealing rooms		
Percentage of hearths	1.8342	0.20
Percentage of storage features	0.1621	0.70
Percentage of sherds	0.2337	0.70
Percentage of manos	1.0000	0.30

[a] *H* statistic is to be compared with a chi-square distribution with *df* = 1.

certain kinds of structures on the sites. Three independent variables—the three types of structural architecture—were defined with two variable states each: masonry rooms present (*n* = 3), masonry rooms absent (*n* = 11); kivas present (*n* = 6), kivas absent (*n* = 8); and mealing pithouses present (*n* = 5), mealing pithouses absent (*n* = 9). Dependent variables and the results of these tests are shown in Table 39. In no case is patterned distribution of the relative percentages of the dependent variables related to the presence or absence of these structures on the sites.

Finally, it was decided to look at sheer abundance of artifacts using a fourth set of tests. Spearman's rank correlation coefficient was calculated using variable pairs, including site size (total number of rooms) with feature or artifact counts (Table 40). The total area of excavation at the sites was not held constant, although this would have been desirable. The expectation that numbers of artifacts would increase as sites become larger was supported, but there were a few notable exceptions to this trend. For example, counts for the variables considered for two Black Mesa sites are listed in Table 41. Both these sites were categorized as small sites for all recodings of the site size variable. However, there are very great differences in numbers of artifacts and features at the two sites. In such cases the difference in artifact inventories may reflect a difference in the total duration of site occupation, whether seasonal or year-round. (The nature of site abandonment may also be reflected in these counts. D:11:348 was exceptional in the large number of storage features that still contained whole vessels.)

Table 40. Spearman's Rank Correlation Coefficients ($n = 14$) for Artifact and Feature Abundance With Number of Rooms.

Variables	r_s	p
Number of rooms with number of features	0.7556	0.001
Number of rooms with number of Tusayan Whitewares	0.7619	0.001
Number of rooms with number of Tusayan Graywares	0.7863	0.001
Number of rooms with number of red-/orangewares	0.5360	0.024
Number of rooms with number of groundstone	0.7331	0.001
Number of rooms with number of lithic artifacts	0.6490	0.006
Number of rooms with number of San Juan Redwares	0.3712	0.096

Table 41. Artifact and Feature Counts for Two Sites With Similar Number of Rooms.

	Sites	
Variables	D:11:348	D:11:1084
Total number of rooms	3	2
Tusayan Whiteware sherds	2,781	210
Tusayan Grayware sherds	10,309	55
Red-/orangeware sherds	427	16
San Juan Redware sherds	20	1
Groundstone tools	86	18
Lithic artifacts	276	50
Total number of features	25	7

Summary and Conclusions

In general, site size, as defined in this study, has not been a good predictor of the patterning of certain artifact types and features on the sites. However, there is some suggestion that San Juan Redwares, hearths, and storage features may appear in different proportions on large and small sites. The appearance of exterior hearths at small sites substantiates the assumptions made by Swedlund and Sessions (1976) that exterior hearths would be more frequently associated with seasonally occupied habitation units, which in turn are generally found on smaller sites. There appears to be change over time in the distribution of storage features on sites. However, the probability associated with the H statistic for these variables is less than 0.10 (the alpha set for rejection of the null hypothesis) in only a few cases.

A major problem with the analysis is group size. The independent variable categories (small and large sites), when controlled for temporal variability, are smaller than the minimal number of five necessary if the H statistic distribution is to approximate that of the chi-square statistic. Ideally, the number of sites excavated would be great enough to permit even greater temporal control. As excavations continue on Black Mesa, sites should be added to an analysis of this sort. If sample size were substantially larger, temporal variation could be controlled.

Additional data that should be considered in the examination of site function and seasonality are floral and faunal remains. Sites occupied for only a portion of the year could be expected to have a different range of such remains than sites occupied year-round. In addition, the nature of floral and faunal remains could be used as evidence to determine what part of the year a seasonal site was occupied.

Two major problems that are confronted when developing a site typology are "(1) the selection of dimensions along which sites vary in a relatively uniform way and (2) the formation of homogeneous groups on the basis of these dimensions jointly considered" (Bruce and Witt 1971:239). It has been shown that previously accepted assumptions about seasonality and site function in the Southwest are not necessarily valid. A new approach to these problems needs to be developed. Concern with the range of variation in the archaeological record and the nature of part-whole community relationships make the development of a functional site typology of interest to archaeologists today.

The Effects of Seasonality on Site Space Utilization: A Lesson from Navajo Sites

Shirley Powell

Interpretations of the function of small prehistoric sites in the American Southwest have depended to a large extent on ethnographic analogy. However, hypotheses concerning site function that have been suggested by these analogies—such as the postulate that many sites were agricultural field houses—are often difficult to test archaeologically. In some cases, the test implications that can be derived from the hypotheses cannot be examined because of the limited material culture inventory at such sites (Gregory 1975). An additional problem relating to the development of test implications is that ethnographers have not collected data with archaeological problems in mind. For this reason, ethnoarchaeology as an archaeological research strategy has become the focus of increasing attention within our discipline.

The research discussed in this paper is the result of one such ethnoarchaeological study. The investigation examined the possibility that patterns of site space utilization might be one index through which the function and season of occupation of archaeological sites in the American Southwest could be determined. The results of this research, which was done using data from abandoned Navajo sites in northeastern Arizona, are discussed below. First, however, the role and development of ethnoarchaeology in archaeological research is considered briefly.

Ethnoarchaeology

Ethnoarchaeological research derived from the direct historical approach to ethnographic analogy.

Methodologically, the direct historical approach involved the elementary logic of working from the known to the unknown. First, sites of the historic period are located. Second, the cultural complexes of the sites are determined. Third, sequences are carried backward in time to protohistoric periods and cultures (Steward 1942:337).

The consequence of such research "provides a point of contact and a series of specific problems which will coordinate archaeology and ethnology in relation to the basic problems of cultural studies" (1942:337).

Explicit in Steward's method is that "historical problems" and the development of historical sequences "are surely the most important consideration of archaeology" (1942:339). He sees the extension of ethnographic cultures into the archaeological past through the method of the direct historical approach as contributing to the data base to be used in studying cultural change.

Interpretation of archaeological data has often been based on the premise that our knowledge of the past is only as good as our knowledge of the present. This assumption implies that explanation results from projections from present to past behaviors, with temporal continuity the justification for these projections (cf. Binford 1968). Over the past 40 years, there has been a shift from using ethnographic analogies as explanations of archaeological phenomena to using analogies to construct models against which to compare patterning in the archaeological record. The change has been from reliance on the ethnographic model as the means of interpretation of archaeological phenomena to a recognition of the need to test such models using independent archaeological data (Binford 1968). An example of the latter approach is Hill's (1970) testing of assumed room function in a southwestern pueblo. Ethnographic analogy suggested differential room functions for puebloan rooms of different sizes and shapes. Rather than accepting these room functions, Hill made predictions concerning room artifact inventories (derived from the ethnographic situation) and then compared the predicted pattern to the pattern observed in the archaeological record. The comparison verified the validity of the ethnographic model in this situation.

Current approaches to ethnoarchaeology are graphically illustrated in Table 42, which presents Schiffer's (1976:4) diagram of the strategies of behavioral archaeology. It is proposed (Reid et al. 1974) "that the subject matter of archaeology is the relationships between human behavior and material culture in all times and places" (Schiffer 1976:4). The types of questions that may be asked about the relationships between culture and human behavior are illustrated in Table 42 and make up the four strategies of behavioral archaeology. Ethnoarchaeology, the examination of present material culture to explain past human behavior, is one of these strategies.

Table 42. The Four Strategies of Behavioral Archaeology (from Schiffer 1976:5).

		Material Culture	
		Past	Present
Human Behavior	Past	1	2
	Present	3	4

One application of ethnoarchaeology has been the investigation of the relationship between archaeological site space and the size of the population occupying that site. Cook and Treganza (1950) and Naroll (1962), using site size measurements from ethnographic and archaeological sites, have demonstrated a general allometric relationship between site size and settlement population.

Total area of the dwelling floors and total population of the largest settlements of eighteen societies show a loglog regression which suggests that the population of a prehistoric settlement can be very roughly estimated as the order of one-tenth the floor area in square meters (Naroll 1962:587).

Naroll's findings have frequently been cited by archaeological researchers making intersite population comparisons. Such researchers have apparently failed to note the several qualifications to which Naroll's regression formula is subject. First, the formula was derived from size measurements on the *largest* settlements of the 18 ethnographic societies used by Naroll to derive his formula. This is not to deny the general utility of the population size-dwelling area relationship, but one could easily imagine different patterns of site space use in functionally distinct settlements of the same society. Second, the question of cross- (or intra-) cultural variability in site space use is not addressed, although organizational patterns are likely to affect the use of interior roofed space (Wiessner 1974). In addition, occupants of sites located in areas of consistently fine weather may make greater use of exterior, nonroofed activity areas than people living in regions of inclement weather. It seems obvious that people would prefer to perform site-specific activities outside during the winter in temperate Mazatlan more than people in Nome. Along this same line of reasoning, differential use of interior and exterior site space might be expected during different seasons of the year and thus may be used to infer seasonal patterns of site utilization.

The Problem

As noted above, a great deal of effort has been expended in attempting to determine the function of small sites in the American Southwest. Ethnographic analogy suggests a summer and/or early fall seasonal occupation of such sites, with an inferred function as agricultural field houses. This subsistence-settlement interpretation has frequently been applied to small sites on the Colorado Plateau. Further examination of the ethnographic literature suggests alternative interpretations that include the following: (1) small sites are a developmental stage in the growth of sites and eventually might have become large; (2) small sites are constituents of a dispersed, noncentralized settlement pattern; or (3) small sites are seasonal, but were used to perform activities other than agriculture (McAllister and Plog 1978). It behooves the archaeologist to consider these and other alternative interpretations of small site function and their behavioral and material correlates.

Interpretation of small sites on the Colorado Plateau as agricultural field houses implies several things about the behavioral patterns associated with such use. Even though it has been demonstrated that a variety of activity sets might have characterized their occupation (Moore 1975), it is generally agreed that agricultural field houses were occupied during those parts of the year when agricultural activities, including planting and harvesting, took place. This in turn suggests a late spring, summer, or early fall period of annual occupation. Thus, the occupation of agricultural field houses took place during a period of comparatively mild weather. In contrast, the "permanently" occupied settlement would have been inhabited during the harsher winter season.

Given this occupational pattern, it seems likely that there was a different utilization of site space on winter- and summer-occupied sites. A population occupying a site exclusively during the winter should use site space differently from the same population living on a similar site during the summer. A larger proportion of the winter-occupied site should be devoted to protected, interior space than the summer-occupied site (assuming a similar range of activities were performed at the two sites). That is, domestic activities that might comfortably be performed outside during the summer should take place inside during the winter. Certainly a modern counterpart to this situation can be seen by a comparison of homes in different parts of this country. Homes in the Sun Belt often include elaborate outdoor living areas: the swimming pool–patio–barbecue complex. Homes in the Northeast, on the other hand, feature analogous interior spaces such as the rumpus room or playroom/family room.

Ethnoarchaeology seems a particularly appropriate technique for testing this hypothesis. Investigating patterns of site occupation extant in the ethnographic record allows the archaeologist to develop models for seasonality and function, as well as to investigate and verify postulated behavioral patterns that might be reflected in the archaeological record. This paper examines known seasonally occupied sites for systematic variation in the use of interior, roofed space. Specifically, it is proposed that fall- or winter-occupied sites will have proportionately greater interior space than sites occupied in the spring and summer seasons.

Data Base

Recently abandoned Navajo sites in northeastern Arizona form the data base for this study. Two functional site types, agricultural field houses and pinyon camps, were examined (Plates 9 and 10). Site functions were verified by one or more Navajo informants. Agricultural field houses are characterized by late spring, summer, or early fall occupation, while pinyon

Plate 9. Navajo shade, typical of structures found on summer-occupied sites.

Plate 10. Navajo winter windbreak, typical of structures found on winter-occupied pinyon camps.

camps are occupied for the period of the pinyon harvest, usually in the late fall.

Nineteen pinyon camps were located during the fall 1975 site survey on the northern extreme of Black Mesa by the Black Mesa Archaeological Project; all were revisited (Figure 7). Each of these sites was mapped using a Brunton pocket transit and metric tapes. All artifactual and faunal material was mapped in exact location. A comparative group of agricultural field houses could not be found on Black Mesa, which is generally considered by Navajo groups to be too high in altitude for the successful practice of agriculture. Instead, 15 field houses (again identified as to function by one or more informants) from the Klethla Valley (to the north and at the foot of Black Mesa) were used (Figure 7). These sites were located by Scott Russell during his ethnographic survey of the valley. The same procedures mentioned above were also used to map this latter group of sites. It should be noted that they were not selected for inclusion in the sample by a probabilistic sampling

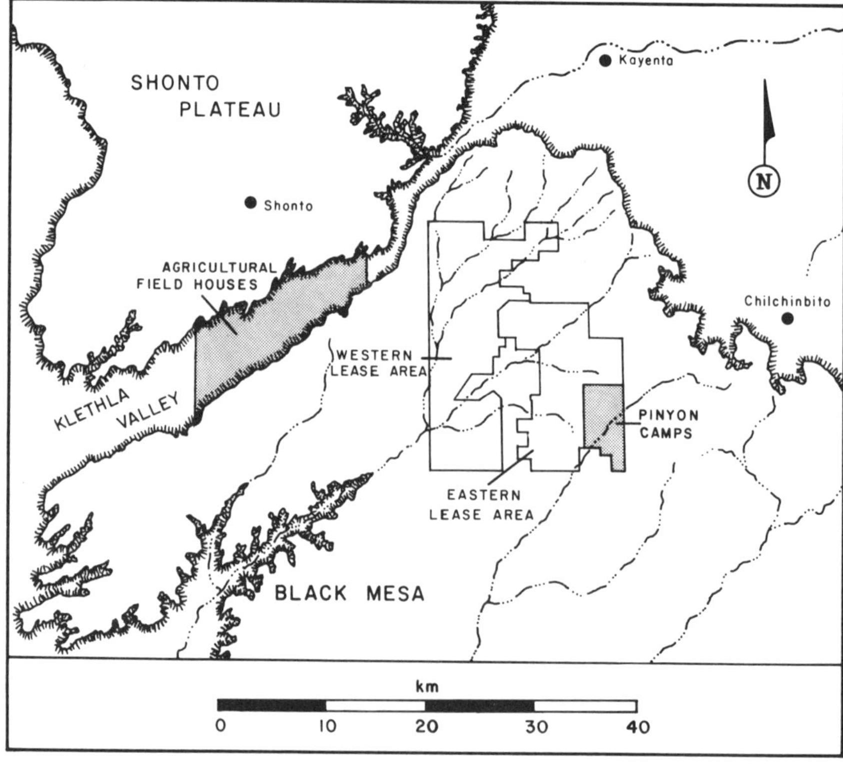

Figure 7. Locations of agricultural field house sites and pinyon camps.

strategy. For this reason, any patterns determined in site space utilization may not be interpreted as being generally characteristic of Navajo sites of these types. Results will simply suggest patterns that may exist.

Controlling for site function by comparing summer-occupied agricultural field houses with winter-occupied ones would be preferable, but it is not possible because of the season-specific nature of the special activities performed at the sites. However, it seems likely for both site types examined that site-specific activities (either agricultural or collecting) took place off the site and that the tools associated with those activities were eventually returned to the "home" site (Binford 1976). If this is the case, the range of domestic maintenance activities carried on at the two types of sites should be similar. For purposes of further analysis, it is assumed that similar activities did take place at these two types of sites.

Measurement and Evaluation

To test the proposition that fall- or winter-occupied sites (i.e., pinyon camps) will exhibit proportionately more interior space than spring- or summer-occupied sites (agricultural field houses), it was first necessary to calculate the total site areas and the area encompassed by shelters for each site. All sites were mapped on 0.5 cm gridded graph paper in the field. The scale for field house maps was 1 cm = 2 m; for pinyon camps, 1 cm = 4 m. Areas were calculated to the nearest meter by simply counting all squares within the site or shelter boundary. Site boundaries were defined by the extent of the artifact scatter; a line was drawn connecting artifacts or faunal debris located farthest from datum. Squares bisected by the boundary lines were treated as follows: squares with greater than 50 % of their area within the site boundary were included, while those with less than 50 % were excluded from the area determination. It was felt that calculating proportions of grid squares would suggest mapping precision that did not exist. Site area measurements and their ratios of interior space to total site area are given in Tables 43 and 44.

Tests

The Wilcoxon two-sample test, a nonparametric equivalent of the *t*-test, was used to examine the proposition that fall- or winter-occupied sites will have proportionately greater interior space than summer-occupied sites. This test examines two samples to determine if they have the same distribution. A nonparametric test was chosen because it makes no assumptions regarding population distributions.

The proportion of interior space to total site area was ranked over both samples from lowest to highest (Tables 43 and 44), and the sum of the rankings for each sample was calculated. If the samples were both derived from populations with the same distribution, the two sums of rankings for both samples

Table 43. Agricultural Field Houses.

Site	Total Area (m²)	Interior Area (m²)	Interior Area Ranks	Ratio	Ratio Rank
1	118	16	9.5	0.136	18
2	2,348	16	9.5	0.007	1
3	231	23	20	0.099	12
4	84	10	5	0.119	16
5	140	21	17.5	0.150	21
6	943	20	14.5	0.021	3
7	560	16	9.5	0.029	7
8	104	10	5	0.096	11
9	533	18	12	0.0347	9
10	2,776	28	25	0.010	2
11	385	9	2	0.023	4
12	561	14	7	0.025	6
13	264	9	2	0.0341	8
14	174	10	5	0.057	10
15	378	9	2	0.024	5

Table 44. Pinyon Camps.

Site	Total Area (m²)	Interior Area (m²)	Interior Area Ranks	Ratio	Ratio Rank
D:11:?	91	29	27.5	0.319	32
D:11:663-1	129	32	30	0.248	27
D:11:663-2	100	29	27.5	0.290	31
D:11:682	80	20	14.5	0.250	28
D:11:683	115	25	21	0.217	25
D:11:685	178	28	25	0.157	22
D:12:223-A	122	34	31	0.279	30
D:12:223-B	147	27	23	0.184	23
D:12:223-C	95	31	29	0.326	33
D:12:223-D&E	431	54	34	0.125	17
D:12:223-F	194	21	17.5	0.108	14
D:12:223-G	277	41	32	0.148	20
D:12:223-H	255	28	25	0.110	15
D:12:258-A	252	51	33	0.202	24
D:12:258-B	67	16	9.5	0.239	26
D:12:258-C	143	20	14.5	0.140	19
D:12:262	70	26	22	0.371	34
D:12:263	188	20	14.5	0.106	13
D:12:264	85	22	19	0.259	29

(W_1 and W_2) would be approximately equal. "The larger the difference between W_1 and W_2, the less likely it becomes that the samples will be random samples from populations" with similar distributions (Thomas 1976:308). The statistical hypothesis being proposed is that W_1 is less than W_2 when W_1 is the sum of rankings for agricultural field houses and W_2 is the sum of rankings for pinyon camps (Tables 43 and 44).

The statistic, U, is calculated as follows:

$$U = W_1 - \frac{n_1\,(n + 1)}{2} \text{ or}$$

$$133 - \frac{15\,(15 + 1)}{2} = 13$$

where n_1 = the number of agricultural field houses measured and n_2 = the number of pinyon camps measured.

Because n_1 and n_2 both exceed eight, the probability value associated with the Wilcoxon statistic is approximated through the normal distribution as follows:

$$\mu_w = \frac{n_1\,(n + 1)}{2}$$

$$\text{and } \sigma_w = \frac{\sqrt{n_1\,n_2\,(n + 1)}}{\sigma_w}$$

The Z score is calculated as follows:

$$Z = \frac{W_1 - \mu_w}{\sigma_w}$$

The probability associated with this value of Z is less than 0.0001. Thus, the null hypothesis that the two samples were drawn from populations with the same distribution may be rejected, and there is support for the proposition that the interior space of agricultural field houses is proportionately less than the interior space on pinyon camps. The time of year during which a site is occupied appears to be reflected in patterning in the use of site space.

It is also probable that the absolute interior area of summer-occupied sites will be less than that of winter-occupied sites, assuming the same number of people occupying each dwelling. To test this proposition, the interior area of each site was ranked (see Tables 43 and 44). Summing the ranks for each sample, W_1 (field houses) = 145.5 and W_2 (pinyon camps) = 449.5. Using the formulas above for calculation of the Wilcoxon statistic, $U = 25.5$. Again, the probability is assigned to this value of U through approximation via the normal distribution ($Z = -8.22$, $p < 0.0001$). These same calculations were also done excluding the values for the pinyon camp D:12:223-D&E, which has two structures. All other sites have only one structure each. With this exception, $W_1 = 145.5$, $W_2 = 415.1$, $U = 2.5$, $\mu_w = 255$, $\sigma_w = 27.66$, and $Z = -8.742$ ($p < 0.0001$). Again, the null hypothesis that the two samples were drawn from populations with the same distribution may be rejected. Structures on agricultural field houses are significantly smaller than those found on pinyon camps.

There are problems with these conclusions, some of which have been mentioned above. Site function is not controlled to the desired degree. It could be argued that the patterning in the use of space on these two site types might be due to differential site functions rather than season of occupation. However, it is likely that most activities taking place on the sites are similar, with dissimilar activities taking place away from the sites. There is also no control for annual duration of occupation or reoccupation of the sites from year to year. It is possible that the differences in the areas of structures on field house sites and pinyon camps may be due to the size of the task group performing these activities. On the other hand, it can be argued that task-group size for the performance of these activities is likely to be variable but to have similar central tendencies. That is, in both cases the task group will be composed of members of a nuclear or extended family. If this is the case, interior area differences for the two types of sites are probably due to seasonal factors. Certainly, additional informant information on the nature of site-specific task groups and duration of site occupation would be helpful in clarifying these points.

The problem of differential task-group size is controlled to some degree by looking at the proportion of interior space to total site area. If interior space increases as the number of people living on the site increases, it is probable that the total site area (here defined by artifactual and faunal material dispersion) will also increase. This increase will be reflected in the ratios used in the first test.

Another problem with the tests is the way in which sites were chosen for the sample. The fortuitous nature of sample selection (if we found the sites, we included them in the sample) violates the statistical constraint of random selection. For this reason, these results must be viewed as suggestive and advisory.

Conclusions

Results of the tests do indicate that season of site occupation may be an important determining factor in the relative size of interior space on a site. It also appears that season of occupation may affect the absolute area of interior space, although this proposition remains problematical and may be related to the size of the group occupying the site (for which no data were obtained) rather than the season of occupation.

The tentative conclusions drawn here certainly have interesting implications for the inference of site function and the determination of the size of populations occupying the sites. The results of the tests suggest patterning in the use of space on seasonally occupied special-activity sites. What is now needed is a comparative measure of site space use for habitation sites. If habitation sites exhibit unique patterning of space, a predictive model of site space utilization may be generated for independent testing against archaeological data. Perhaps the seasonality interpretation of variability in southwestern sites may finally be testable.

8

Ecological Consequences of Early Agriculture in the Southwest

Richard I. Ford

Too often, archaeologists and paleoethnobotanists have discussed and debated early agriculture in the southwestern United States on the basis of the presence or absence of prehistoric plant remains of specific domesticates from sites rather than on the implications of these remains for understanding ecological processes and biocultural adaptations in a particular environment. Agriculture—which in this instance refers to the deliberate planting, tending, and harvesting of domesticated plants whose genetic composition renders them dependent upon humans for their survival, indeed their very existence—is a cultural practice with manifest and latent ecological consequences.

From an environmental perspective, agriculture creates anthropogenic ecosystems. Cultural practices affect the extent of the area and the composition of the biotic taxa in each ecosystem. The land may be cleared and prepared for planting with fire, which will affect the mineral composition of the soil and possibly the succession of plants and animals that will recolonize the abandoned land. The technological means employed to manipulate the new plant community may have planned or expected results (manifest), but there may be unintended or unrecognized (latent) environmental consequences as well. Similarly, the fact that plant classificatory rules are followed while crops are being cared for will guide behavior and determine which plants will be weeded out. Some ruderal species will be eliminated. Others will be cultivated and collected at different stages of their annual growth cycle for various usages, including human food, and of course, deliberately planted seeds will receive care to assure that at least some portion will be harvested. The resulting community of plants and animals is an ecological system defined by cultural rules and beliefs that may be affected for years, if not centuries, by human action. This, in turn, may be significant for the biological maintenance of the human population.

The dietary importance of anthropogenic ecosystems must be assessed according to the biogeography of the plants and animals defined as edible by a particular culture throughout the territory it uses, the technology it employs to prepare and to store its foodstuffs, and the demography of the local human population itself. It almost goes without saying that a sedentary, year-round population in a marked seasonal environment may have to meet its nutritional needs differently from a smaller, periodically mobile group of families who are fissioning and fusing throughout the year. Furthermore, the same plant and animal populations may also have different nutritional values in the economies of the populations briefly exemplified above. The food value of a single species may vary according to the cooking and storing techniques used to prepare it, its biological phenology, and its annual availability. For most prehistoric human populations it is essential to identify as exactly as possible the caloric and protein content of the foods they consumed. If these requirements are satisfied, then most other nutrients such as vitamins, minerals, and other metabolites will normally be fulfilled automatically. (It should be noted that there is debate among nutritionists and physiologists about how much of these nutrients humans require and about their metabolic pathways in the body.) Under this circumstance one must discover, from the autecology of each subsistence item, its availability by season, its predictability in terms of yield and occurrence, and its abundance and density within a catchment area at any given time.

For early agriculture, it is important to recognize that the methods of cultivation probably affected the yield of associated plants in the immediate area of the cleared land. This habitat change also provided forage for animal taxa in greater numbers than natural circumstances could support (Semé, this volume). The ecological consequences are often a concentration of weedy plant species that might otherwise be widely scattered, less abundant, and in insufficient quantity or close proximity for even a seasonally mobile population to gather. The importance of this model of human ecological change can be examined for the higher elevations in the Southwest.

The Upper Sonoran Agricultural Complex

Haury's observation (1945) that the initial domesticates were introduced into the Southwest from Mexico at elevations above 2,000 m where dry farming was possible has been reinforced by more recent research and analysis (Berry 1980; Ford 1980). I have designated this complex the Upper Sonoran Agricultural Complex in recognition of its association with the Upper Sonoran life zone, which is basically dominated by pinyon and juniper forests with various understories of shrubs and herbaceous plants and which is characterized by higher altitudes, shorter growing seasons, and variability in climatic conditions associated with dry farming (Ford 1981). It consists of corn *(Zea mays)*, the pepo gourd *(Cucurbita pepo)*, the bottle gourd *(Laginaria siceraria)*, and the common bean *(Phaseolus vulgaris)*. The date for the introduction of this complex remains controversial. I have argued elsewhere (Ford 1980) in agreement with Berry (1980) that the date is probably around 1000 B.C. or more recent. This complex did not spread everywhere together at the same time. Dry caves of comparable periods of occupation have yielded plant remains indicating these differences. For example, in New Mexico, Bat Cave has corn, pepo gourds, and beans; Tularosa Cave has corn, pepo gourds, and bottle gourds; and Jemez Cave has corn and pepo gourds. These plant data are associated with preceramic or terminal Archaic occupations.

When an ecological perspective is employed to analyze the importance of these introduced domesticates into the economies of previous hunters and gatherers, it is useful to compare the subsistence problems faced by Archaic peoples in the higher elevations of the Southwest with comparable preceramic cultures in the deciduous forest-riverine areas of the East. Disregarding the complexity of calculating Gross Primary Productivity (GPP) and the animal biomass in each area, the relative difference between the areas is striking. The GPP of the East, with its forests of many nut trees, patchy habitats of starchy seeds along floodplains of permanent streams, deer and other mammals, fowl, and fish is 8,000 kCal/m^2/year (Odum 1971:51), and animal biomass is 110 (10^6 t) (Whittaker 1975:226). In the pinyon and juniper forests of the Southwest the number of plant species is fewer, permanent watercourses are infrequent, fish are virtually unavailable, and large game is limited. This gross description is realized by a mean GPP of 2,500 kCal/m^2/year and an animal biomass of only 40 (10^6 t) (Odum 1971:51; Whittaker 1975:226). To better appreciate the impact of corn cultivation in the latter environment, its mean GPP is 3,000 kCal/m^2/year where modern agricultural practices are not followed (Odum 1971:51), a figure slightly higher than the average GPP for a pinyon and juniper woodland shrubland.

To further examine the preagricultural ecological situation, an assessment of several major edible plants demonstrates that they are widely scattered, variable in annual yield, and unreliable as dietary staples. Pinyon nuts, for example, have an infrequent mast, with several years often expiring before even a moderate crop is available. Relying on this resource each fall, despite its high caloric value of 625 kCal/100 g of edible portion, would demand trekking across rather wide expanses of more than several hundred kilometers before trees with nut-bearing cones in quantity might be encountered. Seedy annuals do not cluster in quantity either. They are widely spaced in small patches and are soon succeeded by perennial plants. The absence of rivers with wide alluvial valleys and fresh nursery soil following annual spring floods limits extensive stands of these pioneer annuals to patchy natural openings in the pinyon and juniper forest caused by fire, erosional damage, or the death of older trees. The result is that calories were a limiting factor for hunters and gatherers in the pre-maize Southwest. Plant foods were not sufficiently abundant in any one location to support large populations or even the annual return of small bands.

Cornfield agriculture changed this ecological situation. The corn, even if it was not high-yielding, was predictable in its location, yield, and caloric contribution. The creation of anthropogenic ecosystems enabled pioneer annual plants to invade, and if the farmers permitted them to remain, to form dense patches in harvestable quantity. Even abandoned fields were colonized by food-bearing perennials in greater concentration than otherwise occurred in nature. At the same time, the active cornfield, as well as the abandoned fields, provided herbage ground cover for cottontails, jackrabbits, and other small mammals (Semé, this volume). Previously dispersed plants and animals were at that point concentrated for ease of human exploitation if they took advantage of the opportunity. The prediction is that they did for the ecological reasons stated above. The archaeological evidence provided by modern techniques of fine screening and flotation should reveal the remains of not only cultigens but also the seeds of these invading species and plants reflecting successional stages of human-disturbed habitats.

This view is compatible with Berry's (1980) proposition that corn agriculture was a late introduction into the Southwest and spread rapidly because it was certainly a gift from the gods, and so were the accompanying weeds tended and harvested by these first farmers.

Black Mesa, Arizona: A Case Study

The northeast corner of Black Mesa has been investigated by Southern Illinois University archaeologists, working under contract for the Peabody Coal Company. Twelve Basketmaker II (Lolomai phase) sites have been excavated and analyzed for paleoethnobotanical information (between 1977 and 1980). The charred archaeological plant remains were recovered through flotation following modification systems described by Minnis and LeBlanc (1976) and Watson (1976). A total 851 flotation samples, whose original volume varied in size from one to eight liters, were sorted, identified, and analyzed from these 12 sites. (To date, over 4,500 flotation samples have been described from all sites in the Black Mesa coal lease area [Klesert 1978; Klesert and Powell 1979; Powell et al. 1980; Andrews et al. 1982].)

These Basketmaker II sites date sometime between 700 B.C. and A.D. 100 (Smiley and Andrews 1983), but a more recent inaugural date for most of the sites is more likely. The chronological relationship among the sites has not been established, and the sequence of pithouses within individual sites also remains to be resolved. Consequently, they will be considered as a cultural unit.

The extensive survey of the lease area has located little evidence of occupation prior to the entry of Lolomai people on the mesa. The Lolomai occupants appear to have arrived as corn agriculturalists, although they may have only remained to farm, hunt, and gather on a seasonal basis, as suggested by Powell (1980) for the early ceramic-period occupants. The evidence for the growing of maize is not as overwhelming in the botanical remains as it is for the same area by A.D. 1000. Site D:11:3002 yielded no plant remains from a total of five flotation samples. Site D:7:3003 contained a Pueblo II occupation, and separation of archaeobotanical remains into the two components has been difficult. For the remaining 10 sites, eight had evidence of corn. Table 45 summarizes the results. Very few cultural units from each site actually had corn fragments. A larger number of flotation samples were analyzed for these sites because the evidence for agriculture was so meager, but it should be noted that the volume of the flotation sample does not appear to have been a factor in the low return. Three other explanations are possible. One is that if the sites were seasonally occupied, their inhabitants might have carried the harvested corn-on-the-cob to fall or winter camps off the mesa. A second explanation is that corn was not as important as in the later times. A third is that the disposal of the cobs may have been different, since most features and middens in puebloan sites contain numerous cupules from cobs used as fuel, whereas during the Lolomai phase cobs may not have been a culturally significant source of kindling. In any event, the critical observation is that the Lolomai phase was the initial occupation on northern Black Mesa and was, to a still unknown degree, predicated on the cultivation of maize.

The charcoal from these sites roughly indicates the environment of the region at the time of occupation (Table 46). Today a pygmy forest of pinyon and juniper occupies the hills, and a sagebrush/snakeweed community covers the deeper colluvial soils in the saddles and drainage basins. The extent of the latter community before Navajo sheep raising was introduced is unknown. Along the washes where the water table is high and the alluvium is not deeply dissected, willow and cottonwood grow. Saltbush is common on terraces above these stream channels. Clumps of saltbush, oak, rabbitbrush, cliffrose, fendlerbush, yucca, and an occasional cactus plant grow within the conifer forest. Ponderosa pine, Douglas fir, and Rocky Mountain juniper occupy the extreme northern end of the mesa at elevations approaching 2,438 m (8,000 ft). The ratio of mature juniper to pinyon trees is 60:40, and the yield of Utah juniper berries (fleshy cones) and pinyon nuts is highly variable. Decades pass in some areas without a major crop of either potential human food resource.

The useful plant products from these communities that have been recovered from the archaeological deposits include firewood and potential food (Tables 46 and 47). The pygmy conifer forest community was the source of fuel, with pinyon preferred over juniper despite its more limited availability in the forest. Pinyon is a better self-pruner than juniper, and even the dead limbs that remain are easier to remove from the trunk than are juniper branches. Pinyon has a lower heat value, burns more slowly, and does not spark—three qualities that contrast with juniper. Other wood from this community was much less common; gambel oak was represented by a total of 11 pieces from three sites and rabbitbrush by two pieces from two sites. Both Utah juniper seeds and pinyon nut shells were recovered from six sites, indicating possible use as food, but more important is their lack of abundance

Table 45. Black Mesa Lolomai Phase Sites With and Without Corn (*Zea mays*).

Site	Cultural Units With *Zea*	Total Cultural Units	Kernels[a]	Cobs[a]	Cupule Segments (Attached)[a]	Cupules (Loose)[a]	Rachis[a]	Total Zea
D:7:151	0	30						0
D:7:236	3	61			3(2)	1(1)		4
D:7:239	7	45	1(1)		1(1)	5(5)		7
D:7:713	1	4				2(1)		2
D:7:1108	3	15	1(1)	1(1)		15(3)		17
D:7:1110	0	2						0
D:7:3003[b]	2	49		1(1)		1(1)		2
D:7:3013	4	22	1(1)			3(2)	1(1)	5
D:7:3045	0	7						0
D:11:1161	2	5	3(2)			2(1)	1(1)	6
D:11:1162	7	20	46(6)	4(1)		434(7)	21(3)	505
D:11:3002	0	5						0
Total	29	265	52	6	4	463	23	548

[a]Number of *Zea* anatomical elements (number of units).
[b]Pueblo II contamination expected.

Table 46. Charcoal from Black Mesa Lolomai Phase Sites.

Site	Pinus edulis pinyon pine		Juniperus spp. juniper		Atriplex spp. saltbush		Artemisia spp. sagebrush		Salix/ Populus willow/ cotton-wood		Quercus gambelli gambel oak		Chryso-thamnus nauseosus rabbit-brush		Pinus ponderosa yellow pine		Com-positae		Ring porous		Conifer		Un-identified		Total	
	#	%	#	%	#	%	#	%	#	%	#	%	#	%	#	%	#	%	#	%	#	%	#	%	#	%
D:7:151	307	74.7	89	21.7	14	3.4	1	0.2																	411	100
D:7:236	56	42.8	73	55.7									1	0.8					1	0.8					131	100
D:7:239	435	51.4	299	35.3	7	0.8	5	0.6	3	0.4													98	11.5	847	100
D:7:713	75	36.2	119	57.5			4	1.9							1	0.5					6	2.9	2	1.0	207	100
D:7:1108	253	55.7	149	32.8			1	0.2			9	2.0											42	9.3	454	100
D:7:1110	42	38.5	41	37.6			3	2.8									1	0.9			3	2.8	19	17.4	109	100
D:7:3003[a]	193	49.5	156	40.0	18	4.6	2	0.5	1	0.3													20	5.1	390	100
D:7:3013	196	55.2	158	44.5							1	0.3													355	100
D:7:3045	27	48.2	25	44.6					3	5.4	1	1.8													56	100
D:11:1161	142	47.7	136	45.6	8	2.7																	12	4.0	298	100
D:11:1162	151	44.2	187	54.6	1	0.3							1	0.3							1	0.3	1	0.3	342	100
D:11:3002																									0	
Total	1,877	52.1	1,432	39.8	48	1.3	16	0.4	7	0.3	11	0.3	2	0.1	1	0.03	1	0.03	1	0.03	10	0.3	194	5.3	3,600	100

[a]Pueblo II contamination expected.

133

Table 47. Charred Seeds from Black Mesa Lolomai Phase Sites.

Community *--------Pygmy Forest--------- *-------------Cultivated Land------------ *-----------------------Old Fields------------------- *-----------------General----------------*

Genera	*Juniperus osteosperma* Utah juniper		*Pinus edulis* pinyon pine		*Atriplex canescens* four-wing salt-bush		*Chenopodium* spp. lambs-quarters		*Portulaca retusa* purs-lane		*Kochia americana* red sage		*Amaranthus* spp. pigweed		*Oryzopsis hymenoides* Indian rice-grass		Gramineae grass		*Helianthus petiolaris* sun-flower		*Sphaeralcea* spp. globe-mallow		*Eriogonum* spp. buck-wheat		*Astragalus* spp. milk-vetch		*Opuntia* spp. prickly pear cactus		Cactaceae cactus		Unidentifiable seeds	
Site	#	u	#	u	#	u	#	u	#	u	#	u	#	u	#	u	#	u	#	u	#	u	#	u	#	u	#	u	#	u	#	u
D:7:151	1	1																														
D:7:236			1	1	1	1	47	11	4	4					1	1															6	3
D:7:239	1	1	1	1	1	1	47	22							1	1									6	3					6	3
D:7:713	2	2					23	8																							1	1
D:7:1108	1	1	1	1	1	1	77	6	30	4																					4	3
D:7:1110			3	1			2	2	1	1																						
D:7:3003[a]							13	5	4	2	8	1	2	2	2	2	1	1			1	1					1	1			3	1
D:7:3013							2	2																								
D:7:3045			2	1			1	1																					1	1		
D:11:1161	3	1	1	1	6	2	31	2	1	1			2	1	1	1	1	1	1	1			4	1	2	1					25	2
D:11:1162	13	7					7	5			15	3	1	1	1	1	2	2													9	3
D:11:3002	13	7																														
Total	21	13	9	6	9	5	250	64	40	12	23	4	5	4	6	6	4	4	1	1	1	1	4	1	8	4	1	1	1	1	54	16

[a]Pueblo II contamination expected. # = number of seeds. u = number of cultural units with seeds.

and absence from the remaining sites. Long periods of time between harvestable crops may partially account for this pattern.

Saltbush presents an interesting case. It grows on alluvial terraces and in clumps in the pygmy forest. The wood was used infrequently, most likely as a kindling, but there is evidence that the seeds were collected and processed at four sites. They are not plentiful but do indicate another aspect of supplementing the diet by gathering these seeds in the late summer and early fall.

The pygmy forest also contains *Yucca baccata* fruits and several cacti as potential foods. No evidence for the use of yucca was recovered, and only two cacti seeds were found. The one prickly pear seed is from a questionable Lolomai phase context.

The remaining charcoal fragments derive originally from three distinct communities. One is the sagebrush/snakeweed community with only sage charcoal found. Again, sage may have been used for kindling or for special-purpose fires because it burns very slowly without much heat unless it is in quantity. Sage also forms a heavy ash over its slow-burning embers, making it an ideal camp fire or nightlong fire. The second is willow or cottonwood from the washes, which may not have been the deeply incised channels they are today; a higher water table to support a more expansive growth of these trees in prehistory is a distinct possibility. Charcoal from this community came from three sites in limited quantity. The last is one piece of ponderosa pine from a higher elevation at the northern end of the mesa. No Douglas fir was recognized in the 3,600 pieces of examined charcoal. The conifer category consists of very small flecks drawn from random samples and is most likely pinyon or juniper.

The identifiable seeds provide substantial evidence for cornfield agriculture and the anthropogenic ecological changes induced by the Lolomai phase farmers (Table 47). Seeds characteristic of disturbed land, including cultivated fields and older fallow land, were recovered. Evidence for these ecological associations were derived from a survey by C. Wesley Cowan and me of Navajo fields of various ages on Black Mesa in the coal lease area (Plate 11). Lambsquarters (cf. *Chenopodium Fremonti*) is rarely observed except in nitrogen-enriched sheep corrals and in active cornfields. Purslane (now *Portulaca orleracea* that has replaced the archaeological *Portulaca retusa*) was located in cornfields and rarely elsewhere. Pigweed (*Amaranthus albus* and *Amaranthus retroflexus*) was in fields and other human-disturbed areas. Fallow old fields included Indian ricegrass in fenced areas, sunflowers (although they are also observed on the borders of cultivated fields but not in our sample), buckwheat, milkvetch, and prickly pear (*Opuntia fragilis* var. *fragilis*), which was found in greater numbers in this community than in the pygmy conifer forest. Four-wing saltbush was recorded in old fields on alluvial terraces, and wolfberry (*Lycium pallidum*) was located as well.

The archaeological seed evidence suggests that the cornfields contained several pioneer annuals that were permitted to grow to maturity with

Plate 11. Modern cornfield on northern Black Mesa.

the maize and old fields. They continued to be collected even if they were not planted. Sites D:7:1110 and D:7:3045 did not produce maize but did contain seeds suggesting the presence of cornfields. The most outstanding evidence for an abundance of ruderal plants in active fields are *Chenopodium* and *Portulaca* seeds. Considering the low probability of any seed being preserved, much less recovered, in archaeological contexts, these quantities are significant. They suggest that cleared land in the pinyon and juniper and sagebrush communities were invaded by pioneer annual taxa, otherwise widely spaced and not found in concentration. Some were cultivated by permitting them to grow, while others undoubtedly were weeded out. Purslane provides succulent greens and edible seeds. The lambsquarters and perhaps the pigweed were probably double harvested: that is, they were collected when their first few leaves appeared above ground, and then regenerated plants and late germinating seeds were allowed to reach maturity when the ripened seeds were harvested. Sunflowers may have bordered the fields and provided another edible seed. This pattern suggests a cornfield with numerous potentially useful plants growing intermixed with the corn and complementing the corn in the diet.

The old fields were undoubtedly the source of Indian ricegrass and perhaps cactus fruits. No wolfberry seeds were recovered. The other seeds have little recorded ethnographic use as food in the Southwest, although they may have been consumed by Lolomai people. Buckwheat leaves and stems are eaten by Hopi and Navajo, and the seeds are made into a mush. Some species of milkvetch have edible roots, pods, and seeds, according to Hopi, Apache, and Zuni informants. Similar uses of these may have applied in Lolomai times. Globemallow is commonly used as a medicinal poultice or adhesive. If these were introduced to the archaeological deposit by Lolomai phase inhabitants, then they extend the range of culturally valued old field successional perennial plants.

Cultivated land with its dense herbaceous and low shrub cover improved the habitat for rabbits and other small rodents. The analysis of fauna from D:7:236 by Michele Semé (1980b:468) indicates that cottontail and jackrabbits are the most numerous individuals, 24 and 9, respectively. Other small mammal bones constitute 14 individuals. Remains of one individual (possible) deer, one antelope, and one mountain sheep were recognized as well. These large mammals were probably not numerous in prehistoric times, but the fields helped to increase the edible animal biomass even if it required capturing more individuals relative to large game to satisfy protein requirements (see Semé, this volume).

The Lolomai phase occupation of Black Mesa changed the ecological relationships between the people and their natural biotic environment. The cultivated fields provided a more secure caloric source from maize and starchy seeds than was possible on a recurrent basis in any comparable area in the Upper Sonoran forest areas. Cornfield agriculture, including the continued exploitation of old field perennials, increased the edible biomass of the area within the site catchment, increased the predictability of yield, and improved the nutritional basis of the population. It also permitted larger aggregates of people to assemble, at least seasonally. Early agriculture on Black Mesa is best understood as a series of beneficial ecological consequences.

Conclusions

Research employing nutritional models and ecological analyses is continuing. The archaeological record is admittedly incomplete, and additional plant resources such as pepo gourds may be recovered as additional samples from these sites are examined and new Lolomai phase sites are excavated. The Black Mesa project has given us a qualitative understanding of early agriculture as a series of cultural transactions with the natural environment. Maize and the other conveniently harvested seeds can be appreciated as one solution to a caloric problem, even though protein still had to be derived from animals.

Additional research suggested by this study which will require cooperation with other scientists working with the Black Mesa Lolomai data. The first question, quite rightly, is the degree of reliance on maize. This cannot be resolved simply by noting its presence and the ecological changes its cultivation produced. Analysis of human skeletal parts for $^{13}C:^{12}C$ ratio in human collagen to determine the value of C_4 photosynthetic pathway plants such as corn and chenopods must be undertaken to determine the actual dietary significance of these plants (Vogel and van der Merwe 1977). In addition, faunal analyses and palynology must be employed to understand the permanent changes to the environment and possible expansion of sagebrush communities that resulted from prehistoric agricultural practices. Finally, the cultural adaptations to potentially more secure caloric sources and more efficient patterns of plant exploitation resulting from the ecological consequences of maize agriculture must be investigated through artifact analysis, household composition, village patterns, and regional settlement systems. A start has been made. New ideas about the spread of agriculture as a series of ecological processes and benefits have been presented, but we must test these propositions more rigorously through systemic modelling and concomitant statistical analyses.

9

The Effects of Agricultural Fields on Faunal Assemblage Variation

Michele Semé

Garden hunting refers to human hunting behavior in which animals, attracted to the conditions created by cultivation of plants, can be killed on a regular basis. The concept of garden hunting was first formulated to account for the diversity of relatively large mammals in archaeofaunas in a tropical ecosystem (Linares 1976). However, the empirical evidence on spatially dispersed food resources and on animal responses to the resources suggests that this is a general process and is applicable in temperate areas. It can also involve much smaller animals, such as cricetine rodents. The response of small rodents to human-created environments can be examined by using optimal foraging theory.

In this paper, a model of the ensuing behavioral interaction between humans and rodents is stated. Evidence to support the behavioral interaction model comes from experimental monitoring of human-created environments and anecdotal information on rodent behavior. Expectations on the archaeological visibility of the behavioral interaction model are generated. These expectations are tested against the archaeological record from Black Mesa, Arizona. Although most attention is focused on the response of rodents to agricultural fields, their response to human refuse areas is also examined.

Optimal Foraging Theory and the Human Consumer

Humans, as heterotrophic, or consumer, organisms, must procure energy from their environment. This is accomplished by utilizing the energy stored either in primary producers (plants) or in other consumers (herbivores, omnivores, and carnivores). Humans consciously and selectively garner energy from their environment and thereby use only a portion of the potential sources of energy available in any ecosystem. This resource selectivity has been repeatedly observed in both ethnographic and archaeological investigations (Smith 1975; Cordell 1977; Lee 1979; Styles 1981). This observed selectivity is based on the simple need of any consumer to balance energy expenditure against energy gain. The average energy costs of securing food must always be less than the average net energy gained from the diet (Emlem 1966; MacArthur and Pianka 1966; Charnov 1976; Pyke et al. 1977). The achievement of such an energy balance is accomplished by maximizing or minimizing some aspects of food procurement or foraging behavior. This balancing is termed optimal foraging (Pyke et al. 1977:138).

It has recently been suggested that optimal foraging theory be applied to the study of human diets (Pullinam 1981). However, with humans as the predator under investigation and resource selectivity the research question, certain assumptions of optimal foraging theory cannot be met. In dealing with humans, the model chosen must minimize or eliminate these assumptions. The assumptions of optimal foraging theory nonapplicable to humans as predators are as follows: optimal diet and foraging behavior are the result of Darwinian natural selection; the predator consumes the prey item immediately upon capture; the predator forages only for itself and until some satiation level is achieved; and the predator cannot control the constraints in the system that determine cost-benefit ratios.

I have chosen not to address the problems involved in the assumption of the effects of natural selection, fitness, and optimal diet. Suffice it to say that regardless of biological underpinnings, variations and adaptation can be viewed and studied as strictly cultural phenomena.

The second assumption is that the predator consumes the prey item upon capturing it. Therefore, search and capture as well as handling are mutually exclusive activities: the predator cannot continue searching and capturing additional prey items while handling the initially encountered item. For the study of human predators, the problems involved in this assumption can be resolved by collapsing search, capture, and handling times into one variable defined as "stalking and capturing time" (Pullinam 1981:65). We need not consider actual consumption as a part of hunting behavior.

Under the third assumption, the predator is foraging only for itself, and the stimuli to forage are based on internal physiological factors that determine satiation. This contrasts with foraging humans who are most likely to be procuring energy not only for themselves but also for other individuals. Although some knowledge of a satiation level governs time spent foraging and energy procured per foraging effort, the satiation level is determined in relation to factors unrelated to the immediate, internal physiological state of the human forager. The problems connected with this assumption of foraging behavior can be dealt with if we consider human foraging behavior as the behavior of time minimizers (Pyke et al. 1977:139).

Time minimizers are those animals for whom "the net rate of energy intake while the animal is foraging would be maximized" (1977:139). With humans, the energy demands of hunting activities can be manipulated to decrease energy output (Styles 1981). Procurement of food energy sources by humans can be thought of as active or passive (Greer 1976). Active foraging behavior requires "a fuller degree of involvement, a considerable amount of time, a concentrated individual or group effort, and probably a significant energy output" (1976:2–3). However, humans tend to structure their activities so that levels of involvement, either for the individual or the group, are minimized, hence passive, without sacrificing returns on effort. Even if some hunting requires active involvement, it still does not demand the active involvement of the entire group who stand to gain or receive energy from an act of predation. "[An act of hunting] would be active on the individual level—it [is] a concentrated time-consuming activity requiring . . . full attention and energy. But to the group, [the hunter's] activities [are] passive in the sense of being peripheral to the main efforts of the group" (1976:4). If hunting is accomplished by use of mechanical devices designed to function with the hunter in absentia, search and capture times are no longer exclusive demands on the human predator. Involvement and energy expenditure are sharply reduced. These abilities to manipulate the pursuit time constraints in the systems are accomplished without the necessity of immediate biological or evolutionary changes.

The manipulative abilities of human predators are also related to the problem with the last assumption of optimal foraging theory listed—the assumption that the predator cannot control most of the factors in the prey-predator system. For humans, this is not the case, not only because of the behavioral abilities of humans but also because they perceive their environments as having nonrandom (patchy) distributions of resources.

Organisms structure their behavior through their perceptions of the environment by grain response. They then either randomly or nonrandomly arrange themselves within the ecosystem. A random, or fine-grained, response is one in which "the consumer species encounters [resources] in the same proportion in which they actually occur" in the environment (MacArthur and Wilson 1967:95). The nonrandom, or coarse-grained, response is one in which the consumer species behaves in such a manner as to "encounter [resources] in a proportion different from that in which they actually occur" in the environment (1967:95–96). Humans tend to exhibit a coarse-grained response in their resource exploitation behavior. They are selective in their resource choices to maximize the probablity of encountering a chosen resource as they move across the landscape. If a patch is more productive than other parts of the environment (i.e., has a higher density of prey items), hunting time is then not dependent on food density as it is in a nonpatchy model. Efforts will be concentrated in these productive patches.

I argue that humans' abilities to manipulate and even create patchiness in their environment by horticultural and other activities can result in differing optimal diets of animal food items. This relationship is to be contrasted for agricultural and nonagricultural activities.

Since I have already chosen to classify humans as time minimizers, the process of energy maximization of foraging by humans can be expressed as

$$V = E/H$$

where V, the value of a potential resource item, is the ratio of that item's energy content (E) and handling time (H) (Pullinam 1981:65). This very general statement about optimal choice contains the least number of constraints and makes it very suitable for qualitatively examining human hunting behavior. The implication of the statement is that, in any particular subsistence system, a potential animal prey item will be judged by the criterion of its energy-to-handling ratio. One prey item will be selected preferentially over another if its energy-to-handling ratio is higher. However, it is also the case that for human predators the value of a prey item is relative to other factors in the subsistence system. Changes in one area of subsistence could change handling time, hence value, of a completely separate area of subsistence. Defining handling time for human predators as stalking and capturing (Pullinam 1981), this change in selectivity can be illustrated by the curve described by the statement $V = E/H$ (Figure 8).

For the purpose of illustrating the process of change in a prey item's value, relative to subsistence base, we will consider only a single species. In the statement $V = E/H$, for a particular species, E, caloric worth per gram successfully captured, does not vary, and thus is a constant. Since human foragers or hunters must always expend some energy on the procurement process, H can never equal zero, but we can envision H as possibly becoming very small. As H approaches zero, V would be increasing: V, as a function of H, would become very large. This is shown by the curve in Figure 8.

The possible relative change in value of a prey item is not the result of instantaneous consumer-choice decision making upon each new encounter of a prey item. Rather, it is considered to be a value change that is embedded in changes in the subsistence base of a group of humans. Within a certain subsistence procurement regime, value of item j would be a discrete point (V_j) somewhere on the curve. Under an alternate subsistence procurement regime, given the interrelationship of subsistence energy costs (Flannery 1968), it is possible for item j to attain a second, enhanced value ($V_{j'}$). Under a nonagricultural subsistence base, certain potential resources will not be selected as dietary components because they possess characteristics that give them a relatively lessened value such that their inclusion in the diet lowers overall energy harvest (Charnov 1976). Characteristics could include behavioral patterns such as periodicity of activity, nonassociation with vegetation or other markers on the landscape (which eliminates patch definition around the resource), or lack of easy perception of the prey item by the predator. Such characteristics result in search and/or capture times with prohibitive energy costs. However, under a horticultural or agricultural subsistence base, that same potential resource may interact with humans in a manner unique to that subsistence system, as a patch-defined resource. That resource then has a higher relative value both as compared to other potential prey items and to itself under a nonagricultural subsistence energy regime. This is illustrated in Figure 9.

I am hypothesizing that such changes in selectivity do indeed occur.

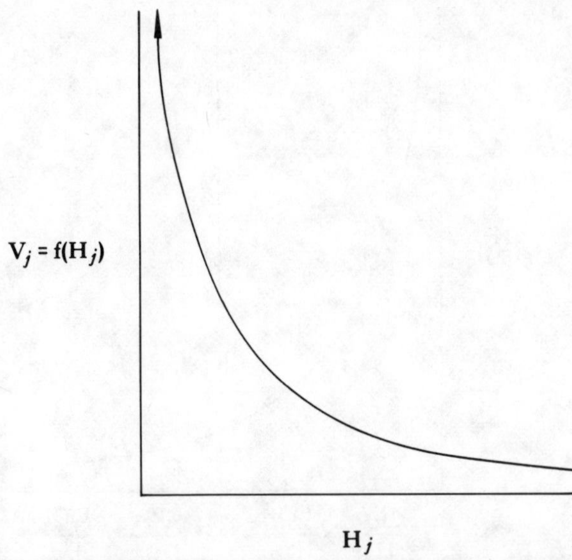

Figure 8. Graph of the relationship of value (*V*) to handling time (*H*) for some prey item (*j*) as *H* approaches *0*. In the statement $V_j = E_j/H_j$, E_j is constant.

In horticultural/agricultural subsistence systems, animal species of little value to the hunter-gatherer can be reassessed as a prey item and selected as a resource or diet item. The reassessed prey item could be a new item to enter the diet; however, it is not necessary that the item be a new dietary item. Changes in energy flow can result in an enhanced value, or importance, of that item at the expense of items previously in the diet (Charnov 1976). The process of the reassessment of the cost-benefit function of animal species in relation to horticultural or agricultural systems has been termed garden hunting (Linares 1976). Garden hunting has been used as an implicit explanation for the selection of prey items (Linares 1976; Emslie 1981). I intend to demonstrate the functioning of this process by presenting empirical measurements of movements of small rodents in and around fields. The animal biomass changes because cultigens and associated ruderal plants are concentrated in an anthropogenic (or human-created) environment. Evidence is offered that practitioners of cultivation, both on a subsistence and a modern commercial level, perceive this change in animal dispersal and respond to it.

The Response of Rodents to Fields

The effects of human-produced environmental patches on the dispersal of rodents was observed for a cornfield in southern Illinois (Turner 1966). In this study, the distribution and movements of *Peromyscus leucopus* (white-

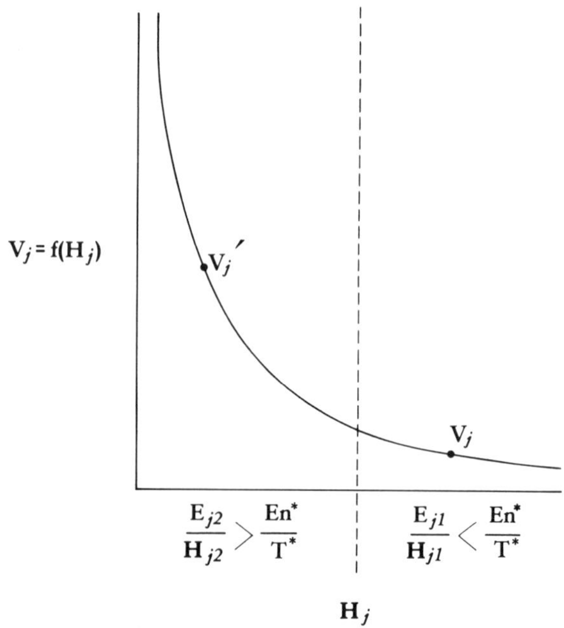

Figure 9. Increase in value of prey item j, such that predator selectivity changes under different subsistence bases. E_{j1}/H_{j1}, value of item j in a hunter-gatherer subsistence system; E_{j2}/H_{j2}, value of item j in a horticultural system. $E_n{}^*/T^*$ is the total energy available from a feeding regime. An item is included in the diet only if $E_i/H_i > E_n{}^*/T^*$.

footed mouse) were monitored for two successive years to determine if the rodents would move from areas of abundant natural foods into the field environment. It was observed that the seed-eating *P. leucopus* had a definite tendency to move out of the surrounding wooded areas into the cornfield.

Movement toward the cornfield was termed positive, and movement away from the cornfield was termed negative (1966:14). The following association between the environment of the field and *Peromyscus* was noted:

> Total positive movements exceeded total negative movements by a small margin. . . . Correlated with the fruiting of the corn, negative movements decreased in August while positive movements remained maximal. The greatest difference between positive and negative movement occurred during August (1966:32).

The activity levels of *Peromyscus leucopus* not associated with immigration (or movement into the field from the wooded areas surrounding the field) were also higher in the cornfield than in the surrounding woodlands. These nondirectional or nonmigratory movements are defined as either neutral (lateral) or nonmovement (successive trapping in the same locale) (1966:14).

> Total negative movement within the cornfield greatly exceeded total neutral movement within the woodland during all months. . . . The zenith of neutral movement within the cornfield was . . . correlated with the fruiting of the corn. . . . Total non-movement within the cornfield exceeded total non-movement in the woodland. . . . Previous to fruiting of the corn, non-movement in the woodland was maximal and was greater than non-movement within the cornfield; thereafter non-movement in the cornfield was greater, and non-movement within the woodland dropped sharply (1966:37).

Turner interpreted these records as documentation of movement of *Peromyscus leucopus* from areas of abundant natural food into the artificial food sources of the cornfield. The invasion of the cornfield was signaled by the high levels of positive movement during the period of maturation of the corn crop. The high level of neutral movement within the cornfield after invasion was the result of a population of *Peromyscus* having established itself within the field rather than there being constant immigration into the cornfield (1966:37). The pattern of established populations versus immigrating populations will be addressed later within the discussion of the implication of a field environment as a constant source of animal biomass.

Turner also recorded other rodents' activity in and around the cornfield, though none were as thoroughly investigated as *Peromyscus*. In decreasing order of observation, the other users of the field included *Mus musculus* (European house mouse), *Blarina brevicauda* (short-tailed shrew), *Tamias striatus* (eastern chipmunk), *Glaucomys volans* (eastern flying squirrel), *Zapus hudsonicus* (jumping mouse), and *Rattus norvegicus* (Norway rat).

Other Observations of Rodent Behavior

Although not quantitative, like Turner's, there is nonetheless a wealth of anecdotal information about the behavior of rodents in relation to planted fields. The additional information includes not only assessment of these animals as crop pests to the modern Anglo farmer in the American Southwest but also information on the damage potential of these animals to the subsistence gardens of southwestern Indian horticulturalists in the nineteenth and twentieth centuries.

Table 48 lists small animals that probably composed the microfauna of Black Mesa during the Anasazi occupation, their dietary preferences, and how these feeding preferences may cause them to come into contact with humans through the agency of gardens or fields.

In the Southwest, ethnographers have noted that fields and gardens must often be rid of small mammals to ensure crop yield.

Table 48. Assessment of Small Rodents as Crop Pests.

Species	Food Preferences	Evaluation as Pest
Eutamias quadrivittus	Pinyon nuts; seeds	Common pest in human settlements.
Ammospermophilus leucurus	Seeds; fruits; green vegetation; wild sunflowers and related plants	"They are at once attracted by grain fields and gardens and do considerable damage to both the planted and ripening grain" (p. 96).
Spermophilus spilosoma	Seeds; sunflowers; *Atriplex*	Responsible for "considerable mischief in the fields" (p. 112).
Spermophilus variegatus	Nuts; seeds; berries; fruits; roots; green vegetation	"At regular camp places they gather to collect scattered grain, and gardens and grainfields always attract them" (p. 105).
Cynomys gunnisoni	Grasses and plants around burrows	Primarily known to reduce grazing potential of range lands.
Thomomys bottae	Underground roots; bulbs and tubers; green vegetation	"Whenever opportunity offers they quickly find a potato patch or garden, and if left alone a few of them will almost destroy either. They also do considerable damage in grainfields by cutting the growing grain or covering it with their mounds" (p. 234).
Perognathus flavus	Almost entirely seeds of composites; grasses	"Some claims have been made that these mice dig up the planted grains. . . . Alone their depredations would be of little consequence, but added to that of many other rodents their might adds to the tax levied upon the products" (p. 276).
Perognatus flavescens	Not listed	Not listed.
Dipodomys ordii	Seeds of sunflowers; legumes; amaranth; purslane	When in the vicinity of fields "where crops of small grain are raised, they feed to some extent on the grain and may carry away and store considerable quantities" (p. 269).
Reithrodonotomys megalotis	Grass seeds; green vegetation	"The dense vegetation [associated with agricultural fields] furnishes such perfect cover and protection that the mice multiply at a rate calculated to do considerable damage to the grain and hay crops" (p. 165).

Table 48—continued

Species	Food Preferences	Evaluation as Pest
Peromyscus crinitus	Not listed	"In the days of the cliff dwellers these mice may have been of great economic importance, and have caused much loss to the hoarded stores of food" (p. 161).
Peromyscus maniculatus	Mainly seeds; esp. of composites; grain; acorns; berries	"Along the borders of fields of wheat, oats, and barley the mice in spring eat or carry away the planted seed and in fall feast upon the ripening grain until the last shock is hauled away and the last stack threshed or used up" (p. 146).
Peromyscus boyelii	Hackberries; juniper berries; pinyon nuts; acorns; seeds of a variety of plants	"They readily enter the borders of grainfields and feed both on the ripening grain and sprouting seed. They may also live in grain shocks or stacks, or gather at granaries or bins" (p. 156).
Peromyscus truei	Pinyon nuts; juniper berries; seeds in general	"Locally when very numerous these mice may do considerable mischief to crops planted near their cliffs or cause trouble by entering houses and . . . barns situated near their homes" (p. 153).
Onychomys leucogaster	Often carnivorous; sunflower seeds; wild bean seeds	"Usually these mice are not sufficiently abundant to be of any great economic importance, and if they were abundant their beneficial [carnivorous] food habits would overbalance the slight mischief they might occasionally do" (p. 138).
Neotoma albiqula	Eclectic diet, may include anything	"They rarely do much harm to grain or other crops . . . and can not be considered a serious pest except in very local and exceptional cases" (p. 180).
Neotoma stephensi	Not listed	Not listed.
Microtus mexicanus	Green vegetation; grasses	Does not occur in what are now agricultural areas, therefore not evaluated as a pest.

Note: Data are from Bailey (1971).

For the Havasupai:

The attention required by the growing crops is not burdensome; of course the fields must be weeded, traps placed for the ground squirrels and rats who would otherwise uproot the corn (Spier 1928:103).

For the Pima:

Rabbits usually came at night and caused some damage; at times the Pima attempted to drive them out of the fields with arrowweed fire brands, but with indifferent success (Castetter and Bell 1942:177).

For the Hopi:

In the trapping of small game such as field mice and the like . . . a man would set many of these [deadfall] traps round the edges of his field when vermin were troublesome at or after planting time (Beaglehole 1936:17).

The organized communal rabbit hunt . . . is still held at irregular but frequent intervals throughout the year, most frequently in early summer and autumn when fields must be protected from the depredations of the rabbit (Beaglehole 1936:11).

The Response of Rodents to Human Refuse Areas

Plants growing in an agricultural field are not the sole human-generated attractant for rodents. The human activities of food storage and refuse accumulation could offer them equally attractive resource patches. A modern refuse dump in Ontario, Canada, was monitored to see what, if any, pattern of rodent movement was discernible (Courtney and Fenton 1976). The dump consisted of common household refuse (kitchen garbage, discarded household furnishings, automotive parts, and other assorted hardware) deposited in a large depression in the ground. During the period of observation it was found that *Peromyscus leucopus* (the specifically monitored taxon) seemed positively attracted to the refuse area. "An analysis of new *P. leucopus* joining the dump and control areas each week . . . indicated that more immigrants moved into the dump area than into the control" (1976:417–418). Courtney and Fenton's overall observation was that certain taxa, not just *Peromyscus*, were encountered more frequently in the dump area. They believed the availability of food and/or resting areas in the dump environment was responsible for observed spatial distributions.

Thus we see that small mammals, including rodents and rabbits, are attracted to anthropogenic environments, environmental patches created by human alteration of the landscape for the purposes of crop cultivation or refuse deposition. This attraction creates a new behavioral interaction between humans and the animals involved.

The Black Mesa Data

Given the model, the main result that should be observable in the archaeological record is that sites associated with agriculture should have a microfaunal assemblage that is more complex than the microfaunal assemblage of sites not associated with agriculture. It is important to note that the microfauna need not be entirely absent in the faunal assemblages of sites not associated with agricultural activity. Certain small mammals can be cost-effective prey items in a nonagricultural subsistence economy. Data for testing the hypothesized association between capturing small mammals and agricultural activities come from the 48 archaeological sites excavated by the Black Mesa Archaeological Project between 1977 and 1980.

Ford (this volume) suggests that the primary productive potential and the dispersed, unreliable nature of annual yields of vegetal dietary items in a pinyon and juniper setting (the primary ecological setting of northern Black Mesa), severely limit the use of these environments by hunters and gatherers. "Plant foods were not sufficiently abundant in any one location to support large populations or even the return of small bands" (Ford, this volume, p. 129). However, this same ecological setting can have an entirely different productivity level if the human groups modify the area for agriculture:

> The corn, even if it was not high-yielding, was predictable in its location, yield, and caloric contribution. The creation of anthropogenic ecosystems enabled pioneer annual plants to invade, and if the farmers permitted them to remain, to form dense patches in harvestable quantity (Ford, this volume, pp. 129–130).

Ford goes on to suggest that these human-altered environments also act to concentrate animal biomass. In light of optimal foraging theory (Pyke et al. 1977) and behavioral data on rodent feeding behaviors (Turner 1966), we can now look for evidence supporting or negating the suggested interaction between field environments, small mammals, and human predatory behavior in the archaeological record of Black Mesa.

The sites were assessed for patterns in their faunal assemblages and in their physical and environmental attributes that may relate to agriculture. The first characterization of the sample of sites was the number of taxa in the faunal assemblages of the sites. The larger-bodied taxa identified in the faunal assemblages of Black Mesa sites are *Erethizon dorsatum* (porcupine), *Canis* spp. (coyote or domestic dog), *Urocyon cinereoargentus* (gray fox), *Taxidea taxus* (badger), *Lynx rufus* (bobcat), *Odocoileus* sp. (deer), *Antilocapra americana* (pronghorn antelope), and *Ovis canadensis* (bighorn sheep).

In addition to the two ubiquitous southwestern leporids, *Sylvilagus auduboni* (desert cottontail) and *Lepus californicus* (black-tailed jackrabbit), the following taxa have also been identified in the microfaunal remains of Black Mesa sites: *Eutamis* sp. (chipmunk), *Ammospermophilus leucrus* (white-tailed antelope squirrel), *Spermophilus spilosoma* (spotted ground squirrel), *Spermophilus variegatus* (rock squirrel), *Cynomys gunnisoni* (Gunnison's prairie dog), *Thomomys bottae* (Botta's pocket gopher), *Perognathus* spp. (pocket mice), *Dipodomys ordii* (Ord's kangaroo rat), *Reithrodontomys* sp. (harvest mouse), *Peromyscus* spp. (deer mice), *Onychomys leucogaster* (northern grasshopper mouse), *Neotoma albigula* (white-throated woodrat), *Neotoma stephensi* (Stephens' woodrat), and *Microtus mexicanus* (Mexican vole).

It is a working assumption in this study that the above microfauna are in fact consumed resources. An occasional rare microfaunal remain exhibits charring from burning or etching from having passed through a digestive tract. Neither, however, constitutes strong evidence for food utilization. Even if the question of consumption is refuted, the general principle of the argument is still applicable: human and rodent behavioral interactions can be modified by human-induced landscape changes.

A second assumption holds constant for this study, the depositional processes affecting faunal assemblage composition. Patterns of faunal assemblage complexity are undoubtedly related to length of site occupation and depositional complexity of the site (Semé 1981). However, in the initial part of the investigation, I have decided to identify patterns while holding the above considerations constant, though I shall try to take these factors into account later.

Not all these taxa are present in the assemblages of every site. Rather, there is a trimodal pattern to their presence or absence. The first mode includes those sites from which no faunal remains were recovered. The second mode is those sites with one to nine different taxa in the faunal assemblages. The third mode is those sites with 12 to 20 different taxa composing their assemblages. It is only these last assemblages that have a microfaunal component. Further, the microfauna are the only significant qualitative differences between Classes II and III. Throughout the remainder of this paper, Class I will designate those sites with no faunal remains; Class II will designate those sites with one to nine taxa; and Class III will designate sites with 12 to 20 taxa. Table 49 lists, by faunal class, the sites used in this analysis. Mean number of taxa for each class are: Class I, 0.0; Class II, 3.6; and Class III, 14.1.

The Model and Predictions

If agricultural field clearing creates new habitats for microfauna, then certain sites may have been the loci of the behavior under investigation (garden hunting), but other factors intervene to distort and invalidate the instrument of observation (microfauna) chosen to measure the target behavior. Because of this, it is first necessary to look more closely at depositional patterns in the sample of sites. Toward this end, the three classes of sites were tested for variation in cultural and physical characteristics.

Table 49. Archaeological Sites Used in Analysis Arranged by Faunal Class.

Class	Site	Number of Taxa
I	D:7:424	0
	D:7:441	0
	D:7:708	0
	D:7:723	0
	D:7:1104	0
	D:7:1109	0
	D:7:1110	0
	D:7:1115	0
	D:7:1118	0
	D:7:1119	0
	D:7:1125	0
	D:7:1134	0
	D:11:1096	0
	D:11:1136	0
	D:11:1152	0
II	D:7:514	1
	D:7:707	1
	D:7:713	1
	D:11:1162	1
	D:7:214	2
	D:7:222	2
	D:7:3038	2
	D:7:263	3
	D:11:215	3
	D:11:381	3
	D:11:1158	3
	D:11:1244	3
	D:7:1108	4
	D:7:3021	4
	D:11:73	4
	D:11:1161	4
	D:7:19	5
	D:7:109	5
	D:11:426	5
	D:7:3055	6
	D:11:320	6
	D:11:2001	6
	D:11:338	7
	D:7:710	9
III	D:7:725	12
	D:7:216	13
	D:7:220	13
	D:11:425	13
	D:7:23	14
	D:7:236	14
	D:7:239	14
	D:7:704	15
	D:7:18	16
	D:11:275	20

It is hypothesized, from the complexity of the fauna in each of the sites, that Classes I to III represent a gradient in complexity of cultural activities performed at the site. Class III would be the group of sites associated with the widest range of cultural activities, and Class I with the lowest. Each site was assessed for the presence of the following physical characteristics: extramural features, jacals, shallow pithouses (floor $<$ 35 cm below ground surface), deep pithouses (floor $>$ 35 cm below ground surface), isolated masonry structures, contiguous masonry or jacal structures (a roomblock), a kiva, a midden, and whether there were clear indications of remodeling or reoccupation of the site (overlapping or superimposed structures). A score for physical attributes was obtained by summing the number of attribute classes present at the site.

An analysis of variance was then performed on the three classes. The physical attribute score, the dependent variable in the test, is a measurement of the diversity of cultural activities carried out on a site. It is assumed that a higher physical attribute score indicates a wider range of behaviors at that site. The lower the physical attribute score, the more limited the behaviors performed at that site. A correlate of the relation between physical attribute score and specificity of behaviors is that the lower the physical attribute score, the narrower the representation of the range of hunting behaviors represented at that site. (Representation is here defined as physical evidence that can be collected during excavation of an archaeological site.) Conversely, the higher the physical attribute score, the broader the range of hunting behaviors represented in the faunal record.

Results of the test showed that all three classes, while originally separated on faunal criteria, were also significantly different in their physical attributes ($F = 30.84$, $df = 2$, $p < 0.0001$). Furthermore, the class means, which are also the points of best fit under the statistical model tested, show a gradient of increasing complexity (Class I = 0.875, Class II = 3.000, Class III = 5.80). Thus the hypothesis is retained. Complexity of faunal assemblages is associated with the variety of physical remains at the sites. The broader the probable range of activities performed at a site, the more complex the faunal record.

We can characterize the range of behaviors or activities performed at a site by the resolution, or clarity, with which those behaviors can be observed archaeologically (Binford 1980). The behavioral resolution of archaeological sites is termed grain and should not be confused with the concept of environmental grain discussed earlier in this paper. Coarse-grained sites have a low resolution of behavior. These types of sites are the accumulated product of a number of activities such that no one discrete behavior is readily visible. Fine-grained sites have a high resolution of behavior because they have resulted from the performance of a minimal number of behaviors. Generally, it is easiest to observe target behaviors in a fine-grained archaeological record. However, it would appear that for this study, a fine-grained archaeological record (Class I sites) is somehow unsuitable for observing the organic remains of hunting behavior (if, in fact, hunting was a behavior connected with these sites). Hunting is only an obvious behavior in a coarse-grained archaeological record, Classes II and III. Because Class II and III sites are coarse-grained behavioral records, I feel it is necessary to explore further the depositional patterns of these sites.

It has previously been observed for Black Mesa that sites with a midden have more faunal remains than sites without a midden (Semé 1981). A similar trend is found for the diversity of fauna in this study. Class III sites tend to have middens, while Class II sites do not ($G = 6.726$, $p = 0.05$). However, within Class III sites, microfauna is as likely to be recovered from nonmidden areas as from the midden itself ($t = 1.2698$, $p > 0.05$). This follows the conclusions I reached in the earlier study: amount of recovered faunal remains relates to (1) greater absolute amount of refuse deposited at the sites due to increased occupational intensity and (2) absolute increase in amount of bone preserved due to creation of protected depositional areas resulting from increased occupational density (1981:67–70). The overall site pattern is that visibility of hunting behavior is related to the archaeological grain of the sites.

Keeping the above patterns in mind, I now would like to proceed to test the site classes for association with agricultural activities. Class III sites, the only sites with a microfaunal component to their assemblages, should be associated with agricultural activity. Conversely, Class II sites should not be associated with agriculture. With Class I sites, the important question is not whether they are associated with agriculture but what other factors, behavioral and preservational, could result in the absence of a faunal record.

Two previous studies utilizing Black Mesa data provide criteria that are relevant measurements of agricultural association. One study (Catlin 1978) assessed the relationship between site types and agriculture by examining the percentage of sagebrush within a 0.5 km catchment. The other study (Powell 1980, 1983) assessed season of site use. Although this second study is not directly concerned with agricultural activity at a site, it can nonetheless be used in such an assessment. Certain seasons of the year, especially the warmer months, are more probably times of agricultural activity. If a site is believed to have been occupied during warm weather, then it is more likely that agricultural activity was associated with it than at a winter-occupied site.

Catlin sought to distinguish limited-activity sites from habitation sites in the eastern half of the Peabody Coal Company lease area on Black Mesa. In his study, physical characteristics available from survey data were used to categorize types of prehistoric sites. The physical characteristics measured were site size, apparent number of structures and features, and artifact variety. Three site categories were discerned. Type 1 sites were considered to be "habitation units due to their relatively large size and structural diversity"

(Catlin 1978:87). Type 2 sites were those sites that seemed to be specialized-activity loci with no apparent structures and of relatively small size. Type 3 sites were sites

> of intermediate capacity relative to limited activity sites and habitation sites. This possibility is indicated by the relatively large variety of attribute states which are included in the site type. . . . Such a range in variability suggests that these types of sites represent a range in cultural activities which falls somewhere in between those occurring on habitation sites and limited activity sites (1978:87).

Unfortunately this last category of intermediate sites was excluded from Catlin's main analysis since his interests lay in the dichotomy between Type 1 and 2 sites. Catlin hypothesized variation between Type 1 and 2 sites in their association with arable land. He predicted that habitation sites should be associated with agricultural activity, hence arable land, while limited-activity sites would be associated mainly with nonagricultural activities and nonarable land. Given the similar soil requirements of sagebrush and cultigens, percent sagebrush within 0.5 km of a site was used as a measure of potential arable land associated with that site. The predicted associations were found:

> The amount of sage around permanent habitation sites was significantly greater than the amount of sage around limited activity sites. . . . [I]t can therefore be stated that permanent habitation sites were located near significantly higher amounts of arable land (1978:94–95).

Since I wished to examine the implications of interaction between fields and hunting behavior, I performed a similar test on the sites in my sample. Since my Classes I and III are apparently analogous to Catlin's Types 2 and 1, respectively, the same relationship should be found. Since Class II sites apparently represent a range of activities beyond limited-activity sites and agriculture is a ubiquitous activity on Black Mesa (Ford, this volume), some association with arable land should be found for this "mixed," highly variable grouping of sites. However, results of a test for differences among the classes in percent of sagebrush in a 0.5 km radius were nonsignificant ($F = 1.43$, $df = 2$, $p = 0.2513$). The class means trend in the expected direction (Class I $= 22.8$, Class II $= 30.0$, Class III $= 36.6$), but the difference between the dichotomous Classes I and III is not significant ($t = -0.156$, $df = 22$, $p > 0.05$).

Although the three classes of sites were distinguished on faunal and physical characteristics, they could not be distinguished on the basis of an environmental characteristic that Catlin believed to be indicative of agricultural activity. While agricultural activity may be associated with sagebrush areas as Catlin contests, it does not follow that sites not associated with agriculture are not associated with sagebrush. Given the variety of behaviors that may be represented by smaller sites, location of limited-activity sites may very well be based on a number of criteria—all of which would be independent of sagebrush. Catlin excluded an entire group of sites, many of which may in fact also have been limited-activity sites that were included in my study. This may account for the lack of congruence in results between the two studies.

Probable association with agriculture was then tested using the criterion of season of site occupation. Season of occupation of a site was inferred from intrasite space utilization and artifact densities established by Powell (1980, 1983) for the Black Mesa study area. Powell discerned four groups of sites: (1) large late sites that were permanently occupied, (2) large early sites occupied during the winter season, (3) small early sites, and (4) small late sites. The last two categories are believed to be temporary or limited-activity sites occupied during the summer months.

I reasoned that Powell's large late sites should be my Class III sites— sites associated with the microfaunal assemblage components (although there are a few early [pre-A.D. 1050] sites in Class III). The early large sites, being winter occupations and therefore not associated with agricultural fields, should not have microfaunal components. They should be equivalent to my Class II sites. It is also the case that if rodents are simply attracted to human activity areas (because of refuse deposits and/or abandoned structures) and not specifically to agricultural fields, both Class II and III sites should have microfaunal components. Powell's small early and small late sites should correspond to my Class I sites, the sites with no faunal remains. This should occur even if some of these small sites were field houses, since faunal refuse deposits at such sites would be surface scatterings of bone. These are situations in which bone would not be expected to be recovered archaeologically.

A G-test to test the level of association between my classifications and Powell's classifications was performed. Results of the test were significant ($G = 23.6018$, $df = 4$, $p < 0.001$). Classification based on faunal assemblage complexity is related to classification based on season of occupation. The trend is that sites characterized by Powell as winter-occupied are also those sites that do not have the small rodent component in their faunal assemblages (Class II sites). Sites characterized as occupied year-round tend also to be those sites with the small rodent component (Class III sites). The small early and small late sites tend to be those sites with no faunal material recovered during excavation (Class I). These results support the hypothesis that much small rodent hunting is dependent on the behavioral interaction that develops between humans and low cost-benefit species in the presence of anthropogenic ecosystems. However, complete understanding of the results comes from the combined work on seasonality and depositional patterns.

Table 50. Summary Characteristics of the Three Site Classes.

Class	Faunal Record	Physical Complexity	Season
I	None	Low	Warm
II	No microfauna	Intermediate	Cold
III	Microfauna	High	Warm and cold

Depositional Patterns

The information on season of occupation, site grain, and fauna is summarized in Table 50. What is evident is that agricultural activity alone is not sufficient to account for the patterns that have been attributed to garden hunting. Rather, several other behaviors must be considered, primary of which is restricted mobility resulting in a coarse-grained archaeological record. A coarse-grained archaeological record, in turn, results in better visibility of faunal remains. Note that although Class I and II sites may be the componental equivalents of Class III sites, their faunal records are *not additive*. If no physical processes of preservation disturbed the faunal record of Class I sites, then the presence or absence of microfauna in their assemblages would be the most critical measurement in the test of the garden hunting model. However, preservation processes do make these sites unsuitable for the model's evaluation. It is only with a secondary (and noisier) contrast that the hunting behavior under question becomes archaeologically visible. That secondary line of evidence, winter-only (Class II) versus year-round occupied sites (Class III), did show the trends predicted by the garden hunting model.

Conclusions

In summary, it was shown that rodents and rabbits do alter their distribution across the landscape in response to the availablity of artificial food sources in fields or gardens, even to the point of migrating from areas of abundant natural food resources into the anthropogenic environment. Populations of small rodents, once estalished within the field, cease immigration movement (Turner 1966). In the Turner study, it was highly desirable *not* to be removing members of the established population from the field. However, in a normal situation, the humans tending the field would be cognizant of these invaders and their potential for damage to the crop yield; trapping with intent to remove the animals from the field should ensue. In fact, if humans trap and remove members of a population that have been attracted to a field, the humans may, in effect, be creating a situation where constant immigration is then possible. The death of a crop pest in a field only stops that particular animal from occupying the field, and other individuals, with the earlier occupant removed, may then invade the field to use the food supply located there until they too are eliminated, and so on. It has been observed that a situation of heavy immigration of rodents into an area results in populations "resilient to large artificial [trapping] mortality" (Middleton and Merriam 1981:703). Therefore, I not only suggest that anthropogenic environments act to concentrate animal (as well as plant) biomass into a highly useful resource patch, but also that the concentrated animal biomass is a renewable resource. As humans trap, remove, and utilize a crop pest, they create a situation of constant immigration of additional animals; hence they have a constant supply of garden game.

For the prehistoric occupation of northeastern Black Mesa, Ford (this volume) has suggested that anthropogenic (or human-created) environments are necessary for human occupation of the area, given its sparse, dispersed biomass. Evidence has been presented elsewhere on how such a system involving cultigens and ruderal plants may have functioned. In this paper I hypothesized that a similiar trend occurs with animal biomass and anthropogenic environments. To support this contention, evidence was presented on rodent behavior in relation to cultivated areas. Since species known to be attracted to modern field environments are consistently present in the archaeological faunal assemblages of sites with more complex faunal assemblages, sites probably associated with agricultural activity, the hypothesis is supported: animals of little or no value to a hunter as a dietary item can have an increased value in an agricultural setting as a result of biomass concentration in and around anthropogenic environments and can enter into the diet.

10

Intersite Variation in Faunal Remains on Black Mesa

David Eckles

An important aspect of prehistoric Black Mesa faunal procurement patterns is the effect such patterns have on the faunal inventories found at various sites. This paper examines site function and site location to investigate how these variables affect intersite variation in faunal remains. Prior to 1978, intersite variation in faunal remains was not considered at length. For example, the analyses of Douglas (1972) and Fagan et al. (1972) grouped sites by phase without regard to location. A number of studies, however, have argued that intersite differences in site type and location do exist and that these differences affected the kind and amount of faunal exploitation carried out by the occupants of each site on Black Mesa.

The general question of intersite variation in site location has been recognized in past archaeological studies. A distinction between upland and lowland settlement has been made throughout work on Black Mesa (Gumerman 1970; Gumerman et al. 1972; Phillips 1972; S. Plog 1977d). The initial distinction between upland and lowland areas focused on the proximity of sites to a major drainage. Sites located very near or on a major drainage were considered lowland sites, while sites located farther away from a major drainage were considered upland sites (Gumerman et al. 1972; Phillips 1972). The major drainages in the study area have a drainage rank of 3 or 4, using a ranking method similar to the Southwestern Anthropological Research Group classification of drainage rank (Gumerman 1972). Gumerman et al. (1972) employed this distinction and noticed more upland settlement through time. Later studies (Catlin 1978; S. Plog 1977d; S. Plog and Klesert 1978) focused on additional ways to characterize site location. In addition to a site's distance from a major drainage, environmental characteristics such as the distance to a minor drainage (rank of 1 or 2), the percentage of sagebrush-grassland around a site, and altitude and relief were considered. These variables were selected to test for associations between site locations and environmental parameters.

Other studies have considered more specific aspects of intersite variation. Phillips (1972) attempted to show a relationship between the larger habitation sites and smaller sites of the Toreva phase. He hypothesized that the larger sites, located primarily in the lowlands, were "mother" sites from which smaller populations emigrated and settled in the uplands. The larger sites also were argued to be the loci of all socioreligious activities. In another study, Catlin (1978) emphasized the importance of studying limited-activity sites. Such sites, the smallest on Black Mesa, consist of a small surface scatter of sherds and/or lithics, have relatively few or no structures, and are abundant on Black Mesa. Catlin's (1978) analysis suggested that such sites were the loci of a more limited range of subsistence activities.

Stephen Plog (1978:33–34 and personal communication) has recently attempted to synthesize data concerning site type and site location. He has suggested that, contrary to the view of a linear movement of sites from the lowlands to the uplands through time, both upland and lowland areas were exploited during all phases. Plog suspects that a subsistence-settlement network existed, with a central habitation site and several subsidiary sites in both lowland and upland environments. The subsidiary sites were located in different areas to exploit seasonally available resources (limited-activity sites) and to maintain a spatially more diversified agricultural base. This is similar to the Hopi method of field location, in which fields are placed in diverse locations to avoid a total crop loss from poor growing conditions in one area.

These specific studies and many general discussions (e.g., Binford 1965; F. Plog 1974) of human adaptive systems show the need to consider intersite variation in site location and function. As noted above, intersite variation in activities may have had an effect on the kinds and amount of bones deposited at different sites. Thus, in this paper I will attempt to test whether or not there are differences in faunal remains from sites of different functions and from sites located in different environmental areas.

Site Type and Variation in Faunal Remains

In light of the hypothesized differences in site functions, the purpose of this section is to test for associations between site types and faunal assemblages. To conduct such a test, a method for creating site types had to be selected. Two previous studies have provided information relevant to that decision. First, Powell (this volume) has shown that sites with differing numbers of structures do not appear to have differed in the activities carried out at the sites. Thus, although the number of structures on a site is often used in creating site typologies in the Southwest, it was rejected for this study. Second, Catlin's (1978) analysis of survey data from the eastern half of Peabody Coal Company's lease area has suggested significant differences between two types of sites distinguished by the types of structures present. Sites with no surface indications of structures, which therefore are likely to have only jacal habitation structures or to lack structures completely, had significantly lower frequencies of manos and features and significantly lower densities of graywares and chipped stone than sites with both kivas and masonry roomblocks (Catlin 1978:90–92). In addition, the latter sites tended to be located near more arable land (Catlin 1978:94–95). Since masonry roomblocks are almost exclusively storage rooms (Bagley-Baumgartner, this volume), this evidence suggests that functional site types can be distinguished by the *types* of structures present rather than simply the *number* of structures. Catlin (1978:87) argues that the sites with kivas and roomblocks were permanent habitation sites, while the sites with no surface indications of structures were limited-activity sites that were occupied for shorter periods of time. These results help to explain some of the differences in artifact abundance that Powell (this volume) found between sites with similar numbers of structures, such as D:11:348 and D:11:1084. Although similar in the number of structures present, more functional types of structures and a greater number of artifacts were present at D:11:348.

Thus, in order to test for differences in faunal procurement at different site types, all sites excavated prior to 1978 for which information on the faunal remains was available were ranked according to the diversity of structural types present. Four different types of structures were distinguished on the basis of inferred function. They are kivas, habitation structures, storage structures, and mealing rooms. Each site thus was assigned a number from zero to four, indicating increasing structural diversity.

One of the major differences between faunal procurement at limited-activity sites and habitation sites should have been in the relative diversity of different animals that were exploited. A greater diversity of animals should have been exploited by populations residing at habitation sites since they were occupied longer. To test this proposal, faunal remains were divided into 11 categories: cottontail rabbit, jackrabbit, mountain sheep, pronghorn antelope, mule deer, large rodents *(Spermophilus, Cynomys, Thomomys,* and *Eutamias)*, small rodents *(Neotoma, Dipodomys, Peromyscus, Microtus,* and other mice), carnivores, domestic dog, birds in general, and turkey (considered to be a domesticated bird). The rodents were divided into "large" and "small" categories so their large numbers would not overrepresent their importance. Both dog and turkey were separated since both are considered to have been domestic animals. Dogs may have been kept as pets and used occasionally for food, and turkeys may have been used as a food source and for their feathers. The faunal index thus ranges from zero to 11, in order of increasing diversity.

Finally, it was decided to examine the relationship between faunal diversity and the diversity of exploited plant resources. Bradfield (1973) has argued that in the Great Basin and northern Southwest the historical exploitation of animals was largely determined by plant resources. Thus, there may be associations among the diversity of structures, floral remains, and faunal remains. Floral remains were also similarly divided into categories primarily on the basis of generic or family-level groups. They include pinyon pine (nuts), juniper (berries), grasses (seeds and greens), weeds (e.g., pigweed and lambsquarters, for both seeds and greens), other edible plants (e.g., chokecherries and hackberries) that occur infrequently, and all cultigens (corn, beans, and squash). Thus, the index for floral remains ranges from zero to seven for each site, indicating increasing floral diversity. Floral remains were not recovered with flotation techniques prior to 1975; thus, a comparable diversity index could not be calculated for these sites. The faunal, floral, and structural diversity indexes for all sites included in the analysis are shown in Table 51.

The Analysis

Analysis of the diversity indexes was initiated by constructing histograms for each category (Figure 10). Because of the results of Catlin's (1978)

Table 51. Relative Indexes Showing Structural, Floral, and Faunal Diversities of Black Mesa Sites.

Site	Structural Diversity	Floral Diversity	Faunal Diversity
D:7:18	4	4	6
D:7:19	3	5	5
D:7:23	3	3	10
D:7:27	3	—[a]	8
D:7:134	3	5	10
D:7:135	2	5	8
D:7:136	3	—[a]	11
D:7:152	2	—[a]	9
D:9:1	3	—[a]	4
D:9:2	1	—[a]	5
D:10:1	2	—[a]	6
D:11:97	3	4	6
D:11:275	3	5	10
D:11:290	4	7	9
D:11:298	0	2	1
D:11:324	2	4	2
D:11:338	2	3	7
D:11:348	3	6	8
D:11:352	4	7	7
D:11:354	1	6	3
D:11:356	4	6	7
D:11:409	3	5	7
D:11:814	1	3	6
D:11:879	1	3	1
D:11:1081	1	4	0
D:11:1084	2	6	1
D:11:1153	2	4	4
D:11:1158	1	3	3
D:11:1161-Lolomai	0	3	4
D:11:1161-Toreva	1	5	2
D:11:1162	1	5	1
D:11:1170	1	2	1

[a]Botanical report not available.

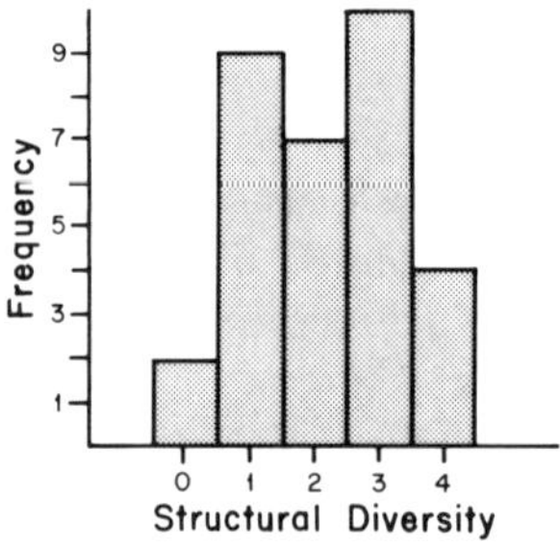

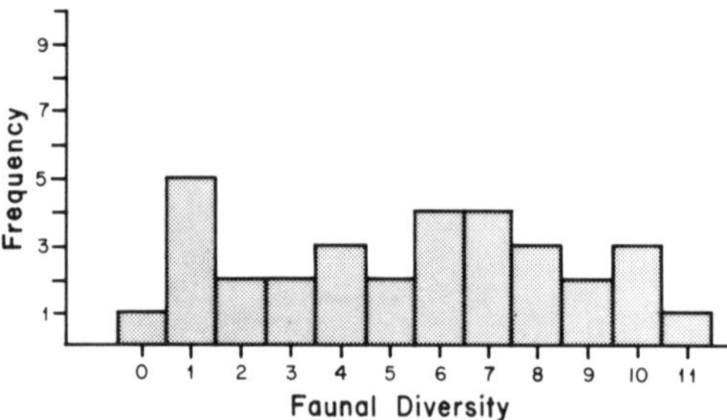

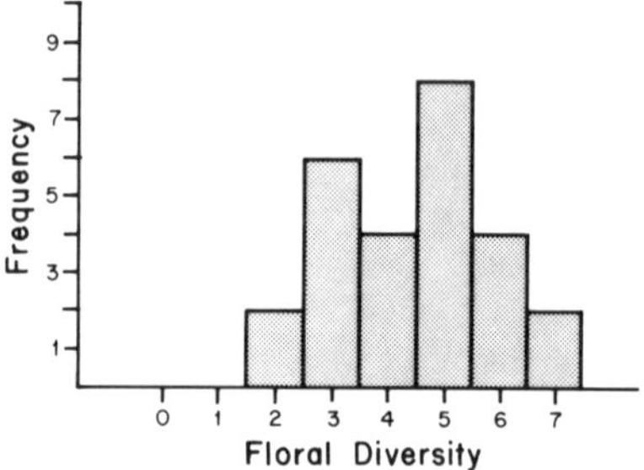

Figure 10. Diversity measures.

analysis of survey data, it was expected that the histogram of structural diversity might have a tendency toward bimodality. The histogram shown at the top of Figure 10 is slightly bimodal with peaks at one and three types of structures. In addition, none of the sites with only one or two structures had either kivas or masonry roomblocks, which is also consistent with Catlin's settlement typology.

To examine the relationship between structural diversity and faunal diversity, cross-tabulations were made. For structural diversity, sites were grouped into two categories corresponding to the two peaks on the histogram: (1) sites with one type of structure or less and (2) sites with three or four types of structures. Because sites with two types of structures fell between the two peaks in the histogram and could not clearly be assigned to either of the above groups, they were deleted from the analysis. Faunal diversity values were also separated into two groups: (1) sites with five or fewer of the animal groups represented and (2) sites with six or more groups. The separation point corresponded to the median of all values and also separated two peaks on the left side of the histogram from one primary peak on the right side. The resulting contingency table is presented in Table 52. The table shows that there is a very strong association between low structural diversity and low faunal diversity and between high structural diversity and high faunal diversity. This is supported by a chi-square value of 11.58 (significant at the 0.01 level) and a phi coefficient of 0.46.

A cross-tabulation of structural diversity with floral diversity was also made. For this table, values of floral diversity were separated into two groups: (1) sites with four or fewer plant groups represented and (2) sites with five or more plant groups present. The separation point in this case again corresponded to the median value and also separated two peaks of floral diversity values on the histogram. The contingency table created is shown in Table 53. The table shows a significant association between values of structural and floral diversity. The chi-square value is 3.82 and is statistically significant at the 0.10 level, although the phi coefficient is only 0.18. The contingency tables show that fewer plants and animals were exploited by the inhabitants of sites with low structural diversity indexes and supports the hypothesis that such sites were limited-activity loci occupied for short periods of time.

In addition to the occurrence of a limited variety of faunal remains at sites with low structural diversity, particular types of animal remains tend to be found at such sites. Rabbit bones as well as small and large rodent remains are common, as they are at sites with high structural diversity. Artiodactyl remains, such as deer, mountain sheep, and antelope, tend to be absent, although they commonly occur at sites with high structural diversity. This is

---

Table 52. Cross-tabulation of High and Low Structural Diversity With High and Low Faunal Diversity.

		Faunal Diversity		
		0 to 5 Animal Groups	6 to 11 Animal Groups	Row Totals
	0 to 1 Structure Types	10	1	11
Structural Diversity	2 to 4 Structure Types	2	12	14
	Column Totals	12	13	25

$\chi^2 = 11.58$, $p = 0.01$, $\phi^2 = 0.46$

Table 53. Cross-tabulation of High and Low Structural Diversity With High and Low Floral Diversity.

		Faunal Diversity		
		0 to 5 Animal Groups	6 to 11 Animal Groups	Row Totals
	0 to 1 Structure Types	7	3	10
Structural Diversity	2 to 4 Structure Types	2	9	11
	Column Totals	9	12	21

$\chi^2 = 3.82, p = 0.10, \phi^2 = 0.18$

Table 54. Cross-tabulation of High and Low Structural Diversity With the Presence/Absence of Artiodactyl Remains.

		Artiodactyls		Row Totals
		Present	Absent	
	0 to 1 Structure Types	2	8	10
Structural Diversity	2 to 4 Structure Types	13	1	14
	Column Totals	15	9	24

$\chi^2 = 10.29, p = 0.01, \phi^2 = 0.43$

shown by the contingency table presented in Table 54. The chi-square value of 10.29 (significant at the 0.01 level) and the phi coefficient of 0.43 show a strong, nonrandom association between low structural diversity and the absence of artiodactyl remains and between high structural diversity and the presence of artiodactyl remains.

There may be several reasons for this pattern in the distribution of different types of animal remains. First, evidence suggests that artiodactyls were probably procured primarily during the fall and winter. At those times, deer, antelope, and mountain sheep tend to group into larger bands (Wood et al. 1970:12, 14; Geist 1971:14; Davis and Taylor 1939:450; Caton 1877; Lechleitner 1969:223; Bailey 1931:26) and could be more easily hunted (Flannery 1968:77). Consistent with this argument is the fact that the Hopi (Beaglehole 1936:4–7, 10–11; Parsons 1936:278), Navajo (Hill 1938:96, 145–148), and Great Basin groups (Steward 1938:34–37; Bradfield

1973:352) primarily hunted these animals from November to February. Second, the procurement of smaller animals may have been associated with and regulated by the procurement of plant resources. Bradfield (1973:348, 352) notes that the movement of Shoshonean groups was determined by the procurement of plant rather than animal species. As densities of small animals, particularly rodents, tended to be high primarily in areas where plants were gathered, "the hunting of these small animals, consequently, dovetailed in with the gathering of seeds and roots" (1973:352). Flannery (1968:77) has noted a similar pattern in data from Oaxaca and Tehuacan during the food-collecting and "incipient cultivation" era in those regions. He argues (1968:77, emphasis in original) that the evidence suggests "that scheduling gave preference to the seasonality of the *plant* species collected; and when conflict situations arose, it was the *animal* exploitation that was curtailed." He also suggests that small fauna were hunted from May to September, while deer hunting was limited to the late fall and winter.

In addition to the evidence presented above, other aspects of the Black Mesa data support the hypothesis that the sites with low structural diversity were areas where populations were residing primarily for the procurement of plant resources. Despite the fact that the faunal diversity index has a wider range in values than the floral diversity index, the average floral diversity value at sites with few types of structures is higher (3.60) than the average faunal diversity index for such sites (2.45). A one-tailed rank sum test indicates that this difference is statistically significant at the 0.10 level. In addition, the floral diversity values at sites with few structural types are much less variable than the faunal diversity values, as would be expected if the sites were primarily established for procuring plant resources. The coefficient of variation (Steel and Torrie 1960:20) for the floral diversity index is 37.5, and for the faunal diversity index the coefficient is 78.1. Higher values of the coefficient indicate greater variation.

The evidence presented above is all consistent with the hypothesis that sites with low structural diversity indexes were limited-activity sites, while those with high structural diversity indexes were occupied more permanently. Furthermore, the evidence suggests that the limited-activity sites were primarily plant collecting stations occupied during the spring, summer, and early fall, although a number of small animals were also exploited at such sites. These sites are thus very similar to the rainy season camps that Flannery (1968:77) described for Oaxaca and Tehuacan. Black Mesa sites with high structural diversity indexes are characterized by the remains of plants and animals that would have been produced during the spring, summer, and early fall, as well as by the remains of animals that ethnographically were hunted during the late fall and winter. Thus, the sites appear to have been occupied during all four seasons. Intersite variation in faunal remains thus results in part from variation between sites.

In conclusion, it should be noted that the faunal and floral diversity values correlate directly with the volume of excavated deposits at each site and thus with the number of faunal and floral remains recovered. In addition, larger samples usually have more types of remains than smaller samples drawn from the same population because of the greater chance of finding remains that occur in low frequencies. However, these facts do not invalidate the conclusions reached above for two reasons. First, the proportion of each site that was excavated was extremely high at all sites. In many cases—and in particular on many of the small sites such as D:11:298, D:11:814, D:11:1081, and D:11:1153—we are dealing with virtually complete populations. The variation amoung sites in the amount of faunal and floral remains recovered is therefore not a result of differential sampling fractions but is a result of variation in the size of the populations sampled.

Semé (1981) has noted that higher amounts of faunal remains recovered from sites with greater structural diversity may in part be a result of better preservation of bone at such sites due to the common association of middens with kivas and masonry storage rooms. She also notes, however, that the high faunal frequencies as well as the presence of middens are probably due to the greater length of occupation at such sites. Thus, the direct correlation between the number of faunal remains recovered and faunal diversity indicates that sites with low and high values of structural diversity differ not only in the diversity of animals that their inhabitants successfully hunted but also in the amount of hunting which took place at such sites.

Second, a hypothesis that the different values of faunal diversity are solely due to the effects of different sample sizes would not be supported by some of the results reported above. That hypothesis cannot explain, for example, why average floral diversity is higher than average faunal diversity at sites with few types of structures or why faunal diversity is more variable than floral diversity at such sites.

Site Location and Intersite Variation in Faunal Remains

Site location may also have played a role in intersite variation in faunal remains, given a least-effort energy capture strategy. That is, animals located closer to the site in question may have been encountered more frequently and thus hunted more often. For example, considerable distances must have been traveled from all sites on Black Mesa to get to antelope or mountain sheep hunting areas, but sites located closer to the antelope area would be expected to contain more antelope remains.

To test the hypothesis that intersite differences in faunal assemblages were caused by differential site location, several physiographic variables used in previous settlement pattern studies on Black Mesa (Catlin 1978; Gumerman et al. 1972; S. Plog 1977d) were selected. These variables are distance from a major drainage, percentage of sagebrush-grassland around a site, and elevation. Another variable, distance from the northern escarpment on Black Mesa, was selected since there may have been greater exploitation of mountain sheep near this area; mountain sheep prefer rugged cliff country (Bailey 1931; Geist 1971; Lechleitner 1969; cf. Semé 1980a). The northern escarpment is an area of steep cliffs with broken, rocky terrain (Gumerman et al. 1972).

Data were collected for each of the physiographic variables (Table 55). The data, arranged by phase and site, include the percentages of the animal species (based on estimates of the minimum number of individuals for each species) from each site. Distance from a major drainage (drainage rank of 3 or 4) is the smallest distance from a site to the nearest major drainage. Drainages of this magnitude are the largest in the study area. Site elevations were taken from U.S.G.S. topographic maps and from 1 inch $=$ 400 feet scale maps provided by the Peabody Coal Company. The percentage of sagebrush-grassland areas within a 0.5 km radius of the site was measured with a polar planimeter, a device that measures area in irregular, planar surfaces. Such areas appear to have contained the primary concentrations of arable land (Catlin 1978:26–29). The choice of a 0.5 km radius is somewhat arbitrary. The original rationale was that this was a likely distance from a site for the placement of agricultural fields. In addition, it was found that circles of that size were the largest that could be used without eliminating intersite variation in the sagebrush-grassland percentages (Catlin 1978:93). This calculation should provide a way to distinguish between sites located primarily in sagebrush-grassland areas or in pinyon and juniper woodlands.

Several categories of animals were isolated to test the above hypothesis. These categories were based on species-level or higher taxonomic categories. They include the following: cottontail rabbit, jackrabbit, pocket gopher, prairie dog, ground squirrel and/or chipmunk, small rodents (rats and mice), carnivores, mountain sheep, mule deer, and antelope.

Correlation coefficients (Pearson's r) were calculated to measure the correlation between the relative frequencies of various animals at a site and the values of physiographic variables. Only the relative frequency of mountain sheep remains was examined in relationship to the distance from the northern escarpment. Two separate series of tests were performed. The first series included all sites analyzed for faunal remains. In the second series, only those sites considered permanent habitation sites were included to control for the functional differences between sites that were demonstrated in the first part of this paper. The results of these correlation tests are presented in Tables 56 and 57. (Antelope are not included since their remains were not present at enough sites to calculate a meaningful correlation.)

In the first series of tests (Table 56), the frequencies of only two animal species showed a significant correlation with any of the physiographic variables. There was a significant negative correlation between the frequency of mountain sheep remains and the distance to a major drainage, indicating that as a site's distance from a major drainage decreases, the amount of mountain sheep bone increases. There was also a significant negative correlation between the frequency of ground squirrel-chipmunk remains and the percentage of sagebrush-grassland. This suggests that these animals were

Table 55. Data on Physiographic Variables and the Relative Frequencies of Animal Species from Black Mesa Sites.

Phase and Site	Distance to Major Drain-age (m)	% Sage-brush-grass-land 0.5 km Radius	Eleva-tion (m)	Dis-tance to North-ern Escarp-ment (km)	% Artio-dactyl (Total)	% Moun-tain Sheep	% Mule Deer	% Ante-lope	% Cotton-tail	% Jack-rabbit	% Ground Squirrel-Chip-munk	% Pocket Gopher	% Prairie Dog	% Small Rodent	% Carni-vore
Lolomai															
D:7:152	200	65.0	1,914	7.1	2.8	0.0	1.4	0.7	40.0	12.4	2.8	10.3	3.5	13.2	2.8
D:11:1161	1,800	12.0	2,097	16.1	0.0	0.0	0.0	0.0	33.3	33.3	0.0	0.0	16.7	16.7	0.0
D:11:1162	1,600	19.0	2,091	16.1	0.0	0.0	0.0	0.0	50.0	0.0	0.0	0.0	0.0	0.0	0.0
Dot Klish															
D:9:2	2,700	100.0	1,798	40.8	14.0	0.0	0.0	0.0	33.3	13.0	0.0	7.0	0.0	7.0	0.0
D:10:1	400	100.0	1,859	28.4	18.2	0.0	3.0	3.0	27.4	15.1	3.0	6.0	3.0	6.0	0.0
Dinnebito															
D:7:23	150	63.5	2,012	3.7	30.0	12.5	10.0	5.0	20.0	17.5	5.0	2.5	2.5	2.5	12.5
D:7:134	400	44.0	2,100	7.4	17.5	13.5	2.2	1.7	42.2	20.9	0.4	9.6	1.7	3.1	4.4
D:7:135	250	53.0	2,073	7.4	3.7	1.8	0.0	1.8	46.3	5.6	1.8	27.8	1.8	7.4	1.8
D:7:136	200	53.0	2,063	7.4	5.4	1.8	1.8	0.9	44.8	9.5	1.8	9.5	2.9	6.6	6.5
D:11:338	1,200	33.0	2,067	16.0	7.1	7.1	0.0	0.0	28.6	14.3	0.0	0.0	7.1	14.2	14.3
D:11:1153	2,500	36.0	2,106	15.8	11.0	0.0	0.0	0.0	67.0	11.0	0.0	0.0	11.0	0.0	0.0
D:11:1158	2,200	23.0	2,112	16.1	0.0	0.0	0.0	0.0	40.0	40.0	0.0	0.0	20.0	0.0	0.0
Wepo															
D:11:814	1,900	32.0	2,085	15.4	7.7	0.0	0.0	0.0	7.7	7.7	7.7	23.1	15.4	15.4	15.4
Wepo/Lamoki															
D:11:290	2,600	21.0	2,140	14.8	2.8	0.9	1.9	0.0	44.5	25.8	4.7	8.1	0.5	16.1	5.3
D:11:1084	2,700	12.0	2,140	14.8	0.0	0.0	0.0	0.0	0.0	0.0	0.0	0.0	0.0	0.0	0.0

Table 55—continued

Phase and Site	Distance to Major Drainage (m)	% Sage-brush-grass-land 0.5 km Radius	Elevation (m)	Distance to Northern Escarpment (km)	% Artiodactyl (Total)	% Mountain Sheep	% Mule Deer	% Antelope	% Cottontail	% Jackrabbit	% Ground Squirrel-Chipmunk	% Pocket Gopher	% Prairie Dog	% Small Rodent	% Carnivore
Lamoki															
D:7:18	300	46.0	2,036	4.0	19.2	0.0	0.0	0.0	34.6	7.7	0.0	7.7	0.0	15.3	15.3
D:11:97	800	100.0	1,981	18.5	6.2	6.2	0.0	0.0	25.0	25.0	12.5	0.0	0.0	12.5	0.0
D:11:352	2,100	18.0	2,118	14.8	0.5	0.0	0.0	0.0	48.7	26.9	6.2	0.5	1.0	12.5	2.0
D:11:354	2,700	46.0	2,109	14.2	0.0	0.0	0.0	0.0	40.0	40.0	0.0	0.0	10.0	0.0	0.0
D:11:409	2,600	28.0	2,121	14.2	20.0	10.0	10.0	0.0	40.0	10.0	0.0	0.0	10.0	10.0	10.0
D:11:1081	2,200	35.0	2,134	14.1	0.0	0.0	0.0	0.0	0.0	0.0	0.0	0.0	0.0	0.0	0.0
Toreva															
D:7:19	300	44.0	2,030	4.0	5.9	5.9	5.9	0.0	47.0	11.8	0.0	17.6	0.0	11.8	0.0
D:7:27	900	65.0	2,024	7.1	8.0	0.0	1.6	3.2	41.9	12.9	1.6	8.0	3.2	19.3	1.6
D:9:1	3,200	92.5	1,798	42.5	16.3	0.0	8.3	8.3	8.3	16.3	0.0	0.0	0.0	8.3	0.0
D:11:275	2,200	14.0	2,128	16.0	2.4	0.6	1.2	0.0	47.7	14.1	7.1	3.5	0.0	14.0	1.8
D:11:348	2,400	38.0	2,121	13.8	2.4	0.0	2.4	0.0	28.5	19.0	2.4	24.0	0.0	14.3	2.4
D:11:356	2,700	69.0	2,112	14.2	2.4	0.0	0.0	0.0	43.4	24.0	0.0	7.2	4.8	14.4	0.0
D:11:298	2,600	9.0	2,115	15.1	0.0	0.0	0.0	0.0	0.0	0.0	0.0	0.0	0.0	0.0	0.0
D:11:324	1,600	36.0	2,085	15.5	50.0	0.0	0.0	0.0	0.0	0.0	0.0	0.0	0.0	0.0	0.0
D:11:879	1,600	36.0	2,097	15.9	0.0	0.0	0.0	0.0	0.0	0.0	0.0	0.0	0.0	0.0	0.0
D:11:1161	1,800	12.0	2,097	16.1	50.0	0.0	0.0	50.0	0.0	0.0	0.0	0.0	0.0	0.0	0.0
D:11:1170	1,600	33.3	2,079	15.1	100.0	0.0	100.0	0.0	0.0	0.0	0.0	0.0	0.0	0.0	0.0

Note: Relative frequencies were calculated using the data on minimum number of individuals represented.

Table 56. Pearson's Correlation Coefficients for Relative Frequencies of Animal Species and Physiographic Variables: Series I.

Animal	Distance to Major Drainage	% Sagebrush-Grassland	Elevation	Distance to Northern Escarpment
Cottontail	−0.140	0.060	0.063	—
Jackrabbit	0.102	0.162	−0.030	—
Ground squirrel-Chipmunk	−0.050	−0.377	0.087	—
Prairie dog	0.068	−0.175	0.137	—
Pocket gopher	0.341	0.189	0.328	—
Small rodents	−0.122	0.189	−0.171	—
Carnivore	−0.207	−0.067	0.056	—
Mountain sheep	−0.503*	0.132	0.043	0.239
Mule deer	0.309	0.021	−0.126	—

*$p \leq 0.05$, $n = 32$, $df = 30$

Table 57. Pearson's Correlation Coefficients for Relative Frequencies of Animal Species and Physiographic Variables: Series II.

Animal	Distance to Major Drainage	% Sagebrush-Grassland	Elevation	Distance to Northern Escarpment
Cottontail	−0.170	0.420	0.480*	—
Jackrabbit	0.320	0.020	0.176	—
Ground squirrel-Chipmunk	−0.040	−0.732*	0.220	—
Prairie dog	0.120	0.180	0.220	—
Pocket gopher	0.310	0.130	0.680*	—
Small rodents	0.353	−0.342	0.280	—
Carnivore	−0.240	−0.757*	0.220	—
Mountain sheep	−0.435	−0.120	0.153	−0.540*
Mule deer	0.309	0.021	−0.126	—

*$p \leq 0.05$, $n = 20$, $df = 18$

exploited more in the pinyon and juniper woodland, as would be expected, since the preferred habitat of most ground squirrels and chipmunks is the pinyon and juniper woodland.

The second series of correlation coefficient tests (run using only habitation sites) showed several more statistically significant correlations. Again, there was a significant negative correlation between the distance to the northern escarpment and the amount of mountain sheep remains found in a site. This suggests that more mountain sheep exploitation occurred in sites closer to the northern escarpment, as would be expected if the inference that mountain sheep on Black Mesa primarily inhabited the nothern escarpment is correct.

The relative frequencies of both ground squirrel-chipmunk remains and carnivore remains were negatively correlated at a statistically significant level with the amount of sagebrush-grassland within a 0.5 km radius of the sites. As noted above, such a correlation is expected for ground squirrel-chipmunk remains. There is also some reason to expect such a correlation with carnivore remains, since many of the species found on Black Mesa primarily inhabit the pinyon and juniper woodland (Bailey 1931; Findley et al. 1975; Lechleitner 1969). In addition to these correlations, it should be noted that there appears to have been more frequent exploitation of antelope by inhabitants of sites in sagebrush-grassland areas.

Significant positive correlations were found between elevation and the relative frequencies of cottontail and pocket gopher remains. Although some studies have suggested that no difference in cottontail population levels would be expected at higher elevations (Bailey 1931; Lechleitner 1969), Stiger (1977) did find on the Kaibab Plateau of Utah that cottontails are almost exclusively in forested areas at higher elevations. The interpretation of the positive correlation with pocket gopher frequencies is difficult because, as Douglas (1969) has pointed out, pocket gophers are notorious for burrowing into archaeological deposits. Therefore, we are not sure if all pocket gopher remains from Black Mesa sites were procured by prehistoric groups. In addition, the significant positive correlation is unexpected, because information on pocket gopher habitats (Bailey 1931; Lechleitner 1969) does not suggest greater populations of these animals at higher elevations.

The second series of correlation coefficients showed several more statistically significant coefficients. In all but one case (ground squirrel-chipmunk frequency and the percentage of sagebrush-grassland), these significant correlations were not significant in the first series of tests in which all sites were included. The inclusion of limited-activity sites in the first series of tests may have obscured significant correlations because such sites were primarily plant collecting stations where few animals were hunted. Thus, even if certain animals were available in the area where the limited-activity site was located, they may not have been exploited because of the priority of collecting plant foods.

There were several significant correlations between various physiographic variables and the relative frequencies of particular animal species, but most of the correlation coefficients proved to be nonsignificant. This may indicate either that animal hunting did not normally follow a strict least-effort strategy or that the prehistoric distribution of animals on Black Mesa was not highly determined by the environmental variables considered. The hypothesis that animal hunting was regulated by the time and place of plant food exploitation may also account for the lack of significant correlations; the animals hunted would reflect the areas from which the plant foods were derived. However, the associations between physiographic variables and relative frequencies of mountain sheep and antelope especially seem to indicate the influence of site location on the hunting of these animals.

Conclusions

This paper has attempted to test some causes of intersite variation in faunal remains. Several conclusions can be drawn from such tests. First, there were intersite differences in faunal remains as a result of differences in site functions. Second, there were differences in the fauna exploited by populations residing in different areas on Black Mesa. Third, this study has shown that animal hunting was largely determined by the time and place of plant food production. Thus, different types of sites with different floral assemblages would be expected to contain different faunal assemblages. These conclusions indicate that some of the previous proposals concerning prehistoric faunal exploitation on Black Mesa may not be valid. For example, Douglas (1972) has suggested there was a peak in artiodactyl exploitation in the Wepo phase. However, the two Wepo phase sites analyzed by Douglas are from two very different areas. D:7:11 is located on the northern bench of Black Mesa, above the floor of Long House Valley, while D:11:18 is in a predominantly sagebrush-grassland area between Coal Mine Wash and Moenkopi Wash (Gumerman et al. 1972). In addition, the two sites are different in structural diversity and complexity. Such differences in site type and site location must be considered in future faunal analysis if we are to make valid inferences about patterns of faunal exploitation.

11

The Relationship of Source Distance to Conservation of Chipped Stone Raw Materials

Margerie Green

Many early publications (e.g., Gumerman 1970; Gumerman et al. 1972) on the prehistory of northern Black Mesa suggested that prehistoric Black Mesa sites were characterized by very few chipped stone artifacts. A typical site report from an early publication generally describes fewer than 20 lithic artifacts. The low frequencies of this artifact class were attributed to the absence of local raw materials suitable for knapping, since the nearest potential sources of raw materials were thought to be the gravel terraces of the San Juan and Colorado rivers (Gumerman 1970:19).

Research conducted in the area since 1975 has shown that these earlier interpretations are incorrect. Survey work and excavations that consistently sifted all excavated dirt through 6.35 mm (quarter-inch) mesh have shown that although the numbers of lithic artifacts on Black Mesa sites do not approach those found elsewhere in the Southwest, they can no longer be considered rare. For example, the average density of lithic artifacts for several hundred sites located during a survey of Black Mesa in 1975 was one per two square meters. In contrast, for 39 sites located on a survey of part of the Chevelon Canyon drainage in east-central Arizona in 1971, there was an average density of one lithic artifact in every square meter (Green 1975).

In addition to finding more lithic artifacts on sites, a chipped stone raw material source survey begun in 1976 by Phil Schafer of the U.S. Geological Survey and me has established that many materials were readily available to prehistoric populations in the area. This paper, which was written in 1977 (Green 1977b), reports on only the first stage of the raw material source survey. A complete presentation of the results can be found in Green (1982). Materials from a variety of other raw material sources in northeastern Arizona were also exploited.

It was felt that prehistoric Black Mesa populations utilized both nearby and distant raw material sources, which offer an excellent data base to test hypotheses concerning minimization of effort in prehistoric activities. General archaeological research (Johnson 1977) and specific studies of the prehistoric American Southwest (Plog and Hill 1971) utilize several models built on the assumption that prehistoric populations minimized effort and maximized gain. However, few archaeological tests of this assumption have been made, and the tests that have been conducted have sometimes suffered from a lack of appropriate data bases. For example, Chapman's (1977) study of raw material procurement and lithic technology in the lower Chaco River of New Mexico attempted to test the effort-minimization and gain-maximization hypothesis. However, he concluded that the test was hindered by the small geographical area he could consider, and he thus suggested that testing the hypothesis on a larger, regional scale would be more appropriate (1977:446). The wide spatial distribution in the raw material sources utilized by Black Mesa populations provides such a regional scale for testing the hypothesis.

The Hypothesis

This research tests the hypothesis that the degree to which chipped stone raw material types were used and conserved is related to the distance between the source of the material and the site at which it is found. Chipped stone artifacts made from distantly obtained raw materials should occur in lower frequencies at sites than those artifacts made from material from closer sources. However, when the former are present, they should have been used to a relatively greater extent than local materials. This hypothesis clearly has a mini-max rationale, since it is based on the assumption that populations strive to maximize gains (in this case, chipped stone raw materials) while minimizing the effort expended in procuring these materials.

Much of the theoretical base of this hypothesis is derived from Binford's (1976) study of Nunamiut hunting trips. Binford tested the assumption that the more important an item, the more apparent it should be in the archaeological record. He found instead that in the technological assemblage of certain societies, specifically the Nunamiut, an important item is maintained and repaired (curated). Thus, it does not appear as frequently in the archaeological record as do less important items. On the other hand, an expedient technological assemblage is one in which items are manufactured, used, and immediately discarded.

The concept of curation is not being tested in this paper; rather, its implications are adopted for the concept of conservation. The dictionary definition of conserve is "to keep in a safe or sound state; preserve from loss, decay, waste or injury." The relevant portion of the definition for this research is "preserve from . . . waste." Rather than expecting either expedient or conservative use of raw materials, I predict a continuum, with locally derived materials reflecting more expedient use and distantly derived materials conforming to the conservation model. More distantly derived materials should show a greater degree of conservation than locally derived materials because more effort must have been expended to procure them.

The effort expended was probably not just in the physical sense of people traveling to get the material, if indeed each individual secured his own supply. Depending on the actual distance to the source and the terrain to be covered, individuals would be removed from the domestic work force for varying lengths of time. This loss of energy to the system must also be considered under "effort expended." On the other hand, certain members of the group may have procured the material for everyone, or it may have been traded for, by individuals or by groups, with people from outside the area. In either case, some form of payment must have been necessary. In contrast, locally derived materials should have been easily available to all, unless other, unknown restrictions were placed on their use.

The second, related hypothesis states that if distance to source was the major factor affecting use and conservation of raw materials and it is held constant, then patterns of raw material use at sites should not differ significantly. However, the effects of factors other than distance to source, if any, should be more apparent among distantly derived materials; the procurement of more distantly derived materials may have presented a more complex situation.

If we assume that the population at each site independently secured its own supply of chipped stone raw materials, several factors may have varied the usage of distantly derived materials. First, the amount of time spent away from home procuring material increases as distance to sources increases. Certain flexible "home" situations may have allowed more time to be spent elsewhere. In addition, knowledge of distant sources may not have been shared. If we assume that populations tend to become extremely familiar with their territory, the location of resources in that area should have been common knowledge. However, the information about more distant sources might not have been shared, especially if sites did not have overlapping occupation spans. Carrying this one step further, even if the distant source was known to all, perhaps it was only through exchange ties, not shared by all, that the material could be acquired.

It may also have been the case that distantly derived materials were acquired through redistribution from only certain sites in an area. If this was the situation, these redistributive centers may be expected to exhibit different patterns of raw material use. For example, raw material might have passed through some primary stages of manufacture before being distributed throughout the area. Some of these situations may eventually be rephrased in hypothesis form and tested. The present research, however, will only be concerned with testing the importance of distance as a major factor governing raw material use. The following sections describe the data base.

Chipped Stone Raw Material Source Survey

The chipped stone raw material source survey has located potential sources for approximately 75 % of the lithic raw material types found on Black Mesa sites. Subsequent investigation has increased this figure to 90 %.

The first priority of the source survey was to identify materials available on Black Mesa, particularly those obtainable within the study area. Thin layers of baked siltstone and secondarily deposited blocks of petrified wood are both found along Dinnebito Wash (Figure 11). Siderite, an iron carbonate, occurs in both nodules and layers in numerous outcrops within the study area. All three of these materials occur in the Wepo formation that caps most of the mesa. Along the northern escarpment is a secondary deposit of quartzite cobbles and small pebbles of chert. Sandstone, which was sometimes used for knapping material, is also abundant on the mesa. Taken together, these materials were used to manufacture about 50 % of the lithic artifacts at the two sites discussed below.

In addition to the above materials, several types of material are available from areas surrounding Black Mesa. Approximately 28 km to the north of the project area are outcrops of limestone and chert in the Owl Rock member of the Chinle formation. Petrified wood from the petrified forest member of the Chinle formation also outcrops beneath the Owl Rock. These occur together in alcoves at the base of Skeleton Mesa. The Navajo sandstone, which is so apparent to the north of Black Mesa, contains chert-producing limestone layers in such areas as the Shonto Plateau, Red Lake, and Cow Springs. These layers are often badly fractured and only several millimeters thick, but were observed to exceed 35 cm in thickness at the Cow Springs locality. The limestone matrix was also used for knapping material. The Owl Rock and Navajo cherts are located approximately 29 and 43 km, respectively, from the project area and together account for about 35 % of the lithic artifacts found at the two sites.

Several gravel terraces and areas with secondary gravel deposits are located between 32 and 71 km from the project area. Middle Mesa and another gravel terrace near Red Lake contain quartzite, chert, chalcedony, and petrified wood. Similar materials can be found in the gravels near Church Rock. Chert gravels, including those found on Black Mesa, account for less than 11 % of the lithic artifacts from the sites.

Site Descriptions

The chipped stone artifacts from two sites, D:11:290 and D:11:356, compose the data for this study. The two sites were located during the 1975 survey. Lithic material recovered during subsequent excavations in 1976 is used for this analysis. The sites are approximately 0.8 km apart, and for the purposes of this analysis, they will be treated as though they were the same distance from raw material sources. In addition to being located in the same area, the sites appear to be functionally similar, since a similar range of structural types is present on both sites.

Site D:11:290 is located in a pinyon and juniper woodland flanked on the north and east by wide, flat areas of sage. A large site, covering over 12,000 m², it had 25 structures, including four masonry rooms, two kivas,

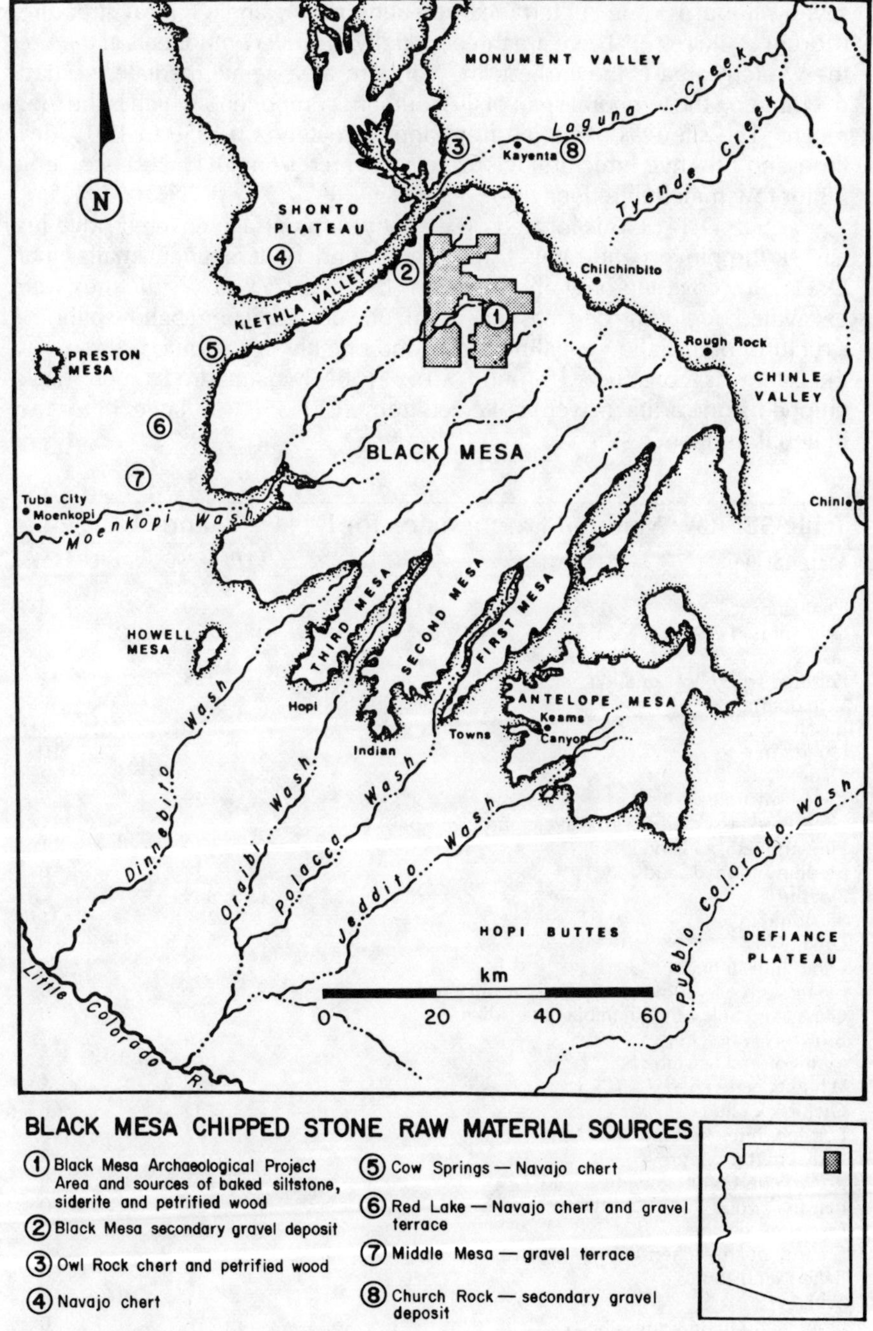

BLACK MESA CHIPPED STONE RAW MATERIAL SOURCES

① Black Mesa Archaeological Project Area and sources of baked siltstone, siderite and petrified wood

② Black Mesa secondary gravel deposit

③ Owl Rock chert and petrified wood

④ Navajo chert

⑤ Cow Springs — Navajo chert

⑥ Red Lake — Navajo chert and gravel terrace

⑦ Middle Mesa — gravel terrace

⑧ Church Rock — secondary gravel deposit

Figure 11. Black Mesa chipped stone raw materials.

seven pithouses, one subterranean mealing room, and 11 jacal structures (Corum et al. 1977). There are three spatially distinct components at the site: the western area is the earliest; the northern area is intermediate, perhaps overlapping the temporal span of the southern component, which is the most recent. The site was occupied from approximately A.D. 950 to 1100. Two thousand fifty-five lithic artifacts were recovered from D:11:290 (see Table 58 for raw material frequencies).

Site D:11:356 is located on a gently sloping sage-covered ridge just east of the pinyon and juniper and sage boundary. It is much smaller than D:11:290, covering only about 680 m^2 (Neily 1977). Five structures were excavated, including one masonry room, one deep and one shallow pithouse structure, one shallow mealing room, and one kiva. Tree-ring dates suggest the site was constructed around A.D. 1118. Two hundred ninety-seven chipped stone artifacts were collected from D:11:356 (see Table 58 for raw material frequencies).

Table 58. Raw Material Frequencies for D:11:290 and D:11:356.

Material Type	D:11:290	D:11:356
Chalcedony	39	6
Unidentified chert	11	0
Jasper	1	0
Petrified wood (low quality)	123	12
Vein quartz	7	0
Basalt	0	1
Quartzite	63	10
Shale	3	4
Baked siltstone	29	9
Limestone (associated with Navajo and Owl Rock cherts)	9	1
Fine-grained sandstone	30	17
Medium-grained sandstone	13	0
Siderite	489	72
Siltstone	296	31
Unknown	25	0
Other limestone	1	0
Opaque green-yellow chert (from Kayenta area)	2	0
Glassy volcanic other than black obsidian	1	0
Brown Navajo chert	115	34
Multicolored Navajo chert	43	2
White Navajo chert	120	15
Owl Rock chert	293	68
Purple-white chert (possibly Owl Rock)	87	7
Gray chert (from gravel)	90	2
Brown chert (from gravel)	111	5
Petrified wood (high quality)	5	0
Fracture-line chert	19	1
Creamy opaque chert	12	0
Baked sandstone	1	0
Schist	1	0
Oolitic and fossiliferous cherts	16	0
Total	2,055	297

Variable Measurement

In the test discussed below, material type was broken down as finely as possible, especially in the case of commonly used cherts that come from a variety of sources. Distance between sites on Black Mesa and sources of raw materials was measured on an ordinal, or relative, scale, rather than on a ratio scale, for three reasons. First, the low frequencies for the majority of material types necessitated collapsing categories for statistical analyses. Thus, sources at different distances from the sites had to be grouped together. Second, although a potential source, meaning an outcrop or deposit, was found during the source survey, we could not establish through visual means that it was the particular source used by Black Mesa populations. It is, however, generally safe to assume that the material came from the vicinity of the source that we found, since the geological formations or conditions under which the materials were produced are, in most cases, very localized. For example, baked siltstone is formed by coal fires, and the major coal-bearing layers are in the Wepo formation that caps Black Mesa. Finally, the type of terrain separating site from source might have been a more important factor than absolute distance in terms of judging the amount of effort necessary to reach that source. Given this proposal, a source on the mesa itself is considered closer than a source off the mesa in the analysis discussed below.

The material types from the two sites thus were grouped into three categories on the basis of distance to source. The first group includes materials available on Black Mesa, and the second is made up of materials that outcrop off the mesa but are within 48 km of the project area. The third category includes all cherts from gravels and other materials from distant sources. Unfortunately, any artifacts manufactured from Black Mesa chert gravel would also be sorted into this category; it appears almost impossible to separate gravels by source. However, it is doubtful that Black Mesa chert was used to a great extent because of the small size of the pebbles (generally less than 2–3 cm in diameter).

Several technological characteristics of the lithic assemblages from the two sites were measured. The first was the amount of cortex present. The amount of cortex was divided into three categories. (1) Primary flakes are those with greater than 90 % of their dorsal surface covered by cortex. These flakes were removed from the core at early stages of manufacture and include the first flakes removed from the core. (2) Secondary flakes are those with less than 90 % and greater than about 10 % of their dorsal surface covered with cortex. The lower amount of cortex is generally taken to indicate flake removal from farther inside the core, presumably at later stages of manufacture than primary flakes. (3) Tertiary flakes are those with little or no cortex on the dorsal surface; they include resharpening and retouch flakes.

In addition to the amount of cortex, the number of dorsal scars was recorded. Dorsal flake scars are evidence of the prior removal of flakes from cores. The number of dorsal scars on each flake generally increases as the knapper gets farther into the core. Finally, general size measures (e.g., length, width, and thickness) were also recorded. These afford some indication of stage of manufacture (e.g., retouch flakes are generally smaller than primary flakes) and are more accurate than raw frequencies for describing the amount of material present.

The amounts of debitage and utilized material were also recorded. Debitage is the debris that results from lithic manufacture and includes unutilized flakes and shatter. Utilized material includes any artifact with evidence of special preparation (manufacture modification) and/or utilization (use modification), including the entire range from utilized flakes to projectile points.

Testing the Hypothesis

Five test implications were derived from the first hypothesis which states that chipped stone raw material should have been used and conserved relative to the distance from its source to the site at which it was found. The first two implications are: (1) frequencies of chipped stone raw materials at sites should be inversely proportional to the relative distance between site and source, and (2) size measures for artifacts made from different raw material types should be inversely proportional to the distance between site and source. The rationale behind the first two test implications is that it is more expedient to carry quantities of rocks over shorter distances, and so more and larger pieces of the easily accessible material should appear on sites.

The observed frequencies of the raw material types are consistent with the hypothesis, showing that more artifacts were manufactured from local materials. The ratios for the two sites (D:11:290 and D:11:356) of the frequencies for the closest to the most distantly derived materials are 3.6:2.3:1.0 and 10.3:8.5:1.0, respectively. Since D:11:290 was occupied prior to D:11:356, these ratios in part reflect the tendency noted by Fernstrom (this volume) for the frequency of material obtained from distant sources to decrease through time. Mean length, width, and thickness were calculated to determine whether the frequencies actually represented greater amounts of material or merely more pieces of material. These measures, shown in Table 59, further substantiated the conclusion, indicating that artifacts manufactured from local materials were generally larger (these figures are discussed in more detail below, and tests concerning the significance of the differences are presented).

The next two test implications that were examined are: (3) there should be significantly more debitage from locally derived material than from more distant sources and (4) evidence of utilization should be greater for distantly derived materials, including significantly more utilized flakes, manufacture-modified artifacts, and more utilized edges on single artifacts. Test implications (3) and (4) address the question of most efficiently balancing material procurement effort and its use. Test implication (3) is expected because locally derived materials require relatively less procurement effort, and therefore,

Table 59. Size Measurements (in mm) for the Artifacts from the Three Source Distance Categories.

| Variable | Site | Source Distance Category | | | | | |
| | | 1 | | 2 | | 3 | |
		$\bar{x}$	s^2	$\bar{x}$	s^2	$\bar{x}$	s^2
Length	D:11:290	38.30	314.63	27.55	127.99	23.81	79.35
	D:11:356	34.92	272.61	29.89	112.67	23.93	77.07
Width	D:11:290	33.09	252.97	23.07	108.11	19.09	61.10
	D:11:356	30.35	245.49	24.36	103.27	18.00	39.57
Thickness	D:11:290	14.42	126.52	8.84	37.68	7.22	43.97
	D:11:356	11.74	66.58	9.53	37.35	6.27	6.07
Sample size	D:11:290	1,055		678		293	
	D:11:356	155		127		15	

there should be less concern for wastage of material. Test implication (4) is expected because increased use of material that is more difficult to acquire should have been more efficient.

To compare the amount of material used relative to source distance, all utilized artifacts, regardless of function, were placed in one category. Cores and manufacturing debris formed the second category. The chi-square statistic was calculated to test for a nonrandom association between material use and distance to source. The test, using data from D:11:290, indicated a nonrandom association that is significant at the 0.001 level (Table 60). Although only significant at the 0.11 level, the frequencies from D:11:356 followed the predicted trend within each source-distance category, as shown in Table 61. There was more debitage than expected from local material, and more of the distant material was utilized than would be predicted under a random model. For test implication (4), proportionally more utilized edges per artifact were expected for raw materials from more distant sources. At both sites, this expectation was met with chi-square values significant at the 0.01 level, as shown in Tables 62 and 63.

The final test implication derived to test the first hypothesis is: (5) there should be more evidence of early manufacturing stages for local material, and the opposite should apply to distant material. This is expected because the transport of waste material should not have been as critical over short distances as over long distances. To test this proposal, chi-square values were calculated for cross-tabulations of (a) flake type (i.e., primary, secondary, and tertiary flakes) and source distance and (b) number of dorsal scars and source distance. The predicted result was that there should be significantly fewer primary flakes from distant raw materials and that these materials should exhibit significantly more dorsal scars than flakes of local material. These tests were significant at both sites at the 0.01 level, as shown in Tables 64—

Table 60. Observed and Expected Frequencies of Debitage and Utilized Flakes at D:11:290 for the Three Source Distance Categories.

	Source Distance Category						Observed Totals
	1		2		3		
	Obs.	Exp.	Obs.	Exp.	Obs.	Exp.	
Debitage	834	773.5	487	498.5	165	214.0	1,486
Utilized Flakes	218	278.5	191	179.5	126	77.0	535
Observed Totals	1,052		678		291		2,021
	52.0 %		33.5 %		14.4 %		

$\chi^2 = 61.2$, $df = 2$, $p \leq 0.001$

Table 61. Observed and Expected Frequencies of Debitage and Utilized Flakes at D:11:356 for the Three Source Distance Categories.

	Source Distance Category						Observed Totals
	1		2		3		
	Obs.	Exp.	Obs.	Exp.	Obs.	Exp.	
Debitage	137	132.8	108	110.0	11	13.2	256
Utilized Flakes	14	18.2	17	15.0	4	1.8	35
Observed Totals	151		125		15		291
	51.9 %		43.0 %		5.2 %		

$\chi^2 = 4.41$, $df = 2$, $p = 0.11$

67. However, the values for the third source-distance category depart from the expected pattern. This discrepancy may be caused by the fact that, by definition, gravels occur with a rolled percussion cortex. Also, in the other two source-distance categories, cortex and weathering are often absent because of natural fracturing of layers. Even with this discrepancy, the results are significant and substantiate the hypothesis.

To test the second hypothesis, that distance was the most important factor governing raw material use, it first was necessary to demonstrate that patterns of raw material use varied significantly among the three source-distance categories. This is necessary because if all chipped stone raw materials used at one site followed the same pattern, regardless of distance, then finding this same pattern at a second site would not provide an adequate test of the hypothesis. However, if it can be shown that raw material use varied

Table 62. Observed and Expected Frequencies of Worked Edges on Artifacts from D:11:290 for the Three Source Distance Categories.

| Number of Worked Edges | Source Distance Category | | | | | | Observed Totals |
| | 1 | | 2 | | 3 | | |
	Obs.	Exp.	Obs.	Exp.	Obs.	Exp.	
0	837	777.5	490	501.1	166	214.3	1,493
1	146	176.0	120	113.5	72	48.5	338
2	61	74.5	43	48.0	39	20.5	143
3	8	22.4	25	14.4	10	6.2	43
4	0	1.6	0	1.0	3	0.4	3
Observed Totals	1,052		678		290		2,020

$\chi^2 = 89.39$, $df = 8$, $p < 0.001$

Table 63. Observed and Expected Frequencies of Worked Edges on Artifacts from D:11:356 for the Three Source Distance Categories.

| Number of Worked Edges | Source Distance Category | | | | | | Observed Totals |
| | 1 | | 2 | | 3 | | |
	Obs.	Exp.	Obs.	Exp.	Obs.	Exp.	
0	143	136.7	109	112.0	10	13.2	262
1–3	12	18.3	18	15.0	5	1.8	35
Observed Totals	155		127		15		297

$\chi^2 = 9.81$, $df = 2$, $p = 0.01$

Table 64. Observed and Expected Frequencies of Flake Types at D:11:290 for the Three Source Distance Categories.

| Flake Type | Source Distance Category | | | | | | Observed Totals |
| | 1 | | 2 | | 3 | | |
	Obs.	Exp.	Obs.	Exp.	Obs.	Exp.	
Primary	47	44.5	22	29.0	17	12.5	86
Secondary	288	261.2	129	170.3	88	73.5	505
Tertiary	699	728.3	523	474.7	186	205.0	1,408
Observed Totals	1,034		674		291		1,999

$\chi^2 = 26.88$, $df = 4$, $p = 0.001$

Table 65. Observed and Expected Frequencies of Flake Types at D:11:356 for the Three Source Distance Categories.

| | Source Distance Category | | | | | | |
| | 1 | | 2 | | 3 | | Observed |
Flake Type	Obs.	Exp.	Obs.	Exp.	Obs.	Exp.	Totals
Primary and Secondary	44	35.0	17	28.6	6	3.4	67
Tertiary	110	119.0	109	97.4	9	11.6	228
Observed Totals	154		126		15		295

$\chi^2 = 11.67$, $df = 2$, $p = 0.005$

Table 66. Observed and Expected Frequencies of the Number of Dorsal Scars on Artifacts from D:11:290 for the Three Source Distance Categories.

| | Source Distance Category | | | | | | |
| | 1 | | 2 | | 3 | | Observed |
Number of Dorsal Scars	Obs.	Exp.	Obs.	Exp.	Obs.	Exp.	Totals
0	114	103.1	61	66.4	23	28.5	198
1	203	176.5	79	113.7	57	48.8	339
2	315	308.7	199	198.9	79	85.4	593
3	236	251.9	173	162.4	75	69.7	484
4	100	114.5	91	73.8	29	31.7	220
5	45	53.1	40	34.2	17	14.7	102
6–7	23	28.1	22	18.1	9	7.8	54
> 7	16	16.1	13	10.4	2	4.5	31
Observed Totals	1,052		678		291		2,021

$\chi^2 = 33.95$, $df = 14$, $p = 0.0025$

significantly according to source distance and that this variation follows the same pattern at a second site, the hypothesis is supported.

The null hypothesis for the tests is that there is no difference in size dimensions or in the number of worked edges among artifacts of materials from sources at varying distances from the site. The alternative hypothesis is that the size and utilized edge variations among source-distance categories are so great that there is a high probability that they are unlikely to be the result of chance variation. Analysis of variance was employed for the variables length, width, thickness, and number of worked edges per artifact. The Kruskal-Wallis test, a nonparametric equivalent of analysis of variance, is used for the cortex and number of dorsal flake scar variables. It was necessary to treat number of dorsal scars on an ordinal scale because bifacially worked

Table 67. Observed and Expected Frequencies of the Number of Dorsal Scars on Artifacts from D:11:356 for the Three Source Distance Categories.

Number of	Source Distance Category						Observed
	1		2		3		
Dorsal Scars	Obs.	Exp.	Obs.	Exp.	Obs.	Exp.	Totals
0–1	30	29.7	25	24.4	2	2.9	57
2	51	43.0	24	35.5	8	4.2	83
3	51	50.6	42	41.5	4	4.9	97
4–8	23	31.3	36	25.7	1	3.0	60
Observed Totals	155		127		15		297

$\chi^2 = 16.77$, $df = 6$, $p = 0.01$

Table 68. Results of Analysis of Variance and Kruskal-Wallis Tests for Differences in Artifact Size Measurements and in Technological Attribute Frequencies Among the Three Source Distance Categories.

Variable	D:11:290		D:11:356	
	Test Statistic	p	Test Statistic	p
Length	$F = 167.84$	0.001	$F = 7.31$	0.001
Width	$F = 187.05$	0.001	$F = 10.96$	0.001
Thickness	$F = 112.66$	0.001	$F = 6.14$	0.003
Utilized edges	$F = 35.85$	0.001	$F = 7.17$	0.001
Dorsal scars	$H = 0.47$	NS	$H = 3.65$	NS
Cortex	$H = 1.34$	NS	$H = 1.76$	NS

artifacts were recorded as "99," which does not represent an accurate count of dorsal flake scars. The level of rejection for all the tests is 0.05.

For both sites, length, width, thickness, and the number of utilized edges per artifact were significantly different among the three source-distance categories (Table 68). However, the tests using the number of dorsal scars and the cortex variables were not statistically significant at the 0.05 level (Table 68). In nonstatistical terms, these results indicate that the size of lithic artifacts from sources of different distances differs significantly. As noted earlier, overall size decreases as distance to source increases. In addition, the number of utilized edges on a single artifact differs significantly according to source distance—again, as indicated earlier, in an inverse relationship.

The hypothesis was not supported by the tests involving number of dorsal scars and amount of cortex. There are two possible explanations for this discrepancy. First, all raw materials, regardless of source distance, were subjected to the same manufacturing stages at the sites. Perhaps it was preferable to leave some, or all, of the cortex on a cobble and carry it back to the site without exposed surfaces or sharp edges. The only differences then would have been the sizes of artifacts manufactured and the number of edges used on artifacts of different materials. The second possibility relates to a problem (mentioned earlier) with the characteristics of the raw material and not to the prehistoric utilization of the raw materials. Not all of the raw materials occur naturally with cortex, particularly those in the two closest source-distance categories. This factor may be skewing the data by producing higher frequencies of distant materials with cortex and lower frequencies of the nearby materials with cortex than expected.

The final step in the analysis involves determining whether the pattern of raw material use for artifacts within each source-distance category was the same at the two sites to see if other factors also affect the variables considered. The null hypothesis is that there is no difference between the means of the variables for the two sites. The t-test was used for the interval scale variables: length, width, thickness, and the number of worked edges per artifact. The Kolmogorov-Smirnov two-sample test was employed for the ordinal scale variables, the amount of cortex, and the number of dorsal scars. The results of the t-tests were slightly more complex than those for the Kolmogorov-Smirnov test, so the latter will be discussed first. The results of both sets of tests are presented in Table 69.

Table 69. Results of t-tests and Kolmogorov-Smirnov Tests for Differences in Artifact Size Measurements and in Technological Attribute Frequencies Between D:11:290 and D:11:356 for Each of the Source Distance Categories.

| | Source Distance Category | | | | | |
| | 1 | | 2 | | 3 | |
Variable	Test Statistic	p	Test Statistic	p	Test Statistic	p
Length	$t = 2.24$	0.05	$t = -2.16$	0.05	$t = 0.02$	NS
Width	$t = 2.00$	0.05	$t = -1.29$	NS	$t = 0.38$	NS
Thickness	$t = 2.86$	0.05	$t = 0.30$	NS	$t = 0.55$	NS
Utilized edges	$t = 4.10$	0.01	$t = 3.29$	0.01	$t = 4.82$	0.01
Cortex	$T_1 = 0.04$	NS	$T_1 = 0.09$	NS	$T_1 = 0.06$	NS
Dorsal scars	$T_1 = 0.11$	NS	$T_1 = 0.11$	NS	$T_1 = 0.14$	NS

For both the amount of cortex and the number of dorsal scars, the null hypothesis was accepted. For the tests comparing the mean lengths of artifacts from the two sites from both the first and second source-distance categories, the null hypothesis was rejected. However, it was accepted for the third category. For mean width, the null hypothesis was rejected for the first source-distance category, but it was accepted for the other two categories. The artifacts from the first source-distance category were significantly wider at D:11:290. The *t*-test results for thickness of artifacts followed the same scheme as that for width: rejection of the null hypothesis for local materials and acceptance for the two categories of distant materials. The pattern again showed significantly thicker artifacts from the first source-distance category at D:11:290. The last set of *t*-tests, those for the number of utilized edges, resulted in uniform rejection of the null hypothesis.

Overall, the results of the *t*-tests for size measures and for number of utilized edges tend to support the proposal that if distance to source was the major factor affecting use and conservation of raw materials and if it is held constant, then patterns of raw material use at sites should not differ significantly. The test results in Table 69 show that in only seven of 18 cases were there significant differences between sites. In addition, four of these significant differences are in characteristics of locally available and presumably abundant materials. Given such abundance, it is not surprising that there were fewer constraints on their manufacture and use, and thus more intersite variation in artifact characteristics. In addition, subjective examination of material types leaves the distinct impression that distant materials (e.g., chert gravels) were sought because of their homogeneity and superior conchoidal fracturing. The materials available on the mesa are generally coarse-grained (sandstone), soft (siltstone), or brittle (siderite). The cherts grouped into the second source-distance category are often in badly fractured layers. Thus, one of the factors affecting flake size is variation in the quality of materials (thicker or wider flakes were from poor-quality material). Other factors that must also be considered include different styles of manufacture and different tool functions (hence the need for differently shaped flakes). Future research will probe these possibilities.

Summary and Conclusions

In summary, not only were local chipped stone raw materials available on northern Black Mesa, but the majority of lithic artifacts were manufactured from these local materials. This analysis has demonstrated that prehistoric use and conservation of material was related to the distance to material source, thus supporting the use of mini-max strategies in the prehistoric Southwest. When material was acquired locally, which was most often the case, there was less regard for wastage. Conversely, when material, perhaps of higher quality, was acquired from a distance, it was used to a greater extent and wasted significantly less than local material.

Although artifacts became progressively smaller at both sites as the distance to material source increased, the sizes of artifacts from local material also varied between the two sites that were examined. The larger size and variation in size for the local materials suggest that they were easily available to all. The lack of variation in artifact size between the two sites for the distant material suggests that it was utilized in the same way at both sites. The fact that the inhabitants of D:11:290 used more of the most distantly derived material and that the site is both larger and earlier than D:11:356 may suggest that exchange ties changed through time and/or that more of an effort was made to obtain higher-quality material earlier in time. The first interpretation matches those reached by Fernstrom (this volume). The patterned degree of use of materials within each source-distance category and the patterned variation between categories suggest that either there was a threshold on how much each material could be used or on how much each material needed to be used.

12

The Effect of Ecological Fluctuations on Exchange Networks, Black Mesa, Arizona

Katharine W. Fernstrom

In this paper I examine the effects of ecological fluctuations on exchange systems. Over the past 10 years, archaeologists have used geographic and communication models (Irwin-Williams 1977; Renfrew 1975) to examine exchange materials and networks, and raw materials and source analyses (Weigand et al. 1977) to quantify and describe the relationships among the participants in those networks. Rather than use one of these approaches here, I use an economic theoretical approach. This involves examining decision-making processes and processes of resource allocation (Burling 1968:176). I argue that choices in the allocation of resources are directed toward a goal that ultimately enhances the physical survival of the groups involved. When ecological fluctuations (defined here as fluctuations in climate, resource availability, and/or population level) threaten the subsistence system, revisions in the allocation of resources enable the system to adapt to those fluctuations.

In this context I suggest that one way to allocate resources is to change the distribution of materials committed to exchange transactions. Although this research focuses on exchange as an economic activity, exchange relations and exchange networks have a variety of functions in a society. Exchange activities supplement productive activities by providing network participants with access to goods and services, thus reducing the physical risk of inadequate supplies. However, in order to benefit from an exchange network, a participant must weigh the costs and benefits of committing goods and/or services to one transaction or another or of conserving them for private use (e.g., Burling 1968).

Exchange systems also provide participants with access to at least four broad, nonexclusive categories of information that reduce the uncertainty inherent in any economic system. Information transmitted through exchange transactions relates to material value systems, available resources, stylistic systems, and a variety of verbal information transmitted during the transaction (Renfrew 1975:22–24).

The structure and content of exchange transactions circumscribe, and are circumscribed by, the social context in which they occur. The flow of goods and information is less inhibited among kin members and close neighbors, and the social rules governing the cost and scheduling of repayment are less rigid. Conversely, the greater the social and geographical distance between participants, the more structured and formalized the transactions. Concomitantly, although formalized, exchange activities can integrate disparate groups by involving them in social and economic obligations (Sahlins 1972:185–230; Wobst 1977).

In terms of extrafamilial relations, exchange networks complement and make possible the recruitment of marriage partners. In discussing hunting-gathering groups, Wobst distinguishes between the "minimal" and "maximal" equilibrium size of a society. The former defines the minimal "number of people which will consistently guarantee the presence of a suitable mate for a group member upon reaching maturity" (1974:154). The latter term defines the maximal number of people that "can be consistently integrated by the cultural mechanisms of a given cultural system and which is consistently required for the successful operation of such a cultural system" (1974:154). The minimal group is "operationalized here as the mean and median number of persons that live in the intervening distance between two marriage partners. These partners are nearest neighbors among the available mates in the mating pool" (1974:154). Because the source of marriage partners, and thus the distance between partners, varies over time and space, a single marriage network will be made up of familial groups that stand at varying social, economic, and geographical distances from ego's family. Thus, marriage ties and socioeconomic ties crosscut and reinforce one another.

In summary, exchange networks are important adaptive mechanisms in every society. They are material transport systems, information systems, and systems of familial and political integration. The ability to change patterns of exchange activities by changing patterns of decision making means that conditions in the natural and social environment that affect resource availability, information flow, and/or mate selection can potentially affect the structure and content of exchange activities, and vice versa.

Researchers have argued that physiological and behavioral changes are frequently made in order to maintain the relationship between the individual or group and the environment (Slobodkin and Rapoport 1974; Hockett and Ascher 1964; Mayr 1976). Slobodkin and Rapoport (1974) have argued that by successfully meeting a variety of ecological challenges, a well-adapted population develops a repertoire of behavioral and biophysical responses that mitigate the effects of most of the ecological perturbations to which it is subjected. Responses in this repertoire vary, both in the types of stimuli to which they are a response and in the intensity of resource commitment that they require in order to be effective.

Slobodkin and Rapoport (1974) have defined two types of response mechanisms: low-stake, rapid-response mechanisms and high-stake, slow-response mechanisms. These stand in hierarchical relationship to one another. The former require little commitment, while the latter involve greater commitment of resources. Response to the failure of low-stake, rapid-response mechanisms to alleviate the pressures of ecological perturbations includes the gradual initiation of high-stake, slow-response mechanisms. Both the initiation of high-stake, slow-response mechanisms and the accumulation of series of low-stake mechanisms can create major change in the system.

Here I am primarily concerned with the effects of increased population density and increased environmental uncertainty. These can have a variety of repercussions on man-man and man-land relationships. Increased population density requires production of greater amounts of food per unit of land. Increased demands on the system of food production can lead to a perceived decrease in the margin of error and a perceived increase in the uncertainty and risk associated with food production.

There are at least three classes of responses for dealing with conditions of increased risk associated with subsistence productivity. In each of these cases, responses can be short-term or long-term, depending on the intensity and duration of the perturbations and the success with which they are initially countered. One, groups can institute or increase existing storage space (Minnis 1981; Powell 1982). Foods stored during highly productive seasons or years would provide a buffer against food shortages occurring in less productive seasons or years when overall productivity was low.

Two, groups can change their repertoire of subsistence resources, their technological basis of production, and/or the structure of task organization. Boserup (1965), Flannery (1968), Glassow (1972), and Ford (1977) have pointed to increased population density as an impetus for increased dependence on more localized resources and domestic plants, increased sedentism, increased organizational complexity, and changes in the tools used to process various resources.

Three, groups can intensify those aspects of their exchange activities that are most productive and secure. These are the localized networks in which participants are related by blood, marriage, shared obligations of reciprocity, and economic interdependence. These correspond roughly to Sahlins' (1972:196–210) spheres of generalized and balanced reciprocity. People participating in generalized reciprocity are related through affinal and consanguineal ties and live in the same household. In this context, material support is given when it is required, and neither the time nor the form of repayment is specified. People participating in balanced reciprocity are related through wider-reaching political ties and live in various communities; Sahlins has designated this an intratribal relationship. In this context, exchange transactions are completed at once, and the payment given equals the value of the materials received. Between these two extremes, economic relationships change from less formal to more formal as one moves physically and socially away from the household and into the broader community sphere.

In the remainder of this paper, I focus on this last set of responses. In the following section I summarize ecological conditions in the Southwest, specifically those perceived to have affected exchange relations in the study area. Then I present the data, analyses, and conclusions.

The Problem

Research indicates that there was considerable ecological variation through time on the Colorado Plateaus, and on Black Mesa in particular. In general, over the greater plateau area, populations tended to increase and expand geographically after A.D. 550. Between A.D. 900 and 1000, populations moved from the northeastern plateau to the western uplands. After A.D. 1150, most upland areas were abandoned, and populations were concentrated along lowland watercourses (Euler et al. 1979). These changes appear to correlate with such environmental changes as moisture level and erosion.

Using dendroclimatological, hydrological, and palynological data, Euler et al. (1979) and Karlstrom et al. (1976) have identified environmental trends at the local level. During the prehistoric occupation of Black Mesa, major mesic cycles probably spanned ca. A.D. 400–700 and A.D. 900–1100. Major xeric cycles appear to have occurred ca. A.D. 100–400, 700–900, and 1100–1300. The mesic cycles were characterized by winter-dominant rain and alluviation. The xeric cycles were characterized by summer-domi-

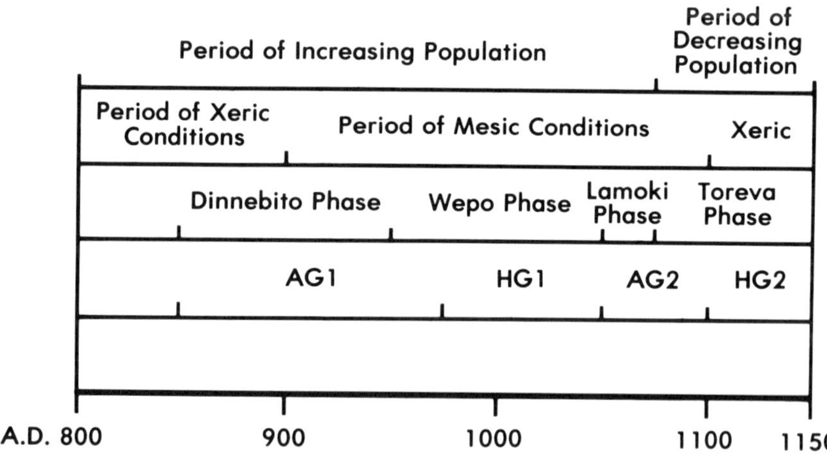

Figure 12. Temporal relationships between cultural phases, subsistence phases, population levels, and climatic fluctuations (Karlstrom et al. 1976; Klesert 1970:33; Layhe 1977:43).

nant rain, low water tables, and arroyo cutting. Within these broad cycles, short-duration droughts occurred sporadically throughout the occupation period in the study area (Figure 12).

Using different samples and methods, both Layhe (1977, 1981) and Swedlund and Sessions (1976) have identified parallel trends in population growth in the study area. In general, the period A.D. 600–800 was characterized by a stable population. After A.D. 800, population increased until A.D. 1075 or 1100 when it peaked. After A.D. 1100, population decreased steadily, culminating in abandonment of the study area by A.D. 1150 (Figure 13).

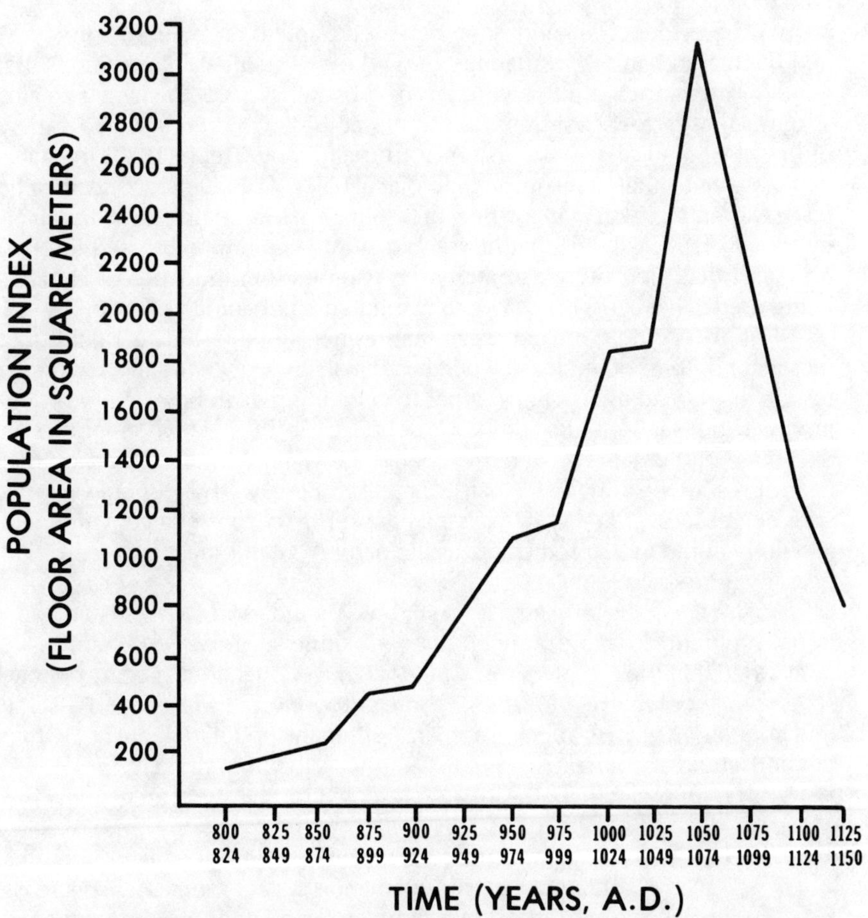

Figure 13. Changes in population level (in m² of floor area) through time (from Layhe 1977:43).

Research on ethnobotanical remains indicates that residents of the study area arrived already practicing corn agriculture. Ford (this volume) and Semé (this volume) have suggested that the domestic cycle focused on harvesting and collecting domestic and wild plants and on hunting animals concentrated around field plots.

Although both domestic and wild resources were present at all periods of occupation, the availability of wild foods appears to have fluctuated. The periods A.D. 850–975 (AG1) and A.D. 1050–1100 (AG2) seem to have been characterized by a decrease in the amount of wild plants being used. The periods A.D. 975–1050 (HG1) and A.D. 1100–1150 (HG2) were characterized by a greater availability of wild plant foods (S. Plog 1978:23–27). The relationships between the environment and subsistence variables are summarized in Figure 12.

The evidence suggests that increased population, sporadic droughts, and fluctuations in the availability of wild foods resulted in conditions that could promote increased perceptions of subsistence risk. The evidence also suggests that residents of the study area met these conditions with a variety of low-stake and high-stake responses. Research by Green (1982) indicates that there were changes in the technological basis of production. Specifically, there was an increase in the variety of the kinds of tools being used. Research by Powell (1982) shows that household storage volume increased through time and that there was also increased variability in the types of facilities being used. These responses would result in greater adaptive flexibility.

In this context I hypothesize that residents of the study area also met these conditions of increased perceived risk by concentrating exchange resources in local transactions rather than dividing them between local and nonlocal transactions. In addition to changes in the relative emphases in exchange participation, overall exchange flow should increase as a buffer against resource shortages. Finally, increased perceived risk should be met with decreased variability in exchange flow. That is, the social environment should become more predictable as the natural environment is perceived to become more risky.

The effect of population growth on demand for resources is an additional problem. I have examined this problem elsewhere (1980) and have concluded that the sample sizes were not large enough to make any definite statement about this relationship. For the purposes of this research, I assume that population growth affected demand within the population but not within the household unit; the focus of this analysis is the household.

The following hypotheses are presented for the study area:

> H_1: If exchange activities are becoming more localized, then the proportions of materials from most distant sources will decrease over time, and proportions of materials from most proximal sources will increase over time.

H_2: If the exchange system is being used as a buffer against perturbations in the natural environment, then exchange activities will increase during periods of perceived risk.

H_3: If the exchange system is being used as a buffer against perturbations in the natural environment, then the variability in exchange flow will decrease during periods of perceived risk.

These changes should be manifested in an increase in the amounts of materials from closer sources relative to those from more distant sources, in an increase in overall importation of materials, and in increased homogeneity of exchange flow.

Data

Chipped stone materials were used to test these hypotheses. Chipped stone was deemed the most appropriate material because its sources and their geographical relationships to the study area were known. Imported stone materials came from sources as close as 30 km and as much as 125 km away; thus it was possible to contrast exchange behaviors with reference to different sources.

Stone materials were identified by Green (1977a, 1982). In general, local materials are sandstone, baked siltstone, siderite, quartzite, and poor-quality petrified wood. Imported materials are cherts and stone of volcanic origin. The specific types of imported stone examined in this study were Owl Rock chert, purple-white chert, and chalcedony, all of which come from sources 30 km from the study area; brown and red/white/blue/black Navajo cherts, which are derived from sources 45 km away; and Chinle chert, which comes from sources 125 km from the study area (Green 1977a, 1977b, 1982) (Figure 14).

The materials were measured both by weight and count because it was not known which measure would be more sensitive to the questions being asked. The measurements were tabulated by percentages to standardize the effects of postdepositional processes. The sites on Black Mesa are sampled according to statistical constraints. Under these constraints, it can be assumed that erosion of materials from the site occurs randomly for all classes of materials. If the excavation units are selected randomly, it can be assumed that the materials retrieved occur in the same *relative* amounts as when they were deposited prehistorically (Chenhall 1975). In contrast, *absolute* counts and weights may have no known relationship to the original population of artifacts as it was deposited prehistorically.

The following ratios were calculated for the counts and weights of materials from each site used in the sample: total imported chipped stone to total chipped stone and total source-specific chipped stone to total imported chipped stone. In each case, total imported chipped stone refers to all

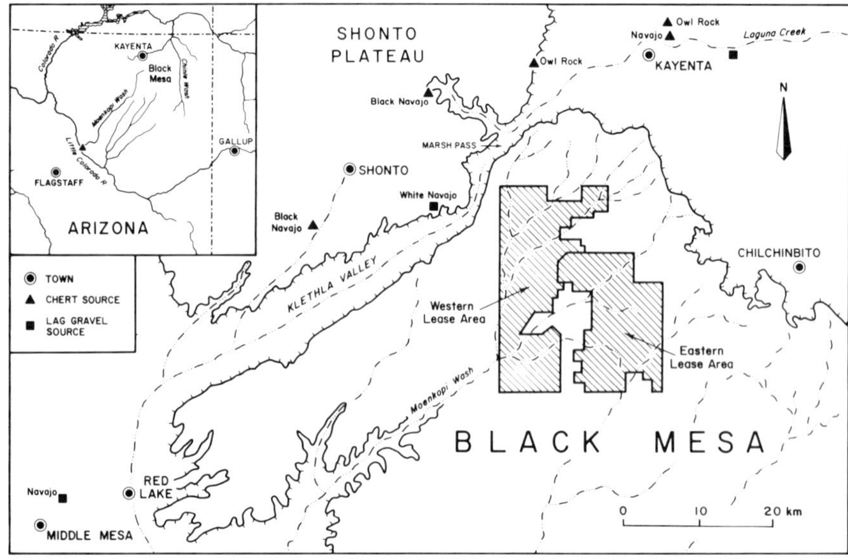

Figure 14. Black Mesa and vicinity showing sources of exotic chipped stone materials.

imported chipped stone found on sites, including those for which sources have not yet been identified; total source-specific imported chipped stone refers to total imports from each of the three source areas mentioned above. All of these proportions can be used to examine trends through time; the source-specific measurements can be used to compare changes in source utilization. Two additional variables, number of raw materials imported and number of different material sources exploited, were created to look at variation in exchange contexts.

Ten excavated sites were selected for the sample on the basis of three factors, although only nine were used in some analyses. One, they are all large sites, qualitatively speaking; that is, they show evidence of at least two of the following four types of features: kivas, middens, pithouses, and masonry rooms. Green (1978) suggested that these sites have a greater range of material types on them than smaller sites. Further, it was necessary to hold intersite function constant so that equivalent patterns of chipped stone procurement could be measured.

Two, they are all ceramic-period sites and almost all fall into phases of the period A.D. 850–1150. No Basketmaker sites were sampled because they cannot be dated closely enough for the purposes here. Dates were assigned primarily on the basis of tree-ring dates; ceramic assemblages were used to corroborate the tree-ring dates. One site was dated using a regression date generated from ceramic attributes (e.g., Hantman and Plog 1978; Stephen Plog, personal communication).

Three, they are all apparently single-component sites. It was felt that the shallowness of the sites limited the chances of accurately separating temporal components in terms of activity areas, where, in addition to the midden, the majority of the lithics are found. A summary of site information is presented in Table 70. (There are no weight measures for materials on site D:11:290S. This information was not available and so was treated as missing data in the analyses. Although the tree-ring date for D:11:1153 is listed as A.D. 815, the ceramic assemblage indicates that the site was occupied during the Wepo phase [A.D. 950–1050] [Table 70]. For this reason, the site was placed in the AG1 phase [A.D. 850–875] for analytical purposes [Fernstrom 1980:111–112].)

Figures 15 and 16 are frequency polygons that illustrate the changes in proportions of total imported chipped stone over time. Figures 17–19 are frequency polygons for proportions of materials coming from three individual source areas: Skeleton Mesa, 30 km distant; the Navajo chert sources, 45 km distant; and Cameron, 125 km distant. These materials will be used to test hypotheses about how the distance of the material source from the study area affects exchange flow. Only materials with known sources were used so that differences in the distances of the sources from the study area could be stringently controlled.

These figures (Figures 15–19) illustrate that number and weight of chipped stone materials were subject to extreme fluctuations among the site samples, particularly during the later phases. However, these later years are characterized by a larger sample than was available for the earlier years. To offset the effects of uneven sampling, phasewide averages were calculated and are included in the figures.

Figures 15 and 16 show that total numbers and weights of imported chipped stone increased through most of AG1 and then decreased gradually. These trends are particularly evident in the graphs of averaged values.

Figure 17 shows that numbers and weights of materials from 30 km sources increased more sharply and over a longer period of time than total imports. Again this is most evident in the graphs of averaged values. This would be expected if participants in the exchange network were interacting more intensely with their closer neighbors.

In contrast, Figures 18 and 19 show that numbers and weights of materials from 45 km and 125 km sources decreased through time. In combination, these support Hypotheses 1 and 2. As population increased and perceived risk became greater, interaction with groups around closer sources increased, and interaction with more distant sources decreased.

Analyses

Spearman rank correlation analyses were used to examine Hypothesis 1 in greater detail. This hypothesis predicts changes in flows of imported chipped stone, relative to one another, over time. Assuming that the total

Table 70. Summary of Site Information.

Site	Occupation Date (Tree-Ring)	Date Excavated	No. of Pithouses	No. of Jacals	No. of Masonry Rooms	No. of Mealing Rooms	No. of Kivas	No. of Middens	No. of Ramadas
D:7:18	1042	1977	0	3	5	1	1	1	0
D:7:19	1117	1977	1	4	2	0	1	1	0
D:7:134	945	1975	4	3	10	0	1	0	0
D:7:704	1098	1978	1	3	6	1	1	1	0
D:11:73	921	1975	0	2	3	1	1	1	0
D:11:97	1091[a]	1976	0	2	0	1	1	1	0
D:11:290S	1083	1976	2	5	3	1	1	1	0
D:11:348	1106	1976	1	2	2	0	1	1	0
D:11:352	1073	1976	1	2	2	0	1	1	0
D:11:356	1118	1976	2	1	1	1	1	1	0
D:11:409	1063	1976	1	5	0	0	1	1	2
D:11:1153	815	1976	3	2	0	0	0	1	0

[a]Regression date, $\pm$ 24 years (Stephen Plog, personal communication).

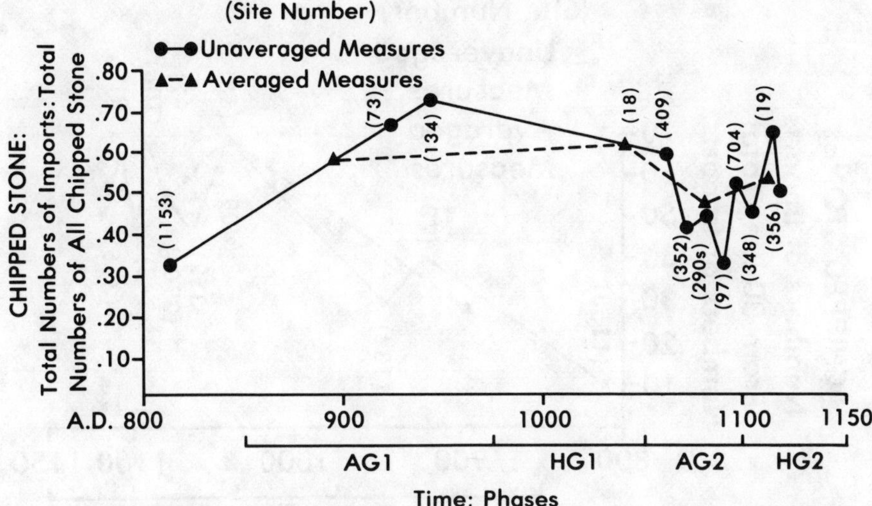

Figure 15. Changes in total numbers of imports: total numbers of chipped stone through time.

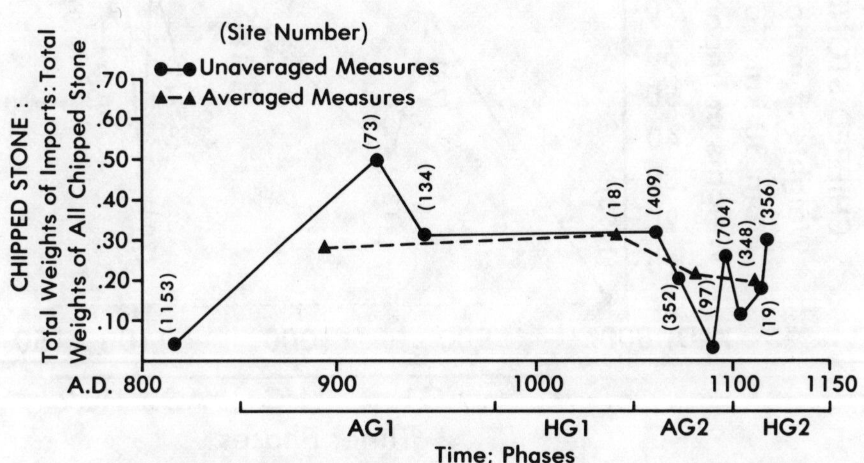

Figure 16. Changes in total weights of imports: total weights of chipped stone through time.

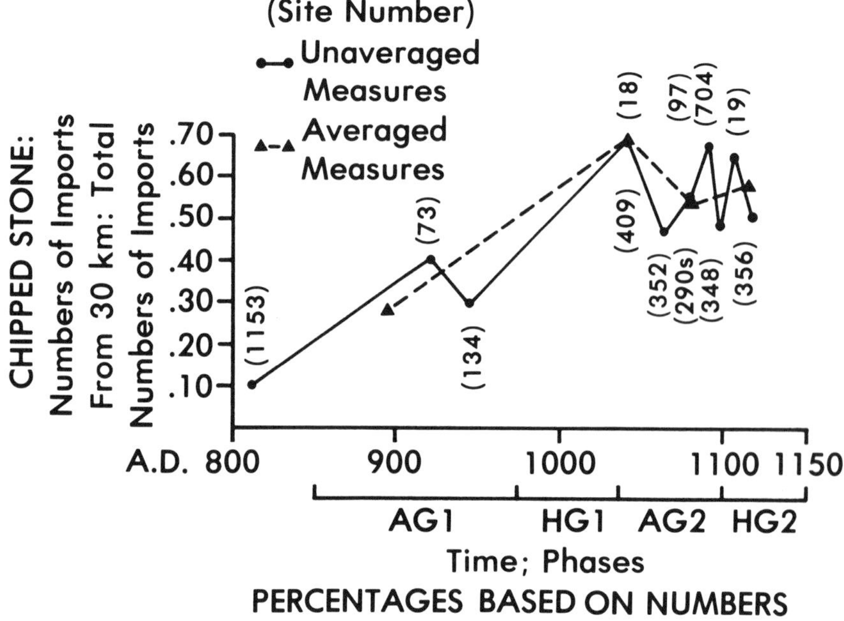

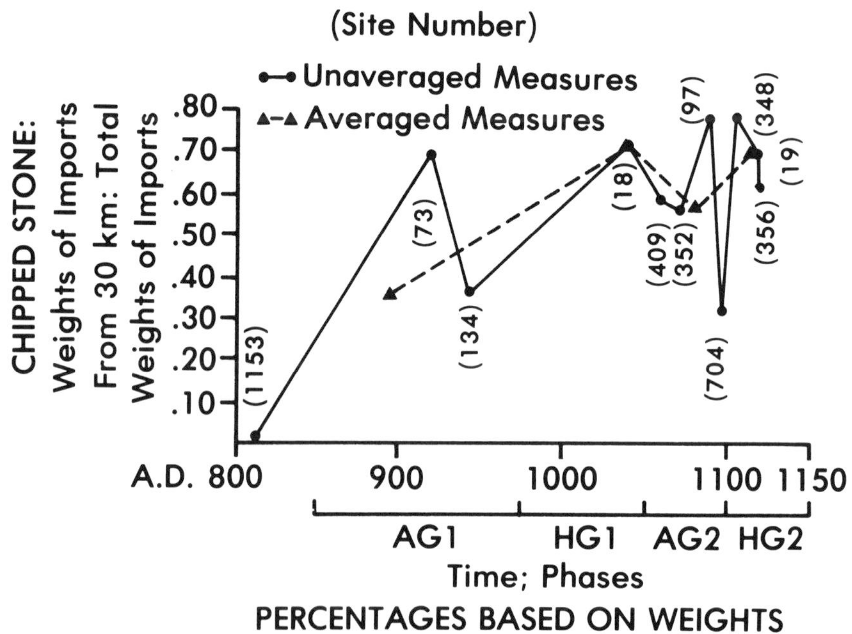

Figure 17. Changes in imports from 30 km sources through time.

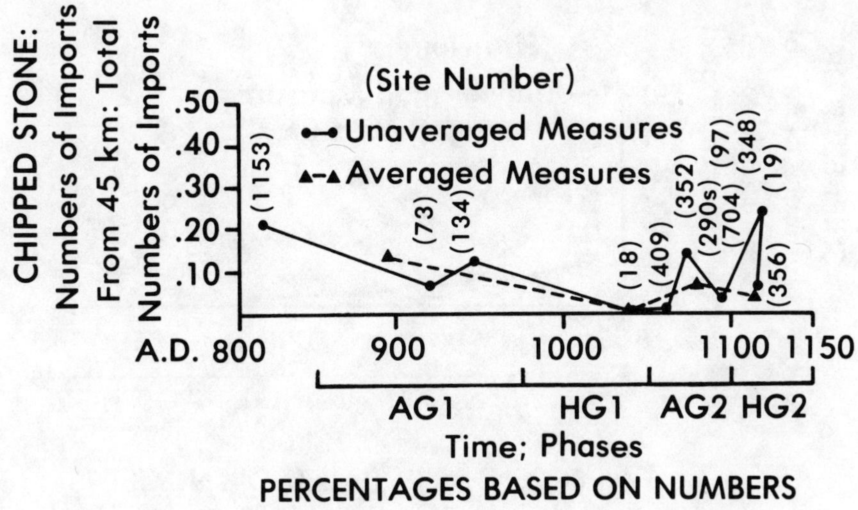

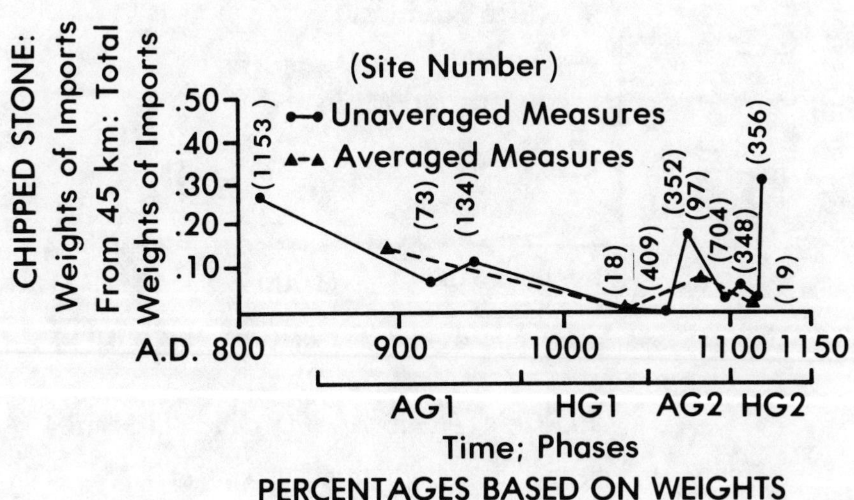

Figure 18. Changes in imports from 45 km sources through time.

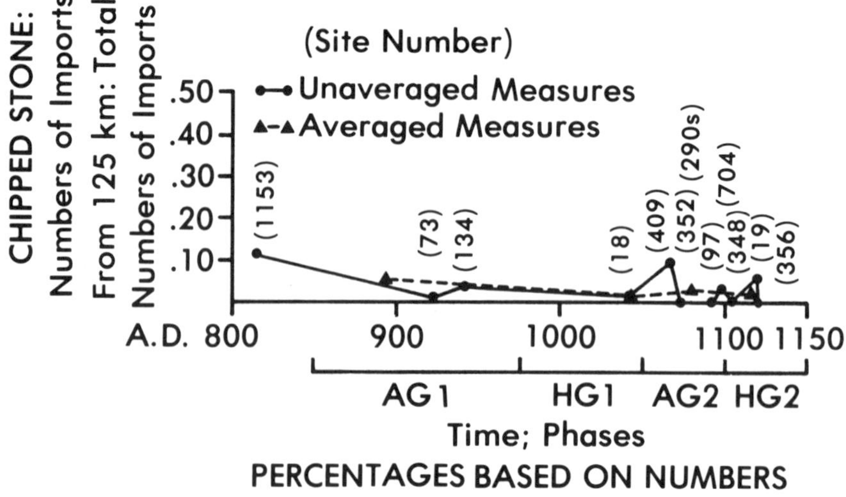

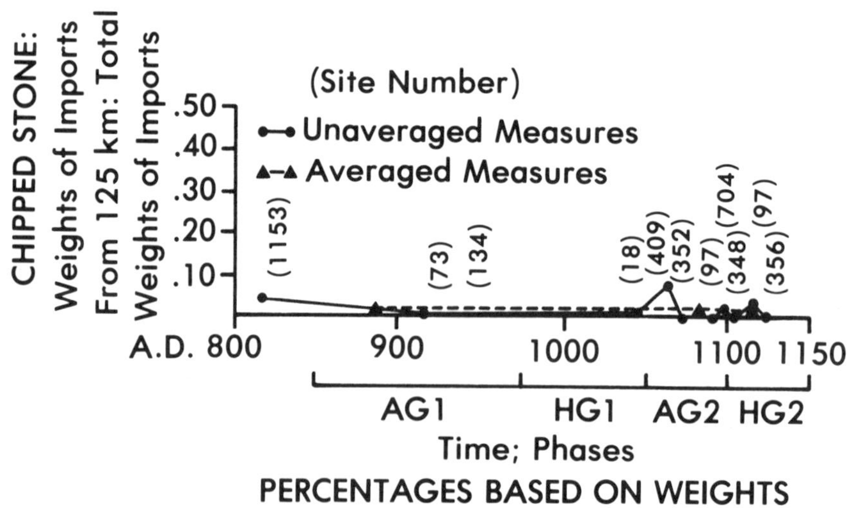

Figure 19. Changes in imports from 125 km sources through time.

flow of imported chipped stone remains constant over time or increases as population (and thus demand) increases, then materials from more distant sources should decrease as total imports increase. Also materials from more distant sources should decrease as materials from more proximal sources increase.

The Spearman rank correlation analyses were carried out using the CORR procedure and the Spearman option from the Statistical Analysis System (SAS) (Helwig and Council 1979:403–417). In the Spearman rank analyses, date and proportional numbers and weights of total imported materials and of materials from the three sources were correlated against one another. The results of these analyses are summarized in Table 71; in general, they support Hypothesis 1.

The Spearman rank correlation analyses yielded six significant r_s values ($\alpha = 0.05$) and two additional values with associated probabilities less than 0.10 (Table 71). Three of the significant r_s values assess the association between proportional numbers of materials from 30 km, 45 km, and 125 km sources with their respective proportional weight measures. Each pair of measures is positively associated. The remaining three significant r_s values measure the association between proportional numbers of 30 km and 125 km materials, between proportional numbers of 30 km materials and proportional weights of 125 km materials, and between proportional numbers and weights of total imports (Table 71). The r_s values with associated probabilities of less than 0.10 measured the association between date and proportional numbers of materials from 30 km materials and between date and proportional numbers of materials from 125 km sources. Date and flows of materials from 30 km sources are positively related; date and flows of materials from 125 km sources are negatively related.

The directions of most of the correlation coefficients meet the expectations outlined above. Although the results are not significant ($\alpha = 0.05$), materials from the most proximal sources (30 km) are inversely related to materials from the more distant sources (45 km and 125 km); materials from intermediate sources (45 km) are also inversely related to materials from the most distant sources (125 km). According to Hypothesis 1, I would expect material flows from 125 km sources to decrease first, relative to all other sources. I would expect material flows from 45 km sources to decrease second, relative to material flows from 30 km sources. However, the sequence in which intersource relationships change is not a problem addressed here.

The tests that do not fully conform to expectations are those that test the relationships between date and total imports (inversely related) and between total imports and materials from 30 km sources (inversely related). Also, in some cases, proportional numbers and proportional weights of materials do not have the same directional relationship with other variables. For example, date is positively associated with proportional numbers of materials from 45 km sources but is inversely related to proportional weights of these

Table 71. Summary of Spearman Rank Tests for Hypothesis 1.

Correlated Variables		r	p
Date	by $n\%$ 30[a]	0.54991	0.0640
	$n\%$ 45	0.05263	0.8710
	$n\%$125	−0.50413	0.0947
	Total Imports	−0.16462	0.6092
	$W\%$ 30[b]	0.40000	0.2229
	$W\%$ 45	−0.06834	0.8418
	$W\%$125	−0.45766	0.1569
	Total Imports	−0.30524	0.3614
$n\%$30	by $n\%$ 45	−0.17926	0.5772
	$n\%$125	−0.71727	0.0086*
	Total Imports	−0.32807	0.2978
	$W\%$ 30	0.76364	0.0062*
	$W\%$ 45	−0.29613	0.3766
	$W\%$125	−0.63405	0.0362*
	Total Imports	−0.25968	0.4406
$n\%$45	by $n\%$125	−0.26762	0.4004
	Total Imports	−0.37258	0.2330
	$W\%$ 30	−0.23288	0.4907
	$W\%$ 45	0.91305	0.0001*
	$W\%$125	−0.37834	0.2512
	Total Imports	−0.30664	0.3591
$n\%$125	by Total Imports	0.43183	0.1610
	$W\%$ 30	−0.50262	0.1151
	$W\%$ 45	−0.25659	0.4463
	$W\%$125	0.97548	0.0001*
	Total Imports	0.21657	0.5224
$W\%$30	by $W\%$ 45	−0.39636	0.2275
	$W\%$125	−0.42906	0.1879
	Total Imports	−0.14579	0.6689
$W\%$45	by $W\%$125	−0.39659	0.2272
	Total Imports	−0.26027	0.4395
$W\%$125	by Total Imports	0.29625	0.3764
Total % Numbers	by $W\%$ 30	−0.03636	0.9155
	$W\%$ 45	−0.37813	0.2515
	$W\%$125	0.40045	0.2223
	Total % Weight	0.76993	0.0056*

[a]$n\%$ = percentage based on numbers of artifacts
[b]$W\%$ = percentage based on weights of artifacts
*significant

materials. Other than the small size of the sample, I have no explanation for these discrepancies.

Kruskal-Wallis one-way analysis of variance tests were used to examine Hypotheses 2 and 3 in greater detail. The Kruskal-Wallis analysis of variance test yields a statistic, H, which approaches χ^2 when $n > 15$. When n is small ($n > 4$ and $n < 15$), the H statistic assumes its own distribution. There are tables of H values and their associated probabilities (e.g., Siegel 1956:282–283). However, these can only be used for analyses with three samples (n_{1-3}) and where values of n range from $n_1 = 2$, $n_2 = 1$, $n_3 = 1$ to $n_{1-3} = 5$ (Siegel 1956:184–194, 282–283; Fernstrom 1980:153–154).

In the current analysis, $n = 12$ but is divided into two to four samples, and values for n range from one to eight. In cases like this, it is valid to refer to the χ^2 distribution, but the results must be regarded with extreme caution (Fernstrom 1980:153–154; Siegel 1956:184–194).

The Kruskal-Wallis analyses were carried out using the SAS NPAR1WAY procedure and Wilcoxon option (Helwig and Council 1979:331–334). This procedure generates chi-square approximations of the H statistic and their associated probabilities. If the associated probability level is greater than 0.05, then the null hypothesis is retained.

Hypotheses 2 and 3 focus on temporally specific decisions to change patterns of resource allocations. These would be equivalent to Slobodkin and Rapoport's (1974) low-stake, rapid-response mechanisms. That is, groups under stress will make short-term adjustments in their patterns of resource allocations; these adjustments are not expected to be permanent.

In Hypothesis 2, I looked at variation in flows of materials from specific sources. Two sets of Kruskal-Wallis tests were used to examine this question. The results of these tests are summarized in Table 72. None of the tests are significant at $\alpha = 0.05$. In the first test I looked at variation in proportional numbers and weights of total imported materials and materials from 30 km, 45 km, and 125 km sources, across the three classes of climatic change summarized above. The tests generated chi-square values that range from 3.81 to 1.70 with associated probabilities that range from 0.1489 to 0.4272. None of these values are significant at $\alpha = 0.05$. However, the tests that generated the lowest probability values were those testing variation in proportional numbers of 30 km and 45 km materials and in proportional weights of 30 km materials. Since these are the more proximal sources, I would expect materials from these sources to increase during periods of increased risk and to decrease at other times. Failure to show variation in materials from more distant sources may be a function of sample size, or it may be a function of the overall rate of exchange with more distant sources. That is, the amount of resources allotted to interaction with more distant sources may have been so small that no drastic revisions were made during periods of stress.

In the second test of Hypothesis 2, I looked at the variation in the same eight variables across the four classes of subsistence change summarized above. The tests generated chi-square values ranging from 7.87 to 1.32

Table 72. Kruskal-Wallis Tests for Hypothesis 2.

Class (*df*)	Variable	H^2	p
Climate (2)	Proportional numbers of materials from:		
	30 km sources	3.10	0.2120
	45 km sources	3.54	0.1703
	125 km sources	2.68	0.2619
	Total imports	1.70	0.4272
	Proportional weights of materials from:		
	30 km sources	7.87	0.0487
	45 km sources	4.58	0.2053
	125 km sources	2.65	0.4486
	Total imports	2.53	0.4702
Subsistence Stress (3)	Proportional numbers of materials from:		
	30 km sources	3.99	0.2633
	45 km sources	3.73	0.2927
	125 km sources	1.32	0.7253
	Total imports	1.52	0.6788
	Proportional weights of materials from:		
	30 km sources	2.95	0.3987
	45 km sources	2.97	0.3969
	125 km sources	0.56	0.9052
	Total imports	4.09	0.2523

and probabilities ranging from 0.0487 to 0.7253. The only significant value is associated with the test of variation in proportional numbers of materials from 30 km sources. This supports the results from the previous test and the results of tests for Hypothesis 1. In general, the results of these two tests indicate that Hypothesis 2 is valid but that the analyses are complicated by problems of sample size and additional, uncontrolled variables.

In Hypothesis 3, I looked at changes in the variety of materials being imported and in the number of sources being used. If people in the study area were focusing their exchange relationships on a limited number of contacts, then there should be decreased variety in the number of materials and sources being used. I used two Kruskal-Wallis tests to examine this question. The results are summarized in Table 73. None of the values generated by these analyses are significant at $\alpha = 0.05$.

In the first test, I looked at variation in the number of materials and the number of sources across the three classes of climatic change summarized

Table 73. Kruskal-Wallis Tests for Hypothesis 3.

Class (*df*)	Variable	*H*	*p*
Climate (2)	Numbers of materials imported	4.27	0.1185
	Numbers of sources exploited	1.04	0.5950
Subsistence			
Phases (3)	Numbers of materials imported	1.18	0.7579
	Numbers of sources exploited	2.91	0.4061

above. Two chi-square values were generated: 4.27 and 1.04. Their associated probabilities are 0.1185 and 0.5950, respectively. The lower probability value is associated with variation in number of materials.

In the second test, I looked at variation in the number of materials and sources across the four classes of subsistence changes summarized above. Two chi-square values were generated, 1.18 and 2.91, with associated probability values of 0.7579 and 0.4061. This time, the lower probability value is associated with variation in number of sources. However, unlike the previous set of results, there is very little difference between the two sets of values.

In general, neither index appears to be very sensitive. Number of sources is a very crude index: it has a small range of possible values (1–3), and each source represents a grouping of possible sources at a given distance from the study area. In general, the results of these tests suggest that Hypothesis 3 is valid but that the indexes used to evaluate it are not sensitive enough.

This problem of crude analytical tools may also be affecting previous analyses. In each case, both analyses yielded a variety of results. This may be due to definitions of subsistence changes: the defined classes may not accurately define socioeconomic trends in the study area.

Summary

In summary, visual assessment and analysis of the diachronic changes in exchange flow support the above hypotheses. The visual assessment indicates that on a site by site basis, the flow of chipped stone increased through time. This is supported by the analysis of variance tests, which showed that there was variation in exchange flow across periods of apparent ecological stress. These conclusions support Hypothesis 2, which argues that exchange flow would increase in response to increased risk in the natural environment.

Although the results are obscured by interference from other variables, the Spearman rank correlation analyses suggest that exchange with varying sources changed according to their distance from the study area. This supports Hypothesis 1, which argued that exchange materials would be committed to transactions with closer participants rather than with more distant ones. This change in allocation of resources is viewed as an attempt to secure local networks as a buffer against risk in the natural environment.

The results of the analysis of variance tests suggested that most exchange flows became more homogeneous during the period of greatest perceived risk. This supports Hypothesis 3; it argued that increased perceived risk should be met by increased homogeneity and predictability in the social environment.

Although residents of the study area met increased uncertainty with localization and intensification in exchange activity, aspects of their overall adaptive strategy failed; the study area was abandoned by A.D. 1150. There are three areas where localization of, and increased activity in, exchange networks may be maladaptive.

First, localization of exchange networks reduces the variability in the information circulating in the network. This may effectively reduce participant access to information about alternative adaptive strategies (Cordell and Plog 1979). Second, increased localization of exchange networks may result in increased localization of marriage networks. This will reduce the potential number of available mates for any individual and thus weaken those socially integrative ties. Third, abandonment of the study area may have been primarily related to factors only indirectly related to exchange (e.g., food shortages and climatic problems). These problems, plus decreasing population, may have increased the exchange obligations for the remaining groups, thus providing an additional reason for leaving the study area.

Conclusions

There is no doubt that exchange systems are an important aspect of every society. Because they integrate several aspects of a given socioeconomic and political system, they are a fruitful topic of study. However, researchers must take care to define those specific aspects of the system that they are analyzing. The way in which exchange systems articulate with systems of production and consumption will be constrained by technological factors and problems of supply and demand. The way in which exchange systems articulate with social and political systems will be affected by the organizational constraints present in the society. Although my arguments and conclusions are valid, my failure to adequately control for each of these variables in the above research has clouded the issues at hand. For example, understanding the effect of population growth on demand, and thus on rates of exchange, has been a recurring problem, one that I have not been able to deal with satisfactorily (Fernstrom 1980). I hope that this research will stimulate increased interest in problems of exchange as an adaptive mechanism; it is important that researchers examine these problems in greater detail.

13

Patterns of Cultural Change: Alternative Interpretations

Stephen Plog and Shirley Powell

Recent research on Black Mesa has changed our views of the prehistory of the area in several ways. Perhaps the most noteworthy change is that variation among sites seems much greater than suggested by initial research. As we noted in the introduction to this volume, most of the papers presented here are attempts to understand the causes of the increased variation that we observed in faunal, floral, and artifactual remains; in architectural types; in site size; and in surface-subsurface relationships. In this paper we briefly discuss the implications of these and other changes in prehistoric adaptations on Black Mesa. In particular, we examine the organization of procurement systems, the development of social networks and exchange systems, and past efforts to explain cultural change on Black Mesa. Recent and forthcoming publications (Powell 1983; S. Plog 1983b) will include much more detailed discussions of these topics.

Procurement Systems and Their Organization

Most previous summaries of the prehistory of our study area have stated that after about A.D. 800, populations relied on cultigens as a major source of food (Swedlund and Sessions 1976:146; Gumerman 1970:118). In addition, a proposed colonization of areas away from major drainages, perhaps begun as early as A.D. 1000 but definitely by A.D. 1050, has been argued to have resulted from increased reliance on dry farming in such areas (Gumerman et al. 1972:194; Gumerman and Euler 1976a:167–169). Although some remains of cultigens had been recovered during excavations, the above statements were primarily based on indirect indexes of farming activity such as the types of groundstone present and the locations of settlements (e.g., Gumerman 1970:118; Gumerman et al. 1972:194).

The initiation in 1975 of an intensive effort to obtain plant remains through the use of flotation methods has provided a more reliable data base than the indirect subsistence indicators noted above. Identification of the recovered plant remains by personnel of the Ethnobotanical Laboratory at the University of Michigan and analyses of these data have altered our understanding of the importance of different procurement systems and of the effect of plant cultivation on local ecosystems. The analyses have shown that in addition to cultigens, a wide variety of other plant resources such as cactus fruits, grass seeds, and pinyon nuts were exploited (Cowan et al. 1978; Ford 1978 and this volume). In addition, while cultigens were important, their contribution to an individual's diet did not increase continually during the period from A.D. 800 until abandonment, but appear to have fluctuated through time (S. Plog 1977d:24–25; Ford 1978 and this volume). However, as Ford (this volume) has argued, the degree of reliance on maize cannot be determined solely from analysis of plant macrofossils recovered from sites. Analysis of trace elements and carbon isotopes in human skeletal parts is needed and is currently being conducted by Debra Martin, Alan Swedlund, and George Armelegos of the University of Massachusetts. In addition, pollen from excavated sites is presently being studied by Robert Murry of Texas A&M University. Integration of the results of these studies should provide a more detailed and more accurate outline of the evolution of procurement systems.

The diversity in procurement strategies suggested by current evidence should not be unexpected, since the Southwest in general, and Black Mesa in particular, is characterized by considerable variation through space and through time in critical environmental parameters such as temperature and rainfall, and thus in resource productivity (Ford 1972; F. Plog 1978; Powell 1980, 1983). When a population practicing diverse adaptive strategies encounters critical environmental changes, "there is a much higher probability that at least some individuals in the population already will be practicing a . . . strategy appropriate to the new conditions" (F. Plog 1974:52).

Additional strategies appear to have been used to cope with variation in resource productivity. Population mobility is one of those strategies. For example, some historic groups in the Southwest and the Great Basin practiced a seasonal settlement round with occupation of distinct winter and summer villages (Bettinger 1978:30–32; Powell 1980:103–131). In other instances, permanent villages were maintained, but temporary camps were established in resource zones peripheral to the permanent villages during periods of resource availability in the peripheral areas (Bettinger 1978:33–36). Both strategies, however, were based on the movement of people to different areas at particular times of the year.

Initial reconstructions of prehistoric settlement patterns on Black Mesa during the period from A.D. 800 to 1000 suggested little or no population mobility. Those reconstructions postulated the presence of permanent habitation sites in lowland areas along the major drainages with little or no utilization of peripheral upland areas (Gumerman et al. 1972:191–192; Gumerman and Euler 1976a:166). However, the empirical support that once existed for this model now appears to have been the result of research strategies that emphasized the excavation of sites with surface indications of structures (see Plog and Powell, Chapter 1 in this volume). Many, if not most, of such sites in areas distant from major drainages date to the period after A.D. 1050. Thus, excavations prior to 1976 revealed little or no evidence of settlements in upland areas that dated prior to A.D. 1050. Recent research strategies, however, have stressed the excavation of sites with a greater variety of surface characteristics and have consistently recovered evidence of upland settlements dating before A.D. 1050 (S. Plog 1977d; Klesert 1978; Klesert and Powell 1979; Powell et al. 1980; Andrews et al. 1982). Most of these fall into Eckles' (this volume) category of sites with low structural diversity. His analysis suggested that such sites were occupied primarily during the spring and summer for plant collecting.

Given the new information on settlement and locational diversity, two alternative models based in part on the historic evidence discussed above have been developed to account for prehistoric Black Mesa settlement patterns. On the basis of her analysis of a variety of data from excavated sites, Powell (1980, 1983) has proposed that prior to about A.D. 1050 both upland and lowland areas of Black Mesa were occupied almost exclusively seasonally. After that time, both permanent habitation sites and seasonally occupied, limited-activity sites were present in upland and lowland areas, although limited-activity sites were concentrated more heavily in upland zones (Powell 1980:254–255,259–260,262,267,271; 1983).

Stephen Plog (1978:34; 1980a:131), on the other hand, has argued that settlements occupied throughout the year were present on Black Mesa by A.D. 800 to 900. He suggests that the period from A.D. 800 to 1000 was characterized by permanent settlements, primarily along major drainages, with seasonal exploitation of resources in other zones such as the upland areas away from the major drainages. After A.D. 1000, he sees increasing evidence for permanent habitation sites in both upland and lowland zones. Thus, while Powell feels that the settlement pattern changed through time as a result of a shift to sedentary villages, primarily after A.D. 1050, Plog suggests that the change simply reflects more intensive use of upland areas as population growth occurred in the region.

Both interpretations, however, imply that mobility was an important part of the adaptive strategy before A.D. 1000 to 1050 but that a significant reduction in mobility occurred after that time. Such a change would have reduced the extent to which populations could cope with variation in resource availability by moving to other areas, by farming areas in different zones, or by exploiting a variety of resources. In addition, the settlement changes and population increase indicate that while per capita consumption of cultigens may not have increased through time, more areas of Black Mesa were being farmed, and many of the new farming areas were marginal for agriculture (S. Plog 1980a:131; Braun and Plog 1980:53). Minnis (1981) has documented a comparable increase in the settlement of marginal lands in the Mimbres River Valley of New Mexico. He has been able to show that the probability of successful farming in areas outside the river floodplain is less than half of the probability for areas along the floodplain (Minnis 1981:199–

222). As a result, variation in productivity is much greater in the marginal zones than in the more optimal areas. While a detailed study comparable to Minnis' has not been carried out on Black Mesa, it is likely that the settlement of marginal areas in the latter region also resulted in a lower probability of successful farming and thus greater variation in annual productivity.

Social Networks and Exchange

Given the reductions in mobility that occurred through time on Black Mesa, social networks would have been altered (Braun and Plog 1980:40–42; S. Plog 1980a:129–132, 1980b, 1980c; Hantman and Plog 1982). Ethnographic studies (Yengoyan 1972; Wiessner 1977) have indicated that mobility requires widespread social ties through which a group obtains access to resources in other areas. These social ties are maintained in part by the regular exchange of goods between trade partners (Wiessner 1977). As mobility decreases, however, the necessity for such widespread social ties decreases, and the scale of exchange systems may therefore contract (Cashdan 1979; Wiessner 1977:373).

The area encompassed by these social networks may also be reduced by additional factors associated with decreased mobility, such as increased population densities and the resultant changes in mating networks (S. Plog 1980c; Braun and Plog 1980:42–44). For example, using Bradfield's (1973:353) estimates of population density for the mobile Western Shoshoni and given Wobst's (1974:154) estimate of a maximum of 475 people for a viable network, the spatial extent of marriage networks should be about 19,700 km², or a radius of 79.2 km around a given community. Using density estimates for the more sedentary Northern Paiute of Owens Valley (Bradfield 1973:353), the spatial extent of the estimated network would be reduced to 2,460 km², or a radius of 28 km around a given community.

Thus, during periods of low population density on Black Mesa, the mating network in which a given community participated may have encompassed most of northeastern Arizona as well as parts of southeastern Utah, southwestern Colorado, and northwestern New Mexico. As population density increased, the spatial extent of such networks may have contracted. If population densities on Black Mesa ever approached those in Owens Valley, mating networks for Black Mesa populations may have covered only a small part of northeastern Arizona.

In addition to changes that can be predicted in the spatial extent of social networks, it also can be argued that the degree of cooperation or integration *within* networks intensified while exchange zones contracted (Braun and Plog 1982:507–508). Although the widespread nature of exchange ties may have decreased in importance as population mobility decreased, local exchange may have become even more important as an aid in buffering productive variation within the increasingly localized areas (Braun and Plog 1980:20). As permanent utilization of upland areas increased on Black Mesa, floodwater farming was carried out in washes with smaller catchment basins. As noted above, agricultural productivity in these areas was thus more susceptible to variability in rainfall. More populous and/ or more cohesive social networks within which food and other resources may have been shared possibly developed as an organizational adaptation to variation in resource productivity (Martin and Plog 1973:327–330).

The above proposals concerning the evolution of social networks on Black Mesa are supported by current information on the exchange of ceramics and of chipped stone raw materials. Recent analyses of these materials (Deutchman 1979, 1980; Fernstrom 1980 and this volume; Green 1982, 1983; Hantman and Plog 1982; S. Plog 1980b, 1980c) have demonstrated that, contrary to previous arguments (Gumerman et al. 1972:198; Gumerman and Euler 1976a:164), there was considerable exchange among Black Mesa populations and inhabitants of surrounding areas. Although no exact estimates of the magnitude of the exchange currently can be made, it is clear that thousands of ceramic vessels and pieces of lithic raw material were involved. In addition, analyses have suggested definite patterns in the spatial scale of the exchange that are consistent with those reported by Fernstrom (this volume). Between A.D. 800 and 900, much more material from distant sources was present on sites than during the period from A.D. 1050 to 1125 (S. Plog 1980b; Hantman and Plog 1982). That is, the spatial scale of the exchange zones was contracting, suggesting that social networks were becoming smaller.

Furthermore, as the exchange zones contracted, there was increasing similarity in the nonlocal lithic materials utilized on Black Mesa sites (Green 1982). This suggests that there was increased sharing of materials among settlements and thus increased integration within networks (Green 1982). Also, as in some other areas of the Southwest, there is a strong pattern of cooccurrence of masonry storage rooms and kivas on Black Mesa sites. This pattern may be due to centralized storage among a group of villages, storage with a religious base or sanction (F. Plog 1974; see also Ford 1977:181–182); however, this is an often-repeated hypothesis that has never been rigorously tested. Synenki (1979) is currently analyzing aspects of survey data from Black Mesa to test more effectively the extent to which sites with kivas may have served as civic-ceremonial centers of social networks.

The "remarkable degree of similarity" between design styles on ceramics from Black Mesa and from nearby areas that has been noted in previous studies (Gumerman 1970:119) may also indicate important changes in social networks (S. Plog 1980a, 1980c; Hantman and Plog 1982). Prior to A.D. 950 or 1000, design styles were similar across broad areas of the American Southwest, but petrographic analysis has shown that this similarity cannot be explained exclusively by ceramic exchange (Hantman and Plog 1982:250). Rather, it has been interpreted as the result of "unbounded, non-hierarchical information exchange, characteristic of low density, mobile populations" that lack discrete social networks (Hantman and Plog 1982:250).

Between approximately A.D. 950 and 1100, however, there is an increase in the number and diversity of design styles in the Southwest as a whole (S. Plog 1980b:127; Hantman and Plog 1982:251). Black Mesa ceramics are highly similar only to ceramics from nearby areas. Similarly, Lofton's (1974) study of ceramics from the Middle Chinle Valley, east of Black Mesa, indicates that while Mesa Verde characteristics are present on ceramics from A.D. 1000 to 1100, Kayenta-style ceramics typical of the northeastern Arizona area dominate after A.D. 1100. Again, petrographic analysis has suggested this pattern is not exclusively the result of exchange (Hantman and Plog 1982). Rather, these stylistic changes, as well as the reduction in the spatial extent of exchange zones, may have been a result of increasing population density and alternative risk minimization strategies such as localized resource sharing (Braun and Plog 1980:50–60; Hantman and Plog 1982; S. Plog 1980c). Social networks appear to have become more discrete and spatially more compact, but population levels within networks increased, as did mechanisms for sharing resources within networks and across social boundaries (Hantman and Plog 1982). Ties that crosscut social boundaries may have been important as social networks became more compact spatially because "the use of established social relationships to acquire food during a shortage is a viable strategy only if the shortage is more localized than the social network" (Minnis 1981:49). Hantman (1983) recently examined ceramics from Black Mesa and from other areas in the Southwest to determine the extent to which style distributions and the adoption of stylistic innovations are related to settlement hierarchies and the number and size of political units.

The above proposals contrast with statements that most Anasazi communities on Black Mesa or elsewhere were independent, autonomous entities. In addition to altering our conception of the degree of autonomy of Black Mesa communities, the above hypotheses concerning the evolution of social networks in the American Southwest have important implications for the nature of archaeological research there, particularly for cultural resource management studies, which often concentrate on small areas. They underline the importance of a broad regional perspective in understanding cultural change. In order to describe and understand prehistoric adaptive systems, we must utilize research universes that are not just hundreds of square kilometers in area, but are thousands of square kilometers. Only with such large study areas will we be able to examine the diverse components of alternative adaptive systems. Thus, our understanding of prehistoric cultural evolution on Black Mesa will be hindered unless we continue to expand the scope of our field research beyond the Peabody Coal Company lease area.

Explanations of Cultural Change on Black Mesa

The information presented above on the development of procurement systems and social networks on Black Mesa also has implications for some models that have been developed to explain prehistoric cultural change in the area. These models (Karlstrom et al. 1976; Euler et al. 1979) heavily, if not exclusively, emphasize the primacy of environmental change in causing cultural change. The population growth and permanent occupation of upland areas occurring between A.D. 850 and 1100 is attributed to a mesic cycle that created favorable farming conditions, while the population decline and abandonment of northern Black Mesa is argued to have been a result of a period of low rainfall (Karlstrom et al. 1976; Euler et al. 1979). This model is based on the assumptions that procurement systems stayed constant (Euler et al. 1979:1090), that population increased continually during the mesic cycle (Euler et al. 1979:Figure 5), and that villages were economically autonomous.

As the above discussion has shown, some of these assumptions are not valid. In addition, the cultural changes that occurred did not necessarily coincide with periods of environmental change. For example, current information suggests that the trends toward decreased emphasis on cultivated plants and toward exploitation of a greater variety of plants (Gasser 1982; Powell 1980:241–248), which characterized the final decades of the Anasazi occupation on Black Mesa, began before the peak of the mesic cycle was reached. Similarly, the changes in patterns of interaction among villages also did not occur exclusively during periods of climatic change, and models emphasizing climatic variables do not account for either the pattern or the nature of the change in social networks.

Finally, recent analyses of population change (Layhe 1977, 1981; S. Plog 1980c) have shown that the rate of population growth was not constant during the mesic cycle but included periods of rapid growth followed by periods of little or no growth. In addition, the peak in population density appears to have occurred between A.D. 1050 and 1100. The population decline, which ultimately led to the depopulation of northern Black Mesa, thus began before the peak of the mesic cycle was reached at A.D. 1100. This information does not support the statement that "major population trends are both parallel and reciprocal to the long-term hydrologic fluctuations" (Euler et al. 1979:1098).

Those who favor environmental explanations of cultural change on Black Mesa have suggested two causes of the discrepancy between the peaks of the population curve and the mesic cycle. First, it has been attributed to possible error in the dates used to generate the population curve (Euler et al. 1979:1099). However, the latter dates are at least as accurate as most of the dates used to construct the paleohydrological curve. It has also been argued (Euler et al. 1979:1099) that the use of different class intervals is the reason for differences between the population curves generated by Layhe (1977, 1981) and by Swedlund and Sessions (1976). This may in fact explain the major differences between the curves. However, it is still the case that the population estimates derived by Layhe, which are based on smaller class intervals and therefore should be a more accurate representation of prehistoric demographic change, indicate that the population decline began before the peak of the mesic cycle.

The above evidence thus indicates that there is not as close a correspondence between cultural change and primary and secondary hydrological pulsations as has been claimed (Karlstrom et al. 1976:160; Euler et al. 1979:1089) and that there is not strong evidence that cultural adaptations on Black Mesa "were largely produced by environmental alterations" (Karlstrom et al. 1976:161).

Although alternative models of cultural change on Black Mesa are not discussed here (see S. Plog 1978, 1980c; Braun and Plog 1980), we do want to emphasize that such models should have several characteristics. First, they must recognize the systemic nature of human ecosystems. While environmental changes can and do have an impact on cultural systems, particularly in arid, marginal areas such as the American Southwest, it is also the case that human populations can sometimes alter the environment in important ways (Ford 1977 and this volume; Semé, this volume). Recent studies have shown that some prehistoric environmental changes once thought to have been caused by climatic change were more likely caused by human alteration of the environment (Minnis 1981:149). In addition, interaction among different human populations can have important effects on cultural systems. Models of cultural change in the prehistoric Southwest and particularly on Black Mesa have too often ignored the social environment. Finally, cultural change is too often attributed to "events" such as short-term climatic fluctuations. We feel that only by analyzing long-term processes of change in variables such as population density and the scale of social networks will we be able to develop adequate explanations of cultural evolution in the American Southwest. It is in that direction that much of the research now being conducted by the Black Mesa Archaeological Project is oriented.

References

Andrews, Peter P., Robert Layhe, Deborah Nichols, and Shirley Powell (editors)
  1982 Excavations on Black Mesa, 1980: a descriptive report. *Center for Archaeological Investigations, Research Paper* 24. Southern Illinois University, Carbondale.

Bagley, Kathy M.
  1979 *Towards a functional classification of nonceremonial structures on Black Mesa, northeastern Arizona.* Unpublished M.A. thesis, Department of Anthropology, Southern Illinois University, Carbondale.

Bailey, Vernon
  1931 Mammals of New Mexico. *North American Fauna* 53.
  1971 *Mammals of the southwestern United States.* Dover, New York.

Bartlett, Katharine
  1933 Pueblo milling stones of the Flagstaff region and their relation to others in the Southwest: a study in progressive efficiency. *Museum of Northern Arizona, Bulletin* 3. Flagstaff.

Beaglehole, Ernest
  1936 Hopi hunting and hunting ritual. *Yale University, Publications in Anthropology* 4.

Beals, Ralph L., George W. Brainerd, and Watson Smith
  1945 Archaeological studies in northeast Arizona. *University of California, Publications in American Archaeology and Ethnology* 44(1).

Berry, Michael S.
  1980 *Time, space, and tradition in Anasazi prehistory.* Ph.D. dissertation, University of Utah. University Microfilms, Ann Arbor.

Bettinger, Robert L.
  1978 Alternative adaptive strategies in the prehistoric Great Basin. *Journal of Anthropological Research* 34:27–46.

Binford, Lewis R.
  1965 Archaeological systematics and the study of culture process. *American Antiquity* 31:203–210.
  1968 Methodological considerations of the archaeological use of ethnographic data. In *Man the hunter,* edited by R. B. Lee and I. DeVore, pp. 263–273. Aldine, Chicago.

1976 Forty-seven trips: a case study in some formation processes of the archaeological record. In Contributions to anthropology: the interior peoples of northern Alaska, edited by E. S. Hall, Jr., pp. 299–351. *Archaeological Survey of Canada, Paper* 49. National Museums of Canada, Ottawa.

1980 Willow smoke and dogs' tails: hunter-gatherer settlement systems and archaeological site formation. *American Antiquity* 45:4–20.

Binford, Lewis R., Sally R. Binford, Robert Whallon, and Margaret A. Hardin

1970 Archaeology at Hatchery West, Carlyle, Illinois. *Memoirs of the Society for American Archaeology* 24.

Blalock, Hubert M., Jr.

1972 *Social statistics.* McGraw-Hill, New York.

Boserup, Esther

1965 *Conditions of agricultural growth.* Aldine, Chicago.

Bourlière, François

1964 *The natural history of mammals.* Knopf, New York.

Bradfield, Maitland M.

1973 *A natural history of associations.* Buckworth, London.

Braun, David P.

1980 Appendix I: experimental interpretation of ceramic vessel use on the basis of rim and neck formal attributes. In The Navajo project: archaeological investigations Page to Phoenix 500 KV southern transmission line, by D. C. Fiero, R. W. Munson, M. T. McClain, S. M. Wilson, and A. H. Zier, pp. 171–231. *Museum of Northern Arizona, Research Paper* 11. Flagstaff.

Braun, David P., and Stephen Plog

1980 *Tribalization in prehistoric North America.* Paper presented at the 1980 annual meeting of the American Anthropological Association, Washington, D. C.

1982 Evolution of "tribal" social networks: theory and prehistoric North American evidence. *American Antiquity* 47:504–525.

Bruce, Grady D., and Robert E. Witt

1971 Developing empirically derived city typologies: an application of cluster analysis. *Sociological Quarterly* 4:238–245.

Bunzel, Ruth L.

1929 *The Pueblo potter: a study of creative imagination in primitive art.* Columbia University Press, New York.

Burling, Robbins

1968 Maximization theories and the study of economic anthropology. In *Economic anthropology: readings in theory and analysis,* edited by E. E. LeClair and H. K. Schneider, pp. 168–186. Holt, Rinehart and Winston, New York.

Cashdan, Elizabeth A.

1979 *Trade and reciprocity among the river Bushmen of northern Botswana.* Ph.D. dissertation, University of New Mexico. University Microfilms, Ann Arbor.

Castetter, Edward F., and Willis H. Bell
  1942 *Pima and Papago Indian agriculture*. University of New Mexico Press, Albuquerque.
Catlin, Mark A.
  1978 *The function of limited activity sites in subsistence-settlement systems on Black Mesa, Arizona*. Unpublished M.A. thesis, Department of Anthropology, Southern Illinois University, Carbondale.
Caton, John D.
  1877 *Antelope and deer of North America*. Field and Stream Publishing Co., New York.
Chapman, Richard C.
  1977 Analysis of the lithic assemblages. In *Settlement and subsistence along the lower Chaco River: the CGP survey*, edited by C. A. Reher, pp. 371–452. University of New Mexico Press, Albuquerque.
Charnov, Eric L.
  1976 Optimal foraging: attack strategy of a mantid. *American Naturalist* 110:141–151.
Chenhall, Robert G.
  1975 A rationale for archaeological sampling. In *Sampling in archaeology*, edited by J. W. Mueller, pp. 3–25. University of Arizona Press, Tucson.
Clarke, David L.
  1972 Models and paradigms in contemporary archaeology. In *Models in archaeology*, edited by D. L. Clarke, pp. 1–60. Methuen, London.
Clemen, Robert T.
  1976 Aspects of prehistoric social organization on Black Mesa. In *Papers on the archaeology of Black Mesa, Arizona*, edited by G. J. Gumerman and R. C. Euler, pp. 113–135. Southern Illinois University Press, Carbondale and Edwardsville.
Cook, S. F., and A. E. Treganza
  1950 The quantitative investigation of Indian Mounds. *University of California, Publications in American Archaeology and Ethnology* 40(5).
Cordell, Linda S.
  1977 Late Anasazi farming and hunting strategies: one example of a problem of congruence. *American Antiquity* 42:449–461.
Cordell, Linda S., and Fred Plog
  1979 Escaping the confines of normative thought: a reevaluation of Puebloan prehistory. *American Antiquity* 44:405–429.
Corum, Joyce, Craig Baker, and Margerie Green
  1977 Arizona D:11:290. In Excavation on Black Mesa, 1976: a preliminary report, edited by S. Plog, pp. 46–62. *University Museum, Archaeological Service Report* 50. Southern Illinois University, Carbondale.
Cottam, W. P., and George Stewart
  1940 Plant succession as a result of grazing and of meadow desiccation by erosion since settlement in 1862. *Journal of Forestry* 38:613–626.
Courtney, P. A., and M. B. Fenton
  1976 The effects of a small rural garbage dump on populations of *Pero-*

myscus leucopus Rafinesque and other small mammals. *Journal of Applied Ecology* 13:413–422.

Cowan, C. Wesley, Josselyn F. Moore, Richard I. Ford, and Michael T. Samuels

1978 Appendix I: a preliminary analysis of paleoethnobotanical remains from Black Mesa, Arizona: 1977 season. In Excavation on Black Mesa, 1977: a preliminary report, edited by A. L. Klesert, pp. 137–156. *Center for Archaeological Investigations, Research Paper* 1. Southern Illinois University, Carbondale.

Cushing, Frank H.

1920 Zuni breadstuff. *Museum of the American Indian, Indian Notes and Monographs* 8. New York.

1967 *My adventures in Zuni.* Filter Press, Palmer Lake, Colorado.

Davis, William B., and Walter P. Taylor

1939 The bighorn sheep of Texas. *Journal of Mammology* 20:440–455.

Dean, Jeffrey S.

1969 Chronological analysis of Tsegi phase sites in northeastern Arizona. *Laboratory of Tree-Ring Research, Papers* 3. University of Arizona Press, Tucson.

DeBloois, Evan I., and Dee F. Green

1978 SARG research on the Elk Ridge project Manti-Lasal National Forest, Utah. In *Investigations of the Southwestern Anthropological Research Group,* edited by R. C. Euler and G. J. Gumerman, pp. 13–23. Museum of Northern Arizona Press, Flagstaff.

DeBoer, Warren R., and Donald W. Lathrap

1979 The making and breaking of Shipibo-Conibo ceramics. In *Ethnoarchaeology: implications of ethnography for archaeology,* edited by C. Kramer, pp. 102–138. Columbia University Press, New York.

Deutchman, Haree L.

1979 *Intraregional interaction on Black Mesa and among the Kayenta Anasazi: the chemical evidence for ceramic exchange.* Ph.D. dissertation, Southern Illinois University. University Microfilms, Ann Arbor.

1980 Chemical evidence of ceramic exchange on Black Mesa. In Models and methods in regional exchange, edited by R. E. Fry, pp. 119–133. *SAA Papers* 1.

Dixon, Wilfred J., and Frank J. Massey, Jr.

1969 *Introduction to statistical analysis* (third ed.). McGraw-Hill, New York.

Douglas, Charles L.

1969 Ecology of pocket gophers of Mesa Verde, Colorado. In Contributions in mammology: a volume honoring Professor E. Raymond Hall. *University of Kansas, Museum of Natural History, Miscellaneous Publication* 51:1–428.

1972 Analysis of faunal remains from Black Mesa: 1968–1970 excavations. In Archaeological investigations on Black Mesa, the 1969–1970 seasons, by G. J. Gumerman, D. Westfall, and C. S. Weed, pp. 225–238. *Prescott College, Studies in Anthropology* 4. Prescott College Press, Prescott, Arizona.

Doyel, David E.
1972 *The Miami Wash project: a preliminary report on excavations in Hohokam and Salado sites near Miami, central Arizona.* Arizona State Museum, Tucson.

Eardley, A., and M. W. Vivavant
1967 Rates of denudation as measured by bristlecone pines, Cedar Breaks, Utah. *Utah Geological and Mineral Survey, Special Studies* 21.

Egloff, B. J.
1973 Method for counting ceramic rim sherds. *American Antiquity* 38:351–353.

Embleton, Clifford, and Cuchlaine A. M. King
1968 *Glacial and periglacial geomorphology.* St. Martins Press, New York.

Emlen, J. Merritt
1966 The role of time and energy in food preference. *American Naturalist* 100:611–617.

Emslie, Steven D.
1981 Prehistoric agricultural ecosystems: avifauna from Pottery Mound, New Mexico. *American Antiquity* 46:853–860.

Ericson, Jonathan, Dwight Read, and Cheryl Burke
1971 Research design: the relationship between the primary functions and the physical properties of ceramic vessels and their implications for ceramic distributions on an archaeological site. *Anthropology UCLA* 3:84–95.

Ericson, Jonathan, and E. Gary Stickel
1973 A proposed classification system for ceramics. *World Archaeology* 4:357–367.

Euler, Robert C., George J. Gumerman, Thor N. V. Karlstrom, Jeffrey S. Dean, and Richard H. Hevly
1979 The Colorado Plateaus: cultural dynamics and paleoenvironment. *Science* 205:1089–1101.

Evans, Ian S.
1970 Salt crystallization and rock weathering: a review. *Revue de Géomorphologie Dynamique* 19:153–177.

Fagan, Kathy, Paula Kux, Gary Miller, Ed Fausel, and Jackie Moore
1972 Seven sites: faunal remains from Black Mesa, Arizona. Ms. on file, Center for Archaeological Investigations, Southern Illinois University, Carbondale.

Fernstrom, Katharine W.
1980 *The effect of ecological fluctuations on exchange networks, Black Mesa, Arizona.* Unpublished M.A. thesis, Department of Anthropology, Southern Illinois University, Carbondale.

Findley, James, Arthur H. Harris, Don E. Wilson, and Clyde Jones

1975 *Mammals of New Mexico.* University of New Mexico Press, Albuquerque.

Fitting, James, and John Halsey
1966 Rim diameter and vessel size in Wayne Ware vessels. *Wisconsin Archaeologist* 47:208–211.

Flannery, Kent
1968 Archeological systems theory and early Mesoamerica. In *Anthropological archeology in the Americas,* edited by B. J. Meggers, pp. 67–87. Anthropological Society of Washington, Washington, D. C.
1976 Sampling by intensive surface collection. In *The early Mesoamerican village,* edited by K. V. Flannery, pp. 58–62. Academic Press, New York.

Fontana, Bernard L., William Robinson, Charles Cormack, and Ernest Leavitt, Jr.
1962 *Papago Indian pottery.* University of Washington Press, Seattle.

Ford, James A.
1951 Greenhouse: a Troysville-Coles Creek period site in Avoyelles Parish, Louisiana. *American Museum of Natural History, Anthropological Papers* 44(1).

Ford, James A., and Gordon R. Willey
1949 Surface survey of the Viru Valley, Peru. *American Museum of Natural History, Anthropological Papers* 43(1).

Ford, Richard I.
1972 An ecological perspective on the eastern Pueblos. In *New perspectives on the Pueblos,* edited by A. Ortiz, pp. 1–17. School of American Research, University of New Mexico Press, Albuquerque.
1977 Evolutionary ecology and the evolution of human ecosystems: a case study from the midwestern U.S.A. In *Explanation of prehistoric change,* edited by J. N. Hill, pp. 153–184. School of American Research, University of New Mexico Press, Albuquerque.
1978 *The significance of archaeological plant remains for interpreting prehistoric adaptations on Black Mesa.* Paper presented at the 43rd annual meeting of the Society for American Archaeology, Tucson.
1980 'Artifacts' that grew: their roots in Mexico. *Early Man* 2(3):19–23.
1981 Gardening and farming before A.D. 1000: patterns of prehistoric cultivation north of Mexico. *Journal of Ethnobiology* 1:6–27.

Forsling, C. L.
1931 A study of the influence of herbaceous plant cover on surface runoff and soil erosion in relation to grazing on the Wasatch Plateau of Utah. *United States Department of Agriculture, Technical Bulletin* 220.

Freeman, Leslie G., Jr., and James A. Brown
1964 Statistical analysis of Carter Ranch pottery. In Chapters in the prehistory of eastern Arizona, II. *Fieldiana: Anthropology* 55:126–154.

Gasser, Robert E. (compiler)
1982 The Coronado Project archaeological investigations, the specialists'

volume: biocultural analyses. Coronado Series 4, *Museum of Northern Arizona, Research Paper* 23. Flagstaff.

Geist, Valerius

1971 *Mountain sheep*. University of Chicago Press, Chicago.

Gile, L. H.

1975 Causes of soil boundaries in an arid region, II: dissection, moisture, and faunal activity. *Proceedings: Social Science Society of America* 39:324–330.

Glass, Gene V., Percy D. Peckham, and James R. Sanders

1972 Consequences of failure to meet assumptions underlying the fixed effects analysis of variance and covariance. *Review of Educational Research* 42:237–288.

Glassow, Michael

1972 Changes in adaptations of southwestern Basketmakers: a systems perspective. In *Contemporary archaeology*, edited by M. Leone, pp. 289–302. Southern Illinois University Press, Carbondale and Edwardsville.

1977 Population aggregation and systemic change: examples from the American Southwest. In *Explanation of prehistoric change*, edited by J. N. Hill, pp. 185–214. School of American Research, University of New Mexico Press, Albuquerque.

Goodyear, Albert C.

1975 A general research design for highway archeology in South Carolina. *University of South Carolina, Institute of Archeology and Anthropology, Notebook* 7:3–38.

Green, Margerie

1975 *Patterns of variation in chipped stone raw materials for the Chevelon drainage*. Unpublished M.A. thesis, Department of Anthropology, State University of New York, Binghamton.

1977a *Analysis of chipped stone raw materials for Black Mesa*. Paper presented at the 42nd annual meeting of the Society for American Archaeology, New Orleans.

1977b Identification and variation in the use of chipped stone raw material for the Black Mesa area. Ms. in possession of author.

1978 *Variation in chipped stone raw material use on Black Mesa*. Paper presented at the 43rd annual meeting of the Society for American Archaeology, Tucson.

1982 *Chipped stone raw materials and the study of interaction*. Ph.D. dissertation, Arizona State University. University Microfilms, Ann Arbor.

1983 The distribution of chipped stone raw materials at functionally non-equivalent sites. In *Spatial organization and exchange: archaeological survey on northern Black Mesa*, edited by S. Plog. Ms. on file, Center for Archaeological Investigations, Carbondale.

Greer, John W.

1976 Some thoughts on faunal procurement: consideration for southwest Texas. *The Artifact* 14:1–20.

Gregory, David
1975 Defining variability in prehistoric settlement morphology. In Chapters in the prehistory of eastern Arizona, IV. *Fieldiana: Anthropology* 65:40–46.

Gumerman, George J.
1970 Black Mesa: survey and excavation in northeastern Arizona, 1968. *Prescott College, Studies in Anthropology* 2. Prescott College Press, Prescott, Arizona.

Gumerman, George J. (editor)
1972 Proceedings of the second annual meeting of the Southwestern Anthropological Research Group. *Prescott College, Anthropological Reports* 3. Prescott College Press, Prescott, Arizona.

Gumerman, George J., Deborah Westfall, and Carol S. Weed
1972 Archaeological investigations on Black Mesa: the 1969–1970 seasons. *Prescott College, Studies in Anthropology* 4. Prescott College Press, Prescott, Arizona.

Gumerman, George J., and Robert C. Euler
1976a Black Mesa: retrospect and prospect. In *Papers on the archaeology of Black Mesa, Arizona,* edited by G. J. Gumerman and R. C. Euler, pp. 162–170. Southern Illinois University Press, Carbondale and Edwardsville.

Gumerman, George J., and Robert C. Euler (editors)
1976b *Papers on the archaeology of Black Mesa, Arizona.* Southern Illinois University Press, Carbondale and Edwardsville.

Hack, John T.
1942 The changing physical environment of the Hopi Indians of Arizona. *Harvard University, Peabody Museum of American Archaeology and Ethnology, Papers* 35(1).

Hanson, John A., and Michael B. Schiffer
1975 The Joint Site: a preliminary report. In Chapters in the prehistory of eastern Arizona, IV. *Fieldiana: Anthropology* 65:47–91.

Hantman, Jeffrey L.
1983 *A socioeconomic interpretation of ceramic style distributions in the prehistoric Southwest.* Ph.D. dissertation, Arizona State University. University Microfilms, Ann Arbor.

Hantman, Jeffrey L., and Stephen Plog
1978 *Predicting occupation dates of prehistoric Black Mesa sites: a comparison of methods.* Paper presented at the 43rd annual meeting of the Society for American Archaeology, Tucson.
1982 The relationship of stylistic similarity to patterns of material exchange. In *Contexts for prehistoric exchange,* edited by J. E. Ericson and T. K. Earle, pp. 237–263. Academic Press, New York.

Haury, Emil W.

1945 The problem of contacts between the southwestern United States and Mexico. *Southwestern Journal of Anthropology* 1:55–74.

Helwig, Jane T., and Kathryn A. Council (editors)
1979 *SAS user's guide: 1979 edition*. SAS Institute, Raleigh, North Carolina.

Hill, James N.
1968 Broken K Pueblo: patterns of form and function. In *New perspectives in archeology*, edited by S. R. Binford and L. R. Binford, pp. 103–142. Aldine, Chicago.
1970 Broken K Pueblo: prehistoric social organization in the American Southwest. *University of Arizona, Anthropological Papers* 18.

Hockett, Charles F., and Robert Ascher
1964 The human revolution. *Current Anthropology* 5:135–147.

Hole, Frank, and Robert F. Heizer
1973 *An introduction to prehistoric archaeology*. Holt, Rinehart and Winston, New York.

Horton, Robert E.
1945 Erosional development of streams and their drainage systems: hydrological approach to quantitative morphology. *Geological Society of America, Bulletin* 56:275–370.

House, John H., and Michael B. Schiffer
1975 Significance of the archeological resources of the Cache River basin. In The Cache River Archeological Project: an experiment in contract archeology, assembled by M. B. Schiffer and J. H. House, pp. 163–186. *Arkansas Archeological Survey, Research Series* 8. Fayetteville.

Hunter-Anderson, Rosalind L.
1977 A theoretical approach to the study of house form. In *For theory building in archaeology: essays on faunal remains, aquatic resources, spatial analysis, and systemic modeling*, edited by L. R. Binford, pp. 287–315. Academic Press, New York.

Irwin-Williams, Cynthia
1977 A network model for the analysis of prehistoric trade. In *Exchange systems in prehistory*, edited by T. K. Earle and J. E. Ericson, pp. 141–152. Academic Press, New York.

Johnson, Gregory A.
1977 Aspects of regional analysis in archaeology. *Annual Review of Anthropology* 6:479–508.

Jorgensen, Julia
1975 A room use analysis of Table Rock Pueblo, Arizona. *Journal of Anthropological Research* 31:149–161.

Karlstrom, Thor N. V., George J. Gumerman, and Robert C. Euler
1976 Paleoenvironmental and cultural correlates in the Black Mesa region. In *Papers on the archaeology of Black Mesa, Arizona*, edited by G. J. Gumerman and R. C. Euler, pp. 149–161. Southern Illinois University Press, Carbondale and Edwardsville.

Kerlinger, Fred N., and Elazar J. Pedhazur
1973 *Multiple regression in behavioral research.* Holt, Rinehart and Winston, New York.
Kidder, Alfred V.
1927 Southwestern archaeological conference. *Science* 66:489–491.
Kim, Jae-On, and Frank J. Kohout
1975 Analysis of variance and covariance: subprograms ANOVA and ONEWAY. In *Statistical package for the social sciences,* by N. H. Nie, C. H. Hull, J. K. Jenkins, K. Steinbrenner, and D. H. Brent, pp. 398–433. McGraw-Hill, New York.
Kirkby, M. J.
1969a Erosion by water on hillslopes. In *Water, earth and man,* edited by R. J. Chorley, pp. 229–238. Methuen, London.
1969b Infiltration, throughflow and overland flow. In *Water, earth and man,* edited by R. J. Chorley, pp. 215–227. Methuen, London.
Klesert, Anthony L.
1979 Black Mesa culture history and research design. In Excavation on Black Mesa, 1978: a descriptive report, edited by A. L. Klesert and S. Powell, pp. 27–54. *Center for Archaeological Investigations, Research Paper* 8. Southern Illinois University, Carbondale.
1980 *Elementary catastrophe theory in archaeology.* Ph.D. dissertation, Southern Illinois University. University Microfilms, Ann Arbor.
Klesert, Anthony L. (editor)
1978 Excavation on Black Mesa, 1977: a preliminary report. *Center for Archaeological Investigations, Research Paper* 1. Southern Illinois University, Carbondale.
Klesert, Anthony L., and Robert Layhe
1980 Black Mesa culture history and research design. In Excavation on Black Mesa, 1979: a descriptive report, edited by S. Powell, R. Layhe, and A. L. Klesert, pp. 47–58. *Center for Archaeological Investigations, Research Paper* 18. Southern Illinois University, Carbondale.
Klesert, Anthony L., and Shirley Powell McAllister
1977 Arizona D:11:1084. In Excavation on Black Mesa 1976: a preliminary report, edited by S. Plog, pp. 121–127. *University Museum, Archaeological Service Report* 50. Southern Illinois University, Carbondale.
Klesert, Anthony L., and Shirley Powell (editors)
1979 Excavation on Black Mesa, 1978: a descriptive report. *Center for Archaeological Investigations, Research Paper* 8. Southern Illinois University, Carbondale.
Lange, Charles H.
1959 *Cochiti: a New Mexico pueblo, past and present.* University of Texas Press, Austin.
Layhe, Robert
1977 *A multivariate approach for estimating prehistoric population*

change. Unpublished M.A. thesis, Department of Anthropology, Southern Illinois University, Carbondale.

1981 *A locational model for demographic and settlement system change: an example from the American Southwest.* Ph.D. dissertation, Southern Illinois University. University Microfilms, Ann Arbor.

Layhe, Robert, Steven Sessions, Charles Miksicek, and Stephen Plog

1976 The Black Mesa archaeological project: a preliminary report for the 1975 season. *University Museum, Archaeological Service Report* 48. Southern Illinois University, Carbondale.

Lechleitner, R.

1969 *Wild mammals of Colorado.* Pruett, Boulder, Colorado.

Lee, Richard B.

1979 *The !Kung San: men, women, and work in a foraging society.* Cambridge University Press, Cambridge.

Leet, L. Don, and Sheldon Judson

1954 *Physical geology.* Prentice-Hall, New Jersey.

Linares, Olga F.

1976 Garden hunting in the American tropics. *Human Ecology* 4:331–350.

Lofton, Delsie

1974 *An archaeological survey of the middle Chinle Valley.* Unpublished M.A. thesis, Department of Anthropology, Arizona State University, Tempe.

Longacre, William A.

1970 A historical review. In *Reconstructing prehistoric Pueblo societies,* edited by W. A. Longacre, pp. 1–10. University of New Mexico Press, Albuquerque.

McAllister, Shirley Powell, and Fred Plog

1978 Small sites in the Chevelon drainage. In Limited activity and occupation sites, edited by A. E. Ward, pp. 17–23. *Contributions to Anthropological Studies* 1. Albuquerque, New Mexico.

MacArthur, Robert H., and Eric R. Pianka

1966 An optimal use of a patchy environment. *American Naturalist* 100:603–609.

MacArthur, Robert H., and Edward O. Wilson

1967 *The theory of island biogeography.* Princeton University Press, New Jersey.

McNeil, Judy, Francis J. Kelly, and Keith McNeil

1975 *Testing research hypotheses using multiple regression.* Southern Illinois University Press, Carbondale and Edwardsville.

McNemar, Quinn

1962 *Psychological statistics.* John Wiley and Sons, New York.

Martin, Paul S.

1964 Summary. In Chapters in the prehistory of eastern Arizona, II. *Fieldiana: Anthropology* 55:216–226.

Martin, Paul S., and Fred Plog
  1973 *The archaeology of Arizona.* Natural History Press, New York.
Martin, Paul S., and John B. Rinaldo
  1960 Table Rock Pueblo. *Fieldiana: Anthropology* 51(2).
Mayr, Ernst
  1976 *Evolution and the diversity of life: selected essays.* Belknap Press,
    Cambridge, Massachusetts.
Middleton, John, and Gray Merriam
  1981 Woodland mice in a farmland mosaic. *Journal of Applied Ecology*
    18:703–710.
Mindeleff, Victor
  1891 A study of Pueblo architecture: Tusayan and Cibola. *Bureau of Amer-
    ican Ethnology, 8th Annual Report* 8:3–228.
Minium, Edward W.
  1970 *Statistical reasoning in psychology and education.* John Wiley and
    Sons, New York.
Minnis, Paul E.
  1981 *Economic and organizational responses to food stress by non-strat-
    ified societies: an example from prehistoric New Mexico.* Ph.D. dis-
    sertation, University of Michigan. University Microfilms, Ann Arbor.
Minnis, Paul E., and Stephen A. LeBlanc
  1976 An efficient, inexpensive arid lands flotation system. *American
    Antiquity* 41:491–493.
Moore, Bruce M.
  1975 Pueblo small structure sites: a digest of ethnographic data. Ms. on
    file, Dana College, Blair, Nebraska.
Moore, Josselyn
  1979 1978 Ethnobotanical and ecological research. In Excavation on
    Black Mesa, 1978: a descriptive report, edited by A. L. Klesert and S.
    Powell, pp. 179–215. *Center for Archaeological Investigations,
    Research Paper* 8. Southern Illinois University, Carbondale.
Morgan, M. A.
  1969 Overland flow and man. In *Water, earth and man,* edited by R. J.
    Chorley, pp. 239–255. Methuen, London.
Naroll, Raoul
  1962 Floor area and settlement population. *American Antiquity* 27:587–
    591.
Neily, Robert
  1977 Arizona D:11:356. In Excavation on Black Mesa, 1976: a prelimi-
    nary report, edited by S. Plog, pp. 100–104. *University Museum,
    Archaeological Service Report* 50. Southern Illinois University,
    Carbondale.
Nie, Norman H., C. Hadlai Hull, Jean G. Jenkins, Karin Steinbrenner, and
Dale H. Brent
  1975 *Statistical package for the social sciences.* McGraw-Hill, New York.

Nunnally, J. C.
   1967 *Psychometric theory.* McGraw-Hill, New York.
Odum, Eugene P.
   1971 *Fundamentals of ecology* (third ed.). W. B. Saunders, Philadelphia.
Parsons, Elsie Clews (editor)
   1936 Hopi journal of Alexander M. Stephen. *Columbia University, Contributions to Anthropology* 23 and 24.
Peel, R. F.
   1966 The landscape in aridity. *Institute of British Geographers, Transactions* 38:1–24.
Phillips, David A., Jr.
   1972 Social implications of settlement distribution on Black Mesa. In Archaeological investigations on Black Mesa: the 1969–1970 seasons, by G. J. Gumerman, D. Westfall, and C. S. Weed, pp. 199–210. *Prescott College, Studies in Anthropology* 4. Prescott College Press, Prescott, Arizona.
Phillips, Phillip, James A. Ford, and James B. Griffin
   1951 Archaeological survey in the lower Mississippi alluvial valley 1940–1947. *Harvard University, Peabody Museum of American Archaeology and Ethnology, Papers* 25.
Pickford, G. D.
   1932 The influence of continued heavy grazing and promiscuous burning on spring-fall ranges in Utah. *Ecology* 13:159–171.
Plog, Fred T.
   1974 *The study of prehistoric change.* Academic Press, New York.
   1975 Demographic studies in southwestern prehistory. In Population studies in archaeology and biological anthropology: a symposium, edited by A. C. Swedlund. *Memoirs of the Society for American Archaeology* 30:94–103.
   1978 The Keresan bridge: an ecological and archaeological account. In *Social archaeology,* edited by C. L. Redman, M. J. Berman, E. V. Curtin, W. T. Langhorne, Jr., N. M. Versaggi, and J. C. Wanser, pp. 349–372. Academic Press, New York.
Plog, Fred, and James N. Hill
   1971 Explaining variability in the distribution of sites. In The distribution of prehistoric population aggregates, edited by G. J. Gumerman, pp. 7–36. *Prescott College, Anthropological Reports* 1. Prescott College Press, Prescott, Arizona.
Plog, Fred, Richard Effland, and Dee F. Green
   1978 Inferences using the SARG data bank. In *Investigations of the Southwestern Anthropological Research Group: an experiment in archaeological cooperation,* edited by R. C. Euler and G. J. Gumerman, pp. 139–148. Museum of Northern Arizona Press, Flagstaff.
Plog, Stephen E.
   1977a Cultural resources of the J23–24 strip areas, Black Mesa, Arizona.

Ms. on file, Center for Archaeological Investigations, Southern Illinois University, Carbondale.

1977b Introduction. In Excavation on Black Mesa, 1976: a preliminary report, edited by S. Plog, pp. 1–30. *University Museum, Archaeological Service Report* 50, Southern Illinois University, Carbondale.

1977c *A multivariate approach to the explanation of ceramic design variation.* Ph.D. dissertation, University of Michigan. University Microfilms, Ann Arbor.

1978 Black Mesa research design. In Excavation on Black Mesa, 1977: a preliminary report, edited by A. L. Klesert, pp. 21–42. *Center for Archaeological Investigations, Research Paper* 1. Southern Illinois University, Carbondale.

1980a *The evolution of social networks in the American Southwest.* Paper presented at the 45th annual meeting of the Society for American Archaeology, Philadelphia.

1980b *Stylistic variation in prehistoric ceramics: design analysis in the American Southwest.* Cambridge University Press, New York.

1980c Village autonomy in the American Southwest: an evaluation of the evidence. In Models and methods in regional exchange, edited by R. E. Fry, pp. 135–146. *SAA Papers* 1.

1983a Estimating vessel orifice diameters: measurement methods and measurement error. In *Measurement and explanation of ceramic variation: some current examples,* edited by B. A. Nelson, in preparation.

Plog, Stephen E. (editor)

1977d Excavation on Black Mesa, 1976: a preliminary report. *University Museum, Archaeological Service Report* 50. Southern Illinois University, Carbondale.

1983b *Spatial organization and exchange: archaeological survey on northern Black Mesa.* Ms. on file, Center for Archaeological Investigations, Southern Illinois University, Carbondale.

Plog, Stephen, and Anthony L. Klesert

1978 Introduction. In Excavation on Black Mesa, 1977: a preliminary report, edited by A. L. Klesert, pp. 1–20. *Center for Archaeological Investigations, Research Paper* 1. Southern Illinois University, Carbondale.

Powell, Shirley

1980 *Material culture and behavior: a prehistoric example for the American Southwest.* Ph.D. dissertation, Arizona State University. University Microfilms, Ann Arbor.

1982 *Food storage and environmental uncertainty: an example from Black Mesa, Arizona.* Paper presented at the 47th annual meeting of the Society for American Archaeology, Minneapolis.

1983 *Mobility and adaptation: the Anasazi of Black Mesa, Arizona.* Southern Illinois University Press, Carbondale and Edwardsville.

Powell, Shirley, and Anthony L. Klesert

1980 Predicting the presence of structures on small sites. *Current Anthropology* 21:367–369.

Powell, Shirley, Robert Layhe, and Anthony L. Klesert (editors)
1980 Excavation on Black Mesa, 1979: a descriptive report. *Center for Archaeological Investigations, Research Paper* 18. Southern Illinois University, Carbondale.

Pullinam, H. R.
1981 On predicting human diets. *Journal of Ethnobiology* 1:61–68.

Pyke, G. H., H. R. Pullinam, and E. L. Charnov
1977 Optimal foraging: a selective review of theory and tests. *Quarterly Review of Biology* 52:137–154.

Read, Dwight W.
1974 Some comments on typologies in archaeology and an outline of a methodology. *American Antiquity* 39:216–242.

Redman, Charles L., and Patty Jo Watson
1970 Systematic, intensive surface collection. *American Antiquity* 35:279–290.

Reed, Charles A.
1957 Observations on the burrowing rodent *Spalax* in Iraq. *Journal of Mammalogy* 39:386–389.

Reed, Marti
1971 Jacal and masonry architecture: functional patterns on Black Mesa. Ms. on file, Center for Archaeological Investigations, Southern Illinois University, Carbondale.

Reid, J. Jefferson, William L. Rathje, and Michael B. Schiffer
1974 Expanding archaeology. *American Antiquity* 39:125–126.

Reid, J. Jefferson, Michael B. Schiffer, and Jeffrey M. Neff
1975 Archaeological considerations of intrasite sampling. In *Sampling in archaeology,* edited by J. W. Mueller, pp. 209–226. University of Arizona Press, Tucson.

Renfrew, Colin
1975 Trade as action at a distance: questions of integration and communication. In *Ancient civilizations and trade,* edited by J. Sabloff and C. C. Lamberg-Karlovsky, pp. 5–39. School of American Research, University of New Mexico Press, Albuquerque.

Rick, John W.
1976 Downslope movement and archaeological intrasite spatial analysis. *American Antiquity* 41:133–144.

Rogers, Malcolm
1936 Yuman pottery making. *San Diego Museum, Papers* 2. San Diego Museum of Man, San Diego.

Roscoe, John T.
1975 *Fundamental research statistics for the behavioral sciences.* Holt, Rinehart and Winston, New York.

Ruppé, Reynold J.

1966 The archaeological survey: a defense. *American Antiquity* 31:313–333.

Sahlins, Marshall
1972 *Stone age economics.* Aldine, Chicago.

Scheffé, Henry
1959 *The analysis of variance.* John Wiley and Sons, New York.

Schiffer, Michael B.
1972 Archaeological context and systemic context. *American Antiquity* 37:156–165.
1975 Behavioral chain analysis: activities, organization, and use of space. In Chapters in the prehistory of eastern Arizona, IV. *Fieldiana: Anthropology* 65:103–119.
1976 *Behavioral archeology.* Academic Press, New York.

Schiffer, Michael B., and William L. Rathje
1973 Efficient exploitation of the archeological record: penetrating problems. In *Research and theory in current archeology,* edited by C. L. Redman, pp. 169–179. John Wiley and Sons, New York.

Schoenwetter, James, and A. E. Dittert, Jr.
1968 An ecological interpretation of Anasazi settlement patterns. In *Anthropological archeology in the Americas,* edited by B. J. Meggers, pp. 41–66. Anthropological Society of Washington, Washington, D. C.

Schumm, S. A.
1964 Seasonal variations of erosion rates and processes on hillslopes in western Colorado. *Zeitschrift für Geomorphologie, Supplementband* 5:215–238.
1967 Rates of surficial rock creep on hillslopes in western Colorado. *Science* 155:560–561.

Sellers, William D., and Richard H. Hill
1974 *Arizona climate 1931–1972.* University of Arizona Press, Tucson.

Semé, Michele
1980a *Analysis of faunal remains from archaeological sites, Black Mesa, Arizona.* Unpublished M.S. thesis, Department of Biological Sciences, University of Texas, El Paso.
1980b Faunal analysis of material from the 1979 field season. In Excavation on Black Mesa, 1979: a descriptive report, edited by S. Powell, R. Layhe, and A. L. Klesert, pp. 465–508. *Center for Archaeological Investigations, Research Paper* 18. Southern Illinois University, Carbondale.
1981 *Methodology in archaeological faunal analysis: an example from Black Mesa, Arizona.* Unpublished M.A. research paper, Department of Anthropology, Southern Illinois University, Carbondale.

Shaffer, Jimmie Gray
1972 *Arizona U:2:29 (ASU): a Honanki phase site in the southern Verde*

River Valley, Arizona. Unpublished M.A. thesis, Department of Anthropology, Arizona State University, Tempe.

Shepard, Anna O.
1974 Ceramics for the archaeologist. *Carnegie Institute of Washington, Publication* 609. Washington, D. C.

Siegel, Sidney
1956 *Nonparametric statistics for the behavioral sciences*. McGraw-Hill, New York.

Slobodkin, Lawrence B., and Anatol Rapoport
1974 An optimal strategy of evolution. *Quarterly Review of Biology* 49:181–200.

Smiley, F. E., and Peter P. Andrews
1983 An overview of Black Mesa archaeological research. In Excavations on Black Mesa, 1981: a descriptive report, edited by F. E. Smiley, D. L. Nichols, and P. P. Andrews, pp. 43–60. *Center for Archaeological Investigations, Research Paper* 36. Southern Illinois University, Carbondale.

Smith, Bruce D.
1975 Middle Mississippi exploitation of animal populations. *University of Michigan, Museum of Anthropology, Anthropological Papers* 57. Ann Arbor.

Smith, Watson
1952 Excavations in the Big Hawk Valley, Wupatki National Monument, Arizona. *Museum of Northern Arizona, Bulletin* 24. Flagstaff.

Speth, John D., and Gregory A. Johnson
1976 Problems in the use of correlation for the investigation of tool kits and activity areas. In *Cultural change and continuity: essays in honor of James Bennett Griffin,* edited by C. Cleland, pp. 35–50. Academic Press, New York.

Spier, Leslie
1917 New data on the Treton argillite culture. *American Anthropologist* 18:181–189.
1928 *Havasupai ethnography*. The Trustees, New York.

Steel, Robert G. D., and James H. Torrie
1960 *Principles and procedures of statistics*. McGraw-Hill, New York.

Steward, Julian H.
1938 Basin-Plateau sociopolitical groups. *Bureau of American Ethnology, Bulletin* 120.
1942 The direct historical approach to archaeology. *American Antiquity* 7:337–343.

Stewart, Marilyn C.
1975 *A typology of pits on the Englebert site*. Ph.D. dissertation, State University of New York. University Microfilms, Ann Arbor.

Stiger, Mark A.

1977 *Anasazi diet: the coprolite evidence.* Unpublished M.A. thesis, Department of Anthropology, University of Colorado, Boulder.

Styles, Bonnie W.

1981 Faunal exploitation and resource selection: Early and Late Woodland subsistence in the lower Illinois Valley. *Northwestern University, Archaeological Program, Scientific Papers* 3. Evanston.

Sullivan, Alan P.

1974 Problems in the estimation of original room function: a tentative solution from the Grasshopper Ruin. *The Kiva* 40:93–100.

Swedlund, Alan C., and Steven E. Sessions

1976 A developmental model of prehistoric population growth on Black Mesa, northeastern Arizona. In *Papers on the archaeology of Black Mesa, Arizona,* edited by G. J. Gumerman and R. C. Euler, pp. 136–148. Southern Illinois University Press, Carbondale and Edwardsville.

Synenki, Alan T.

1977 *Explaining the relationship between surface and subsurface remains: a multivariate approach.* Unpublished M.A. thesis, Department of Anthropology, Southern Illinois University, Carbondale.

1978a Arizona D:11:879. In Excavation on Black Mesa, 1977: a preliminary report, edited by A. L. Klesert, pp. 103–108. *Center for Archaeological Investigations, Research Paper* 1. Southern Illinois University, Carbondale.

1978b Arizona D:7:19. In Excavation on Black Mesa, 1977: a preliminary report, edited by A. L. Klesert, pp. 51–64. *Center for Archaeological Investigations, Research Paper* 1. Southern Illinois University, Carbondale.

1978c *A multivariate approach for examining the relationship between surface and subsurface remains.* Paper presented at the 43rd annual meeting of the Society for American Archaeology, Tucson.

1979 Ritual, organization, and production: monitoring variability in aspects of societal complexity. Ms. in possession of author.

Thomas, David Hurst

1975 Nonsite sampling in archaeology: up the creek without a site? In *Sampling in archaeology,* edited by J. W. Mueller, pp. 61–81. University of Arizona Press, Tucson.

1976 *Figuring anthropology.* Holt, Rinehart and Winston, New York.

Thompson, Raymond H.

1958 Modern Yucatecan Maya pottery making. *Memoirs of the Society for American Archaeology* 15.

Tolstoy, Paul

1958 Surface survey of the northern Valley of Mexico: the Classic and Post-Classic periods. *American Philosophical Society, Transactions* 48(5).

Tolstoy, Paul, and Suzanne K. Fish

1973 Excavations at Coapexco, 1973. Ms. on file, Department of Anthropology, Queens College, Montreal.

1975 Surface and subsurface evidence for community size at Coapexco, Mexico. *Journal of Field Archaeology* 2:97–104.

Tricart, J., and A. Cailleux
1962 *Le modèle glaciaire et nival*. Sedes, Paris.

Trigger, Bruce G.
1968 The determinants of settlement patterns. In *Settlement Archaeology*, edited by K. C. Chang, pp. 53–78. National Press Books, Palo Alto, California.

Tschopik, Harry
1941 Navaho pottery making: an inquiry into the affinities of Navaho painted pottery. *Harvard University, Peabody Museum of American Archaeology and Ethnology, Papers* 17(1).

Turner, Christy, and Laurel Lofgren
1966 Household size of prehistoric western Pueblo Indians. *Southwestern Journal of Anthropology* 22:117–132.

Turner, Ronald W.
1966 *Effects of a cornfield upon the movement of* Peromyscus leucopus. Unpublished M.S. thesis, Department of Zoology, Southern Illinois University, Carbondale.

Underhill, Ruth
1946 Work a day life of the Pueblos. *United States Indian Service, Indian Life and Customs* 4, Phoenix, Arizona.

United States Department of the Interior
1964 *Summary report of the soil and range inventory for the 1882 Executive Order area (Arizona)*. Washington, D. C.

Vivian, R. Gwinn
1970 An inquiry into prehistoric social organization in Chaco Canyon, New Mexico. In *Reconstructing prehistoric Pueblo societies*, edited by W. A. Longacre, pp. 59–83. University of New Mexico Press, Albuquerque.

Vogel, J. C., and Nikolaas J. van der Merwe
1977 Isotopic evidence for early maize cultivation in New York State. *American Antiquity* 42:238–242.

Washburn, A. L.
1973 *Periglacial processes and environments*. Arnold, London.

Watson, Patty Jo
1976 In pursuit of prehistoric subsistence: a comparative account of some contemporary flotation techniques. *Midcontinental Journal of Archaeology* 1:77–100.

Weigand, Phil C., Garman Harbottle, and Edward V. Sayre
1977 Turquoise sources and source analysis: Mesoamerica and the south-

western U.S.A. In *Exchange systems in prehistory,* edited by T. K. Earle and J. E. Ericson, pp. 15–32. Academic Press, New York.

Whallon, Robert

1969 Reflections on social interaction in Owasco ceramic decoration. *Eastern States Archaeological Federation, Bulletins* 27 and 28:15.

1972 A new approach to pottery typology. *American Antiquity* 37:13–33.

Whittaker, Robert H.

1975 *Communities and ecosystems* (second ed.). Macmillan, New York.

Wiessner, Polly

1974 A functional estimator of population from floor area. *American Antiquity* 39:343–350.

1977 *Hxaro: a regional system of reciprocity for reducing risk among the !Kung San.* Ph.D. dissertation, University of Michigan. University Microfilms, Ann Arbor.

Wilcox, David R.

1975 A strategy for perceiving social groups in Puebloan sites. In Chapters in the prehistory of eastern Arizona, IV. *Fieldiana: Anthropology* 65:120–159.

Wobst, H. Martin

1974 Boundary conditions for paleolithic social systems: a simulation approach. *American Antiquity* 39:147–178.

1977 Stylistic behavior and information exchange. In Papers for the Director: research essays in honor of James B. Griffin, edited by C. E. Cleland, pp. 317–342. *University of Michigan, Museum of Anthropology, Anthropological Papers* 61.

Wood, John E., Thomas S. Bickler, Wainright Evans, John C. Germany, and Volney W. Howard, Jr.

1970 The Fort Stanton mule deer herd. *New Mexico State University, Agricultural Experiment Station, Bulletin* 567.

Wood, W. Raymond, and Donald Lee Johnson

1978 A survey of disturbance processes in archaeological site formation. In *Advances in archaeological method and theory* (vol. 1), edited by M. B. Schiffer, pp. 315–381. Academic Press, New York.

Woodbury, Robert B.

1954 Prehistoric stone implements of northeastern Arizona. *Harvard University, Peabody Museum of American Archaeology and Ethnology, Papers* 34.

Yengoyan, Aram A.

1972 Ritual and exchange in aboriginal Australia: an adaptive interpretation of male initiation rites. In Social exchange and interaction, edited by E. N. Wilmsen, pp. 5–10. *University of Michigan, Museum of Anthropology, Anthropological Papers* 46.

Index

Numbers in italic indicate pages with tables.